W9-CWW-382

863 3897

AN ECONOMIC HISTORY OF SPAIN

AN ECONOMIC
HISTORY OF SPAIN

JAIME VICENS VIVES

With the Collaboration of JORGE NADAL OLLER

Translated by FRANCES M. LÓPEZ-MORILLAS

PRINCETON UNIVERSITY PRESS
PRINCETON, NEW JERSEY
1969

NOTE: Most of the maps and charts for this
English language edition were supplied by the
Spanish publisher; hence, geographical terms
appear with their Spanish spelling.
All captions are in English.

Translator's Note

The late Jaime Vicens Vives (1910–1960) was Professor of Modern History at the University of Barcelona and Director of the Center for International Historical Studies there. Recognized as one of the most brilliant of recent Spanish historians, he has been responsible for many new interpretations in Spanish history, especially of the fifteenth century. Among his works are *Aproximación a la historia de España* (*Approach to the History of Spain,* Barcelona, 1952), *Juan II de Aragón; monarquía y revolución* (*John II of Aragon: Monarchy and Revolution,* Barcelona, 1953), *Historia crítica de la vida y reinado de Fernando II de Aragón* (*Critical History of the Life and Reign of Ferdinand II of Aragon,* Zaragoza, 1962), and, in the Catalan language, *Els Trastàmares* (Barcelona, 1956) and *Notícia de Catalunya* (Barcelona, n.d.). He was also general editor of the monumental five-volume *Historia económica y social de España* (Barcelona, 1957–1959).

The present volume, which grew out of Professor Vicens Vives' course in Economic History of Spain at the University of Barcelona, first appeared in 1955, and a second edition was issued in 1959. After Vicens Vives' untimely death it was edited for a third time in 1964, revised by Dr. Jorge Nadal Oller, a former pupil and colleague at the University of Barcelona, who had also collaborated in the first two editions.

This English translation has been made from the third edition. The translator wishes to express special gratitude to Professor Robert S. Smith of Duke University, a specialist in Spanish economic history, who patiently edited the manuscript with the eye of a trained economist, and whose labor was an indispensable step in the preparation of this edition.

Thanks are also due to Laura H. Mapes for valuable help in repaging the Index, as well as at many other stages in the preparation of the manuscript.

F.M. L-M.

Providence, Rhode Island
1968

Author's Preface to the Second Edition

In 1955 and 1956, the lectures I had given during those two years from the chair of economic history of Spain in the School of Economic Sciences at the University of Barcelona were collected and published under the title "Notes for the Course on Economic History of Spain." Because of the nature of the subject and the lack of available textbooks, I accepted the idea of immediately supplying the students in the course with a text which would help them in their work. It was an arduous task, and one that did not turn out just as I had hoped. The notes I gave to the printer were too general in scope and needed careful revision. A number of unsupported value judgments and some gross errors slipped into them. That was inevitable. But I took the precaution of stating that these notes should be considered only as a teaching guide and not as a completely finished work.

In spite of these drawbacks, the "Notes" in question soon spread outside the strictly academic area and began to circulate among a public increasingly interested in learning more about the subject. This tempted me to prepare a manual of the economic history of Spain which would elucidate the present state of the many problems that cluster about this particular discipline, and which would also serve as a point of departure for new scientific accomplishments in the understanding of our economic past. This task, naturally, would have been an exceedingly lengthy one. But in view of insistent and kindly suggestions from friends and colleagues, and of the needs of students, I have decided to relinquish for the moment a more definitive project, which would have occupied me for many years, and to send to the press a somewhat more detailed and, insofar as possible, more exact revision of my original "Notes."

Like any manual for the use of university students, the present volume attempts to gather all the information available within the area treated. This means that it contains the inevitable generalizations in those fields in which I have not done direct and personal research. However, with the aid of Dr. Jorge Nadal Oller, my associate in the chair and a specialist in 16th and 17th-century Spanish economic history, this volume has been able to count on firsthand information from the second half of the 14th century to the end of the 19th. The material which concerns previous periods is based upon both fundamental bibliography and recently published articles.

My constant concern has been to trace with accuracy the dynamics of Spanish economic history. To do so has been, perhaps, the most exhausting work of all. I have also been concerned with eliminating nonessentials in order to stress fundamentals. Many of my working notes have not been included in this volume. Some have been omitted in hope that they can be utilized at a better time—that is, in a more detailed work; others in the hope that new monographic material will appear which will place them in a truer perspective. I hope that this always thankless task of selection has not been inadequate, and that I have not chopped down more than the necessary number of trees in the attempt to show the forest more clearly.

The original text has been twice revised, first by Dr. Nadal and then by myself. Thus we have succeeded in presenting a really different work, although here and there the umbilical cord connecting it with the "Notes" can be detected. Some chapters have been totally recast; others, rewritten. Changes have been made throughout. Among these I wish to point out the new orientation given to monetary subjects which in the original were rather sketchy because of lack of basic information, and the inclusion at the end of the volume of bibliographical resources which will serve to guide and supply points of reference for those wishing to explore in more detail the problems treated in the book.

Anyone who has been concerned with studies on the economic history of Spain will realize the difficulty of the task I have undertaken in these pages. Therefore, I shall gratefully accept any indications and suggestions for improvement which may be offered, if in the course of time a further edition appears.

J. V. V.

Barcelona
November, 1958

Note to the Third Edition

When the need became clear for a new edition of *An Economic History of Spain,* and in view of the untimely death of Professor Jaime Vicens Vives, we thought that it would be most appropriate to turn over revision of the text to one of his most highly regarded disciples, Dr. Jorge Nadal Oller, who had already collaborated in the revision of the original text, and whose brilliant work in the teaching of this material as well as in research make him one of our best specialists in that discipline.

Fortunately it has been possible to keep this revision within the bounds established by the two previous editions, for during the four years that have passed since the appearance of the second edition, the structure of our information on Spanish economic history has not substantially altered.

In fact, publication of the "Notes" was the first step toward an objective which is already being achieved, that of a totally new—and fascinating because hitherto unknown—view of our Spanish economic past.

We hope, then, that this *Manual* will continue to guide coming generations of students, and that it will open before the general reader the new horizons offered by study of the problems of Spain's economic history.

Table of Contents

Translator's Note   v
Author's Preface to the Second Edition   vii
Note to the Third Edition   ix

1. Stages in the Spanish Economic Process   3
2. Infrastructure of Spanish Economic History   9
3. Man in Spanish Economic Life   21

PART I · PRIMITIVE AND COLONIAL ECONOMY
4. Economy of Prehistoric Spain   39
5. Economy of the Hispanic Colonizations   46
6. The Economy of Roman Spain, I   57
7. The Economy of Roman Spain, II   71
8. The Economy of Visigothic Hispania   83

PART II · FEUDAL AND SEIGNIORIAL ECONOMY
9. General Indications   95
10. The Economy of Al-Andalus   102
11. Economy of the Western Hispanic Kingdoms from the 8th to the 12th Centuries   122
12. Economy of the Pyrenean Kingdoms from the 8th to the 12th Centuries   138

PART III · URBAN ECONOMY
13. Reconquest and Resettlement in the 12th and 13th Centuries   155
14. The Evolution of Urban Economy   167
15. Economy of the Catalan Urban Patriciate; Demography and Social Structure   175
16. The Economy of the Catalonian Urban Patriciate; Labor and Industry   187
17. Catalonian Trade   201

18. Prices, Money, Banking, and General Economic Conditions in the Crown of Aragon   223
19. Public Power and Financial Organization in the Crown of Aragon   232
20. Structure and Expansion of the Castilian Herding and Agrarian Economy from the 13th to 15th Centuries   241
21. Castilian Industry and Trade from the 13th to 15th Centuries   258
22. Money, Usury, and Public Finance in Castile   278

PART IV · MERCANTILIST ECONOMY
23. The Economy of Ferdinand and Isabella's Reign   291
24. Expansion of the Spanish Economy in America After the Discovery   315
25. Demographic and Social Structure in the 16th Century   330
26. Labor and Production in the 16th Century   344
27. Trade and Currency in the 16th Century   357
28. American Colonial Economy from 1550 to 1700   385
29. Demographic, Agricultural, and Industrial Decline of Spain in the 17th Century   411
30. Commercial Stagnation, Tax Pressure, and Currency Inflation in the 17th Century   432
31. Study of the Trade Cycle Under the Hapsburgs   456

PART V · ECONOMIC TRANSFORMATION IN THE 18TH CENTURY
32. Bourbon Reform Policies   471
33. Population and Labor   483
34. Agricultural and Livestock Production   505
35. Industrial Revival   524
36. The American Economy   540
37. Commercial Development   552
38. Economic Policy   566
39. Money and Finance   581
40. The Business Cycle in the 18th Century   598

PART VI · THE IMPACT OF THE INDUSTRIAL REVOLUTION
41. 19th-Century Spirit of Reform   607
42. Population and Property   617

TABLE OF CONTENTS

43. Agricultural and Livestock Production   644
44. Industry   657
45. Transport and Trade   679
46. Economic Policy   702
47. Money, Credit, and Banking   713
48. Survey of the 19th-Century Business Cycle   733

    Bibliography   747
    Index   803

AN ECONOMIC HISTORY OF SPAIN

1 · Stages in the Spanish
Economic Process

PERIODIZATION IN ECONOMIC HISTORY. As we begin the study of historical phenomena, we are faced, inevitably, with the problem of their periodization. The philosophers of history establish certain periods in human events in order to study them better. However, what societies come to be is not confined to watertight compartments nor closed-off periods. Neither Man nor Humanity can be crammed into periods, not even into the oft-described stages of youth, maturity, and old age. Thus we cannot speak of ages in history; it cannot be said that there were culturally backward Middle Ages, nor a Modern Age with an ultra-advanced civilization. For just as there are young people who seem to have been born old, and old people who always stay young, so there are peoples and societies which continually renew themselves or remain permanently senile. Therefore, to speak in terms of periods is only a pedagogical device and has value only as a point of reference.

Historical life is a movement of societies toward spiritual and material perfection. In this process the important factor is the rhythm of the action, the speed with which social structures achieve their full dimensions. Sometimes the rhythm appears to slow down; at other times, conversely, it accelerates noticeably. Each of these phases can be thought of as historical periods, but we must not lose sight of the fact that they make up a coherent and uninterrupted whole.

PRINCIPAL STAGES IN SPANISH ECONOMIC EVOLUTION. Applying this criterion to the economic history of Spain, we can point out several broad phases or chronological periods. But in order to do this we must keep in mind (1) the progress of economic evolution in general, and (2) the evolution of the Hispanic social structure.

In fact, when we speak of the economic history of a nation, we must remember that its development cannot be thought of as isolated, but rather as taking place within the so-called *intelligible framework of history,* that is, in relation to the cultural structure of which it is a part. In the case of the Iberian Peninsula, it naturally must be located within the orbit of Western society. And since economic life is above all a matter of relationship, Spain undoubtedly exercised a decisive influence on this group of nations at many points in history. And it is likewise obvious that at other times particular nations and even continents, such as America, had a powerful influence on Spanish economic development.

As for the use of the social structure as a basis for periodization, we must point out that there is an intimate connection among economic, social, and political structures. And since it is often the case that economic progress is so slow that periodization is difficult to establish (as in the case of the progress of agricultural techniques and their advance or retrogression in relation to factors of climate) and, on the other hand, since social structure reflects more clearly the modifications caused by the cyclical waves of the economy, we can sometimes have recourse to social structural forms in order to achieve a panoramic view of Spain's economic history.

PRIMITIVE COLONIAL ECONOMY. The true birth of Hispanic economy took place in antiquity, when the more advanced peoples of the Eastern Mediterranean undertook colonization of the outlying lands of the then known world. In the historical process of control over the metal routes by Eastern peoples, Hesperia or Hispania was the mythical country of riches and the marketplace where the metals of the North Atlantic and the gold and marble of Africa came together. The economic factor was, therefore, the chief incentive for the incorporation of Spain into the Mediterranean world.

Thus Hispania came little by little into the system of Mediterranean colonizations. Of these, the most important were the Punic and the Greek. The colonization of *trading posts* and *fortified places* predominated, established on islands, coasts, and straits. We find this same system in more modern times in the colonization carried out by European nations. Holland in South Africa and the East Indies, England in Asia and other parts of the world are obvious examples of it during the 16th to 19th centuries.

We know how Rome joined the ranks of the colonizing powers in Hispania by defeating her rivals the Carthaginians. The dominion of Rome in the Hispanic Peninsula for more than six centuries was the basis of an economic system founded on exploitation of mines and the olive oil produced by the large landed estates, a system which has lasted to the present day. Roman Hispania therefore gives us an excellent example of a colonial economy based on settlement and primary exploitation, within the larger compass of ancient Mediterranean economy.

FEUDAL AND SEIGNIORIAL ECONOMY. When the Germanic peoples overran the Roman Empire, Mediterranean economy began a gradual decline which became precipitous around the 9th century. During this period a new economic system, feudalism, was established.

In Spain, as in other parts of the Western world, the collapse of mercantile and monetary economy led to the establishment of a family-type economy based on two elements—wheat and sheep. This type predominated from the 8th to the 12th century, especially in the Christian zone, for the economy of Moslem Spain had taken an entirely different turn, and Al-Andalus was one of the few European centers in which a commercial type of economy persisted longest.

We must understand the Christian reconquest, especially in the early centuries, in its economic aspect; that is, as an attempt to resolve the people's concrete and direct problems. Very often the expeditions carried out by the Asturian, Castilian, and Leonese kings had a double purpose, economic and political, insofar as they were an attempt to protect pastures and grazing routes, the basis, as we have seen, of the Hispanic economy at that time. Again, the raids of the Christian armies often carried off men and money to the North, where both were badly needed. This much will suffice to make us understand that during the feudal period the Christian kingdoms of the Meseta, or central plateau, were mere satellites of the great Moslem economic center of southern Spain.

COMMERCIAL EXPANSION OF THE BOURGEOIS PATRICIATE. A profound change took place in the peninsular economic picture during the 12th century with the rise of a new mentality, that of the bourgeois patriciate, which contrasted sharply with the mentality of the preceding centuries. This urban bourgeoisie established new living standards and new economic systems. Among the Hispanic regions Catalonia quickly distinguished herself by her economic impetus, stimulated by a flourishing trade in gold, slaves, spices, and the manufacture of cloth. During the 13th, 14th, and part of the 15th centuries, Barcelona was the most important Spanish economic center. Somewhat later than Catalonia, about the beginning of the 14th century, Castile entered the arena of commercial expansion by exploiting the excellent wool from her sheep. Her international outlet was supplied by the Basque and Cantabrian coasts. Castile became the chief export market for wool—a veritable Australia of the Late Middle Ages—and because of her great wealth could aspire to political and economic supremacy in the Peninsula.

MERCANTILIST PERIOD. The mercantilist period comprises the 16th and 17th centuries, beginning with the establishment of the Spanish monarchy under Ferdinand and Isabella, and the discovery of the New World. Two facts essentially define it—survival of the economic mentality of the bourgeois patriciate (though transferred to the State), and the opening of the gigantic American market. It is the period when Mexican and Peruvian silver arrived in Spain, breaking all the old economic molds and quickly leading to capitalism.

However, the golden age of Castilian economy under mercantilism did not last long. Castile did not adapt to capitalistic ways and created a fictitious economy in which wealth in precious metals, instead of benefiting her, led her into unfortunate paths. And on the other hand, Spain was forced to maintain a very large military establishment, greater than her resources warranted. The situation deteriorated after the beginning of the 17th century, coming to a climax in the financial collapse of 1680, one of the basic dates in the Spanish economic process.

ECONOMIC TRANSFORMATION DURING THE 18TH CENTURY. After a long hiatus, the early governments of the Bourbon Philip V managed to stabilize the Spanish economy by the second decade of the 18th century. From then on Spain went through a period abounding in reforming energy and economic activity. Just what happened in the 18th century? The fact is that Spain fell into line with the rest of Europe. Until then the Spanish economy had followed one path and European economy another. While in Europe the technological inventions which marked the beginning of the industrial era were appearing, while the concept of large-scale capital was being developed and the idea of commercial enterprise was taking rational shape, the most important part of Spain continued to be bound to the old routine systems of farming and herding. When the two currents met, Spain experienced a rapid rise in her economy, based on the activity of the State, the development of American commerce, and the industriousness of Catalonia and the Basque region. But this very flowering, when it broke up the archaic social structure, brought Spain face to face with the constitutional problem of the 19th century and with it the fact of political and social revolution.

IMPACT OF THE INDUSTRIAL REVOLUTION IN SPAIN. The Industrial Revolution, which began in England about the middle of the 18th century, did not become apparent in Spain until early in the 19th, and then not everywhere but only in some marginal, peripheral zones where the Peninsular War—disastrous for the Spanish economy as a whole—had been unable to kill prosperity or the spirit of industrial progress. These regions survived not only the collapse of the war against Napoleon but the loss of the American empire. The result was, however, that loss of the former colonies deprived these regions of an extraordinary chance to compete with the principal economic powers during the 19th century.

Impoverished by internal wars, the selfishness of her ruling classes, and the backwardness of her masses, Spain achieved only an underdeveloped stage of capitalism during the 19th century. Although the cotton industry made great progress, metallurgy was obviously retarded and the national economy was dominated by foreign capital. However, some elements in the agricultural and industrial fields made tremendous efforts to achieve positive progress with Spanish resources. The actions of some industrialists and landowners of the last century, in the face of corrupt and deficient administrations and a conformist and stagnant country, are worthy of admiration and respect.

CONTEMPORARY ECONOMIC HISTORY. The contemporary phase of Spanish economic history begins in 1917. The First World War not only seriously disturbed the Spanish social system, raising the question of capitalism versus socialism as acutely as in other countries, but, by mobilizing the country's economy, it emphasized the enormous discrepancy between what had been done and what remained to be done. It became necessary to establish a balance among agriculture, grazing, and industry that would make possible the full development of the industrial and technological revolution. The contemporary period, in spite of its dramatic failures, exhibits the most determined collective effort to discover a viable channel for realizing those aims and for bringing Spain's economy into the general framework of the economy of the West.

2 · Infrastructure of Spanish Economic History

GEOLOGICAL FORMATION OF THE HISPANIC PENINSULA. The basic infrastructure of Spain's economic history is determined by the nature of the land masses which appeared in southwestern Europe as the result of an extremely long tectonic process. What are the chief stages in this geological history, and what have their consequences been for the Spanish economy?

In the Paleozoic era a gigantic land mass (*Hesperia*) appeared which formed the southern boundary of a large continent. This mass took on its definitive shape during the Silurian, Cambrian, and Hercynian periods. It was during this last period that the principal axes of the Meseta's structure were established, in a northwest-southeast direction, forming high mountain ranges now worn down by erosion. When, as a result of various folding actions, geological upheavals submerged the accumulations of lush vegetation created by the warm climate of the epoch, the foundation was laid for the rich carboniferous deposits of some Spanish coalfields, notably those of Asturias and Puertollano. At the same time, the Hercynian upheavals cracked the initial nucleus, and through these cracks important mineral layers appeared, such as those found throughout the southern lip of the Meseta, or Sierra Morena (copper in Huelva, lead and silver in Sierra Morena, mercury in Almadén, etc.).

The important consequences of this Paleozoic movement, therefore, were (1) establishment of the Meseta, the essential nucleus of the Hispanic Peninsula, (2) northwest-southeast direction of the principal topographical alignments and of the hydrographic system, (3) relative abundance of soft and hard coal formations, and (4) presence of mineral layers in some mountain sectors.

During the Mezozoic era the structural lines of Hesperia were maintained, despite the fact that several times during this period the region was flooded by seawater. The result was the deposition of large quantities of calcareous alluvia around its edges. There was no essential change, except for the rather unfavorable role which these deposits later exercised on Spanish agricultural soil. In the strictly mineralogical sphere, the marshy system which followed the Cretaceous sea resulted in numerous lignite deposits. These, apart from the typical calcareous and marble formations, are the only manifestations of the Mezozoic which have economic importance in Spain.

In the Tertiary period the tectonic process was more important. As the continent of Gondwana, or Africa, advanced against the northern continent, in the process destroying the geosyncline which separated them, its deep folds came into violent contact with the edges of the primary Spanish and French land masses. This collision, known as the Alpine, produced a number of tectonic upheavals which have given the Peninsula its shape: in the south, the Baetic system; in the north, the Pyrenees. Simultaneously, it produced the elevation of the old calcareous sediments on the edges of the Meseta, giving rise to the Iberian System and the Cantabrian mountains at the same time that a series of fractures and mountain resurgences brought about the present configuration of the Central System and Sierra Morena.

After the Alpine mountains were formed, the Meseta became covered by a series of lakes connected with the shallow seas covering the valleys of the Ebro and Guadalquivir; these slowly became filled in by sediments from the great Tertiary mountain chains. Also, the phenomena of compression and decompression gave rise to numerous mineral deposits (iron in Biscay, lead in Cartagena).

At the end of the Tertiary, and after the opening of the Strait of Gibraltar, the Peninsula took on its present outlines. Only the plains of the Levant and the Andalusian and Portuguese coastlines continued to be partly submerged.

In the Quaternary era the superficial coverings of alluvia, clay, and sand were laid down. At that time huge glaciers covered the Pyrenean region and the high peaks of the Cantabrian, Iberian, and Baetic systems. The most fertile agricultural lands date from this period.

It should be kept in mind that the Tertiary compressions and decompressions took place in a generally northeasterly-southwesterly direction; that is, in a direction diametrically opposed to that of the Hercynian period. This fundamental texture is still to be observed in the hydrographic network and natural routes of the Peninsula.

SPANISH SOIL. Two sets of facts can be observed from the tectonic process we have just described, one which has to do with the general structure of the Spanish land mass, the other with the quality of its agricultural soil.

Geographers point out the presence of four main structural elements in the Peninsula: the Meseta; the mountains which surround it; the depressions adjoining it on the northeast and south; and the outer mountain ranges. The surrounding mountain systems are the Cantabrian to the north, the Iberian to the east, and the Sierra Morena to the south, although the last is less a mountain range than the result of erosion of the Meseta's southern edge, graded down by the fault which opened up early in the Tertiary. The adjoining depressions are the Iberian, or Ebro, valley to the north, and to the south the Baetic or Guadalquivir valley. The exterior mountain ranges are the Pyrenees to the north and the Baetic to the south. This geographical structure determines, at first glance, the specific characteristic of the Hispanic Peninsula: its natural unity, modified by marked regional compartmentation.

Modern research has revealed that the soil of the Peninsula can be separated into two great subdivisions which we shall call, following Hernández Pacheco, "siliceous Spain" and "calcareous Spain." This important difference arises as much from the geological nature of the soil as from the climatic and physiographic accidents which have taken place in recent times.

In this regard, a work of Lucas Mallada's entitled *The Evils of Our Country and the Coming Spanish Revolution* (*Los males de la patria y la futura revolución española*), published in 1890, is still of some interest. He divides the national territory into the following types of soils: bare rock, 10%; low-yield land, 35%; moderately productive, 45%; and highly productive, 10%. These figures substantially alter the eulogy usually made of the fertility of Spanish soil, derived from the *Laudes Hispaniae* written by St. Isidore in the 6th century and repeated by Alfonso X, "the Wise."

In fact, only 55% of Spanish soil is suitable for agriculture, which in comparison with the European average is a disappointing proportion. Fernando Martín Sánchez-Juliá has recently taken issue with these figures in an article entitled "Fundamental Truths About Spanish Agrarian Economy" (*Verdades fundamentales sobre la economía agraria española*), in which he has attempted to dispute the pessimistic theory of Spanish agriculture. But if we examine his figures we see that his conclusions are similar to those of Lucas Mallada, for the truth is that the Hispanic Peninsula cannot be compared with countries like France or Holland, but rather with other Mediterranean countries such as Italy or Greece, whose agricultural shortcomings are well known.

MORPHOLOGY OF THE PENINSULA. If we are to understand the economic infrastructure of Spain, the study of its relief is essential. It is well known that Spain occupies the second place in Europe, after Switzerland, for the ruggedness of its terrain. But this fact is still more important if we keep in mind the blocked-off and compartment-like arrangement of this relief. To use Salvador de Madariaga's happy phrase, the whole Meseta is like "the citadel of a Spanish castle," indicating that the plateau occupies the position of a castle in relation to a block of territory which separates it, like a bastion, from the European continent.

If we examine a hypsometric, or altitude, table of the Hispanic Peninsula, we will observe the following: 15% of the territory has an altitude between 0 and 200 meters; 17%, between 200 and 500; and the rest, 68%, more than 500 meters. And 42% falls between 100 and 500 meters. Such a geographical structure gives rise to unfavorable conditions for agricultural and commercial life, all the more so when the extreme abruptness of the relief is an additional complicating factor. If we leave out the Ebro and Guadalquivir valleys and some few highlands in New Castile, León, and Old Castile, the mountain ranges cross the territory of the Peninsula like barriers, and sometimes like actual walls. If the Pyrenees rise like a mountain frontier between Europe and Spain, access to the sea from the Meseta is no less difficult, on the Cantabrian side as well as on the Mediterranean or the Atlantic.

To sum up, then, we should keep in mind three chief facts about the tectonics and morphology of the Peninsula: (1) geographic cantonalism; that is, division of the territory into separate compartments not easily accessible among themselves, (2) the unconnected nature of the hydrographic system, which confers geographic reality on the tectonic division, and (3) the abnormal relief picture. The constant and enormous differences in altitude offer great difficulties to the development of communications.

HISPANIC CLIMATE. The study of climate is of prime importance in any consideration of economic history. Our point of reference must necessarily be that of the present-day climate. However, when we study the possibilities of the Spanish economy in the past, we must keep in mind that our climate is not necessarily that of former times. There is a dearth of data on this subject, but we do know that ever since Neolithic times, that is, since about 4000 B.C., there has been a prolonged period of desiccation in our peninsula and in general all over the tropical zone. This phenomenon has given rise to the steppe-like character so typical of the country. It is possible that this desiccation became more pronounced at the beginning of the 14th century, as certain changes which took place in the southernmost regions of Spain (in Almería, for example) seem to indicate. But we cannot trace its development exactly. On the other hand, modern studies indicate that during certain periods in modern times Spain experienced long periods of drought. One of them probably occurred at the beginning and toward the middle of the 16th century. Others took place in the course of the 17th and 18th centuries. The economic history of Spain would make great progress if we could learn the exact nature of these oscillations between humidity and aridity, which constitute the essential problem for proper comprehension of our agricultural past.

At the present day, a major part of the Hispanic Peninsula is arid. The French geographer Brunhes divided it into two regions, *humid Iberia* and *dry Iberia*. To do so he used the 500 mm. isohyetal line, which runs, approximately, to the north of Barcelona, follows the southern slopes of the Pyrenees, extends almost to the Picos de Europa, surrounds the Cantabrian System and the mountains of Zamora and León in a great arc, descends toward the southwest, penetrates deeply into the Meseta by way of the Central System, and then, returning to its northeasterly-southwesterly direction, disappears in the Algarve, in southern Portugal. To the north of this dividing line humid Iberia receives more than 500 mm. of precipitation yearly, and dry Iberia, to the south of it, less than 500

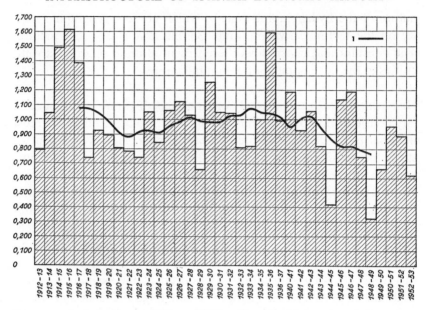

RAINFALL INDEXES FROM 1912 TO 1953.—*Key:* 1, nine-year moving average. Numbers at left indicate total annual rainfall in millimeters.

mm. This division is rather rough, for what really matters is not the quantity of rain but its distribution over the course of the year and its retention in the soil. Two geographers, Dantín and Revenga, have established a map of the mean annual dryness of the Peninsula, which corrects Brunhes's and makes it more accurate. Humid Iberia is composed of three zones: one in the North which includes the Pyrenees, the Cantabrian System, the mountains of León and Zamora, Galicia, the Central System, and northern Portugal as far as the Tagus; and two in the South, that of the Sierra de Cazorla (sources of the Guadalquivir and Segura rivers) and that of the Sierra Grazalema in the province of Cádiz. The rest of Spain is included in dry Iberia, which has four zones of extreme aridity (Ebro valley, the middle basin of the Duero, the plains of New Castile, and the lower Guadalquivir basin) and one almost desert zone (the southeastern coast from Murcia to Almería).

It is said that humid Iberia comprises less than 32% of the Spanish territory, while the dry zone makes up more than 68%. Actually, the most accurate figures are the following: the arid region contains 314,000 sq. km., of which 66,000 receive from 500 to 600 mm. annual rainfall, 180,000 from 400 to 500 mm., and 68,000, less than 400 mm. If we keep in mind that these last two portions have a total area of 248,000 sq. km., or almost half of the territory, we will realize the extraordinary importance of the problem of aridity in Spain.

The causes of this situation are to be found in the excessive evaporation characteristic of regions situated along the 45th parallel latitude north, and also in the lack of moisture resulting from the climatic mechanism. Three climatic centers influence Spain: to the northeast the Siberian low-pressure area, which is cold and dry; to the northwest the Icelandic low, which is damp and temperate; and to the southwest the Azores high, which is hot. The rains produced by these two low-pressure areas, which are responsible for the fertility of Western Europe, rarely reach our latitudes; the Azores high-pressure area keeps them away from the Peninsula. Only in very favorable circumstances, especially during equinoctial periods, when the Azores high approaches the equator, do rains from the Atlantic lows reach the Peninsula. The success of a given harvest depends on these rains, and so, consequently, does the prosperity of the country.

As a result of this climatic situation, steppes (or rather, those regions which have been rendered barren by man) occupy 7% of the peninsular territory. The Spanish steppes can be classified in the following groups: (1) southeastern, from Cape Gata to Cape Nao, (2) the Baetic steppes, (3) those of New Castile (from Albacete to Madrid, including La Mancha), (4) the region around Valladolid, and (5) the steppes of the Ebro valley.

There is no doubt that these steppe-like zones have played a decisive role in the evolution of Spanish economic history.

HYDROGRAPHY. As can be deduced from the foregoing, the arrangement of the hydrographic network derives from two factors, (1) the course of the great tectonic lines which form the northwest-southeast pattern, caused by the movements of the Hercynian period, and the northeast-southwest pattern formed by the Pyrenean movements, and (2) the geographic cantonalism arising from tectonics in general.

These two phenomena, together with the factor of humidity, act to determine the three essential characteristics of Spanish hydrogra-

MEAN ANNUAL ARIDITY IN THE IBERIAN PENINSULA.—This maps shows aridity in terms of the thermo-pluviometric index, relating temperature to rainfall; index rises with temperature and with deficient rainfall. Figures

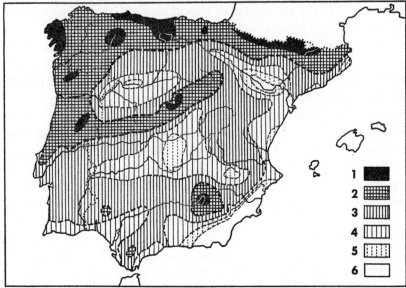

between 0 and 1 indicate extreme humidity and no aridity; between 1 and 2 it is still possible to speak of areas without aridity problems; aridity is slight between 2 and 3 and very noticeable between 3 and 4; between 4 and 5 it is extreme, and above 5 it is desert-like (*after* DANTÍN *and* REVENGA).

phy. In the first place, rivers have little volume. We need only compare a few statistics of Spanish rivers with other European rivers to realize how little water flows into the former (the largest Spanish river, the Ebro, flows at the rate of 700 cubic meters per second at its mouth, while the rate of the Po is 1,800 and the Rhône, 1,880, not to mention the great rivers such as the Rhine, Danube, Volga, etc.). In the second place, there is variation of flow: because of the unpredictable character of the rainfall, the volume of Spanish rivers is extremely irregular. This variability, ranging from double volume to fifteen times, reaches enormous proportions during high-water periods and leads to catastrophic floods. This is especially true of the rivers and streambeds of the Mediterranean littoral, where water volume can rise from almost nothing to 3,000 and 4,000 cubic meters per second. This fact presupposes great difficulty in the natural exploitation of rivers. Only at the price of enormous effort has man been able to reduce these wild variations partially and make use of river water for irrigation.

The third characteristic is the abruptness of the hydrographic contour. No Spanish river presents a gentle course between its source and its mouth; on the contrary, a number of steep drops occur. The rivers of the Meseta usually have two, one when they emerge from the mountains where they originate and another at the place where they encounter the change of altitude between the Meseta and the Portuguese zone. The Ebro is still more complicated, for it experiences three drops: the first when it reaches the Meseta, the second when flowing out of the Meseta through the Pancorbo passes, and the third when it encounters the gorges of the Catalan shoreline system.

With rare exceptions, then, Spanish rivers are not suitable for irrigation because their waters are confined between steep banks. Some have been used along part of their course, and are still being used, for navigation; but this is not common. To utilize them for hydroelectric or agricultural purposes necessitates huge regulatory systems such as reservoirs and dams, and even in these cases there is a problem with the large volume of mud and sediment deposited in them because of their great tendency to flood.

PLANT COVER. Spain's plant cover corresponds in general to that of other Mediterranean steppes. Lack of forests is characteristic, although in this regard we should not base our opinion entirely on present figures, for it is evident that before the 19th century—that is, before large areas of communal and mortmain land were brought under cultivation—there were more forested zones in Spain than there are today. Descriptions which have come down to us from the 13th, 14th, and 15th centuries speak, in fact, of large forested zones where today we find only steppes or moorland.

Generally speaking, meadow land is found in humid Iberia and steppes and subtropical plants in dry Iberia. Forests of characteristic mountain type exist in the Pyrenees, the Cantabrian System, the mountains of León and Zamora, in the Central System, the Sierras of Moncayo, Oca, and Demanda, and in the Montes Universales and similar chains.

In this connection the limits of the spruce and beech tree and the esparto plant are important. The southern limit of the European spruce takes in all of the Pyrenees region and extends toward Catalonia, including the Montseny massif. The southern limit of the beech tree is also significant; it covers almost all of Catalonia, then turns to the north of the Montes Universales, runs along the entire crest of the Central System on its western side and reaches as far as the Sierra de la Estrella in Portugal. The northern limit of esparto grass is typical of a large part of the steppe regions, for it begins near Tarragona, crosses the Ebro region to the north of Saragossa, curves toward the south of the Central System, and takes in a large part of La Mancha and the whole northern portion of the Baetic System.

Throughout these zones we can observe a considerable difference between the plant cover of Spain and the rest of Europe. But in addition to this natural plant cover, there exists another which is manmade. We refer here essentially to the *vega* * and the *huerta*,** both creations of man in the face of Nature. We shall speak of these later, when we discuss man's reaction to the unfavorable soil of Spain.

NATURAL COMMUNICATIONS. Even though we admit that Spain's geographical relief has always made collective life difficult, we can easily see that mountain defiles and passes must have had great influence as natural means of communication, for such passes have been used from earliest times for travel and commerce.

Our mental picture of the present communications network is a radial one, branching out from Madrid; but in fact the natural routes of communication in the Peninsula run from north to south and divide it into four great zones. The first joins Galicia to Portugal, especially by means of the Atlantic coastal plains; the second joins Asturias to León, Extremadura, and western Andalusia, through the pass of Pajares and the valley of the Alagón; the third connects the province of Santander with Old Castile, New Castile, and Andalusia by means of the passes of Reinosa, Guadarrama, and Despeñaperros; the fourth, much more limited, connects Catalonia with Valencia and Murcia by means of the passes along the Mediterranean coast.

Among these four zones, there are a number of centers of con-

* Intensively cultivated flatland, often a river valley.
** A plot of irrigated land, intensively cultivated.

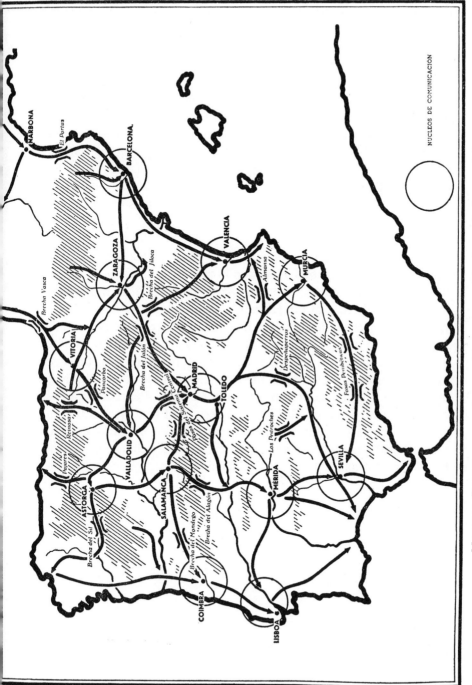

NATURAL ROUTES IN THE IBERIAN PENINSULA.—The large circles stand for the chief centers of communication. The most important mountain passes are shown on the map by two parallel lines.

nection which correspond to the isolated compartments into which the Peninsula is divided. Between the first and the second zones there are few important connections, and this explains up to a point the political division of Spain and Portugal. However, between the second and the third, numerous points of connection exist, especially in the north between Castile and León. Aragon occupies a prominent place between the third and fourth zones and serves to connect Castile with Catalonia by means of the Jalón valley and the passes of Fraga. And finally we must stress the role of general correlation played by the territory to the south of the curve of the Central System, that territory whose capitals have been successively Toledo and Madrid. It is in this region that the routes of communication of all four zones come together.

GEOPHYSICAL POSITION OF SPAIN. The geophysical position of a country is determined by its location in respect to the great mercantile, trade, or political routes in any particular period. In this regard it must be realized that the Hispanic Peninsula enjoys a wholly favorable geophysical position, for it is at the center of the crossroads formed by the two great lines of communication of Western Europe and the Mediterranean, from France to North Africa on the one hand, and from the Atlantic to the Near East on the other. This axis of communications has meant that the Hispanic Peninsula always exercised a very important role in all periods of history, and that in consequence its situation in regard to large-scale international commerce has been preponderant at times, enabling the Peninsula to benefit from outside stimuli or influencing its economic and financial life.

3 · Man in Spanish Economic Life

FORMATION OF POPULATION IN HISPANIC ANTIQUITY. Historical anthropology is a new science which was introduced in Spain by Professors Aranzadi and Bosch Gimpera. They blazed a trail which has later been followed by their pupils and by a number of excellent researchers (Pericot, Caro Baroja, Alcobé, etc.). It is through the work of these men that today we are beginning to glimpse part of the truth. It is to be hoped that in the future this partial knowledge will be sufficiently expanded to cover completely the panorama of Hispanic ethnological history. But for now, any evolutionary sketch such as the one we present here is subject to many corrections.

We shall make no mention of Neanderthal man. He left few traces in the Peninsula and disappeared at the end of the Lower Paleolithic period; one branch in the evolution of the hominids disappeared with him. He was probably eliminated from the historical scene by the so-called Cro-Magnon man, who belonged to the modern human species, *Homo sapiens*. Cro-Magnon man arrived in the Peninsula at the dawn of the Upper Paleolithic period, bringing with him a typical tool culture, the same as has been found in certain deposits at La Gravette in France. Therefore the Cro-Magnons are known as *Gravettians*. This means that by 50,000 B.C. Spain was inhabited by groups of modern men of a homogeneous race and culture. They were nomadic hunters, the first Hispanic peoples in the strict sense of the word.

During the Upper Paleolithic period the Gravettians continued to be the chief basis of population, but then a series of emigrations occurred which lasted many years, sometimes hundreds of years, and which were related to the slow shifting of the hunting grounds. The first and heaviest infiltration was of a race of hunters who had adopted an arrowhead of a special type with which they hunted very successfully. These were the so-called *Aurignacians*. They were near relatives of the Gravettians. These groups have achieved considerable fame, for they created the type of art known as Franco-Cantabrian, among whose masterworks are the cave paintings of Altamira. During this same epoch, though at an uncertain date, Spain was invaded by very warlike men, inventors of the bow and consequently of the swift arrow. They are called *Solutreans*. We know relatively little about this people, for prehistorians are still not sure whether they came from the north of Europe or from North Africa. Originally, by one route or another, they must have come from Asia. As a result of the fusion of these contrasting types, an important culture was formed on the Atlantic side of Europe, the one called *Magdalenian*. To this culture belong the highest achievements of the cave art of Altamira, of other places in the Cantabrian region, and in southern France. But it does not seem that the Magdalenians were a differentiated people.

After the Solutreans, we should make some mention of *Capsian* man. Some years ago it was believed that the first African tribes emigrated to Spain sometime at the end of the Paleolithic period. This emigration was that of the Capsians (so-called from the site of El Gafsa, in Tunisia). It was thought that they had produced the paintings in the caves of the Levantine and Catalan coasts, with scenes of men dancing, fighting, and hunting, which contrast so strongly with those of Altamira. But today even their existence is somewhat in doubt, and in any case their influence has been moved forward to the beginning of the Neolithic period.

After Neolithic man we are on much firmer ground, although there are many problems and questions still unsolved. By that time there was a mass of population in the Peninsula which can be called Mediterranean, and which represented the racial type that came to be dominant in the country. To say "Mediterranean race" means a dolichocephalic people of medium height, with more or less curly hair, slender and fairly dark-skinned. This man, the probable successor of the Epigravettians of the Paleolithic period, was faced by a sensational new situation. Several warrior and commercial peoples from the Eastern Mediterranean had become established in the southeastern part of the Peninsula (4,000 B.C.) and had established some fortified castles there, organized a political system and had begun to cultivate the soil. These people soon broke out from the Almería region where their strongholds were located and advanced toward the west (Andalusia) and north (Valencia and Catalonia), and for more than a thousand years (2,000–500 B.C.) were masters of the country (Bronze Age). This Almerían people, probably of Oriental origin, aided a slow immigration into the Peninsula of North Africans, who were the catalyzing element of the so-called *Iberians*. In fact, it appears that these latter people were the result of the fusion, in Andalusia and the Levant, of the North Africans with various Neolithic groups (probably the descendants of the Epigravettians), all dominated by an Almerían minority of Oriental origin.

At the beginning of the first millennium B.C., this situation changed radically. The Pre-Iberians who had dominated the Peninsula during the Bronze Age were submitted to formidable pressure from a European people. These brachiocephalic people, blond, blue-eyed, and tall, were the *Celts*. The first invasion was that of the people of the so-called "Rhine urn culture," who appeared in Catalonia about the 9th century B.C. But the two great Celtic invasions belong to the period between the 9th and the 6th centuries. The immigrants advanced by stages along both sides of the mountain barriers. Some invaded the northern part of the Catalonian region. But the greatest Celtic infiltration was the one which, breaking through the Fuenterrabía pass, went toward Galicia on the one hand and on the other toward the south of Portugal, and finally, by way of the two Castiles, to Andalusia. The new settlers were different from the Iberians, not only in their physical but also in their mental makeup. Some authorities believe that it was the Celts who gave the peoples of the central mountains of the Peninsula their qualities of command and their sense of political organization. But there is room for much argument about this.

Such was the situation encountered by the colonizing peoples, the Phoenicians, the Carthaginians, and the Greeks, when they successively arrived in the Peninsula from the 10th to the 5th centuries B.C. And it is the situation which they have described for us in their works. However, it would be audacious to say that thanks to them Spanish ethnography is perfectly clear today. Speaking in general terms, we can state only that the Iberians were dominant in Andalusia and the Levant, that the Celts predominated—at least as a ruling minority—in the rest of Spain, and that in one place in the Peninsula, namely the Iberian System, there existed a fusion of peoples from which the Celtiberians originated.

One question remains to which we have not alluded before—that raised by the Pyrenean race. Traces of it exist from remotest times in the dolmen culture of the Pyrenees; in modern times we find a proof of its survival in the Basques and in the people of certain Pyrenean valleys extending into Catalonia. What is the origin of this special human type characterized by specific anthropological traits and an archaic language of mysterious ancestry? There are many theories but few proven facts.

PEOPLES OF THE HISTORICAL INVASIONS. Spanish anthropology has changed very little in its basic structure since the end of the 5th century B.C. There have been, however, certain changes in the ruling classes, but they are neither so numerous nor so important as was once believed. Let us take a look at them:

The *Romans* ruled the Peninsula for seven centuries (2nd century B.C. to 5th century A.D.), but their only contribution to the Spanish *ethnos* was in the form of small groups of retired colonial functionaries, some merchants, military garrisons, and the like. There was no question of Roman infiltration *en masse*. It was a colonization of an urban type and even so was limited to peripheral regional centers.

In the second place, there was the *Jewish* element. It is well known that there are theories, such as that of the German professor Werner Sombart, which make the history of the capitalist movement revolve around this race. And related to these theories there is a general opinion which holds that the economic prosperity of the country ended at the moment when Ferdinand and Isabella expelled the Jews from Spain. We shall leave until later a scientific assessment of this problem, but it is of interest to make a few observations about the development of the Jewish population in Spain. The Hebrews became established in the Peninsula during the period of Roman domination, as a consequence of the general movement of dispersion known as the *Diaspora*. After the 2nd century A.D. we find Jewish colonies in Hispanic port cities, especially in those of the South, where commerce was most active. These groups developed considerably and, in spite of the hostility shown them by the Visigoths (who even tried to expel them during the 7th century), survived the Visigothic period and acquired great power during the Moslem period, which was one of great prosperity for them. Indis-

pensable in the finances and economic life of the Christian kingdoms, the Jews were the real rulers of the economy during the 12th
and 13th centuries. After that time they began to decline, although
the *conversos* (renegade Jews) took over their economic power.
The only—but very important—anthropological investigations
which have been carried out in medieval Jewish cemeteries in Spain
show that there was absolutely no anthropological difference between an "old Christian" and a Jew. This is a scientific proof which
should be kept in mind. The Spanish Jew of the 13th century was
identical to a Spanish Christian of the same time, except in two important things—he had a different religion and a very different
economic mentality. This latter quality was the one which the Jews,
when Christian pressure was most intense, passed on to the *conversos* and *judaizantes* (Jewish-leaning Christians). How many
Jews were there in Spain? As a maximum (and we shall study this
figure at the appropriate time) there were some 200,000 at the time
of their expulsion by Ferdinand and Isabella. They were few in
number, but the number is an unimportant factor. What was important was their wealth and their economic capacity; and thus it is possible that the financial and mental drain caused by the loss of the
Jews was difficult to recoup within the historical circumstances of
their expulsion.

The third group which we must include in our ethnographic
study is that of the so-called *Visigoths*. It is a common misconcep-
tion that during the 5th, 6th, and 7th centuries all the inhabitants of
Spain were Visigoths. Nothing could be farther from the truth.
There never was a Visigothic Spain, but only a Visigothic people
who infiltrated the Peninsula during the 5th century A.D. As a
demographic element we can estimate their number at some
200,000. The majority of these people settled in the Castilian
mountains and in the eastern plateau region of the Duero river. The
nobles and the military class carried out some duties at court and in
the provinces, where they represented no more than a bureaucratic
superstructure. They became in large part absorbed by the Hispanic
inhabitants, that is, the ancient population made up of Mediterranean men who had been civilized by Rome. Some survived over the
course of the centuries to become an integral element in the great
landholding nobility.

The fourth group is the *Moslems*. Anthropologically it is extremely varied. Among its members are Arabs, of pure Semitic stock; Syrians, who were also within the Semitic area; and Berbers, settlers from the other side of the Strait of Gibraltar. This last group not only crossed the Strait with the first Arab armies, but through trade and later invasions had prolonged contact with the peoples of the Peninsula. We should like to know just how large the number of Moslems was. Probably there were also relatively few of them. At that time an invasion such as the Moslem one in Spain could be carried out by armies of 10,000 men. But this does not leave profound traces in the anthropology of a country, and though it is possible that throughout the Emirate and the Caliphate of Cordova there were frequent demographic relationships between the two sides of the Strait, infiltration was probably a purely local phenomenon confined to Andalusia.

But this is not quite the end of the story. A fifth racial element began to be introduced into the country starting in the 11th century. It was a slow demographic infiltration, but undoubtedly a more important one than those of the Romans, Visigoths, and Moslems. We refer to the *Franks* (Languedocians and French). Beginning in the 10th century the greatly overcrowded population of Gaul scattered in all directions, and one of these directions was toward the south. By the 11th century we find the Franks established not only in the cities, such as Pamplona, Jaca, Toledo, and Ávila, but great tracts of agrarian repopulation in Castile were the work of Frenchmen as well as Aragonese and Navarrese, or Basques. But if we consider the situation from the 11th century to our day, we will find that a great wave of Frenchmen crossed the Pyrenees starting in the second half of the 15th century. The intensity of this phenomenon reached its highest point at the end of the 16th century, but continued in succeeding centuries in the form of a slow infiltration of a mercantile and artisan character. A precise study of French immigration into Spain, about which we have relatively little data, would help us to comprehend certain essential phenomena in modern Spanish economic history.

CONQUEST OF THE SOIL: AGRICULTURE AND HERDING. The successive racial waves we have been discussing all had to face a single reality—Spanish geography. For man as an economic entity, geography means soil, especially plant-producing soil that must be conquered, for utilization of mineral wealth is a phenomenon which comes after occupation of the territory. And this action can take place only through cultivation of the soil or through grazing. And, as we have already pointed out, there are two clearly differentiated botanical landscapes in Spain as well as two mineral ones (humid Spain and dry Spain; siliceous Spain and calcareous Spain); therefore the types of life are also dual—on the one hand agricultural, and on the other herding.

Given the climatic conditions of the Peninsula, the conquest of the soil through agriculture has been slow and difficult work and has taken place, specifically, along the coastlines. The classic phenomenon goes under the name of conquest of the Mediterranean "hoyas," or basins. In the course of this process a perfected agriculture has been developed, based on the utilization of water and of fruit trees. Vineyards and olive groves require less care, but all these types of planting need an uninterrupted tradition, with a tendency toward a stable homelife and individual agrarian enterprise. This was clearly shown in Italy, by a similar process of geographical adaptation, in the special principles of Roman law, which is based on that of individual property.

Grazing exists side by side with this type of life. In the Mediterranean countries grazing is divided between steppes and mountains. In the Iberian Peninsula, this involves a relationship between the people of the North (Pyrenees, Cantabrian mountains) and the steppes of the South, especially La Mancha and Extremadura. The typical kind of life is nomadic and is exactly opposite to the life we defined before: in place of stability, nomadism; in place of uninterrupted tradition, chance; instead of the individual principle, collectivism (in regard to livestock as well as to agrarian concepts).

If these types of life are indeed true, for so they have been studied by geographers and recognized by historians, it is legitimate for us to ask whether they have created and defined a mental attitude. We consider that this is in fact the case. Every primary human process creates a mental structure in the course of time. In the case of the Mediterranean and Andalusian farmers, such a mental attitude has been developed by successive groundbreakings of this inhospitable shore, infertile in comparison with other agricultural regions of the earth. That is, it has not arisen out of a simple type of agricultural life but by an uninterrupted process of occupation and improvement of the soil. As I have mentioned in one of my books, *Brief Survey of Catalonia (Noticia de Cataluña)*, the Catalans have colonized and conquered the soil eight times since the 2nd century A.D.; and the same could be said of Valencia, Murcia, and even, perhaps, of Andalusia, although in the last case the cultural and mental succession was interrupted by the Castilian conquest of the 13th century.

In regard to the mentality created by a herding type of life, we should accept the opinion of Professor Ramón Carande, who has studied the problem posed by the extension of Castilian nomadic pasturing into Andalusia and America. Carande holds that nomadism in the Meseta has given rise to those great environmental structures, those great desires for space, which obviously go along with this type of life, and at the same time to the spirit of command, of colonization, and of hopeful anticipation which characterize Castilian expansion not only in Spain but everywhere in the world. All this has worked to the detriment of spiritual application to practical realities, and we will not be surprised to discover, in the course of the present pages, that in many ways Castile has never been able to go beyond the precapitalist stage in her economic mentality.

THE SPANIARD'S CONCEPT OF WEALTH. Let us understand by the concept of wealth the system of mental attitudes regarding material values. The problem raised by this concept is very profound, especially in regard to Spain, for it affects nothing less than the role which she has played in Western civilization. Ever since this role was disputed in the 18th century by Masson de Morvilliers, in the famous article on Spain in the *Encyclopédie Française,* the controversy it has aroused has recognized neither limits of prudence nor periods of truce. Leaving this polemic to one side, we shall contribute a series of concrete facts to a future critical study of the Spaniard's behavior in regard to economic life.

It is obvious that the differing process of conquest of the soil and the dual type of life which arose in Spain out of the numerous immigrations and the utilization of agricultural land have given birth to a concept of wealth, elementary if you will but dual also. What characterizes the *peasant?* Traditionalism in his concept of the value of land; limited resources; tireless and individual labor; an economy based on the family; a sense of continuity; thrift. What characterizes the *nomadic herdsman?* Relativity of economic values; tendency toward monopoly; adoption of a more or less well-organized collectivism; a group economy; discontinuity of effort; and finally, repugnance for rationalized forms of economic life.

There is a third concept of wealth, that of the *merchant.* This is the typically European concept, the one that links the individual to the business enterprise; continuity to ambition; thrift to investment; the ambition for power to the social necessity of that power; the individual to collectivity. This is the concept of wealth which created the modern economy in England, the United States, France, and Germany. However, it has appeared in Spain very infrequently. Even today we resist such a concept, to the point that it can be said in public, "Spain's genius is anti-economic." This is the attitude of a nomadic mentality. Many other signs reveal to us, however, that in opposition to this rather Quixotic attitude there is an everyday reality which tends to overcome it. One of the tasks of Spanish economic history is to capture the development of the normal concept of wealth in Hispanic man.

THE TECHNICAL SENSE. The problem of the concept of wealth is connected with that of the technical sense. It is evident that the Spanish contribution to the general development of technology, so vital to economic coherence, has been minimal. The controversy aroused by this point has come to be linked with Spain's role in the whole order of Western civilization. Some have lamented the fact that her contribution has been so meager; others, giving more value to spiritual than to material factors, have applauded the triumph of Spain's genius over the materialism of technology. All of this seems mere verbiage to us. Today we are able to see the problem a bit more clearly, since Professor López Ibor has faced it honestly and has presented the question from a scientific point of view.

López Ibor follows two essential lines of reasoning, one related to historical time and the other to Spanish psychology. According to him, at the very time when the taste for science, and secondarily for technology, began to develop in Europe, Spain and the Spaniards were in a very difficult situation. In the 17th century the Spaniard was tired; his great world undertaking had been a failure; he lacked spirit, had no energy, and all of this caused a feeling of backwardness which he subsequently found hard to overcome. So much for the chronological position. As for the factor pertaining to the Spanish temperament, a number of points should be noted, he says. (And when we refer to López Ibor and the Spaniard he speaks of, let us remember that he is referring specifically to the Castilian Spaniard, the one he knows best and to whom he alludes most frequently.) What, then, does Professor López Ibor see in the Castilian?

First, a total indifference towards Nature, physical nature, that gentle and attractive landscape which man constantly encounters except in a spot so monotonous, though of such lofty spiritual values, as Castile (the Castile of the Duero and La Mancha, be it understood, not the Castile of the mountains). In Catalonia, and in general all along the Mediterranean coast, the situation is quite different; there we find overflowing natural beauty, and everything which turns toward the esthetic and sensuous is lost in a concern with purely technological matters. In the Basque region and the Cantabrian littoral, Nature in general exercises the same balancing role as in the rest of Europe: she predisposes man to admire and study her.

Second, the Castilian's temperamental preference for human and personal values, not those which are cosmic and abstract; he cares nothing for the figure and the symbol. The Spaniard wants to encounter the person, to know who he is, to find out who is hidden behind those figures and those symbols. This is why Spain's economy, like her politics, is a purely personal factor. All this undoubtedly represents a fundamental value which Spain has maintained against, or in the face of, or surrounded by, that technological civilization which Europe has created. But in the economic sphere the difficulty of seizing these abstract values has made the task of the Spaniard infinitely more difficult.

Third, the bigotry of the concept of the *hidalgo* (which we consider to be an acquired historical mentality rather than a temperamental factor): the Spaniard's vocation for glory, both in battle and in literature; the sense of what is noble and hidalguesque; contempt for servile occupations and anything representing sustained labor.

Fourth, social disinterestedness. Rather than disinterestedness —that is the word used by López Ibor—we would define this concept as *an absolute lack of curiosity.* It stems from the conviction that either we are the best, and furthermore the cleverest, of men, or that our affairs are going very well and that we need only copy what others do in order to have them go even better. This enormous lack of curiosity, which has characterized Spanish history since the 16th century, is obviously one of the most essential features of Spanish psychology.

Professor López Ibor has omitted one point which, in our opinion, is essential and serves to complete his exposition of the problem—that of the Spaniard's repugnance for confronting intellectual problems which touch on orthodox positions. We need not mention the Inquisition, that focal point of the "Black Legend." The Inquisition is only one of a number of myths which have been put forward to explain obscurely what is clearer than daylight. If the Spaniard had felt the necessity of saying something to the world of technology, he would have done so with or without the Inquisition. The fact is that he had little to say. And the cause of this was the loss of cultural contact between the Spanish universities and those of Europe decreed by Philip II, expressing the general feeling of a country which demanded "waterproofing" the frontiers in the face of the risk of heresy (1565). And since science is the product of collaboration among minds which are *a priori* dissident and nonconformist, and technology is the result of this collaboration applied to practical matters, a slow retardation set in regarding the acceptance of new scientific ideas and new systems and methods of work. Therefore, when the more progressive Spaniards came into contact with Europe in the 18th century, they found that they suffered from a formidable technological deficit.

The history of the 19th century in Spain has been studied as a great conflict between rival political factions. This is a purely superficial view of history. In reality, the shape of the 19th century in Spain is the bitter struggle of the few to master technology, that technology which had been forged in Europe and which was continually slipping out of our grasp.

THE SENSE OF ORGANIZATION. The modern world has combined wealth and technology into a system of capitalistic organization (and in certain countries a socialistic organization, according to the mode of understanding concepts such as property, distribution of national income, and organization of business).

What characterizes the development of capitalism in Europe? Three facts. First, the depersonalization of business. Business becomes something apart from the individual businessman. A man became a capitalist when he was able to separate his capital from his operating fund and to invest it as an abstract sum which would gain or lose money by itself. This depersonalization is essential to the understanding of capitalism. Second, the mystique of business. Capitalism thinks of the prosperity of a business enterprise as a sign of the blessing of Providence. Thus various authors (Troeltsch, Weber, etc.) have been able to write and sustain the proposition that capitalism is linked to the birth of Protestantism, for the latter had changed the character of works of redemption, making it consist not only in spiritual good works but in the favorable progress of business. And the third point is the necessity of business as a mark of social distinction. Beginning in the 17th and 18th centuries, men went into business not only to make money, but also because it conferred solidity, security, and comfort; it came to be felt that a person who possessed neither a factory nor money nor social position was a failure.

If we contrast these three principles with those we have previously mentioned as defining the Spaniard's economic psychology, we will find a diametrical difference. It is very difficult for the Spaniard to depersonalize himself in regard to business. The home, the business, and the owner form an unbreakable circle. The business mystique does not exist. There has always existed, and there exists in Spain today, a mystique of humanity, a mystique of religion, a mystique of lofty spiritual values, but not one of business. Only a handful of Spaniards have ever believed that Paradise could be attained by way of business. And as for the third point, until the 18th century there were laws forbidding any noble, or any *hidalgo,* to engage in manual labor. Here we have a radical incompatibility between the concept of nobility of blood and that of money.

What Spain *has* had through the centuries, ever since Ferdinand and Isabella came into contact with the New World, has been the bureaucratic concept of business organization. This is a very different thing from the capitalistic concept of organization of the economy.

SPAIN AND EUROPE: HISPANIC ISOLATIONISM. Does this mean, as has been asserted so many times, that Spain is an Oriental country in her economy? No, although in principle this is not an untenable theory. The fact is, however, that the Spaniard, by virtue of geographic structure, of type of life, of historical mentality, of links with other European countries, is a full member of Western culture. But within that culture, and precisely because of those psychological characteristics, he is someone apart. He is a disturbance, an abnormality; but he is necessary and vital. Spain cannot be condemned for being an abnormality. The world needs to be abnormal in order to progress; that is, it needs contrasts in order to advance along the road to perfection, which is not only material but ethical. But the basic Spanish tendency is toward what is European, and this not because the Europeans are different, but rather because the Spaniard himself is European and therefore cannot escape from that orbit into which he was drawn by Rome and within which, through the ages, he has found himself located, at some times comfortably, at others uncomfortably, but always recognizing it as his true home.

How can we explain this abnormality? Undoubtedly through the factor of Hispanic isolationism. For long periods in her national life Spain has lived isolated and ignored. Her mountain walls, less high than the spiritual ones she has erected, have contributed in some degree to produce this phenomenon. And this has brought on a series of problems which gave rise to economic tensions and eventually to important revolutions once those barriers were broken down.

Hispanic isolationism was notorious between the 8th and 10th centuries, although at that time it had little importance. It was overcome in the course of the 11th to 15th centuries when, starting with the French emigrations, Spain was in close contact with the rest of Europe. But ever since the middle of the 16th century and almost to the present day, the process has dragged considerably. There have been cases, of a political and military nature, in which Spain has intervened in Europe and vice versa, but they have relatively little weight. What is important is the attitude of ignorance which has prevailed, despite the development of a spirit of imitation in clothing styles and intellectual thought, in science and economics, and despite the minority groups who, ever since the end of the 17th century, have considered it their essential function to put Spain solidly in the European mainstream.

CANTONALISM AND REGIONAL NUCLEI OF ECONOMIC ACTIVITY. The geographical compartments into which the Spanish territory is divided have resulted in economic cantonalism. In fact, one can hardly speak of an economic history of Spain up to the end of the 18th century, and even until well into the 19th. Even in the 17th century regional economies still existed which were unmistakable and were in fact differentiated by law and custom: a Castilian economy, a Valencian economy, a Catalan economy, etc. If we go back to earlier periods, this regional economic diversity corresponds to the division of the peninsular territory into independent kingdoms.

Hispanic economic cantonalism has been imposed by three conditions. The first of these is geography, the second history, and the third the mentality arising from the social structure. In connection with geography we have already mentioned the existence of regional frameworks which give personality to each one of the zones into which the Peninsula can be thought of as being divided. As for history, economic cantonalism developed as far back as the earliest prehistoric times, persisted during the entire ancient period, and finally acquired consistency during the Middle Ages when the regional economies took on very different rhythms. And as for mentality, since it is the product of both history and geography, it tends to concentrate in what we might call regional nuclei.

We believe that four such nuclei can be distinguished: the Castilian, the Catalan, the Northern, and the Andalusian. Everything we have been saying corresponds to the first of these, for general considerations pertaining to the concept of wealth, and to economic organization and the technological capabilities of the Spanish people, have been formulated on the basis of peculiarly Castilian attitudes.

As a regional nucleus of Hispanic economic activity, the Catalan contribution is distinguished by a number of typical factors: strong will, aptitude for work, curiosity, a technological turn of mind, and a family type of capitalism. These conditions have not always obtained. For example, the aptitude for work which is so characteristic of the Catalans of today was not in evidence during a large part of the modern age; during the first two centuries of this period all historical evidence combines to deny it. Only after the last years of the 17th century did this aptitude begin to be considered as typical by travelers in the country and by those who studied working life and commerce. Similarly, curiosity seems to have been awakened at the same time as aptitude for work—around 1680. As for the technological spirit, we should point out that the Catalan has real *adoration* for technology and that he is especially clever at solving mechanical problems. His adoration for the machine is a phenomenon of collective psychology. On the other hand, the Catalan has not entered fully into the ultimate form of capitalistic organization (the large incorporated company), for in Catalonia the medium-sized personal business is typical. But against the opinion of those who have theorized about this (Pi y Sunyer, Tallada, etc.), holding that it is a defect in the individual and collective temperament, we think we have proved that it was an accidental condition which appeared during the course of the 19th century and became fixed by the colonial crisis at the beginning of the 20th.

The Northern economy is characterized by vital curiosity, by a spirit of technological progress very much in the European mold, and in particular by capitalism in business. This trait, principally associated with the Basques, possibly derives from their capacity for large general concepts. St. Ignatius of Loyola is an example of the union of the mystic spirit with that of a great undertaking, creating a large militant organization at the service of the Church. In much the same way, the great Basque (and North Castilian and Asturian) businessmen of the 19th and 20th centuries have united the mystique of business with an impressive industrial and financial capability.

Andalusian economic psychology requires careful examination, and indeed we do not know whether this has ever been done. The Andalusian mentality apparently results from the submission of the people's economic needs to the interests of the dominant classes; therefore, it has been said, an enormous gulf exists between the ruling minority and the great mass of workers. The subordination of the former class to the exigencies of social tradition, the absence of curiosity, the lack of technological spirit, the scanty development of any sort of business enterprise, all have left a very special mark on the Andalusian mentality. However, in other periods of historical life the Andalusian has been in the forefront of peninsular economic activity (in the 10th century, under the Caliphate; in the 16th, immediately after the conquest of America). The true nature of the Andalusian regional nucleus can only be understood after a radical revision of the myths which at present obscure its meaning.

I · PRIMITIVE AND
COLONIAL ECONOMY

4 · Economy of Prehistoric Spain

THE NATURAL ENVIRONMENT. If we push history back to the appearance of man on the planet and accept the evidence that this appearance dates at least from the Quaternary period, what we might call primeval history begins at the end of the Pliocene (warm climate, luxuriant vegetation, many mammal species), when the temperature begins to fall and the first glaciation is about to take place. However, since this primeval or prehistoric age goes back farther than the Quaternary, we should point out some traits of the natural environment at different periods.

Quaternary (from 600,000 or 500,000 to 10,000 B.C.*).* Its chief characteristic is the alternation of climatic phases (four periods of glaciation, or periods of intense cold, and three interglacial periods), the probable cause of which was variation in the intensity of solar radiation.

In those times the Peninsula had a shape similar to that of today, and the Strait of Gibraltar was already open. The effects of glaciation had less influence on the Peninsula than on the rest of Europe, though some did occur: perpetual snows descended to the 1,700–1,800 meter level in the Pyrenees, to 1,400 in the Picos de Europa, and to 2,400 in the Sierra Nevada; the climate of the Meseta was similar to that of Poland today, the Cantabrian coast's was like Scotland's, and in Andalusia the climate resembled that of southern France; rivers carried much more water, and volcanic phenomena were very common; the flora and fauna resembled those of the Nordic countries.

Transition to the modern geological period (from 10,000 to 5,000 B.C.*).* This period, about which we know little, was also one of transition in the cultural sphere (Mesolithic or Epipaleolithic). Great geological disturbances occurred which marked the transition from the Pleistocene, or late Quaternary, to the Holocene.

Fully modern period (beginning about 5,000 B.C.*).* The upheavals of the previous period finally produced recession of the ice to its present limits and the definitive configuration of coastal levels.

FOOD-GATHERING ECONOMY: NOMADIC HUNTERS OF THE PALEO-LITHIC. When he faced the day-to-day problem of living, the most primitive man, in the most elementary stages of technology, was limited to the use of the spontaneous elements which Nature had placed within his grasp—the simple gathering of wild products and the hunting of wild animals. It was, therefore, a destructive economy of a negative type: consumption of resources without replacement and, consequently, a forced nomadism. Once the resources of the place where they were staying became exhausted, the Paleolithic tribes found no other solution than to move somewhere else in search of the nourishment they needed.

In this type of life hunting played the main role, for it supplied meat in abundance as well as skins for clothing. The preeminence of hunting is undoubtedly related to the first known manifestation of spiritual life in man. In fact, the great cave paintings of animals can be explained by sympathetic magic, a concept found in all early hunting peoples which identifies the desired animal with its pictorial representation. Primitive man used for this early hunting activity the arms or tools provided by chipping waterborne stones; he also made use of wood treated with the aid of fire, already known at the dawn of humanity.

Who were these hunting peoples of a nomadic type of life and a rudimentary tool culture, who occupied the Peninsula for the space of half a million years? Our knowledge of them goes back only as far as the second phase of renewal of cold, within the last glacial period, during which the ancient Neanderthal inhabitants, of whom we know almost nothing, were forced into oblivion by new men whose physical characteristics were not essentially different from those of modern man. This phenomenon took place at the same time as the arrival in Western Europe of new peoples, probably of Asiatic origin, who raised the level of material culture very notably by perfecting the use of flint.

There were two groups which came into Spain. One is called the *Gravettians,* a people of Mediterranean type who spread over almost the entire Peninsula; they are known for their variety of small stone implements (microliths). They and their successors, the *Epigravettians,* are our most remote ancestors; it is thought that they entered Spain about 100,000 B.C., at the end of the Lower Paleolithic. Another group, the *Aurignacians,* became established later in the Basque-Cantabrian zone. These people, more advanced culturally, are known especially for their skill in hunting and their use of bone for tool-making.

During the last stages of the Paleolithic, other ethnic groups came to join this first surviving substratum. They were the *Solutreans,* armed bands of possible African extraction; they introduced the bow and with it long-range hunting. They circulated among the earlier peoples, sometimes mingling with them, and surviving in certain places until the arrival of the *Magdalenians.* This people reached Cantabria and the northern part of the Peninsula in pursuit of the reindeer and bison of northern Europe, which had been pushed southward by the last period of intense cold, in the fourth glacial period. The Magdalenians had a well-developed industry of bone implements and spears.

AGRICULTURAL AND HERDING ECONOMY IN NEOLITHIC TIMES. A series of new discoveries, known as the Neolithic revolution, took place in the region between the Nile and Mesopotamia within a cycle of only 2,000 or 3,000 years, at the beginning of the fully modern geological period. These discoveries changed the whole direction of humanity and marked its entrance into a new civilization. Agriculture was the focal point of this new progress. The discovery of cultivation of the soil is a landmark in human culture second only to the discovery of fire.

The introduction of agricultural techniques implies a waiting period between sowing and reaping and therefore implies a sedentary type of life, for it makes possible the renewal of resources without having to move from place to place. At the same time, since living in one place made it impossible to follow large game on its long migrations, it required domestication of the more necessary animals; thus herding came about as an adjunct to agriculture. And then the settling down and living together of a group of persons in the same area made a certain amount of political organization necessary. Finally, let us point out, as a supplement to agriculture, the appearance of other important civilizing elements such as pottery, the wheel, weaving, etc. In short, we can see that the introduction of agricultural techniques revolutionized the way of life of prehistoric man, raising him to heights undreamed of during the Paleolithic era and opening the way to subsequent improvements, among them metallurgy.

Now that we have described the economy of the Neolithic period, it is only necessary to add some details about its development within the Hispanic setting. In the Peninsula the Neolithic begins about 4,000 B.C. under the influence of outside groups who came from the East, by what route we do not know. Even lacking such data, we do know that this foreign element enriched the extremely low cultural level of the Peninsula at a time immediately preceding the appearance of the Neolithic movement on its soil. As for the rest, the Neolithic agrarian innovations, which arrived in Spain rather belatedly, gave a decided impulse to the incorporation of the country into the cycle of more advanced civilizations.

INTRODUCTION OF METALLURGICAL TECHNIQUES: LOS MILLARES. The Neolithic period in Spain lasted a relatively short time, and is thought of as the period immediately preceding the age characterized by the discovery of metal and its possibilities as a working tool and a technical instrument. This discovery had been made in the Near East about the year 4000 B.C., but there was considerable delay before it spread to the rest of the inhabited world. The first metals used were those which are found in their native state (gold and copper especially) and which can be worked, to a certain extent, like stones. Copper in particular was the metal *par excellence* of the early period. It was extracted from pits and mines by the use of fire and stone wedges; next, by the action of heat on the ore, the metal-bearing particles were loosened, then separated by means of washing. Finally, to unite the particles of metal, they were smelted in clay bowls.

A later discovery was the alloying of copper with tin, which was known in the form of impurities in the former metal; and this gave rise to the use of bronze, a harder metal and one easier to smelt than copper.

The introduction of metallurgy, really the first transformation of matter which man had accomplished, opened the door to the making of tools which were conventional in form yet more resistant and easier to produce than stone ones. In Spain, which was rich in copper (Andalusia and Asturias) and tin (Galicia), the impact was extraordinary. This took place about 2000 B.C. and marks the incorporation of Spain into the civilizing commercial currents of the Mediterranean.

Given the cultural state of Neolithic men in Spain, it seems probable that they learned metallurgical techniques from some Mediterranean people whose identity is unknown to us. This belief is strengthened by the site of Los Millares, a typical Bronze Age settlement near Almería on the Spanish Levantine coast and a foreign colony in Hispanic territory. We shall omit here the different stages in its development, but Los Millares is essentially a fortified town on a hill, with a well-developed water supply system, an extraordinary variety of tools made of stone, metal, bone, and other materials, and a very complex religious life.

A foreign bastion in hostile territory, an advance base of a much richer civilization, a mercantile and cultural crossroads, and the focal point of a very mature spiritual sense—that is Los Millares. With its walls and moats, its utensils and ornaments of Egyptian and Minoan origin, its alabaster vases, bone needles and buttons, its necklace beads of calcite, turquoise, jadeite, and amber (from the Baltic, perhaps?), and its enormous burial chambers each large enough for a hundred graves, there is no possible doubt that it indicates a culture brought from the Near East.

REGIONAL ECONOMIC GROUPS IN THE BRONZE AGE: EL ARGAR. Los Millares is the most representative site of a cultural circle called the Almerían, which comprised the southeastern part of the Peninsula and was settled by a people from the Sahara. This circle, the Mediterranean outlet of prehistoric Hispanic territory, reached its highest point of development later, well within the Bronze Age, when the rise of metallurgy made the expeditions of Eastern merchants in search of Spanish minerals more frequent. The site of El Argar is symbolic of this period.

The Almerían culture spread along the shore of the Levant as far as Catalonia. Then it reached into the Ebro valley by way of the Maestrazgo passes and attained the Meseta through the Jalón valley. In Catalonia it coexisted with the Pyrenean culture, which had been developed by a herding people of possible Caucasian origin with characteristics similar to those of the modern Basques. The Pyrenean herdsmen of the Bronze Age lived a poor existence, a mere reflection of the life of more advanced peoples to the north and south of the mountains, and buried their dead in dolmens. They were grouped around two centers—the Catalan and the more isolated Basque—whose point of union was the highlands of Huesca.

In the south, the Almerían culture spread very rapidly into the Guadalquivir valley. Andalusia's greater agricultural and mining wealth, and the fact that it was on the Atlantic tin route, gave it a separate personality. This special character of Andalusia was to give rise to the extraordinary fame of one of its economic and cultural elements, the bell beaker, which is recognized today as a product of the fusing of the Hispano-Mauritanian and Almerían cultures. This bell-shaped beaker went beyond regional and peninsular limits and spread all over Europe.

The Meseta, shut away in the center of the Peninsula, formed a sort of substratum in which the cultural manifestations of the peripheral zones left their deposits. For the period with which we are dealing, historians usually lump its culture with that of the caves, which is meaningless. In reality, judging by the very small chink opened by a few inadequate archaeological investigations, the only significant development in the center of the Peninsula during the Bronze Age is the extension and perfection of the bell beaker (Ciempozuelos).

Although the economic groups we have just mentioned lived in isolation from each other, economic and cultural relations did exist among them. The best proof of these links is the occurrence of the megaliths—great funerary constructions of stone—probably of foreign (Mediterranean) origin, which appear almost throughout the country, and their establishment in such diverse places as among the Basque-Catalan herdsmen and the farmers of the Guadalquivir valley.

First Commercial Relations Among the Penninsula, the Near East, and the Atlantic. When we dealt with the introduction of agriculture, and later metallurgy, into Spain, we spoke of the Eastern origin of these discoveries. This is a fact which has not been proved in any concrete way, but one which has been

44

deduced—on the positive side because of the existence in Egypt and Syria of very advanced cultures capable of stimulating such phenomena, and negatively because the indigenous Hispanic inhabitants would have found it impossible to reach such high forms of culture from levels of civilization which were considerably lower.

Once such relations are admitted, it would be interesting to know the extent of contacts between the two ends of the Mediterranean. Authorities are divided on this point into Orientalists and Occidentalists, according to the greater or lesser weight given to the East in the evolution of the forms of life of peninsular prehistoric peoples. In any case, however, it has been possible to establish a certain parallelism between the Spanish Eneolithic cultural centers and those of the Near East, especially Egypt (ornamental objects and ceramic decorations) and the islands of the Aegean, which leaves little doubt of the influence of these peoples in Spain.

It remains to be determined which people it was who established the bridge between the two coasts. Siret's theory, favorable to the Phoenicians, has been abandoned, and today the Cretans are thought to have carried out the role of intermediaries.

On the other hand, very late in the second millennium B.C., the old Eneolithic culture reached a high point in Galicia and nearby Portuguese regions. Since this same phenomenon took place simultaneously in Brittany, Cornwall, and Ireland, it is felt that underlying this coincidence there may exist an ethnic or at least a cultural unity. Active navigation even in simple hide boats would result in close links among these countries.

The abundance of metal—especially gold and tin—in the countries mentioned explains the prosperity of this Atlantic period. Tin in particular was the object of active commerce with the southern part of the Peninsula, which served as an intermediary with the more advanced countries of the Mediterranean and even with faraway Egypt. The benefits which the North Atlantic countries drew from this export of metals were both cultural and technological in nature. Proof of this is found in their entrance into the circle of the megalithic phenomenon, their use of the bell beaker, and the fact that the important British metallurgical industry must have derived from that of Almería and the Algarve, in southern Portugal.

5 · Economy of the Hispanic Colonizations

MEDITERRANEAN COLONIZATIONS IN THE PENINSULA. We have just seen that economic relations certainly existed between the peoples of the Eastern Mediterranean and the Peninsula before the first millennium B.C.; but they cannot be defined exactly. The Egyptians, Myceneans, and Cretans must have reached the coasts of Spain in search of metals, especially copper and tin. But there is no proof of the fact, nor can we have sure knowledge about it today.

However, beginning with the year 1000, the Peninsula came fully within the orbit of Mediterranean colonizations. For this period we do have concrete and coherent information, both archaeological and written. But this information is not always definitive.

First the Phoenicians, later the Greeks and Carthaginians, brought the Peninsula into the great international trade of the period. To what can this fact be attributed? In the first place, there was an economic motive. After the so-called invasions of the seafaring peoples, which affected the politics and economy of the Near East around the first millennium B.C., several great empires were established in that area, notably those of Assyria and Babylonia. Their needs, of all kinds, grew rapidly, and to supply them the peoples of the Syrian coast and Palestine increased their mercantile activity. These seafaring peoples, especially the Phoenicians, gradually conquered the sea routes and established direct relations with the Western Mediterranean. As in former centuries, metals were the chief inducement to this economic renewal.

At the same time, population increased over the entire Eastern Mediterranean littoral. This brought about a demographic and political crisis, particularly noticeable in Greece after the 8th century, which gave rise to civilization in the modern sense of the term. Masses of people emigrated from one place and established themselves in another, first in nearby places, later in more remote ones. This led to: the *factoria,* or trading post, established on faraway coasts; then to the *colonia,* an imitation of the mother city, with the same language, religion, and laws; and finally to the *clerukia,* or establishment of a strategic base whose purpose was to control access to an important trade route.

Throughout the Mediterranean area, the Eastern colonizations caused economic and political struggles. The Greeks and Phoenicians vied for control of Sicily, key to the central Mediterranean, the former from their positions in Magna Graecia (that is, southern Italy), the latter from Carthage and North Africa. This struggle was transferred bodily to the Western Mediterranean. The Phoenicians progressed slowly along the North African shore and by way of the islands, notably Sardinia and the Balearics. The Greeks advanced along the northern coast from Cumae, a settlement near Naples, to Marseilles. But the objective of both was the same: the metal market of southern Spain. This antagonism was to last for centuries, and would be resolved only by the integration of Spain into the Roman Empire, successor of the Greeks in its antagonism to the Punic peoples.

THE INDIGENOUS PEOPLES. Simultaneously with the process we have described, the ethnography of the Peninsula acquired its definitive traits, which can be followed by means of the texts of various geographers of Mediterranean antiquity.

The most characteristic features of this process are: invasion of the Indo-European Celts into the center and north of the Peninsula; definitive formation of an Iberian community in Andalusia and the Spanish Levant; and fusion of these two ethnic groups in the center of the country.

If we take a panoramic view of the indigenous peoples during their period of greatest stability and at a time when our sources of information are most accurate, that is, shortly before the Roman conquest, we can sketch an outline which will include the most important of them. We give them here as a simple reminder.

In the Andalusian region were the *Turdetani,* successors of the *Tartessians,* and undoubtedly identified with them in spite of the difference in name. On the Levantine coast the principal groups were the following: in the southeast, established in the present-day provinces of Almería and Murcia, were the *Bastetani.* The *Iberians,* strictly speaking, began in the Segura valley and included the

Contestani, established in Alicante, the *Edetani,* located in Valencia and in the Maestrazgo region as far as Saragossa, and then the Catalan tribes (*Ilercaoni* and *Cesetani* in Tarragona; *Laietani* and *Lacetani* in Barcelona; *Ausetani* on the plains of Vich and Gerona; *Indigetes* in the Ampurdán region; and a number of tribes on the spurs of the Pyrenees, such as the *Ceretani*). In the Ebro valley, the *Ilergetes* were established to the north of the river, and the *Iacetani* on the slopes of the Pyrenees.

Established from the upper Duero region to the Jiloca, and in control of communication between the Ebro and the Meseta, were the *Celtiberian* tribes. They were made up of four great groups, the most notable of whom were the *Arevaci,* whose capital was Numantia. In the Rioja region were the *Verones,* also forming a link between the Ebro valley and the Meseta.

Along the Cantabrian shore, from the Pyrenees to Galicia, lived the *Vascones* in the Basque region, the *Cantabri* in Cantabria, the *Astures* (who were found not only in Asturias but also all over León), and the *Galaici,* who spread out toward northern Portugal.

In the northern Meseta, besides the Celtiberians and Astures already mentioned, the most important people were the *Vaccei,* who inhabited the middle Duero region. Three peoples predominated in the southern Meseta: the *Vettones,* the *Carpetani,* and the *Oretani.* On the Atlantic side, from north to south, lived the *Lusitani* and the Celts.

PHOENICIAN, GREEK, AND CARTHAGINIAN COLONIES IN SPAIN. After the crisis of 1000 B.C., the Phoenicians were the first Near Eastern peoples to advance toward the Western Mediterranean. During the apogee of the city of Tyre, Phoenician expeditions reached the Pillars of Hercules and founded *Gadir* (modern Cádiz). We do not know the exact date of its founding, but even though we do not find archaeological remains of the city earlier than the 6th century, it is evident that the sources which speak of a foundation dating back to about 1000 B.C. are substantially correct. In any case, it seems that Cádiz was a small trading post up to the Carthaginian period; that is, till the 6th century. Besides this strategic colony which controlled Atlantic trade and kept an eye on the important kingdom of the Tartessians, the Phoenicians founded on the southern coast the trading posts of *Sexi, Malaca,* and *Ab-*

dera, though some doubt exists about these (the name Abdera is of Greek origin).

As for the Hellenic peoples, we know that settlers from the cities of Chalcis and Rhodes were in contact with the Peninsula in the 9th and 8th centuries B.C. The Chalcidians founded Cumae, an important colony in Italy, while the Rhodians were the sailors who spread the myth of the Pillars of Hercules and those who certainly established in the 8th century the colony of *Rodhae,* probably located very near present-day Rosas. To judge from the large number of coins found there, Rodhae must have had its period of greatest splendor in the 4th century B.C.

The first authentic trace of Greek commercial activity in the Western Mediterranean is the voyage of Kolaios of Samos, who sailed as far as Tartessos in the 7th century B.C. This trade became brisker during the 6th century because of the fall of Tyre to the Assyrians and the increasing contact between the Hellenic peoples and the Tartessian kings. At that time the Greeks used the route of the islands, that is, Sardinia, Minorca (Mahón), and Ibiza, and founded a number of southern colonies such as *Mainaké,* probably near Málaga, and *Hemeroskopeion,* very close to present-day Denia, at a place where iron mines existed, according to Strabo. His testimony confirms the name of "Ferraria" given by Pomponius Mela to Cape Nao, near the colony. The founding of the first Greek city of *Emporion,* also on the gulf of Rosas, seems to have taken place at the same time. This expansion, spurred on by the great colony of Marseilles (founded in 600 B.C.), was interrupted by the battle of Alalia in 535, a famous struggle in the annals of Western Mediterranean colonization. In that battle the Greeks were victorious over the Carthaginians and Etruscans, but at so great a cost that they had to reduce their activity in the Hispanic Peninsula. The southern lands were abandoned to Carthaginian occupation, and the Greeks, in place of their original project of extended colonization along the shoreline, substituted one encompassing a smaller area, but which was equally intensive.

Under the leadership of Marseilles, foundation of the new city of Ampurias (Neapolis, on the mainland) belongs to this *second phase of Hellenic colonization.* Vitalized by refugees from the southern colonies, Ampurias immediately (end of the 6th century) gained very great importance as an advance base of Hellenism in the West. We have evidence of this in the minting of coins and in the considerable traffic with Attica (ceramic evidence) and the rest of the Eastern Greek world. This phase of prosperity was to last throughout the 5th century, and was made possible because the Punic enemy was engaged in the dispute over Sicily. The same situation went on for another century, the 4th, especially during its second half, when the treaty of 348 between Carthage and Rome specified their respective zones of influence and thus guaranteed the security of the Greek colonies. Hemeroskopeion, at that time the farthermost colony in the Western Hellenic world, was at last out of danger. In line with this fact, archaeological findings of the period just after 348 in this zone show a considerable rise in Greek imports, particularly noticeable in ceramic objects, the majority of which come from the south of Italy and Sicily (direct commerce with Attica fell off sharply from the time of the Peloponnesian Wars at the end of the 5th century). As García Bellido has pointed out, it is likely that under the protection of the terms of the 348 treaty, and subsequent commercial prosperity, the Massiliots, or even the colonists of the peninsular establishments themselves, should have risked the founding of new trading posts in the zone closest to the line of demarcation between Carthaginians and Romans. The fact is that the earliest remains of two new colonies belong to this period: *Alonis,* near Benidorm, and *Akra Leuké* (Lucentum, later Alicante). Both were located in a region rich in silver, lead, and iron, and especially as close as possible to Sierra Morena, which was even richer in minerals.

In the third place, we should mention the Carthaginians. Successors to the Phoenicians in the control of North Africa and southern Spain, they destroyed Tartessos about the year 500 and took over Mainaké. From that time onward, horrific legends about the Atlantic spread over the eastern Mediterranean, propaganda which the Carthaginians used to avoid competition on this profitable route. *Ibiza* gained exceptional importance as a point on this route. A Phoenician colony had been founded there, probably about 660 B.C., and it served the Carthaginians as a strategic spot to cut the island route of the Hellenes and keep an eye on the Western Mediterranean. Aside from this advantage, the island had economic value as a producer of Tyrian purple. Ibiza was one of the chief Carthaginian colonies in the Western Mediterranean. A little later, in the 6th century B.C., the Carthaginians advanced toward the interior of Andalusia, where numerous Punic archaeological remains can be found (Osuna, Carmona, Marchena, etc.). This was the prelude to what later became the Barcide colonization; that is, the colonization undertaken by Hamilcar Barca after the defeat of his troops in the first war with Rome (ending in 241). The Barcide colonization took the form of a military occupation of the country and especially the establishment of new cities, the most important among them being *Alicante* and *Carthago Nova* (Cartagena).

The impetus of Carthaginian domination was shown in the storming of Saguntum (219 B.C.) by Hamilcar Barca's son, Hannibal, an action which brought Spain into the Second Punic War and, eventually, into Rome's orbit.

OBJECTS OF TRADE. The chief activity of the colonizing peoples in Spain was undoubtedly aimed at gaining control of the Peninsula's metals, as well as of those products which reached it through the Atlantic lines of communication. The metalliferous products exported to the Near East were silver (the most important lodes were in Cartagena), gold (which abounded in the gold-bearing river sands), copper (the metal-rich zone of Huelva), tin (abundant in Galicia and Andalusia because of the Atlantic trade), and lead. Iron ore began to be exported during this period, for excellent veins of it were found in Galicia and Baetica. Salt was also an export product. The fishing establishments of southern Spain (Gadir, Carteia, Sexi, Abdera, etc.) furnished dried fish as an additional item in the export trade. In connection with this we can cite *garon,* a fish sauce (tuna, mackerel, etc.) which was consumed in great quantities in the Eastern cities.

Keeping in mind that the Iberians were bad sailors and that Cantabrian trade with the British Isles was slight, the principal marine activity centered around the colonizing peoples. On the other hand, it must be noted that although they were essentially seafaring peoples, their merchants sometimes went into the interior of the country. This is proved by the discovery of Ampurian coins in a number of places in the Ebro basin, such as Renieblas, and in Osma, in the present-day province of Soria.

As for imported goods, they consisted mostly of luxury objects such as perfumes, certain stuffs and cloths, Tyrian purple, and artis-

51

tic products, jewels, and other such luxuries. The heavy importation of wine and oil in the early period of colonization gradually disappeared (except for high-grade brands) as planting of vineyards and olive groves developed around the outskirts of the colonies.

TECHNOLOGICAL AND CULTURAL INFLUENCE. Although we have no precise data on the subject, it is obvious that the Phoenician and Greek peoples made substantial contributions to the primitive Hispanic economy. Thus, in the field of agriculture it was certainly the Greeks who introduced the vine and the Phoenicians—or perhaps also the Greeks—who introduced the olive tree. In industry, certain textile processes, the salting of fish, and in particular advanced metallurgical techniques were taught to the natives of the peninsular littoral by the colonizing peoples.

Perhaps the most important influence had to do with writing, for which the Greeks very possibly were responsible. Writing took two forms—that of the South, belonging to the Tartessians, and the Iberian form, whose use began south of Alicante and included the Valencian region, Catalonia, the Ebro zone, and the south of France, forming a great cultural unit.

Another interesting innovation in the mercantile field was the diffusion of money. The Punic peoples as well as the Greeks showed the native inhabitants the value of metal in commercial exchange. The Barcide mintings are magnificent and so are the Greek, especially in Ampurias, whose coins were dispersed over a large radius from Narbonne to Alicante. As we said before, Ampurian coins are a good index for judging the area of economic penetration of the Greek colonization in Spain.

TARTESSOS. The history of the kingdom of Tartessos raises a whole series of insoluble problems because of the absence of any archaeological testimony which might corroborate the abundant literary references to it. In its early period Tartessos can be considered as a way station in Phoenician trade, which exported in its great ships the tin of Brittany and Cornwall and the silver, copper, and gold of the Andalusian mines. In fact, the name of Tarshish or Tartessos begins to be heard after the establishment of the Punic peoples at the mouth of the Guadalquivir. Later, the export of those metals through Cádiz gave rise in the East to the mythical notion of a fabulously rich country located beyond the Pillars of Hercules, on the edge of the Sea of Shadows.

At any rate, the relationships between Phoenicians and Tartessians are confused. First there was a stage of rivalry, culminating in the burning of the ships of Gerion, king of Tartessos, by the Phoenicians. There followed a shorter stage of Punic domination, characterized by a great exploitation of the wealth of southern Spain: Posidonius assures us that the Phoenicians even made the anchors of their ships out of silver when, already heavily loaded, they were about to depart. Later, during the 7th century B.C., the crisis in Phoenician affairs meant the recovery of Tartessos, this time as an independent kingdom. One of her monarchs, Argantonios, extended his dominions as far as Cape Nao, and at the same time established a firm alliance with the king of Samos and especially with the Greeks of Phocis, whom he invited to come and settle in his territory.

The 7th century, then, marked the second stage of the legend of Tartessos, with Greek friends substituted for Phoenician rivals. Exploitation of the metallic treasures of the southern part of the Peninsula continued as intensively as before, though under the new sign of collaboration with the Greeks. This state of affairs continued until the year 500, approximate date of the destruction of Tartessos by the Carthaginians, which clinched Carthaginian power in the Western Mediterranean. The destruction of Tartessos was a postscript to the naval battle of Alalia (535 B.C.), which broke the naval power of the Phocians, allies of the Andalusian kingdom.

INDIGENOUS ECONOMIC AREAS. Tartessos constitutes an exception in economic development among the indigenous peoples affected by colonization. The rest of the Peninsula carried on a much less brilliant existence, more or less modeled on the expansion of technical knowledge imported from the Eastern Mediterranean, and ranging from the zones of superior culture in the Levant and Andalusia to the extremely backward areas of the Cantabrian North. Caro Baroja has established the existence of some regional groups whose principal characteristics will be summed up as follows:

CANTABRIAN CULTURE AREA. This took in the Cantabrian zone and the northwestern part of the Peninsula. Its economic base was

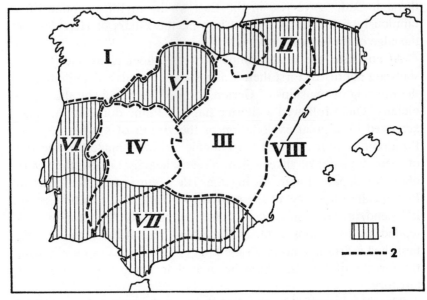

CULTURE AREAS.—Numbers: I, Cantabrian; II, Pyrenean pastoral culture; III, fundamentally pastoral culture of the eastern Meseta; IV, Vettonic pastoral culture; V, collectivist agrarian culture of the western Duero valley; VI, upper Lusitanian agrarian culture; VII, upper Tartessian culture. *Key:* 1, territory of culture areas II, V, VI, and VII; 2, boundaries of areas I, III, IV, and VIII.

fundamentally agricultural and its social system was a matriarchate, with daughters inheriting and sisters giving dowries to their brothers. As regards agricultural techniques, they practiced a system of cultivation with *hoes* and other similar, extremely rudimentary implements. When Augustus conquered this region, the Romans made great efforts to change the system, obliging the men to work in the fields. They also made the people come down from the hills, where they cultivated tiny parcels of land, and settle on the plains, permitting more fruitful labor.

The Cantabri, Astures, and other groups were not acquainted with money, and transactions were made by the use of pieces of cut metal or by simple barter. In contrast to these symptoms of backwardness, we should point out the existence in the Cantabrian area of some elements stemming from other, higher cultures, in particular the herding of sheep and goats which, in principle at least, is characteristic of other cultural types.

As a modern reminder of this culture there is still a narrow belt in this area where agricultural tools more primitive than the plow have survived. This is the case of the Basque "laya," an iron stake used for cultivating the soil.

THE MESETA AREA AND THE WEST. This includes not only the Meseta and a large part of Portugal, but also the Pyrenees and the Ebro basin. It takes in five different areas:

(1) *Pyrenean pastoral culture.* Its limits are harder to fix than in the case of the Cantabrian region because its characteristics are less outstanding, especially on its edges, where it runs into the agricultural Cantabrian culture (Basque Country) or the colonial Catalan culture. The essential economic base of this area was the flock, and the dolmen its highest spiritual manifestation.

(2) *Fundamentally pastoral culture of the eastern Meseta.* This is fundamentally but not exclusively a herding culture. Although flocks of sheep and even herds of cattle were the basis of the food supply, agriculture also existed, but it was basically different from that of the northern area; cultivation was done with the *plow* instead of the simple hoe used by the Cantabrians.

(3) *Vettonic pastoral culture area.* Its origins were within the Meseta, like the culture previously described, but its pastoral traits were more sharply accentuated and more archaic. In this area a number of animal sculptures have been found (serpents, boars, bulls, and so on) which can only be the work of cattle herders. On the other hand, the finding of wheat together with the absence of plowshares makes Caro Baroja think that the Vettones, essentially a warrior people, must have stolen the cereals they needed from their northern neighbors.

(4) *Collectivist agrarian culture area of the western Duero valley.* This was so called because of the Vaccei's custom of dividing up the fields by lot every year, working the parcels of land according to the lottery and using the harvest in common, according to the needs of each family. But it seems that we need to qualify this definition somewhat, for in a system of total agrarian collectivism the distinction of classes (rich, poor, and slaves) which actually existed would have been impossible. It is to be supposed, therefore, that the

annual distribution of land affected only the rich, who turned over its cultivation to the poor and the slaves. In regard to agricultural techniques, the use of the *curved-sheath plow* (typically Mediterranean, in contrast to the *quadrangular plow* of European origin) is characteristic of this culture, as is the existence of large granaries and storehouses for cereals.

(5) *Upper Lusitanian agrarian culture area.* This included the Portuguese zone between the Tagus and the Duero. In this territory, which seems to have been one of the oldest centers of plant cultivation, there existed a sharp contrast between the mountain people, who were poor shepherds, and the inhabitants of the plains, who were rich farmers. The names of Viriatus and his father-in-law Astopas symbolize, respectively, the two types.

To the Greek Polybius (2nd century B.C.) we owe a list of Lusitanian prices, the oldest in the Peninsula. It confirms the existence of an important trade in agricultural and animal products.

MEDITERRANEAN-ANDALUSIAN AREA. This was the zone most affected by the Punic and Hellenic colonizations. Caro Baroja subdivides it into the following areas:

(1) *Upper Tartessian culture area.* Originally it had the same economic basis as the Lusitanian culture; that is, cultivation with the plow; but to this was added a growing wealth in the herding of cattle. Tartessian coins reflected these elements by being marked with the curved-sheath plow, a spike of wheat, and a kind of yoke typical of the region. Later, with the first colonizations, exploitation of the great mineral deposits of the region was added to the original agricultural and herding base. We have already spoken of the role of Phoenicians and Greeks in the utilization of Andalusia's mineral wealth.

(2) *Upper Mediterranean culture area.* This was intimately connected—indeed, often interfering—with the culture previously described, and it shared the same characteristics. "However," says Caro Baroja, "the autonomy of the Mediterranean culture in respect to the Tartessian can be appreciated in the fact that they differ in imported elements as significant as the alphabet, for here a phonetic language existed which was apparently very distinctive." On the other hand, the culture of the Levant did not present traits as marked as that of Tartessos in the area of organization of the state.

6 · The Economy of Roman Spain (I)

ECONOMIC CAUSES OF ROMAN COLONIZATION. Most authors, when they weigh the motives which led to the extraordinary expansion of Roman rule, put the greatest emphasis on mercantile concern or military advantage.

In the concrete case of Hispania, the first Roman conquest was merely an episode in the Second Punic War. But once Carthage was defeated and expelled from the country by the treaty of 201, the Romans had no intention of abandoning it. The economic value of the Peninsula, especially its mines, naturally had something to do with this decision. But all in all, the essential reasons were more of a political and military nature than an economic one. To evacuate Spain would have been an invitation to the Carthaginians to re-occupy it. For this danger there was only one solution: permanent occupation, at least in regard to the Mediterranean side. The difficult advance toward the interior of the territory, of which the Celtiberian and Lusitanian wars make up the best-known episodes, was undertaken in spite of Rome's repugnance to extend her zone of action in Spain. It can be explained only as a security measure designed to guarantee her permanent occupation of the coast.

A consequence of that same Second Punic War which brought the Romans to Spain was the formation of a powerful group of capitalists in the mother country. Imperial expansion converted Rome into the chief Mediterranean capital market; under many forms —war booty, indemnifications, licit or illicit exploitation of conquered countries—money flowed into Rome in enormous quantities. In the course of two generations Italy became the richest country in the Mediterranean.

Once they had reached this point, the Romans realized that in order to preserve their privileged position they would have to put their acquired assets to work by exporting them and making them reap profits in countries where money was scarcer. Thus, the exportation of capital was the chief instrument in the progressive conversion of Roman imperialism, political in its origin, into an imperialism which was clearly economic.

It is within this overall picture that we must place Rome's final decision, subsequent to the initial entry of her legions, to extend her sway over all the Hispanic territory, admirably suited for capitalistic expansion because of its natural wealth.

HISTORICAL EVOLUTION OF ROMAN RULE IN SPAIN. In relation to the foregoing, we can distinguish two essential stages in Roman domination of the Peninsula. The first, principally of a military nature, includes the period from the landing of the legions at Ampurias (218 B.C.) to the days of Caesar and Augustus. The second, characterized by a desire to colonize the country effectively, takes in the period of the Empire. In both these periods we can distinguish various phases, which we shall summarize as follows:

Phases of military conquest: (1) Extension of Roman rule along the coast of the Spanish Levant (218–195 B.C.). (2) Penetration toward the interior as a guarantee of possession of the coastal zone. The Celtiberian and Lusitanian wars, the central episode of this phase, ended in treaties of federation which laid the groundwork for pacification, not rule, of the Meseta.

Phases of colonization: (1) Creation of Roman colonies and transformation of indigenous cities into *municipia,* but *only on an individual basis;* a process begun by Caesar, broadened by Augustus, and continued without any qualitative change during the Claudian and Flavian dynasties, up to the time of Vespasian. (2) Concession of Roman law to *all* the Hispanic territory, as the instrument of definitive settlement by Rome (74–75 A.D.). The author of this measure, Vespasian, initiated a real revolution in the politico-administrative and social system of the Peninsula. The Spaniards were given the *ius latinus minus;* that is, they continued to live under their own system of law, minted their own money, and were not even subject to the *tributum* of the Romans. But their cities were organized on the Roman model. They were autonomous, federally united to the Roman state, and their subjects continued to be foreigners, that is, aliens within the Empire. Thus, the essential feature of the *ius latii* given to the Spaniards, apart from its usefulness in accustoming the natives to Roman life, customs, and law, was its value as an instrument for attaining Roman citizenship. By means of this law, the *duumviri, quaestores,* or *aediles* of any Latin city, and their descendants, automatically became Roman citizens at the end of a year. Vespasian's concession increased the number of Roman citizens in the Peninsula and opened the way for a long period of collaboration between Spaniards and Romans (2nd century A.D.), and Caracalla's final equalitarian measure. (3) Extension of Roman citizenship to the entire Empire by Caracalla in 212. This was the culmination of the process begun by Caesar and Augustus and so firmly helped along by Vespasian in the 1st century. After this time, when the legal obstacles which had hindered the cohesion of the different Imperial territories had disappeared, Rome's effective rule over almost all of Spain became a fact. However, Caracalla's measure should not be understood as the finishing touch to native administrative organization. The process we have just described was in many ways more formal than real, more of law than of fact. Some rural centers continued to exist (often situated within the very administrative territory of the Romanized cities), which eluded the efforts of Vespasian and Caracalla and preserved their original native regimes. This fact is of great significance, for it was precisely these rural native strongholds which rose to importance in the latter period of the Empire, when the cities, strangled by taxation, began to decline, thus putting an end to the country's traditional dependence on them.

EVOLUTION OF SOCIAL STRUCTURE AND WEALTH IN ROME. Before going into the analysis of Hispanic economic structures under Roman rule, we need to have in mind the general lines of the evolution of society, and of wealth, in Rome.

The Republic had been plagued by rivalry between *patricians* and *plebeians.* The former, protected by the State which they controlled, were divided into *senatores* and *equites,* who held the respective monopolies of agrarian wealth and business.

The end of the Republic came about because of the alliance of the plebeians—bourgeoisie and proletarians—against the patricians. Thus, the Empire begun by Augustus (period of the Principate) was an expression of the victory of the middle and lower classes, supported by the army. The middle classes made particularly good use of the circumstances until, under the successors of Augustus, the bourgeoisie became the spinal column of the Empire. The remarkable rise in urban Spanish life under the Claudians and

Flavians (1st century) fits in exactly with this process. And its culmination led to the liberal monarchy established under the Antonines.

But this bourgeoisie depended on the labor of the lower classes —peasants and urban proletariat—who had been its old allies but were now the object of exploitation. The old antagonism between patricians and plebeians turned into opposition between *honestiores* (bourgeoisie) and *humiliores* (masses), increasingly polarized around the contrast between city and country.

The intervention of public power and the army in favor of the *humiliores* led to social civil war in the middle of the 3rd century. The result was the annihilation of the bourgeoisie and the upper classes of society in favor of military men, bureaucrats, and peasants. A new political formula arose during this last stage of Rome's social evolution (the so-called Dominate): the despotism of her emperors.

The variations which we have observed in the social structure correspond to an equal number of ups and downs in the monopoly of wealth. Thus, the transition from Republic to Principate involved the change from a *feudal capitalism,* developed by the great Republican landholders, to an *urban capitalism,* Hellenic in origin, based on trade, industry, and systematic agriculture (high point of grape and olive cultivation in Spain), which got its start as a result of the decay of the aristocracy's great fortunes. The development of this type of capitalism coincides with the urbanization of the Empire.

Later, the phenomenon of the conversion of the middle-class entrepreneur into a rentier, that is, the immobilizing of wealth through purchase of real estate to the detriment of industry, trade, and even agriculture, resulted in a stagnation of economic life and, in the long run, the degeneration of urban capitalism and the middle class which had supported it.

In the last stage of the Empire (the Dominate) the collapse of urban capitalism, coincident with the constant growth of the State's needs, resulted in deterioration of economic life. State intervention in the organization of commerce and industry, and the terrible tax pressure on the urban middle class, decreased the circulation of money, weakened the spirit of enterprise, and brought the economy back to its original agricultural level: great tracts of land (*lati-*

fundia) were tilled by peasants tied to the glebe (*coloni* and serfs). Thus the last phase in the evolution of wealth came to pass in Rome, *state capitalism,* weighing heavily on the lower classes who had become the only producers.

DEMOGRAPHIC DEVELOPMENT. The population of the Graeco-Roman world, including Spain, has been studied by Julius Beloch. He uses the yardsticks of production and price of cereal grains, and the military contingents of various countries. This method has been severely criticized, but Beloch's work is in fact the only way in which we can approach the demography of antiquity with any degree of precision.

Insofar as Roman Spain is concerned, the only figures we possess are those which refer to the three northwestern districts of the province of Tarraconensis. According to Pliny, who was in Spain as a *procurator* about the middle of the 1st century, the *Conventus Asturianus* (Asturias and León) had 240,000 freemen; *Lucus Augusti* (Lugo), 166,000; and *Bracara* (Braga), 285,000. This totals 691,000 persons, not counting slaves, for an area of 85,000 sq. km.; that is, a density of eight persons per sq. km. in the most inhospitable part of the Hispanic province.

Beloch believes that this same density would be applicable to the interior of Tarraconensis and Lusitania, less densely populated than the rest of the territory, as is attested by the extraordinary cheapness of food (in Lusitania, prices were one-fourth as high as in the more populated regions) and the abundance of game. The regions mentioned, with an area of about half a million sq. km., probably had an overall population of some 4 million inhabitants.

The province of Baetica and the Levantine coast, however, were doubtless much more densely populated: a relative density of twenty inhabitants per sq. km. and a total of 2 million persons. Since this zone was more Romanized, it offered better living conditions and had received large groups of Italian immigrants, especially political refugees, during the civil wars in Rome.

To sum up, during the period of Roman domination Hispania probably had some 6 million inhabitants and a population density of ten-twelve persons per sq. km. (cf. Italy, twenty-four; Sicily, twenty-three; Sardinia, fifteen; province of Narbonensis, fifteen; rest of Gaul, six–seven).

DISTRIBUTION AND SETTLEMENT OF POPULATION. We shall begin with the traditional distinction between urban and rural population, keeping in mind that in Roman organization the *vici,* or rural settlements, were considered to be dependencies of the cities within whose *territoria* they were located.

Since the *municipium* was the unit of administrative organization set up by Rome, we should not be surprised to see the proportion between urban and rural centers which appears in the following table, referring to the time of Augustus:

	Tarraconensis	Lusitania	Baetica	Total
Rural centers	114	35	?	149 + ?
Urban centers	181	46	175	402

On the other hand, politico-administrative groupings of an urban nature took many forms. An essential difference separated the demographic entities organized in the Roman mold from the foreign or indigenous ones. The proportions of the two kept changing in favor of the former as the country became more Romanized, as can be observed in the following table:

THE CITIES OF HISPANIA

	Time of Augustus			Time of concession of *ius latii*		
		Foreign				
	T.	L.	B.	T.	L.	B.
Free	—	—	6	—	—	—
Federated	—	—	3	—	—	—
Tributary	—	—	129	—	—	—
Totals	138 + 38 + 129 = 305			—	– + 100 = 100	
		Roman				
Colonies	12	5	9	—	5	10
Roman municipia	13	—	10	—	1	—
Latin municipia	18	3	27	—	3	41-54
Totals	43 + 8 + 46 = 97			50 – 55 + 9 + 51 – 64 = 110-128		

T. = Tarraconensis   L. = Lusitania   B. = Baetica

Excavations now in progress are giving us an idea of the real importance of the Hispano-Roman cities. The perimeter of their walls gives a clue to their area in each case. By using this measurement we know that Mérida, with 49 hectares, had the largest population. Tarragona had some 36 hectares, and at the time of its greatest splendor, around the 2nd century, probably had only about 30,000 inhabitants (slightly fewer than today, when it has become a small provincial capital). Among lesser cities Osma measured 28 hectares; Termantia, 17; Calahorra, 16; Barcelona, 12; and Gerona, 6. Clunia (130) and Saragossa (55) were exceptional in exceeding fifty hectares, but these cases were due to fairly sparse construction inside the city walls.

AGRICULTURE. The Romans were a farming people. Agriculture occupied most of the labor force and furnished Rome with the largest part of her resources.

The peculiar features of the Hispanic Peninsula fitted in wonderfully well with this agrarian orientation of the Roman economy. Thus, both the State and private Roman citizens began very early to invest their capital in agrarian exploitation of the conquered country. A considerable benefit arose from this interest: the introduction of Roman techniques of cultivation, at that time the most advanced ones; specifically, the system of fallowing in a three-year cycle, use of fertilizers, extension of the use of plows and the perfecting of a varied number of implements, such as harrows, long-handled hoes, mattocks, spades, and pickaxes. In reference to this, Caro Baroja has been able to identify the threshing procedures used in different areas at the end of the Imperial period: in the south the thresher with a wheel or roller; in part of the same zone and in the center of the country, the thresher composed of beams and flints; in the rainy lands of the north and west the flail, after the end of the 4th century. Threshing was also done with draft animals who trod the grain by moving in circles.

Agricultural prosperity coincided, in particular, with the early period of what we have called urban capitalism, in which the middle class turned to systematic cultivation of the countryside; Hispania, which had been thought of simply as a cereal-producing province, became acquainted with large-scale cultivation of the grape and the olive. Hispania's olive oil, more expensive than the African variety but much finer in quality, immediately began to be exported in large quantities, while Spanish wine, together with that of other provinces, flooded the Italian market.

By a process of natural evolution, the countries which had been the chief consumers of southern Italian wines—Spain, Gaul, and Africa—became producers in their turn. The same thing happened in the eastern countries of the Empire. This fact carried a double risk: the virtual ruin of Italian viticulture and the possibility of a wheat shortage.

Realizing this danger, the emperors adopted various measures, of which the most famous was that of Domitian (81–96 A.D.), prohibiting the planting of new vineyards in Italy and the provinces besides decreeing the uprooting of half the existing ones. To what extent was this order carried out? In the specific case of Spain, it appears that Baetica was able to keep its grapevines, while the northern part of the country was obliged to submit to the restriction. At least this is what is usually deduced from Probus' counterorder, laid down 200 years later, again permitting the cultivation of vineyards in the provinces of the Danube, Gaul, and Hispania.

The production of Italian olive oil, however, did not receive the benefit of such protection. On the contrary, Spain and Africa enjoyed entire liberty to extend their olive cultivation, and came to be the main oil-producing countries of the Empire. As testimony of Hispanic supremacy in this area we have the majority of the *amphorae* found at *Monte Testaccio,* just outside Rome. Since some of these amphorae carry the mark of the exporters, we know even the names of some of the great Hispanic families who engaged in the olive oil trade; for example, those of *Aelius Optatus* and the *Caecili,* established in Ecija (Astigi) in the heart of Baetica in the middle of the 2nd century, a period of extreme prosperity for the region. The mark of the Aelius Optatus family, still frequent on amphorae of the early 3rd century, has also been found at Autun, far inside Gaul, thus proving the wide circulation of Andalusian oil.

Besides cereals, wine, and olive oil, three plants used in industry should also be singled out from the agricultural production of Roman Spain: flax, esparto grass, and cotton, this last probably introduced by the Phoenicians or Carthaginians. Flax and esparto in particular nourished a considerable textile industry which extended outside the province.

SYSTEM OF EXPLOITATION OF LAND: LATIFUNDISM AND COLO-
NATUS. Land could be held either by private individuals or by
groups. The two systems were commonly combined. Each proprietor had the use of his private lot of land and in addition some
rights of use which he shared with his neighbors, generally in regard
to grazing grounds and forests (*compascua*).

The proprietor could cultivate his land himself or rent it out to
one or more tenant farmers. Whether one or the other system was
used depended on the size of the holding. In the case of a small
piece of property, its utilization was the task of the owner himself,
with his family and slaves, and its center was the farmstead or isolated grange in the country, the *villa,* which became the widespread
type of habitation in Roman Spain. We should point out that later
on this system gave rise to more important kinds of settlement,
which have persisted to the present day. Thus, in the hinterland of
Ampurias, that is, in the present-day Ampurian district, there are at
least fifty localities in which either the prefix or the suffix of the
name is *villa.*

Latifundism is a topic of great importance. In Spain the existence
of large landholdings or latifundia arose from the very fact of the
conquest, which facilitated the extension of the State's *ager publicus.*
Once in possession of these great tracts of land, the State turned
them over in usufruct for exploitation by a beneficiary in exchange
for the payment of a land tax (the *ager vectigalis*), which soon
ceased to be paid. Thus mere use, if prolonged over a certain period
of time, could lead to the conversion of a public estate into a private
latifundium. In other cases the latifundium might have been private
from the beginning, perhaps because Roman capitalists had taken
the place of the old manorial owners, perhaps simply because of the
application of the *ius occupandi,* without previous concession by the
State.

In any case, in the course of time the latifundium brought about
the failure of small properties which, unable to compete with it,
were simply absorbed. In some instances this produced a new type of
latifundium characterized by the consolidation of scattered small
properties.

This phenomenon of concentration of agrarian property did not,
however, imply single-handed exploitation of the latifundium. The
proprietor kept only part for himself and rented out the rest. The

65

renters had full liberty to carry out utilization of the land in any manner they wished, and often did not even live on the rented property but on their own—this in the case of small proprietors —or in neighboring *vici.* However, the rental contracts which linked the farmer to the proprietor gradually became permanent, at first as a privilege favoring the renter, later as an obligation which could not be escaped. In this way adscription to the glebe, or *colonatus,* became established, at the same period when the artisans and tradesmen in the cities were also losing their freedom and being restricted to guilds. In the country this restriction was greatly strengthened by Diocletian's tax reforms (end of the 3rd century), which turned over to the proprietors of latifundia the collecting of taxes owed by their own tenants, or *coloni,* and later by an Imperial statute of the 4th century which, in order to avoid difficulties in tax collection arising from changes of domicile, explicitly prescribed binding farmers to their land.

The *coloni* received lands which they could cultivate on their own in any form they wished, in exchange for a tax and for helping the proprietor to work the piece of land he had reserved for himself. Later, in the latifundia located outside the city districts, or even inside them when decay of municipal organization had set in, an even tighter link was produced than the merely territorial one represented by the *colonatus:* the practice of *commendatio* (service in exchange for protection), which also involved a personal relationship between proprietors and *coloni.* This practice continued to grow in the measure in which the poor farmer felt himself less and less protected by the public power. *Colonatus* and *commendatio* are two Roman institutions of great interest in connection with the later, feudal world.

LIVESTOCK AND FISHING. The Romans introduced few novelties into these branches of the Hispanic economy. Wealth in livestock was no different, in fact, from former times. However, as an indication that the conquerors were not wholly indifferent to improvement in animal husbandry, we can cite a reference made by Strabo to some crossbreeding of sheep done by an uncle of Columella who lived in Cádiz.

Sheep, horses, and pigs stand out in importance. Sheep in Baetica produced a reddish-golden wool of high quality, while those of the Meseta gave a blackish wool of inferior grade. Spanish horses were valued for their swiftness; hence their fame within the Roman army. A famous ham industry arose in the Pyrenees region, where there were many pigs. The abundance of wild animals in Cantabria also deserves mention, and there are numerous references to different regions' wealth in oxen and cows, a survival from pre-Roman times.

Fishing shows a few more new procedures in Roman Spain. Fish abounded along her coasts and in her rivers, and were the object of active commerce. On the Atlantic side the oysters of the Duero and the Tagus were famous, while on the coast of the Levant salted fish were processed and marketed, especially in Cartagena (where an inscription recalls the existence of a fishermen's guild).

In the south, even more favorable conditions existed. The fishermen of Cádiz risked long voyages along the west coast of Africa and even on the open sea, while those of other cities such as Málaga, Mellaría, and Bailon fished in nearby waters for the oysters, lampreys, eels, and tunny in which, Strabo says, the waters of Baetica were so rich. In Belo, pits and receptacles have been found which were used for preparing *garon,* a fish sauce much appreciated in the ancient world. To sum up, then, Spain was the rival of Pontus (Black Sea region) in supplying Rome with seafood.

MINING. Rome's mining policy relied much more on the exploitation of provincial deposits than on Italian ones. To the scarcity of mining resources in the home country was added a desire to avoid the disadvantages of large-scale exploitation there: on the one hand, the danger of large concentrations of slaves was feared, and on the other the lack of manpower for agriculture if freemen were used instead of slaves.

Within this framework, then, the wealth of Hispania played a very important role. Mining assumed such importance in the picture of Hispano-Roman relationships that some authors have held that this wealth was the only purpose of the conquest. However, no technological improvements went along with the intensive exploitation of Spanish mineral lodes. Romanization, insofar as the metal industry was concerned, did not result in lowering of costs, but only in the intensity and extent of exploitation.

The fortunate discovery of an inscription with the text of the *Lex*

Metalli Vispacensis, setting forth the organization of the mining district of Vipasca (Aljustrel, in Portugal), has given us a fairly exact knowledge of the mining system in Hispania and, by extension, in the whole Empire.

In no case did Rome exercise a monopoly over the exploitation of mines. What did happen was that the State, because it was the principal holder of land, was also the chief proprietor of mines. Once in possession of them, it began to lease them to private individuals who together formed powerful companies (*publicani*), which exploited them by the use of slaves. Gradually a progressive tendency began to appear everywhere—in Spain, during Flavian times (end of the 1st century)—to exclude these companies of concessionaires and to concentrate the exploitation of the mines in the hands of government employees (*procuratores*) who could carry this out by a system of subleasing. This system was the one followed in the Vipasca district: the State and the concessionaires made an equal division of the product taken from the mine. Finally, when the excessive taxes imposed on them produced too few *metallarii,* or leaseholders, there was a change to direct exploitation by the State, using slaves or personal service by individuals who were theoretically freemen.

There were also mines which were private property, exploited by their owners or leased to others. The State respected these, except in a few cases of confiscation, as in the case of the mines at Almadén. But this measure was not employed in any widespread way.

The Vipasca law also reveals the placing of the mining district outside normal administrative organization. The procurator of Vipasca was in charge not only of the apportionment of pits and lodes and of overseeing the work, but also exercised effective control over all public services in the district: markets, schools, baths, etc. The importance of the mining districts within the Roman economic system no doubt explains this exceptional jurisdiction.

As for Hispania's wealth in metals, we have many references to it but no quantitative data. *Gold* was extracted from the lodes of Baetica (north of Cordova), Lusitania, and especially Asturias; it was also produced from the Tagus, Duero, Betis, and Tader rivers, the last-named near Cartagena. The principal deposits of *silver* under exploitation were found in the *Saltus Castulonensis,* or Sierra

Morena, which separated the Citerior province from the Ulterior; there were also deposits in the Ebro valley, Cantabria, and Celtiberia. Silver exports to Rome were heavy. The *iron* mines of the Moncayo region gave rise to the famous metallurgical industry of Bilbilis (Calatayud) and Turiaso (Tarazona). Toledo was also the seat of an important iron industry. Other mines in various parts of the country are also mentioned, especially on the Cantabrian coast, where Pliny places "a craggy mountain, a marvelous thing, all made of iron," probably referring to Somorrostro.

Ríotinto was already in Roman times the chief *copper* mine, a metal which was also produced in Vipasca, while *lead* was extracted especially in the Cartagena region (40,000 miners, according to Polybius) and in Sierra Morena. Finally, the *mercuric sulfide* and *mercury* of Sisapo (Almadén) complete the list of Hispano-Roman mining activity. We need only add salt from the salt deposits of Cardona and Egelaste (in the Carthaginian *conventus*), center of a very prosperous salting industry.

Though all sources are unanimous in stressing the importance of Spanish mining during this period, we lack precise data which would enable us to evaluate its production. We can only cite the estimates made by a group of British engineers in the Ríotinto mines of the copper ore processed by the Romans: to judge from the 20 million tons of slag found there, the quantity of ore extracted in the course of five centuries of Roman domination can probably be set at about 60 million tons.

INDUSTRY AND INDUSTRIAL LABOR. Development of industry in Roman Spain was the result of a general process of economic decentralization undergone by the Empire. When the Western countries, whose economic level was much lower than that of Rome, became absorbed, Italian industry had to assume a different character: people in the provinces were not interested in luxury or high-priced articles; the rural mass of population, with minimal buying power, needed cheap goods which could be mass-produced. And there was also a problem of transportation. No matter how low the prices of Italian industrial products were, they cost more in the provinces because of the transport factor. These circumstances explain the process of industrial decentralization; that is, development of industry in provincial centers to the detriment of production in the mother country. Industry became consolidated in Spain by the 2nd century, when extension of the highway network was added to pacification of the country. In any case, however, the industry of Hispania was never able to compete with that of neighboring Gaul.

It was essentially a local industry, located in the main population centers, and its primary purpose was to supply the most pressing needs of those centers and the districts surrounding them. It would be useless to enumerate these industries, therefore, for there were as many industries as there were necessities to be satisfied in Hispano-Roman life. Only a small number expanded beyond the local and provincial ambit and enjoyed export status. Such industries were a complement to natural production. Thus the enormous success of the olive tree gave rise to the oil industry. Something similar occurred with the weapons of Bilbilis, the cord and rope manufactured out of the esparto grass of the Levant, the salting of pork and fish located respectively in the Pyrenees and in various coastal spots, and, on a lesser scale, with the linen cloth of Saetabis and the woollens of Baetica.

As for industrial organization, the greatest change which took place was the transition from a system of free organization of the artisan classes to one of binding a worker to a trade. Here we are dealing with a phenomenon similar to the adscription of the farm worker to the glebe. When labor was still developing along liberal lines, the *collegia* of artisans arose as free associations of a beneficent and religious nature: inscriptions give us a good deal of information about these bodies in Spain, such as the guilds of the masons (*collegia fabrum*) in Tarragona and Barcelona, those of the bronze-workers in Itálica, of carpenters in Cordova, fishermen in Cartagena, Syrian merchants in Málaga, and so on. During the later Empire these "colleges" became an instrument of State control and of restriction to a trade imposed by public decree. This happened at the very time when the Roman State, exhausted and without resources, began to demand forced labor. Thus the only solution was to prevent the artisan from freely changing his trade in order to find another more to his liking, or simply emigrating to the country. And so the artisan and his descendants became bound to the corresponding "college," with no possibility of leaving it.

7 · The Economy of Roman Spain (II)

TRADE: OBJECTS, VOLUME, AND ROUTES OF HISPANO-ROMAN TRADE. In the countries which composed the Roman Empire, its consolidation meant a great commercial development favored by peace, by development of communications, and by the practice of a liberal economic policy. After Augustus, the State in fact adopted a hands-off attitude in regard to mercantile competition, letting economic life evolve freely. During this phase the only restrictive measures were some very moderate customs duties, imposed on traffic among the provinces, and a few mild taxes. This policy of almost total commercial freedom is in contrast to the state of affairs which had prevailed in Egypt and the Hellenistic world.

There were four chief currents of Roman trade. First was the one linking the countries on either side of the *limes* (frontier), making possible an interchange of products between Romanized and barbarian countries—manufactured goods in exchange for raw materials. In Hispania this current is identified with the famous tin route dating back to prehistoric times, which had brought the precious ore from Cornwall and Brittany into the Mediterranean through Gades. The tin route had made Gades one of the great cities of the Roman Empire in the Republican period: the third in number of *equites* (knights), according to Strabo. But later the consolidation of Roman rule in Gaul and the consequent detour of the tin route by way of Bordeaux and Narbonne marked the decline of the Baetic city. During the Empire, Spain's only relations with countries outside the frontier were with the Eastern nations. From the East came precious stones and spices, while Spanish lead and tin were shipped as far away as India. It is known that a pearl merchant had an establishment in Mérida, and that in Málaga there was an important Syrian colony.

The second current of Roman trade linked the various provincial territories. In the case of Hispania, we have evidence only of a considerable interchange with neighboring Gaul. We have already mentioned proof of the existence of Andalusian olive oil in Autun (vicinity of Lyons). There is also evidence that olive oil was exported to Germany. To this may be added the fact that there were Spanish colonies engaged in the importation of food products in Bordeaux, Nîmes (a colony of settlers from Calagurris, modern Calahorra), and Narbonne. Gaul, a more industrialized country, reciprocated by sending ceramic objects in particular. Thus in southern regions the oil lamps were imported from the great factory at Iol Caesarea (Cherchel).

Third, we should mention mercantile relations with Italy. The volume of this trade changed in proportion to the Romanization of the country. In fact, imports from Italy decreased as the process of urbanization begun by Caesar and Pompey led in Spain—as in Africa and Gaul—to the rise of a capitalistic economy similar to that of Italy and the East. On the one hand was scientific agriculture, which encouraged cultivation of the vine and the olive, to the detriment of the export possibilities of Campania (the ruins of the port of Puteoli clearly show this phenomenon); on the other was the industrialization of the province, which worked against Italian manufactured goods, of too high a grade for the modest provincial consumers, and which were further burdened by the weight of long and costly shipping.

This awakening of the provinces to economic life explains the fourth great current of Hispano-Roman trade, interior commerce, which linked the different points within Hispania. It began to develop in the 2nd century when industrialization of certain cities, and especially extension of the highway network, offered both products and a means of exchanging them.

Now that we have indicated the principal currents of Hispano-Roman trade, we need only point out the special importance of the exportation of minerals and food products—wheat, wine, olive oil—from Spain to Rome. The Imperial *annona,* or official supply service of the Roman people, was the foremost client of Spanish agricultural production. The emperors' obsessive preoccupation with keeping Rome's lower classes satisfied explains this virtual monopoly, as well as the State's growing intervention in the regulation of transport and all activities related to it.

ROADS AND TRANSPORT. Before the Roman period the only means of large-scale transport had been by sea or river. Although this type of traffic was notably improved—for example, by systematic construction, begun in the 1st century, of lighthouses to guide navigation, as represented by the magnificent Tower of Hercules in Corunna—credit is especially due to the Romans for having constructed an extraordinary network of highways linking all the important points in the Empire.

Rome was the center of the network, and roads branched out from there in all directions. The link with Spain was assured by the famous Via Augusta, constructed in part on the old Via Hercules of the Carthaginians. It ran along the coast except in a very few stretches and led from Rome to Gades. Other secondary roads, of a military nature, branched off this main road into the interior of Hispania. Augustus himself, who as its name indicates was responsible for the great coastal route, ordered the construction of the road which led to Saragossa from Tarragona, by way of Lérida and Huesca. From Saragossa the road was prolonged by Domitian as far as Olisipo (Lisbon), passing through Toledo and Mérida. This latter city was the point of departure for the "silver route" which passed through Salamanca and went to Zamora. Here it met the road which, starting from Saragossa, followed the course of the Ebro and then went into the regions of Burgos, Palencia, and Valladolid. Astorga, terminal point of the "silver route," was an important highway junction, where the highways to Lusitania and the Cantabrian coast crossed (Santander, Corunna, Padrón and Braga branches), and also joined the great trans-Pyrenean route which led to Bordeaux through Logroño, Pamplona, and Roncesvalles; it later became the famous medieval road to Compostela. In the south, Mérida was linked to Gades by the Hispalis (Seville) road; in Seville the Hispalis road joined the branch of the Via Augusta which started in Guadix and which, instead of turning toward the coast, went inland through Cordova, Ecija, and Carmona.

This was the essential layout of the Hispano-Roman roads. Of course many other, lesser ones also existed—what we might call the network of local roads—and taken together they made up a total of some 13,000 miles, or 20,000 kilometers.

Transport was carried out along these roads in carts. These carts were of two types, light and heavy, and their loads varied, respec-

HISPANIA IN THE LATE ROMAN EMPIRE.

tively, between 200 and 600 pounds and 1,000 and 1,200 pounds. That is, a Roman cart could carry only about a fifth as much as a modern cart. This difference is important because it explains the large number of teamsters, animals, and carts necessary to large-scale transport at that time, and consequently the unfortunate system of requisition and forced labor imposed by the State on this branch of activity; for though the State could not take direct charge of the means of transport, it nevertheless needed to assure their effectiveness. As the Imperial *annona* was the chief customer of Hispanic economy, the State had no recourse but to intervene in the ordering of land transport; and therefore, since the drivers had no defense, in the end they became subject to a system of forced labor.

RIVER AND MARITIME TRANSPORT. Roman Spain, like Gaul, had a superb means of communication in her rivers, which complemented the land routes. Let us recall the most important of these, all on the Atlantic side of the country: the Duero was navigable, even for ships of deep draught, for more than 150 km. from its mouth; the Tagus, with its gold deposits and abundant fish, was navigable for smaller ships; the Betis, or Guadalquivir, was normally navigable as far as Seville and could be used by smaller ships as far as Cordova.

As for sea traffic, Tarraco (Tarragona), Cartagena, and Cádiz monopolized the greater part of commerce with the Roman homeland. Since it was the seat of the Imperial governor, military replacements and official messengers arrived at Tarraco, and this makes it easy to suppose that the city was linked to Rome by a regular service. With favorable weather the trip between the two cities took only four days, while seven were needed to reach Cádiz. But aside from these three large ports there were many others in which active commerce was carried on: Málaga, which had relations with the nomadic tribes of the African coast; the island of Escombreras across from Cartagena with its fisheries; Denia with its iron exports; at the mouth of the Ebro, Tortosa, outlet for the products of an important agricultural region; Corunna, an important mining port (tin), etc.

The same tendency toward State control was also observable in sea transport. Efforts made to control the *navicularii* were particularly noticeable after the time of Alexander Severus. But because of their greater economic potential and their organization into powerful associations—there is evidence of associations of shipowners in Olisipo, among other peninsular cities—the shipowners offered more stubborn resistance to control.

HISPANO-ROMAN MARKETS. So long as the Empire enjoyed indisputable military supremacy and a solid economy based on the military factor, the State was a believer in "laissez-faire" in the economic sphere. The Senate—and later the Emperor—had sole authority to concede the *ius nundinarum* or right to hold markets; it gained some profit from these by means of certain taxes and intervened to guarantee the material security of men and merchandise. This security—what in medieval times came to be called "the peace of the market"—found its authorization in a supervisory system headed by the *aedile*. This special peace of the market protected merchants not only in the marketplace itself, but during their travels to and from it.

Markets were held inside the cities every nine days (*nundinae*), generally in the Forum itself, seat of judicial sessions, and at an early stage were merely an instrument to facilitate mercantile exchange. But later, with the transition from a free economy to a system of controlled economy, the market gradually gained importance until it ceased to be a simple commercial instrument and became the only place where business could be done. Finally, a decree of Valentinian III, promulgated in 444 or 445, shortly before the Visigoths became independent of the Empire, put the seal of approval on this process by establishing the obligation not to sell outside the marketplace. In parallel fashion, the initial taxes which the State had originally laid on the holding of markets—the *portoria,* customs duties on circulation of merchandise, which gave rise to the medieval *telonea*—were increased by others that were much more onerous. Among these the most important was the *siliquantium,* imposed beginning with the reigns of Theodosius and Valentinian and consisting of a twentieth of the price of sales, and which was levied on both buyer and seller.

COINAGE. Roman supremacy put an end to the monetary chaos of the Greek world. After Rome the prevailing tendency was one of monetary unity, to the detriment of the minting of local currency.

The Roman *denarius*—a silver coin—which was already international currency throughout the known world by the time of the Republic, was officially converted by Augustus into the basis of all accounts and public budgets. Continuing in this same direction, by the beginning of the 2nd century the Roman State alone had the right to mint silver and gold, save for a very few exceptions made in favor of exceptional cities (Alexandria and Antioch, among others). During the early Empire a gold piece, the *aureus,* was minted, and an attempt was made to establish a constant relationship between it and the silver coin; but this could not be done, for the loss of Dacia and the mines of Transylvania which occurred at the end of the 2nd century resulted in a dearth of gold. The *aureus* became an unstable coin, accepted only by weight.

In Spain the old Greek mintings of Ampurias and Rodhae disappeared at the beginning of the conquest, and the Roman monetary system was accepted; in Tarragona first, later in Huesca and then in many other cities, coins identical to those of Rome were minted. At the time of the Republic coins of Iberian types, though adapted to the new system, still survived side by side with those which had been copied from the coins of metropolitan Rome. These are the Ibero-Roman coins. But during the Empire Nero decreed the suppression of these local mintings. This measure was effective in regard to coins of higher value (those of gold and silver), but Rome continued to tolerate the minting of fractional copper coins in the western provinces. In spite of this, there continued to be a scarcity of small coins, and the use of tokens and scrip, tendered by merchants, bankers, and the like, was widespread.

As the State continued to use up its private capital (this process was speeded by the defects of its own financial organization, by the rise in expenditures occasioned by maintenance of the army, and by foreign wars), all efforts to restore the public treasury were reduced to the extraction of money in any manner whatever. The system of *liturgiae* became general; this meant that the *humiliores* were forced to work for the State, while the *honestiores* were obliged to pay extraordinary taxes. This system shows us the Roman Empire in the process of regression to a state of natural economy because it had not succeeded in amassing the necessary quantity of stable money.

Caracalla's attempt to restore the coinage by introducing a new type of coin called the *antonianus,* equivalent to two denarii, was another failure. After that time the buying power of Imperial coinage continued to drop: the denarius which in the 1st century was worth 85% of a gold peseta was scarcely worth 25% by the 3rd century.

Prices rose, good money was hoarded, and the denarius diminished in value, very often obliging the State to accept payments in kind. The first efforts to put an end to this chaotic situation belong to the second half of the 3rd century, to Aurelian in fact. Thinking more in terms of a reform in the process of manufacture than in the money itself, the Emperor simply decreed unification of coinage by means of a sweeping suppression of local autonomous mintings, even those of the Senate of Rome. But the malady had deep roots, and when Diocletian was unable to correct it, he put an end to a situation in which real money was threatened with substitution by fiduciary money (accepted only by State recognition) by means of a reform of the coinage itself. Since the gold which had evaporated during the period of military anarchy had now reappeared, coins of this metal could again be minted. This was the origin of the *solidus,* equivalent to one-sixtieth of a pound (5.45 grams). As for silver coinage, he replaced the antonianus by a new denarius, the *silico* (3.41 grams). Finally, Diocletian created a vellon coin, of silver-plated copper, the *denarius communis* or *follis,* the purpose of which was to facilitate small buying and selling transactions. This reform was completed by Constantine, who lowered the weight of the solidus to one seventy-second of the Roman pound, or 4.55 grams. Constantine's solidus survived as a stable monetary unit. However, public favor inclined to give preference to a smaller gold piece, the one-third solidus or *tremis,* minting of which lasted into Visigothic times.

FINANCIAL REGIME AND FISCAL POLICY. Within the Empire, the provinces paid three types of taxes: direct, indirect, and the product of the monopolies.

Starting as far back as 167 B.C., the conquered countries—that is, the provinces—paid only the direct tax, symbol of conquest and submission. This tax was levied on the soil, not on the person of the proprietor. At first the federated and free cities were exempt from this, but other foreign cities, known as *stipendiariae* or tributary cities, had to pay it. This land tax could take two forms—the *decuma,* or tithe on agricultural sales; and the *stipendium* or *tributum,* which was levied by apportionment. After Caesar's time the tithe disappeared and the *stipendium* became universal.

On the other hand, we must point out that the tax on properties, though it was the chief one, was not the only type of direct tax imposed on the provinces, for it was supplemented by two others, one which affected individuals—the *tributum capitis* or poll tax—and another levied on sales in commerce and industry.

The main indirect tax was customs. The Empire was divided into great customs districts. Spain was included with the provinces of Narbonensis, Sicily, and Africa—not including Mauretania—in the so-called *Quattuor publica Africae.* Merchandise transported across the borders of this district was subject to a payment equal to 2% of its value. Customs duties were, therefore, moderate.

Finally, the provinces as well as Italy paid taxes on state domains and monopolies. This provincial public domain included numerous elements: cultivated lands, pastures, forests, salt marshes, and, concretely in Spain, silver and lead mines.

But besides these regular taxes, the system of *liturgiae,* or extraordinary taxes, became prevalent as the financial situation grew worse. These were demanded of wealthy citizens in order to take care of the most urgent necessities: feeding the people in times of famine, forced loans, aid in constructing ships or equipping soldiers, feasts and commemorations, etc.

Little by little these *munera,* or *liturgiae,* became inherent in the *honores* (public offices) until they were regular obligations. It was a heavy burden, though it was tolerated by the wealthy classes so long as it did not become excessive. But this came to pass by the 1st century. In Spain, when the process of urbanization reached the poorer regions of the country, it was necessary to adopt the severest measures to assure the necessary number of citizens willing to serve as officials. Nobody wanted the *honores,* for to accept meant paying the *munera* which went with them.

As time went on, the participation required of the cities in the empire's financial reorganization aggravated the situation still more. The Republican system which had consisted in farming out direct taxes—both the land and the poll tax—to private persons (*publicani*) was abandoned, making the responsibility for collecting them fall back on the magistrates and senates of the cities. So long as the taxes were moderate the new procedure worked satisfactorily, and the cities accepted the responsibility because it meant that they could free themselves from the abuses of the *publicani,* who often banded together into powerful companies.

The onerous task of the municipal authorities and the capitalists (there was a close bond between these two groups, the same bond which linked the *munera* to the *honores*) was then extended to other sectors of society. Vespasian, faced with the demands of the companies to whom collection of indirect taxes was farmed out, supplanted them by rich persons (*conductores*) who were responsible for the total collection of some particular tax. The drawbacks of such an occupation explain the growing difficulty in finding *conductores* by any means other than coercion. The end result was that collection of taxes came to be thought of as a *munus,* according to which the rich taxpayer was responsible for the poor one. This system spread until it became general after the 3rd century. The magistrates and senates of the cities ceased to be jointly responsible for collecting taxes, and this responsibility was transferred to wealthy persons (the *decemprimi,* or "first ten" citizens in each town) who were obliged to pay delinquent taxes or face confiscation of their private properties.

The transition from collective responsibility to individual responsibility—begun in the 2nd century—produced dire results. Chief among these was a material as well as moral decline among the most active elements of the citizenry, which had evident consequences in the decline of the cities.

CRISIS OF THE 3RD CENTURY AND TRANSFORMATIONS IN ECONOMIC AND SOCIAL MENTALITY DURING THE DOMINATE. Social antagonism between the bourgeoisie and the proletarian classes—former allies against the Republican aristocracy—grew more and more acute until it resulted in the crisis of the 3rd century. The lower classes emerged victorious from this crisis owing to the fact that the army, made up essentially of poor farmers, eventually set itself up as the representative of their interests. The internecine struggles aroused by this social revolution gravely compromised the stability of the Empire and, therefore, the development of economic life, which had been slowly declining since the 2nd century. Taking advantage of the civil wars, Germanic tribes broke through to the Mediterranean for the first time, leaving destruction and terror in their wake. The period of military anarchy which began with the capture of the emperor Valerian by the Persians (259–260) was particularly influenced by this fact. While the process of secession of the western from the eastern provinces was already under way, bands of Germanic warriors were crossing Gaul and arriving in Hispania. Recent studies permit us to date the irruption of the Franks and Germans at about the year 262; the invaders destroyed Tarragona, devastated the Levant, and, after sacking Baetica, crossed the Strait of Gibraltar. A second invasion, which took place about 275, carried the devastation to the interior of the Meseta. The German successes seriously compromised the economy of the Western Mediterranean. It is significant that the last dated proof we have of the Spanish olive oil trade in Rome is from the year 257.

The result of this double social and economic process was the destruction of the bourgeoisie and economic ruin. Labor was disorganized and production began to decline. The progressive waning of markets and the buying power of the people were the prelude to industrial decay. For its part, agriculture was caught in a terrible dilemma, for the ruin of trade and industry deprived it of necessary capital, and the exigencies of the State took away a major part of its produce as well as a labor force it could not do without. There was a dizzying rise in prices and a simultaneous drop in the value of money. In this situation, further aggravated by a corresponding rise in the needs of public power, relations between the State and the taxpayers took the form of organized plunder: forced labor, seizure of supplies, compulsory levies, etc. These new procedures, born of economic decadence, could lead only to greater decay.

Lacking any stimulus and confused in all its manifestations, the economic activity of the Dominate became limited to a few elementary forms which served only to supply the most pressing needs. Oppressive taxes led to the enslavement of farmers, artisans, and merchants, by means of their forced adscription to glebes or guilds. Thus the class which might have been able to exercise a guiding function, the bourgeoisie, was eliminated.

The bourgeoisie of the early centuries of the Empire had been the soul of business and of economic enterprise. The bourgeoisie of the later period, however, was a class whose only desire was to invest the income of previous efforts in some rural property which would furnish a refuge for a quiet life. With their traditional ambitions to create fortunes destroyed by the tax system, the bourgeoisie of the 3rd and 4th centuries sought only to retire from active life and to take refuge in the security of some small agricultural income which would permit them to spend their lives unnoticed and untroubled.

This decline in the bourgeois class, its destruction as such, was decisive. In fact, deprived of their most active element, the people of the Dominate gave themselves over to resignation. Though the spread of the Christian religion may have had something to do with it, we must point out that this new attitude was inevitable because of the very fact that any independent effort was doomed to failure in advance, since the more an individual produced, the more the State took away from him.

The farmer knew that if he managed to improve and enlarge his holdings he would be promoted to *curialis*—that is, to the position of a person likely to be named a municipal councilor or magistrate—which simply meant financial oppression. Faced with this example, the *colonus* or tenant farmer had no incentive to better his fortunes and become a free farmer. The same situation obtained in all branches of the economy. The only rebellion possible against the situation we have just described was to take refuge in banditry or in the army; and certainly these were not satisfactory solutions.

The lesser evil, adopted by the majority, consisted in abandonment of the city for the country, where in hard times it had always been easier to get along. Thus there was a recovery of the rural element at the expense of the urban one; and in the provinces this represented the indigenous peoples' retaliation to the Romanizing process which had stemmed from the cities.

8 · The Economy of Visigothic Hispania

VISIGOTHIC INTRUSION INTO HISPANO-ROMAN SOCIETY: SOCIAL AND ECONOMIC REPERCUSSIONS. A few years ago it was believed that the invasion of the Visigoths had signaled the start of the Middle Ages in Spain. This opinion was in line with the general thesis that the Germanic invasions had renewed the decadent Mediterranean world by bringing in new blood and new ideas. Today, research of all kinds and archaeological research in particular have demonstrated that we must take an entirely different view of the matter.

Seen from any angle, the Visigoths in Spain were only an appendage of the Roman Empire; therefore, instead of speaking of Visigothic invasions and a Visigothic state, we prefer to allude to the Visigothic intrusion, a wedge introduced by peoples of Germanic origin into the living tissue of Hispano-Roman society. Naturally this wedge caused social and economic repercussions, though they were not so great as once was believed. Thus, from the social point of view, the most important thing we should attribute to the Visigoths was the contribution of a cycle of relationships between man and man which overturned the political and social principles of the classical world and which later, on the collapse of the Mediterranean economy, came to fruition in so-called feudalism. In the same way, in the matter of economic repercussions, the Visigoths merely accentuated the tendency toward ruralization in the Peninsula which had begun in the 3rd century, as we have just seen, with the Frankish invasion.

POPULATION. The most important information we need in order to understand the precise influence of the Visigoths on Spain's economy is undoubtedly that of population.

Until very recently it was believed that the barbarians had been very numerous and that they had occupied all the territory of the

Peninsula. But since the investigations of certain scholars, notably Rheinhardt, we know that the number of German invaders in the Peninsula was very small and that they occupied an inconsiderable portion of it. Once the 80,000 Vandals under Genseric had crossed over to Africa, some 200,000 Visigoths and 100,000 Suevi (isolated in Galicia and northern Portugal) remained in Spain; they were a very small percentage compared to the 6 million Hispano-Roman inhabitants at the time of the invasion.

In contradiction to the theory of those who believed that the Visigoths settled everywhere in the Peninsula, it is known today, thanks to the research of the scholar mentioned above, that in the 4th century, the period of greatest Visigothic immigration into the Peninsula, they occupied only one region, the one whose central nucleus is the present-day province of Segovia, surrounded by those of Burgos, Soria, Guadalajara, Madrid, Toledo, Valladolid, and Palencia. In this region, all of which falls within Old Castile and represents only about 10% of the peninsular territory, the new emigrants received land to live on, in accordance with the laws then existing. This does not mean that there were not Visigoths in other places on Spanish soil. These were mainly the nobles, and the officials and warriors who lived either in the provinces or at the royal court.

The ruling Visigothic class was called *Goti* in the texts and was carefully distinguished from the old inhabitants, who were called *Romani*. Ethnic circumstances, reinforced by political, social, and juridical causes, made this distinction very clear in the 5th and 6th centuries. Things changed after that time. The most accepted theory is that there was a slow mingling of Goths and Hispano-Romans after the end of the 6th century. The probable stages in this process were: the authorization for mixed marriages given by Leovigild; the conversion to Catholicism, which took place during the reign of Reccared; unification of the law code in the middle of the 7th century with the promulgation of the Code of Recceswinth, or *Liber Iudiciorum*. This process can also be noted in the texts, for the use of the word "Hispani," or Spaniards, becomes more and more frequent and is symbolic of the unity between the Goths and the former Romans.

This theory, though, is not in agreement with the number of Visigoths who settled in the Peninsula, nor with the actual facts observable in the evolution of Hispano-Roman society. On the other hand, it is quite possible to understand the historical evolution of Visigothic society by keeping in mind the following double phenomenon: first, conquest of the State by the Hispano-Roman upper class, accomplished through the Church; and second, assimilation of races exclusively at the top of the system—that is, among the land-owning aristocracy, both Gothic and Roman. This process was well advanced but not complete at the time of the Moslem invasion.

In consequence we will have to believe that the Gothic minority continued to form, throughout the period we are studying, a group apart from the authentic Hispano-Roman society—that is, a military state upon a former structure which was strongly autochthonous. Only by keeping this fact in mind can we explain how readily disaster befell the Visigothic state in 711, when the Moslem invasion took place.

Beside this Gothic minority and the enormous mass of Hispano-Roman population, other important racial groups also existed. In first place among these were the *Jews,* who formed a vigorous commercial caste in the principal cities of the Levant and South of the Peninsula and who firmly resisted any fusion, even in spite of the threats with which the Visigothic state tried to exclude them from society in the 7th century. We should also mention the *Frankish* element, which had become established in Galicia beginning in the second half of the 6th century, and in witness to which we have some fifty place names (Francos, Franco, Francelos, Francia, Franza, and those which bear the Latinized Germanic suffix *-ingus*), most of them in the Miño valley. Bröens, who was the first to study the Frankish colonization in Galicia, related it to pacts between the successors of Clovis and the administrators of the old Gallo-Roman *civitates,* which tended to limit immigration of the Germanic element into those places. The same author attributes to this ethnic group the introduction of purebred Aquitanian cattle, which predominate in the Portuguese region between the Duero and the Tagus and nowhere else. Lastly, the *African* merchants who settled in the cities of the southern littoral are worthy of mention, as are the *Byzantines,* who formed an important group in Andalusia and along the Mediterranean coast as far as Cartagena. Though they were expelled by Swinthila, the Byzantines persisted in the country and undoubtedly became mixed with other indigenous elements.

ESTABLISHMENT ON THE LAND AND FORMS OF AGRARIAN EXPLOI-TATION. The Visigoths became established in the Peninsula as a result of the system of *foedus* or military agreement reached with the Romans, who, since they had no army to oppose the invasions of the Vandals, Alani, and Suevi, accepted the Visigoths' offer, considered them as auxiliary armies, and gave them lands the better to accomplish this function.

This system, known as *hospitalitas,* was set up in 418, and in spite of the fact that it is mentioned in legal texts, it has not yet been properly interpreted. Some authorities believe that when the Visigoths became established in the country, it was probably only the latifundia which were divided, giving the Goths a third of the lands called *dominicatae,* those cultivated directly by the owner; the Goths received two-thirds of the *indominicatae,* or lands belonging to the landlord but given over to cultivation by *coloni.* This last type of land was called *sortes goticae.* Other authors, however, believe that small landholdings were also divided and that, in general, one-third of the property stayed in the hands of the Roman inhabitants while two-thirds was given over to the Goths. In any case, the unit of distribution was the *fundium,* or parcel of land large enough to maintain one family, while highlands, pastures, and woodlands remained undivided. Some of these passed into the hands of the State, and others remained as lands of common use among those who had previously enjoyed possession of them.

We must, however, keep in mind the evolution of Visigothic settlement in the Peninsula when we try to discover which of the theories is of greater value.

We know that distribution of lands among the Visigoths began about the middle of the 5th century, but it was not widespread until the times of Theodoric II and Euric, and especially not until, after Alaric I, the Goths were expelled from Gaul and had to fall back on the Peninsula. The distribution affected only the provinces in which they had already become established, and since we know that this territory was really very small, we must accept the fact that the previous social and economic structure, especially in regard to agrarian property, continued without great changes.

In general terms, Visigothic distributions of land tended to break down the latifundia which had been formed in the times of the Roman Empire; but this phenomenon did not last long. In reality the latifundia were very soon reconstituted: in the first place because a large number of them passed into the royal patrimony and were increased by successive conquests, confiscations, and usurpations; in the second place because ecclesiastical lands continued to grow through donations, little by little forming extremely large holdings in the old pattern; and finally, they were reconstituted by the kings' donations to the nobles and magnates who had been faithful to them during the constant civil wars which marred the history of the Visigothic monarchy in Spain.

As for the exploitation of land, it did not undergo great changes, at least no changes other than those which had come to be the norm during Roman times. We have ample proof of this, in techniques as well as in organization, from the *Etymologies* of St. Isidore.

In fact the center of agricultural exploitation was the rustic *villa,* where the owner had his residence, called the *curtis* or *atrium.* The owner, however, did not personally take charge of running the villa; rather the lands were exploited by men called *villici, actores,* or *procuratores,* who were the real administrators. The distribution of land to the peasants is very interesting, for beside the old remnants of Roman agrarian organization there are new elements, which correspond to the new concept of relations among owners and workers. Thus, the main groups who cultivated the land on the large estates were the *coloni,* deriving from the old Roman *colonatus* system; the more or less short-term *renters,* also subject to the same rules of labor and relationship as in the previous period; and then two new types. These were the holders of *precaria,* made up of those who, having asked the owner for land ("precarium" meant begging or asking), obtained a temporary grant by means of a rescript which they signed in due time; and the recipients of *commendatio,* those who received lands by means of a pact of fealty linking them to their lord by personal service. This class is important, for from the practice was to spring a series of formulas between landlords and farmers which would have great influence on agrarian relationships during the Middle Ages.

Besides the lands subject to the landlords, there were also uncultivated and vacant lands, woodland, and communal pastures. All this derived from Roman times, but there is one new fact nevertheless. We can now speak of the existence of a *conventus vicinorum*—that is, a kind of neighborhood meeting, an agrarian and herding council—which took care of such things as distribution of woodlands, pastures, and vacant lands among those who could use them for agriculture and herding. Some authorities believe, and it seems not unlikely, that medieval municipal organization arose from the "conventus."

AGRICULTURAL PRODUCTS. There are no novelties in Visigothic as compared to Roman agriculture, though some philologists have believed that certain words adopted by Castilian farmers reveal innovations brought in by the Germanic peoples. But the truth is that, except for artichokes and spinach, which some believe (with little justification) to have been imported by the Visigoths, the agricultural horizon of Visigothic Hispania corresponds exactly to what it had been in Roman times. And it stayed so because, in reality, the great mass of farmers and peasants continued to be made up of the same Hispano-Romans as in previous centuries.

Consequently, the basis of Visigothic agriculture was cereal grains, grape culture, and vegetable crops on irrigated land. Cereals, among them wheat, were the chief base of nutrition in Visigothic Spain; vineyards were widespread, for in almost all the known documents, when an inheritance or donation is being dealt with, vineyards are mentioned along with farmlands. As for irrigation farming, it is obvious that the irrigating system begun by the Iberians and Romans continued to exist.

In addition to vineyards there are also references to the apple tree, which was used for the production of cider. The apple tree was, however, considered to be inferior to the olive, for in the laws pertaining to indemnification the latter tree has a value of 5 solidi as opposed to 3 for the apple.

LIVESTOCK. In this area there was an evolution of major importance. The most accepted theory is that the preferred occupation of the Goths was stockbreeding, and that in consequence they developed it all over the Peninsula; both private and public texts substantiate this. There is no doubt that in Visigothic times large flocks of sheep existed, and that they emigrated from one place to another in the practice of a type of nomadism which, with the passage of time, came to make up the economic occupation of a large part of the Meseta.

Because of this advance in livestock, a competition developed between it and agriculture that was to affect the social and human relations of the Castilian peoples for so long. We read in St. Isidore of the necessity of having the grain cut before the flocks were allowed to graze, which means that there must have been cases in which the flocks were let into the farmers' fields without any concern as to whether the grain was ready to harvest or not. Rental agreements are also extant which provided for the pasturing of certain flocks on the property of other owners; this agreement was called *pascuarium*.

Besides raising sheep, a good deal of prominence was given to swine, the chief source of meat supply. The principal draft animals were the horse, ass, and ox. The horse, however, was not as important then as later, during the Middle Ages, when it became the primary instrument of war.

EXPLOITATION OF MINES. We have little documentation concerning mining activity during the period. But everything we do know leads us to suppose that the Roman tradition was continued; that is, that fundamentally the exploitation of mines was the concern of the State, and that they were leased out. Mining labor was provided by those who had become serfs through nonpayment of taxes, for work in the mines was very hard. This does not mean that there were not some individual concessions; from the legal point of view, at least, private persons were authorized to exploit the mines. We do not, however, have any documents which would prove the existence of this type of mining concession.

As for metals, St. Isidore speaks of the gold-bearing sands which were found in various places, near Toledo for example. The existence of lead mines is known in different places in Lusitania, Galicia, and Cantabria. We are also aware of the importance of the salt beds of the province of Tarraconensis, but in general the volume this industry may have had is not known.

INDUSTRY AND LABOR CONDITIONS. Once Mediterranean commerce had fallen into decay and Hispano-Roman society had been impoverished by the invasions, it follows that industry declined. The most important industrial activities were reduced to satisfying elementary necessities. Thus, in the field of metallurgy, the most outstanding industries were those useful to farming and those which produced arms for war. But in general, activity of a domestic type predominated in the textile industry and in occupations related to the sea; these were the only ones which were at all widespread.

Industrial labor underwent some changes in comparison with Roman times, for the invasions broke up the *collegia,* or guild organizations, which had been characteristic of the later Empire. Two types of artisans existed—those who were subject to some noble and lived on his farm lands, generally as slaves, and free artisans who lived in the cities. Some texts are extant which prove the existence of private workshops, but the usual practice was for the artisan to offer his work in different places and to charge a separate fee for each job. However, there is evidence of the survival of a system of wage earners—that is, of workshops where a number of free artisans worked for a single master. The pay was known as *merces.*

TRADE AND TRADE ROUTES. Trade did not disappear under the Visigoths, for it was engaged in by colonies of foreign merchants, Jews, and Hispano-Romans, who were especially numerous in the different Mediterranean seaports. These groups maintained an exchange, which, although it could not be called active, was at least constant, with various places in Europe.

The principal trade routes were connected with North Africa (particularly with Carthage), Italy, Greece, Asia Minor, and Septimania, the commercial outlet for the Gallic countries. It is also known, through the discovery of coins, that the Visigoths traded in the Atlantic. This commerce, however, was probably not in their own hands but in those of Hispano-Roman merchants who continued the old traditions of the Atlantic metal route.

Exports consisted of cereals, various kinds of metals, salt, wine and vinegar, olive oil, and honey; imports tended to be luxury goods: silks, Tyrian purple, ivory, jewels. The chief importers were the nobles and the clergy.

One special peculiarity of Visigothic commerce is the existence of exchanges, or *cataplus,* in which merchandise was bartered or sold. The so-called *negotiatores transmarini,* or merchants from overseas, came to these exchanges, and the tax on the transit of merchandise (*toloneus*) was levied in them. There were also small marketplaces, the so-called *conventus mercantium,* where exchanges between the cities and nearby localities were carried out. All this was, as can easily be supposed, a survival of the Mediterranean economy's period of prosperity under the Roman Empire.

Lastly, we should point out the presence of *argentarii,* or bankers, who traded in the money which served as exchange for the payment of products.

COINAGE AND SURVIVALS OF IMPERIAL FINANCE. The Visigothic monetary system was only a copy of the Roman one, though somewhat simplified, for the barbarian chieftains came into the Empire as simple auxiliaries, without the right to take over any of its essential prerogatives, among them the coining of money; and also because Hispano-Roman private persons, accustomed to Imperial coinage, were reluctant to engage in money-changing. This double circumstance explains the fact that for a long time Visigothic coins bore the likeness of the reigning emperor, or, if that could not be procured, the likeness of an earlier one. Only at the end of the 5th century did King Leovigild dare to mint coins with his own portrait. We believe that this innovation is probably related—as M. Bloch has pointed out in the case of the Franks—to the king's desire to affirm his sovereignty in the struggle against citizens of the Byzantine Empire who occupied part of the Spanish soil.

Having described their basic similarities, we must now look at the differences between the two systems. Essentially these were: (1) reduction of the Visigoths to a gold monometallism (they minted only gold, although at times, especially toward the end of their period of domination, it was of such low fineness that it was worth little more than silver), (2) the weakness of the Visigothic economy supplanted the *solidus* in favor of the *tremis,* which was worth only a third of the former, (3) progressive loss in weight of these coins, and (4) breakup of the State monopoly of coinage, which had been so rigorously imposed by Constantine. As a symbol of the confusion of the Visigothic mintings, we need only cite the figure of seventy-nine mints scattered over the country.

As for the Visigothic treasury, there is great technical confusion in comparison with Roman practice. For two centuries the patrimony of the king was lumped with what belonged to the State. Later, in the 7th century, a certain amount of separation began to be made between the king's funds and the State's, but the monarchy never really assimilated the idea that two types of funds existed, personal and public. And for this same reason, there never came to be a clear distinction between the system of collection of private and general taxes, to the point that the State gave the lords in their villas the right of collecting the taxes which were owed to it. This implied the intervention of a third element between the taxpayer and the State—the landowner, who undoubtedly benefited from such a system. This was one of the profound causes of the development of the feudal system.

TOWARD MEDIEVAL AGRARIAN ECONOMY. To sum up, the subsidiary Visigothic economy in the Peninsula represents a moment of transition between Roman mercantile economy and the domestic type of economy which was to predominate in the early medieval centuries.

After the 3rd century, when the cities had experienced the rude shocks of the Frankish invasion, the economy had tended to become ruralized. The world had come to be divided into little fortified city centers and small manorial villas, in which the agrarian economy was centered. After the invasion of the Visigoths had increased the demoralization of commercial economy, the tendency toward ruralization became ever more noticeable. This fact, emphasized by the Visigoths' inclination toward livestock breeding, gradually led to the system of closed economy typical of the 8th to 12th centuries.

II · FEUDAL AND SEIGNIORIAL ECONOMY

9 · General Indications

Society and Feudal Economy in the West: Origins and Development. Between the 9th and 12th centuries Western Europe built up a system called "feudal." Until quite recently these centuries were considered as a murky period, situated between the radiant sun of classical civilization and the showy brilliance of the Renaissance civilization and economy. Today we know that this impression is not accurate. With the feudal system, in fact, we come into contact with the birth of our own civilization, and with a period of very interesting features, in the course of which we begin to see the outlines of a social and economic process destined to accomplish great things.

Feudalism was a total organization of society and economy, imposed for two main reasons—lack of personal security and the collapse of economic circulation. It should not be believed that this second cause, the purely materialistic one, the diminution of exchange of products, was what brought about the birth of feudalism. In reality we are dealing with a complex process in which the exhaustion of the ancient world is mingled with the beginning of the modern one.

The lack of security was caused by the impact of peoples generally labeled barbarians. In modern terminology, following Toynbee, there are two types of barbarians, external and internal. The former were the Germanic peoples, who in two successive waves completely destroyed the economy of the ancient world. But two waves were necessary, not a mere Germanic incursion over the frontiers of the powerful Roman Empire. The first great impact occurred in the 5th century and began with the well-known invasion of the Suevi, Alani, and Vandals; but the decisive blow, the one which spelled the downfall of the old Mediterranean civilization, belongs to the 8th and 9th centuries, when the Hungarians and Normans in particular completed the destruction of the remnants of the Empire in the West.

Coincident with this factor of insecurity produced by the invasions was the confusion caused in the minds of the Empire's peoples by those who cared nothing about the culture and economy of the preceding civilization. The Christian proletariat is a good example of this. Contempt for material goods, the profound feeling that an afterlife existed which would make up for the unhappiness and meagerness of the earthly life, were elements which worked against many incentives of the classical world's economy and contributed to its weakness.

The feeling of insecurity gave rise to the following process: when individuals were faced with a lack of the protection which the State owed to each of them, they sought among the powerful a support which would at least offer them the possibility of being defended against their adversaries. Thus, between the 6th and 8th centuries a number of ties of dependence were formed which eventually made up, through a series of juridical and social events, what we call feudalism.

The essential link in interpersonal relationships was *fealty*. One person declared fealty toward another when the lord offered protection and aid; and the one who came under this protection, the vassal, offered for his part service and counsel. It is obvious that this relationship in itself has almost nothing to do with economics, for it is a bilateral pact resting on a moral principle. It is legitimate, then, to ask ourselves: what was the economic factor in feudalism which turned it into the prototype of a system of organization of man's life?

Before answering this question we must examine the decline in interchange of products and the diminished monetary circulation at the end of the Roman Empire. Commerce and production had been in decline since the 3rd century, after the first great Germanic incursion into Imperial territory (invasion of the Franks), to such a degree that citizens who possessed money, oppressed by the tax structure, preferred to move to their villas in the country, and by this means to establish a position of strength in the interior of the country against any possible demand of authority. But at the same time, many peasants left the country to take refuge in the walled cities. This double movement destroyed agricultural production, paralyzed trade, and produced a decline in the circulation of money. Naturally the whole economic complex of Mediterranean antiquity did not collapse at one stroke. The Viennese professor Alfred Dopsch showed in a famous study the survival of ancient society until the 8th century. And as for the Mediterranean economy, Professor Henri Pirenne, in one of the most fundamental treatments of the history of medieval economy, has proved that until complete control of the island of Sicily by the Moslems, or well into the 9th century, total paralysis of trade was not possible.

However, from the 8th century onward we find a situation characterized by lack of money, the collapse of trade, and a rapid slide toward an agrarian economy. Therefore—and now we return to the question we formulated before—when insecurity led a man to make himself the vassal of a powerful lord, the latter could compensate him for his services only by offering land. It was land which became the basis of interpersonal relationships, involving the *benefice,* or act of giving land, the act of admitting a vassal into the circle of relationships of a lord. Gradually, in the course of the 9th and 10th centuries, this land received a name—*fief.* We shall not go into a philological investigation of the word here, but we do need to remember that many attribute it to a development of the early Germanic word *vieh,* meaning cattle, and thus we find ourselves from the outset within the same economic line of descent: fief always meant a payment to ensure that the recipient of *commendatio* (later vassal) would maintain his fealty to the lord who offered him protection.

Thus we can define feudalism as *an organization of the social and political structure of Western Europe during a period of great economic contraction, characterized by an economic system of a family, agrarian type.* It is natural that this system should have evolved in the course of time, so that, in addition to becoming a specific social and economic form of agrarian structure in Europe, it was likewise a system of organization of labor. Feudalism enclosed the rural masses in a system of attachment to the land called *service to the glebe.* This occurred between the 11th and 12th centuries, and after that time it represented an organization of labor, added to the original factors of the social, economic, and political structure of the country.

To sum up, feudal society deserves the reproach which has been leveled at it for so long, that it was the organization of the many for the benefit of the few. But we must also think of the harsh conditions of the times, when there was neither order nor possibility of organization, when everything was in ruins. It was, then, an emergency system in Western society, accepted by the majority of the common people, first because it responded to the need for seeking security at any price, second because it meant coming to terms with the brutality of the few, also at any price.

SPECIFIC CIRCUMSTANCES OF THE SPREAD OF FEUDALISM IN SPAIN. In the Peninsula the expansion of feudalism showed very distinctive features which we must keep in mind, for they constitute a notable difference in comparison with the general European prototype. The Moslem invasion was undoubtedly the factor which contributed most toward altering Spanish feudalism. But we should not forget other physiographic and morphological factors which also combined to give it new directions.

Professor Claudio Sánchez Albornoz, a leading figure in the historical investigation of the Early Middle Ages in Castile, has advanced the theory, among others, that in the 6th century prefeudal organization was more advanced in Spain than in France, so that if the Moslem invasion had not occurred the Visigoths would by their own process of development have achieved a feudal system very similar to that of the Franks. But when Islam burst onto the scene the process was violently interrupted.

What social and economic phenomena did the Moslem invasion bring about? In the first place, brutal rupture of the prefeudal bonds which had been forming. Everything fell apart. At the time of the invasion there were neither victors nor vanquished, generally speaking, for the Moslems, too few in number to restore order and assume power over the country, immediately granted pacts of freedom and autonomy to everyone who wished them. In consequence, the system of protection and vassalage was broken in favor of a mystical concept called Islam—that is, the community of all believers—and as all believers had necessarily to be free, no feudal or prefeudal bond could survive. On the other hand, these same Moslems were part of a Mediterranean mercantile organization, a difficult, and perhaps poor, organization, but the only one which maintained commercial relations between East and West. For this reason Moslem Spain was, until the 11th century, the last bastion in Europe where there was still a flourishing monetary economy, especially one based on gold. The introduction into the Peninsula of gold coinage, which also spread into the Christian kingdoms, explains why monetary collapse was not so complete there as in France; and it also explains why the necessary conditions for the formation of feudalism did not occur in the same form. Even in Catalonia, the most thoroughly feudal section of the Peninsula, *feudalism took an atypical form because of the factor of monetary circulation.*

On the other hand, there is one fact which must be taken into account. Though it seems paradoxical, the Moslem invasion, following as it did the harsh experience of the 8th century, implanted a feeling of security in Spain. It is usually held that the Reconquest was a constant battle. Sánchez Albornoz stresses the extraordinary number of campaigns recorded in chronicles of the time. But if we exclude the upper Meseta region between the Duero and the Cantabrian mountains, where the struggle was carried on with real violence and the country was devastated by war, things were quite different in other parts of the country. Until the time of the Almorávid invasion, what we call the Reconquest was unbroken contact between the farmers of the South and the herdsmen of the North, with its large and small antagonisms to be sure, until in the 11th century the idea of a crusade, Nordic in origin, changed the Christian kingdoms of the North into fierce enemies of the Moslems of the South. But up to that time the bonds uniting the inhabitants of Spain were of such a nature that one noted historian prefers to call the period that of the *Slow Reconquest.*

The influence of the Moslem conquest on evolution of the feudal system in Spain is, of course, evident. However, the difference in geographical location of the early Christian states in the Peninsula explains the fact that there existed two typical modes of political and economic organization. One, which was properly speaking feudal, belonged to Catalonia; the other, called the seigniorial system, characterized the Meseta.

In the *Marca Hispanica,* or Catalonia, Charlemagne's conquest (about 800 A.D.) caused the introduction of feudal precepts and the establishment in the country of a feudal superstructure, which meant that this part of the Peninsula did not evolve at the same rate as the rest. This is an extremely important fact, for not a few of the differences which exist between Catalans and other Hispanic peoples stem from it. As for the Cantabro-Asturian group of peoples, they not only kept at a distance from Carolingian and Frankish influences (which did not begin to affect that part of the country until the 11th century), but further, the territorial pattern of the Reconquest left them an ample margin of land for cultivation and for raising their flocks. It was not likely that an Asturian or Cantabrian shepherd would fall into feudal servitude when from the Picos de Europa as far south as the Duero there was plenty of land to settle in, especially after the middle of the 11th century. The expression "broad is Castile" comes from that time, when any man who dreamed of liberty, who wished to flee from a system of personal dependence, could find a place to settle in the river valleys of León and Castile. Therefore we can state that although it seems paradoxical today, the birth of Catalonia's economy was characterized by a structure of an aristocratic type, while the birth of the Castilian economy gave rise to a democratic structure.

PENINSULAR MODES: FEUDAL ECONOMY AND SEIGNIORIAL ECONOMY. Taking a close look at what feudal economy and seigniorial economy actually were, we find two types of economic mentality which were similar and yet different. The chief characteristic of the first is found in the *linking of jurisdiction to property*. This is very important. We are not speaking now of person-to-person relationships, but those of worker to master. This is true to such a degree that the feudal lord, besides being the manager, was the administrator of justice and the man who decided about the system of cultivation, the system of sales, and, in short, the man who organized the whole economic production of the territory under his jurisdiction. We can imagine, then, how impossible it would have been for one of these rural workers to escape from the economic circle into which he had been thrust by the course of events. Subject to the administration of his lord, judged by his lord, and under the restrictions imposed by his lord, he was blindly subjected to an oppressive economic system. For the feudal lord acquired, moreover, in the course of time, the right to mint money in his own name, and with this money he could defraud his subjects at any time. Even if we leave aside the ominous moral question raised by feudalism, it was the harshest kind of life, with the exception of slavery, that laboring humanity has ever known.

Seigniorial economy was somewhat different. In principle the lord also had jurisdiction over the land, but it was *a jurisdiction limited by the power of the monarchy,* which reserved to itself certain special cases known as "Court cases." Among these, in addition to those of a legal nature, there was one which was very important: the lord could not mint money, and if he did so he was immediately haled before the king's justice. And the fact that the monarch always had control over this precious privilege gave the lord much less chance to harass his subjects. But there is another, still more remarkable fact. In the system of feudal economy the laborer could not free himself from the vicious circle into which his vassalage had drawn him; in the seigniorial economy of the Meseta, by contrast, the existence of ample zones of reconquest gave rise to very important forms of freedom in the agreements relating to labor.

Many examples corroborate this principle. The essential one is that of the Castilian *behetrías,* or free towns. A *behetría,* a word which comes from the Latin *benefactoria* and consequently is connected with the word "benefice," meant a group of towns or villages which had the right to elect their own lord. There were two types of *behetrías,* those "from sea to sea," which were free to choose a lord from wherever they pleased, and those "from line to line," which could select a lord only within a certain aristocratic family. Now we can understand the difference between the peasants of Asturias, Cantabria, León, and Castile, and the Catalonian peasant, for while the former were able to renounce their lord, at least in early times, the Catalonian peasant was confined to the feudal bonds which limited his working opportunities.

10 · The Economy of Al-Andalus

MOSLEM SPAIN UP TO THE CALIPHATE. Politically, the history of Moslem Spain (Al-Andalus) comprises four stages: in the first, between 711 and 755, the invaders respected their political and religious dependence on the Omayyad caliphs (*dependent Emirate*); during the second, from 755 to 912, religious dependence continued but political independence from the new Abbassid dynasty became a fact (*independent Emirate*); in the third, from 912 to the beginning of the 11th century, independence was extended to the spiritual sphere (*Caliphate of Cordova*); and in the fourth, the Caliphate broke up into a number of *Taifa kingdoms,* more or less subject to the control of the African empires (Almorávides and Almohades) which maintained them in existence. One of these kingdoms, Granada, survived till the end of the 15th century.

The establishment of Islam in the Peninsula was initially a movement of liberation; the peasants, administrative class, and even the Visigothic nobles were freed from their old dependent status, some of whose roots can be traced to Roman times. The transfer of part of the agricultural soil was the only important change. In the course of half a century, while the army of Islam was off marauding in the south of France in an attempt to conquer Gaul, a new society took shape in the Peninsula, based on religious tolerance and a considerable degree of equality in social life, especially in Andalusia, which had always welcomed foreigners since the times of Tartessos, Rome, and Byzantium.

During the second stage, that of the independent Emirate, the great Moslem dream of conquest beyond the Pyrenees came to naught at the battle of Poitiers. After that, organization of the Hispanic territory as a state became a necessity; this permitted the rise to power of Abderrahman I, a scion of the Omayyads and consequently related to the legitimate succession of Islam. The Moslem state had many problems to face. Some of these problems were external to the territory of the old Hispania, and were connected with the foreign auxiliaries (Berbers and Syrians) who had participated in the conquest; others were internal and involved, among Christians, both those who adopted the Moslem faith and those who did not; third, there were problems relating to the Christians on the northern frontier. Abderrahman's political tactics were based on centralization, in an aristocratic and Arabic sense. This provoked strong currents of resistance. Syrians, Berbers, and Mozárabes fought many times for their independence within the framework of the Emirate. Thus, when a particular Emir was weak, resistance groups tended to divide the state. This situation went on for nearly a century; with the accession to the throne of Abderrahman II (822–852), Al-Andalus changed direction. In the political sphere, the Hispano-Moslem state was modeled closely on the Caliphate of Baghdad, and its economy and culture became strongly Orientalized. However, native resistance continued to be a threat for another half-century, as native revolts in upper Andalusia demonstrated, especially that of Omar-ibn-Hafsún during the reign of Abderrahman II's grandsons.

The third phase, inaugurated by Abderrahman III in 912, is called the Caliphate. This was the apogee of the centralized state, whose bases were an army composed of mercenaries, middle-class economic power, a tendency toward expansion to the East and North Africa, and the culmination of the system of tolerance begun in earlier periods. This phase of tremendous prestige for Spanish Islam ended with the ascendancy of the mercenary army and the fall of the Caliphate, after the period of tension under Almansur.

POPULATION AND SOCIAL STRUCTURE. What was the population of Spanish Islam? This question is very difficult to answer. The first invaders probably comprised a maximum of 35,000 men, divided into the following two groups—the 10,000 to 17,000 African Berbers who made up Tarik's army, and the 10,000 to 18,000 Arabs and Syrians who came with Musa. To these initial groups we must add those who arrived in the Peninsula later, and about whom we have no reliable information. We also lack statistics on population growth, for although we have some quantitative data, much of it comes from exaggerated accounts, either by Arab geographers who visited Spain or ambassadors from medieval Europe. These considerations make the truth hard to determine, though we should not be too far off the mark if we stated that the *6 million* inhabitants who remained within the Moslem zone probably experienced a certain growth in numbers during the 9th and 10th centuries, owing to the general prosperity of the country at that time.

Now let us examine the *composition of the social structure*. This depended on two factors, one which might be called religious and racial, the other economic and political. As for the first factor, we must think of the population of the Moslem state as being divided into two great groups, Moslems and non-Moslems. The first of these included the Arabs, called *Baladíes,* who made up the ruling aristocracy of the country and were also the great landholders of the Moslem zone. Next were the *Syrians,* who as auxiliary troops of the invading armies of Islam's early period had been rewarded with distribution of lands; these lived in the cities and were also concerned with cultivation of the soil. The Syrians were acquainted with the irrigation and farming techniques which had worked well in the Eastern Mediterranean. We must keep in mind that this social class was very important in the development of agriculture in Moslem Spain. Next came the *Berbers,* a North African people who were established as shock troops on the northern frontiers of Al-Andalus, confronting the Christians. Their establishment there produced severe internal difficulties, until at last the Berbers were confined to the mountainous part of the Central System, in Extremadura and New Castile, where they carried on their traditional economic life based on herding. Another important layer of Moslem society was composed of *Slavs,* or freedmen of foreign extraction; these formed part of the army, whose allegiance was owed to the Caliphs, and consequently they scarcely count as an important economic factor, but they do have importance as a group tending to stabilize the regime.

This Moslem population would have been insufficient had it not been able to count, in addition, on the *Muladíes,* Visigothic or Hispano-Roman renegades and country dwellers, who abandoned the Christian religion *en masse,* perhaps because they were insufficiently instructed in it, and embraced Islam in order to enjoy the economic and social advantages of their conquerors. This enormous mass of population is, strictly speaking, the Hispanic one; after having been dominated in turn by the Tartessians, the

Romans, and the Visigoths, it ended by being the lowest social layer of Moslem Spain.

In addition, the *Jews* and the *Mozárabes* did not count as Moslems. The Jews enjoyed great freedom and tolerance. They were always respected, were given considerable advantages and prospered mightily, in the pursuit of the sciences as well as within the economy. As for the Mozárabes, this was the name given to those Christians who, unlike the Muladíes, had not renounced their faith. They were usually artisans and lived in the principal cities of Al-Andalus. The influence of the Mozárabes, in the religious as well as in the political and economic spheres, is crucial if we are to understand the relations between Islam and peninsular Christianity during the Early Middle Ages.

On the other hand, in regard to the *hierarchy of the social structure,* the Moslems considered themselves as divided into three great groups in order of their wealth and political importance; the upper class was called *jassa,* the mass of the people *amma,* and the slaves *sagaliva.* There also existed a special class of believers called *mawlas,* who always enjoyed considerable prestige because, as dependents of the princes, they formed an important part of the army; civil servants were recruited from among them.

THE HISPANO-MOSLEM CITIES. After the splendid urban civilization of the Roman Empire, Western Europe passed through many centuries of decadence. During this period, with communications disrupted, industry virtually dead, and commerce at a standstill, the cities became depopulated and were reduced merely to semirural religious and political centers. Especially between the 8th and 10th centuries, the prevailing agrarian type of economy was symptomatic of the decline of urban life.

Later, starting with the end of the 10th century, there was a slow rebirth of city activity, leading to their great development in the 12th and 13th centuries. What was the role of the cities of Moslem Spain in the resurgence of those of Western Europe? Nearly all historians have neglected this point, but Torres Balbás has pointed out that the Andalusian cities constituted an exception within the general process of decadence during the Carolingian period, and that they were very advanced by the beginning of the Romanesque period. From early in the 8th century there was brisk communication both by land and sea between Al-Andalus and the Eastern Mediterranean, owing at first to their political interdependence and continually maintained by their ties of religion, language, and civilization. Sea trade between both ends of the Mediterranean was never interrupted, and thus the Moslem world did not suffer the fate of Western Europe, where urban life almost died out.

Consequently, the cities of southern Spain enjoyed a life of their own during the Early Middle Ages, and for a long time they were at a considerable advantage compared to the most important conquered Christian centers. Lacking exact figures, Torres Balbás has estimated the population of different urban centers by the extent of their respective walled areas. Leaving out Cordova, to which this method is not applicable but which judging from other sources must have had a population of some 250,000 inhabitants during its period of greatest splendor (end of the 10th century), the results obtained from other great cities are: Toledo, 106 hectares in area and 37,000 inhabitants; Almería, 79 and 27,000 respectively; Granada, 75 and 26,000; Saragossa, 47 and 17,000; Valencia, 44 and 15,500; and Málaga, 37 and 15,000. The true value of these figures can better be appreciated if we compare them with those of the largest European centers of the period (end of the 11th century and beginning of the 12th): in Flanders, Ghent and Bruges with 80 hectares each; in France, Reims with 20 to 30, Paris and Rouen about 20, Soissons 12, etc. There are no figures available for Italian cities, but it is known that their peak of development did not come until the 13th century.

DISTRIBUTION OF LAND AND FORMS OF AGRARIAN EXPLOITATION. In order to understand the Moslem economy, we need to consider first of all how land was distributed after the conquest. At the beginning of his campaigns, Mohammed had set up the practice of dividing the booty—both lands and chattels—among the warriors, keeping back only a fifth (*jum*) for the Caliph. But when Islam spread through the Near East, especially Syria and Egypt, and the need arose to divide spoils based particularly on rural lands, Caliph Omar excluded these from the booty in order to preserve his troops' fighting spirit. Omar decreed that the conquered lands should not be divided, and so, though in theory they became part of the common property of Islam (*fay*), they in fact remained in the possession and use of their former owners. Only when the spread of Islam had reached its limit—that is, after the conquest of Spain—would this restrictive practice need to be revised: once the limit of expansion had been reached it was no longer necessary for the Moslems to continue their nomadic habits. From that time on the soldier could become a peaceful farmer and owner of the conquered lands.

In Spain, Tarik and Musa distributed some parcels of land. However, this division could be made only on a very small scale because of the small number of Moslem invaders and the widespread practice of private agreements between Moslems and natives, by means of which many of the latter managed to keep their old properties. This type of agreement favored the survival of latifundism, a system which had been established by the Romans and had prospered during Visigothic times. Essentially, once the first disturbances brought about by the conquest had passed, landholding property changed very little, and in consequence the social structure of the country did not change either. Cultivation of the land stayed in the hands of the native inhabitants and the rents came into the possession of either the former landowners or persons other than these—in either case, at any rate, into the hands of the upper class.

On the other hand, contractual arrangements for exploitation of the land changed a great deal. While in Europe the forms of feudal landholding we described before were predominant, the Moslems introduced into conquered Spain the *partnership* system, which they in turn had inherited from the Byzantines. This partnership established a contract between two freemen—the owner of the land and the tenant, who was not considered to be a slave. Therefore, between the owner and the *amir,* or farmer (sometimes called the *xaric,* or partner), there existed a series of relationships based on the farmer's delivery of a greater or lesser share of the harvest. This share was usually not more than half. The man who divided the harvest equally with his lord was called a *munasif,* or sharecropper; but there were also peasants who contributed only a fifth, and these were called *mujammis.* In these circumstances there is no doubt that the farmers, those who tilled the fields, were much better off under the Arabs than under the Visigoths.

This also reflects a very different mentality from that of the Romans and Visigoths, and it consisted in the fact that the Arabs loved Nature, gardens, orchards. A very old tradition, based perhaps on the concept of the oasis and further developed during their stay in Syria and Egypt, had made the Arabs a people who thought very highly of agriculture. Delight in the countryside, so often celebrated by their poets and sages, was translated not only into their predilection for country villas surrounded by grape arbors, vineyards, and olive groves, but also into the growing refinement of agricultural systems, as shown in a series of almanacs, notably the Cordovan one written and edited by Arib-ibn-Saab.

AGRICULTURAL PRODUCTS. The agricultural production of Al-Andalus was very interesting. Not only did the Moslems take advantage of and develop the crops which they found in the Peninsula, but they also introduced new plant species and encouraged agricultural techniques until they reached a point of great perfection.

Among the *cereals,* wheat was most widely cultivated. It appears that the supply was always sufficient for the Moslem population; yet there were famines, inevitable at that time, such as those of 915 and 929. In spite of them, however, Spanish Islam enjoyed complete independence in this important aspect of food supply.

As for *cultivation of trees,* fostered by the Arabs' extraordinary love for them, we must separate these into two classes—olive trees and fruit trees. The development of the olive was so great that it can be said that the farthest limit of Islam's expansion in Hispania coincided with the northern limit of practicable cultivation of this tree. Therefore olive oil was, as in Roman times, one of the Peninsula's chief export products. Among fruit trees the most important were the fig, lemon, and almond. The Arabs, extremely fond of sweets, took particular pains to extend cultivation of the almond tree; and development of the orange tree, which came to acquire so much importance in Spain, undoubtedly followed that of the lemon.

Another aspect of Moslem agricultural production was that of the grape. The question inevitably arises of why we can speak of the grape in Moslem Spanish agriculture when one of the rules of the Koran specifically forbids use of alcoholic drinks and stimulants in general; but it was one thing to preach in Arabia and another to stick to the commandments in Spain. The fact is that the vine, which had been seriously cultivated in Roman times and the products of which were famous not only within the country but beyond its borders as well, also strongly attracted the Moslems. From the 9th century onward there are indications that at literary gatherings more drink was consumed than poetry composed; and in confirmation of this, the case is often cited of a judge who, walking along a street in Cordova and encountering a drunken man, instead of taking him to jail and sentencing him as duty demanded, took the man home with him so as to care for him better. This spirit explains the failure of antialcoholic measures such as those decreed by Alhakem II, who ordered the grapevines uprooted to avoid the constant infraction of the Koran's prescriptions.

Still more important than cultivation of the olive and the vine was the use of *irrigated land,* which is thought to be an innovation brought into Spain by the Arabs. Here an unsolved, or only partly solved, problem appears which has given rise to a great deal of debate: whether the Moslems were indeed the ones who introduced irrigation into Spain. Some authors insist that it was they who brought in the irrigation system. Two reasons are given for this—first, that the Moslems must have been acquainted with such systems in Mesopotamia and that with the conquest they brought them to Spain, where they had not previously existed; second, that in the vocabulary of this type of agriculture the majority of the words are of Arabic origin. Those who hold the opposite view believe that the Arabs did not change the state of irrigation in Spain, and point out the fact that conduits and canals are found in excavations of Roman sites. But in fact the question can be settled in the form of a compromise, for the truth probably lies between these two extremes. It is quite possible that Roman irrigation systems existed not only in Spain but also in Egypt and Syria, and that in the latter countries the Moslems learned of the great progress which these peoples had made in their agriculture, and that they then transferred this progress to Spain where, finding a primitive irrigation system, they developed it extensively and linked it directly to agriculture.

All manner of things were grown by irrigation. We possess a book on agriculture, written in Seville in the 12th century by Aben Alawanz, in which more than 120 species of fruits and vegetables are mentioned: green beans, peas, lettuce, turnips, melons, watermelon, squash, etc; and also the two important products introduced by the Arabs, which are identified with irrigation farming, rice and sugar cane.

As for *utilization of forests,* the Arabs took great pains to develop them in parts of the Peninsula where such development was favorable. It is possible that tree cover in the Peninsula acquired its greatest extension at that time. Live oak trees, grown for furniture manufacture, and pines from the mountain slopes of Cuenca and Soria, for shipbuilding, were the species most widely utilized.

Industrial plants were also cultivated by the Moslems, precisely because these plants furnished the raw material for a handicraft industry which was, as we shall see, extremely well developed. The principal ones were flax, cotton, silk, and esparto grass. Flax was cultivated especially in the Genil region, and its quality was admired throughout the Mediterranean area, so much so that linen was one of Moslem Spain's principal exports. Cotton grew in the lower Guadalquivir region, down the river from Seville, and was vastly superior to Nile cotton. It too was exported (to Morocco). It goes without saying that silk, which had been introduced very early by way of China and Rome, became extremely popular in Moslem times and was cultivated in several regions of Al-Andalus (Granada, Murcia). Esparto grass was obtained throughout the southeastern region. But apart from these plants we must mention three products which the Moslems developed extensively for their usefulness in dyeing cloth. The red color was produced by the plant called madder, or *rubia tinctorum,* which is still found in certain parts of Castile, and which in the 18th century, as we shall see, was used on a large scale in the Catalonian textile industry. Blue was obtained from woad. This was a highly valued plant, native to the southern countries, and there was active commerce in it. Lastly, cochineal produced very beautiful tints.

And finally, a reference to *saffron:* this was the first spice plant cultivated in Europe, and Al-Andalus became the first place to give competition to the ascendancy of the East Indies over European cuisine.

LIVESTOCK. The problem also arises here as to whether migratory pasturing of sheep, which was current in Spain and especially in Castile during the Early Middle Ages and survived into the 18th century, was something the Moslems found in the country or whether they brought it in themselves. There are two theories: the anti-Moslem one holds that migratory pasturing existed at the time of the earliest inhabitants, that it continued to develop, especially under the Visigoths, and that any procedures introduced by the Islamic invaders added nothing to it; the Orientalists, however, claim that it was in fact the Berbers, a North African people accustomed to seasonal pasturing between the high mountains of the Atlas and the Atlantic plains, who introduced the migratory procedure into the country and who, especially, established the rules for seasonal migration.

This question has not been settled, nor do we believe that it can be; and here again we must take the middle position; that is, admit the existence of migratory pasturing in Spain from earliest times, and later the growth of migratory activity owing to the Berbers who settled in the mountains of the Central System and later in nearby regions of Castile and Extremadura.

Two other problems exist in regard to the horse and the ass. The former is much more important, for it lies at the center of a controversy, carried on for a long time, concerning the origins of feudalism. In the 9th century a horse did not have the same value as it does today: then it was considered a war "machine." The man who had a horse and the means to maintain it was a powerful lord, for there was a world of difference between fighting on horseback and on foot.

One theory, held by German historians in particular, claimed that European feudalism stemmed from the necessity felt by the Franks in the middle of the 8th century to organize a social system which would make use of cavalry as shock troops against the Moslem cavalry. This theory has been disproved, for it has been realized that the Moslems did not bring large numbers of horses into Spain; in fact, the army of Islam was composed essentially of foot soldiers, and therefore it was not likely that the Franks needed to establish a social system based on cavalry in order to check it. This does not mean that Spanish Islam paid no attention to horsebreeding. A breed of horse—the Andalusian—was developed at that time in Al-Andalus which had fine qualities, a handsome appearance and great spirit, and which was derived from imported strains but attained its final characteristics in Spain.

As for the ass, we know that it came from Egypt. We also know that there were asses in Spain before the Emirate. But the Moslems converted this animal into the fundamental one for agricultural work, especially on small farms, where it is particularly useful. The ox continued to be essential to large farming operations and undoubtedly was partly responsible for the prosperity of Moslem agriculture.

This summary of Moslem livestock would not be complete without some reference to the breeding of fowl. The Moslems were men who, generally speaking, had great fondness and affection for all God's small and humble creatures. Mohammed was especially fond of blue doves, and consequently every good Moslem felt it an honor to have dovecotes in his home. This is the basis of the zeal and pleasure with which the Moslems raised not only doves but also chickens and every kind of domestic species; and later, as a special luxury imported from the East, peacocks. As for bees, beekeeping had very ancient traditions in the Mediterranean and the Moslems merely continued them; but they did so with the same meticulous care which they employed in the upkeep of their villas and farmsteads.

EXPLOITATION OF MINES AND INDUSTRY. It appears that mines were not the property of the State, as in Roman and Visigothic times; instead, they were privately exploited. There were mines of various kinds all over Spain, and it would be useless to itemize the large number of minerals utilized by the Moslems. We shall mention only five, those which were most important to the economy of Al-Andalus.

Gold, which had been sought in river sands during Roman times, continued to be exploited in the same localities, especially in the Segre, Tagus, and Guadalquivir rivers. *Iron* had an important zone of exploitation in lower Andalusia, especially in Constantina and Huelva. *Lead* mines were also worked in the same region, particularly in Cabra. *Mercury* was extracted in the locality called for this reason Almadén, which in Arabic simply means "the mine." Finally, there was *rock salt,* always very much in demand, and in competition with sea salt, to supply the enomous requirements of the peoples of northern Europe. It would be very interesting to study the salt trade between southern Spain and northern Europe. But as yet we lack precise information about this commercial operation of the Moslem world.

As would be expected, industry gave priority to production of food and alcoholic beverages, and was related to the principal agricultural crops—on the one hand, milling, or the transformation of cereal grains into flour; and on the other, the olive, turned into oil by the presses; and finally, wine.

Industry, properly speaking, was subject to the craft system, of which we will speak later as a form of labor organization. For the moment we shall refer only to types of industrial production. The most important was the *wool industry,* which was pretty generally scattered over the country; this industry, of a domestic type, was to persist in the Peninsula until the middle of the 19th century, when the mechanized Catalonian industry would concentrate it in a few cities. The *flax industry* was based in Aragon, more particularly in Saragossa. Until the 18th century the Aragonese flax and hemp industry occupied an important place in Spanish industrial life. As for *silk,* it was manufactured almost everywhere in Al-Andalus, though the principal centers of production were Almería and Cordova. In this latter city Caliph Abderrahman III built a large factory that produced *tiraz,* a kind of brocade which required a very specialized type of workmanship, and which the traveler Mohammed-ibn-Ubaid had introduced on his return from a trip to the East in 929. It had an enormous vogue all over Europe, and the richer Europeans were heavy consumers of Al-Andalus' silk fabrics. Nor is it necessary to say that the Spanish Christians were also important customers of the Moslem factories. In short, the high-grade *textile industry* in the 9th, 10th, and 11th centuries was established in the South.

In regard to *leather,* it is sufficient to recall the importance of the cordovan work of Cordova, and the *guadamecíes,* or stamped leather products. And the excellence of Moslem workmanship is also evident in the development of minor arts related to *construction:* gilded tiles and ceramic decorations such as those of Calatayud.

Another industry which achieved great fame was *arms manufacturing.* It had two main centers, Toledo and Cordova. The temper of the steel of Al-Andalus was highly appreciated in the entire Mediterranean area. It derived, if not from the Moslems themselves, from a previous metallurgical development which they took over and improved. Arms from Andalusia and Toledo went to North Africa and even farther, to Egypt and Syria.

In *gold work* the production was extremely varied. But, properly speaking, this is a chapter in the history of fine arts rather than economic history. The Moslem Andalusians imitated Oriental types. This activity gave rise to a certain amount of export trade with Europe and Asia Minor.

In the *glass industry* a really notable invention was made, a step in technical progress which we owe to the Spanish Moslems: flint glass was discovered during the second half of the 9th century by Abbas-ibn-Firnas of Cordova.

We should also mention the *paper industry*. We know that paper came from China in the 4th century of our era, and that its use was diffused in the West by the Moslems. It began to be manufactured in Spain in the 9th century, and by the 10th the paper industry of Játiva was considered to be one of the most important in Europe. Paper was exported to Italy and the other European countries. The expansion of this product can be followed today by means of ancient texts and codices.

LABOR. We have already mentioned agricultural labor. Therefore it is not necessary to stress the labor situation in the countryside at large, which was much more favorable for the Moslem tenant farmers than for their Christian counterparts in the North at the same period.

In regard to labor in the mines, there are certain texts which show the existence, especially in Almadén, of specialized teams which relieved each other in shifts. This seems to indicate a fairly complex organization in this important economic field, but we lack more precise data on the subject.

A good deal more is known about artisan labor. For the Moslem, handicraft was felt to be closely identified with an attitude toward life and religion, just as the good Moslem farmer also fits into that same ideal framework with which we tend to surround the entire Islamic civilization. This artisan, who lived, as we will describe later, in the *souk* (*suq,* in Arabic), or marketplace, where he sold his products, had the moral obligation to do a good piece of work at a reasonable price. This rule of conduct regarding labor was called *hisba,* and had been laid down by the Prophet himself—that is, within the general framework of the Moslem religion, there was a separate chapter concerned with the artisan's standards of professional ethics. This gave rise to the formation of guilds or corporations, or better still to *communities of a trade,* which were presided over by the most respected person in the community, the *amin* or *arif,* designated by the authorities to watch over the integrity of the fellow-members of his trade. These communities were merged into a coherent whole which formed the industrial class of the population, governed by an important personage, the *almotacén,* whose responsibility was to carry out energetically the regulations pertaining to sales and workmanship in the marketplace. Sometimes he was called the *zabazoque* (master of the marketplace).

Now that this religious characteristic of labor has been noted, we must point out its principal manifestations. Those who belonged to the food-supply trades—butchers, bakers, millers, innkeepers, and so on—had a special status. The clothing industry was equally important. It included carders, bleachers, weavers, dyers, and shoemakers. Besides these there were the perfumers, who were renowned throughout Christian Europe. The construction branch was very important. In addition to the corporation of the *banná* (masons), we find that of the ceramists and glassmakers. Nor should we forget the guilds of the paper and parchment sellers, nor the powerful corporations of goldsmiths in the Moslem cities.

TRADE AND TRADE ROUTES. There is one essential basis of Moslem trade: traffic between city and country, that traffic which had been interrupted in Christian Europe but which continued in Moslem Spain. Apart from this typically local commerce, however, there existed one of greater scope which we might call national and international. National commerce was served by a network of highways, a Roman legacy which the Moslems had done much to maintain. The principal nucleus of communications was Cordova, and important lines went out toward all the peripheral points of Al-Andalus; for instance, to Lérida, Valencia, Toledo, Mérida, Seville, and Almería.

The center of this large-scale commerce was the *souk.* We have detailed descriptions of what a souk was like in Cordova, Seville, and Almería. It was a number of little streets grouped around the principal mosque, each occupied by the artisans of a particular trade. These streets, extremely narrow but occasionally widening into a small plaza (*tarbiat*), teemed with activity, for the shops and workrooms of the artisans and luxury tradesmen opened onto them; these were called *bazaars,* occupied two or three stories, and engaged in wholesale trade. In certain places, near the port or the principal highway, were the *alfóndigos* or warehouses (*funduk,* in Arabic) where the merchandise of nonlocal businessmen was stored, and the *jan,* or inns, where they were housed. The *alfóndigo,* or *alhándega* as it was sometimes called, was imitated all over Europe in medieval times.

In this animated atmosphere of the *souks,* in continual *algarabía* (the constant gabbling of the vendors, who called customers to the *almoneda,* or "sale in the open air"), the most important people were the *challas,* or middlemen, usually persons connected with the trade in foodstuffs, speculators of grain in lean seasons, who redistributed their wares among the retail sellers.

As for international trade, the maritime factor and the development of a postal service must be taken into account. News, which is a basic ingredient in international economy, was given a good deal of importance by the Spanish Moslems. In the caliph's court there was a minister whose special concern was the postal service. We possess other information which reveals the constant communication and curiosity that existed among the different countries of the Arab world, and from which Spanish Islam benefited in the long run.

The most purely international port of Al-Andalus was Almería. Ships from Syria, Egypt, and Byzantium, and later from Genoa and Pisa, gathered there. One traveler states that in the 11th century there were no less than 970 warehouses in the city. This figure, though no doubt exaggerated, gives an idea of the intensity of the commercial life of that particular port. As for Seville, it was the central point for the commerce of Al-Andalus with Morocco.

Al-Andalus' chief markets for export were in North Africa (textiles, olive oil, and arms), and for import in the Near East (spices, luxury goods). As a market Christian Spain exceeded all of these. It could well be said that for five centuries northern Spain was a colony for the export of Moslem products.

COINAGE. The Moslems adopted an original monetary system, though the elements of it were based on systems already in existence. It was a bimetallic system based on the *dinar,* a gold piece which was an imitation of the Byzantine solidus, and on the *dirhem,* a silver coin copied from the drachma of the Sassanid Persians. The ratio of value between these two types of coins was 10:1—that is, a dinar was worth 10 dirhems. The *amisfo* (one-half dinar) and *atsolso* (one-third dinar) circulated as fractional coins.

This was the basic standard. But a few variants, depending upon different stages of political rule, must be pointed out. During the dependent Emirate all the types of coins described above circulated, but in small quantities and as imitations of North African mintings. In the period of the independent Emirate, when there was political but not religious self-determination in regard to Baghdad, silver dirhems were "naturalized" in Spain but coinage of gold ceased, for this was reserved as a privilege of the Eastern prince. After 912 (the Caliphate), the minting of gold coins was resumed, and these gradually became more numerous than silver ones, to the point that Abderrahman III struck 200,000 dinars in the mint at Cordova, a figure which reveals a large circulation of money and obvious commercial prosperity. During the period of the Taifa kingdoms a devaluation of money took place, revealed in the diminution of the amount of gold in circulation and the debasement of silver dirhems, which eventually were made of copper (*feluses*). During the restoration of Moslem power under the Almorávides (1086–1146) the financial splendor of the period of the Caliphate was also restored (much minting of gold, the reestablishment of silver, and, consequently, almost complete disappearance of copper coins). Under the Almohades the system was reformed by introducing coins of lesser value; the *dinarín* replaced the dinar (2.36 grams weight instead of 4 grams). The *dobla* (4.60 grams) was minted as a multiple of the dinarín, with twice its value. On the other hand, the old dirhem of 2.72 grams was reduced to 1.50 grams, though the denomination remained the same, and the half dirhem, at a weight of 0.75 grams, was minted as a fractional coin. The system established by the Almohades survived in the kingdom of Granada up to the time of its conquest by Ferdinand and Isabella.

Beginning early in the 10th century, one of the characteristics of

Moslem coinage was its extension, especially into Christian Spain. This problem has not been studied in any great detail, though it is obviously an interesting question. Professor Mateu Llopis has studied it from a point of view which seems accurate. He speaks of the influence of Al-Andalus' monetary economy on the development of the Christian kingdoms in the North. In fact, the gold and silver produced in Andalusian mints easily crossed the borders and directly stimulated the economy of the Christian kingdoms, especially since these kingdoms, starting in the 10th century, had begun to sack the cities of the South and demand tribute from the Taifa kingdoms. Later on we shall speak of the circulation and subsequent imitations of dinars (Catalan *mancusos,* Castilian *maravedís* and *doblas*) and dirhems in the Northern kingdoms of the Peninsula. Here it is only necessary to add that this influence of Moslem coinage operated not only on the monetary economy of the Christian territories but also on their general economic resources. It is evident that the great period of Romanesque church construction in Catalonia begins in the 11th century. Is it not equally evident that this architectural high point is related to the Moslem money which came just at the right moment to spur economic growth in the Christian countries? After the year 1000, therefore, and up to the end of the 13th century, Moslem money continued to stimulate the economy of the Christian kingdoms, in spite of the unfavorable factor of military struggle.

THE FISCAL SYSTEM. A number of fundamental ideas must be taken into account. The exchequer of the Caliphate was extremely rich; it is estimated that Abderrahman III's revenues amounted to some 20 million dinars annually. This revenue was collected under three different categories: (1) the personal income of the Emir or Caliph, (2) by means of taxes levied on movable goods (crops, merchandise, flocks), real property (land, and buildings in general), and mercantile transactions; in this regard we must keep in mind two kinds of taxes established by the Moslems which later passed into the practice of the Christian communities, especially in Castile—customs duties (Moslem customs had the name of *al-mojarife,* and from this arose the so-called *almojarifazgo* duty which survived so long in the Castilian economy), and taxes on buying and selling transactions, called *gabela* in Arabic, (3) the poll tax to which non-Moslems were subject in addition to the other taxes mentioned.

ECONOMIC PREPONDERANCE AND TECHNOLOGICAL INFLUENCE OF SPANISH ISLAM. The debate between defenders and opponents of the thesis which attributes to the Moslems a preponderant role in Spanish economic development can be settled by accepting the theory of historical reality, which does not recognize abrupt changes in social, economic, or technological matters. It is obvious that the pro-Arabists made use of a very important point, that of philology. When they maintained that the Arabs had been responsible for everything, they pointed out the great number of Arabic words in Spanish in order to make clear that the Christians had depended on the Arabs in art, industry, commerce, and agriculture. But to the modern historian the question of vocabulary is not particularly important. A given technique may well have been discovered by the Iberians and Romans, later accepted by the Moslems, given an Arabic name and passed on to the Christians under that name.

However, and in spite of this critical attitude, the number of nouns in the economic sphere which modern Spanish owes to Arabic is impressive. Let us quote A. Vilanova: in agriculture, "When the Arabs perfected the Roman irrigation system, they laid out *acequias* (canals), built *albercas* and *aljibes* (cisterns and reservoirs), raised water from wells by means of *norias* (irrigating wheels), and the earthen jars attached to these were called *arcaduces;* they took water from rivers by means of *azudes* (sluices). On their garden plots and farms, or *almunias,* they cultivated *alcachofas* (artichokes), *alubias* (green beans), *alcaparras* (capers), *alpiste* (canary seed), *altramuces* (lupine), *albaricoques* (apricots), and *albérchigos* (peaches), *berenjenas* (eggplant), *acelgas* (chard), and *almendras* (almonds). In Andalusian fields were raised *alcacel* (barley), *alfalfa, caña de azúcar* (sugar cane), and *algodón* (cotton). Land was measured by *almudes,* grain by *caíces, arrobas, quintales,* and *fanegas,* and liquids like wine and *aceite* (olive oil) by *azumbres.* Straw from the harvest was kept in *almiares* (stacks) and in storehouses, or *alfolíes;* grain was milled in *aceñas* (water mills) and *tahonas* (horse-powered mills), while olive oil was pressed in *almazaras.*

"The Arabs' proverbial industriousness, which, significantly, introduced into Spanish the word *tarea* (task), not only gave rise to a great deal of terminology relating to agricultural labor and products but left traces in all the arts and trades. Their skill in embroidery has left us the word *recamar* (a kind of raised embroidery) and *alamares* (button-loops). The tanning of leather gave us *badana* (dressed sheepskin), *guadamecí* (stamped and gilded leather), and *tahalí* (leather belt). The dexterity of the Moslem *alfareros* and *alcalleres* (potters) resulted in the manufacture of *alcancías* (money boxes), *jarras* (jugs), *alcarrazas* (pitchers), and *tazas* (cups). Jewelers, masters in the art of *ataujía* (damascening), made *ajorcas* (bracelets), *arracadas* (earrings), and *alfileres* (pins), and necklaces with inlaid *aljófar* (raw pearls). Beautiful coffers of *azabache* (jet) and *marfil* (ivory) were made, this last being the material of which were fashioned the pieces in the game of *ajedrez* (chess), among them the *alfil* (bishop).

"The Arabs' commercial activity has left the Spanish language a legacy of some special terms, such as *aduana* (customs), *arancel* (tax schedule), *tarifa* (tariff), *almacén* (warehouse), *almoneda* (auction), and *zoco* (souk). Some of their mintings, after long circulation among the Christians, gave their names to Spanish coins, such as the *maravedí,* the old gold dinar minted by the Almorávides."

We can see, then, the number of terms which Spanish adapted from the Moslem tongue. This is impressive, but it is not a definitive argument. What does become clear is the role played by Islam in the transmission of knowledge from Arabia and the Near East to the Christian world. This role was made easier by a common religious attitude and the activity of a single ethnic group. In regard to the former, the Moslems did not feel that fundamental incompatibility between faith and science which other religions have experienced at certain periods. Because of this, it is possible that the Moslems, with the broad sense of tolerance we mentioned before, were the ones who brought to European science that fruitful contact between reality and scientific speculation which was to result in the technology of the Western world. It cannot be said that the Arabs created technology, for they had inherited it in their turn from the Alexandrine world of which they had become a part. Technology as such begins in the 2nd century A.D. in Egypt—that is, in the Hellenistic world. But the Moslems, who became masters of Egypt, grasped the essence of this technology and transmitted it to Europe by way of Spain.

It should be kept in mind, however, that this transmission did not always take place simply by psychological and scientific contact, but in general was carried out by the Mozárabes—that is, the population of Christian origin which refused to deny its religion and which was eventually expelled, forced to emigrate from Islam as a consequence of the repressive measures taken by Abderrahman II and Alhakem I. In the 9th and 10th centuries a very large number of Mozárabes emigrated toward the north and became established in various places in León and Castile. Mozarabism had a perceptible influence on the Christian economy. But up to what date is it permissible to consider that its influence lasted? This is a very debatable question. It is possible that it survived up to the onset of the great Christian conquests of the 13th century, when Mozarabism was definitely eliminated by *Mudejarism*—that is, the subjugated Moslem population. As authentic Moslems, the Mudéjares had the same technological and economic characteristics as the original colonizers of Al-Andalus.

11 · Economy of the Western Hispanic Kingdoms from the 8th to the 12th Centuries

HISTORICAL EVOLUTION OF THE RECONQUEST IN THE MESETA KINGDOMS UP TO THE 12TH CENTURY. During the five centuries of the Moslems' apogee in Spain, the economy of the kingdoms in the Cantabrian regions and the Meseta was far from brilliant. But before we point out its chief traits, we should have some idea of how the struggle against Islam developed. And for this we must single out three facts.

First is *geographic cantonalism*. The fact that the Moslem invasion completely destroyed the Visigothic regime meant that the territories in which the Christians had thrown off the Moslem yoke returned to a type of life very similar to that of pre-Roman times. Over the course of the centuries these northern regions, never thoroughly Romanized, had preserved an internal tribal organization. It was this structure, as Sánchez Albornoz has demonstrated, which reappeared in the 8th century, when the invaders met firm resistance from the Christian centers in the Cantabrian mountains. With the reappearance of the tribal system in the form of small counties and states, there also reappeared a geopolitical cantonalism which had been a special characteristic of Spain's organization before the Romans. And so, just as an Asturian kingdom was established which was linked with the Cantabrian valleys and with the Galicians on its western side, some defensive positions began to take shape on the lower edge of the Cantabrian System which came to be, successively, the kingdoms of León and Castile, not to mention the Basque people who, on the eastern end of the mountains, continued to live with the same degree of independence they had enjoyed up to the time of Leovigild—that is, until a hundred years before the Moslem invasion.

This fact is important, for if geographic cantonalism exists, so does economic cantonalism. Therefore, the points which we make in the course of this chapter should be understood as a simple outline, and only along general lines can they be applied specifically to Galicia, Asturias, Cantabria, León, and Castile.

The second point is the *chronological evolution* of the Reconquest. There are four periods in the struggle against Islam, corresponding roughly to each of the centuries involved. The first (8th century) is simply resistance behind the mountain barriers of the Cantabrian System. In the 9th century, between Alfonso I who begins the century and Alfonso III who ends it, there was a gradual advance toward the Duero. Alfonso I at least succeeded in forcing the Moslems to move out of the Leonese mountains, leaving the whole region between the Cantabrian System and the course of the Duero as a "no man's land." For a whole century this Duero region, which later came to be León and Castile, was completely abandoned. It was a land given over to struggle and combat, in which withdrawals were frequent and skirmishes constant. But at the end of the century Alfonso III consolidated the territorial and military situation, so that after his reign the Meseta kingdoms had a firm line at the Duero and furthermore carried out a series of small advances which protected this line from possible Moslem incursions through the passes of the Central System. Zamora, Salamanca, Avila, Simancas, Sepúlveda, Roa, and Osma, among other places, were the key points on this frontier.

The situation was maintained, along general lines, throughout the 10th century. But at the end of it Islam, reorganized by the Caliphs, surged toward the north and at one moment even threatened to undo the progress achieved during the previous two centuries—for example, during Almansur's summer raids at the end of the 10th century. However, this confrontation turned out favorably for the northern kingdoms. The Moslems realized for the first time that they had to fight not with a few near-tribal groups, but with real states which had achieved organization—a dangerous situation which arose in the 11th century at a time when the Caliphate had lost its power. This century marks a progressive advance of the Christian armies toward the south. It is the period of Ferdinand I of Castile, and especially of Alfonso VI, who conquered Toledo in 1085. In spite of the subsequent counteroffensive of the Almorávides, the conquest of Toledo permitted resettlement of the lands between the Duero and the Central System, which was carried out in a very different spirit.

The third problem which we must consider in the Reconquest is the *ideological* one. What was the ideology of these Christians who fought against the Moslems? It is indeed important to ascertain their ways of thinking, even from the economic point of view. Up until about fifty years ago the theory was that the Christians of Asturias, León, and Castile, fired by religious faith, had fought against the Moslems—that is, that from the first moment of the struggle against Islam it was the differing religious concept of Christianity which had inspired the Christians of the North to fight against the Moslems of the South.

Since this idea is anachronistic, because the idea of a crusade does not belong in the 8th, 9th, and 10th centuries, it has been necessary to change direction and seek some other motive, some other impetus. Since 1925, when Don Ramón Menéndez Pidal published his famous *The Spain of the Cid* (*La España del Cid*), this religious idea has been supplanted by one which we might call Neo-Gothic —that is, that the peoples of the North had fought during this period not to recover any kind of religious supremacy, but to reestablish the Visigothic kindom of which they felt themselves to be the successors. This Neo-Gothic idea is related to the theory of the Leonese empire, which developed in the 11th century and culminated in the 12th.

As for the Neo-Gothic idea, we feel that it does not correspond to the true realities of the country at that time. We do not deny that there may have existed upper-class governing groups—bishops and abbots for example, or royal secretaries—who had this idea, and who from their sanctuaries in the court, the monasteries, or the cathedrals, may have believed that what the kings were trying to do, in fact, was to restore the Visigothic state. But actual events, as demonstrated by the constant lack of unity among the kingdoms, show that in the practical reality of daily life this imperial idea did not exist at court. It is possible to observe, on the other hand, in Castile as well as León, in Asturias as well as Galicia, the predominance of rural life and the difficulties of communication which made it impossible to maintain any coherent idea of a state; for this idea belongs to a higher culture than the Christian kingdoms actually possessed at the time.

Therefore, and even without completely discounting the religious and Neo-Gothic ideals which may have existed at certain moments, what really characterizes the early times of the Reconquest is much more modest; it is something as modest—and heroic—as the simple desire for a livelihood. This desire imposed, on the part of the tribal organizations of northern Spain, an attitude of resistance to Islam just as they had showed it against Augustus' legions during the Cantabrian wars. Superimposed on this ideal, that of economic expansion came later; it was the result of the nomadism which existed between the mountains and the mesetas. Gradually, it was the herdsmen who imposed the necessity of resettlement on the kings, and not because of any religious or political ideal, but simply out of a desire to live, and to live in better circumstances than those which had existed during the early period of the Reconquest. In other words, what the Christian cared about was to resettle, to reconquer better lands and make them fertile for his children, creating a new spiritual climate which was impossible in the steep lands of the North.

POPULATION AND SOCIAL CLASSES: THE MOZÁRABES. It is absolutely impossible to determine the population of the Meseta during this period. Not only do we have no information on the size of the cities, but we have scarcely any idea of the rural population. It is possible that as a consequence of studies begun by Professor Torres Balbás we may some day know what the population of the cities was, with their different elements, Jews, Christians, and Moslems; but we will need many years of research to obtain approximate data. In any case, it appears that one essential idea can be accepted: at that time the mountainous region to the north of Castile had a very dense population, denser perhaps than it ever had had or would ever have again until our own times. The same situation obtained in the Pyrenees. Certainly, in the valleys of Asturias, Santander, and Galicia, the population was much greater than it was later on, when the impetus of the Reconquest led these people—in a "hallucinatory call," as Sánchez Albornoz puts it—to emigrate from their valleys and settle in the lands to the south.

What was the social structure of that population? This question can be answered only along very general lines, for it is here that local differences play a preponderant role. But taking the situation as a whole, the social classes were distributed in the following manner: at the peak of the social hierarchy were the *magnates,* descendants of the old Visigothic *seniores*. However, among these magnates we do not find the great lord, owner of vast estates, such as was to develop in the Meseta after the 12th century; land was still scarce, and in spite of the fact that large proprietors did exist, there was no possible comparison with the later medieval estate owners. Lower than the magnates were the knights (*equites,* in the documents), those who fought from horseback and who consequently had special predominance at the time of the struggle against the Moslems. The knight represented the democratic element in the society of the period, especially in Castile, for as the proverb says, "The *infanzón* (or son of the magnate) is born, the knight is made." This reveals that any person endowed with courage and gallantry in combat could come to occupy a privileged position in society. Beneath the knightly class were the *ingenuili*—that is, people considered to be free. These were persons who had absolutely no tie of dependency to any lord. There were few of them originally, but later they grew in number as a result of the resettlement. And finally, as the lowest social layer still free, were the so-called *patrocinati,* really "the people" in the strict sense; they were those who had a dependent relationship to a lord, either because they worked on his land or simply because of military occupation. The lowest class of society was made up of *serfs;* these were divided into two groups, those who tilled the fields and those who gave personal service. The latter, who were simply servants, enjoyed more prestige than the former. The rural serfs made up the labor base, and consequently the economic activity of the period fell upon their shoulders. They were the ones who worked for the *patrocinati,* the knights, and the magnates.

On the fringe of these social classes were the *Mozárabes.* We have already mentioned that this name was applied to Christians who had remained in Al-Andalus, and who had refused to deny their religion. As a consequence of the restrictive policy of the 9th-century emirs, they emigrated toward the north, where they settled first with the support of the Asturian, and later of the Leonese, kings in a number of cities and regions: Astorga, Zamora, Asturias, Galicia, Castile, and even the Basque country. The importance of Mozarabism is triple. In the first place, the Mozárabes had an ideal notion, sublimated by their resistance to Islam, of what the Visigothic kingdom had stood for, and in consequence the Neo-Gothic faction grew as a result of their intervention in the policies of the Christian states. But apart from being conscious of their political existence, the Mozárabes carried into the North the torch of religious intolerance against the Moslems who had persecuted them. This mystique, which was transmitted to the Christians of the North, had something to do with implanting the idea of a crusade.

But we are particularly interested in what the Mozárabes represented as an economic element. In the economic history of this period, between the 8th and the 12th centuries, the Mozárabes occupied an essential place, to the point that there is a clear line of division between the 8th–9th and the 10th–11th centuries. When the Mozárabes became established in the towns and cities of the Christian kingdoms, they introduced certain arts, trades, and an economic concept which the Christians did not possess, or rather, one which they had neglected for a long time.

RESETTLEMENT OF THE DUERO VALLEY: PRESURA. We have noted that in the Cantabrian mountains there were no owners of great landed estates. In the valleys, especially in Asturias and northern Castile, early forms of distribution of land were preserved. But when in the 9th century, after the conquests of Alfonso I and Alfonso III, the enormous expanse of territory between the Cantabrian System and the Duero became free and available for resettlement, an inevitable phenomenon occurred: emigration of the mountain peoples to the plain. Magnates as well as *ingenuili,* and even serfs, were tempted to leave the valleys in order to seek fortune and freedom in the Meseta. However, as Sánchez Albornoz has said, if it was possible to bring to life the desert places of the Duero region, this was due to the colossal displacement of great numbers of human beings who came not only from Galicia, Asturias, and Cantabria, but also from the Basque region; nor should we forget the Mozárabes of the South, who played an important part.

There was a resettlement policy. Whenever the fortunes of battle offered an opportunity, a string of advance posts began to be occupied on the line easiest to defend; in this way Astorga (854), León (856), and Amaya (860) were resettled in one initial push; then Coimbra (876), Lancia (882), Castrojeriz (893), Zamora (893), Burgos (896), and Simancas (899); and later Clunia, Gormaz, and Osma (912), and Salamanca, Avila, and Sepúlveda (940).

127

Once fortresses were established in the repopulated district, efforts were made to connect it to the center of the kingdom through a network of strategic positions (castles and military posts). Finally, the essential part of the operation was undertaken: colonization of the land which up till then had been "no man's land," the conquest of the soil by the peasant. This process was called *presura,* or "taking over."

Following the Romano-Visigothic tradition, unclaimed land (*bona vacantia*) belonged to the treasury and was at the disposition of the king, who was consequently the only person with authority to confirm its colonization. Therefore, *presura* was regulated by the monarchy.

Presura could be of two kinds, depending on whether it resulted from the direct or delegated initiative of the monarch, or from private initiative. In the first case, the king organized an expedition, which he might direct in person or—as was more frequent—put under the orders of a *comes* (count). Among the members of the expedition were soldiers and simple farmers. Like a caravan, this expedition would travel along the course of one of the tributaries of the Duero looking for a place to settle, though in most cases there was already a concrete idea of the site to be repopulated. Once there, the lands were divided, and after the count had had the royal horn sounded and the oriflamme, or royal standard, displayed, it was considered that *presura,* or colonization, had taken place. Astorga, Amaya, Burgos, Toro, Oporto, and Coimbra, among many other cities, were resettled in this way.

At other times private persons—magnates, bishops, and abbots—went to the king to ask permission to resettle. The king consented, and then the procedure was similar to the one we have just described. It was usually the abbots who carried out this system of colonization, and in fact the southern bank of the Duero was colonized by monasteries.

In addition to these forms of *presura* originating with the king, there were also occupations of territory which were controlled by no one—perhaps groups made up of several families who asked permission from nobody, neither the count nor the monastery nor whatever Ramiro or Ordoño was reigning at the moment, but who set out on their own initiative from the valleys of the North in search of freedom and settled in some corner of the Meseta plains.

Once they had spent a certain number of years there, they called on the king to recognize their *presura*. But the king would not do so until it was demonstrated that they had actually tilled the soil, a procedure called *escalidare,* from the Vulgar Latin word *escalio,* meaning "to cultivate."

Therefore resettlement, or the act of *presura,* is found at the very base of the economic organization of the Meseta states during this period. Its essential importance arises from this, but it has additional importance which we must emphasize: *presura* and resettlement created in the Castile of the earliest period a social structure of a democratic type; for given the extent of the territories to be cultivated, when the mountaineers descended into the plain, no sort of feudal organization could be imposed on them. They were free men, as pioneers have always been.

LOCAL ECONOMY. The most important fact to be observed in the economic history of the Early Middle Ages in the Meseta kingdoms is the lack of what is usually called a closed agricultural economy, or what Professors Karl Bücher and Werner Sombart have termed *Hauswirtschaft* (domestic economy), set up on an independent base with no medium of exchange and consumer of its own products within the restricted area of the manorial establishment which produced them. If the falsity of this thesis insofar as Europe is concerned has recently been demonstrated, it is even more false in the case of the Meseta kingdoms, where, by the normal process of contact with the Moslems and especially because of the influence of the dinar economy, monetary exchange existed to a certain degree. Nor can we forget that we are dealing with the 9th, 10th, and 11th centuries, and that consequently an economy of true exchange could not exist when systems of communication and provisions for the safety of merchants were lacking, and the people cultivated their fields under threat of enemy attack. In consequence, it will be preferable to adopt the term *local economy* to describe this period, for it includes a sort of village autonomy, more or less related to that of other villages by means of a rudimentary sort of market.

In the Meseta a typical arrangement of this kind can be sketched as follows: the center of economic life was the *vicus,* or hamlet. It included two types of property, individual and collective. The individual part, called *fundus* or *hereditas,* had as its center the house (*domus*), sometimes called *fumus* (from the smoke which came out of the chimney). Any stable kind of agricultural operation needed at least four units of land: the *terra* or *serna,* where grain was grown; the *ferregenalia,* or land where fodder for the stock was raised; the orchard, or *hortus;* and the *curtes,* or place where stock was kept.

As for collective exploitation, such lands generally were not the property of the village but of the king or lord, and the village paid a tax on them. They were used for the following purposes: the *defesa* (in modern Spanish, *dehesa*), the grazing grounds for cattle; the *cotus,* a forest for hunting; the *mesta* (a name which attained extraordinary importance in Castilian economic life), where flocks of sheep were taken for grazing; and finally the *piscaria,* the lakes and rivers where fishing was done on a collective basis.

What was cultivated on these private lands? The documents concerning leases and sales give us concrete details about the plants that were grown: principally *cereals*—wheat, barley, and millet, and in the more mountainous regions rye; very few garden vegetables—turnips, onions, and garlic; among the fruit trees were apples, cherries, figs, and, after the 11th century, olives. We must keep in mind that the olive groves were towards the south, in the zone occupied by the Moslems, and that only when the Christians advanced toward the southern territories could they take advantage of the olive trees planted there. There were *vineyards,* especially in the zones most favorable for their cultivation, such as the Rioja region. In reality, the growing of grapes in the Meseta formed a complement to the lands of basic cereal economy. And in a few favored places, *flax,* the only textile plant, was also grown.

LIVESTOCK ECONOMY: ITS IMPORTANCE. The livestock economy at this time is of great importance. This much is obvious, but the fact is that we know nothing about it. An extremely important book on Spanish grazing is that by an American, Julius Klein, called *The Mesta.* But Klein placed the beginning of his researches in the 13th century, when the Mesta was already a formal organization. We know absolutely nothing about its origins. Therefore, though we can state that the development of livestock in the Cantabrian and Meseta regions is of interest, we are guessing rather than relying on documentary evidence. We can, however, make one sure deduction; for if in 1273—the year of very important statutes concerning the Mesta promulgated by Alfonso the Wise—great flocks and a complex organization existed, we are justified in believing that grazing was a fundamental activity at least from the 10th century onward. And the opinion of present-day medievalists, with Sánchez Albornoz at their head, supports the view that the Reconquest can be explained in large part by the warriors' need to take their flocks to the south to pasture them.

We shall not return to the problem of who developed nomadic pasturing in Spain, of whether it was the Iberians, Visigoths, or Berbers. What does seem evident is that after the conquests of the 9th century, grazing gained importance in the kingdom of Asturias. It must have developed at that time through two fundamental institutions, the *cañada,* or sheepwalk, and the *Mesta,* or organization which cared for the flocks during their migrations.

The origin of the *cañada* is known. The texts tell us that *cañadas* were any kind of path situated between the fields (either vineyards, wheat fields, or garden plots). Then, as the flocks grew in number, the *cañadas* began to become specialized; that is, some which served principally for the passage of sheep gained in importance. The flocks traveled from the mountains of the North to the *extremes,* or grazing grounds, on the banks of the Duero. These *extremes* are so essential in the process of the Spanish Reconquest that they have even given rise to a concrete name—Extremadura, the *extreme* of the Duero. It was first applied to the districts of Soria and Segovia, and at last came to give a specific name to one of the regions of Spain.

As for the second element, the *Mesta,* it arose out of local collective grazing. It is obvious that the villagers in a given community must have had to come to some agreement for organizing the pasturage of their lambs and sheep in the *mesta,* or common grazing grounds. The origin of such an organization must have been to avoid litigation among those who reclaimed strayed sheep. Then some conflict arose among four or five localities, and a committee was formed to patrol the mesta. There occurred a transposition of names: mesta, the name of the grazing ground, was given to the committee, and thus arose those small groups called mestas, which later grew larger and which in the 13th century must have banded together in the great Castilian Mesta which ruled the wool trade in Europe for three centuries.

ARTISAN LABOR AND THE ORIGINS OF TRADE. Thanks to the studies of Sánchez Albornoz, we have some idea of what economic, industrial, and commercial life was like in the Meseta during the 10th and 11th centuries. Compared, for example, with the economic structure of the Pyrenean kingdoms of the period, it was not very rich. This is fundamentally due to the atmosphere of struggle which enveloped the Leonese and Castilian settlements. Until the year 1200 the cities of León and Castile contained herders, farmers, and soldiers. In charters granted during the 11th and 12th centuries, there is virtually no mention of mercantile and industrial activities. And when they do appear, the exception confirms the rule: there are references to the Franks of Sahagún (1084), the shoemakers of Burgos (1124), and the craftsmen, undoubtedly Mozárabes, of Escalona (1130). On the other hand, these same charters give minute details on everything pertaining to the cultivation of grain, to farm lands and market gardens, to irrigation, pasturing, hunting, and forestry.

In general terms, we can distinguish two kinds of artisan labor, one within a local manorial economy, or that of the inhabitants of a village subject to some lord, and another in the local economy properly speaking, that of the *behetrías* (in which only the land was subject to the lord) and the cities. In the local economy properly speaking are found the so-called *ministeriales*. As will be remembered, one of the lord's prerogatives was to monopolize economic life, and as a result of this he also exercised a monopoly over industry. These *ministeriales,* then (weavers, smiths, carpenters), carried on the various trades required by the group. The name is important, for from it derives the word "menestral," which has been so prominent in the vocabulary of the West, especially in Catalonia.

In regard to the artisan economy either in the city or the town, it was very limited. The chief trades had to do with clothing (weavers), food (bakers), the manufacture of various working tools (smiths and carpenters), construction (masons), and finally the goldsmiths, who made luxury objects for the church and the lords. Two types of artisans begin to be distinguished; one is called *artifex* (craftsman) and the other *operatorium* (worker). At that time the craftsmen were those who traveled from place to place, earning their living as best they could, generally in exchange for payment in kind, but sometimes in money when the occasion arose. As for the workers, they had established workplaces, small shops in which they served a very limited clientele. There is no evidence in either class of a desire to make money. All they cared about was earning a living.

MARKETS, SHOPS, ALFÓNDIGOS. The word "market" begins to be heard in the Cantabrian mountains about the 10th century, when security appears to have been regained, at least in the North. The market is a very important element which goes far to explain the economic life of a district, especially in medieval times when it was the center of the commercial activity of a region.

Professor Valdeavellano has been the principal researcher into the origins of the market, and he has formed a theory not only of the economic value of markets but also of their legal significance. Here, however, we are not interested in the market as the manifestation of any legal principle, nor even as an urban development, but solely as an economic institution.

The market required something which had not existed in the early times of the Reconquest; namely, peace. There could not be a weekly or annual market attended by the inhabitants of different villages unless someone maintained peace. That someone could only be the sovereign, but the real sovereign, not the local lord; the king in Asturias and León, the count in Castile. Therefore the monarch, as soon as he succeeded in imposing reasonable order, insured the defense of the market, especially of the roads leading to it. And at the same time, he insured the overseeing of the transactions which took place there, as well as weights and measures.

We must imagine the market of those times as a periodic transaction between sellers and buyers after the manner of the Eastern markets, crowded and noisy, with sellers crying their prices and buyers trying to argue down the price of the desired object as far as they could. It was all presided over by an appointed official, the *zabazoque* (a Romance form of the Moslem word *sahib al-suq*), who supervised prices and measures.

Situated in certain places at junctions of the old Roman highways (*viae antiquae*), which continued to be the basis of the road network, or at the junctions of other, secondary roads, the market acquired a wider economic importance. Besides the villagers from nearby places, these markets attracted itinerant vendors, mostly Jews and Moslems, who brought with them *tiraz* from Cordova, Byzantine brocades (*pannos greciscos*), Persian woven goods, and French cloth (*saias franciscas*), in addition to perfumes, jewels, and trinkets of all kinds.

Gradually, a few shops and workshops became established in the vicinity of the market, the *operatoria*. Two conditions were necessary for these; first, that the artisan could count on enough money in circulation to guarantee his sales and his economic survival, and second, that within the town there should be a group large enough to consume articles made by others than themselves. As these two conditions did not exist until the 11th century, it is understandable that shops did not appear in the Meseta kingdoms until the beginning of this century.

As for the *alfóndigos,* they were nothing less than the Moslem *funduks.* As the markets developed, it became necessary to have warehouses for merchandise and inns for those who dealt in it. Both the pattern and the name of these establishments were Moslem.

CIRCULATION OF MONEY. Natural economy and monetary economy coexisted during the early centuries of the Reconquest. This fact reveals the difficulties of a monetary circulation reduced to the survival, on a very small scale, of the types of coins of the previous period (Visigothic *tremises* and the *solidus* of the Suevi). The kings of Asturias and León did not mint money.

Then there was a second phase in which monetary circulation increased because of exogenous factors. The first cause was contact with the Moslem economy (especially the arrival of the Mozárabes to resettle the Duero valley). They introduced the gold dinar and especially the silver dirhem, known in Christian territory as the *solidus argenteus.* Later, the replacement of gold by silver as the essential monetary base must have been reinforced by Carolingian influence, which seems to have been a fact by the reign of Alfonso II (791–842). The new Frankish monetary system—whose influence was so great not only in Spain but in all the Western countries—was based on adoption of the *silver denarius* as real currency, and relegation of the old gold solidus to the status of money of account (1 solidus = 12 of the new silver denarii). It seems that the kingdom of León, when it adopted this system, introduced as a variant the *denarius brunus,* or fractional copper coin, whose exact relationship to the silver one is unknown. We must emphasize, however, our original statement about the scanty circulation of coinage in the western territories, which lasted for a very long time. The *Poem of the Cid,* which is an excellent witness to the life of the period, tells us, for example, that when the princes of Carrión had to return the 3,000 silver marks they had received as dowry for their wives, whom they later repudiated, they paid in *apreciadura* (kind)—horses, palfreys, mules, and swords—because they had no money.

There is another point which it would be well to make clear: the value of things in those times, in the kingdoms of the Meseta, had a significance very different from that of today. For us land is an important value; but for the Leonese and Castilians of that period, who had land to spare from the Cantabrian mountains to the Central System and even farther to the south, the value of agricultural property was insignificant. The principal value was assigned to luxury goods. To possess a chalice, an ivory box, brocade made of special silk, a piece of Cordovan *tiraz,* was what was most prized. Next in the scale of values came the horse, as an element which defined a profession—the military career—and a social category. On a lower scale were fur robes and livestock: cows, sheep, goats, and pigs. Land came at the bottom of this list, and even lower than land all foodstuffs, which theoretically were worth nothing because they were not sold.

ORIGINS OF THE FISCAL SYSTEM IN THE CHRISTIAN KINGDOMS OF THE MESETA. The scarcity of minted money and the decline of monetary circulation resulted in the existence of a fiscal system very different from anything we can imagine today. And if we add to this the confusion between personal property and state property in the person of the monarch, we will realize that, in general, both the Asturo-Leonese monarchy and later the Castilian one, acted simply like any other great landowner. Only after the middle of the 11th century, with the development of the market, did the monarch begin to collect taxes in money, and these constituted the basis of the treasury in later times.

As chief lord of the kingdom, the monarch should have received from his vassals taxes in money or in kind on the lands they possessed. But things did not always work out that way—in the first place, because the monarch was in the habit of alienating from his patrimony large portions of his holdings in payment for services rendered or, as a mark of devotion, for churches and monasteries. And further, this cession was usually accompanied by *immunity,* that is, exemption from all types of taxes to the Crown. Consequently, those who paid in the last instance were the peasants, the village folk.

Peasants paid two different types of taxes, in case they were free and did not have to pay in addition the poll tax of the serfs. The first was connected with land and included the *tributum, funcio,* or *censo* (later, it would also be called *infurcio, foro,* and *pecho*). The second type included the *regalías,* such as payment for common utilization of highlands and forests (*montaticum, herbaticum*) and the privilege of holding markets.

This brings us to the development of taxation on merchandise and trade. At this time we begin to see the outlines of what would come to be an improved system of tax revenue. The most important tax was the one levied on the right of transport: *portaticum* (porterage) and *pontaticum* (bridges); these were divided into *pedaticum* (referring to persons) and *passaticum* (having to do with animals). Another interesting chapter was the customs duty, derived from the Moslem *almojarifazgo,* and that on the buying and selling of merchandise, which was imposed in the form of a tax called *maquila,* a term still used today in Castilian agricultural terminology.

THE ROAD TO SANTIAGO. One of the most important factors contributing to the change undergone by the Castilian and Leonese economies at the end of the 11th century is linked to the development of pilgrimages to Santiago. Historians have told us much about the heyday of European devotion to the Apostle venerated in Compostela, about the roads which led to this center of Christendom, and about the spiritual, cultural, and religious phenomena related to the pilgrimages. But they have barely touched upon the economic repercussions of this most important movement, which represented the dawn of a commercial revolution for western Spain.

Lacarra is the only scholar who has treated this theme, when he emphasizes the demographic value of the "French road" (establishment of Estella as an exclusively "Frankish" town in 1090 and of whole sections of the cities along the route inhabited only by people of French extraction). Through his studies we can infer the influence of the pilgrimages on the preservation of roads and bridges, the building of hospitals and inns, and especially on the birth of a powerful middle class. For along with the pilgrims came a veritable army of merchants, artisans, innkeepers, and money-changers who, when they were assimilated at the end of the 12th century, became the motive force of the country's economic evolution. But in Navarre the fusion of these two elements, Spanish and French, took place considerably later (with the Privilege of Union, laid down by Charles III the Noble in 1422), for in addition to the proximity of the frontier there was the circumstance of occupation of the throne by French dynasties.

These indications are sufficient to show that it would be most useful to study thoroughly the economic effects of the Road to Compostela.

12 · Economy of the Pyrenean Kingdoms from the 8th to the 12th Centuries

HISTORICAL EVOLUTION OF THE RECONQUEST IN THE PYRENEAN KINGDOMS UP TO THE 12TH CENTURY. When we spoke of the economy of the Christian states of the Meseta during the first five centuries of the Reconquest, we had in mind that we were dealing with a geographical complex encompassed by three features: to the north, the Cantabrian Sea, whose waters were hard to navigate and which at the time offered no commercial connections; to the south, the axial line of the Cantabrian mountains; and finally, even farther to the south, the great barren plain of the Duero stretching to the Central System, the passes of which were controlled by the Moslems until the end of the 11th century. This geographical configuration is of supreme importance, for a very different range of values operated in the Pyrenean economy.

What lay beyond the Christians who had taken refuge in the Pyrenees? Not a tempestuous sea, but France and Europe. Then there was the axial line of the Pyrenees, which exercised the same function of resistance as in the case of the Cantabrian part of Spain. Toward the south, once the pre-Pyrenean ranges had been crossed, there was a zone of a steppe-like character, though it contained many rich spots such as the valleys of the Ebro tributaries and certain districts in southern Catalonia. This explains how eager the Moslems were to hold on to these regions, which guaranteed them the use of valuable economic resources. Therefore, a line which we might draw through such places as Tudela, Saragossa, Lérida, and Tortosa was a very firm Moslem frontier which for 500 years, from the 8th to the 12th centuries, kept the Christian kingdoms of the Pyrenees shut away in their mountain valleys.

But if this was an unfavorable circumstance, two positive factors did exist in the Pyrenean world, especially on its eastern, or Catalonian, side: the first was the Mediterranean, in whose waters remnants of the sea traffic of antiquity still survived; the second was the corridor formed by the central section of Catalonia—that is, the part called the *prelittoral depression,* from the Panadés region to the Roussillon. At that time this corridor was the umbilical cord which connected the economy of Al-Andalus to that of the rest of Europe. Along this corridor passed both money and economic concepts, while Moslem culture, imbued as it was in the culture of the classical world, expanded into the European continent.

The result was, and we must keep it very much in mind, that one of the points of economic tension in Europe was created in the Pyrenean region beginning in the 10th century—not in the whole region, but in the eastern end of Catalonia, bordered by the Mediterranean and crossed by the great coastal corridor. Without this point of tension it would be impossible to explain the importance achieved by Barcelona, a city which in the 3rd century was still an insignificant place compared to the great Hispano-Roman cities.

Now we shall refer specifically to the historical evolution of the Reconquest in this zone and point out its principal stages. In the 8th century a number of Pyrenean valleys, especially those in the center, escaped the Moslem avalanche; but the Christians who retreated toward the north took refuge in the kingdom of the Franks and created a community of exiles there. Their eventual influence was decisive, for when they returned they brought back a new social, political, and economic mentality: feudalism.

The 9th century saw the beginnings of political consolidation among the refugee Christian groups in the valleys. Some points of crystallization, both social and economic, began to appear: Navarre, Aragon, Sobrarbe, Ribagorza, and Pallars. In the eastern part of Catalonia, Carolingian expansion initiated the Carolingian period with the capture of Barcelona in 801, the creation of the Spanish March and its integration into the Frankish and European imperial structure. However, the Moslem zone of resistance along the pre-Pyrenean barriers kept this progress from continuing. During the 10th century the struggle was fairly equal, although Islam made some sensational advances, as in the case of Almansur's raids. In the following century the tide of battle turned. During its first phase Sancho the Great of Navarre tried to set up a Pyrenean kingdom, an attempt at unity which corresponded to the economic unity of the mountain region, and to which we shall refer again. In the second half of the century the Christians made an effective advance toward the south which was to culminate in the 12th century with the capture of strategic towns in the Ebro valley; Saragossa, Tortosa, and Lérida were all to fall, and when the economic, political, and military system of the Moslems fell with them, it was possible to unite the Pyrenean world in a great economic and political entity, the Crown of Aragon.

POPULATION AND SOCIAL CLASSES. Thanks to recent studies by Ramón d'Abadal, the noted specialist in the historical origins of Catalonia, we have an approximate idea today of the population density of the Pyrenean region, especially as a result of investigations carried out in the districts of Pallars and Ribagorza, and in Ripoll and Vich.

If it is difficult to rely on modern statistics, it is an impressive accomplishment to have arrived at a population figure not through statistics but by studying the few documentary references in the 9th and 10th centuries. And this has been carried out in an absolutely scientific manner. By following the theories of Ramón d'Abadal, we find that the population of the Pyrenean valleys was already stabilized by the end of the Hispano-Roman period, and that from then on into the 19th century, when highways and railroads advanced into the mountains, this population remained more or less stationary; so much so, that if in the highlands of Pallars and Ribagorza, in the very heart of the Pyrenees, there were 6,000 persons in the 19th century, this same number can be estimated to have lived there in the 10th century. This is an exceedingly important fact, for it shows that in the Pyrenean valleys there was a concentration of biological energy which, as it slowly spread down onto the plains following the flow of historical circumstance, must have contributed to creating the future population of Catalonia.

In the pre-Pyrenean zone—that is, the one situated between the axial line of the mountains and the pre-Pyrenean ranges, the zone most exposed to Moslem attack—Ramón d'Abadal's figures show that the population doubled between the 10th century and the beginning of the 19th, from some 1,500 inhabitants around the year 1000 to about 3,000 around the year 1800. The density of population, therefore, was maintained in a relatively normal state: 6.5 inhabitants per sq. km. for the lower mountain zone and 5.5 for the higher one.

The figures which this same researcher has deduced from documents for the population of the valleys of San Juan de las Abadesas and Ripoll coincide with previous estimates. In the first of these valleys he has located some 1,000 persons, which represents a farming population considerably higher than the present one. This means that the mountain region was saturated with people, although historical forces constantly drained off the surplus in order to repopulate the southern parts of the region. This seems to be the case of Cerdaña, which in the 10th century was the base for resettlement of the districts of Ripoll, Vich, and Guillerías.

This population is reflected in a concrete social structure, though there are two separate stages in its evolution, corresponding to the period before and after the Frankish influence. Before the Carolingian invasion, and certainly in the most remote valleys of the Pyrenees, the population maintained a rate of evolution very similar to its previous one. This is true to the point that, as d'Abadal himself points out, the word "fief" is very rare before the 10th century, though it is a word which came to have a great deal of importance in the Catalonia of later times. There did exist a social upper class, formed by the rulers, who were called counts, and their followers, called *fideles;* then came the class of the free population, the so-called *ingenuili,* and at the lowest level the *serfs,* whose situation is still somewhat unclear because of the difficulty of gauging the expressions used in the texts, for they employ the word "serf" to designate the peasants who had no liberty as well as those who had entered into a certain degree of dependence through landholding procedures.

This first phase, then, which lasted until the 10th century, was wiped out in Catalonia by the establishment of feudalism, the general characteristics of which it will not be necessary to repeat. Let us recall that the feudal system implied the distribution of property in exchange for military service; there were some who fought and others who worked so that they could be defended. In this concept the land was of such importance that it could be broken up through successive vassalages only to the point where a given plot of land could still maintain a horse. Land was the elemental unit—economic, social, and political—of feudalism.

A clear feudal hierarchy existed in Catalonia, with a structure similar to that found in the rest of Europe. At the top was the *count,* then came the *viscounts, comitores,* and *valvasores,* and, finally, the *knights (milites).* The upper group received the title of *barons* and were the ones who really dominated the social structure of the country. Underneath this feudal hierarchy of a warrior type were the *payeses,* or peasants, those who lived on the *pagus,* or land. In this regard, Eduardo de Hinojosa has stated that the *payeses* had passed without any change in status from the Roman *colonatus* to Visigothic serfdom and thence to a type of serfs of the glebe, or *remenças* (men who had to ransom themselves in order to be freed from subjection to the land). This theory is not confirmed by the actual facts. Documents are our witness that, until the 11th century and well into the 12th, a class of men subject to the glebe was unknown in Catalonia. There were a great many men, known as *propios* and *sólidos,* who, from the 10th century onward, depended on some person by virtue of the land which that person, on payment of a certain rental, had given to them to cultivate.

Consequently, in the early times of Frankish rule and the rule of the counts in Catalonia, there was no rigid system, as was believed until recently, but a constantly shifting situation in which economic facts responded to a given social structure, and in which this social structure did not affect the system of land tenure and wealth, as has been believed up till now. In fact, establishment of the feudal system in Catalonia coincided, as we shall soon see, with the beginning of a monetary economy, resulting in a mixture of social values unknown in a pure type of feudalism.

We should make some reference to social elements different from those we have just listed—on the one hand the *Moslem* population, which became incorporated into the Pyrenean states after the conquest of the Ebro valley, and on the other, *slaves.* From the very beginning the Moslems represented an economic contribution of the greatest importance, which was to develop especially during the Late Middle Ages. Slaves were the object of a good deal of trade, as we shall see later on. And finally, the *Jews* must be mentioned; from the 10th century onward they formed one of the most economically active groups in Catalonia, Aragon, and Navarre.

DISTRIBUTION OF PROPERTY: APRISIO. In those valleys of the Pyrenees least affected by the Moslem invasion, distribution of the land continued as in earlier times, on the basis of private property.

This system received the name, also common in Castile and León, of *hereditas*. In Catalonia, because of its location as a frontier area and a corridor between France and Spain, distribution of land underwent more noticeable changes as a result of the aftereffects of the Moslem occupation and the necessity of resettling a number of districts which the struggle had left almost deserted. Shortly after Charlemagne's conquest, the basis of property was the *allodium,* or freehold. This could be of two types, either a family inheritance or a holding acquired by the act of *aprisio,* as a result of the agreements *pro hispanis* decreed by Charlemagne. This system fundamentally resembled the *presura* system in Castile. It consisted of a concession made by the monarch under the terms of which the beneficiary, in addition to having the right to occupy empty lands, was granted royal protection, exemption from taxes, and hereditary rights over the land he had acquired. Thus, public property conceded to the Spanish refugees in Septimania could easily become private property. The greater part of the cultivated land in Old Catalonia derives, even today, from the holdings acquired by Spaniards in the 9th century.

Three types of *aprisio* agreements were made: those carried out directly by the counts, with their followers and servants; those given by these authorities to monasteries, to the end that the monasteries would aid them in a difficult and often onerous task; and finally, direct agreements, the majority, usually made with humble people who became owners of the land by the double fact of being its first occupants and of having colonized the wastelands. But in this last case freehold did not confer any authority at all.

Both types of *allodium,* as we said before, concerned free private property. There also existed the *honores,* compensation in land given to certain public functionaries so that they would give a service which could only be rewarded in this manner. *Honores* were at the very foundation of the development of feudalism for they, together with *benefices* and *immunity,* produced the fief. Feudalism did not appear in Catalonia until the 10th century, a little later than was previously believed.

How, then, were freeholds, *honores,* lands in payment for services, fiefs, and lands already hereditarily linked to a single person, distributed? If it is a fact that latifundia did not exist because the mountainous and broken character of the land did not permit it, there were also great proprietors who owned parcels of land scattered over a wide area. Oddly enough, the most important monasteries are to be included in this group.

EARLY MOUNTAIN ECONOMY OF THE 10TH CENTURY: PYRENEAN MONASTERIES. In the works of Ramón d'Abadal, we have an equivalent to Sánchez Albornoz's study of this theme in relation to León. Making use of documents which at first glance seem mere catalogues, d'Abadal has been able in these works to reconstruct a good part of the economic activities of 10th-century man.

In general terms, we find in Catalonia, very much as in Castile, an economy of a local type. We can notice differences from district to district: whereas in the less Romanized territories the center was the *castrum,* or castle, at whose feet had grown up a hamlet of military origin ruled by a representative of the count, in the more Romanized places such as the Ampurdán region the population was concentrated into *villae,* or towns, usually under ecclesiastical jurisdiction. Some of these villae became the seat of a parish. In the future the *parochia* was to become the demographic and economic unit of Catalonia. For the rest, we must mention the place occupied by an isolated house, the *domus, casa, casale,* or even *mansio,* from which was to come the modern Catalan word *mas* (farmstead), which today is at the very center of rural Catalonian economy.

In this domestic type of economy, the variety of crops grown is also very similar to those we have mentioned for the Meseta kingdoms. There was the house with its lands, its vegetable garden, its barns, and the surrounding fields. The *cereals* produced on these fields were wheat, rye, barley, and millet; the gardens produced cabbage, onions, and garlic, as in the Meseta, which means that there was no fundamental difference; among *fruit trees* (with the generic name of *pomniferi*), the apple (*poma,* in Catalan) and fig were prominent. Nor should we forget the vine and the olive tree. It appears that both of these were cultivated farther to the north than they are today, even extending into the pre-Pyrenean districts. But this statement, proved for the vine, is less certain when applied to the olive tree, so it is more prudent to consider that its limit was less extensive and that it was for a long time coincident with the limit reached by the Moslem invaders.

There is another new feature in the economy of the Pyrenean

region of Catalonia during the centuries of the Early Middle Ages: whereas in Castile and the Leonese mountains agriculture and herding formed the essence of the rural economy, in Catalonia there was an incipient development of industry because of the abundance of water and forests; for example, water (or hydraulic) mills appeared in the Pyrenees in the 9th century. As a result the economy evolved quite rapidly. And thus we should not be surprised by the appearance of the word *fabrica*. In the 9th and 10th centuries it was applied to metallurgical workshops, which would come to be called *fargas* and would have such importance during the 13th, 14th, and 15th centuries. As examples of toponymy we might mention Sant Joan de *Fábregues,* midway along the river Ter, and Vall-*ferrera,* in the Pallars region.

In addition to the word *fabrica,* the word *fornus* appears in documents, applied to lime-kilns. This shows the establishment of an activity which would be greatly expanded later.

All of the foregoing applies to small hamlets and parishes. But the monasteries are the most interesting if we are to understand the Catalonian economy of the 10th and 11th centuries. The monastery was an entity which was not only religious but economic, nor can we speak of a closed economy when we refer to it. For when a monastery like that of Cuixá—with its flocks of sheep (500), cows (100), mares (50), its agricultural establishments, and its many smallholdings spread out over more than twenty villages—extended along the river Ter from the Cerdaña region to the Roussillon, occupying the whole Conflent valley, we are in the presence of an active district economy, which was soon to spill over its own borders and reach the coast of the Roussillon.

DEVELOPMENT AND EVOLUTION OF GRAZING. While in the Meseta grazing became the fundamental base of Early Medieval economy, in the Pyrenean kingdoms it was far from attaining a similar importance because the Moslems controlled the steppes of the Ebro. For two centuries, in fact, livestock movement was limited to the comings and goings between mountain and valley which even today are typical of Pyrenean economy. Only when Sancho the Great of Navarre extended his conquests to the far side of the Ebro could the livestock of the Pyrenees reach the steppe region of the South. Here we have a socioeconomic explanation for the Navarrese expansion toward Castilian territory which was characteristic of this monarch's policy.

In the same way, when Alfonso I the Battler forced the mountain passes and conquered Saragossa, a current of migratory pasturing was immediately established, as mentioned by Lacarra in his book on the resettlement of the Ebro valley. The little Aragonese kingdom soon became a livestock-raising region, especially for sheep, and the movement of its flocks explains its rapid expansion through the mountains of the Iberian System.

To sum up, we may say that grazing in the Pyrenees acquired a definite pattern in the 12th century. On the one hand was the typical Pyrenean herding activity with its small-scale movement from the valleys to the high mountain pastures, which made possible the economic unity of the two sides of the mountain ranges in the form of agreements for common utilization of grazing grounds. And on the other hand there existed an organization of a pure nomadic type which in Catalonia would give rise to the *carreratge* (known in Castile as the *cañada*), the same type of nomadic movement as in the Castilian Mesta, but on a smaller scale.

ORIGINS OF URBAN ECONOMY. Catalonian urban economy began rather feebly about the middle of the 10th century and developed out of the marketplace, as in the Meseta kingdoms. But in Catalonia the market evolved more rapidly, so that from the outset it was divided into two types, rural and urban. The rural market was subdivided in its turn into weekly and annual markets. The first type is known in the texts under the name of *mercatum,* whence the Romance word "mercadal," and the second under the name of *firas nundinas*—that is, the typical fair.

During the course of the 11th century the market came under the monarch's protection, just as had happened in León and Castile, and thus there is in the *Usatges* (*Usages*) of Catalonia a chapter dedicated to the overseeing of roads, entitled "Camine et Strate," by the terms of which any person who committed armed assault or violence on a highway became an outlaw.

As for the urban market, our first knowledge of its existence dates from the year 986, when the town of Cardona—just resettled for the second time—was given the right to engage in *negotium rectum* and *mercatum perfectum.* Upright business dealings and a "perfect market" were to be the two basic factors in the mentality of the Catalonian bourgeoisie for five centuries. These markets were very well attended, especially by Jews, Moslems, and Franks, whose transactions enlivened their proceedings. There were also artisans, established in *operatoria* in streets near the "mercadal," and local businessmen who traveled from market to market. Thus, from the 11th century onward we encounter the *mercerii* and *negotiatores,* or men engaged in business transactions, who began to acquire economic importance at that period because of a fundamental fact which we shall take up in due time.

ORIGINS OF CATALONIAN MERCHANT SHIPPING AND TRADE. This is a subject which has not yet been investigated, but it should be studied authoritatively, for it affects not only Catalonia and Spain but is a paradigm of the origin of a great mercantile city within the compass of Western culture. In the medieval world of Western Europe there were only nine or ten cities similar to Barcelona, and therefore it seems logical that this theme should excite the interest of scholars. So far we do not have a theory of the causes for Barcelona's initial prosperity; we shall attempt to set forth the problem here.

The Mediterranean was Moslem up to the 11th century. In these circumstances, the potentialities of Christian trade were very small. There was only a bit of coastwise traffic among the ports of the Levantine coast, an echo of the age-old seafaring tradition of Ampurias. This does not mean, however, that Catalan fishermen did not take to the open sea and sail about, especially trying to plunder ships which they found drifting or caught unawares. So that along the Catalonian coast there was a double life; that of the fisherman and that of the "corsair," as we might call it (although this word did not come into use until later on). In addition to these there were the great warrior expeditions like the one carried out by Count Suñer II of Ampurias in the 9th century against the Almerían coast, for example; but this is misleading. Catalonian maritime power simply did not exist, for when Ramón Berenguer III tried to conquer Minorca in 1115, he did so with the aid of ships from Pisa. Therefore, and approximately up to the year 1230, we cannot speak of a real Catalan fleet. The important factors were, we repeat, fishing activity and semipiratical raids along the coast-line.

However, the situation we have just described was reversed about the year 1000. The Caliphate of Cordova collapsed, and subsequently the counts of Urgel sent a great expedition to Cordova. This enterprise did not achieve the hoped-for political victory, but those who participated in the expedition did come back with fabulous sums of money, on a scale such as Catalonia had never known. This money could be particularly well applied in Barcelona, at the point of the wedge which Western Europe was driving into the South. No other city could boast the same conditions: it was still part of the Carolingian empire, or Frankish kingdom, for its counts were legally linked to France, but ruled as autonomous sovereigns. This meant that its inhabitants had citizenship in the heart of the Europe of that time. On the other hand, to the south lay the Taifa kingdoms (Tortosa, Valencia, Denia), rich and prosperous but politically weak. The counts of Barcelona collected *parias,* or tribute, from them in cash. And finally, in this advanced zone of Europe a specialized market existed, that of gold and slaves. The gold came from the Sudan, went to the northern coast of Africa, and was distributed from there all over Mediterranean Europe, which was avid for this metal. Its distribution was carried out chiefly through the kingdoms of Denia, Valencia, and Tortosa, and it flowed into Europe by that open door which was the port of Barcelona. The slave market had its origin in those same semipiratical activities to which we have alluded. It is quite possible that, when this problem is carefully studied, Barcelona will turn out to have been one of the great slave centers of the early medieval period.

Now we can understand the fact that Benjamin de Tudela, a Jew who was making a journey about the world, found a seaport with ships from Alexandria, the Holy Land, Greece, Africa, Pisa, Genoa, Sicily, and Marseilles when he arrived in Barcelona in 1150. What did these ships come to trade in? Gold and slaves. And this was, in our opinion, long before the organization of the cloth trade, which became possible only in the 14th century and was the basis of Barcelona's flowering. It was an extraordinary flowering; from a small city, almost unknown in the 3rd century, struggling for existence in the 5th, reconquered at the beginning of the 9th century by Charlemagne, it became by about 1150 one of the great international trade marts of the period.

And all this explains why in 1062, for example, the merchants of Barcelona owned slaves, why in 1104 Ramón Berenguer III collected a tithe on the profits from the capture and sale of slaves, and why in 1148, when Ramón Berenguer IV was planning the conquest of Tortosa, he found support among the *burguenses barchinonensis,* or the bourgeoisie of Barcelona, in the form of large sums of money. All of this justifies our thesis that between the 9th and 11th centuries Barcelona was one of the great points of contact in the Western Mediterranean between the Christian world on the one hand, and the Moslem world on the other.

COINAGE. In Catalonia the double monetary influence of Franks and Moslems was much more marked than in the Asturo-Leonese kingdom. In the first place, there had been a firm establishment of the Carolingian system starting in the 9th century as a result of the Carolingians' installation in the Spanish March. Let us recall that this system was based on the exclusive circulation of silver (soon supplanted by the use of vellon, a silver and copper alloy) of a single unit, the dinero, and its multiples, which existed only as money of account; these were the *sueldo* and the *libra.* The relationship among these types of money was established in a formula which eventually became classic:

$$240 \text{ dineros} = 20 \text{ sueldos} = 1 \text{ libra}$$

The coining of Catalonian dineros, originally linked to that of Frankish money, gradually became independent as the counts of the March tightened their effective rule over the country. And to complete this process, the second half of the 10th century saw the total disappearance of any likeness of the Frankish kings on the coins minted in Catalonia. The great variety of mintings which resulted from the fragmentation of political power—for the Spanish March broke up into a large number of counties—eventually led to the necessity of linking payments to a precise and specified coin. After the 11th century the libra of Barcelona triumphed as a universally accepted standard.

But if the Spanish March fell fully within the Carolingian monetary system, it also came into the area of Moslem gold coinage.

Coincident with the drop in circulation of Carolingian coinage, the mintings of the Caliphate—the gold dinar—invaded Catalonia in the 10th century; and sometime before 1035 Ramón Berenguer I began to coin *mancusos* (the name given by the Christians to the ordinary dinar) in his own kingdom, imitating those of the Taifa kingdom of Málaga. This minting is extremely important, for it foreshadows the full return to gold coinage—begun in the 13th century by the Italian republics—and marks a great advance by the Catalonian economy in comparison with other peninsular economies. In fact, it was only at this time that the first mintings of copper, or silver and copper coins, were being produced in Navarre, Aragon, and Castile. The beginning of Castilian imitation of Moslem dinars was not to take place until the reign of Alfonso VIII in 1172, when the first *marabetís,* or *maravedís* (dinars of the Almoravid type), appeared.

Fiscal System in Navarre, Aragon, and Catalonia. The fiscal system in the two Pyrenean countries was not conceived of as a survival of the old Roman *aerarium,* or public exchequer, but as a further link between lord and vassal, with the peculiarity that, since a system of bilateral dependency existed, the fiscal system was not applied by the lord to the vassal, but the vassal had to comply with the demands of the lord. Therefore, the Pyrenean fiscal system displayed an almost total divergence from that of the Meseta kingdoms. And this difference consisted in the fact that the king did not levy a tax on the vassal, but the vassal was obliged to carry out his strict military and feudal duties, and once these were carried out, any gift had to be freely bestowed. This principle gave rise to a system of *fiscal pacts,* which became very well developed in Catalonia.

Unity of the Pyrenean World. Isolated data, applied to the early economy of Navarre, Aragon, and Catalonia, should not mask a general principle: the unity of the two sides of the Pyrenees for a period lasting nearly a thousand years. From the 8th to the 17th centuries, the inhabitants of both sides of the mountain range formed a compact block, quite apart from any differences between Frenchmen and Spaniards.

This unity had three aspects:

GEOGRAPHIC UNITY. The valleys of the Pyrenees, especially those at high altitudes, form almost without exception transversal fissures which, open to the level country below, lead gradually from terrain favorable to an agricultural economy to one favorable to a herding economy, from a geography conducive to the life of the peasant of the plains to one suited to the life of the mountaineer. Therefore the valleys are linked to the lowland regions by close ties, and take part in their activities. All these valleys communicate with those on the opposite side by means of passes which, though they are higher than the Alpine ones, yet offer easier transit. From one side of the Pyrenees to the other, exchange is possible everywhere. The Pyrenean valley, then, lends itself to easy communication.

ECONOMIC UNITY. In spite of the resemblances we have indicated, the two faces—French and Spanish—of the Pyrenees chain have very different characteristics. The French side, rich in water and in pastures, produced cattle and horses, flax and the textile industry derived from it. The Spanish side, which is dryer, yielded wine and olive oil, wool, salt, and produce. That is, it was a question of two complementary economies having need of each other. And if relations between the Spanish portion of the Pyrenean world and Moslem Spain were impossible, the territories on the French side, especially in their western parts, were also isolated from the rest of the country by the no man's land of Les Landes in Gascony, avoided by traders and travelers. Thus, the interchange possible among the Pyrenean valleys was a necessary one.

DEMOGRAPHIC UNITY. Inevitably, the circumstances we have just described led to a constant process of demographic osmosis. When there was a dearth of people on one side, settlers from the other side came to fill the gap, and vice versa. As examples of this compensatory phenomenon we might cite the resettlement of the Ebro valley by French colonists, the establishment of Spanish groups in Aquitaine after it was depopulated by the Hundred Years' War, and the wave of Gascons into the depopulated Catalonia of the 16th century.

The importance of this triple unity is reflected in the numerous pacts of *lies* and *passeries* (in Spanish, *facería*) into which all the Pyrenean valleys entered with the valleys of the opposite side. These pacts go back at least as far as the 13th century and were independent of relations between France and the Hispanic kingdoms.

They assured the permanence of the two regions' relationship (*lies,* from Spanish *ligar,* "to tie") and freedom of passage (*passeries*) between them, quite apart from political contingencies. In the same way, the Crown of Aragon's expansion over the Pyrenees, which was to culminate in the actions of Alfonso the Chaste, also responded to a desire to uphold the unity of the Pyrenean world.

III · URBAN ECONOMY

13 · Reconquest and Resettlement in the 12th and 13th Centuries

We shall now take up urban economy; that is, the economy which developed in the Peninsula from the 12th to the 15th centuries under the aegis of the mercantile recovery of the Mediterranean world, of which the prime movers were the Italian cities.

Before taking up this subject, we must cast an overall glance at the Peninsula to see what the situation was after the great Christian conquests of the 13th century, and at the same time to study a very important problem for the economic life of the period—resettlement of the country and the distribution of agrarian property.

GEOPOLITICS OF THE RECONQUEST. In general the Reconquest followed the lines of natural geographic communication; that is, of those great zones between the Cantabrian System and the southern part of the country. From west to east, these zones are: the Galician-Portuguese, the Leonese, the Cantabro-Castilian, the Pyrenean, and the Catalonian.

During the course of the 12th century, geographic affinity reduced these five great zones to three: the Portuguese, the Castilian (which had absorbed the Leonese zone), and the zone corresponding to the Crown of Aragon, which resulted from the combined efforts of the Aragonese and Catalonians. A residual region remained in the North: Navarre, remnant of a nucleus which had failed to prosper, surviving as a Pyrenean enclave between Castile, the Crown of Aragon, and France.

The Christian armies' advance toward the south does offer one peculiarity, the chronological delay in the progress of certain zones of reconquest compared with others. The explanation of this is that the Moslems' most tenacious resistance took place in the east, where there were bastions (the pre-Pyrenean ranges, the valleys of the Ebro and its tributaries, the mountains of the Iberian System) which resisted conquest by the Aragonese and Catalans. Thus, the

155

CHRONOLOGICAL DEVELOPMENT OF THE RECONQUEST.

Christian advance was not simultaneous, but was carried out first by the Portuguese, who reached the shores of the Algarve region in southern Portugal before Ferdinand III conquered Seville; the Castilians, in their turn, advanced more rapidly than the Catalo-Aragonese group, for Ferdinand III conquered Seville in 1248, only ten years after James I the Conqueror had captured Valencia. In other words, if we imagine the Peninsula as divided by a diagonal line running northeast-southwest, we will see that at the same time, about the year 1238, the Portuguese were already in Tavira, near the mouth of the Guadiana, while the Catalans and Aragonese were still north of the river Júcar.

This fact is of extraordinary importance because: first, it permitted the Castilians an outlet to the Mediterranean through Cartagena, thus hindering the natural tendency of Catalonia and Aragon to spread toward the south and possibly to conquer Almería; and second, it meant that the whole Spanish South, together with all it represented in terms of economic power and agricultural wealth, came within the exclusive orbit of Castilian resettlement.

RESETTLEMENT: DIFFERENT TYPES IN TERMS OF SPACE AND CHRONOLOGY. We have previously studied two similar types of resettlement, Castilian *presura* and Catalan *aprisio*. Both belong to a difficult period, when advances were being made into empty lands and colonization rather than conquest was necessary.

After the beginning of the 13th century, when Moslem resistance, supported by African Berber troops, was finally broken, and the way was clear for the northern Christians to take over Extremadura, New Castile, Andalusia, Valencia, and Murcia, a very important phenomenon came into being. It was the existence of two reconquests, the one which figures in the history books, or *Military Reconquest*, which was accomplished in giant strides after 1212 and which brought the Castilians to Cádiz in fifty years and the Catalans and Aragonese to take control of Valencia in twelve years; and the real reconquest, or *Slow Reconquest*, which took place later and was based on resettlement and true colonization of southern Spain. This began in 1230 and lasted until 1609, when Philip III decreed the expulsion of the Moriscos.

The Slow Reconquest took different forms in different regions. Therefore we shall study it in relation to the conquest of the *cities* of Aragon, the *huertas* of Valencia and Murcia, the *herding zone* to the south of the Central System, the *commercial base* of Majorca, and *Andalusia,* which presents a number of extremely interesting social and economic problems.

As for the chronological sequence, although we will examine the demographic process in greater detail later on, we can state here that this colonizing type of reconquest, the Slow Reconquest, got a firm start about the middle of the 13th century and continued at a constant rate until the second half of the 14th; then the process was interrupted as a result of the Black Death (in 1348), which caused a tremendous demographic vacuum in the Crown of Aragon as well as in Castile. It was not until a century later that biological losses were recouped, permitting the work of reconquest and resettlement so typical of the period of Ferdinand and Isabella to go forward once more. However, the great drain of population to America again weakened the Castilians' capacity for internal colonization and made inevitable the decree expelling the Moriscos early in the 17th century, for they presented the dilemma of a refractory and prolific population which could not be assimilated by the Christians.

RESETTLEMENT OF THE ARAGONESE CITIES. As a general rule, the Moslem cities of the Ebro valley were conquered by capitulation: the Moslem population could stay in their homes for a year, after which they had to move to settlements outside the walls (the famous *Morerías,* or Moorish quarters), keeping their movable goods and any cultivable land they possessed within the municipal boundaries of that or any other city. The consequences of these agreements are obvious: the problem of resettlement came up only in relation to urban centers, while no substantial change took place in the countryside.

In the cities, once the walled area had been cleared pursuant to the surrender of the Moslems, it was necessary to find Christian settlers either from inside or outside the kingdom. Since there was no native bourgeois class, the new population which was to make its living by the trades and by commerce had to be recruited from foreigners, just as had been the case in the cities of the pre-Pyrenean zone. Thus, the "Franks," who for fifty years had occupied separate quarters of Jaca, Sangüesa, Pamplona, Estella, and Huesca, were the ones who resettled Saragossa, Tudela, Tarazona, and so on. Consequently, the early Aragonese city dwellers were of foreign origin, and came attracted by the special privileges offered them.

On the other hand, Moslems predominated in the countryside and were given the name of *exarchs*. Their position, very little altered at the beginning of Christian rule, slowly worsened with the spread of the Roman law system, which changed them from free partners into tenant-serfs restricted to the glebe, like the *coloni* of the later Roman Empire. Also contributing to making their fate harder was the arrival, in 1126, of 10,000 dispossessed Mozárabes from the South, who disputed their ownership of the land.

OCCUPATION OF THE HORTICULTURAL ZONES: VALENCIA AND MURCIA. Compared with the resettlement of the Aragonese territory, that of Valencia presented the following disadvantages: it was accomplished with considerably more urgency (reconquest of the kingdom lasted only fifteen years, from 1230 to 1245) and without any foreign aid, so that the intensity of the problem was greater and the possibility of solving it smaller.

This dual circumstance meant that mere occupation prevailed over true resettlement, which was put into practice only in the exceptional instances of places taken by force, where considerations of security required the substitution of Christian settlers for Moslem ones. In other places it was deemed sufficient to intersperse some Christian elements among the Moslem mass of population. Thus, when a "measurement," or census, was made in 1272 there were only 30,000 Christians in a Moslem population of 200,000. This disproportion (which meant that every one of the new settlers— each of whom was at once warrior and producer—was of special value) explains why the king was so anxious to control the terms of their settlement. So, instead of general donations made to great lords, in Valencia the monarchy preferred the system of *individual distribution,* giving each occupant a house, an orchard, a vineyard, and some few *fanegas* of land, in parcels of about three, nine, or twelve acres. This type of *royal resettlement* was imposed especially in those urban centers and their hinterlands that were of the greatest strategic value. It gave rise to a type of medium-sized rustic property which has been a definite factor in the prosperity of the *huertas* up to the present day.

But because manpower was lacking to supply this type of resettlement to the whole kingdom, the monarchy was obliged to cede the greater part of the rural lands to the lords who had aided in the conquest. The *seigniorial lands,* occupied almost entirely by Moslems, were administered in the same manner as the Aragonese lands (where most of the new owners came from), and this implied the serfdom of those who cultivated them.

The plight of Levantine resettlement was even worse in the case of Murcia. The reconquest of this territory took place at a time when the biological potential of the Northern settlers—Castilians as well as Aragonese and Catalans—had been almost exhausted. Therefore, when Prince Alfonso (the Wise) conquered Murcia during the reign of Ferdinand III, in 1243, the kingdom was turned over to him in token of submission; in other words, the Moslems continued to carry out the same functions as before and only a few cities (Murcia, Cartagena, Lorca, Mula) were occupied militarily by Castilians. For thirty years, until the great rebellion of 1263-1264, Murcia was a dependency of Castile, though this was purely nominal since the Moslems in fact continued the same organization they had had before. This fact demonstrates that there was a lack of settlers from the North to occupy strategic places in the region; for if the Castilians had been able to count on reserves of manpower, they obviously would have sent people there to occupy the land. The scope of the problem was such that when the Moslem rebellion broke out in 1263-1264, it was not the Castilians who reoccupied Murcia, but James the Conqueror and his son Peter the Great. They brought in new people, and therefore Murcia was in large part resettled by subjects of the Crown of Aragon. Figures referring to the *Repartiment,* or distribution of lands, in Murcia show that 10,000 Catalans and Aragonese settled in the region.

Later, after the revolt had been put down, the policy of Alfonso X the Wise was to send new Castilian contingents to Murcia. Then a distribution of lands took place, the Moslems were removed from the cities, and the countryside was turned over to Christian knights, following the system of colonization used in Andalusia. But in fact, up to the 16th century Murcia was a Moslem world pressing in on a certain number of Christians who lived in the cities, ruling by force of arms and also by virtue of their ownership of the land.

RESETTLEMENT OF THE CENTRAL CASTILIAN ZONE. The conquest of Toledo in 1085 marks the end of the first wave of Castilian resettlement in the Duero region of the Meseta, the section which included the "outlying lands" from the Cantabrian mountains to the river Duero. For a whole century, the 12th, the field of battle was transferred to the southern part of the Meseta, from the Central System to Sierra Morena. While the region contiguous to the Tagus and Guadiana rivers was suffering the consequences of a war carried out with great harshness, the districts to the south of the Duero were receiving definitive resettlement.

Two sets of criteria prevailed at the time. One was to leave the Moslem and Jewish population in the conquered cities undisturbed. This was the resettlement policy of Alfonso VI in Toledo. The other was to turn over the task of resettlement to municipalities or town councils. Thus, the old system of *presura* disappeared, and new Castilian communities, with extensive territories and a forward-looking spirit, began to arise between the Tagus and the Duero. Here the powerful Castile of the 14th and 15th centuries was formed, with its great centers in Avila, Valladolid, Medina, and Segovia.

OCCUPATION OF THE HERDING ZONE. For the kingdoms of the North, one of the most important events of the Reconquest was the occupation of the grazing lands in the South. After the battle of Las Navas de Tolosa (1212), when it became possible for Christian arms to advance toward Al-Andalus, large grazing areas were opened up for Castilian flocks: the Alcarria region, the Toledo mountains, a large part of La Mancha, and all of Extremadura. But even at the outset there was a certain lack of initiative on the part of the settlers of northern Castile to move south. And it was for this reason—to guarantee the security of the conquered zones—that the kings of Castile turned over the region to the military orders: the Order of Alcántara, which occupied the western part of Extremadura; that of Santiago, established in the center; and the Order of Calatrava, which occupied the La Mancha region.

The system of distribution of property was very simple: the king donated lands to the masters of the order; these turned the castles and fortified places over to the commanders; the commanders brought together groups of officers, who defended the population against the Moslems and availed themselves of the peasants' labor and rents, but profited especially from passage of flocks and sale of wool.

It is a proven fact that, although the French military orders carried on important economic activities—in this regard we should not forget that the Order of Templars was the first banking organization in the medieval world—the Spanish orders, by contrast, had absolutely nothing to do with the economic sphere. We should recall here the hypothesis of Américo Castro that although the Spanish military orders adopted a system of the French type, their ideology, on the other hand, was learned from the Moslem resistance communities. That is why we find predominating in them a mystico-religious ideal which sets them apart from the Frankish orders.

Be that as it may, it is evident that the Castilian military orders did not represent any economic organism of importance, and that from the beginning they turned the handling of their finances over to the Jews. We find the Jews serving their interests after the 13th century.

RECONQUEST AND RESETTLEMENT OF ANDALUSIA. The downfall of Moslem power in Andalusia delivered to Ferdinand III, within the space of a very few years, what had been the most prosperous region of medieval Spain. Therefore we must take up the problem of how the region was resettled, and how the economic heritage left by the Moslems was utilized. In principle, the system was one of pure military occupation. The territory being occupied was too large, its cities too densely populated, to even dream of a system of coexistence like that established in Toledo by Alfonso VI. Consequently, the Moslems were forced to evacuate the cities (Ubeda, Baeza, Jaén, Cordova, Seville), which were then organized as redoubts for defense of the territory. But this system of military colonization failed in 1263, for since the country population continued to be Moslem, a great rebellion took place similar to the one in Murcia. It seemed that the Castilian system of occupation was going to fall apart. But once the crisis had passed, the vanquished ppercase:

Moslems were forced to emigrate to Granada or Africa. It was then that real colonizing measures were taken, and there was a systematic resettlement of the region. Julio González, who has studied this question, affirms that there was intensive Castilianization of Andalusia from this time onward. Undoubtedly, this Castilianization depended on the survival of the great latifundia of Moslem times, and on others which were created to meet the demands of the border wars with Granada.

The process was the following: first, the Moslems were expelled from the countryside, just as they had been pushed out of the cities in the early stages of conquest. Second, a special system was set up on the borders of the kingdom of Granada, the purpose of which was to oppose any possible counteroffensives by the Moslems of that region, supported by the African Berber kingdoms. This *frontier* arrangement is extremely important because it established the large latifundia of the military orders and the great Castilian families all along the borders of the kingdom of Granada. All the dukes, marquises, and counts who figured importantly in the history of Spain from the 15th century onward had the basis of their power in this latifundia system. The third consequence of the rebellion of 1263, and the subsequent expulsion of the Andalusian peasant population, was the impossibility of maintaining the high technological level which had characterized Al-Andalus up to that time. After 1263, according to the extant documents, the type of intensive economy which had prevailed in the Guadalquivir valley since Roman times was supplanted in Andalusia by an extensive economy in which the raising of sheep and the cultivation of the olive were to occupy a preponderant position, to the detriment of more specialized crops.

In consequence, any theory about Andalusia requires a profound knowledge of the system of resettlement and the effects which it produced. It requires the realization that the transformation of the Andalusian economy was not accomplished under favorable circumstances: a rebellion, followed by a hasty expulsion, led it into a situation from which recovery was to be very slow.

RECONQUEST OF MAJORCA. In the case of Majorca there were no agricultural or livestock interests involved. The conquest of Majorca was undertaken as a result of the growing needs of the Catalonian merchants, who wanted to take over this maritime redoubt of such great importance in the Western Mediterranean, and which constantly menaced their activity in the trade routes to Sardinia, Sicily, and the North African coast.

This was the motive which led the cities of the Catalonian coast to demand that the monarchy conquer the Balearic Islands, and to proffer the necessary funds to do so. And further, they provided the fleet necessary for the operation.

It was, therefore, a reconquest very different from the one that had been carried out in the Peninsula. In fact, the principal interests were mercantile. As a result of this, Majorca was organized from the very first by bringing in essential seafaring men and working people. This made possible Majorca's conversion into one of the chief bases of Catalonia's political and economic expansion in the Mediterranean.

There was also a distribution of property in Majorca. The Moslems who lived there lost their lands, and most of them emigrated. Then an exhaustive *Repartiment* was made (1232), resulting in the transfer of the island's smallholdings to the new settlers; the majority of these were men from the cities and towns which had contributed to the conquest. Therefore the case of Majorca is something unique in the process of resettlement; it is an example of total colonization carried out in a minimum period of time.

SPECIAL ECONOMIC ENTITIES: THE MONASTERIES AND MILITARY ORDERS. Until the 13th century the great monasteries in Catalonia, Aragon, and Castile were centers of resettlement and the technological organization of agriculture. A visit to any one of them would have disclosed a large agrarian operation of a collective type, centered on the monastery and divine worship. However, this type of farming operation declined in the 14th century because the monks, instead of seeking out the humble country people, preferred to instruct the rich in the cities. This work was done by Franciscans and Dominicans in particular. Thus the monasteries ceased to exercise a role of technological advancement, leaving it to the bourgeoisie of the cities. It was for this reason that modern agriculture did not get a start in places remote from the cities, but in the horticulture areas around them, where the bourgeoisie established summerhouses, gardens, crops, and orchards.

As for the military orders, their role in the economic sphere was far from brilliant. They believed that the country should be organized into a warrior system, and they never really emerged from the feudal environment which had created them. This attitude contributed decisively to consolidation of the Andalusian latifundia system, especially on the frontier of the kingdom of Granada, where the king, in a disagreement with his nobles, had conceded to them the following lands: to the Order of Santiago, the Segura region; to the Archbishop of Toledo, the district of Cazorla, almost to Baza; to the Order of Calatrava, ample domains and fortresses in Martos and Alcaudete; to the Order of Santiago, Estepa; to that of Alcántara, Morón; and finally, to the Order of Santa María, Medina Sidonia, Vejer, and Alcalá de los Gazules. These last-named cities passed into the rule of the Order of Santiago when the Order of Santa María disappeared. As a general rule, the military orders paid no attention to the technical problems of agriculture, and this was why, at the time of the great reconquest of Andalusia, the Castilian state found it did not possess the elements essential to take full advantage of an occupation so vast as that of the old Roman Baetica.

RESETTLEMENT OF RURAL AREAS AND RESULTING SOCIAL CLASSES. The great conquests of the 13th century radically changed the social structure which had predominated on Hispanic soil during the early medieval centuries. The rapid expansion of the Christian peoples toward the south, the enormous wealth which they seized (cities, towns, farms, properties, mills, etc.) subverted the principles on which the organization of the Reconquest had been based, for up till that time it had been in essence a liberation movement, particularly in Castile.

The nobles benefited greatly from this sudden broadening of the Christian kingdoms' agricultural horizons. They were given generous royal concessions and inherited the great Andalusian properties, which became further enlarged by indiscriminate expulsion of the Moslems, converting the old wheat-growing lands into grazing grounds. This accounts for the rise of the *landholding nobility,* which would soon become an element of resistance against the State itself and would give rise to a long struggle with the monarchy, in the course of which it would emerge in large part triumphant. Even within the Crown of Aragon, Aragonese and Catalan nobles found a source of power in the rural regions of Valencia, though not under the excessive conditions which so greatly benefited the Castilian aristocracy.

The *knightly class* also grew in power. The old *hidalgos* of the North were rewarded with parcels of urban land and properties situated on the outskirts of the conquered cities. Many of them entered into a relationship of vassalage with the great titled aristocracy, especially through the practice of *soldada,* or payment made by the monarchy to secure an effective army. Thus the seigniorial system was strengthened and the influence of the nobility on the cities guaranteed. During this period the cities lost their democratic character, eventually falling into the hands of an oligarchy of *hidalgos.* The knights lived off their *soldadas* and from the income of the rents and services of the peasants who cultivated their holdings.

The farmers, however, found themselves in a worsening situation. Contrary to the theories held until fairly recently, affirming the existence of a process of emancipation throughout the Late Middle Ages, we know today that there was an intensification of serfdom beginning in the latter part of the 13th century. The constant migratory movement toward the South which prevailed during the great conquests of Ferdinand III and James I gravely threatened the revenues of the landholding lords of the North. In Catalonia as well as Castile we can observe a process of adscription to the glebe which was to result in the problem of the Catalan *remença* serfs and that of the *solariego* serfs in Castile, not to mention another very important manifestation—the appearance of *jornaleros,* or day laborers, landless peasants who offered their labor, either with or without a team of oxen, to the lords of the latifundia of Extremadura, New Castile, and Andalusia.

14 · The Evolution of Urban Economy

CHARACTERISTICS OF THE COMMERCIAL REVOLUTION. About the middle of the 12th century an astonishing economic development took place in the Mediterranean countries, as much deserving the name of Commercial Revolution as the term we apply to the change undergone by the European economy in the 18th century, led by England, merits the name of Industrial Revolution.

This early revolution is called commercial because the basic factor in the prosperity of the economy is the mercantile traffic which became established among the different Mediterranean countries. Its fundamental cause is to be sought in the movement of the Crusades, which reestablished the unity of the Mediterranean world; for it was the rupture of this unity by the expansion of Islam that had brought about the downfall of the ancient economy. Consequently, when the Crusaders set up in Palestine not only military orders to combat the Moslems, but also colonies and trading posts, it was then that mercantile traffic, which had been interrupted in the 10th century, recovered and took on extraordinary vigor.

The basis of this prosperity centered around the activity of the Italian cities, especially those, such as Venice, Pisa, and Genoa, which for centuries had carried on a more or less regular traffic with Byzantium and the Near East. The Italian cities served as a way station for the Crusaders who went from Western Europe to Palestine and established mercantile colonies in the conquered cities. Thus a fruitful commerce was begun which sent merchandise and spices back to the mother cities. Genoa and Venice reshipped these goods to the rest of Europe and at the same time developed an incipient cloth industry. Little by little this mercantile expansion affected other European areas, especially the great delta of the Rhine and its tributaries.

Consequently, the economy of the Commercial Revolution was based on reconstruction of the unity of the Mediterranean world. It shows two characteristics. First, it was an economy of an urban type; that is, it renewed the ancient tradition that made the city the center of activity in social and economic life. That great vacuum which feudalism had represented, when the countryside was the basis of European economy, was broken by the Commercial Revolution; from then on until the present day, the cities were to have the effective power, and this is extremely important because to speak of cities is to speak of the social class that ruled them—the *bourgeois patriciate.*

The second characteristic is that the Commercial Revolution was inspired by but one end; namely, to make money. It represents the bourgeois' vocation not only to produce enough to live on, charging a just and equitable price for his work or his commercial activity, but to earn enough money to satisfy certain comforts of life. At the beginning of the Commercial Revolution, when the bourgeois dared to expose himself to all kinds of risk and danger by embarking for the Near East on a voyage which often lasted a year, it was because he expected to gain a profit for his enterprise many times over, to a point well beyond the limits permitted by the Church. This is why, from the earliest times of the Commercial Revolution, there is a very interesting moralistic literature concerned with resolving the bourgeois' problems of conscience.

CAPITALIZATION OF URBAN WEALTH. If the city was indeed the center of the new economic style in Europe, it is essential to recognize it as such. We have already said that the germ of the renewal of commercial economy in the Late Middle Ages had been the marketplace. For in the majority of cases, from the marketplace, next to a church or castle, arose a small group of houses or a hamlet. This first urban grouping was the *bourg,* cradle of the city. From it the inhabitants received a name that was to have a significant historical future: *bourgeoisie.*

The process which governed the transition from bourg to city is highly important. Before it could take place, a concentration of capital was first necessary. Any number of theories attempt to explain this phenomenon. We can only be eclectic when we try to pass judgment on them, for all contain true and positive elements.

Capital was formed in the cities by the concentration of three types of revenue. First, that which came from *rural property,* income enjoyed by the bishops, nobles, and knights. Little by little these groups accumulated capital which they then applied, at the opportune moment, to the financing of commerce. In the second place, there was revenue from *transactions on urban properties.* In early medieval times the city had a population far below its capacity; probably only about a third of the urban area was settled. And so the bourgeoisie who owned the unpopulated two-thirds were able to add to their capital the fabulous profits they received from selling their properties during the period of demographic growth and urban concentration of the 12th and 13th centuries. This phenomenon is equivalent to that of *surplus value,* which took place as a result of the cities' growth in the 19th century.

Finally, the third source of capitalization was, naturally, from *mercantile transactions.* There has been a great deal of discussion about this. Those who do not admit the hypothesis insist that medieval mercantile transactions could capitalize no more than 5 or 10% profit. But in reality, if we keep in mind the huge profits earned in some cases and the concentration of these profits in some dozen Mediterranean cities, it can be admitted that the mercantile transactions concentrated in those cities would have afforded profits a certain freedom of movement for investment, and thus would have promoted both business activity and the acquisition of wealth.

THE CITY AS AN ECONOMIC ENTITY. Under what conditions did the city exist as an economic entity? We think this can be summed up in two essential traits. First, the economy of the city was, from the very beginning, an economy based on privilege. The feudal world was a world of privileges: for the noble, for the knight, for the Church, for all those who enjoyed exemptions. So, in this atmosphere the urban economy grew as a privileged body, demanding favorable laws from the outset: exemption from taxes; control of commerce; guarantees of supplies; restriction of competition. In short, it was a protectionist group. The city was born as a privileged entity, and this fact is very important, for such a situation led the patriciate which ruled the city's fortunes to think of itself as a chosen caste. All the bourgeoisie have given ample proof of this attitude, from the 13th century to the 20th.

The second characteristic of the city as an economic entity was the corporative system which directed its life and its economy. The origins of the corporations must be sought not in imitation of the Moslems, as some insist, nor in certain processes of a religious type, but in the humble origin of the city as a market. When the market became stabilized in the form of shops, the artisans who occupied them could live and be assured of work only by joining together in a group. The corporation was born of this necessity for intimate cooperation, as an inevitable corollary of the search for security. Formerly a peasant had attained it by offering his person to the lord, but in the 12th century city dwellers achieved it by forming associations to defend their interests, and by means of a statute which guaranteed their existence as a social class outside the world of feudalism. From this association, first in their work and later within the city, the corporations came into being as the natural result, not of some mystical corporation or theological development, but from the very circumstances of the environment.

DEVELOPMENT OF THE BOURGEOIS PATRICIATE: CHARACTERISTICS. Theoretically, the city was the "universitas" of its inhabitants, and that is why it was often called "university." That is, the city was the commonwealth. All those who lived in the city were the people of the city. But this is true only in theory, for in fact power was held by the bourgeois patriciate.

Generally speaking, these patricians were descendants, at least up to the 14th century, of the original founders or settlers of the city—that is, a patriciate of blood. We know the names of a number of families (twenty, thirty, or forty of them), who had engaged in the same business without interruption, sons inheriting from fathers, and who eventually built up a fortune and a respectable position: *they formed an oligarchy.* They were the ones who ruled the city and defended its freedoms, and in the last instance were those who gave it the essential momentum to triumph in its enterprises.

Beneath these citizens, who in Barcelona even had a name which defined them exactly (*ciudadanos honrados,* or honored citizens), was the world of the people who engaged in various tasks: the merchants, the artisans, and the *menestrales,* or common workmen. In this regard we should recall the origin of the words "artisan" and "menestral," for they were already characteristic of two distinct social classes: the artisans were masters of the most important crafts, and people of a certain social category such as doctors, lawyers, jewelers, and goldsmiths; the *menestrales* made up the "little people," the humbler folk in the guilds.

Very well then: to what did this oligarchic patriciate aspire? What did it want to do with the city? What did it in fact do with it? In the first place, the bourgeoisie arose out of a clear spirit of self-assertion, without which it would never have triumphed. It has often been criticized on the grounds that it was selfish and passive, but no social class can triumph on the basis of selfishness and passivity, especially not the one which has imposed its character on Europe for more than eight centuries. The bourgeoisie triumphed because from the very outset it was able to derive stimulation from business, because it recognized a fine art, *a style of life,* in the making of a product, the sale of that product, and in the whole sequence of commercial transactions—even in haggling. It saw this style of life often as an adventure, often as a pleasure, often simply as a speculation. But it did so not out of a selfishness derived from the mere pursuit of money, but rather by incorporating into this occupation one of many vital needs.

Apart from this creation of business as a style of life, the bourgeoisie brought to the social and economic process two essential characteristics. The first was a *realistic criterion:* the bourgeoisie were, are, and always will be the men who care least about the myths, or fine words, or great formal structures so easily cultivated by the knights, the nobles, and even the workers; for the bourgeoisie are the least sentimental people in the world and therefore want concrete and attainable things. This factor was translated into a certain social conservatism, not free from dissidence in the political sense, and later into a zeal for economic innovation. It is for this reason that the first impulse toward *continuous technological progress* was produced within the bourgeoisie.

Finally, the bourgeoisie was also responsible, even in the economic sphere, not to mention the social and political spheres, for *tolerance;* for even though its members were oligarchic representatives of the "universitas," the commonwealth, they never forgot that the commonwealth should be for everyone. They were the first since the Greeks to understand that the affairs of life had to be settled in the form of coexistence; and in the same way in which one bourgeois in his business dealings gave his word to another, and the gesture represented a lifelong pact, so the bourgeoisie considered that in public relations there was a pact involving mutual obligation, and that on this pact depended, for them and for their ruler, something called "the common good."

MUNICIPAL GOVERNMENT AND ADMINISTRATION. City government was delegated by the king from the beginning; that is, all the privileges the city possessed for its government were conceded by the king (or lord). When the cities became powerful in the course of the 13th and 14th centuries, the tendency of each was to set itself up as a totalitarian republic in which the political, social, and economic functions of government were carried on. This final stage was reached only in the Italian cities and a few German ones. In France, England, and Spain, the cities never achieved an absolute degree of autonomy.

The government of the city was a synodal or collegial system: one group represented the city, while another group, delegated by the first, dealt continually with problems as they arose. We have not the time to set forth the medieval municipal theory, nor to explain in detail the different procedures used to make such a system work. It always consisted of two levels, one of which was made up of between 50 and 100 representatives elected not by the people but by the bourgeois patriciate; the authority of the city resided in these representatives.

This rudimentary government, however, became more efficient after the 14th century, which marks the appearance of public administration. In the 12th century, when the interests of the patrician oligarchy coincided exactly with those of the city, the city assumed a number of responsibilities which were in harmony with its economic development: urban improvement, outside enterprises, etc. All this required money, and the control of money was what brought about the birth of administration in the following century. The aims of city administration were: to assist in the governing tasks of the municipal council; to organize municipal finances (accountants, collectors, depositors, etc.); to undertake public works and defense (bridges, walls, canals); to supply the city with food, especially wheat; to regulate the produce market; to oversee and regulate the industrial and commercial system. These different tasks required growing specialization and the creation of municipal offices in the modern sense of the term. The impetus came from Italy and quickly took shape in Catalonia and, following its example, in the other cities of the Crown of Aragon.

THE CITY AND EARLY PUBLIC FINANCE. Urban taxes were retained by the sovereign until the 14th century. Gradually, from the 11th century on, the cities began to free themselves from the taxes imposed by the Crown, and acquired the ability to create new taxes or duties. The importance of the cities in the Middle Ages and the omnipotence of their upper classes really stems from this financial autonomy, not from their municipal privileges, which have been so much vaunted, but in their right to have a treasury that did not depend on the State. It was there, in the heart of the treasury, that the power of the bourgeois patriciate was made manifest.

Municipal public finance was supplied from the following resources: taxes on property; taxes on mercantile transactions of any type; duties imposed on entry and departure of merchandise; and finally, warrants of quality on manufactures.

Early municipal finance became modified after the first half of the 14th century by the appearance of what today would be called the public debt. The city had money, its citizens possessed capital; but sometimes, in the face of a contribution to a king or the necessity of meeting some possible danger, large sums of money had to be raised at a given time. Since there were no banks, it was logical to resort to direct loans, either from Jews or from persons with liquid funds on hand. Thus the floating debt was born, which in the course of the 14th century became a funded debt. Barcelona was, in fact—as we shall see at the proper time—one of the first cities in the world where this important change took place.

THE CRISIS OF THE 14TH CENTURY AND URBAN STAGNATION IN THE 15TH. The medieval cities' apogee was in the 12th, 13th, and 14th centuries. In this latter century occurred a *profound demographic crisis* (due to the Black Death); but at the same time, it appears that everything connected with the world of the bourgeoisie entered a phase, if not of decadence, at least of stagnation. Until recently it was believed that the Renaissance in Italy had arisen out of a period of booming economy. Today we know that the Renaissance was made possible by great fortunes accumulated in the 14th century, during a period when nobody knew how to employ them, or dared to do so.

This profound decline of the spirit of risk among the bourgeoisie of the great Mediterranean cities is shown in the *lack of technological inventiveness;* in the *deflection of the process of investment of capital,* which no longer went into commerce but into improvement of the countryside (as in the case of the bourgeoisie of Barcelona, who took their money out of commercial enterprises in order to improve the Pla de Llobregat and Maresme regions) and into the purchase of public securities.

On the other hand, late in the 14th century a sudden business paralysis took place, producing grave economic crises and resulting in a radical change in general economic conditions, which passed from a phase of prosperity to one of contraction. The crucial moment everywhere in Europe was the year 1381, the first certain date we possess for far-reaching changes in the business cycle.

The result of this crisis of the cities was that the people became unhappy. The humble folk and the artisans, who looked on the bourgeois patriciate as the very incarnation of the city and saw in that class the prestige of the community, felt defrauded. Now *they* wished to govern, for they felt that the patrician oligarchy was attending only to its private interests. In consequence, a democratic social current arose which manifested itself in violent political upheavals in Italy, Flanders, and Catalonia. These upheavals, all the more noticeable because they were intertwined with the ambitions of the aristocracy and with religious antagonisms, form the backdrop of the 15th century. In Spain, for example, the social conflict led directly to the massacre of Jews in 1391.

These circumstances caused the star of the great medieval cities to grow dimmer, until at the end of the 15th century they were only pale reflections of what they had been a century earlier.

15 · Economy of the Catalan Urban Patriciate; Demography and Social Structure

DEMOGRAPHIC STRUCTURE OF CATALONIA, VALENCIA, AND THE BALEARIC ISLANDS BEFORE THE BLACK DEATH. In the demography of the later medieval centuries, an important factor appears which serves as a demographic dividing line. This factor is the Black Death, which occurred in a number of waves during the second half of the 14th century. Between the period previous to this great calamity and the period subsequent to it, an important change took place in the demographic structure of all Europe. The beginning of a new era, after the plague, is clearly shown in the documents of the time.

Before 1348, when the epidemic began, the population of the Hispanic Peninsula, like that of the rest of Europe, was in a very favorable phase of constant and progressive growth. In spite of the scarcity of precise figures, those available to us allow the suggestion that over the course of the two centuries between 1130 and 1340 the population of Spain almost doubled. This phenomenon is comparable to the sensational advance achieved in the 19th century, and was probably related to the winning of the first great struggle against the death rate. In fact, it appears that the period of the Commercial Revolution coincided with a lengthening of the human life span. The proofs of this brought forward by anthropologists are most suggestive, though insufficient. Anthropologists, on the basis of a study of the skulls, have been able to establish for different periods the distribution by age of adult corpses:

Age	Neo-eneolithic (Spanish Levant)	Hispano-Roman	13th-century Jews (Barcelona)
13–20	16.5	18.1	12.2
21–40	57.2	42.9	31.6
41–60	24.1	22.0	28.5
61—	2.0	16.8	27.5
(Undetermined)	0.2	0.2	0.2
Total	100.0	100.0	100.0

This table shows very clearly the ground which had been gained, in the course of time, by the older age groups. It is sufficient to point out the increase in the number of sexagenarians—practically nonexistent during the prehistoric period but comprising more than a fourth of the adult population in the 13th century—to make acceptable the idea of a decisive prolongation of the life span at the beginning of the Late Middle Ages. After that time, severe losses take place only at the base of the demographic pyramid, for only half the number of children born survive past the first stage (0–13 years). Success in the fight against infant mortality does not come until our own time.

Aside from the gains made by the development we have just described, the population of the Crown of Aragon was also augmented by incorporation of territories reconquered from the Moslems. However, we should not take a static view of this fact, for a double current existed: *Moslem emigration toward the South* and *Christian repopulation*. If we make an approximate calculation of the demographic result of this dual process, we can state that after the conquests of the 13th century some 150,000 souls were incorporated into the Crown of Aragon, a rather considerable number.

Keeping in mind the data provided by the first census, taken shortly after the initial inroads of the Black Death, and making the necessary adjustments, it appears that in about the year 1348 Catalonia had some 450,000 inhabitants, Valencia and Aragon some 200,000, and Majorca some 50,000. In regard to the population of Catalonia, it should be noted that the figure mentioned is probably not very different from that of a century earlier—the middle of the 13th century—which in the case of Catalonia runs counter to the general tendency to increase. This anomaly is due to the constant demographic expansion of the Catalans during a period in which they had to repopulate Majorca, Valencia, and part of Murcia, and, further, had to conquer the islands of Sicily and Sardinia, not to mention a series of battles which took them as far away as Greece and the Near East. These factors account for the apparent stagnation of Catalonian demography. But it is only a relative stagnation, brought about by historical causes which scattered its population, generally speaking, all over the Western Mediterranean.

Among this population we must single out the *Jews*. We do not know exactly the number of Jews in the Crown of Aragon during the Middle Ages, but approximate calculations permit us to realize that they represented an active artisan and commercial segment of the population which carried considerable weight in the total activity, for they regulated or supervised the economic and scientific life of the country. It is estimated that Jews made up 6.5% of the total population of the Crown of Aragon, a higher percentage than in Castile. In the middle of the 13th century this population was distributed in the following manner: 25,000 Jews in Catalonia, 20,000 in Aragon, 10,000 in Valencia, and 5,000 in Majorca. These are important figures; the 5,000 Jews in Barcelona, for example, comprised one-seventh of the total population. Other notable *calls,* or Jewish communities, were those of Gerona, Besalú, Cervera, Montblanc, Tortosa, and Perpignan.

In Aragon, the largest concentration of Jews was found in the cities of Saragossa, Calatayud, Tarazona, and Huesca.

The precise effects of the massacres of 1391 on the Jewish population are unknown. The numbers have been enormously exaggerated. Studies of documents reveal that barely 5% of them died, although in specific cases (Barcelona, Palma de Mallorca, and Gerona) the figures were probably lower.

What became of those 50,000 Jews in the Crown of Aragon after the massacres of 1391? A great many became converted, and others continued to inhabit the Jewish *calls,* especially in the areas more favorable to them, such as Aragon. At the end of the 15th century, that is, at the time of the expulsion, the Crown of Aragon certainly contained 30,000 Jews. And there was an equal number of *conversos,* or converted Jews.

The *Mudéjares* comprise another demographic level; these were the unconverted Moslems, agricultural workers who lived in the regions of Lower Aragon, Lower Catalonia, and especially Valencia. In this last kingdom the Mudéjar population at the end of the 14th century was two-thirds of the total; in Aragon it was 35%, and in Catalonia a tiny proportion, approximately 3%.

THE BLACK DEATH AND ITS DEMOGRAPHIC CONSEQUENCES. About the middle of the 14th century a great epidemic spread over Europe: bubonic plague. It was an epidemic that followed the routes of ships and caravans. The great seaports and coastal areas were particularly hard hit. Every ship that sailed from the Near East brought danger with it. From Alexandria and Constantinople it moved to the Italian ports and spread out from there throughout Europe. The Mediterranean coast began to be attacked by the plague after 1348.

In Catalonia the disease came on the heels of a period of famine which had begun in 1333, the "first bad year" of the chronicles, and this may explain its particular virulence in the region. It is impossible to give a figure for the number of deaths, which some chroniclers put at as much as two-thirds of the entire population, an obviously exaggerated figure, yet not grossly so when viewed from a modern perspective. We learn with surprise, as a matter of fact, that in three urban centers (Albi, Castres, and Millau) in the neighboring French Midi, the number of dead in the plague came to 50% of the population. Is it not likely that this same percentage would apply to the Catalonian cities, whose demographic characteristics were so similar to those of France? In any case the documents, which never tire of applying the most horrific descriptions to the epidemic, add very significant details to our knowledge of the catastrophe. A body of documents recently published by Srta. López de Meneses shows among other things: general remission of taxes owing to lack of taxpayers; attacks on many Jewish *calls* (which were held responsible for the disaster); construction of new cemeteries; amalgamation of two farming districts, Ausona and Ripollés, because they had been depopulated by the epidemic; and so on.

We must emphasize, however, that though the damage done by the first onslaught of plague was very serious, it was not irreparable. Through new marriages made by persons who had lost their spouses during the course of the plague—ordered by the king as part of an incipient demographic policy—the population of Catalonia succeeded in regaining, in the short space of six years (from 1359 to 1365, date of the second census), more than 50,000 persons, equivalent to an annual increase of 2%. This increase meant that the loss in population would have been rapidly recouped had it not been for the later appearance of new setbacks. But, as Pierre Vilar has observed, no sooner had Catalonia recovered from the plague than it was beset by new difficulties. Following an invasion of locusts in 1358 which destroyed the crops, there were further outbreaks of plague (in 1362–1363, resulting in heavy infant mortality, and in 1371, in which many young people died) which dealt a definitive blow to the country's biological reserves. Thus, the population of 430,000 persons in 1365 dropped to 350,000 in 1378, a loss of 1.2% each year.

Furthermore, in addition to the demographic loss, the Black Death resulted in the *undermining of the social structure,* as we shall soon see. Land was left unpopulated and uncultivated, and it became necessary to seek new human resources to till the soil. Rural landholdings lost value because no labor was available to make them productive, and consequently there was no farm income with which to pay taxes to the lord. These two factors operated so profoundly on the economy and the rural mind that they explain the social upheavals which followed.

DEMOGRAPHIC DECLINE IN THE 15TH CENTURY: CAUSES AND REPERCUSSIONS. With 10 % of its younger age groups dead in the second and third waves of plague, the biological potential of Catalonia was in constantly increasing danger of a new calamity. In fact, from the end of the 14th century to the end of the 17th century, the plague recurred in an infernal, almost cyclical, rhythm with famine, death, and war (the four horsemen of the Apocalypse): in 1375, epidemic in Barcelona and famine in the Ampurdán; in 1381, an epidemic mentioned in the chronicles of Gerona; in 1396, flight of the king for fear of the plague, which had struck Barcelona; in 1397, epidemic in the country districts. Later, recognized outbreaks of plague: 1410, 1429, 1439, 1448, 1465–1466, 1476, 1483, 1486, 1493–1494, 1497. . . .

The result of this permanent impact of the plague was demographic stagnation, at a very low level. Certainly, after the beginning of the 15th century we can observe some demographic recovery in a few regions of the Crown of Aragon. But in many places it was too late to recoup the population loss. This was the case of Catalonia, where in addition to the Black Death there occurred commercial decline, emigration to other parts of the Mediterranean, the revolts and wars of the *remença* serfs, and the revolt against John II (1462–1472). At that time a good number of Catalans settled in Valencia or Majorca. We have figures to prove this adverse rhythm: Barcelona had 50,000 inhabitants in 1340, 38,000 in 1359, 20,000 in 1477, and then picked up again with

28,500 in 1497; Perpignan fell from 18,000 to 15,000, Gerona from 7,000 to 4,500, etc. All the cities of Catalonia, with very few exceptions, experienced a loss in population. Along general lines, the *fogatje,* or census, of 1497 gives a clear picture of the country's decline. At that time Catalonia had only 278,000 inhabitants, which means that in the course of a century and a half it had lost from 35 to 40% of its entire population.

In Aragon, where the rhythm was more normal because it was an inland region and did not experience the plague with the same intensity as Catalonia, the demographic process did not suffer this abrupt setback; but neither did it equal the clearly-marked growth of the 14th century. From 1429 to 1496 the Aragonese population rose from 200,000 to 250,000 inhabitants.

The two processes of growth and decline were combined in Valencia. On the one hand, the whole maritime area was affected by the Black Death, and consequently there were great ravages and a drop in population; but on the other hand, in certain places such as the city of Valencia, where Catalans exiled by the war became concentrated and where agriculture and commerce found a particularly favorable atmosphere after the beginning of the 15th century, the population curve shows a rise from 40,000 to 75,000 inhabitants in the course of some seventy years (1418–1483). It is one of the most spectacular population gains for the period, not only in Spain but in all Europe. But certain cities experienced a drop. Roca Traver states, for example, that Alcira lost population at the following rate: in 1418, 8,000 inhabitants; in 1461, 6,000; in 1473, 4,500; in 1483, 2,500. And the case of Burriana is similar.

Along general lines—and this is a very serious problem—the shrinkage of the Crown of Aragon's demographic potential in the 15th century was the fundamental cause of its disappearance as an independent state in the great constellation of Renaissance powers. In the 15th century the Crown of Aragon was in an inferior position, compared with a France which was overpopulated for the period and a Castile which, with 6 or 7 million people, was a decisive factor in the balance of peace and war. (At the end of the century, the population of Catalonia had not reached 4% of the total Hispanic population.) The danger that France and Castile might divide the territory between themselves led the Aragonese kings to ally themselves with the Castilians, for their dynasty had come from the main branch of the Castilian kings.

From the economic point of view, the demographic decline disorganized production and consumption and caused the establishment of foreign immigrants in the country.

FOREIGN IMMIGRATION: ITALIAN COLONIES AND THE START OF FRENCH IMMIGRATION. The study of foreign immigration into the Crown of Aragon is just beginning; therefore, we cannot give exact figures but can only present a general picture of what is known, which will give us some background for the subsequent great wave of immigration in the 16th century.

Data available to us at present show that foreign immigration, which had been going on to some degree since earliest times, acquired considerable importance at the time the Jews lost their influence in the cities and the Black Death depopulated the countryside. These two great demographic and economic factors were influential on the one hand in establishing the Italians in the cities, and on the other in the settlement of the Gascons of southern France in the countryside.

The first mention we have of the presence of *Italians* in Catalonia seems to go back to their collaboration in the reconquest of Tortosa (1148), where a colony of merchants became established. Later, at the end of the 14th century, the Italians colonized the Catalonian and Valencian littoral in great numbers. The pragmatic decree of Martin the Humane in 1402 was decisive in this regard, for it permitted them to settle and to trade in all the cities of the kingdom. The Genoese settled especially in Tortosa and Valencia, while the Florentines, who came next in importance, had a considerable colony in Barcelona. Here they lived side by side with the Milanese, who had carved out a niche in Catalonia for their dealings as agents of the great Lombard international banking activity. To sum up, then, although we do not have exact figures, we have reason to believe that the Italian colony in Barcelona was large, effective, and especially very rich.

Early in the 15th century the *Germans* also made an appearance. They have not been studied in detail either, in spite of the fact that large and weighty tomes have been written about their trade with

Catalonia. In general, they formed an economic bridge with southern Germany, which was then in a phase of great human expansion. We know that in the times of Alfonso the Magnanimous they, together with the *Savoyards,* paid a special tax. The assimilation of the Germans into this latter group merely confirms their mercantile character.

The *French* immigrants, however, were not merchants and men of wealth, but shepherds and farmers. The beginnings of French immigration can be explained if we recall the unity of the Pyrenean world and the drastic depopulation produced in Catalonia by the Black Death. The Gascons came south with their flocks and saw that there were fallow lands and deserted farmsteads (*masos rònecs*). Then the shepherd became a farmer. This was the beginning of the process that was to culminate in the 16th century with heavy French immigration into Catalonia.

We should point out the extremism of this mass of foreigners. With no profound ties to the country, uprooted from their own land, the Gascons contributed to the growth of social unrest in the Catalonian countryside. Some took part as leaders in the revolt of the *remença* serfs; others were chiefs of the gangs of bandits who infested the principality from that time onward.

SOCIAL EVOLUTION: THE PROBLEM OF THE REMENÇAS AND THE URBAN ARTISAN CLASS IN CATALONIA; CITIZENS AND "FORANS" IN MAJORCA. Demographic instability as well as economic collapse in the 15th century led to widespread social movements in Catalonia and Majorca. Valencia did not experience these because the Moslems, who had preserved their religion, lived in a world closed and impenetrable to the series of convulsions produced by demographic and economic stagnation.

The classic theory about the agrarian social evolution of Catalonia held that, because of the occupation of large territories, an uninterrupted process of liberating the rural serfs was initiated after the 13th century. This theory has been proved to be erroneous. On the contrary, it is evident that all over Europe a new type of restriction to the glebe took place in the later medieval centuries. So long as the peasant had no place to flee, it was not necessary to enact legislation to tie him to the land; only when there was a possibility that he might leave the land and go to some city where he could find protection, would it be worthwhile for the lords to convince the public authority to decree his immobility.

The first repressive legislation passed in Catalonia in regard to the peasants was the Constitution of Peter the Great in the Cortes of Barcelona in 1281, entitled "Com per lo Senyor," by the terms of which any peasant was prohibited from leaving the land unless he had first paid for his release.

The changes made after that time must have been considerable, for there is a great deal of testimony to the transformation of free farms into serf farms. The lords used the procedure of *cabrevación,* or inspection of the condition of each of their holdings, and did so to their own advantage and in accordance with their own interests. But this social mechanism was interrupted by the great epidemics which broke out in the middle of the 14th century. The Black Death killed off a tenth of the rural population, and the lords had no recourse but to lease the farmsteads to the survivors. Thus there came into being a class of peasants who worked three or four holdings and enjoyed very low rental terms, which the lords readily conceded because of the sudden lack of manpower. At the same time, the inflationary movement of prices, which became very noticeable after 1370, favored the peasant enormously in the "payment of rent–sale of products" equation. Therefore, the peasant who lived through the successive assaults of the plague became rich within the space of a few years. After 1380 we begin to find a more prosperous peasant, resembling the Russian *kulak* but with the paradox that even though he had more money he was more restricted to the glebe than his predecessors; for the legislation of the period brought him down to the level of the Roman *colonus.*

The rich peasants, who deeply felt the injustice of their legal situation and were capable of fighting for a genuine social movement, sought aid among the lawyers—that is, in the liberal element at Court—and in the notaries, educated in the contractual rules of human freedom. Beginning late in the 14th century, both of these groups formulated a series of claims for redress. These claims, for which the *remença* peasants would continue to do battle throughout the 15th century, until they were in part recognized by the Sentence of Guadalupe (1486), were of two kinds: first, those presented by the rich peasants, who wished to suppress unfair practices, abolish a number of seigniorial abuses, and bring about the disappearance of personal *remença*. But they accepted the survival of the feudal system insofar as the peasant enjoyed the right to effective use of the land and could not be forced off it by the direct or titular proprietor. The rich peasant was interested in extending indefinitely the existing types of lease or rental, for with a long-term lease he could look forward to a noticeable improvement in his economic condition. The second type represented the radical wing of the *remença* serfs, who wished, purely and simply, to annul the rent they paid to the lords and to appropriate the land on which they toiled.

The struggle was cruel after 1462. The first *remença* revolt created real political turmoil, followed by unrest in the cities, and the groundwork was laid for the Catalonian revolution of the 15th century. The problem was not resolved by the end of the war; on the contrary, another uprising was necessary during the reign of Ferdinand the Catholic before the conservative wing of the *remença* peasants could attain their freedom by the famous Sentence of Guadalupe in 1486. Some 50,000 peasants were liberated at the end of the 15th century. This figure, which represents one-sixth of the entire population of Catalonia, permits us to judge how important the suppression of serfdom to the glebe really was. There has been no Catalonian agrarian agitation from that time until quite recently, with the problem of the "rabassaires" and sharecropping farmers. This means that the solution given in 1486 satisfied the contemporary needs of the Catalonian country dweller.

As for the problems of the city folk, the same uneasiness observed in the country can be noted among the urban lower classes after 1430, not only in Barcelona but in all the Catalonian cities, as well as in Valencia and Majorca. The thesis of this movement went as follows: the oligarchy had brought the cities to the brink of poverty; it therefore had become necessary to exclude the oligarchy from the municipal system, or at least to impose a majority of artisans and humble people. It was necessary to establish a protectionist system that would guarantee work for all. In the third place, it was necessary to devalue money and move in the direction of inflation in order to increase consumption, and with consumption, work. In spite of the vast difference in time, these ideas have a marked socialist cast, for the rise of the lower classes has always gone along with a protectionist system of social guarantees to combat the oligarchy, which always wants a social system less subject to the authorities. These reforms provoked great political disturbances in Barcelona. The city was divided into two opposing factions: the "Biga," or aristocratic party, and the "Busca," or popular party. Their struggles, together with peasant unrest, led to the Catalonian revolution of the 15th century. And the problem was not really solved even then. The oligarchy's lack of courage in the defense of its interests, and the equal lack of courage of the artisan classes to impose their will on the oligarchy (as the peasants had done with the lords) left the issue undecided and resulted for this very reason in a social stagnation from which the city of Barcelona, and with it all of Catalonia, was to suffer in the 16th century.

As for Majorca, the struggle there was more unified; that is, there were claims both by the artisans and the peasants, called "forans" or outsiders. More drastically than in Catalonia, the State put down a revolt (1451–1454) against the Majorcan oligarchy that would certainly have led to a favorable change in the social structure of the island. The revolt, whose chief objective was the reduction of rents paid by peasants to city dwellers and inclusion of the citizens in the government of the city, flared up all over the island, and it was necessary to use troops sent by Alfonso V from Naples to put it down.

Decline of the Feudal Aristocracy and Appearance of the Renaissance "Entrepreneur." Under these circumstances, it is comprehensible that the feudal aristocracy in the Crown of Aragon declined notably throughout the 15th century. Catalonia offers the most typical example. When we read contemporary chronicles, such as Monfar's, we can see that the 200 great families which existed in 1414 were reduced to ten or twelve by the end of the century. This was due to three factors: first, the economic crisis; then, the devaluation of money; and finally, demographic losses. This last factor is related to the participation of the noble class in the struggle to acquire Sicily and Sardinia at the end of the 14th century and beginning of the 15th. Many nobles died in these campaigns; there were families, for instance, who lost sons in Sardinia, others in Sicily, others in North Africa, and others in Almería and on the coasts of Málaga. If we add to this the fact that the revenues of landowners were extremely small throughout the 15th century (for after the interlocutory decree of Alfonso the Magnanimous in 1455 no one collected a single penny from the Catalan peasants, and this means that the whole aristocratic economy, based essentially on agriculture, crumbled), we will understand that by the end of the century a noble had to resort to extreme measures in order to live. This can be verified by consulting the documentation in the archives of judicial records in Barcelona. Only some 200 or 300 nobles of second rank were left, and they lived in poverty, continually quarreling among themselves, and thus laying the foundations of the fateful Catalonian brigandage of the 16th century. Above these were the few great families—very few—who had managed to escape the disaster either by the lucky survival of family fortunes or by their settlement in Sardinia or Sicily, from which they could extract fat incomes, or by marriage into the reigning royal family; thus, the counts of Cardona, Prades, Módica and Pallars, the viscounts of So and Castro, the Baron d'Erill, and so on.

For all these reasons, the aristocratic structure, which was to represent the strength of Castile in the 16th century, came tumbling down in Catalonia, with nothing to take its place. There might have existed some real hope had not the revolt of 1462 cut off a branch of the nobility which was in a stage of full development: the so-called Renaissance "entrepreneurs." There were families of knights, like the Requesens de Soler, who engaged in piracy, trade, and moneylending. But these cases were few, not because their example might not have been followed, but because the civil war of 1462 blocked the opportunities for an increase in the kind of man who, in France, Italy, Germany, and England, was to embody the great adventurer—the great commercial entrepreneur of the 16th century.

16 · The Economy of the Catalonian Urban Patriciate; Labor and Industry

AGRICULTURAL LABOR AND ITS ORGANIZATION. It is indeed a pity that we do not possess a history of agriculture for a country as essentially agricultural as was the Crown of Aragon (with the exception of the coastal area) in the Middle Ages. All we have is a mere catalogue of what was produced. But we do not know the value of those products, nor the direct relationship of man to the land through labor. The present paragraphs, then, are merely a surmise as to what agricultural labor and its organization must have been like in the 13th, 14th, and 15th centuries.

In the first place, techniques did not undergo any substantial changes, except those brought about in the course of the 15th century when the bourgeoisie began to invest in land and brought a spirit of innovation to its cultivation. Roman, and even pre-Roman, farming practices continued to prevail, along with Germanic habits which had developed in Visigothic times. For this reason the majority of working tools, such as sickles and harrows, continued to be furnished with stone cutting edges, since those made of metal were extremely expensive.

The organization of agriculture was centered on the independent unit of the *mas* or *mansio,* called *alquería* in the Aragonese and Valencian regions. In this *mas* there was a principal unit called the *capmas,* surrounded by fields. In Catalonia and Aragon the chief crops were cereals (wheat and barley), and also the vine and the olive. In Valencia and certain parts of Catalonia *rice* was cultivated, and in some places *saffron,* which was a highly prized export product. *Cereals* were particularly abundant in the Aragonese and Urgel regions, which were closely connected, by way of the Ebro tributaries, with Tortosa, the great seaport of the district. The *vine* was particularly well developed, and contracts for planting vineyards became very numerous after the 14th century. These were carried out according to the procedure which later came to be called "rabassa morta," or "dead root." It was a contract by the terms of which the leaseholder had the use of the land for as long as the stock he had planted survived. This method of cultivation became highly developed in modern Catalonia.

As for agricultural tasks, the documents reveal that they were the same as those our immediate ancestors knew two or three generations ago: *batudes, podades, femades, segades,* and *trajines* (or clod-breaking, pruning, fertilizing, reaping, and transport). These were the principal occupations of those farmers, who worked at their routine tasks from sunup to sunset.

We may note that in the documents there are frequent references to stabled animals, which allow us to define this type of agriculture as a combination of farming with the raising of domestic livestock.

In contrast, a new type of agriculture appears in the *irrigated lands* that shows signs of greater development. It is related to the techniques achieved by the Moslems and inherited by their immediate successors the Mudéjares. The main problem in these areas was the use of water, and undoubtedly the spread of a control system dates from this period, whose highest achievement was the so-called "Tribunal of the Waters" in Valencia. We have no record of its deliberations. It was, however, a court which gave, and continues to give to this day, on-the-spot decisions on problems arising from the division of irrigation water among the farmers of the area.

CONSEQUENCES OF RURAL IMPROVEMENT BY THE URBAN PATRICIATE. About the end of the 14th century the bourgeoisie began to invest in improvement of the countryside. We shall not take up here the question of whether this process preceded commercial decline or whether commercial decline was its cause; the fact is, however, that we possess reliable documents and proofs that after this time the bourgeoisie began to acquire a good many rural properties, and that through these their interest in agriculture grew progressively greater.

It is easy to imagine that possession of these properties by the bourgeoisie occurred in three stages. In the first, pleasure retreats were acquired in the vicinity of the principal cities, in response to that enthusiasm for Nature characteristic of the 14th century in many Provençal and Italian cities. This stage led to the second, acquisition of land during the initial phases of the business crisis. Typical of the third stage was an effort to make a profit from rural revenues.

The consequences of this process were: first, those of a *technical* nature, the tendency to make farming more scientific so as to obtain the best possible yield. It was, of course, the merest beginning, but this beginning was to lead later to the astonishing flowering of agriculture in certain regions, especially in Northern Europe. Second, those of an *agricultural* nature; increase in the area under cultivation, especially by means of reclamation of marshes. In this regard the drainage of regions in the vicinity of Barcelona, such as the Llano de Llobregat and the Maresme, is particularly notable. Third, those of a *social* order; the bourgeoisie became owners of lands worked both by free farmers and by serfs, with the result that their interests became identified with those of the aristocracy. Thus we should not be surprised to learn that at the end of Ferdinand the Catholic's reign, honored citizenship acquired the same privileges as those of the second-class nobility, while this latter class was admitted to municipal government as a member of the urban patriciate.

ARTISAN LABOR. Until recently we have possessed only fragmentary information on artisan labor in the later medieval centuries, through the studies of the famous 18th-century economist Antonio de Capmany. Today, however, thanks to the researches of Pierre Bonnassié, we have a more concrete and very largely a new idea of what the labor situation in Barcelona was like.

Labor was organized in an urban and corporate form. This means that the city had the last word in its organization, and that the corporation laid down the conditions of work carried out by the community.

As for the workers, we must point out that only two types were known within the municipal community, masters and apprentices.

Let us first take a look at the master, or *mestre*. The essential condition for achieving this rank was that of "parar obrador y haver senyal"—that is, to have a recognized retail shop and to possess a trademark. The first prerequisite had to do with the prohibition on work carried on in the home; this took place in the 15th century when, in the first attempts to concentrate capital in the hands of individual entrepreneurs, it was decided to prevent any attempt against corporate organization of labor. As for the trademark or hallmark, it could be transmitted by inheritance and consequently was one of the qualifications most prized by those who, besides being workmen, took pride in the perfection of their work.

An examination was necessary in order to attain the rank of master. When was the examination established? We know that in Europe the corporations or guilds began to employ examinations in the middle of the 14th century. In Barcelona they are mentioned for the first time in 1389; the custom became general between 1430 and 1462. The last guild to adopt the examination system was the dyers' guild in 1497. We can therefore state that in the course of the 15th century a master's examination became inevitable as a means of establishing any artisan business in Barcelona.

The subject matter of the examination was of two kinds, professional skill and sufficient assets. The first showed aptitude and the use made of materials; that is, the technical capacity of an aspirant to the category of master. However, this proof was not demanded in every case. Sometimes, for example among boatmen, the examination consisted of a simple physical inspection to see if the candidate enjoyed good health; this was considered to be as important as skill in handling the oars or stowing merchandise on board ship. As for the second qualification, assets were estimated on the basis of fees paid or on the accumulation of a stock of merchandise. Payment of fees certainly preceded the qualifying examination. Through coordination of labor in the later medieval centuries, a fee came to be fixed for these examinations, one that varied according to the importance of the guild. There were some, for example the jewelers' guild, in which the fee was so large that it was almost prohibitive. Another case is that of the important coral-workers' guild, whose members had to possess a certain stock of coral before they could pass the examination. These qualifications had a discriminatory side, for it was agreed that outsiders should pay more than natives; on the other hand, sons of masters were usually exempted from paying any fee, thus establishing a precedent that was to become fatal to future development of the guilds' technical and industrial activities.

However, and taking the whole situation into account, the organization of the examinations was fairly liberal. There were few cases of limitation of this rank (among the pharmacists, for instance, only two new members could be admitted annually), while the practice of allowing credit for payment of the examination fees in fact made the mastership accessible to many journeymen, even though they lacked means.

As for the apprentice, called *aprenent* or *mosso* in Catalan, Bonnassié's studies give us information about his geographical and social provenance and the length of his term of service. It is known that 75% of the apprentices were natives of Barcelona and only 25% outsiders, of whom the greater number were from the dioceses of Gerona and Urgel, the most densely populated Pyrenean regions, and from the diocese of Tarragona. Foreigners, those who were not natives of Catalonia, were in a distinct minority. In regard to their social position, 60% came from the industrial class, 33% from among the merchants, and only 7% from the peasants. This means that the artisan class was replenished by the artisans themselves, while it was virtually impossible for a peasant to become an industrial worker.

The apprenticeship contract was for three or four years, and its terms could be fulfilled either in the city of Barcelona or outside it, though in the latter case there had to be an affidavit that the work had been done in the house of another master. The trades requiring a longer apprenticeship were also the more complex ones: six years for silversmiths; four for tailors, dyers, and carpenters; on the other hand, the apprentices of the textile branch had to serve only three years. The master had complete authority over the apprentice, who not only had to promise total obedience in matters of his trade but also in domestic tasks, for the formula "famulus et discipulus" was specified in the contract and governed the interior of the house as well as the workshop. The apprentice's submission was so complete that he could not leave the house without his master's permission. In this regard the terms of the contract were perfectly clear: "absque fuga" was the formula.

Now let us look at the workers; namely, that group of laborers who grew up in and with the cities as they developed. It became necessary to offer a foothold within the original organization, the community of masters and apprentices, to the more experienced journeymen, as well as to day laborers and unskilled workers.

In this first group, that of the so-called *oficiales,* or journeymen, we must mention the "joves, macips o companyons," who were the men employed in Barcelona during the 14th and 15th centuries. These men, who had already finished their apprenticeship and were seeking a living in other cities, or who worked when necessary on some specific industrial job, were usually hired in public places designated by the city itself. However, in the Barcelona of the 14th and 15th centuries, where there was no abundance of manpower, the once daily spectacle of a master going out on the street to find a journeyman to help him in his tasks became far from frequent. Journeymen were paid a daily wage, which was usually decided on verbally; sometimes a share in the profits was agreed upon. Seen overall, the labor situation was good, but neither should it be forgotten that at certain moments there were attempts at social change, and that real workers' coalitions existed. Thus, in 1419, in a franchise given to the tailors' guild, any coalition of "youths" for the purpose of asking for a raise is prohibited.

As for the *unskilled workers,* in Barcelona they were called "bergants" or "manobres." The word "bergant" means rogue, and its very use bring us into the world of the unskilled worker, who offered his brawn when it was necessary and worked no more than he had to. These men were employed as porters and boatmen, and worked in the shipyards and also in the construction trades. The "bergants" were hired in the square bearing their name, and in general were chronically out of work. This social stratum was indeed the poorest of all, and was the one that contained the most refractory elements in the whole city.

Now a reference to *slaves,* who also made up an important sector of the working-class world of the period. They were used in certain trades, but there were some from which they were excluded. Coral-workers could use two slaves in their workshops; boatmen, as many as they wished, as could bakers; but many other guilds excluded them from their roster. The slave's position was quite favorable, for the masters realized that as a forced worker he produced very little; to encourage him, he was treated like a free man. So there really existed two systems: the legal one, which was naturally highly unfavorable, and the true one, in which the slave was a good deal more fortunate.

Women also worked, not only as domestics, where they were contracted for when very young and generally lived under very bad conditions, but also in various trades. Generally speaking, they could manage a workshop and even aspire to a mastership. This feminine labor was developed especially within the textile arts, but we find examples of women masters in other businesses. The husband's authorization was always necessary for this.

As to the *conditions under which work was carried out,* these were not excessively rigorous. The documents which Pierre Bonnassié has examined show that working hours were arranged in the following manner: in the morning, from daybreak until ten o'clock, followed by a three-hour interval, with work resumed at one in the afternoon and continuing until an hour before sunset. This means that a working day was composed of nine or ten effective hours. As far as holidays were concerned, there is a widespread notion that the medieval artisan did not work very hard because of the large number of civic and religious holidays. But in reality the documents indicate that the artisan worked when he felt like it (or when he had work in hand); that is, he did not necessarily pay attention to Sundays or even to the feast-day of the patron saint of the guild.

THE GUILDS AS A LABOR STRUCTURE. We must make a distinction between the guild and the confraternity. The former is essentially an association of trades or crafts, while the latter is the whole community of workers in a given trade, united to carry out certain social and spiritual aims. Because of this, the confraternity stood out as: a political organization, taking part in municipal public life; a military organization, furnishing urban militia to the city; a religious instrument, proffering devotion to its patron saints; and, in the last instance, as an organization of assistance and social service, through a number of provisions which covered the principal episodes of its members' lives from birth to death.

The corporation's social projection is very interesting, but here we shall concern ourselves solely with its economic side. The guild was a *privileged corporation,* and we must keep this very much in mind if we are to realize what it represented in medieval economic life. Above all, it established a guarantee for consumers, excluding so-called "adulterated" products and also avoiding competition among producers. By sustaining these two principles it represented the essence of the medieval attitude.

As for the regulation of labor, the guild was especially concerned with the distribution of raw materials; then, with offering credit to those masters who did not have sufficient funds for a particular piece of business; and finally, with setting technical standards of work and overseeing the prices of products and their intrinsic quality. In this respect we should mention one of the most important organizations in Barcelona in the 15th century, and one that was undoubtedly a predecessor of the modern trade unions: this was the woollen-workers' guild, whose center of operations was the so-called "Casa del Pont d'en Campdurà," where the masters met under the supervision of *ad hoc* guild officials to examine the different facets of production. Dyeing was supervised from there, the threads in woven goods were counted, and finally, the quality of cloth was judged in accordance with set standards.

The Urban Market: Imported Agricultural and Forest Products. The medieval city had developed on the foundation of the market, which in consequence formed the center of its commercial and economic life for a number of centuries. But beginning with the Commercial Revolution of the 13th century the market underwent a notable change. Not only did it disappear as such from the large cities, but it became specialized as a result of the continuity of consumption and the increased buying power of the masses. This phenomenon coincides with the appearance of a magistracy created to solve the different problems that arose in regard to prices, weights, and the quality of goods sold in the market.

Let us choose the case of Barcelona in order to focus this process in a single place. The *mercadal,* which, as we have said, was the place where markets were held in the Catalonian cities, disappeared in the 13th century. At the same time, a number of *plazas,* or marketplaces, were set up, usually located in the vicinity of the walled urban perimeter, in which specialized goods were sold: wheat, wine, fish, etc.

The *alfóndigos* likewise disappeared. They had been an essential feature of the markets in the Early Middle Ages because merchants coming from foreign countries lodged and stored merchandise in them. They disappeared because the comings and goings of foreign merchants were constant, and the system of large collective hostelries became inconvenient. *Hostels,* the small inns typical of the urban life of the period, took their place.

Also about the middle of the 14th century—in 1339 in fact—the *mostazaf* makes his appearance in Barcelona. This was an urban magistracy, derived from the Arabic *almotacén,* which had spread from Valencia through the different kingdoms of the Crown of Aragon. Since he was the official in charge of overseeing the marketplace, the decisions of the *mostazaf* preserved in municipal archives are very important, for they permit us to take up the study of prices and of what we might call the local trade cycle in the Late Middle Ages.

What products were consumed in the domestic market? We find the following references in documents relating to the office of *mostazaf,* and in the study of taxes paid: vegetable products, properly speaking, and their by-products (wheat, olive oil, wine, and dried figs); animals and their by-products (meat, milk, fowl, and two types of fish, dried and fresh); and forest products (kindling and charcoal).

Of these basic goods, there were very few which came from places near the city. In general there was great dependence on long-distance trade. And this was true not only of wine, but even of wheat and wood, which were the three basic elements of consumption in the medieval city.

Wine did not present serious transport difficulties, and was usually carried in wooden casks or tuns. To realize the importance of wine in medieval trade, we need only remember that at that time the capacity of ships was measured in tuns, which has given rise to the use of the word "ton." And there is one fact that should be pointed out in regard to the geography of wines. About the middle of the 14th century the Mediterranean wines, of high alcohol content, lost their reputation in the market owing to the invasion of Burgundy wine, low in alcohol and very fine, which came in as a result of the influence of the Popes' court in Avignon.

Wheat was the basic element of subsistence in the great medieval cities. Therefore, one of their fundamental privileges was the franchise for importing wheat, including the right to seize it in transit, either by sea or by land, in the vicinity of the city in times of emergency. In the case of Barcelona, where it was given the name of "vi vel gratia" (by force or free will), this privilege took the form of privateering permits issued by the city to its merchants, giving them the right to take over any shipment of wheat during periods of scarcity. To understand better the nature of this troublesome problem of wheat supply, we need only add that there was one city in the Crown of Aragon that grew and prospered thanks to the monopoly it exercised over wheat—Tortosa. Tortosa controlled the mouth of the Ebro and with it the great centers of wheat production; that is, Urgel and the Ebro basin. This is why Tortosa enjoyed exceptional importance during the 14th century; it was the city that regulated the price of wheat over a large part of the Western Mediterranean, not only for Barcelona and Valencia, but also for Genoa and Marseilles. It is easy to understand why the Catalonian cities, especially Barcelona, made efforts to put an end to this monopoly. In 1398 Barcelona acquired from the Crown the town of Flix, which controls the passage of the lower Ebro between Aragon and Catalonia. Thanks to this move, Barcelona was able to open and close the gates of the wheat trade from Aragon and Urgel.

But in spite of these measures, the ups and downs of wheat production were so great that recourse often had to be made to shipments from abroad, especially from Sicily. This resulted in a fabulously profitable business, and municipal financial administration arose out of the necessity for financing the loans necessary for these ventures. The wheat trade was one of the causes of the discrediting of the cities' oligarchic governments, for many leading citizens were morally ruined by it. Their business dealings were such that later they had to answer the well-founded accusations of the popular party that they had soiled their hands in the wheat trade.

Another important foodstuff was *fish,* either fresh or dried; it was even more important than meat, since people were committed to abstinence for a large part of the year. It would be interesting to investigate the distribution of dried fish in Catalonia, for there is no doubt that such a study would contribute greatly towards clearing up the beginning of the relationship between the Mediterranean and the sailors of the Atlantic, especially the Basques, who were certainly intermediaries between the great fishing fleet of the Hanseatic League and the southern markets.

As for the supply of *wood* and *charcoal,* we should keep in mind that, because of the limited use of iron, wood was the indispensable material for constructing anything, ships as well as both private and public buildings. This explains why, when we examine the cargoes of ships coming into the ports of the period, we are astonished at the enormous amount of wood and charcoal that was imported. In

Catalonia, for example, there was constant coastwise trade which carried the logs of the Montseny region from the Maresme to Barcelona.

EXPORTED MINING PRODUCTS. Since the economic revolution of the Late Middle Ages was essentially mercantile, it did not result in a decided change in industrial techniques, and therefore was not reflected in the exploitation of mines. Except for some few minerals, the Crown of Aragon was not in the forefront of either export or production. It might have been, though, if it had possessed that important mineral used in dyeing, *alum,* which was a particularly desirable product during the 14th and 15th centuries. There was, however, a compensation in the exploitation of *salt.* There were a number of salt beds centering around Alicante, and especially in Ibiza. They were considerably more valuable then than now. The salt of Ibiza and Alicante entered into the great plans of the international mercantile companies of the period, as is shown by many contracts signed between Italian financiers and the great magnates (and even the kings themselves) of the Crown of Aragon. In this way profitable monopolies were established for the contracting parties. Salt from Ibiza was usually transported in ships of small tonnage, and consequently freightage was inexpensive. Basques usually took charge of this. The sudden appearance of the Basque merchant fleet in the Mediterranean is related to the Atlantic fish trade and the Mediterranean salt trade. By means of this traffic many Basque skippers, with their small ships, gained control of coastwise trade in the Western Mediterranean, as has been conclusively proved by Heers' recent studies on the port of Genoa.

Comparable to mining products was *coral.* Besides the important coral reefs on the present-day Costa Brava, Catalonia enjoyed a monopolistic position in the Western Mediterranean by controlling the coral of Sardinia and cornering a large part of the trade in Tunisian coral.

THE CATALAN FORGE AND ITS DEVELOPMENT. There are a large number of seams of iron in the Pyrenees. Part of this ore, which was of excellent quality, was exported from the seaports of the Roussillon and Costa Brava; the rest was used in the furnaces of the so-called *farga catalana,* or Catalan forge.

The development of metallurgy in the Pyrenees was due, first, to the presence of iron ore; second, to technical skill; and third, to the existence of an international market (especially Barbary and the rest of North Africa) that could easily absorb the products manufactured by this highland metallurgical industry. These three conditions gave rise to the Catalan forge, of whose origins we know little, though we cannot doubt that it was Catalonian in origin, for the term "Catalan forge" was widespread and used in many parts of Spain and Western Europe.

We do not, however, know exactly what technical conditions existed in the furnaces of the medieval "fargas." The more advanced were characterized by a special structure: the arrangement of the various layers of coal and iron; the draft which activated combustion (first by means of bellows, later by water power); the introduction of supplementary air by the device known as the *tolra;* and the hydraulic power which moved a drop hammer. Nor do we know the place of origin of this procedure; it was probably along the course of the rivers Ter and Freser (Ribas, Ripoll, Camprodón, etc.).

This type of production, which gained great fame in the 14th century and up to the middle of the 15th, collapsed completely as a result of the Catalonian civil war of 1462–1472. In 1480, when the Catalonian economy made a recovery, there was only one metallurgical establishment in the whole country, that of Ribas.

URBAN INDUSTRIAL PRODUCTION. Industrial production in the cities of the Crown of Aragon had many facets, as is shown by the number of guilds established during the 14th and 15th centuries. The *silversmiths* occupied a very important place; they were wealthy, and carried on business of a high quality. Barcelona had a virtual monopoly on jewelry in the Crown of Aragon for two centuries, the 14th and 15th, and up to the end of this period its products had a well-deserved success all over Spain. This situation later changed and other types came to the fore, especially the jewelry of Toledo and Seville, which in the 16th and 17th centuries enjoyed a vogue inspired by its popularity at Court.

Activities related to *metallurgy* were an important group: blacksmiths, makers of knives, bows, crossbows, lances, scabbards, shields and helmets, etc. As we shall see, wrought metal was one of the principal export products of the city of Barcelona. The next most interesting group had to do with *wearing apparel,* which was also important in the life of the city: the makers of hats, purses, hose, belts, doublets, gloves; furriers; tailors; shoe and clog makers; and cobblers. Another widespread activity was *transport:* boatmen and porters of every sort, not forgetting the couriers, for whom Barcelona was the center of correspondence for much of Western Europe. We should also mention the *construction trades:* shipwrights, carpenters, brick-makers, potters, masons, etc. Two special groups that maintained an active export trade were the coral merchants and the rope-makers; the latter's ropes and cords were sold successfully throughout the Mediterranean area. The group of the *tanners* and *leather-workers* also deserves mention. It included those who prepared skins for gloves, tanners, harness- and saddle-makers, leather-dressers, parchment-makers, etc.

And finally, we should mention the *textile industry,* which included some especially privileged guilds having to do with the weaving of wool; others of the second rank, such as the weavers of cotton; and still others which were more or less distinguished by the auxiliary operations they performed, such as the dyers and cloth-shearers, the carders and female spinners.

DEVELOPMENT OF THE TEXTILE INDUSTRY IN CATALONIA. One would suppose that the Catalonian textile industry would have a basic bibliography. There are certain works, among them those of Capmany and Ventalló, which deal with the evolution and development of the wool industry in Catalonia. But they are either out of date or do not give us a satisfactory view of the problems with which we are concerned. For example, all current histories consider that the wool industry began to develop in Catalonia in the 11th or 12th century. The truth is that up to 1300 it was a purely local occupation and had no special value as an industry of the first rank. Its development was no greater at that time than that of the wool industry in Aragon, Valencia, Asturias, Andalusia, or any other place where there were a few sheep to be sheared, some spinners, and a small loom.

The establishment of the great textile industry in Catalonia is more recent. Until the beginning of the 14th century Catalonia and the other kingdoms of the Crown of Aragon were importers of high-grade cloth, especially from France and Italy. Only at the end of the 13th century, when the French trade in woollen cloth was interrupted by war, could a textile industry of a certain importance be established in Barcelona. It was set up with foreign workers, financed by commercial companies, and used the very best tools available.

Therefore, the birth of the great Catalonian textile industry should be related to three events: first, the war with France, which began in 1284 and lasted until 1304; second, the establishment in Barcelona of foreign technicians, whose nationality we cannot ascertain with any accuracy; and in the third place, the simultaneous development of export markets which were able to absorb Catalonian production—North Africa, Sardinia, and Sicily, not to mention an Andalusia which had been taken over by Ferdinand III and Alfonso XI and reorganized by Sancho IV.

After Barcelona became dominant in this sphere, there was considerable imitation by the various cities and localities which had traditionally produced woollens for local markets. There were six chief groups: the Pyrenean, with Puigcerdá, Ripoll, Vich, Olot, San Juan de las Abadesas, Berga; the Roussillon, with Perpignan, Ceret, and Tuir; the Gerona region, including the city of Gerona and Bañolas; the Vallés region, with Granollers, Tarrasa, and Sabadell; and Valencia and Majorca, which actually were complementary to Catalonian production.

As for the quality of Catalonian cloth, it was believed until recently that it consisted of cheap stuffs made for mass consumption in the countries of the Western Mediterranean. But an analysis of the Sicilian market in the first third of the 15th century by C. Trasselli has brought out the fact that Catalonia also manufactured cloth of medium and even of superior quality, though it never came to be as fine as the black cloth of Bruges, the blue of London, or the Florentine sky-blue. The black cloth of Perpignan was of highest value, followed by the black of Vich and Majorca and the mixed cloth of Gerona. Barcelona, and in imitation Valencia, produced only cheap stuffs, usually in the spectrum of red or mixed colors.

All of the foregoing refers to woollen cloth, which was the most important by far. But a complete index of the Catalonian textile industry cannot omit other types. A good sample of the development of these is to be found in the famous *fustanys* (fustian), a fabric containing a mixture of cotton and linen or hemp.

17 · Catalonian Trade

CATALONIAN TRADE IN THE LATE MIDDLE AGES. As we take up this theme we must keep two factors in mind. In the first place, it has aroused interest among scholars of economic history. And so, beginning with the work of Capmany, which is basic to the subject, we have a copious bibliography. The works of Gonzalo de Reparaz, Nicolau d'Olwer, Rubió y Lluch, and, nearer to our own time, those of Marinescu, Verlinden, Masià de Ros, Dufourcq, Carrère, Heers, Trasselli, and Del Treppo, among numerous others, have contributed toward giving us an exact and up-to-date view of the subject.

The second point is the fact that when we speak of Catalonian trade we shall include in this term Aragonese, Valencians, and Majorcans. This is not simply a geographical grouping, but because we believe that from the 13th to the 15th centuries the mercantile activity of the other peoples of the Crown of Aragon was necessarily implied in this term. This is also the juridical version of the facts. When a Catalonian consul was named in any Mediterranean city, it was understood that this consul was also empowered to act for Valencians, Aragonese, and Majorcans, and even for Sardinians and Sicilians. This in turn demonstrates the extraordinary importance of Catalonian trade at the time.

In order to study the subject in a systematic way, we have grouped its spheres of influence into two large areas: the Mediterranean, which is older, and the Atlantic, which is more recent. Within the first grouping, there is a sharp division between what we might call the *Christian Mediterranean area* and the *Moslem Mediterranean area.*

This division is imposed not only by the differing geographical location of the Christians, in the North, and the Moslems, in the South, but also because of the characteristic differences in trade, not only in the type of goods dealt in, but especially in the mental attitude toward it. Trade among Christians was a normal type of trade; but that carried on with the Moslems had a special characteristic from the beginning: it was in some degree illicit trade, contraband. We find proof of this in the attitude adopted by the Papacy after the Moslem conquest of the fortress of St. John of Acre. Immediately afterward, in 1291, Pope Nicholas IV prohibited trade with the Moslems in arms, foodstuffs, and ships, on pain of excommunication. When we think of what excommunication meant at that time—to be completely excluded from the bosom of the Church—we can understand that any man who dared cross the imaginary line dividing the Mediterranean into North and South to trade with the Moslems would have many struggles with his conscience every time he did so. And for this very reason, those who did flout the moral frontier earned enormous profits. During the 14th century, when Catalonian trade with all these countries was at its height, a special tribunal, with powers granted by the Pope, had to be created in Barcelona to absolve the numerous ships' captains, merchants, and sailors who constantly broke the edict of 1291, which had been confirmed by each successive Pope. And indeed the Catalan merchants had become accustomed to thinking of the bulls with which they bought forgiveness for having trafficked with the infidel as a sort of tax on this trade.

TRADE WITH THE CHRISTIAN MEDITERRANEAN COUNTRIES. *Route of Languedoc and Provence.* This route deserves to be studied first because it was also the earliest one used by Catalan sailors. It was linked with Catalonia culturally and linguistically, to the point that in the 14th and 15th centuries the commercial language of the region was Catalan, and we are not surprised to find that commercial records in Marseilles or the accounts of a merchant in Toulouse were written not in the tongue of Languedoc but in a Catalan very similar to that used by a merchant of Barcelona at the time. This influence even came to be felt in the Gascon tongue of Bordeaux.

The products which circulated along this route were cereals, exchanges among the different Mediterranean regions, depending on where wheat shortages occurred; and spices, which were redistributed from Barcelona and Perpignan. It is fair to say that Cat-

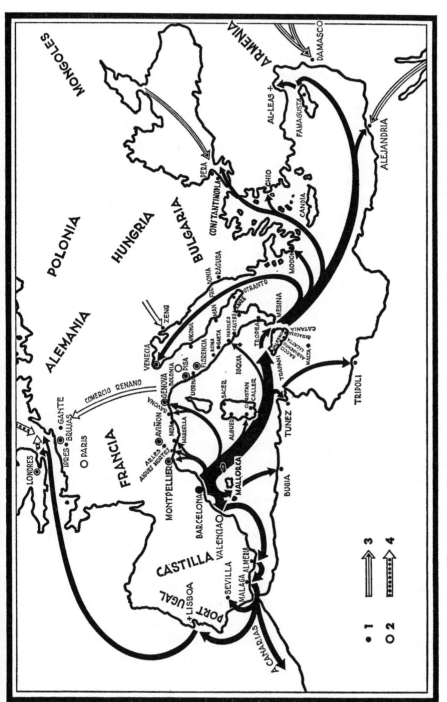

CATALONIAN TRADE IN THE MEDITERRANEAN.—*Key:* 1, consulates of Barcelona; 2, banking centers; 3, routes of Eastern trade; 4, Hanseatic trade.

alan traders monopolized the market of the rich Languedoc country, and even the Provençal market to a certain degree, up to the middle of the 15th century.

The most important stages along this route were, first, Montpellier, which as a possession of the Crown of Aragon was the strategic base established by Catalan merchants in the heart of the economic bloc of Languedoc; then, Avignon, Arles, and Marseilles. They also used the port of Nice, which served to bring in certain products, especially spices, for the Duchy of Savoy and Switzerland.

ROUTE OF THE ISLANDS. The route of the islands, the one which joined Corsica, Sardinia, and Sicily, is not a theoretical subject created by historians. In the documents of the period, especially after James II, it appears as a vital fact which forms part of the policy of the king and the merchants. Even if we leave out the importance of Sardinia as a strategic point in the Western Mediterranean, and of Sicily as a base for wheat, this route was the backbone of the Crown of Aragon's Mediterranean trade; the spice trade was an offshoot of it, and so, more importantly, was control of the African coast.

The chief stages on this route were Cagliari and Alghero, in Sardinia; Palermo on the west coast of Sicily, and Messina and Syracuse on the east side. But the heart of the route, the colony that controlled this Catalonian zone of activity, was in Trapani, located on the west coast of Sicily near Palermo. Catalonian textiles and coral were brought in and Sardinian silver and Sicilian wheat taken out, comprising the chief objects of trade on this route.

TYRRHENIAN ROUTE. This route had one main objective: to supply Naples, especially with textiles. We must remember that Naples was, up to the 15th century, the largest city in Europe, and consequently represented an extraordinary market for consumer goods. Therefore, to bring Catalonian cloth to Naples was a project progressively carried out until the Catalans achieved a monopoly at the end of the 15th century. They took advantage of the voyage to Naples to make a tour of the Tyrrhenian Sea; that is, the Catalonian ships, after arriving in Sicily and buying wheat, went on to Naples where they sold it and their cloth, and then proceeded to the different ports along the Tyrrhenian shore, especially Pisa, Genoa, and Savona. Then they returned by way of Marseilles, rejoining the route of Provence.

The Tyrrhenian route was dangerous, for there was a great deal of competition and it was not always peaceful. But after a certain time in the 14th century, Barcelona was able to compete advantageously with Genoa. It was not until 1435, as a result of the naval battle of Ponza, that the Catalans lost part of the hegemony they had enjoyed up till then; but they quickly regained it, as is shown by the siege of Genoa in 1458 by Alfonso the Magnanimous, and the failure of the support given by Genoa to the claimants for the throne of Ferdinand I of Aragon in Naples.

The importance of Catalonian trade in the Tyrrhenian Sea can be judged by the large number of documents concerning it in the Datini Archive in Prato, near Florence.

ADRIATIC ROUTE. This route had two objectives, Venice and Ragusa. Venice was the chief city for Mediterranean trade at the time, and Ragusa, on the east coast of the Adriatic Sea, was the open door to the Balkans.

There was no real trade with Venice because Barcelona was competing with the same products and in the same trade areas: but Catalonian ships took advantage of the scarcity of wheat in Venice to bring Sicilian wheat there in transit. Once they had reached the end of the Adriatic, they returned by way of Ragusa. There they bought Eastern products which had come from Hungary and Russia, thus completing a profitable trade circuit.

ROUTE OF THE BYZANTINE EMPIRE. The Catalans arrived in the Byzantine Empire, which monopolized trade at the crucial point between Asia and Europe (Constantinople) during most of the Middle Ages, at a time when their chief competitors, Genoa and Venice, were already firmly established there. It was almost impossible to wrest from the two Italian rivals the trade in which they were engaged. It was a most important traffic, for one of the open doors to trade with the Far East was none other than the Black Sea, which gave access to the Crimean Peninsula and then, through the Strait of Kerch, to Tanais, terminal for the trans-Asian caravans which brought in silk, gold, slaves, and the most precious spices. To be in Constantinople, then, was to be in the New York of the period.

Catalans came into the Byzantine Empire as warriors (the *almogávares* of Roger de Flor). In consequence, they gained a bad reputation there. But after the middle of the 14th century we find Catalans established not only in Pera, a quarter of Constantinople, but also in the Crimea, as the French scholar Bautier has discovered. This was medieval Catalonia's most remote mercantile outpost.

The presence of Catalans in this part of the world produced serious tensions. There was open war in 1351, with serious consequences for the Catalonian merchant fleet. After 1380 there was an incipient, though undeclared, state of war, in which Genoese, Venetians, and Catalans sank each other's ships. This struggle produced such severe losses that we can even find in it one of the causes of maritime decline in the Western Mediterranean. However, in spite of this war, which was harshly fought and often went badly for the Catalans, the merchants of the Principality remained in Constantinople until 1453, when the city was conquered by Mohammed II. In this action Catalans shared the glory of dying with Constantine IX for the defense of Europe.

ROUTES OF THE ISLANDS OF THE CHRISTIAN LEVANT. This was a most important area, not only because of its own mercantile activities but because the islands of Candia, Cyprus, and Rhodes were in themselves strategic points for control of the important commercial shorelines of Syria, Palestine, and Egypt.

At first sight it would seem that the Catalans' interests there were limited; however, Catalonian trade always showed an inclination to seek control of this vital area, which has played such a decisive role in the history of the Near East. We find Catalonian trading posts on the Venetian island of Candia (Crete); in the cities of Cyprus, during the period when the island was ruled by the Lusignan family, which was united to the house of Barcelona by two marriages (James II of Aragon to Maria of Lusignan, and Leonor, granddaughter of James, to King Peter of Cyprus); later, in Rhodes, we find Catalans in the service of the Order of St. John of Jerusalem; Catalan names appear more than once in the list of its masters. From Rhodes and Kastellorizo, an island in the Dodecanese group where Admiral Vilamarí built a fortress in the 15th century, Catalonian trade reached the kingdom of Armenia (14th century) and nearby Chios, the island which served as a bridge for commerce with Anatolia.

TRADE WITH THE MOSLEM MEDITERRANEAN COUNTRIES. We shall divide this large area into three parts in order to clarify certain geographical and commercial differences.

EGYPTIAN ROUTE. This commercial traffic, which in the nomenclature of the time was called "trade with the sultans of Babylonia," and in fact was carried on with the Mamelukes, who ruled Egypt at the time, was extremely important, for the most valuable market for Eastern products—chiefly spices, followed by drugs and dyestuffs—was concentrated in Alexandria. Venice, Genoa, and the other Mediterranean cities were especially interested in obtaining a foothold in Alexandria. The first evidence of the presence of Catalans in that city dates back to 1219, when a ship of Hugh IV, Count of Ampurias, traded in the port of Alexandria. Later we find Catalans established there (1264) under the authority of a consul (1272), a date previous to the period of expansion under Peter the Great. With these antecedents the Catalan colony developed so much that by the end of the 14th century it exercised an unquestioned economic ascendancy in the city, as we are told by indisputable Italian sources. The only critical episode took place in 1365, when the participation of some sailors from Barcelona in the assault and sack of Alexandria by Peter I of Cyprus caused the expulsion of the resident Catalan merchants; but good relations were reestablished almost immediately. The fact was that, while Genoese and Venetians were dominant in Constantinople, Catalonian trade was preponderant in Egypt for most of the 14th century. Later, at the beginning of the 15th, acts of piracy, stimulated by an immoderate greed for money, brought about the rupture of good relations. After 1411 the Sultan of Egypt took restrictive measures against Catalonian trade, and this was one of the causes contributing to its decline. However, mercantile traffic was reestablished between 1438 and 1458, until finally the revolution against John II broke out. Then it was completely ruined and was not renewed until the period of Ferdinand and Isabella; but by then, what had been a constant coming and going of vessels was reduced to a mere trickle.

SYRIAN ROUTE. Complementary to Egyptian trade was that carried on with Syrian ports, also controlled by the Sultanate of Babylonia. Little is known of this traffic, but it must have been considerable, for we know of the existence of a Catalan consul in Beirut (after 1347), transferred to Damascus after 1379.

NORTH AFRICAN ROUTE (Ifriqa and the Moghreb). Here Catalonian trade had the character of a monopoly. In 1291, by the terms of the treaty of Monteagudo between Castile and Aragon, their joint zone of influence in North Africa was established to the east of the river Muluya, taking in an area extending from the western Moghreb to Tunis. This enormous territory was at that time under the rule of the successors of the Almohades, the Beni-Marins, who were in a state of total political decay. New kingdoms were to arise from this decay, and the Catalans established fruitful relations with them.

Even before this, at the time of the Almorávid rulers, the Beni-Ganias, Majorca had decisively influenced political events in Tunis and the kingdom of Tlemçen; so, when James I the Conqueror took over Majorca, it was natural that Majorcans and Catalans should follow the path already open.

After 1258 we find the Catalans trading in *Tunis*. In 1301, after a half-century of tension, James II forced the Bey to sign a customs treaty (the so-called Treaty of Tunis) by the terms of which half of the customs revenue brought in by the normal traffic of Catalo-Aragonese subjects went into the coffers of the monarchy in Barcelona. This control of customs permitted two things—first, the export of iron products and cloth to Tunis; second, the importing of gold and coral intended for manufacture in Barcelona. Trade with Tunis was largely favorable, except during the middle of the 15th century, when good relations between Tunis and the Crown of Aragon were broken off because of piracy by a few Catalan noblemen. In any case, trade was reestablished at the end of John II's reign, and continued favorably under Ferdinand the Catholic.

As for *Bougie,* a territory that had formed part of the empire of the Tunisian Hafsid dynasty, it was a kingdom which appeared in the middle of the 14th century, brought into being largely by the Crown of Aragon, and where the Catalan colony did exactly as it pleased for nearly a hundred years. Ambassadors, *truchimanes* (translators), merchants, and later warriors ruled in Bougie as well as in the neighboring kingdom of Tlemçen. And when we recall that one branch of the African gold route ended in the port of Oran, we will realize the implications of Catalonian supremacy in the country.

As for the *Moghreb* (Morocco), the westernmost part of Ifriqa, all the ambitions of the Western powers were concentrated on the stronghold of *Ceuta*. Ceuta was the key to the Moghreb and also to the Atlantic. These two factors make it easy to understand why the Catalans tried a number of times to take over Ceuta. They attempted it from 1227 to 1415, but without success; the latter date marks its capture by the Portuguese. After that, Moroccan trade was in the hands of the Portuguese, Andalusians, and Genoese, as Ricard's studies have demonstrated.

In regard to North Africa, we should mention the Catalans' daring explorations into the Dark Continent, that is, into the huge zone of the Sahara, the Sudan, the Chad and Uganda. This exploit, totally unknown until recently, has been brought to light by the French historian Charles de la Roncière, who has showed how the Catalans contributed to the discovery of this part of the world by means of the caravan routes which went in search of the gold and slaves of the Sudan.

The trade routes of the Dark Continent debouched into the Mediterranean through Tunis, Bougie, and Tlemçen. This fact explains the Catalans' monopolistic tendency in these three important cities of the North African coast. The change of direction in the gold traffic, which took place in the middle of the 15th century after the establishment of the Portuguese on the coast of Guinea, was a serious blow to the Catalonian economy.

ATLANTIC ROUTES. The Atlantic routes of Catalonian trade should also be divided into two areas, European and African.

(1) Traffic in the *European area* was essentially trade in tin and wool with England, and herring and textiles with Flanders and the Hanseatic League. A few years ago a debate arose over whether the Catalans had been the first Mediterranean seafaring people to launch out into the Atlantic. There were some cartographers who defended this opinion, and others who rejected it. It is perfectly clear today that this honor belongs to the Genoese. The Catalans followed them about the middle of the 13th century. They became established particularly in *Bruges,* which was a way station in trade between the Atlantic and the Hanseatic League. There is an important coincidence here: it was Bruges and Barcelona which dominated the structure of Atlantic trade for a large part of the 14th century. When Barcelona declined, Bruges also fell into economic ruin, and its supremacy as economic capital of Northern Europe passed to Antwerp. This fact has a political confirmation: the

friendship between the Crown of Aragon and the Duchy of Burgundy was very noticeable after the time when the struggle with France began; in the face of a common enemy, Burgundy and the Crown of Aragon necessarily became allies. It was for this reason that the Burgundian dukes always strongly supported Catalonian export trade, as Verlinden has proved. In Bruges, the Catalan colony was second in importance up to the beginning of the 15th century. Then it slowly declined, and by about 1460 very little of its old splendor remained. The cause of this phenomenon has as much to do with piracy as with the progressive decline of Catalonian trade.

Lisbon and Seville also deserve mention as way stations on the Atlantic trade routes. By the middle of the 14th century, according to accounts by Portuguese chroniclers, the Catalan colony in *Lisbon* was exceeded in importance only by those of the Genoese and the merchants from Prato, in Tuscany. We say the Catalan colony because here a distinction was made between Catalans and Majorcans. The latter were much admired, especially for their nautical skill. This was so much the case that at the very foundations of the Portuguese discoveries we can discern the techniques brought by Majorcan cartographers to the court of Henry the Navigator.

As for *Andalusia,* the Catalans became established in *Seville* at the beginning of the 13th century, in stern competition with the Genoese. Partly for this reason, and partly because of the alliance that existed between Genoa and Castile, Catalonian commerce never prospered in Seville. After the 14th century the Catalan colony became less and less important, and eventually was supplanted by the Genoese colony. In this struggle for control of Seville it is easy to observe the decline in Catalonian activity. It was there that commercial interests in the Atlantic were at stake; and when the Catalans gave way to the Genoese, it meant that the discovery of America benefited not only the Castilians but also the Genoese, for trade with America in the 16th century was a Castilian-Genoese monopoly.

(2) *African Atlantic area.* The inexorable decline of Catalonian trade at the beginning of the 15th century is also shown in this direction. The *Canary Islands* were conquered at the beginning of the century by the Bethencourts, as a fief of the Castilian crown; but long before, in the middle of the 14th century, Majorcans had sailed toward the Fortunate Isles in search of gold and slaves. We

possess geographical charts which have permitted us to ascertain the names of the Majorcan sailors who carried out these discoveries. We know that in 1342 Francesc dez Valers made a first voyage, and that during the course of the same year one Doménec Gual followed him. From then until 1386 voyages to the Canaries were frequent. The most sensational of these voyages was that of the Majorcan Jaume Ferrer to Rio de Oro, on the coast of Senegal, in 1346.

At the end of the 14th century, coincident with the crisis year of 1381, Majorcan explorations began to be less frequent. The Canaries, which had seemed to be a very appropriate area of colonization for the Catalans and Majorcans, were conquered by a Norman and colonized by Castile. Thus Catalonia gave up in advance the conquest of the Atlantic and the discovery of America.

ARTICLES OF TRADE. When we spoke of the routes of Catalonian trade in the preceding pages, we mentioned certain products which were characteristic of it. Let us proceed to an analysis of these.

Among agricultural products we find *wheat,* sometimes exported but more often imported, according to the fate of the harvest. We should keep in mind the importance of Sicily as a base of wheat supply for the Crown of Aragon. After the middle of the 15th century, Valencian *rice* gained a certain importance. A large part of Valencia's prosperity was owed to this grain, which was exported in large quantities not only to Italy but also to the south of France. The relationship between Marseilles and Valencia derived particularly from the rice trade. There was also regular export of *wine* (Catalonian and Valencian).

Besides these agricultural products, and in addition to *olive oil,* we have evidence even in that remote period of trade in *dried and preserved fruits.* Thus, for example, as early as the 14th century we find *almonds, filberts, walnuts* and *dried figs, raisins, oranges,* and *pomegranates* as the preferred products for ships making the northern journey from Barcelona and Valencia to Flanders. *Saffron* was also included in these shipments.

As for livestock and animal by-products, the three chief items were: *salt pork,* called "cansalada" in Catalan; *honey,* of which considerable quantities were exported; and *wool.* Although trade in this fiber never attained the importance it did in Castile, as we shall see, both because there were fewer head of sheep and because the existence of a powerful wool industry absorbed a large part of the production, it still merits some attention; for a considerable quantity of wool from the Maestrazgo region was exported through the ports of San Mateo and Valencia to Liguria, Lombardy, and Tuscany. This trade was in the hands of the Genoese, who in the course of time came to monopolize it completely.

Among textile fibers, *silk* and *esparto* occupied a favored place in Valencian trade. These types of fiber enjoyed a great reputation abroad, and Valencia had almost a monopoly on them in the Western Mediterranean, in competition with Castile and the Nasrid dynasty of Granada.

The third group of trade items consisted of *spices:* this was the typical kind of "tramp" trading engaged in by the Catalans. They bought spices in the Levant and then supplied them to Barbary, the south of France, Aragon, and Castile. There were large profits in this trade.

Among the spices, drugs, perfumes, and pharmaceuticals distributed through Barcelona we find the following: pepper, ginger, cinnamon, clove, nutmeg, lac, sugar (which was used in pharmacy), incense and myrrh, mastic, musk, camphor (which came from Formosa and had to be shipped through the Malay Peninsula, India, and Alexandria), rhubarb and benzoin, aloes, and so on.

The Catalonian spice trade began to decline about 1430, owing to competition from the French. When the Thirty Years' War in France came to an end, the great financier Jacques Coeur, counselor of Charles VII, made a successful attempt to shut the Catalans out of the spice trade with the southern part of the country; to do this he first constructed some ships in Colliure with the permission of the king of Aragon, ships which the Catalans built without any suspicion of the damage they were doing to themselves; then he vigorously protected the trade operations of Marseilles. After twenty years he had succeeded in completely excluding the Catalans from the spice trade with the south of France.

The fourth group is that of *fabrics*. Wool for making cloth was imported from many places: the Pyrenees, Aragon, Castile (after the 14th century), and finally, England, which exported wool of the highest quality. Besides wool, cloth already woven was imported for dyeing and finishing. Fabrics of fine quality were also bought in

Flanders, France, and Italy for the aristocratic classes of society.

The typical cloth produced in Catalonia was *drap,* of ordinary quality, which found excellent markets in the Western Mediterranean (Barbary, Sardinia, Sicily, and Naples) and even in the Eastern Mediterranean (Egypt, Syria). Catalonian wool production did not fall off as sharply as in the case of the spice trade, for it actively resisted foreign competition throughout the 15th century. However, after the appearance of the English in the Western Mediterranean in 1416, especially in Sicily, production and sale of Catalonian "draps" began to decline.

Another group of export products included *cordage,* that is, rigging for ships; *iron,* in the form of chests and anchors; *paper, ceramic objects,* and *esparto products* from all over the Valencian region; and *coral,* almost a Catalonian monopoly since Catalonia had absolute control over the centers of production (a popular adornment throughout Europe, coral made Catalonia the chief producer of fine costume jewelry); and finally, *hides,* which until the end of the 15th century comprised, together with fabrics, iron, and coral, the four principal Catalonian export products.

As for typical imported products, they consisted, apart from foodstuffs, principally of dyes and metals. Among the former we should mention *alum, woad, indigo* from Baghdad, and the blue dye of Acre; and among metals, *lead* and *copper,* which was imported from Rumania, *tin* from England, and *iron* from Northern Europe. *Cotton* was also imported.

HUMAN TRAFFIC. There is one aspect of Catalonian trade which has not been much emphasized, in spite of its importance and the fact that it had great influence on the economic attitude and the future of commercial activity in Catalonia. We refer to the slave trade. Thanks to the studies of Professor Verlinden, we have today an almost complete view of the problem. From the 9th century onward, Barcelona's fortunes were closely linked to the development of contraband trade and trade in human beings. After the great conquests of the 12th and 13th centuries the slave traffic declined, for it was much easier to buy a Moslem who had been made captive in the conquest than to go a-pirating at sea or to buy slaves in Eastern markets. But in 1348 the Black Death began to make inroads on the population of the country. With the reduction of native manpower, it became absolutely necessary to seek slave labor, either in the markets existing at the time in the Eastern Mediterranean or by acts of piracy along the coasts of North Africa.

The development of slavery is so great in Catalonia, Aragon, Valencia, and Majorca after this date that Professor Kovalevsky of the University of Kiev has set forth the theory that a kind of "Sklavenwirtschaft," or slave economy, became established in the Crown of Aragon as a result of the Black Death. Verlinden denies this. Actually, there did not exist in the 15th century in Catalonia and Valencia an agrarian capitalistic economy based on the working of latifundia by slaves, though it is evident that in Valencia, for example, many rich people owned as many as forty or fifty of them. What is obvious, however, is the rapid increase in their numbers.

The large *extent* of the area where slaves were sought is surprising, though. The main point of acquisition was North Africa. This was where the *Moors* came from (so-called even though they might be Negroes). Besides these, there were Greeks, Russians, Caucasians, Crimeans, Tartars, Turks, Armenians, Albanians, Bosnians, Bulgars, and Wallachians. The heaviest traffic in this Eastern Mediterranean area came between 1380 and 1440, with the peak about 1411.

The number of slaves was extraordinary. Though it is difficult to gauge the size of the slave population, Verlinden has been able to estimate, on the basis of a census of insured slaves and the statistics of sales in the public market of Barcelona, what their approximate number was in Catalonia. He finds 4,375, a figure which, he states, "would have to be multiplied many times." We can estimate, then, some 10,000 slaves for Catalonia, many more for Valencia, and a much smaller number for Majorca—a total of some 20,000 to 30,000 slaves, a truly impressive figure.

When we take the volume of trade into account, we can understand why traders were so anxious to engage in the traffic of slaves, especially since their price was continually on the rise, owing to the depreciation of money, in spite of their abundance in the market. Let us cite a few figures: in 1370 a man was worth 40 libras; 50 libras in 1411; 54 in 1424; 42 in 1441; and 59 in 1445.

For an adventurous trader of the period the slave traffic offered—as it did to so many other, later traders (Dutch, Portuguese, and English in the 17th and 18th centuries, and Spaniards in

the 19th)—one of the most profitable forms of investment. Therefore, the Catalans not only went to buy slaves in the markets of
Naples, Genoa, Palermo, Venice, and especially Candia, the center
for the great slave traffic of the Eastern world, but also went out
and captured them directly, often breaking the successive peace
treaties and truces which their kings had signed with the North African kings. After 1380 the Catalans unleashed in the Mediterranean a piratical reign of terror which, because of their disastrous
greed for immediate profits, ended by destroying the trade. The
causes of this phenomenon have not been clearly understood until
now. But the vicious circle is perfectly obvious: the close relationship that existed between the Black Death and development of the
slave traffic, the consequent great rise in piracy, and finally, the attraction which piracy exercised on traders, thus opening up an abnormal path which eventually would destroy the very trade they
were trying to enrich.

TECHNICAL ORGANIZATION OF TRADE: FLEET, SEAPORTS, CAR-
AVANS, AND ALFÓNDIGOS. The great medieval trade was essentially maritime. Therefore, we must take up the construction of
ships and the development of seafaring techniques in the Late
Middle Ages.

The true Catalonian fleet came to life in the 12th century, developed in the 13th, reached a peak in the 14th, and declined in the
15th, though its total ruin did not come about until the 16th century. As shipbuilders the Catalans were outstanding among those of
the Western Mediterranean. Proof of this is the existence in Barcelona of shipyards (the "draçanes" of Regomir, the "draçanes reials,"
or Atarazanas) whose size and magnificence astonish archaeolo-
gists even today. Together with those of Genoa, the Atarazanas
of Barcelona were the chief pillars of marine construction in the
Western Mediterranean. If we note that in 1378, when Barcelona
and King Peter the Ceremonious decided to fortify and refurbish
the Atarazanas, they spent the fabulous sum of 17,000 florins, we
can judge the importance of these shipyards.

To demonstrate their technical excellence we need only note two
facts belonging to the 15th century and therefore subsequent to the
great period of Catalonian shipbuilding. The first reference is to
Jacques Coeur, minister of the French king Charles VII, whose first

ships were built by Catalans. The second is the treaty signed by Florence in 1461 with Admiral Vilamarí, appointing him naval "condottiero" and leasing his fleet. The powerful city government of Florence, when it wished to guarantee the traffic of its merchants on the Tyrrhenian Sea, appealed to the fleet it considered to be the strongest.

As for the types of ships, most authors have followed Capmany in classifying them in the following manner: among *warships,* there were *galeras, gabiotas, leños,* and *corces;* among *merchant ships* were *naus, cocas, fustas,* and *taridas.* Today, thanks to the researches of Mlle. Carrère, we know the true structure of the Catalonian fleet, which was somewhat different from what has generally been thought.

There were three groups of ships; first, those used for coastwise trade, which were less than 11 meters long and whose burden was less than 10 "botas" (about 4 tons); these were *lauts, esquifes, gróndolas,* and *barcas.* Then came the medium-sized ones, which traded between Barcelona, Majorca, and Valencia. These ships were of some 50 "botas," or about 20 tons; they were called *leños* and *barcas.* They could be distinguished from those of the first type not only because of their larger tonnage, but also because they had a "bridge"; that is, they were covered and could better withstand the onslaught of the seas. For *long-distance trade* there existed four types of ships: the *balener,* the *coca,* the *nau,* and the *galera,* or galley, which, as Mlle. Carrère rightly points out, was the one preferred by Catalonian and Valencian shipbuilders.

These last-named ships had a displacement of 100 to 900 tons, with the preferred mean at 250 to 500 tons. The Catalan merchant's fortunes rose with the development of the galley and fell with it too, in spite of the fact that there was an important change in the techniques of naval construction, in which the shipyards of the country undoubtedly participated. We refer to the introduction into the Mediterranean of the *coca,* a ship of the type for Atlantic navigation, which was round and had a square sail; it had a great deal of cargo space and was not very well-suited to the irregular winds of the Mediterranean. The *coca* appeared there at the beginning of the 13th century. Early in the 14th it was strengthened by the introduction of the *coca* of Bayonne. In the course of two centuries it became transformed into the famous caravel, the ship of the great ocean discoveries.

As for the ports, they were simply landing beaches. Not until the middle of the 15th century do we begin to notice a concern for the building of jetties which would serve to protect customary anchorages against the pounding of the sea. The first port whose construction was attempted was that of Barcelona (franchise granted by Alfonso the Magnanimous in 1438); work on it was suspended as a result of the civil war of 1462–1472 and could not be resumed until considerably later.

It would also be interesting to know more details about caravans, for a large part of continental traffic was carried out by this means. We do not possess descriptions of their organization, as the Italians have; but we do have graphic reproductions of them. We need only to glance at any map of the Majorcan school to see drawings of Catalan merchants with their camels loaded with merchandise. The Catalonian caravan obviously must have been important, for if we keep in mind what La Roncière has said about the discovery of black Africa, it is only logical to suppose that Catalans must have taken part in caravan traffic across the Sahara, between the Sudan and the seaports of Tlemçen, Bougie, and Tunis.

In the Late Middle Ages the *alfóndigos* served as a base for the colonies of Catalans residing in the different Mediterranean ports with which they traded. The *alfóndigos* were really an extraterritorial concession. The Moslem rulers would grant to the merchants a place where they could put up a church, open a bake-oven and a tavern, have the use of some baths and a cemetery, and establish living quarters and merchandise depots. The *alfóndigos* even had notaries and priests, and were placed under the supervision of a special functionary called the consul. This consul attained so much importance in the commercial operations of Catalonia that he deserves special mention. From this institution was to arise an extremely important type of mercantile practice which eventually culminated in the so-called *Consulado de Mar,* or Consulate of the Sea.

FAIRS AND COMMERCIAL EXCHANGES. Fairs were not particularly important in the Crown of Aragon. Unlike those of Castile, which were the heart of commercial and financial activity, the Catalonian fairs, though very numerous, rarely had more than local importance. One of the first appears to have been that of Moyá, which was already being held early in the 13th century. The small scope of the fairs is due to the fact that exchange of goods went on daily, and there was no need to convoke large annual fairs. On the other hand, the *lonja,* or commercial exchange of an Italian type, is characteristic of Catalonia, Valencia, and Majorca.

Originally the exchanges were places under a portico (*loggia,* in Italian) where merchants met to carry on their business. They soon became large and luxurious buildings. In their spacious rooms the merchants attended to the buying and selling of all kinds of products. In the 15th century the so-called "corredors d'orella," or brokers, appeared in them; these not only moved about, bringing together buyers and sellers and exchanging offers on merchandise and properties, but they also speculated on shares of the municipal debt (called *censales* and *violarios*), and thus were the originators of the Stock Exchange which developed in the following century.

From this point of view, we should mention the architectural magnificence achieved by the exchanges of the three great mercantile cities of the Crown of Aragon. The Barcelona exchange was begun in1350 and finished in 1392. Those of Majorca and Valencia were built somewhat later. The splendor of the construction, the richness of the materials used, and the spaciousness of the architects' plans, all show the economic potential of the mercantile class which made these buildings the very center of its activity. Nor shall we describe the exchange in Saragossa, for it was built somewhat later; but it also is connected with this great commercial and financial movement in the Crown of Aragon in the 14th century.

THE CONSULATE OF THE SEA: ORGANIZATION AND FUNCTIONS. Though we are dealing with two closely related organizations, we must distinguish between consuls established in foreign lands and the Consulate of the Sea, an institution set up in the home country.

Originally, a consul was the delegate of the royal power on some ship or commercial fleet sent to a particular spot. Later, when expeditions became more frequent and the *alfóndigos* began to develop, the consul left the ship and set himself up as the authority delegated to fix prices, settle disputes among the merchants of his country, and, especially, to defend their interests before the local authorities. The consul was named by the king up to the year 1266, when James I granted the city of Barcelona the right to elect consuls for all Catalans and those who traded in their name, such as

Valencians and Majorcans. This privilege, confirmed by the same king in 1268, was never to be withdrawn, though at the end of the 15th century the authoritarian monarchy began to make appointments on its own account or to control those made by Barcelona. A consul's post was much sought after, for it gave the right to a high income derived from a certain percentage of the receipts from sales made in the respective *alfóndigos*.

Parallel to the evolution of Catalonian consuls in foreign countries was the development of the Consulate of the Sea in various port cities of the mother country. The Consulate as an institution had an immediate precedent in the *Universidad de los prohombres de ribera* created in 1257 by James I in Barcelona as a society of merchants and shipbuilders of the port area, to provide for overseeing and repairing the *ribera,* or port. Twenty-six years later, in 1283, the first real Consulate of the Sea was established in Valencia. This Consulate, which must have been ruled by the maritime usages then in force in Barcelona, showed even at the outset the definitive dual character of the institution: in the first place, it was a professional corporation which brought together people connected with the sea (merchants and shipowners) in the defense of their economic interests; that is, it was an organization very similar to the present-day Chambers of Commerce, a happy comparison we owe to Professor Font Rius. In the second place, the Consulate was a special tribunal designed to resolve the disputes that came up in maritime commerce. Thus defined, the institution was extended to Majorca in 1343 and Barcelona in 1347. We must point out, however, that the Consulate in Barcelona did not come into being at this date as a new entity, but as a simple reconfirmation of the old *Universidad,* which had evolved by its own efforts into a true Consulate. From Barcelona the Consulate was extended to other Catalonian towns such as Gerona, Perpignan, Tortosa, San Feliu de Guixols, etc. Characteristic of the Consulate in Barcelona was its dependence on the municipal government, which annually elected the two consuls—one citizen and one merchant—charged with running the institution. In other cities the Consulate was an autonomous organization.

In witness to the efficacy of the Consulate of Barcelona we have the *Code of the Consulate of the Sea,* which has exceptional importance as the basis of the Catalonian maritime movement. This code shows us the essence of such trade, its extent and the standards of justice which informed it. Although the oldest code of maritime customs in the Western Mediterranean was that of Pisa (12th century), the Code of the Consulate of the Sea was undoubtedly the one that, beginning in the 13th century and drawing in part on the *Ordinances of the Port of Barcelona* of 1258, on the *Customs of the Sea,* the *Statute of Affairs of the Sea,* and the *Constitutions* of Peter the Ceremonious (1340), made up the most complete body of doctrine then in existence concerning navigation and maritime commerce. For this reason the Code of the Consulate of the Sea had legal application not only in Barcelona, Valencia, and Majorca, but also in many places in Italy and the south of France.

MERCANTILE PRACTICE: BILLS OF EXCHANGE, JOINT-ENTERPRISE COMPANIES; REGULATION OF MARINE INSURANCE. There is a theory concerning mercantile practice which derives from the studies of Sayous, a French professor who studied the problem about 1930–1935. Sayous held that the Catalans were very backward in the matter of commercial practices, and even placed them below the Provençal merchants in this respect. Recent studies by Usher, Roover, Lapeyre, Mitjá, and Noguera have somewhat modified this idea, showing that Catalonia, Valencia, and Majorca quickly followed up the innovations in mercantile practice introduced by the Italians, who at that time were the most advanced in this field. There is no doubt that the Catalans were not innovators in many matters, but the influence exercised upon them by Florentine and Genoese financiers became apparent very quickly. Nor should we forget that during the whole course of the 14th century Barcelona was a very important financial center, included in the circuit of mercantile and financial relationships between Flanders and Italy. Barcelona was situated in one angle of the triangle that it formed with Florence and Bruges, so we are not surprised to find its name among the foremost centers of mercantile practice.

This was the case, for example, of the *bill of exchange,* which appeared at the beginning of the 13th century when European trade became more sedentary and was localized in some few cities. Barcelona had no part in the birth of this basic instrument of mercantile practice. However, from the moment its use became established at the end of the 14th and beginning of the 15th centuries, we find Barcelona always mentioned as a center of reference. The first reliable evidence we have of bills of exchange of a modern type comes from the year 1400, and is in the form of a draft on Barcelona originating in Bruges. Lapeyre has recently discovered the earliest endorsement in the history of such bills of exchange: it is of the year 1247 and appears on a bill from Florence on Barcelona, which was to be transferred to Valencia. These facts demonstrate that the technical level of the merchant of Barcelona was very high.

The same phenomenon appears in the history of the development of joint-enterprise companies. Three stages are known. The first stage is one of simple *comanda*. In Catalan, "comanda" means to confide, to commend, to delegate to a person in whom one has confidence. *Comanda,* then, consisted in a person's commissioning a ship's captain to sell his merchandise in far-off markets. The delegator, therefore, turned over his product to the skipper of a ship and gave him authority to sell it and to collect the proceeds.

There was a second stage, in the 14th century, during which the so-called *Societas Maris* developed. This society of the sea was no longer made up of a single merchant who turned over the sale of his products to someone else, but of two or three persons who got together for some concrete operation, such as chartering a ship, buying fabrics, selling them in faraway lands, and dividing the profits thus obtained; with this division the association came to an end. There are many examples of this type of "societas."

The third stage in mercantile association is represented by the *company,* called "companya" in Catalan. Here there was no intention to found a permanent company, but it was a society formed by four or five persons, sometimes more (there are documents in which as many as thirty associates are named), who agreed to join together for a certain period of time (a maximum of five years) in order to engage in some commercial or industrial enterprise, with periodic distribution of the profits. This means that a mental attitude had developed very different from that existing at the inception of the "comanda."

As for the *regulation of marine insurance,* we must recall the famous ordinances laid down by the city of Barcelona in 1438, which justly belong in the forefront of their class. It is a very brief text, in which we can discern the importance of insurance on ships, merchandise, and any article likely to run some risk. The importance of insurance at the beginning of the 15th century shows the characteristic good faith of the Catalan merchant in his period of greatest maturity.

Later, insurance continued to develop, and to such a degree that in 1484 the definitive ordinances concerning insurance in Barcelona were promulgated; a good many later ordinances in other cities, both Italian and European, came to be based on these.

SCIENTIFIC INNOVATIONS AND COMMERCIAL PROGRESS. The basis of Catalonian trade was, in the last instance, a special skill in the knowledge and mapping of coasts. When the art of cartography was in its infancy a small group of cartographers in Palma de Mallorca, inspired by Italian precedents, made a new art out of the map. This art was known as the art of the "portulanos" (those who charted ports and harbors). All the ports visited by merchants were set down and described in these charts for the first time. But aside from making maps, those who specialized in this work also studied, scientifically, astronomy and the arts related to navigation.

We must take note, however, of one essential thing: these people were Jews. They formed a specialized group which, by gathering up the traditions of medieval science, brought together in Palma a great deal of extremely important information. Undoubtedly, the fact that in 1391 the Jewish *calls* were attacked and the Jewish colony emigrated to Portugal is closely related to the decline of the Catalans' spirit of adventure and their subsequent incapacity for undertaking the great Atlantic ventures.

However, all through the 15th century we find names connected with geographic science, though they become progressively fewer as the century wears on. The last name we know is that of Jaume Ferrer of Blanes, who was called upon by Ferdinand and Isabella to give his opinion on the famous line of demarcation of the Atlantic between Castilians and Portuguese. This was the last act of Catalonian medieval science: helping to divide the world.

18 · Prices, Money, Banking, and General Economic Conditions in the Crown of Aragon

PRICES AND WAGES IN THE CROWN OF ARAGON AND NAVARRE. Thanks to the research of Hamilton, we can follow closely the development of prices and wages in the kingdoms of Aragon and Navarre in the period of the Late Middle Ages. Catalonia is not studied in his work, but this is no obstacle to our using his studies to reconstruct the general trend of prices and wages there during the same period. The graphs on these pages illustrate the point.

Let us examine prices and wages separately. The evolution of *prices* underwent the following stages:

Sharp rise, from 1340 to 1380. This corresponds to what Hamilton calls the Commercial Revolution, and deserves the name of the first price revolution (the second came in the 16th century). According to Hamilton, the exclusive cause of this rise was an increase in the stock of gold, as a consequence of exploitation of the goldfields of Silesia and Hungary, development of trade with northwest Africa, and even the return to a favorable balance of trade in commerce with the Levant (though this last hypothesis is difficult to prove). However, this explanation neglects other causes of an internal nature such as, for example, breakdown of the production system—a result of the Black Death—which was undoubtedly more serious than the demographic loss in itself.

Instability, from 1380 to 1425. This phenomenon is particularly evident in Aragon, where agriculture was more predominant than in other parts of the country, and where prices were almost exclusively linked with the yield of the harvests. But instability was general following the sharp rise in prices and was a product of the necessary readjustment to this situation.

First phase of the secular downward trend, from 1425 to 1460. Beginning in Aragon, the drop occurs in all the kingdoms after 1445. This time internal factors are also of first importance in Hamilton's explanation that demographic recovery was cancelled out by the development of industry and trade, and a less rapid increase in stocks of precious metals.

Crisis, from 1460 to 1480. As a result of the war in Catalonia, prices again begin to oscillate violently, with a tendency to rise. The Aragonese figures are the ones most affected by the Catalonian crisis.

Second phase of the secular downward trend, from 1480 to 1500. That is, consolidation of the trend which began after 1425, although this time, when we consider the drop, we must especially take into account the scarcity of gold circulation.

Wages also show a similar development. There was a sharp rise, especially in Navarre, between 1340 and 1400, a consequence of the lack of manpower and the vertical rise in prices; then a period of adjustment from 1380 to 1420, with sharp oscillations but a general tendency to rise; a long phase of drop in wages beginning between 1420 and 1430 and lasting generally until the end of the century. We should point out, however, concurring with Verlinden, that wages stayed higher and not lower than prices during the last three-quarters of the century in Aragon, and from 1448 to 1466 in the kingdom of Valencia, while in Navarre wages rose much more rapidly than prices during the last ten years of the century. We can deduce from this that, for the mass of wage-earners, the period was not one of retrogression.

Taking the entire situation into account, we must emphasize the similarity among the curves of Navarre, Aragon, and Valencia between 1400 and 1500. This similarity can only be explained by the existence of a common labor market, and it is in this area that Catalonia clearly appears as the great economic motive force of the whole area. Along general lines, its evolution must have been similar to that of the territories studied in the graphs, but with greater alterations between 1460 and 1480.

MONETARY CIRCULATION IN THE 14TH CENTURY: INTRODUCTION OF THE FLORIN. The Commercial Revolution was ushered in by an event of the greatest importance: the adoption of gold as a monetary standard. This reform took place in the cities of Genoa and Florence in 1252 and 1253. Certainly, gold had not disappeared during the Early Middle Ages, and we know of a number of gold mintings. Ever since the Carolingian era, however, silver had been

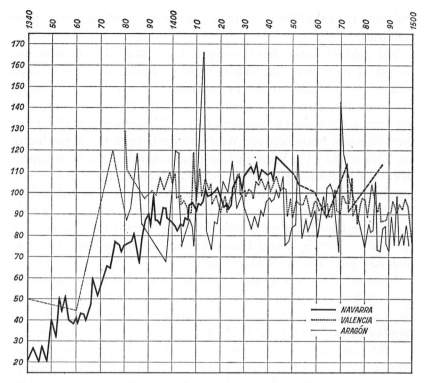

GRAPH OF PRICES IN VALENCIA, ARAGON, AND NAVARRE (*after* HAMILTON).

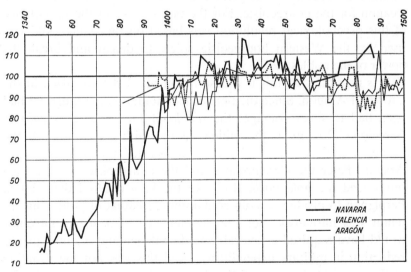

GRAPH OF WAGES IN VALENCIA, ARAGON, AND NAVARRE (*after* HAMILTON).

the metal typical of the economies of the various Western European countries.

The gold revolution has been very closely studied by modern historians of economics. According to Marc Bloch, who has devoted some very intelligent studies to the subject, it was due to a number of causes: the opening of the Black Sea to the Italians as a result of the Fourth Crusade (beginning of the 13th century); a change in the balance of trade between West and East (until the beginning of the 13th century the Western European countries had been dependent on Eastern trade, sending gold to Levantine ports and receiving finished goods from them; but the development of industry in the West meant that the countries of the Levant now paid in gold for the merchandise they bought from the West); the discovery of gold mines in Silesia and Hungary; and the heavy importation of Sudanese gold into the Mediterranean.

Professor Robert S. Lopez states, however, that these causes are not sufficient to explain the change of attitude which led the men of the 13th century to exchange silver for gold. After setting forth a number of hypotheses, he holds that the change took place when, for the first and only time in history, the ratio between the two metals, gold and silver, came to be 1:9; that is, gold being worth nine times more than silver. Then gold was adopted as a standard because it represented a greater degree of nobility, and also a weapon for the bourgeoisie. For the fact was—and the importance of this psychological revolution was based on that fact—gold was used by the Western bourgeoisie solely to defeat and break the power of the nobles.

It is possible that this is a description of what took place in the Crown of Aragon. Since the time of its foundation the kingdom had been tied to silver coinage: the *sueldo* of Jaca and the *sueldo* of Barcelona. But about the middle of the 14th century, when the island of Majorca was definitely incorporated into the Crown of Aragon, Peter the Ceremonious and the bourgeoisie of Barcelona introduced the *gold florin*. In 1346 the king ordered the mint at Perpignan to produce a coin containing 22 carats of gold. This attempt was unrealistic, for the maintenance of a strong currency would have required a favorable trade balance and a simultaneous reduction in military expenditures. And this was not the situation at the moment, because of the demographic, economic, and mili-

tary crisis of the mid-14th century. Therefore the florin was devalued in 1351, 1363, and 1365. At this last date the weight of 18
carats of gold was fixed; that is, 75% of its original content. This
event hampered the development of capitalism in Catalonia, for the
bourgeoisie clung to the current silver coin, the *croat,* which had
been the symbol of their strength for the preceding two centuries.
They refused to devalue it, and this caused a mass flight of silver,
which could be bought advantageously with foreign gold money,
since the European monetary ratio was 1:10.5 compared to the
Catalonian ratio of 1:13.1. This short-sighted traditionalism at a
time when money was undergoing great changes explains the
origins of Catalonia's economic decline.

CATALONIAN BANKING: THE CRISIS OF 1391 AND THE FOUNDING
OF THE "TAULA" OF EXCHANGE IN BARCELONA AND VALENCIA.
The most recent studies, among them those of the American
scholar Usher, assure us that in the 13th century the so-called
campsores or *canviadors* already existed; they were those who engaged in money-changing. As coins were of different metals and
fineness, and local and foreign money were used indiscriminately,
the business of the money-changers was to weigh and appraise
them. The profits they realized were considerable, and it was from
the accumulation of these profits that the banking business, or the
business of lending money, arose. The Jews had monopolized this
type of operation up to the 13th century, for the Church completely
opposed all forms of interest, which it considered usury. The
bankers found a means to flout the canonical strictures by dealing
in bills of exchange. Banking and commercial bills began their
dazzlingly successful career at this time.

The importance of Catalonian banking began to grow within the
13th century itself. It appears for the first time in the legislation of
1284. Later, in the Cortes of 1300–1301, banking business became organized, and laws were passed concerning the rights, functions, responsibilities, and guarantors of the money-changer or
banker.

The second function of the *campsores* was to serve as deposi-
taries for the assets of certain persons, especially merchants, who at
times found it necessary to engage in credit operations and needed
to draw money on a "taula" (in Catalonia the bank was named

"taula," meaning "plank" or "table"). Very soon these exchangers had another function: that of lending money, sometimes to the monarchy, sometimes to the cities, as often for purposes of war as for problems of supplying the country in case of a grain shortage.

During the reign of Peter the Ceremonious, constant warfare with Genoa and Castile caused an enormous development among the bankers in Barcelona, and in their train those of Valencia, Perpignan, Gerona, Lérida, and Tortosa. So much was this the case that in the last third of the 14th century Catalonian banking began to enter a phase of great prosperity. But just as it was about to achieve the stability necessary to assure normal functioning of the country's economy, the contraction of 1381 took place. This was characterized by a paralysis of business, reduction of the investment market, the ruin of *rentiers* owing to the breakdown in municipal finance, over-production, etc. In the face of this brutal shock, the slender stock of theoretical knowledge of the practicing economists of the day failed them completely. Then two sets of parallel events occurred. The first was the massacre of Jews in 1391, to which we have already referred; it was an explosion of popular anger against those who were being accused of the collective disaster. The second was the collapse of private banking. The bankers who had lent money to the king, unable to make good on the deposits which had been left with them, declared themselves bankrupt. Between 1381 and 1383 the chief bankers of Barcelona (Descaus, D'Olivella, Pasqual, and Esquerit), Gerona (Medir), and Perpignan (Garí) went into bankruptcy. This was a hard blow to the confidence placed in them by the public, as is shown by the edict published in Barcelona in 1397 reorganizing the system of money-changing.

As a result of the bankruptcies, the financial relationships which until that date had made up the normal network of public finance in the Crown of Aragon changed. The kings placed the credit of the Crown in the hands of foreign bankers, especially Genoese and Florentines, and in those of the families of converted Jews, particularly Aragonese, who had close ties with their friends and relatives, the *conversos* of Castile. As for the cities, the crisis resulted in the setting up of communal banking deposits known as "taules" of exchange.

When the historians of two or three generations ago spoke of the

Taula de Canvi in Barcelona, they presented it as a product of our ancestors' creative genius, which had followed by only a few years its Genoese predecessor, the Bank of St. George. In fact, the origin of the famous *Taula* was the crisis of confidence which shook Barcelona after the events of 1381. So far from being an idea of genius, it was an event that demonstrated the financial insecurity of the bankers of Barcelona and their imitators in Valencia and Gerona. It was a short-sighted solution, for once they had lost confidence in the bankers and in national finance, the citizens and merchants decided to found the new institution (1401) by basing it on municipal credit and on the money which they were forced to deposit in the communal bank, whether its source was court orders, guardianships, estates, or attachments (edicts of 1412). In this way a great deal of capital was immobilized in the *Taula,* to the obvious detriment of the money market's flexibility in the crises subsequently to arise. It was, then, a blockade which froze money in Catalonia at the very moment when it should have been most fluid.

The *Taula de Canvi* of Barcelona, imitated in Valencia and Gerona, was under the control of the urban oligarchy. Its circle of operations included the *Bailía Real* (office of the king's bailiff), the *Clavariado* of the city (municipal treasurer's office), the small banks which had survived the catastrophe of 1380–1410, and foreign money (after 1446). Extremely careful regulations governed its workings in order to avoid any kind of fraud. Thus a period of financial conservatism was inaugurated which did not bode well for the future of Catalonia.

DEVELOPMENT OF THE ECONOMIC CRISIS IN THE FIRST HALF OF THE 15TH CENTURY; CRISIS OF 1427 AND DEVALUATION OF 1454. All efforts made after 1412, date of the definitive organization of the *Taula de Canvi,* to combat the economic crisis were fruitless. In 1427 there was a new collapse of the investment market and an even greater decline in economic activity. This was shown as much in the sharp drop in collection of taxes in the *Generalitat* of Catalonia and the city of Barcelona as in the *Bailía Real* of Valencia. The amount of the drop was extremely serious, ranging from 25 to 75%. At the same time, mercantile activity and shipping declined. It is estimated that from 1432–1434 to 1454, shipping in the port of Barcelona declined by 75 to 80%.

A currency reform was undertaken in order to offset these unfavorable conditions. It was an inevitable measure. The Valencians and Majorcans adopted it between 1426 and 1427, the Valencians by starting to mint the *timbre,* a 20-carat coin equivalent to 10 *sueldos,* supplanting the florin, which was worth 11. In Barcelona the monetary reform provoked a real battle between the two great urban parties, the aristocratic and the popular. The latter—the *Busca*—called for devaluation of the *croat* by dropping its ratio to the florin from 15 to 18 dineros. This measure, the *Busca* claimed, would prevent the flight of silver to France, increase the volume of trade, and stimulate industrial production. The other party, the *Biga,* opposed this on the grounds of the city's financial prestige, though in fact it was defending its own immediate interests: rural and urban revenues, bank deposits, debts, etc. It was necessary for some of the more adventurous aristocrats, like the Requesens de Soler family, to join the *Busca* before the Crown decreed devaluation of the florin in 1454. This measure was accepted by the bourgeoisie very much against their will, to the point that it was one of the causes which led the country into civil war in 1462. Then the value of money dropped to a point undreamed of by the conservative elements in the city.

THE PROBLEM OF ECONOMIC DECLINE IN CATALONIA. Throughout this chapter we have observed the development of the stages of very unfavorable conditions in the Catalonian economy. After the inflation of 1340 to 1380 and the crisis of 1381, we came to the collapse of 1427 and the total breakdown produced by the civil war of 1462–1472. This process, as we have pointed out, was typical of Western Europe during the same period; but if in Catalonia it was serious enough to result in total stagnation of the economy, this was due to a number of specific circumstances which we would do well to examine. However, we must keep in mind that the heart of the problem was the inability of the oligarchy in Barcelona to see economic problems from a fresh point of view. This does not constitute a reproach to the oligarchy, for all such groups have failed when confronted with the same problem: namely, that of coping with depression conditions by truly adequate measures. Oligarchies have always taken refuge in the memory of the past, which brought them power and wealth.

There are a number of theories concerning the overall problem of Catalonia's economic decline, some working hypotheses, and a few proven facts. Let us sum up the main theses here:

Loss of control of the investment market. It went over into the hands of *conversos* and Italians. Consequently, the Catalonian bourgeoisie could not operate with its own assets; others handled them, and manipulated them for private ends. The country did not have money available to make productive investments during the whole long period of crisis in the 15th century.

Maritime terror and counterterror. The desire to make money rapidly caused the loss of the traditional markets for Catalonian trade in the Mediterranean. The slave trade, piracy, and privateering severely damaged Catalonia's commercial relations with other countries.

Closing of traditional markets in Barbary and Egypt. This was a direct consequence of the terrorism at sea that we have just mentioned.

Foreign competition. French on the one hand, English on the other. The French in the fields of textiles and spices, the English in shipping and the wool trade.

Lack of technological and social stimuli. People left Barcelona because trade was impoverished and because there was a climate of tension. In Barcelona, men fought in the name of theories which masked selfishness and personal antagonisms; but there was no view that looked toward the future. The protectionism of the popular party did not contain the seeds of positive reform in the industrial field. The fact was that the spirit of enterprise which had made Catalonian trade so powerful in the 14th century had been halted.

Lack of economic resistance in Catalonia's own commercial hinterland. This hypothesis of Robert S. Lopez deserves serious consideration. Catalonia had neither the human resources nor a sufficiently powerful consumers' market to allow her to resist the onslaughts of the crisis. And the same was true in the south of France and the Crown of Aragon. On the other hand, Catalonia was faced with sharp competition from Valencia, a city which, by allying itself with Barcelona's enemies (Genoa and Marseilles) became the financial capital of the Crown of Aragon after 1462.

19 · Public Power and Financial Organization in the Crown of Aragon

THE MONARCHY AND PUBLIC ECONOMY: TAXES AND LEVIES. The Commercial Revolution, which was accompanied all over the West by the spread of Roman law, resulted in a tendency toward an authoritarian monarchy. This was a perfectly logical phenomenon, for once the monarchy had emerged from feudal disunity, it attempted to be one that would truly govern; and to govern it needed an army, an administration, and a number of public officials. All of this was translated into greater fiscal greed, in order to lay hands on the funds necessary to carry out these purposes. And so it was that the Commercial Revolution and Roman law contributed toward strengthening the authoritarian monarchy, whose development was parallel to that of precapitalism. It was to result, in the 16th century, in absolute monarchies and in mercantilism as the economic form of those monarchies. This transformation began to take place in the south of Italy, with Frederick II of Sicily, early in the 13th century, and very soon spread to the states of the Hispanic Peninsula.

In the kingdoms of the Crown of Aragon, then, this growth of financial necessity on the part of the sovereign was not accompanied by an increase in financial resources. The king received a number of taxes in his capacity as feudal or seigniorial lord. As sovereign he had the right to receive the contributions, of a feudal type, which every vassal owed to his lord: on his coronation, on his marriage, for the royal table, etc. Since he was commander-in-chief of the army he was owed a number of services, such as the supplying of horses, military service, escort duty, and the like. And as chief of administration he received taxes on merchandise, road tolls, the levy on horned cattle, etc.; that is, everything which stemmed more or less directly from the old Roman fiscal system. These taxes, however, amounted to very little, for they were based on the herding and agrarian economy of the 10th and 11th centuries, while the economy of the Commercial Revolution was based on mercantile exchange and manufactured products, which the seigniorial and feudal system had not foreseen. Consequently the monarchy took in little money. But in addition to this, since in the course of the 13th and 14th centuries the king needed large sums of money to carry on wars and foreign enterprises, he gradually sold the few sources of income he did have to the cities and the nobles. That is, while the country continued to prosper, the sovereign had progressively fewer resources to fall back on.

For this reason, by the middle of the 13th century the sovereign had to surrender to the representative organization of the country's bourgeoisie, the Cortes. When the king asked for money from those who really had control of it, the bourgeoisie, they in turn demanded a political and economic participation in the State's decisions. In Europe this development took place in only two countries—England and the Crown of Aragon. The other monarchies, for various reasons, were able to weather the storm and always had, as in Castile, a free hand to obtain money in cases of great need.

The Aragonese monarchy could count on the royal patrimony in its economic difficulties. But even in this matter it sometimes had to give ground, alienating vast properties, either partially or totally, at critical moments. This was the situation at the time of Peter the Ceremonious. In other cases, recourse to a number of dubious procedures became inevitable; for example, obtaining money from the warring parties by promising favors which then were not forthcoming. This was the ill-starred fiscal policy of Alfonso the Magnanimous.

In any case, one fact should be kept in mind; the aristocracy and the Church were exempt from most taxes, as were honored citizens. Those who really paid were the people, the working men and peasants.

Aside from this general idea, we must keep in mind that, in tune with the circumstances, the financial organization of the Crown was becoming increasingly more complex, and this made necessary the intervention of royal administration in treasury matters. The three chief posts established, beginning in the 13th century, were those of *treasurer, bailiff,* and *"maestre racional."* The first-named official administered the public treasury in the name of the king, the second administered the royal patrimony, and the third handled the central accounting.

THE CORTES AND FISCAL POLICY. The Cortes, as representative to the State of bourgeois policy and the economy created by the corporations, achieved its greatest splendor in the 14th century, after 1283, when it wrested from Peter the Great the famous statute of "una vegada a l'any," obliging him to convoke it—as the name indicates—once a year. After that time, and in spite of the fact that the arrangement was not carried out to the letter (indeed, after 1301 the Cortes was held triennially), it exerted a real influence on the government of the country. In fact, the Cortes reserved to itself the enormous power of granting the "donatiu"; that is, it voted to give a donation in response to the request presented to the assembly by the monarch on the day it opened.

It might seem that in possessing a resource so important as that of holding the country's purse-strings, the Cortes—and here I am referring specifically to the Catalonian Cortes, since it was undoubtedly the one with the strongest personality among those of the kingdoms of the Crown of Aragon—forced the monarch to pursue a particular economic policy. However, study of its deliberations reveals that the Cortes never had a very solid idea of what the best economic policy for the country was. This can be attributed to the opposition of the aristocracy and clergy to the interests of the bourgeoisie, as a result of the composition of the Cortes by these three estates. But it can also be attributed to lack of a guiding principle either in the royal branch or among the bourgeoisie. It is depressing to read how, in the Cortes, where such important mercantile and industrial interests were at stake, the bourgeoisie was sometimes on the side of the nobles, sometimes on the side of the clergy, in deciding small questions of a purely jurisdictional or legal kind. And as these questions were given more importance than any possible concession of the donation, the Cortes' work was consequently paralyzed by bitter debates on the *greuges,* or complaints brought by the representatives of each estate.

In spite of this, during the 14th century the mechanism of the Cortes came to function quite well; but after 1427, when the crisis in Catalonia grew more serious, it became a reactionary organization in which selfish interests stifled collective ones. By following this path, after 1439 the Cortes became an instrument of the political passions which had been unleashed in the country, and therefore its influence was unable to stem the decline of Catalonia.

THE CATALONIAN DIPUTACIÓ DEL GENERAL AND ITS ECONOMIC ROLE. One of the inalterable principles of the Catalonian Cortes' policy was that the monarch should never find out where the money it voted for his donation came from. It preferred to erect a wall of silence between the royal officials and the people who paid and collected the sum agreed upon. This attitude is very Catalan: to separate the person who has to administer the money from the one who has to collect it.

In the period previous to the reign of Peter the Ceremonious, when the Cortes voted a donation it named a commission to parcel out its collection among the inhabitants of the country (which was done by means of a census, or *fogatje;* from *foc,* hearth). The same commission was in charge of appointing the special and general collectors, liquidating the accounts, and prosecuting delinquents. Once its functions were accomplished the commission was dissolved, after burning its papers. During the reign of Peter the Ceremonious, because of the constant struggles with Castile one commission followed hard on the heels of another, to such a point that it became necessary to create a *permanent organization,* which assumed the responsibility for collecting the donation and making the payment to the monarch. This commission, founded in 1359, was called *Diputació del General de Catalunya;* that is, Deputation of the Cortes of Catalonia, the word "General" meaning the community of citizens who came together in the Cortes. The Deputation was, therefore, a permanent commission of the Cortes for matters relating to finance and taxes.

The Deputation was the supreme instrument created by political "pactism" in Catalonia, and by the practical sense of the different estates. There is no corporation in medieval history which so clearly represents the country, and this is the reason why it was imitated in the Crown of Aragon (in Aragon and Valencia at the beginning of the 15th century, in Navarre at the end of this same century) and even extended to Sardinia and Sicily.

In 1413 the Deputation of Catalonia received its definitive structure of laws. Then it became a body with a triple objective.

First—and foremost—was collecting taxes, those taxes which at first went into the king's pocket but which after 1413 became one of the chief revenues of the Deputation itself, now transformed into a powerful political organism with a purpose of its own. In the second place, it had the duty of defending the statutes which had been approved in the Cortes. Its third purpose was to encourage commerce, or rather, to advise on measures which could benefit the economy in general. To carry out these aims, the Deputation created a very complex body of officials, presided over by three local deputies. All this made up a kind of pyramid, with a network of influence very much greater than the monarch himself possessed.

The golden age of the Deputation of Catalonia is the 15th century. In spite of having lost the war against John II and having been reorganized by Ferdinand the Catholic in 1493, it retained a good part of its fiscal and political power up to the year 1714.

CUSTOMS DUTIES: GENERALITATS AND BOLLA. "Generalitats" or generalities were the taxes collected by the Deputation to pay its own expenses and to lay up moneys which could be turned over to the king in case of need. They were of two types: "entradas i eixides," that is, "entrances and exits," which came within the area of customs duties, and the "bolla i segell," a mark placed on cloth when it was manufactured or sold.

There is a lamentable confusion about these "Generalitat" taxes, in spite of their extraordinary importance and the length of time they were in force (four centuries). To clear up the matter we shall only say that the tax on "entrances and exits," since it was related to the successive customs duties set by the Cortes, covered not only cloth production but any import or export product included in the customs. As for the "bolla," it was a piece of metal placed on the loom when weaving was begun, and which remained attached to the cloth during its short existence, to prove the payment of certain taxes on manufactures by the transporter, the tailor, and the eventual purchaser. It also represented a tax on the buying and selling of cloth in the market. All over the country there was a network of officials of the *bolla* to oversee the proper working of these arrangements, and this further slowed the normal development of trade. This tax was so fundamental that it even survived the corporation which had established it, and was not lifted until the time of Charles III (in 1770).

LOANS: CENSALES AND VIOLARIOS. Mobilization of the investment market was the task of the monarchy because it required extraordinary sums which, since they could not immediately be supplied by the country, were loaned by those who had money, nobles and churches as well as bankers and *conversos*. However, regulation of this market was in the hands of the municipal governments. By the 14th century these governments came to have a number of permanent requirements: wheat supply, city improvement, defense, contributions to the Crown, etc. This obliged the city councilors to give up the occasional loan and to organize public credit on the basis of taxes.

This is why, about the year 1340 and as an immediate consequence of the war with Genoa, the public debt of the city of Barcelona was put in order and funded. It is the first case in all Spain of organization of the investment market by means of municipal revenues, closely following Venice and Genoa. The public debt of Barcelona was known by the generic name of *censal,* and simply meant income. There were two types—the *censal* strictly speaking, or permanent debt, and the *violario,* or amortizable debt. Both offered a healthy rate of interest: 7.5% for the first type, 15% or double, for the second. The investor recovered his capital in a short time.

The most important feature of the situation, however, was not the creation of a funded debt but the problem of *interest* related to it. The Church had roundly prohibited illegal gains from money in an attempt to combat usury. But when it was realized that dealings in money under the municipal debt system were honorable as well as lucrative, a campaign in favor of such interest rates was begun. The Church had no recourse but to come to terms with the new financial world. By the middle of the 14th century the theologians and moralists had reached the conclusion that interest on the municipal or royal debt was not to be considered as profit on a *convenio mutuo* but on a sale.

MUNICIPAL TAXATION. About the middle of the 14th century some new taxes were established in the Crown of Aragon which had nothing to do with the seigniorial or royal type of tribute that had prevailed up till then, but were instead related to the need to meet payments on the public debt. Among the more important of these, we shall mention those levied on *foodstuffs:* "vi i verema" (wine), meat, flour, and olive oil. These were the four cardinal supports of the treasury, followed by the tax on fresh fish, and at intervals the so-called "cuartera," levied on wheat flour, or the tax known as "bèsties," falling on animals and fowl. A group of taxes on *manufactured products* is also interesting, for thanks to these we are able to analyze the industrial development of the city. Chief among them were the so-called "cuiram" (on leather), "draperia" (on cloth in general), "pelliceria" (on hides), a tax on grindstones, one on "fusta obrada" (worked wood), and a weapons tax paid on military equipment. Three taxes on textile manufactures deserve mention: "fustanys," on high-grade cloth; "peia," on cloth of medium quality; and "flassades," on a kind of sackcloth. There were also taxes on *buying and selling transactions.* One of them was called "pes del Rei" and affected any merchandise sold by weight; another had the name of "honors i possessions" and had to do with transactions on real estate.

The tax called "navilis i nòlits," which was levied on ships and cargoes, is likewise of interest.

THE MONARCHY'S INTERNATIONAL AND ECONOMIC POLICY: ITS CONSEQUENCES. We cannot find a politico-economic spirit in the monarchy at this time. It is useless to try to discern in the royalty of the 13th and 14th centuries a general economic system or a guiding idea for the development of the economy. In general, the kings simply went on solving daily problems as best they could.

However, as we approach modern times we begin to see a certain relationship, constantly growing closer, between the interests of the monarchy and those of the merchant and laboring classes. Just as after the reign of James II a certain amount of protection began to be given to the guilds because the king profited from them to the degree that they gave him money, a broader concept of the State's financial and economic relations gradually crept in. This took place as a result of the serious economic crisis during the reign of Peter the Ceremonious. But this attempt to organize the economic policy of the State came to grief in the 15th century, especially during the reign of Alfonso the Magnanimous (1416–1458). In Sicily, Naples, and Catalonia, the three great economic centers of his empire, one because of its wheat, one for its population, and one for its industry, this monarch carried out a fiscal policy so oppressive that it brought about violent crises, civil wars, and in the end the collapse of the kingdom on the very threshold of modern times. It is sufficient to recall his irresponsible policy of naval protection for Jacques Coeur, the chief enemy of the Catalonian spice trade, to realize his total ineptitude in managing the affairs of his Crown.

The protectionist attitude that developed in the 15th century was not connected, therefore, with the monarchy but with the cities, and particularly with the popular party formed in them during this period.

DEVELOPMENT OF A PROTECTIONIST ATTITUDE. Protectionist policy began in the privileged urban economy as soon as it became organized into guilds and corporations. Eventually this attitude, aided especially by the demands of the bourgeoisie after the general crisis late in the 14th century, passed from the city to the State. In Catalonia the first protectionist edicts were issued in 1422 by Queen Maria, regent for Alfonso the Magnanimous, in the Cortes of Barcelona. A decree of this date prohibited the importing of any kind of foreign cloth. Later, as the economic crisis worsened, the cause of protectionism was taken up by the popular party, the *Busca,* which considered itself inspired by God to redeem working-class humanity. Just as it had advocated the devaluation of the croat, the *Busca* believed that only protectionism at all costs could save the Catalonian economy from disaster.

Consequently, when it came to power in 1453, it obtained from Alfonso the Magnanimous the famous ordinances of the 24th of August of that year, which constitute the first body of protectionist doctrine previous to the famous 17th-century British Navigation Acts. The decrees of 1453 specified that no goods could be loaded in any Catalonian port, or shipped to Catalonia, except in a Catalan ship, if a vessel bearing that flag were available in the port. The only condition imposed was that the same shipping fees should be offered as those of competing foreign ships.

This law, which should have had a desirable effect on the Catalonian economy, could not be enforced. The chain of events was such that the revolution against John II broke out eight years later, and the interests of the country were so much damaged that it became impossible to think of restrictive measures of such broad scope.

In 1481, once the revolutionary crisis was over, a less drastic solution was sought. Seeing that it was very difficult to apply a Navigation Act in favor of a fleet which in fact did not exist, the Cortes of 1481 decreed a complete set of customs duties to protect Catalonian industry. The importance of these duties is considerable, not only because they involved the first well-developed tariff in Catalonia, but also because they implied a mercantilist attitude which the monarch, Ferdinand the Catholic, would not hesitate to apply to Castile later on.

20 · Structure and Expansion of the Castilian Herding and Agrarian Economy from the 13th to 15th Centuries

GENERAL FEATURES. In the later medieval centuries the Castilian economy went through a phase of obvious expansion. Though we do not share the overflowing optimism that one of its historians, Viñas Mey, has recently demonstrated, considering this expansion as a model of the West's advance toward capitalism, it is certain that we are dealing with a well-defined evolution which gave the kingdom of Castile an important, though not preeminent, place in the aggregate European economy. This vigorous flowering prepared Castile for the great undertaking of the discovery of America; but the preparation involved a special configuration of the economic attitude which, once the time came, was to be reflected in the abnormal response given to the American venture.

The expansion of the Castilian economy shows certain fundamental traits.

In the first place, it was not a uniform movement, but one involving the fabulous *development of the wool trade*. Therefore, from the very outset we are in the presence of a unilateral development of the Castilian economy, based on export of a raw material.

Second, this economic prosperity, besides not being general in the sense of taking in all sectors of the economic structure, *was not general either in regard to the participation of the various regions of the kingdom of Castile*. It was a peripheral development, with one center in the Montaña region of Santander and the Basque Country and the other in Andalusia; and both these centers were in close contact with, and even dependent on, foreign activity.

Third, *the technical organization of the Castilian economy was noticeably backward* in comparison with the mercantile and industrial practices of the Western world. Castile was farther from the centers where this development had arisen than the Spanish lands of the Mediterranean shore, and therefore this backwardness is not surprising.

Fourth, *the social structure of Castile was not well articulated,* and this was a drawback for any change in the economic structure of the country. In Castile there had not been a commercial and urban revolution connected with the bourgeoisie, and consequently the Castilian economy continued to be a primary economy, of a basically agrarian and herding type, in which the urban and industrial element counted for very little.

The persistence of these traits was to have a very unfavorable influence on the great Castilian venture of the 16th century.

DEMOGRAPHIC STRUCTURE IN THE 13TH TO 15TH CENTURIES. It would be rash to put forward any specific figures on the demographic development of the Meseta kingdoms during the later medieval centuries. Only at the end of the period, at the time of Ferdinand and Isabella, was there a population census, and its figures, furthermore, were exaggerated. Under these circumstances we can only cite the general European evolution (a probable 200% increase in the Late Middle Ages) and point out the peculiar situation of Castilian development, which was similar but came later than the rest of Europe. What we can state is that the population of Castile made greater gains than that of the Crown of Aragon during these centuries.

In this demographic process, there is one phenomenon that immediately attracts our attention. The *Mudéjar* group, that is, the *Moslem population assimilated by Castile,* was very small. We already know how the resettlement of Andalusia took place; first the Moslems were expelled from the cities, and then, when the rural revolt broke out in 1263, a systematic elimination of the Moslem element was carried out. Approximate estimates disclose that some 300,000 Moslems were left. This was one-tenth of the total population of the Castilian kingdom in the middle of the 13th century, an extremely low figure if we realize that the area incorporated into the kingdom after 1212 represented almost 50% of the total. An enormous demographic gap, therefore, was produced in the South and had to be filled—as in the case of Valencia in relation to Catalonia—by a constant inflow of people from the North: Galicians, Asturians, Cantabrians, Basques, Castilians, and Leonese, who successively occupied the southern regions during a whole century, from 1250 to 1348, date of the Black Death. We must keep in mind, however, the fact that some cities, such as Badajoz, were re-settled with difficulty and that even at the end of the Middle Ages their population was very low.

Emigration to the South produced the same demographic loss in Castile and León as took place in Catalonia, but it was probably less noticeable, for the point of departure was more extensive and more densely populated than Catalonia.

Another fact which should be noted is that northern emigration to the South was not uniform, but *benefited the cities in particular.* This change in Castile's demographic structure is very important. It altered the whole picture of Castilian Early Medieval life, based on *presura* and rural democracy, and gave rise to an urban gentry which lived on revenues from the surrounding countryside. For this reason the Andalusian cities had a growth which was disproportionate compared to that of other cities in the kingdom. Thus, for example, at the end of the 15th century Seville had 75,000 souls; Cordova, 35,000; Jerez, 35,000; Murcia, 25,000; Baeza and Ubeda, 20,000 each; and Andújar and Carmona, 15,000. In the North, by contrast, the ancient Castilian cities showed smaller figures: Toledo, Valladolid, Medina del Campo, and Salamanca varied between 20,000 and 25,000 inhabitants, while cities which were considered to be among the most economically powerful in the Meseta had barely 10,000 inhabitants, or were only slightly above that figure (for instance Burgos, Segovia, Cuenca, and the budding Madrid).

The Black Death invaded Castile in 1348 and produced the same ravages as elsewhere. The number of victims was large, and included Alfonso XI. But while the effects of the plague were extremely grave in the Mediterranean Levant, the loss was not so heavy in Castile because it was farther away from the great sea routes. Nevertheless, there were notable epidemics in the last 150 years of the medieval period, such as those of 1400, 1422, 1435, and 1468. None of them have been thoroughly studied.

Jews made up an important sector of the Castilian population in the Late Middle Ages. It is impossible to form a judgment on their number, for the figures are so divergent that it seems many authors have been guided more by emotion than by reason (Lea, 5 million; Amador de los Ríos, 1 million; Millás, 20,000). One basic point of departure is the fact that the number of Jews expelled during the reign of the Catholic Monarchs was 150,000, which perhaps enables us to estimate the Castilian Jewish community at the end of the 14th century as being composed of some 200,000 persons. In 1391, however, as a result of the economic crisis, there were anti-Semitic pogroms in Castile as well as in the Crown of Aragon which caused noticeable losses. There is room for all sorts of conjecture in this regard, for there are some authors who estimate Jewish deaths at 500,000 and others who say that nothing at all happened to them. It does seem, however, that quite a number of Jews perished, though not as many as has been supposed; between 5,000 and 10,000. More important is the following: that half of the Jewish community, composed of some 200,000 persons, was converted to Christianity, while a considerable number of the remainder emigrated to Granada (the majority of Jews were Andalusian). Even so, the Jewish colonies which did remain in the country continued to be numerous, for in the Segovian census of 1474, 305 Castilian towns are mentioned as having Jews. But contradictions again appear when we try to interpret this statistic, for some authors state that this represented only 45,000 individuals, a figure that must necessarily be smaller than the true one. If we consider the problem dispassionately, we gain the impression that after the massacres about 75,000 unconverted Jews must have been left, and that this number, in the normal process of population growth, probably doubled by the end of the period. These 150,000 Jews, then, plus the 100,000 *conversos,* were the backbone of the financial and artisan class in Castile.

As for the *Mudéjares,* the figure we gave before, some 300,000, represents a very low proportion: one twenty-fifth or one thirty-fifth of the total population, while in the Crown of Aragon the proportion of Mudéjares to Christians was one in five.

GENERAL OUTLINES OF SOCIAL EVOLUTION: CREATION OF THE GREAT SEIGNIORIAL DOMAINS. One optimistic theory, very characteristic of the 19th century, tried to apply the stereotype of Western Europe to the social evolution of the Castilian nobility in the Late Middle Ages, holding that it declined after the 14th century when the monarchy became allied with the bourgeoisie, thus undermining its power. This version of the situation has absolutely no relation to the facts. For it is precisely in this regard that we begin to discern the abnormality which characterized Castile's social and economic evolution during the Late Middle Ages.

Furthermore, the facts prove the contrary. In the 14th and 15th centuries the Castilian aristocracy reached a peak of power, an importance so overwhelming that it became the ruler of the State. The Castilian nobles did not adopt a defensive position as in the other Western kingdoms, but quite the contrary; they changed dynasties, took over the royal patrimony, and made the royal power an instrument of their ambitions. This phenomenon came about because the monarchy could not count on solid support from the cities. Many Castilian town councils were on the side of the aristocracy, and many more were subjugated by it.

This fact delineates one of the essential traits of Spain's economic future. The triumph and splendor of the nobility created a pro-aristocratic attitude throughout Castile; not because of any attempt to emulate the deeds of the great lords, but because the aristocracy was exempt from all taxes, and the greatest ambition of the poor Castilian commoner was to some day attain the rank of *hidalgo,* in order to free himself from the ever more onerous taxes.

The extraordinary progress of the Castilian aristocracy resulted from a number of causes: (1) *the great land grants in Andalusia.* These grants doubled the economic potential of the old Northern nobility and settled them in the South, and in consequence they enclosed the monarchy, whose patrimony lay along the banks of the Duero and the Tagus, in a dangerous aristocratic vise.

(2) *The fabulous development of the wool trade.* Since the nobles controlled, in their territories in both the North and the South, the terminal routes of migratory pasturing, they naturally were the chief beneficiaries of this trade.

(3) *The establishment of the so-called "juros de heredad";* that is, cession of lands in fee simple, transmissible by inheritance to the eldest son. Castilian law prohibited this type of transmission, but by the reign of Alfonso X we can observe the creation of certain *mayorazgos* (inheritances by primogeniture) in exceptional cases. These cases slowly became more general. The aspiration of every Castilian noble in the 14th and 15th centuries was to be able to leave his possessions entailed within his own family.

(4) *The distribution among second sons of public and ecclesiastical offices.* As inheritance tended more and more to be linked to

245

the firstborn, it became necessary to provide for the sons who followed him. Thus, every noble aspired to providing the lieutenantcy of a castle, or a commandery in one of the military orders, or perhaps some abbey lands, to his second son. This movement reached its greatest proportions in the 15th century and turned the nobility into a sort of parasitic ivy on the country.

(5) *The Castilian civil war of the 14th century.* Such advantages could not have been preserved if in the 14th century the aristocracy had not won its war by triumphing over Peter I the Cruel. He represented interests opposed to those of the nobles: on the one hand the Jews, *conversos,* and the financial fortune of Andalusia; on the other, the town councils, which believed in a social system different from the one that had prevailed up to that time. Henry II of Trastamara was on the side of the Castilian nobility, and his nickname, "king of the concessions," means that it was he who turned over to the nobles the tremendous booty represented by the Castilian royal patrimony. All the great families were formed after that time—those of Pimentel, Ponce de León, Guzmán, Mendoza, Súarez de Figueroa, Fernández de Córdoba, Álvarez de Toledo, etc.—who in the course of two generations came to be called "grandees of Castile" in the documents of the period.

(6) *The ineffectiveness of the Trastamaras in the 15th century.* Throughout this century civil war was endemic in Castile, owing to the preponderance of the aristocracy. The monarch took one side or the other according to the course of events, trying to counterbalance the power of the strongest faction and thus to find an equilibrium which might save the State. The achievement of Ferdinand and Isabella, in fact, was just that: they stabilized the equilibrium attained by the Castilian nobility in the last struggles of the second half of the 15th century.

Enormous domains came into being, for example those of the "ricahembra" Leonor de Alburquerque, who could go from Aragon to Portugal, from Belorado in the Rioja region to Alburquerque, crossing all of Castile, without setting foot on anyone's property but her own. And what of Don Enrique de Sotomayor, who died at the end of the 15th century leaving a fortune equivalent to 50 billion pesetas (almost as much as the present budget of the Spanish State), plus 50,000 hectares of land—some 5,000 sq. km.—or half the size of an average Spanish province? Let us add some other examples. The Count of Haro ruled almost all the Rioja and aspired to annexation of the Basque Country; the Enríquez family, admirals of Castile, had possessions everywhere: in Galicia, León, Castile, and Andalusia; the Pimentels, counts of Benavente, owned a large part of the Esla basin; the Mendozas owned the Alcarria, not counting their possessions in the North, where the family had originated, and the vast territories of the lesser branch of the family in Andalusia; the Álvarez de Toledo family, counts of Alba, owned a large part of the lands in the Salamanca region; the Estúñigas, later counts of Plasencia, half of Extremadura; the Medinasidonias, a large part of the modern province of Cádiz; the Pachecos, marquises of Villena, nearly all of La Mancha.

Furthermore, and this is very important, these nobles not only had lands and money, and could permit themselves the luxury of sending 2,000 lances to a war (something the king of Aragon was unable to do), but they also held all the lucrative public offices, for one was Admiral of Castile, another constable, and yet another the royal standard-bearer, and all their sons and brothers were masters and high commanders in the military orders. This accumulation of power explains Spain's political history and throws a great deal of light on her economic history.

LATIFUNDISM AND ARISTOCRACY IN EXTREMADURA AND ANDALUSIA. It is Professor Carande's opinion that the nobles' seizure of land did not immediately produce the creation of latifundia in Extremadura and Andalusia, but that this phenomenon of agrarian concentration belongs in the 16th and 17th centuries. This may be true from a legal point of view; but it is impossible not to recognize that the great landholdings, the nuclei of what later came to be enormous latifundia, were already in existence at least as early as the 13th century, as can be proved by analyzing the grants made by Ferdinand III in Cordova and Seville.

Therefore, though we cannot speak of legal establishment of latifundia at this time, we can point out that they existed as the backbone of agrarian property in broad areas of southern Castile. How did they come into being? First by primogeniture; then by marriage; and finally, by means of usurpations carried out by the nobility from the royal patrimony and the military orders. It was very easy, given the impotence of the monarchy, to pass from the lieutenantcy of a castle to ownership of it, or to pass from being commander of an order to seizing a territory from that order. This is why, if we could compare the seigniorial map of Spain in the 15th century (a map that does not exist) with one showing modern latifundism (a map that does exist), we would see that the possessions of the *terratenientes* (that very Castilian word) in the 15th century correspond to those of their successors in the 20th.

JEWS AND CONVERSOS AS AN ECONOMIC FACTOR. The weakness of the middle class in Castile during the last centuries of the Late Middle Ages is an obvious fact. There was no urban bourgeoisie, as in the other countries of the West. This gap was filled by a social class outside the Christian religion: the Jews. Américo Castro speaks of them in his book *The Structure of Spanish History* (*La realidad histórica de España*), basing his argument on the data of Amador de los Ríos and Baer, and says that "crafts, trade, and what was equivalent to banking institutions were in the Middle Ages an almost exclusive concern of the Spanish Jews." To explain this abnormal situation, he establishes the principle of the Christians' "technical incapacity," which caused the Jew to become firmly rooted in the area of technical and administrative service to the State, and placed him in the Castilian social hierarchy midway between the upper and lower classes; he flattered the first by servility at the same time as he boldly exploited the second, thus meriting the hatred which the majority of the people felt for him.

The controlling presence of the Jew can already be observed in the early period of the Reconquest, especially in the procurement of supplies for the hosts who set out yearly to do battle on the frontiers. From functioning as a contractor to the armies he went on to be a tax farmer and from there to a manipulator of large sums of money, with which he could make loans to the monarchy and thus round out his sphere of economic and financial influence. One is inclined to ask—as Américo Castro does also—why the Christians did not amass capital and take the Jews' place in loans to the king. But if we study the Cortes after 1367, when there are frequent complaints on the part of representatives of the Castilian cities and the nobility about the admission of Jews to bids on tax farming, we can observe that the kings always gave the same answer: that they preferred Christians to Jews, but that the Jews were always the best bidders and in many cases the only ones. It is clear that the monarchy made this affirmation truthfully, as can be seen in matters affecting the military orders and the Church; the bishopric of Toledo, which had enormous properties, the orders of Santiago and Alcántara, were the first to want to farm out their taxes to the Jews.

Américo Castro adds that Spanish Christianity, "for good and for ill, was rooted in a productive ineffectiveness for material values." The phrase is not a happy one, for a "productive ineffectiveness" is meaningless. But in fact, what Américo Castro is trying to say is that Castilian Christianity did not respond to the material values of the time. And then he roundly affirms the Jews' effectiveness, shown in every branch of the Castilian economy, to the point that even the artisan trades of the cities were in their hands.

This thesis has undergone some modifications. Carlé has studied several censuses of artisans, and has been able to point out that Christians predominated over Jews. However, this conclusion cannot be accepted without reservation, for if we examine the names of Christians who engaged in artisan trades in Toledo, we will realize that they were Mozarabic surnames; that is, of people separated from the Old Castilian economic mentality. Then we find the same vicious circle as before. Whether they were Jews or Mozárabes, it was people foreign to the native Christian tradition of the North who controlled the medieval Castilian artisan trades; this was as true in Seville as in Cordova, in Toledo as in Burgos.

The reference to Burgos brings us to the subject of the *conversos.* When the Jews were violently eliminated from Castilian life in 1391, about half of them were converted to Christianity. Continuing in the footsteps of their forefathers, they became great financiers, good artisans, and excellent public officials. All those who have studied 15th-century life and society in Castile recognize this fact. There has been a certain amount of argument about whether the merchants of Burgos were of Jewish stock. Carlé states that they were Old Christians. This seems doubtful, for if we study carefully Professor Cantera's book on Álvaro de Santamaría, the chronicler of John II, we will be struck by the number of *conversos* in the city and the fact that they controlled large amounts of capital and had a network of influence all over Spain. Later, these same *conversos* were to form the aristocracy of the Emperor Charles' business empire.

AGRICULTURAL EXPLOITATION: VITICULTURE. During the 13th, 14th, and 15th centuries Castilian agriculture was in a stagnant phase, and did not partake of the slow but widespread development of other Western countries. It was only sufficient to supply the local market, or at most the so-called *acarreo* markets, centers which served to redistribute the products of a given region. Such, for example, was the case of Avila.

One fact which proves the backwardness of Castilian agriculture at that time was the underdevelopment of irrigation. In spite of the fact that suitable crop land existed, the peasants never grasped the principles of irrigation which gave such happy results in the Spanish Levant. Therefore, irrigated lands were found only in the Rioja region.

One of the most widely cultivated agricultural crops was the vine. Wine was an item of export to Flanders, England, and the north of Europe in general. On the other hand, it was also a very important item of local consumption, for, as the *Siete Partidas* remarks, "men love it well." There were any number of quarrels between cities, for each of them protected the wines of its particular district with special zeal. However, by the end of the 15th century the zones which were to become the great wine-producing areas of the future are clearly apparent: Andalusia, with its vineyards in the hills of Cordova and Jerez; La Mancha, the Rioja, and the banks of the Duero from Valladolid to Zamora and Toro. Among all the regions Andalusia stood out especially, favored by its proximity to the sea, which was then the chief means of transport; Andalusian wine went to Flanders, for at that time England was the exclusive market for Gascon wines.

LIVESTOCK: THE WOOL REVOLUTION OF 1300 AND ITS CONSEQUENCES. As we have already mentioned, the structure of the medieval Castilian economy was centered on one product, wool, and one producer, the sheep. How to explain this phenomenon? We already know that migratory pasturing was an inherent fact in the economic history of Castile, and that it can be traced back to the

Iberians. Nevertheless, the history of the incredible development of wool production is something which has concerned all historians, who have formed various hypotheses about it. The one which had widest currency before Klein's studies of the Mesta was that the Castilian territory, as a result of the Black Death in 1348, became so depopulated that a sensational increase in the number of sheep was made possible (Sarmiento, for example, in 1765 called the sheep "daughter of pestilence"). This fact was considered to have coincided with the economic difficulties of Peter I, who is supposed to have paid extraordinary attention to herding as a source of income. But Julius Klein, in his book entitled *The Mesta,* states that fifty years before 1348 Castilian wool was already being exported to England and Flanders. Therefore, he does not believe that the expansion of the wool economy can be attributed to the Black Death. But he does not give any solution to the problem.

Consequently, we shall have to take a rather detailed look at the economic scene of the time, to see how it was possible for Castile to become a sort of Australia of that period. In the first place, the Commercial Revolution, in its demographic aspect, brought into being markets which consumed large quantities of wool, especially in Italy and Flanders. There were more people to be clothed, and more who wished to dress in clothing of luxurious and high quality. In the second place, English wool, which until then had been the great supplier of the European market, suffered a series of reverses because of the English kings' political rivalries with France and Flanders. This opened the way to use of Castilian wool for cheap fabrics, especially in Flanders and Italy.

It was precisely at this time, between 1290 and 1310, that an exceptional breed of sheep, the merino, appeared in Spain. How did it get there? Very little light had been thrown on this question until Robert S. Lopez put forward a very suggestive hypothesis based on the study of documents in the archives of Genoa. According to this hypothesis, Genoa was faced with the danger of being cut off from English production, and sought a solution in importing wool from the merino sheep of North Africa. This happened about 1280. But since regular supply was very difficult, it is quite probable that the Genoese who were established in Andalusia imported merino sheep for breeding purposes, and that they showed the nobles in the Seville region the advantages of crossbreeding such sheep. In the course of a generation Castile was able to offer the first high-grade merino sheep to the market.

A number of factors coincided, then, to explain the fact that by 1300 Castile became the chief wool producer in the international market. By that date Castilian wool was even being exported to England—that is, to the very seat of Late Medieval wool production. As for Flanders, Castilian wool largely eliminated English wool from the market there, and from Flanders it was redistributed through central Europe.

The chief consequences of this wool revolution were: the wool trade became the backbone of Castilian economy; flocks increased enormously (we do not know exactly the number of head of sheep, but in 1467 there were some 2,700,000, which means that there must have been about a million and a half by 1300, and that these continued to increase, especially when the Black Death made it easier for herders to impose their influence on the countryside); and agriculture became stagnant. After the Black Death there was no possibility of a reaction from the peasants, for the interests built up in the wool trade were of such magnitude that it was impossible to restore agriculture to the position it had previously occupied.

ORGANIZATION OF THE MESTA. We shall have to study this organization in some detail, for it was perhaps the most important and most original feature of Castilian economy in the Late Middle Ages.

In the Early Middle Ages there existed local *mestas* for the flocks; these were small common fields where sheep grazed. As the needs of these local mestas grew, cooperative groups of neighbors developed whose purpose was to look out for strayed sheep. In the course of time, mestas comprising more territory grew out of these local ones. These mestas must have coincided with the organic division of the Castilian flocks: the *Mesta of León,* which took in the whole mountain region in the north of that kingdom; the *Mesta of Soria,* including the highland zone of the Duero; the *Mesta of Segovia,* with the pastures of the Central System nearby; and the *Mesta of Cuenca,* on the slopes of the Iberian System. Soria especially contributed to the organization of the Mesta.

In 1273, Alfonso X the Wise consolidated the various Mestas and founded what later came to be called *El Honrado Concejo de la Mesta de los Pastores de Castilla,* or Honorable Assembly of the Mesta of the Shepherds of Castile. The motive was merely one of the king's financial embarrassments; he realized that it was much easier to assess taxes on livestock than on men, and formed the mestas into an organization that would provide considerable sums to the monarchy. In exchange for these taxes the herders wrested a series of privileges from Alfonso X, the most important of which was the extension of supervision over all migratory flocks, including stray animals, in the whole kingdom of Castile. This supervisory function was gradually extended, in time, even to "permanent" sheep pastured in local mestas and to the "riberiegas," animals which were pastured along the river banks within the district of a particular town.

The Mesta's principal function was to organize the *cañadas,* that is, the sheep highways which led the flocks from the mountains of the North to the *extremes* of the South, or from the summer pasturing grounds to the winter ones. The royal *cañadas* numbered three: the Leonese, the Segovian, and the Manchegan. These corresponded, generally speaking, to the three great areas of natural communication. The first brought together in León the flocks which were scattered in the northern mountains of the kingdom, and took them to Plasencia, Cáceres, Mérida, and Badajoz by way of Zamora, Salamanca, and Béjar. Béjar is important because it was a junction for one branch of the Segovian *cañada.* This one started in Logroño and went to Béjar through Burgos, Palencia, Segovia, and Avila, that is, along the northern slopes of the Guadarrama range. Another path branched out from this *cañada* to Talavera de la Reina, after which the flocks went on to Guadalupe and then to the regions of Almadén and Andalusia. This same Segovian *cañada* included another eastern branch, which led from Cameros to Soria, Sigüenza, and El Escorial, and from there over the southern side of the mountains to join the western branch in Talavera de la Reina. Finally, the *Manchegan cañada* served the flocks raised in the mountains of Cuenca, which were then brought down to La Mancha and from there took one of two directions, toward Murcia or toward Andalusia.

The *cañadas* were protected by officials called "alcaldes entregadores de la Mesta," or judges of awards. Their maximum width was 90 Castilian *varas* (or about 250 feet). The officials seized every

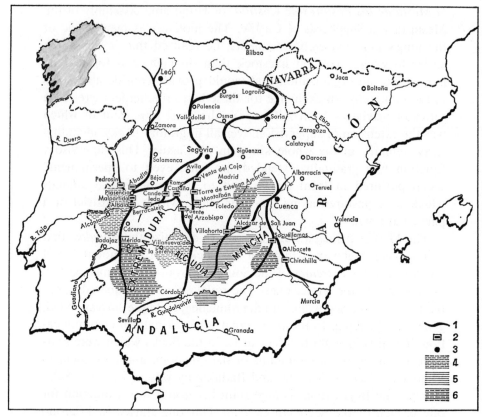

MIGRATORY SHEEP ROUTES IN 16TH CENTURY SPAIN.—*Key:* 1, cañadas; 2, royal passes; 3, headquarters of cuadrillas of the Mesta. GRAZING GROUNDS OF THE MILITARY ORDERS: 4, Order of Alcántara; 5, Calatrava; 6, Santiago.

opportunity to remove the boundary stones from their places and widen the *cañadas* illegally. This produced long-drawn-out lawsuits with the farmers and teamsters.

According to rather late sources, for our knowledge of this matter dates from the reign of the Catholic Monarchs, the flocks were grouped together in *cabañas,* or droves. Each of these was in the charge of a chief herdsman. A drove was composed of at least a thousand head. The *hatos,* or flocks, were smaller. Each drove also included fifty *moruecos,* or stud rams, twenty-five *encencerrados,* the bellwethers which kept the sheep in line, and then one herder, four boys as assistants, five sheep dogs, and five pack animals carry-

254

ing salt. Salt was an indispensable product for the good nutrition of the sheep.

The distances covered by these droves along the *cañadas* were: 830 km. for the Leonese and 270 to 370 for the Segovian and Manchegan routes. They traveled some 30 km. a day when going along the assigned path, and 10 in open country. The flocks left the South about the middle of April, and the sheep were sheared on the trip north, either while they were crossing the mountains or in the so-called *agostaderos,* or summer pastures.

The Mesta's legal position is also interesting. The earliest code, dating from 1379, has been lost, and we know only the text of the statute of 1492 issued by Ferdinand and Isabella. But probably the situation had not changed much. The essential basis of the organization was the "brothers of the Mesta," those who paid the tax or *servicio del ganado* because they owned a migratory flock. Anyone who paid this *servicio* was a "brother of the Mesta," and as such had the right to attend the assemblies which were held twice a year, one in the South and the other in the North. The southern one occurred in January and February, most often in Villanueva de la Serena (where the Mesta's archives were kept), Don Benito, Guadalupe, Talavera de la Reina, Montalbán, or Siruela. In the North they met in September and in autumn, especially in Ayllón, Berlanga, Riaza, Aranda de Duero, and Buitrago, and sometimes in Segovia and Medina del Campo. In order to be valid these assemblies had to have a quorum of forty brothers; generally 200 to 300 herders attended, representing a tenth of the total, so that by the end of the 15th century some 3,000 individuals were members of the Mesta. Voting was done by *cuadrillas,* or groups.

The decisions taken were of various kinds: internal organization, petitions to the king, protests, etc. The chief ones had to do with the duties and offices of the Mesta. On this point, Klein states that, following the ancient custom in Castile of choosing offices by lot, balloting by drawing members' names out of an urn was common in the Mesta. This is not true. In Castile this type of balloting was never used until the time of Ferdinand and Isabella, who brought the system from the Crown of Aragon. Therefore, before 1492 the common system must have been direct election to the various offices, except for that of president, who after the decrees of Alfonso the Wise was appointed by the Crown and generally had some connection with a person of high rank at court.

After the president, or *entregador principal,* the most important officers in the Mesta were the four *alcaldes de cuadrilla,* or *alcaldes de la Mesta,* who presided over the four *cabañas,* and then the judges, representatives, collectors, etc.

It is interesting to look at the social situation in the Mesta. Klein upholds a theory which might be termed a democratic one, saying that the flocks of the nobles represented only a very small proportion of the migratory flocks, and implies that the Mesta was an organization of small herdsmen. This theory, however, is in disagreement with the proven fact that the wool trade was controlled by the great Castilian lords. In support of his assertion Klein brings forward a lawsuit of 1561, in which there are declarations by a number of proprietors of flocks pastured on land owned by the Order of Calatrava. According to this document, of a total of 53,451 head, flocks of 50 head made up 32%; those of 50 to 100 head, 35% (that is to say, small flocks represented 67% of the total); from 100 to 500 head, 23%; from 500 to 1,000, 6%; and more than 1,000, or whole droves, 11%.

To Klein's opinion, which he bases on this lawsuit, we should have to object that these numbers are local, that they affect only one year, and that in consequence it is impossible to make generalizations from them. But on the other hand we must keep in mind that in 1561 the economic and social climate of the Mesta was at a peak, and that the concentration of great flocks had probably also reached its highest point; so that it is possible to believe that before the 16th century the percentage in favor of small proprietors compared to owners of large droves may have been greater.

Nonetheless, the existence of enormous flocks is evident well within the 15th century. For example, the monastery of El Escorial owned 40,000 head of sheep; that of Santa María del Paular, near Segovia, 30,000; the future Duke of Béjar, 25,000; the Duke of the Infantado, some 20,000. In view of the size of these flocks, it must be admitted that such numbers were very influential in the affairs of the Mesta. Therefore we may state without fear of contradiction that, in spite of the number of small proprietors who made up the Mesta, it was the great lords who ran it, who occupied the presidency and the offices of *alcalde de cuadrilla,* and those who, in short, had most to say in the autumn and winter assemblies. And finally, the person who controlled the money from the livestock *servicio* was neither the president of the Mesta nor the king but, after the time of Prince Henry, the Master of Santiago. Henry's father, Ferdinand of Antequera, had made him a donation of the taxes on sheep and cattle. Therefore, the structure of the organization may have been democratic, but the barons of Castile were those who really held the power. This was seen in 1462 with the failure of the Castilian cities' attempt to break the monopoly, which the herders were using to hinder development of the urban cloth industry.

21 · Castilian Industry and Trade from the 13th to 15th Centuries

INDUSTRIAL ACTIVITY: CRAFT LABOR. We possess little information about Castilian industrial activity in the 13th, 14th, and 15th centuries. This lack of data permits various interpretations in Castile: are there few documents because the municipal chanceries were not sufficiently developed, or is it because industrial activity was slight? Castilian municipal documentation, because of its technical backwardness, does not give us the large amount of information which the archives of the Mediterranean area do, but it also seems that, in general, industrial activity did not have the importance in Castile which it acquired in other places in the Peninsula.

There is no doubt that, if he consults the documents having to do with Seville, Avila, Segovia, Toledo, etc., the scholar will find a large number of names showing a variety of trades. Thus, for example, butchers, bakers, blacksmiths, horseshoers, strap-makers, millers, coopers, silversmiths, dyers, cobblers, leather-dressers, tailors, and tile-makers are mentioned. But the fact that such lists exist does not prove that industrial activity measured up to this proliferation of trades; what we need to find out is whether each of these trades had considerable industrial scope. And in this regard, we find only one industry which typically developed in Castile: the *woollen industry*.

We begin to have information about this activity starting in the 12th century. At that time the Castilian weavers worked for a very local market and produced low-grade cloth, especially *sayal* or sackcloth and *frisa de cuatro sueldos,* a kind of frieze, intended for the peasants of the surrounding country. The wealthy and the nobles got their clothing and fabrics from abroad, especially Flanders, whence came the types of cloth known as *escarlata, camelín,* and *blao.* In the 13th century, as a result of the conquests, population growth, and the expansion of wool production, we notice a proliferation of the textile industry, not only for supplying the local market

258

but also for export. This phenomenon is related to the conquest of the Portuguese markets. The first Castilian export area was, as a matter of fact, the kingdom of Portugal, and its center was the market held in Guimarães, where the Portuguese acquired the cloth which was beginning to be manufactured in considerable quantities in the four cities mentioned by the Cortes of 1268: Segovia, Zamora, Avila, and Soria—four cities located on the main routes of the Mesta, and consequently in direct contact with the wool traffic.

Later, during the course of the 14th century, other cities are mentioned as engaging in the cloth industry: Palencia, Murcia, and Cordova. In the 15th century both foreign and domestic demand increased so much that many small places in Castile began to weave wool. But as they did not know how to size and dye the cloth, they sent their fabrics to be finished in different textile centers in the Crown of Aragon and Navarre. This was the case of the cloth industry of Osma, Calahorra, and Sigüenza. The chief centers established at this time were Toledo, Cuenca, and Baeza.

The real extent of this industry is unknown, not because there are too few data but because they are too numerous. When we read in Colmeiro that there were 13,000 looms in Toledo at the end of the 15th century, or when the Marquis of Lozoya states that in Segovia at the same period 38,000 persons were employed in weaving woollens, the only thing we can say is that research in economic history needs to be done over, at least to the point of making the number of inhabitants in a city agree with its possibilities for manufacture.

The fact that the cloth industry had attained considerable development in the 15th century is shown, in fact, by the proposal of the Cortes of 1348, held in Madrigal, requesting a ban on imports of foreign cloth and on exports of Castilian wool. This decidedly protectionist policy was not accepted by John II because of the firm intervention of the Mesta and all those who were profiting from the wool trade: merchants, collectors, traders, and usurers. It was then that a violent struggle was begun by the great landowners to prevent the development of the Castilian bourgeoisie. This is the sense in which we must understand the agreement made by the Cortes of Toledo in 1462, when Henry IV fixed at one-third the proportion of the Mesta's total exports that could be retained by the Castilian cloth industry. This was a low proportion if there was any intention of keeping inside the country the wealth which was going abroad and making the fortunes of so many aristocrats.

Aside from cloth production, other industries can be mentioned, though all of them were either local or of a high-grade artisan type. For example, we know that in Segovia and Toledo there was an important production of *hats,* which were very popular in Portugal; but it was not large enough to supply Castile's internal needs and could hardly have been a large-scale industry, for French and Flemish hats were sold at the Castilian fairs. Another industry that had been very important in Moslem times was the *leather* industry of Andalusia. Castilian hides, therefore, retained a certain international reputation, though not in the sense of a manufactured product but simply as a raw material.

Still within the framework of local industry, it appears that the *soap* of Seville, made from olive oil or perhaps from tallow, achieved a certain amount of development. It must have been an important industry, for after 1427 it was taken over by the Andalusian grandees. By the end of the 15th century the Enríquez family, Admirals of Castile, received annual revenues of 120,000 maravedís from Sevillian soap.

The *wax* industry, related to the lighting of homes, was also well-developed, but even here there was importation from abroad. Then, we need only cite the *arms* industry of Toledo, *ceramics* (Andalusian tiles, the pottery of Toledo), and the *glass* industry, whose chief centers were Murcia and a few Andalusian cities. To sum up, the catalogue of industrial products in Castile during the Late Middle Ages was quite meager, even if we include *naval construction* in the list, for which the most important shipyards were on the Cantabrian Sea and in Seville.

THE CASTILIAN BROTHERHOODS AND ORIGINS OF THE GUILDS. We cannot use the term "guild" for the Castile of Late Medieval times with the same weight we give it in the Crown of Aragon and the rest of Europe, for in spite of the many statements referring to the existence of these brotherhoods in Castile from the 13th century onward, it is doubtful that they were true guilds. In the majority of cases they were simply religious brotherhoods or incipient craft associations, without a special legal, economic, and labor structure.

It is perfectly clear that brotherhoods of artisans did exist in Castile. We find them, for example, in the Soria region at the end of the 12th century (brotherhood of shopkeepers), and at the beginning of the 13th in the city of Soria itself (brotherhood of muleteers), and in Atienza (also muleteers, in 1219). But a brotherhood is a very different thing from a guild, because the former is a religious, social security, and mutual aid organization; a guild, on the other hand, involves the organization of work and in particular regulation of prices, in the acquisition of raw materials as well as in sales.

When Alfonso X conquered Seville in 1248, he published an edict giving certain types of trades *alcaldes,* or magistrates, for the purpose of overseeing them. These *alcaldes* exercised the same role as the Moslem *almotacenes.* But this does not mean that the trade corporations to which Alfonso X assigned *alcaldes* were really organized as guilds. This is proved by the fact that in 1250, when Segovia actually did try to appoint *alcaldes* by act of the city council, Alfonso X prohibited this attempt and said that the existence of "brotherhoods and bad associations" could not be permitted. This decision reveals a peculiar attitude toward guilds on the part of the Castilian monarchy.

Ferdinand III, father of Alfonso X the Wise, had consented to the formation of the brotherhoods we spoke of before if their purposes were religious, beneficent, and decorative. That is, the Castilian monarchy saw these bodies from the beginning, as one author says, as associations "to bury the dead, aid the poor, and pay for festival illuminations." Alfonso X showed the true attitude of the monarchy toward the guild type of brotherhood by prohibiting them in his *Siete Partidas,* saying specifically that workers could not "set prices among themselves." For the Castilian monarchy, the brotherhood was equivalent to "setting" or "fixing," a word used to describe the corporations' attempt to organize municipal economic life through a privileged monopoly of prices and wages.

During the 14th century we find scarcely any mention of brotherhoods in Castile, a proof of their slight development. They are spoken of again in the 15th, but always with the same suspicion shown by the monarchy in the 13th century. This fear of monopoly and of the corporation in fact reflects the absence of a powerful industrial bourgeoisie, and also how far from the Castilian mentality of the Late Middle Ages was the idea of the corporative State which developed with such typical characteristics in Catalonia. In Castile the king wanted to erect no barriers to his authority, either by favoring the Cortes or by assisting the guilds. This is why trade corporations were not destined to appear in Castile until the time of Ferdinand and Isabella, and then not in imitation of Flanders, as the Marquis of Lozoya insists, but simply through application of the Catalonian corporative attitude by Ferdinand the Catholic.

INTERNAL TRADE: ROADS. The Castilian *fueros,* or town charters, give a certain amount of attention to roads, and some prescribe their width, setting it at that of two loaded animals for roads going out of farms, and at two women carrying water jars for those leading out of towns. These measures show us how precarious land transportation was at the time.

The fact was that the country was traversed by mere footpaths, which occasionally made use of Roman roads and bridges. From the 14th century onward some simple but obvious improvements were made, such as construction of bridges and the use of two-wheeled oxcarts for long journeys. This improvement had to do with the Mesta. In the same way as flocks traveled from North to South and South to North, the transport carts used the same route. They spent the winter near Toledo and when spring came set out for the North, loaded with wool. In Vitoria they added iron to their load. After descending the passes of the Cantabrian System, they reached the ports where the wool and iron were put on shipboard. They returned almost empty until, when they reached Poza de la Sal (Burgos), they were loaded with salt, which they sold in Valladolid, Avila, Salamanca, and Zamora, ending their journey in Toledo.

As for the southern route, the carts left Toledo when spring came and carried wood for the kilns of Talavera. Here they took on a load of pottery for Seville, whence they returned with salt for the flocks which grazed in the Andalusian fields. Sometimes they brought wood for the mines of Almadén as well as salt. They returned to the South with quicksilver, which was shipped from

Seville, and here the circuit ended, for then they would go North again with salt, joining up in Toledo with the carts which had made the northern circuit of the country.

The rate at which these carts traveled was very slow, no more than 40 km. a day.

CASTILE AND ATLANTIC-MEDITERRANEAN TRADE. The development of international trade came somewhat later in Castile than in the Crown of Aragon. Catalonia, Valencia, and Majorca participated very early in the revival of Mediterranean traffic. Castile, on the other hand, suffered from the fact that the Strait of Gibraltar, in Moslem hands, set up an obstacle between the Mediterranean and the Atlantic, separating a world which was renewing its mercantile activity from one in which the primitive practices of fishing or piracy persisted. The situation changed radically after the conquest of Andalusia by Ferdinand III, and after Alfonso X and Sancho IV gained control of the Strait, thanks to the fleet and maritime skill of the wealthy Zaccarias family of Genoa. The alliance between Genoa and Castile never lapsed after this time, and constituted the pivot on which Seville's fortunes turned. From the 13th century onward this port saw the passage of Genoese, Valencian, and Catalonian ships which sailed north in search of wool and metals; Breton and Portuguese ships also landed there, as well as other vessels which trafficked with North African ports.

However, this Castilian mercantile prosperity could not be completely understood on the basis of the Andalusian factor, were we to forget the separate development of a maritime force which we shall call Castilian because it belonged to the king of Castile, but which really deserves a special name: that of "Hermandad de las Marismas," or "Brotherhood of the Coast" of the Cantabrian area.

ORIGINS OF THE CANTABRIAN MERCHANT MARINE. Apart from some rather dubious statistics brought forward by Fernández Duro on the presence of Basque whaling ships in the Faroe Islands in the 9th century, the first documents concerning the origins of the Cantabrian merchant marine go back to the 12th. In 1130 a large number of Cantabrian ships took part in the siege and blockade of Bayonne, and in 1150 Sancho the Wise of Navarre granted a charter founding San Sebastián, with very detailed marine ordinances which presuppose a flourishing naval establishment in the Bay of Biscay. We have proof from the year 1190 that the sailors of Santa María de Santoña engaged in whaling. After that time the evidence becomes more frequent. Alfonso VIII, lord of the Montaña and Basque regions, protected the ports along the northern shore, so it can be stated that the rise of Santander, Laredo, and Castro Urdiales began in his reign. This monarch's achievement was to free these ports from their economic subjugation (maritime tithes, ferry tolls, etc.) to the monasteries of the interior.

The four ports of the Montaña region (Castro Urdiales, Santander, Laredo, and San Vicente de la Barquera) rose rapidly during this period. We know that they traded in cloth, arms, and hides. We have good reason to suspect, on the other hand, that it was at this same time that the Basques began to develop the transit trade so characteristic of them in later medieval centuries, going with their ships to Bordeaux to take on Gascon wine which they then traded to the insatiable ports of chilly Albion (the Bordelais were poor sailors, and Bretons and English, in addition to Basques, carried on their sea trade for them). Alfonso VIII's marriage to the daughter of the king of England, who brought him the duchy of Gascony as her dowry, must have been a decisive factor in the origins of this trade. Later, Ferdinand the Saint continued to offer the Cantabrians the same protection his grandfather had given them. The first evidence we have of the appearance of Cantabrian sailors in the Mediterranean comes from the early years of his reign. One of them, Roy García of Santander, who had participated in the siege of the port of Cartagena in 1245 and later became established in Seville, served as head of a flotilla which guarded the coast between Cádiz and Cartagena. It is well known that men from Santander, Castro Urdiales, and Santoña took part in the assault of Seville (1248); it is possible that the Castilian fleet was outfitted in San Vicente de la Barquera.

This success resulted in the creation of the Admiralty of Castile, which was established in Burgos and was given jurisdiction over the four ports already mentioned: Santander, Laredo, Castro Urdiales, and San Vicente. The paradoxical fact that a naval office should be located in a city of the interior can be explained by the religious and economic relationship of those towns with the capital of the archdiocese, the secular center for the collection of tithes and other levies and taxes. We should also keep in mind that at that time Burgos had already attained a certain importance in the incipient wool trade.

In the next stage, a generation later, Cantabrian trade appears to have been very well developed. The earliest extant customs schedule of one of these ports dates from 1295; it is that of Laredo and lists French merchandise, especially dry goods from Limoges, and Flemish merchandise such as cloth from Ghent, Douai, Ypres, Cambrai, Bruges, and Valenciennes. A year later (1296) the famous Brotherhood of the Coast was set up, its precise title being "Brotherhood of the Merchant Fleet of Castile and Vitoria." Such is the official title used by the ports of Santander, Laredo, Castro Urdiales, and San Vicente de la Barquera when they allied themselves with those of Bermeo, Guetaria, San Sebastián, and Fuenterrabía. The name of Vitoria appears because those ports belonged to the diocese of that city.

The declared reason for the founding of this Brotherhood shows us three important facts. First, one of an international nature: France was at war with England and the Brotherhood wished to maintain a highly profitable neutrality. Second, of a financial character: a protest against the tithes which Burgos continued to demand. Third, of an economic nature: a monopoly on the export of iron by the Cantabrian and Basque sailors themselves, without having to submit to the decisions of the Admiralty in Burgos.

In order to defend its common interests, the Brotherhood decided to meet in Castro Urdiales once a year, and at any other time when it might be necessary to protect its interests from possible attack by the archbishops and admirals of Burgos. And this is how that great commercial force, the Cantabrian merchant marine, appeared on the international scene.

THE WOOL TRADE AND THE ATLANTIC MERCHANT MARINE: BURGOS AND BILBAO. It is possible that up to the time of the foundation of the Brotherhood of the Coast, the two principal products traded in by these people were wine and iron. At first the Bretons had come to Castile for wine, arriving in Seville; but as soon as the Basques and Cantabrians emerged from the stage of being merely deep-sea fishermen, they made a great deal of money by taking part in the wine trade between Bordeaux and England. There is documentary proof of this trade, to which we have alluded before, after 1221. Of equal importance with wine was Biscayan iron, of high quality, which was much appreciated in the northern countries because it was easy to work and very durable. Anchors and chains were made of it.

The wool revolution in Castile was established on these two essential bases. Maritime trade in wool must have got started about the middle of the 13th century, for we know the names of Castilians in Bruges from 1267 onward, while the Basques must have been there before them at a date we do not know. This can be deduced from contemporary documents (Basque names are the first listed in the *Registry of the Ancient Consulate of Spain in Bruges,* published by L. Guillodts van Severen). But the Basque-Castilian colony did not really take root until after 1300. After this critical moment, the wool trade enjoyed extraordinary prosperity. And although this traffic was centered in Burgos, following the tradition of the Admiralty of Castile and the diocese of Burgos, Cantabrians and Basques were in fact the ones who transported the wool. The port of Bilbao received its charter of settlement at this time (June 15, 1300) and very soon came to be the central nucleus of Basque maritime trade, thus initiating a glorious industrial, mercantile, and seafaring history.

It is within this framework that we must think of Castile's intervention on the side of France in the Hundred Years' War. From the economic point of view this was a war of wine, having to do with the Gascon markets; but essentially it was a war of wool which mobilized the four great Atlantic powers: England and Castile as producers, and France and Flanders as purchasers and weavers. Castile helped France against England, who was her outright rival in the supplying of wool.

Therefore, when King Edward III of England signed the treaty of London with the Brotherhood of the Coast, in 1351, granting and guaranteeing peace and neutrality to the Basques and Cantabrians, it meant a capitulation by the English merchant marine to the Cantabrian fleet, for after this treaty its "open sea" rights in the English Channel were recognized, and it could reach the ports of Flanders, especially Bruges, without hindrance.

The development of the wool trade culminated in the foundation of the *universities* (or brotherhoods) *of merchants* in Burgos and

Bilbao. An interesting argument is brought up in this regard. The fact that in 1336 a certain consulate of Castilians is mentioned in Bruges (though the decree of Louis de Nevers mentions only a legal authorization for one) has caused some authorities to state that the brotherhood of merchants of Burgos goes back to the middle of the 14th century. However, no documents relating to this brotherhood of merchants, which was to reflect so clearly the spirit of the merchant bourgeoisie of Burgos, antedate the year 1443; on the other hand, the Consulate of Burgos dates from 1494, at a still later period. The Basques insist that the brotherhood of merchants of Bilbao must have appeared in the 14th century. In fact, we know that the brotherhood of merchants of Bermeo was established in 1353, and that Bermeo was then the chief town of Biscay (*caput Vizcaiae*); but the first authentic references to Bilbao date from 1489. If we study the earliest texts carefully, it can be proved that the guild of Castilians in Bruges was formed not in 1336, but on the twenty-third of April, 1441; the delegates of Burgos also represented the interests of Toledo and Seville, and all of them made up what was called "the nation of Spain." As for the Basques, the guild of Bilbao in Bruges goes back only to 1451. Thus, the supposed early Castilian guild development in the 14th century, related to the wool trade, simply does not exist (at most, we can refer to the formation of a Burgalese brotherhood of gentleman merchants of Santa María de Gamonal, in 1305). We must locate this event a century later, when it corresponds with the real development of commercial life in Castile, Cantabria, and the Basque region.

There is another fact worth noting, for it later was to develop on a large scale: the economic rivalry between Burgos and Bilbao. Bilbao rose in the 14th century, competing with the other Northern ports, grew unexpectedly prosperous, and became a rival of the Castilian merchants who held the monopoly on wool. We have proof of this, for as early as 1453 Burgos promised preferential duties on wool shipments to the port of Santander, as if it were trying to ruin Bilbao. All this is related to the dispute between Castilians and Basques, the question of whether the Basques formed a separate colony in Bruges or whether they should be represented by the Castilians. In 1451, by a decree (later recognized by the king of Castile) of Duke Philip the Good, the merchants who had settled there were divided into two guilds—that of Burgos, called the guild of Spain, and that of the Biscayans. The rivalry between Burgos and Bilbao continued throughout the great period of prosperity of Castilian wool, increased as the sums of money involved grew larger, and came to an end only when the two cities fell into the economic stagnation of the last third of the 16th century.

In addition to the traffic in wool, iron, and wine characteristic of Basque-Cantabrian trade with Flanders, England, and France, we should mention a not unimportant economic factor: the appearance of ships of the Hanseatic League in Spanish Cantabrian ports. Their route customarily ended in Lisbon. The Hanseatic cities traded in wheat, cloth, salt fish, amber, and other Northern products, and their ships brought much trade into the small ports of the Cantebrian shoreline from the 14th century onward.

ANDALUSIA'S POSITION IN INTERNATIONAL TRADE: SEVILLE. The development of the Atlantic-Mediterranean routes and the gold trade enhanced Seville's constant and uninterrupted progress throughout the Late Middle Ages. This progress was accentuated during the 15th century, affecting not only Seville but the whole Atlantic coastline from Cádiz to Huelva. The enthusiasm which Columbus' enterprise aroused can be understood simply because of the fact that the whole region teemed with seafaring folk.

In the 15th century Andalusian sailors had three essential goals: the Canaries, where they could barter for gold and slaves, not to mention the profitable sugar trade; North Africa, theater of the wars of "furto," or piracy, and the source also of profitable trade relations stemming from the strongholds controlled by the Portuguese; and then, Genoa and the Western Mediterranean. During the course of the 15th century we can find only one mention of a voyage to Alexandria by Andalusians. This means that the great spice trade in which Barcelona, Genoa, and Valencia were engaged did not interest them.

The essential axis of this growth was, as we have said, Genoa. After Seville was reconquered, the Genoese made it, along with Lisbon (in the 14th century there were three generations of Portuguese admirals who bore the Genoese name of Passegno), their advance commercial outpost on the Atlantic. It was the Genoese, interested in maintaining the Seville-Genoa connection, who had a free hand in setting policy governing the Strait of Gibraltar during

Sancho IV's reign. Thus they were able to form an Andalusian economic and political establishment, which became solidified at the time of Peter I. It was made up of Genoese, Jews, and the sailors and merchants of the region. By the middle of the 14th century this combination, taking advantage of the war between Peter I and Peter the Ceremonious of Aragon, was on the point of controlling the Western Mediterranean. Castilian ships even threatened the port of Barcelona, to the discomfiture of the city's bourgeoisie. But the reaction was unexpected, for since Peter I supported the Genoese and the Jews, feudal and agrarian Spain, supported by Aragon, rose up against him. On the battlefield of Montiel the struggle was not only a rivalry between two half-brothers (Peter I and Henry Trastamara), but also over which system was going to prevail in Castile—that of the nobles or that of the merchants. The nobles won, and the Andalusian fleet received a setback as a naval force with aspirations toward control of the Western Mediterranean.

From then on the principal concern of Seville and the Andalusian seaports was the Atlantic: Morocco, the Canaries, Guinea. The history of trade between Andalusia and the Canaries in the 15th century has not yet been written, and this is a pity, for it foreshadows the American venture. All along the African coast there was sharp rivalry between Portugal and Castile, of which we know the essential facts. What we do not know is its economic background, which was, from the outset, linked to a mystical concept. Just as Henry the Navigator, prince of Portugal, created the famous Order of Christ to convert the Africans, the Order of Santa María de España appeared at this time. Its purpose was "the exploit of the sea," a reference to conquest of the Strait. We have no details about the development of this institution. It would be interesting to see how this "exploit of the sea" was connected with the mystical spirit of the continental military orders.

Castilians and Basques in Mediterranean Trade. Castile's Mediterranean vocation is owed to Cartagena, not to Seville. Suárez Fernández has emphasized this point. He believes that after the failure of Peter I's military offensive, Castilian activity in the Mediterranean was not renewed until the end of the 14th century, and then had to do with trade in wool and hides, which were exported to Italy. Valencia and Majorca frequently served as intermediaries, but Barcelona never did. These trade relations flourished with the loss of the Eastern markets (Tamerlane's conquests in the Near East), which made the Genoese, Florentines, and Venetians decide to seek compensation in the West. The Italians brought luxurious fabrics (of silk and gold), other luxury goods, worked metals, and spices. One of the main trade routes led to Málaga, the great port of the kingdom of Granada, which was a market for silk and sugar, dried fruits, and saffron.

This movement coincided with the penetration of the Basque merchant fleet into the Mediterranean. This is a most important phenomenon. From the year 1351 we find proof of the Basques sailing to Barcelona. They expanded their activities little by little, favored by their position as neutrals in regard to the warring cities and by the high quality of the ship they used, the *coca* of Bayonne. At the beginning of the 15th century the Basques, pushed out of the Atlantic by the Hundred Years' War, became the great carriers of merchandise for the Western Mediterranean. After 1426 they began to frequent the port of Marseilles, whose fleet had been ruined by the Catalans in the sack of 1423. For twenty years Basque ships were frequent in the Provençal trade. Later, in the heat of the struggle between Genoa and Barcelona, they were intermediaries in trade between the Crown of Aragon and Italy. They carried the salt of Ibiza and the wheat of Sicily, Apulia, and Seville in the service of Genoa. In the service of Barcelona they transported herring and silk to the city, but more often Andalusian and Portuguese leather, wool, and cochineal. This traffic was so profitable that Galicians, Portuguese, and Andalusians followed them into the Mediterranean. The Portuguese became masters of the Mediterranean sugar trade, with the Genoese as their accredited agents. As for the Andalusians, their activities at this time were often piratical.

This world of shipping, which developed as a result of the conversion of the Mediterranean seaport cities into centers of high finance, began to decline in the last third of the 15th century. All of the carriers felt strongly the call of the Atlantic. And there was also the definitive establishment of the Spanish bloc of supremacy in the Western Mediterranean. After 1495, documents show that Basque traffic in the Mediterranean became limited to the Spanish Empire's lines of communication with Italy.

AREAS AND OBJECTS OF CASTILIAN TRADE. After this historical survey of the origins and development of Castilian trade (in which we can distinguish two great stages separated by the turning point at the end of the 13th century, the wool revolution, resulting in a surge of commercial activity), we shall proceed to a rapid analysis of the areas and objects of trade which were typical of it. In large part it will be a summary of what has gone before, though this time from a regional and homogeneous geographical point of view.

The chief regional area of Castilian trade was *Flanders*. The beginning of relations with this part of Europe can be placed before the year 1267. Flanders was important because of its location at the mouth of the Rhine, and because it was at the center of a densely populated area having good trade connections with the Black Sea and the Baltic region and producing excellent manufactured goods. It was in 1267 that Castilian officials were appointed in Bruges for the first time, in relation to trade with Burgos and Biscay. This traffic, however, had little importance until the expansion of the wool industry took place. After the beginning of the 14th century the Castilians became one of the chief foreign colonies in Bruges, and received a number of privileges from the counts of Flanders.

The first of these dates from 1336 and was given by Count Louis de Nevers. It granted powers to the Castilian merchants to settle lawsuits among members of their own nation. Seven years later, in 1343, Count Robert of Flanders granted an important privilege having to do with organization of Castilian commerce. Finally, in 1367, after the crisis of hostilities with England was over, Louis de Mâle confirmed these privileges and established them definitively. In the 15th century the importance of the Castilian colony in Bruges grew so fast that it was soon larger than the Catalan one, which occupied second place, and surpassed the Hanseatic colony as well. It was during this period that the dukes of Burgundy recognized, as we have mentioned, the merchants' guild of Burgos (1441), and shortly afterward the guild of Biscay (1451).

Generally speaking, Castile's trade with Flanders consisted of

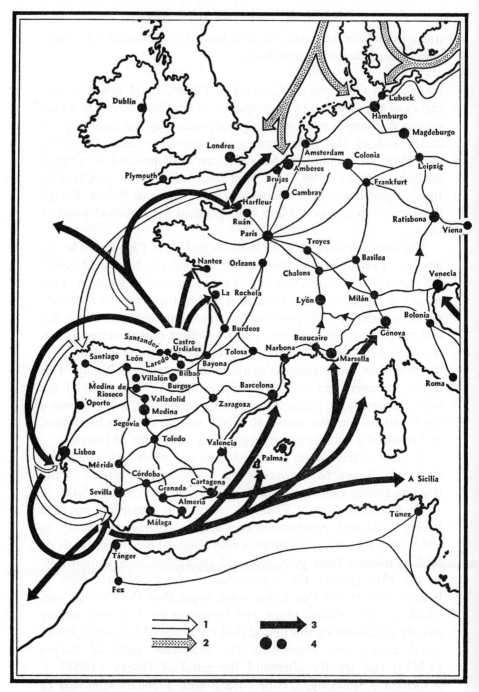

CASTILIAN TRADE.—*Key:* 1, Northern trade; 2, Hanseatic trade; 3, Castilian trade; 4, most important fairs and economic centers.

exporting wool and iron and importing luxury goods. These exports were complemented by others—some minerals, such as alum and salt, and others that were largely agricultural: wine, olive oil, lemons, almonds, fruit, and rice. But there was a new product after the middle of the 15th century: sugar from the Canaries, which soon invaded the Northern market and took the place of Eastern sugar.

What did Castile receive in exchange for these substantial exports? Luxury goods in particular, aside from fabrics and textiles. Castile imported lace from Bruges and Mechlin; from Ypres, the fabrics known as *bruneta* and *blanqueta;* high-grade stuffs from Poperinghe and Tournai; from Ghent, the types of cloth called *tinto* and *viado;* from Lille and Blois, the famous *camelin;* from Douai, the fine cloth known at *tiritaña;* and linens and fabrics from Arras, Abbeville, and Cambrai.

Beyond Flanders, on the shores of the North Sea, Castilian trade connected with that of the *Hanseatic League* and England. We do not know a great deal about relations between the powerful Germanic mercantile league, with its center in Lübeck, and Castile. But we do know that there was direct traffic between the Hanseatic League and the Cantabrian seaports from the 14th century onward. The two economies were complementary and benefited mutually (wool and iron going to the North; fish, wheat, and luxury goods to the South). However, frequent rivalries broke out between the Hanseatic and Basque-Castilian merchants, no doubt owing to the former's aggressive policy of expansion. The struggle was very intense in the middle of the 15th century, in connection with trade in the port of La Rochelle. The peace of 1453 marked the victory of the Cantabrian sailors and merchants.

Trade between *England* and Castile was hampered by the conflict of economic and political interests. England and Castile were both producers of wool, and this fact made them rivals for the market in Flanders. Furthermore, the alliance with France placed the Castilian merchant fleet in opposition to the English one. Consequently, the early and peaceful relations between the two kingdoms—facilitated by the shipping of Gascon wine to England—gave way to a long period of rivalry at the time of the Hundred Years' War. After the end of the 13th century, the period of the wool revolution, English kings often complained to the Castilians of the Cantabrians' and Biscayans' constant depredations. After a series of complaints (the first in 1292) and truces, the peace of 1354 was achieved, giving the four cities of the Brotherhood of the Coast great advantages in trade with England. But this breathing spell ended in 1369 with the outbreak of the war, in the course of which the English tried to expel the Basques and Castilians from North Sea trade. At the beginning of the 15th century, after a new period of truce, they expelled the Basques from Harfleur, in the Seine estuary, one of the way stations in wool traffic with Flanders. We have already observed the consequences of this occurrence in the expansion of the Basque fleet toward the Mediterranean. For several decades trade with England was interrupted and was at the mercy of military events. It was only reestablished on a fairly large scale during the reign of Ferdinand and Isabella.

The *Atlantic coast of France,* on the other hand, was one of the most favorable places for Castilian trade. From this region, the outlet for the densely populated and industrious Seine and Loire basins, an enormous number of manufactured products reached Cantabrian ports (nails, furs, trinkets, needles, mirrors, etc.), in addition to the usual fabrics and high-grade cloth. And wool and iron ore went from these ports to France. Using La Rochelle as a starting point, and with the exception of the Gascon coast (enemy territory, since it belonged to England), the Castilians became established in the principal seaports. After 1363, when Charles V of France granted perpetual security and peace to the Castilians who traded in his realm, we find them in Nantes and Dieppe. These colonies prospered after the end of the Hundred Years' War. A whole string of active Basque-Castilian centers became established along the French Atlantic coast: Bayonne, Bordeaux, La Rochelle, Nantes, Rouen, and Dieppe. The most important of these way stations was Rouen, capital of Normandy, where recent researches have located Castilian, Basque, and Andalusian immigrants.

As for *Portugal,* we must remember the attraction which this market had had from the very first as a place of export for Castilian cloth. Aside from the two countries' competition for the African trade routes during the 15th century, they frequently cooperated in a very friendly manner in Morocco, where Portuguese garrisons often doubled as Andalusian trading posts.

We have already spoken of the *Mediterranean* when we mentioned Basque expansion in the 15th century. We need only add that it played a secondary role in Castile's international trade, except for the important branch linking Seville, Cartagena, Majorca, and Genoa, which carried gold, slaves, and wool on the outward journey and brought back high-grade manufactured goods.

FOREIGN MERCHANTS IN CASTILE: THE GENOESE. The Castilian kings showed themselves to be favorable to contact and negotiation with foreign merchants, to whom they owed so many political, military, and economic benefits. This was a tradition whose roots are to be found in the road to Santiago, and which was confirmed in the 13th century by a number of important legislative acts. In 1287 Alfonso X gave a general safe-conduct to any merchant who wished to trade in Castile, with the sole condition that the value of his imports and exports be equal; he further declared an exemption from all customs duties on objects imported for personal use. This basic law was extended in the 14th century by the Decree of Alcalá, issued by Alfonso XI, which declared that foreign ships trading in Castilian ports were not subject to seizure.

Among foreign traders, those who received special benefits were the Genoese. In 1251 Ferdinand III granted them a special statute in Seville, later extended to the colonies established in Cordova, Cádiz, Jerez, Murcia, and Cartagena. This fact proves that the bourgeoisie of the Republic of St. George controlled the ports used for the export of wool as well as strategic points on the Strait of Gibraltar. These colonies had differing legal status, depending on whether their members were temporary or permanent. They were considered permanent when they actually inhabited a city, and in this case might live in a separate quarter, as in Seville and Cádiz, or scattered about the city, as in Jerez, Murcia, and Cartagena.

The French predominated in the northern regions of Castile. We find them established particularly in Toledo and Burgos, in the latter city living side by side with English, Germans, and Lombards.

DEVELOPMENT OF THE GREAT CASTILIAN FAIRS. At the beginning of the 13th century, the local or regional markets which had become established during the early period of the Reconquest continued to develop in Castile. The fair—that is, the mercantile institution and activity distinguished from the market by the fact that it lasts a number of days, has more privileges, is more subject to regulation, and takes in a larger radius of economic action—appeared in the 13th century, not in the north, as it would be logical to suppose, but in the south. In fact, the first privileges granted to fairs were given in New Castile, Extremadura, and Andalusia during the reigns of Alfonso X and Sancho IV: in Seville in 1254; Badajoz in 1258; Alcaraz, 1268; Cádiz, 1284; Talavera, 1294; and Mérida, 1300. This phenomenon must be thought of as closely related to the commercial activity stimulated by the incipient wool trade.

As for the creation of fairs in the north, great confusion reigns, since the date of establishment of many of them is unknown. It is said that those of Valladolid and Sahagún date from the 12th century, and that it is not known exactly when the fairs of Palencia, Segovia, Toledo, and San Sebastián were established. This leads us to think that these places probably had markets of more or less importance, and that at a given time which we can locate sometime during the 14th century they received the status of a fair. This is what happened at Compostela, which in 1351 received an authorization to celebrate a fair, extending its duration from two to fifteen days. The date for Burgos is 1339, and our first information about the very famous fair of Medina del Campo comes from the year 1321. This tends to confirm the theory that the southern fairs were the first to appear, owing to contact with the new commercial methods introduced by the Genoese and related to the Mesta.

This resistance to the development of fairs is linked to the position of the Castilian monarchy, which was never in favor of what was called a "free market." In the 15th century especially, when Castile's population was increasing rapidly, wool was selling well, and the textile industry was beginning to flourish, there was a tendency on the part of the nobles and clergy to concede one market to each town, the purpose being to stimulate trade and particularly to collect taxes from the merchants who attended the fairs. This practice cut down on the amount taken in by the royal treasury and threatened the privileged position of the old established fairs and markets. This is why "free" fairs and markets were banned by the Cortes of 1430, except for those which already possessed a royal dispensation.

After the middle of the 15th century the fair of Medina del Campo became more important than the others, for after its unsuccessful attempt to establish fairs all over Castile the monarchy was determined to concentrate the wool trade, and especially the money trade, in that fair. As the Castilian court was an ambulatory one and the flocks of the Mesta also traveled about, Mesta sales and payments to the monarchy were usually stipulated as payable in a certain place; and it was then that the famous phrase "to be paid in Medina del Campo" began to appear on bills of exchange. The concentration of the wool trade and the investment market made Medina del Campo, after 1450, the great financial center of the Crown of Castile. We must note, however, that after the end of the 14th century the great lords of the Mesta had excellent sources of income in Valladolid as well as Medina.

Merchants from Burgos, Seville, Lisbon, Valencia, and Barcelona, among those of the Hispanic Peninsula, traded in Medina del Campo. And among the foreigners were Irish, Flemings, Genoese, and Florentines. As for the types of goods exchanged, in Medina del Campo wool was sold and luxury articles were bought, for Castilian import trade was essentially in this kind of merchandise. There was no other luxury market in all Europe, not even in the courts of the Italian princes, that could compare with the one of Castile. This is understandable in view of the economic potential of the country's aristocratic class.

The financial role of the fairs was so important that, when the time of the monarchy's weakness arrived, the revenues brought in by Medina del Campo were usurped by the Archbisop of Toledo and the Count of Alba.

The taxes collected at the fairs were of two types, municipal and royal. As for the first type, the chief tax was the "fee of the ground of the fair"; that is, the one collected for putting up a stall there. In addition, there were taxes for guarding the merchandise ("constable's fee") and those paid on weights and measures. As for the royal taxes, the chief ones were the *alcabala* and the *sisa,* which appeared at the end of the 13th century, as we shall soon see.

22 · Money, Usury, and Public Finance in Castile

CASTILIAN COINAGE AND ITS FLUCTUATIONS. We have previously (pp. 134–135) referred to the meager monetary circulation of the Astur-Leonese kingdom, based as it was not on coins of its own but on the introduction of Frankish, and especially Moslem, coins. The advances of the Reconquest merely reinforced the entry of the kingdom, now Castilian-Leonese, into the dual monetary orbit of allies and invaders. *Dineros* and *dinars* from beyond its frontiers circulated more and more freely until the economic development of Castile brought about an emancipation. The first Castilian dineros were minted in Toledo shortly after its capture by Alfonso VI, and the first dinars (with Arabic inscriptions) much later, in 1172, after the Moslem king of Murcia, the habitual supplier of the Castilian-Leonese market, had stopped minting gold.

Let us survey the history of the two foreign coins transplanted to Castile.

GOLD COINAGE. The first Castilian version of the dinar, which we owe to Alfonso VIII, was called a *morabetí* or *maravedí,* taking its name from the Almorávides who at that time had restored the unity of Moslem Spain. Following the prescription of the Koran, this gold maravedí had a ratio of 1:10 in terms of silver; that is, it was worth 10 dirhems. A little later the monetary reform of the Almohades, the new invaders, also had repercussions on the Christian system. The *dobla* appeared, taking the place of the maravedí; this coin was equal to two dinarins (the name of the new Moslem dinar, of less value than the old) and was divided into half-doblas, or *mazmudinas.* As usual, the first doblas to circulate in Christian territory were foreign-minted, until, when the power of the Almohades was crushed in 1212, Alfonso X was obliged to mint them in his own kingdom. This Castilian version added to the existing coins a new fractional piece, the *cuarto,* or quarter-dobla. Also (though this did not influence specific coins, but did reflect the monetary evolution of Western Europe), it should be noted that Alfonso the Wise introduced the *mark* of Cologne as a unit of weight (233 grams of fine gold), as a substitute for the traditional Roman libra.

The dobla became firmly established (up to the time of Ferdinand and Isabella) as the Castilian gold unit. The only modification in it, a fairly unimportant one in the long course of its history, was its adaptation to the maravedí by Alfonso XI, who converted the latter into a simple money of account without any real value. Alfonso XI divided the dobla not into equal parts but into two fractions of 20 and 15 maravedís, the cause of this unequal division being the inequality of value between gold and silver. In fact, while the dobla was worth 35 maravedís in gold coin, it was worth 1 maravedí more, 36, in silver because of the difference in metal. This duality of value, depending on whether one counted in gold or silver, made the division into equal parts impossible, hence the separation into coins of 20 and 15. But what is really interesting with regard to the transplanted dobla in Castile is the fact that it survived until the end of the 15th century, outside the great European current which, beginning as early as the 13th century, caused the general adoption of Italian coins, with the florin at their head. Castile's fidelity to the Moslem system was to mark a profound divergence from the territories of the Crown of Aragon, which had joined the European movement, and would finally lead to the reform of Ferdinand and Isabella.

SILVER COINAGE. In contrast to what happened with gold, the silver coinage of the Western kingdoms developed within the orbit of European, that is to say French, mintings. Certainly the Moslem dirhem circulated in Castilian and Leonese territories, but at the time of the first Castilian mintings Alfonso VI introduced the *dinero,* a vellon coin (that is, a mixture of copper and silver containing 76 grams of fine silver). Although in France the dinero was worth one-twelfth of the *solidus* or *sueldo* (the ancient gold coin reduced after Charlemagne's time to mere money of account), in Castile the continuation of gold mintings permitted relating the dinero to the gold coin (the maravedí), using the same proportion. That is, the dinero was a twelfth, not of a fictitious sueldo, but of an actual coin, the maravedí.

Later, the amount of silver used in the dinero diminished so that the *pepiones,* the name given to these coins at the time of Ferdinand III, contained only 22 grams of silver. To correct this tendency and to revalue vellon, Alfonso the Wise instituted his reform. The basis of this was the introduction of the *maravedí blanca* or *maravedí burgalés* (note how, when it was replaced by the dobla, the old gold maravedí gave its name to a silver coin at the time of Alfonso the Wise), valued at one-sixth the original gold maravedí; that is, double the value of the dinero and pepión. But the "Burgos" coin did not last long, and the very king responsible for it was obliged to devalue its silver content by a third, bringing into existence the *alfonsíes* or *prietos* (that is, "dark in color"), or *coronados* and *cornados,* as they were called at the time of Sancho IV. The failure of Alfonso X's reform was underscored by Ferdinand IV when he minted the *novenes,* equal in value to the old pepiones.

At last Peter I achieved a true readjustment of silver coinage, so necessary after the confusion produced by repeated inflationary measures. In the middle of the 14th century this monarch established a new silver coin that was stronger than its predecessors. This was the *real,* the Castilian version of the Catalan *croat,* which in its turn had been inspired by the *gros* of St. Louis. The real, which contained 3.5 grams of silver and was worth 31 maravedís, was destined to attain great popularity, confirmed by Ferdinand and Isabella's reform. However, between the two great reforms of Peter I and Ferdinand and Isabella, a long period of monetary convulsions and disorders intervened. Thus, in the time of Henry II, whose reign coincided with an extremely serious crisis in the Castilian monarchy, inflation knew no limits. The silver in vellon coins was reduced by half. Henry III minted a new coin, called the *blanca,* which was worth 5 dineros and contained 15 centigrams of silver. This new monetary unit was again debased by John II, whose blancas contained only 10 centigrams of silver. This plunged the country into a monetary chaos from which it did not emerge until the reign of Ferdinand and Isabella.

If we compare the course of the ordinary maravedí with the price of gold, we can establish two great inflationary periods in Castile, one between 1252 and 1258 (value falling from 4.22 to 2.87), and another at the moment of the European crisis of 1380 (1388, 0.90; 1390, 0.47). The Castilian monarchy's tendency towards inflation was enormously prejudicial to the industrial classes. The nobles had their real estate, and furthermore had infiltrated all the places where money was worth something, by means of the "vellum" of wool if not on the basis of "vellon." The constant devaluation of the currency was one of the essential reasons why Castilian industrial structure never solidified during the 15th century as it should have done.

ROLE OF THE KINGDOM OF GRANADA IN THE CASTILIAN MONETARY ECONOMY. The majority of the Moslems who fled from Andalusia after the great rebellion of 1263 had become concentrated in Granada. A large number of farmers and many artisans from the cities emigrated to the little kingdom, defended by its high mountains, and with its rich flatlands and long coastline. Therefore Granada had a dense and industrious population, though it never reached the total of 1 million inhabitants which has so often been attributed to it. However, agriculture was prosperous, workshops were active, and a very remunerative trade was carried on with Africa through the ports of Almería and Málaga. Granada exported wheat, grapes, fruit, sugar, cochineal, and silk; manufactured goods, among which were velvets, damasks, and gold jewelry; and minerals such as gold, silver, and lead.

This wealth clearly benefited the Castilians. After 1430, the Nasrid dynasty of Granada undertook to pay a tribute of 20,000 gold doblas annually. It would be interesting to establish a graph of Granada's gold payments to the Castilian monarchy. And it would also be very significant to study the psychological process which accustomed the Castilian monarchy to count in its budget on a share of income which did not come from the labor of its vassals, drained off through taxes. Therefore, when it is stated that the treasures of America perverted the procedures of the exchequer and the royal officials, this important precedent is forgotten: that before the 16th century there was also a treasure which came to Castile from outside—the treasure of Granada.

THE GOLD ROUTE. The flood of gold that inundated Castile from Granada brings up the subject of the gold route. The trade which Granada carried on with Morocco and the countries of the Barbary Coast (especially with Tlemçen) brought in gold from the Sudan. A very large amount of this metal constantly flowed into the ports of

Almería and Málaga. At the beginning of the 15th century, however, the Castilians as well as the Portuguese, no doubt stimulated by the discoveries of the Majorcans who had reached Senegal, began a series of voyages of discovery along the coast of the Sahara in hopes of bartering for gold, slaves, and ivory. There was some romanticism in the voyages of Henry the Navigator of Portugal and the Andalusian sailors, but there was also a good deal of commercial activity. The grants given by Portugal to Henry the Navigator, and those which Castile offered to the Andalusian sailors on the Canaries route, were fundamentally grants for trading operations.

We do not know much about this struggle because each court, and each seaport, took great care not to announce its findings to its neighbors; a geographical discovery was a state secret. The Castilians' main way station was undoubtedly the Canary Islands, from which they sailed to barter for gold, slaves, and ivory on the nearby African coast. In consequence, gold arrived on the Andalusian coasts not only along the route of Granada (through Tlemçen) but also from Senegal, through the Canaries and Cádiz. And from Cádiz it found its way into the pockets of the Genoese. This means that, long in advance of Columbus' discovery, we have an exact precedent for the gold route of the American treasure. Gold arrived in Castile only to be siphoned off by foreign powers, especially Genoa.

GENOESE, JEWS, AND CONVERSOS IN THE CASTILIAN MONEY TRADE. One of the studies which should be undertaken with the greatest urgency, if we are to understand something of the modern economic history of Spain, would have to do with the role played by the Genoese in the 15th century, not only in the Crown of Aragon but especially in Castile. There does exist a conviction that it was important; we know that the colonization of Spain by the Genoese after the 13th century marked a fundamental stage for the discovery of America, and that Valencia and Seville were their chief strongholds in the two Crowns of Aragon and Castile. But we know almost nothing about the precise manner in which they operated. Their role as great intermediaries between Andalusian Atlantic trade and that of the Mediterranean and Central Europe has not been properly clarified. And in particular, we do not know how they managed to get Sudanese gold into their country. Financiers rather than merchants, the Genoese of the 15th century must have financed the voyages of Atlantic exploration by Andalusians; they must have gained control of the Southern wool trade and lent money to the great Andalusian landowners. All these are mere working hypotheses. What is perfectly clear is that they established in Andalusia the mercantile and capitalist base which gave them such a leading role in the Castilian money trade of the 16th century.

A similar operation of cornering the money market, or rather, another concentration of capital, was in the hands of Jews and *conversos*. Since there was no long-term capital in the hands of bankers, and since the Jews, and later the *conversos,* were collectors for the military orders and the Church, it was logical that all the money which escaped from Genoese control wound up in their hands. From time to time there was a pogrom, and money went back into circulation; but it soon returned to its old owners. By the middle of the 15th century money was in the hands of the *conversos,* except for the small proportion under control of the Mesta (that is, of the great lords who engaged in the wool trade).

To sum up, the circulation of gold in Castile at about the middle of the 15th century can be reconstructed as follows: Granada and West Africa, as the great gold routes flowing into Seville; from there, disappearance of part of it to Genoa; the other, smaller part went north. In Medina del Campo it served to pay for luxury goods bought at the fair. Finally, when it reached Burgos it was swallowed up by the *conversos* in payment of their loans to the king, the nobles, and the magnates of the Mesta.

So the gold followed a straight line, without the country's profiting from it. And if we compare this circulation with that of the 16th century we will find the situation exactly the same. So the constant inflow of gold in the Late Middle Ages was the necessary precedent to the great machinery of the 1500's, which also swallowed up the treasure of America without the Castilian commoner's receiving any benefit from it.

USURY IN CASTILE. Usury was calamitous in the early times of the Commercial Revolution. As neither capital nor credit institutions existed, money was very costly. The Jews in particular profited from this business, and it was then that they gained the reputation of usurers. But after the end of the 14th century their role declined all over Western Europe, with one notable exception—Castile—where their influence grew daily, to the point that, as we have said, they obtained control of most of the money in circulation.

Among the causes of this phenomenon was the incapacity of the Castilian bourgeoisie for creating banks and banking deposits. But more important than this was the immoderate desire for luxury and ostentation which characterized their society and was, as Sánchez Albornoz points out, one of its chief vices. The nobility, the clergy, and the bourgeoisie ruined themselves because of their desire to dazzle others with jewels, clothing, and ornaments. Chronically in need of cash, they found it in the tight purse of the Hebrew. Early in the 13th century, sumptuary statutes like those of Cuenca authorized the Jews to charge interest at the rate of one-eighth of a maravedí or one-twelfth of a solidus per week. This means a *monthly* interest of 50 and 33⅓ % respectively, a truly fabulous amount. Alfonso X limited this interest to 33⅓ % *annually* (1268), a tremendous reduction which was often flouted. Private documents prove this. The kings, urged on by the nobles, the clergy, and the municipal councils, repeated Alfonso's decrees. In vain. Money continued to be very costly in an ambitious society little given to work. Hence the violence of the upheavals of 1391, when Jews, accused of the high cost of living and the ruin of many important people, were persecuted everywhere in Castile. But really, as we know, the cause was a change in the general economic outlook. During the 15th century *conversos* took the place of Jews in loaning money to kings and aristocrats, churches and town councils. Burgos was the center of this business.

Usury came to a peak because the Jews had attained the rank of treasury agents of the Crown and the military orders. We have already mentioned this several times. The financial difficulties of the Castilian Crown gave wide scope to the activities of this group. After the 12th century the monarchs had a Jewish *almojarife,* or taxgatherer, at their side. A century later these *almojarifes* had taken over the administration. The family of Zag de la Maleha played an important role in this respect at the time of Alfonso X, and that of Abraham de Barchilón (the Barcelonian) during Sancho IV's reign. From that time on, collection of taxes was the task of Jews and *conversos*. The Castilians hated them passionately. But their *raison d'être* is clear: they alone were the ones who understood the value of money in Castile.

TAXES AND LEVIES BY THE STATE. Along general lines, the same principles for the collection of taxes and levies that had existed in the early period of the Asturian, Leonese, and Castilian monarchies were still in force; that is, the main weight of taxation fell, on the one hand, on those who owned land and, on the other, on those who worked or engaged in business. So it is no novelty to encounter again the fees, tithes, poll taxes, and war levies we spoke of before.

During the Late Middle Ages the most important new feature was the application of the country's growing economic resources to the royal treasury. This was achieved in two ways, by broadening the old taxes and by obtaining various grants and loans from the Cortes. The position of the aristocrats is also interesting. Since they were exempt from all taxes, they attempted—and partly succeeded in the effort—to wrest from the monarch the money which came in from taxes and levies. A large part of the social struggle in Castile in the 14th and 15th centuries was due to the nobles' eagerness to obtain control over the chief sources of collection of taxes on commerce.

Because of their nature, these can be divided into two large groups, taxes on *transit* and on *buying and selling*. In the first group we find the bridge tax, the turnpike tax, the ferry tax; the castle tax, paid by those who used a road under the jurisdiction of a castle; the road tax, which was paid for the safeguarding of highways; and the duty on the passage of animals. The *almojarifazgo,* or customs dues, can be related to these.

Taxes on buying and selling transactions were more important; these developed as commercial expansion took place, particularly expansion of the wool trade. In the 13th century two famous taxes appeared which were to persist in the history of the Castilian exchequer almost to the threshold of our time—the *alcabala* and the *sisa.* Both grew out of difficult moments for the monarchy, one in the time of Alfonso X and the other during Sancho IV's reign. The *alcabala* was a certain percentage on sales in the marketplace: first it was 5% (in 1269), and later (in 1377) it was raised to 10%. As for the *sisa,* or deduction made by the treasury from the sale price of a product, it was first applied during the time of Sancho IV at the rate of 1%; shortly afterward, about the middle of the 13th century, it became fixed at 3%.

To have an idea of what this constant succession of taxes, duties, and fees represented for the businessman, we must add to them the municipal and seigniorial levies.

We have left to the last any mention of the Crown's fattest source of income: the tax on sheep, or the fiscal organization which was set up over the great migratory flocks of the Mesta. From the earliest times of the wool revolution, the Crown had a very convenient area in which to collect taxes. When the general charter of the Mesta was granted by Alfonso X, one of its chief purposes was to establish the fiscal responsibility of livestock breeders. Four years earlier (in 1269, in fact), the so-called *servicio* had been established, voted by the Cortes, under the terms of which each flock of the Castilian drove was obliged to pay a certain amount. This service, voted for three or four years, kept on being renewed. In 1343 the *montazgo* was added to it. This was a purely municipal tax, but the Crown converted it into a general one, cancelling the local *montazgos*. "Servicio y montazgo," after that, became one of the chief resources of the Crown. Thus, it is logical and comprehensible that when Ferdinand of Antequera of the house of Trastamara, a very prudent man, exercised the regency of Castile for a few short years, he tried to insure the prosperity of his house by causing his third son Prince Henry to inherit, along with the mastership of Santiago, the right to collect the duties of *servicio* and *montazgo*. Hence the Castilian prince had an immense fortune in his hands: he controlled the uncultivated lands of the southern Meseta, many more in Andalusia, and furthermore had the right to collect taxes from the Mesta and turn them over to the Crown. Since Prince Henry turned out to be a good administrator, he formed quite a flawless tax organization; so when Don Álvaro de Luna took his job away from him, his system was adopted by the State. In 1457 a schedule of "servicio y montazgo" taxes was approved which remained in force until the end of the 17th century.

THE CASTILIAN CORTES AND FISCAL POLICY. In the Crown of Aragon, and more especially formulated in Catalonia, it had been a principle of political law that any economic relationship between the sovereign and the people had to be based on a pact which closely linked the sovereign with the Cortes to impose taxes, and the Cortes with the sovereign to vote them. In Castile this pactist theory, characteristic of a flourishing bourgeoisie, was formulated only by the Cortes of Henry IV, and then rather timidly. This is logical, for the Castilian monarchy never had to face a guild organization like the Catalan one, and at the same time it enjoyed much broader financial resources.

It is true, though, that in spite of the fact that the Castilian monarchs had large sums of money at their disposal, there were certain moments when they were not able to meet their responsibilities. This meant that they had to apply to the Cortes for grants and levies, and that the Cortes tried to take advantage of the situation to wrest from them certain special concessions on taxation.

During the reign of Alfonso XI (14th century) the Cortes obtained from the king the promise that he would not assess any tax or levy without its authorization. This law appeared in all the fundamental codes of Castile, but in spite of it the monarchy never paid much attention to a concession which had been extracted from it at a tight moment. On the other hand, when the Cortes did vote a tax, it was the royal officials who collected it, thus giving an opportunity for the indefinite perpetuation of a tax granted for a special and transitory purpose.

Since no regulatory mechanism existed for the tax payments of the subjects to the monarch, the Castilian Crown quickly fell into the hands of moneylenders or issued certificates of indebtedness pledged on certain Crown incomes. These certificates were the so-called *juros*. There has been no careful study of the origins and development of these *juros*. We know that three types existed— those payable on demand, perpetual, and on one life—and that all of them were state issues of paper to legalize a debt or guarantee a loan. After the beginning of the fifteenth century the practice of issuing *juros* led the Castilian public treasury to the verge of inflationary anarchy.

ECONOMIC POLICY OF THE MONARCHY. If the Aragonese monarchy sometimes had political whims in the economic field and often sacrificed material realities to the pursuit of a fanciful objective, as in the case of Alfonso the Magnanimous, the Castilian monarchy scarcely had any idea of the country's real economic situation. Taken up with warlike enterprises, dominated by the feudal and seigniorial superstructure of the great landowners, it paid scarcely any attention to commercial relations, which were almost entirely the work of its more enterprising vassals. Fluctuating as it did between contradictory ambitions, its solution was always to seek the easiest path, and the easiest thing was to bow to the monopoly of the Mesta and the interests of the wool exporters: *conversos,* Genoese, and Flemings. The result of this was an internal contradiction between the needs of a country with a growing population and a burgeoning textile industry, and those of a monarchy accustomed only to solving its own selfish problems and the quarrels of those who grew rich from their connections with the throne.

Isolated figures opposed to this general trend, which was governed by the idea of consumption and freedom of external trade, were Alfonso X and Henry III. One author even speaks of a "controlled economy" when he refers to Alfonso the Wise. It was hardly that. It is true that this monarch reformed the currency standard and set up a severe tariff law (1268) which banned the export of precious metals, livestock, wool and silk, leather, wine, and wheat. It is also true that he favored the Castilian merchant marine and rescued it from foreign dependence. But this same Alfonso X was the monarch who created the Mesta, and was the adversary of the guild organizations. He was, therefore, not a very convinced protectionist. And in the end his efforts were a total failure.

His successors allowed themselves to be led by circumstances. They were incapable of dealing with economic factors. Only Henry III dictated an order in 1398 urging foreign merchants to embark their goods in Castilian ships. This was a measure taken in a period of crisis, no sooner published than flouted. Only during the reign of Henry IV—that king so little known to history—did an effective and intelligent protectionist policy begin to be practiced, and it was to be continued by the Catholic Monarchs.

IV · MERCANTILIST ECONOMY

23 · The Economy of Ferdinand
and Isabella's Reign

DEMOGRAPHIC RISE: EMIGRATION OF RELIGIOUS MINORITIES. The period of Ferdinand and Isabella seems to have produced a noticeable rise in population, probably due to the end of the civil wars both in Castile and Catalonia and the reestablishment of a normal economic situation.

There is much evidence of this state of affairs, though the figures are scanty and unreliable. Thus, Quintanilla's census (1482), the only one we can make use of for the whole period, gives the Crown of Castile a total of 1,500,000 households (6 to 7 and a half million inhabitants), a frankly exaggerated figure. To the central nucleus, composed of Castilians, we should have to add the inhabitants of the old kingdom of Granada (from 500,000 to 750,000) incorporated into the nation in 1492, and the subjects of the Aragonese Crown (probably 1 million, in round figures) and the Crown of Navarre (100,000?). In fact, the only proved increase is that of the Principality of Catalonia, which rose from 55,541 households in 1497 to 59,435 in 1516.

This bright demographic picture in Castile probably made up for losses through emigration, which were considerable. In first rank among these we must place the departure of the *conversos,* which took place as a consequence of the establishment of the Inquisition. It is impossible to give exact figures for the numbers involved in this movement. Next comes the departure of the *Jews,* which according to Baer affected some 150,000 persons; and also that of the *Moriscos* of Granada after the revolt of 1502, a group which can be estimated at 300,000 individuals. To this we must add the emigration of the *discoverers of America,* which up to 1520 was a very small contingent. We can estimate, then, for the whole kingdom of Ferdinand and Isabella, a total of some 500,000 persons, a number whose real importance must be measured, as we shall see, more by the emigrants' economic quality than by their quantity. As for immigrants, they were few in number—select *colonies* of foreign businessmen and artisans, and in the Pyrenees the first evidences of the growing avalanche of *Gascon* shepherds and peasants.

Let us emphasize the question of *confessional minorities,* which were so important in Ferdinand and Isabella's religious and economic policy. At the beginning of their reign the Jews numbered some 200,000. Of these, 150,000 emigrated and the rest became converted, especially in certain regions of Catalonia and in Majorca. We must point out that the majority of expelled Jews settled in lands controlled by the infidel (Cairo, Alexandria, Aleppo, Tripoli in Syria, Salonica, and Constantinople), where they very soon formed a basic economic community, so that their departure from Castile not only deprived the country of this community, but benefited the enemies of the Faith, against whom the drastic measure of the Inquisition had been intended.

In regard to the *conversos,* we must handle all the figures with care. If we start with the approximately 130,000 Jews who had renounced the Hebrew religion at the beginning of the 15th century in Castile and the Crown of Aragon, it can be supposed that their number by 1480 was about double: some 250,000. These people made up the most powerful, most vital and active segment of the Castilian population in the 15th century. Everyone, both attackers and defenders, agrees on this point. When the Inquisition began to function all over Spain, between 1480 and 1486, the *conversos* accused of Judaic tendencies fled *en masse.* How many emigrated? We do not know. How many were burned at the stake? This too is unknown. There are figures to suit every taste. The most likely possibility is that in the period with which we are dealing some 2,000 Jewish-leaning *conversos* were burned and about 20,000 returned to the Church. The rest probably emigrated. This is the impression given by reading the documents of the time. The mercantile cities of the Catalonian and Valencian coasts, along with many cities in Aragon, Castile, and Andalusia, felt the departure of the *conversos* as something which profoundly damaged their economic vitality. This was the basis of the resistance made to the establishment of the Inquisition—not in its aspect as a defense of dogma, but to what it represented in the way of trials without legal guarantees, seizure of property, and paralyzation of mercantile life. The cases of Saragossa, Teruel, and Barcelona are proof of this.

The number of *Moriscos* came to 1 million, of whom there were 50,000 in Aragon, 160,000 in Valencia, 10,000 in Catalonia, and 15,000 in Majorca, a total of 235,000 for the Crown of Aragon; and in Castile some 700,000, distributed in the following manner: 200,000 in Castile before the conquest of Granada, and 500,000 in the kingdom of Granada. Some 300,000 of these departed, as we mentioned before, leaving a remainder of 400,000 in the Crown of Castile. We must keep in mind that in 1502 this group of people lost their position as a legal minority and became a dissident minority within the country, dissident in a different, but no less profound, sense from the Jewish-leaning *conversos*.

POPULATION DISTRIBUTION. How were the inhabitants of Spain distributed at the time of the Catholic Monarchs? The vast majority lived in the country. More than 80% of the total Spanish population were peasants. Urban workers, including Jews, *conversos,* and so on, amounted to 10 or 12% before the expulsion. The urban middle class, counting citizens, merchants, and ecclesiastics, made up some 3 to 5%. And finally, the nobles, taking together the aristocracy of both Castile and Aragon, represented less than 2%, divided into 5,000 magnates (dukes, counts, barons, etc.), 60,000 knights, *hidalgos,* and so on, and 60,000 urban patricians, or aristocrats of the cities. These 125,000 individuals were at the summit of the social scale and controlled the country from above.

It was at this time that the countryside, especially in Castile, first began to show signs of depopulation. When we seek the origins of the unfavorable situation in the 17th century, with deserted lands and an army of vagrants and beggars infesting the country, we tend to put the responsibility on the Hapsburg government. In reality the phenomenon goes back to the time of Ferdinand and Isabella, as can be observed in several famous contemporary chronicles, such as Carvajal's. The peasant classes, unable to make a living from the soil, began their exodus to the cities. Thus, the urban population grew at a rate higher than the general rhythm of the country. Seville and Valencia were famous for having 80,000 inhabitants; Barcelona had 35,000; Cordova, Toledo, Granada, Valladolid, Salamanca, Murcia, Málaga, Saragossa, Majorca, and Perpignan between 15,000 and 25,000; and there was a large group of cities with 10,000 to 15,000 inhabitants.

STABILIZATION OF PROPERTY: RISE OF THE CASTILIAN ARISTOC-
RACY. During the 15th century property and revenue from land had
passed from hand to hand all over Spain, in Castile as well as in the
Crown of Aragon. In the greater part of Spain, around 1476, no
one could say "this is mine" and "this is yours," for the luck of a
battle, the favor of a sovereign, a change of sides, were enough to
cause a person's property to be confiscated and given to someone
else. It was a state of general chaos. Ferdinand and Isabella reestablished peace and stabilized property. This fact is very important, for
property, as Ferdinand and Isabella left it, underwent very few
changes in the succeeding centuries, until the disentailment laws of
the 19th century.

When Ferdinand and Isabella are discussed, one of the common-
est statements made about them is that they put the nobility in their
pockets; it is true that, from the point of view of authority, they let
no one raise his head. But in the social aspect they maintained the
economic advantages to the aristocracy stemming from the ownership of land. This fact is supremely important if we are to understand the future of the Castilian economy.

Let us look at what happened. In Catalonia the civil war had
ended in 1472, but John II allowed the confusion to continue. In
1479, when Ferdinand the Catholic took over the government, he
began to bring a little order out of chaos. In 1481 he decreed a
general restitution of property, issuing, with the compliance of the
Cortes, a pragmatic sanction setting forth the restitutions which
were to be made. For this purpose he exacted from the Cortes a
donation of 100,000 libras with which to pay his supporters for the
property they unjustly occupied and were going to have to give up.
The result was that with a fairly moderate sum of money, the country was able to blot out the past errors of the civil war. If we also
keep in mind the publication of the Sentence of Guadalupe, in
1486, and that it very cleverly gave the peasant effective possession
of his land, leaving jurisdictional control to his lord, we will understand that Ferdinand the Catholic's accomplishment was truly
democratic, for it gave some 50,000 individuals access to a fair-
sized property. This is why there have not been, up to the contemporary period, any attempts at agrarian revolt in Catalonia.

What happened in Castile? There the Cortes of Toledo met in
1480, and the necessity was recognized of putting the exchequer in

order. Estimates were made, and it developed that enormous quantities of maravedís were owed. It was then decided to cancel the gifts and hereditary pensions enjoyed by the nobles. Thanks to the studies of Matías Usón, it has been proved that the nobles, who possessed some 63 million maravedís of revenue, in fact had to give up some 30 million. However, in Castile this reduction was very superficial; the nobles lost half of the income they had violently and unjustly usurped after 1464, but the order was explicitly given to preserve the properties, grants, and pensions they had possessed before the upheavals of Henry IV's reign. That is, the destructive work performed by the Castilian aristocracy during the reign of Henry II, and completed during that of John II, was formally respected. Since these usurpations were the most important ones, it can be stated that the law of 1480 served only to ratify the absolute social and economic control of the noble class over the State and the rest of the country. The known figures could not be more conclusive: about the year 1500 the nobles owned 97% of the territory of the Peninsula, either directly or by jurisdiction. This is the same as saying that 1.5% of the population owned almost the entire Spanish territory. This fact is of capital importance.

Of this 97%, 45% belonged to bishoprics, high ecclesiastics, cathedral chapters, canonries, the urban aristocracy, and the knights. The rest belonged to the grandees and formed true latifundia. We shall mention a few names. Andalusia was divided among the following landowners: the Guzmáns, dukes of Medinasidonia; the Cerdas, dukes of Medinaceli; the Ponce de Leóns, dukes of Arcos; the family of Fernández de Córdoba in both branches, as counts of Cabra and lords of Montilla, the latter soon elevated to dukes of Sesa; the Mendozas, counts of Tendilla and Priego. The archbishopric of Toledo was sole owner of the rest. Extremadura was divided, almost half-and-half, between the family of Súarez de Figueroa and the Order of Alcántara. In Murcia the largest landowners were the Fajardos; in Salamanca the Estúñigas, dukes of Béjar, and the Álvarez de Toledo family; in La Mancha, the Orders of Santiago and Calatrava, the archbishopric of Toledo and the Marquis of Villena; in the Alcarria, the Duke of the Infantado.

The remaining 3% had to be shared by some 4 or 5 million Castilians. We can easily understand that Ferdinand and Isabella's social reform amounted to nothing, for in addition the following took place: first, the monarchs confirmed and extended the right of establishing *mayorazgos* (Laws of Toro, 1504), that is, the right of hereditary transmission which entailed property to the firstborn of a family; second, they approved a policy of matrimonial connections whose only result was to produce a concentration of property in the hands of those who already had it; and third, in Granada they carried out a policy favorable to the aristocracy. Granada was a new conquest, but with the exception of the western regions of the kingdom (Ronda, Málaga, Alora, Coín), which were given to peasants and workmen from lower Andalusia, the rest was turned over to the nobles in compensation for what had been taken away from them in 1480. So to those who had was given—practically the whole kingdom of Granada.

To these facts we must add another which was no less important: the sale of the lands of free farmers because of the agrarian crisis at the beginning of the 16th century, followed by depopulation of the countryside and the appearance of the specter of famine. This movement could only benefit those who had money with which to buy; namely, the aristocracy again.

The sum total of the events we have just described explains the enormous fortunes of the Castilian lords of the period. As Marineo Sículo says, one-third of the country's revenues belonged to the king, one-third to the nobility, and the other third to the Church, which is like repeating "the aristocracy," for its second sons owned the choicest part of the ecclesiastical benefices. Sixty-one nobles enjoyed an average annual income of 20,000 ducats (1 ducat = 375 maravedís = 8 days' wages of a specialized worker). The wealth of the grandees can be estimated at 1,245,000 ducats annually; that of the Church, 6 million overall—fabulous sums, which render comment unnecessary.

THE MIDDLE AND PEASANT CLASSES IN CASTILE, ARAGON, AND CATALONIA. We have just described the result of Ferdinand and Isabella's social policy: the consolidation of the nobility's economic potential. If it is really true that they tried to weaken the aristocracy's political power by bringing the educated middle class into the royal councils, it is no less true that subordinate executive power was turned over to the grandees, in viceroyships as well as in high military posts. On a larger scale, it was from the ranks of the lower nobility that Ferdinand and Isabella recruited the royal governors of the cities, who formed the Castilian State into the rigid mold characteristic of an authoritarian monarchy.

As for the middle class, we cannot say that it particularly benefited. Order and authority, combined with a relative economic prosperity, made up for loss of liberty in the Cortes and in municipal government. This is why the Castilian town councils recalled the times of the Catholic Monarchs with special affection. The same occurred in the Crown of Aragon. But now a particularly grave problem arises: the elimination of the dissident middle class—Jews, and Jewish-leaning *conversos.* Both groups occupied three key positions: in the first place, they were the financiers; in the second place, they held the chief public offices related to the court and the municipal governments; and last, they represented an artisan class which was lively, intelligent, and alert.

It is difficult to take up this problem from a purely economic point of view. Knowing the number of *conversos,* their vitality and influence, it is understandable that their wealth and preponderance should have aroused hatred among certain social classes in Castile. Generally "the hatred of the people" is spoken of, but the facts we possess limit the acceptance of this term to certain concrete classes which were, as a matter of fact, the aristocracy and the Church. Though we admit the animosity of part of the Castilian population for the *conversos* who refused to abandon the religious practices inherited from their ancestors, we will have to state that Ferdinand and Isabella were totally intransigent when they decided to sacrifice the country's economy to its spiritual well-being. There can be no doubt whatever on this score, for in the face of the reasonable arguments made to them by the city governments of Seville, Toledo, Barcelona, Valencia, and Saragossa, in the face of the serious dislocation which the establishment of the Inquisition and the consequent flight of the *conversos* meant for these cities, the king and queen always replied that in the first place, they were taking into account the religious benefit of the country, that they had the economic factor well in mind, and that in consequence they were sacrificing it to the spiritual policy which had been decreed.

In view of all this, it is possible to state that the elimination of religious dissent was due to an inalterable desire to maintain orthodoxy, over and above all material concerns. However, this feeling

297

was not the only one, but was perhaps accompanied, in circles connected with the Court, by less lofty purposes. There is a historiographic tendency, lately centering around Américo Castro's work *The Structure of Spanish History* (*La realidad histórica de España*), which insists that the Inquisition was created under the sole pretext of "robbing" the *conversos*. A number of texts are quoted in support of this thesis which would seem irrefutable were they not a product of the violent polemics of the period. At any rate, we cannot reduce the elimination of the Jewish-leaning *conversos* to such an uncompromising word as "robbery." On the other hand, it is possible to state that at the time the Inquisition was established the State was undergoing a profound financial crisis, and that the voices of those who counseled economic measures against the *conversos* prevailed. But even in this case the problem cannot be solved in such a simplistic manner; for although Ferdinand and Isabella could attack the *conversos* in order to take over their wealth, their elimination from national life was prejudicial to the treasury's future revenues; that is, it was an operation which quickly brought in a certain amount of money, but which resulted after a time in the stagnation of the sources of public revenue (this was what happened in a number of Castilian cities, which obtained tax exemptions by pleading the departure of the Jews and *conversos*, the only ones who really contributed to the public treasury). We need to weigh matters carefully, therefore, and admit on the one hand the spiritual necessity felt in the Castile of the time to avoid all religious dissent, and on the other the urgent need to face the undeniable necessities of the public treasury.

If we accept as approximate figures the 20,000 who returned to the Church, the 2,000 burned at the stake, and the 120,000 who fled, among whom were commanders of the military orders, canons, friars, city magistrates, people of all classes, for the *conversos* were imbedded in the very fabric of Castile, we will realize what an enormous paralyzation of the country's resources took place; not only because a vital sector of the nation fled, but because even before the introduction of the Inquisition, which was established slowly, first in Andalusia, then in Castile, and finally in the Crown of Aragon, the *conversos* were responsible for the flight of capital on a large scale. This brought about a stagnation in the capitalization of the middle class that, in combination with the preponderance of the aristocracy, was on the point of causing the monarchy's financial collapse between 1485 and 1490.

A no less serious problem was the expulsion of the Jews; the apologists for this measure thought that it was necessary in order to eliminate the element which controlled the Castilian *conversos,* while its critics felt it was only an excuse to seize the Jews' property and wipe out the debt incurred by the war in Granada. These opinions could be reconciled if we possessed impartial critical studies. The documentation is in the archives, but no one has yet had the courage to tackle this material, which is abundant but scattered.

As for the peasant classes, the policy of Ferdinand and Isabella varied from region to region. In Catalonia, where a social doctrine existed in regard to the *remença* serfs (a total of 15,000 to 20,000 households, or one-fourth of the total population), Ferdinand the Catholic assured their liberty and stability by means of the Sentence of Guadalupe (1486), which eliminated the problem of serfdom and evil practices. The keystone of this measure, to which the nobles and the cities were stubbornly opposed, was to give freedom to the peasant by assuring him effective possession of the land that he tilled. In Aragon, however, where the analogous problem of the *exarchs* existed, not only was the situation of this group not improved but, conversely, it was changed in favor of the lords. As for Castile, in 1481 the right of landed serfs to abandon their lord was confirmed. If we keep in mind that this right was theoretical, since it appeared in legislation but not in the reality of the social fabric (for, as we have observed, 97% of the land in Castile belonged to the civil and ecclesiastical aristocracy), the freedom of 1481 meant only the freedom to die of hunger, as was immediately shown during the great crises of 1502 and 1509 in Castile.

STAGES IN THE CONTAINMENT OF CATALONIAN ECONOMIC DECLINE. The economic decline of Catalonia had reached a new low at the end of John II's reign, so much so that Ferdinand's accession to the throne was awaited as if it were the coming of the Messiah.

It has been said over and over that Ferdinand the Catholic's policy brought about the economic ruin of Catalonia. This statement, made by the romantic school of Catalan historians, has gone over into Castilian and foreign works. But the truth is exactly the opposite: during Ferdinand and Isabella's reign there was economic recovery in Catalonia.

In 1479 and 1481 the first step was taken to arrest Catalonian economic decline. In the Cortes of 1481 two important measures were taken for this purpose; the first was general restitution of property, of which we have already spoken, and the second was the restoration, or "redreç," of trade. This consisted of a long catalogue of protectionist measures, in which a schedule of customs duties was established, the entry of certain foreign products was forbidden, measures were taken to safeguard the coral industry, and the monopoly of Catalonian fabrics in Sardinia was decreed. This atmosphere of recovery received a setback in the years immediately following, between 1481 and 1488, owning to the double phenomena of social revolution in the countryside and the establishment of the Inquisition in Barcelona. In 1486 Catalonia was really exhausted. But after 1488 Ferdinand's good will, plus the people's desire to live and the artisans' will to work, resulted in a visible rebirth of mercantile and industrial activity in the Principality.

In 1488 a number of measures were taken which were to affect the total situation: stabilization of the currency, a study of the establishment of a monopoly on Catalonian cloth in Sicily, and the fight against privateering. Piracy had been one of the causes of Catalonian economic decline, especially because of the reprisals it provoked from the affected countries. In 1491, however, all safe-conducts and privateering licenses were suspended, and in 1492 a pragmatic decree was issued freeing the galley slaves. This event contributed toward calming relations between Barcelona and Genoa, and permitted both to concentrate their efforts on eliminating the pirates who infested the Barcelona-Valencia-Balearic triangle. At the same time, an order was issued prohibiting the traffic of ships from Genoa and Nice in Catalonian ports (1491), and the export of Catalonian wool was limited so that local industry, stimulated by the monopolies in Sardinia and Sicily, could be better supplied.

The problem of the Catalonian textile industry's monopoly in Sicily was slowly solved. First an entry tax (5%) was placed on French cloth (1498), and then it was totally banned not only in Sicily but also in Naples (1506). So by 1506 Catalonian cloth had preferential rights in Sardinia, Sicily, and Naples, three great consumer markets. There is no doubt that these facts influenced Catalonian mercantile recovery, revealed in the resumption of trade with Egypt. In 1495, after half a century of paralysis, the fleet of Juan Sarriera, general bailiff of Catalonia, again reached Alexandria. The Catalan consulate was at once reestablished in that city. After 1495 this profitable trade was not interrupted, though it declined in proportion to the growing success of the Portuguese in their voyages to India and the Spice Islands.

The last stage, from 1503 to 1516, was one of clear prosperity: the cities' population grew, Barcelona recovered, sea trade with the Atlantic countries was renewed, Catalonian ships traded with Flanders and England, the insurance companies did excellent business, and finally, the Crown of Aragon's great traditional market in North Africa was reopened. In 1511, after Bougie, Oran, and Tripoli were taken, a pragmatic decree issued in Burgos on the eighteenth of December granted the Catalans the right to impose a duty of 50% on any non-Catalan article imported into those seaports.

On the other hand, we should point out that Ferdinand's improvements in Catalonian industry and trade also affected agriculture. In this regard, the Sentence of 1486 which resolved the *remença* problem was complemented by the decree of the Cortes of Monzón in 1511, prohibiting the passage of flocks through cultivated lands. This was a measure of utmost importance for the future of Catalonian agriculture, which, compared with the radically opposite policy decided upon ten years earlier in Castile, shows that the decrees of Ferdinand and Isabella should not be considered simply as royal decisions, but as responding to social structures in existence in the two countries. What was possible in Catalonia was not possible, as we shall see, in Castile.

To sum up: except in the matter of trade with America, which we shall take up shortly, it is proved that during the reign of the Catholic King, either because of the monarch's favorable attitude or because of the country's vital recovery, Catalonia progressively regained the stature she had lost in the middle of the 15th century.

AGRARIAN AND GRAZING POLICY IN CASTILE: EXPANSION OF THE MESTA. The fundamental fact of Ferdinand and Isabella's economic policy in Castile is the solution, favoring livestock over agriculture, of a problem which had existed since the beginning of the 13th century.

No historian, no matter how great an apologist he has been for the Catholic Monarchs, has been able to defend this decision. Ballesteros Gaibrois states in a work on Queen Isabella, "The result was permanently harmful for the Spanish economy." And, trying to find some excuse, he adds, "This was one of the subjects which the great policy-makers of the time simply did not have within their mental range." This conclusion seems unfounded to us, for the problem of famine in Castile was one that Ferdinand and Isabella lived with daily, and it was intimately related to the dilemma which they found already in existence and solved in favor of livestock.

The fact that Ferdinand and Isabella favored the Mesta is obvious. This appears not only in the legislation we are about to describe, but also in the less important decrees of their government. Torres Fontes speaks in a recent article of a disagreement that developed over a grazing ground in Murcia which some good farmers had planted with trees, sowed with grain, and then fenced in to prevent the passage of flocks; he shows that the royal decision condemned this act, and tells of the solemn moment when the herdsmen destroyed the fence and chopped down the trees. There is something here—a negative element, which must have been very deeply rooted—which strikes very deep in Castilian economic history and explains the anguish of the farmers. And this is not a personal, subjective impression. It is borne out in hundreds of texts. Let us choose one of these: the protest of the delegates of the city of Cáceres in the courts of Valladolid in 1501, when, referring to these attempts against agricultural property, they exclaimed, "Such things cannot be called just nor honest, since they are not for the public good but for the private advantage of a few favored men."

Let us examine a number of decrees issued by Ferdinand and Isabella favorable to herding, detrimental to agriculture.

The *royal cedula of 1480* ordered evacuation of the enclosures set up by farmers on communal lands during the time of Henry IV.

The *ordinance of 1489,* called *Defense of the Cañadas,* decreed the redrawing of the boundaries of these sheepwalks in order to expel from them the farmers who had settled there during the previous fifty years. This law caused considerable losses, for it greatly widened the paths along which the flocks passed, and especially banned the setting aside of land for enclosures.

The *edict of 1491* banned enclosures in the kingdom of Granada.

A law of the same year, confirmed in succeeding years, authorized shepherds to "lop"; that is, "to cut down the smaller trees for their branches during the winter or when pasture is scarce." This measure, together with the absence of any measure stipulating punishment for the burning of forests to encourage growth of grass for grazing, resulted in deforestation of the country in spite of the interest shown by Isabella the Catholic in perpetuating the forests. As Julius Klein writes, "This reign was indeed the crucial period in the history of Castilian forestry; and the desolation which was wrought in the wooded areas of the kingdom had its beginnings in the uncompromising partiality of Ferdinand and Isabella for the pastoral industry."

But all these edicts pale into insignificance if we consider the famous *land lease law* of 1501. When the law in defense of the sheepwalks began to be enforced, the herdsmen tried to invade the farmers' fields and the city councils defended themselves. A fundamental solution had to be found: the law of 1501. By its provisions the Mesta could extend the lease of a field indefinitely, paying for it the sum originally agreed upon, and keeping for its own purposes any grazing ground it had occupied for a few months, without the owner's knowledge. This last decree implied a presumption of legal usufruct in favor of the herdsman, a presumption established independently of the desires of the owner of the land, who was obliged to lease it for a ridiculously low rent. Great stretches of Andalusia and Extremadura were thus linked to the Mesta and to the interests of the Mesta's ruling minority. For agriculture, the result could not have been more unfavorable.

What were the reasons for Ferdinand and Isabella's policy toward the Mesta? Its first motive is crystal clear: *monopolistic regulation of the wool trade.* Over and above any other consideration, they were ruled by the need for obtaining "great quantities of gold and other advantages from abroad" (J. Klein). And the reason for this was that the monarchy was the chief beneficiary of the Mesta. In fact, since 1466 indirectly, and 1493 directly, the Crown had controlled the great masterships of the military orders. This means that it received, through the Order of Santiago, 100% of the *servicio y montazgo* taxes which constituted the Crown's chief financial resources. Therefore, instead of waiting for a few years until the development of agriculture would bear fruit, the monarchs chose to follow the easy path of their predecessors and collect money on something as tangible and easily taxable as sheep. This brings us to the second motive: *the financial crisis undergone by the Crown after 1484.* Owing to the expansion of the Inquisition and the flight of capital in the hands of the *conversos,* and subsequently, in 1492, to the expulsion of the Jews, quick remedies were needed; and none was closer to hand than the wool which was exported. Hence the protection of the Mesta. Hence too, after the time of Ferdinand and Isabella, it could be said that, "The exploitation and preservation of sheepherding is the chief support of these kingdoms."

It now seems hardly necessary to add more details on the state of agriculture in Castile at the time of Ferdinand and Isabella. But does evidence of the decline of Castilian agriculture at the time derive solely from legal testimony?

No. It is a fact based on the conscientious studies carried out by Ibarra and Hamilton on the evolution of the grain problem in Castile. And as their findings agree, and are incontrovertible, we can state that in 1504 Ferdinand and Isabella's agrarian policy began to bear fruit in the form of a frightful crisis in the grain market, resulting in the massive importation of wheat, called "bread from oversea," after 1506.

If we study production during this period, we find an uninterrupted series of insufficient harvests from 1502 to 1508. Scarcity had been known before (1486 and 1491) and had forced the placing of a ceiling price on the *fanega* of wheat, setting it at 124 maravedís (the normal price in years of a good harvest was 50). But after 1502 this price-fixing not only failed to correct the scarcity of wheat, but its price rose out of all bounds: 600 maravedís in 1504 and 1506. Only the prompt importation of wheat avoided continuation of the ravages of famine; but the fatal result was that the fall in prices ruined the farmers who had sowed wheat under great difficulties in 1505.

The very serious threat of famine in 1506 was not the result of a series of adverse climatic circumstances, but of a deficient agrarian structure, produced by one-sided protection of livestock, absenteeism in rural areas, the expulsion of the Moriscos from Granada, latifundism, and the growth in power of the aristocratic class.

DEVELOPMENT OF INDUSTRIAL ECONOMY IN CASTILE. The traditional thesis holds that the Catholic Monarchs fomented Castilian industrial activity in every direction, and that they brought it to an extraordinary level of expansion. We must confess that we do not find evidence to confirm this statement. The industries usually mentioned in the books were either luxury items or had only a local market. The only flourishing industries worthy of the name were the iron production of the North and the fabrics of the central Castilian zone: Segovia, Soria, Avila, and Toledo in particular. And even in the development of the cloth industry we can observe two sharply differentiated phases—the first, a stage of crisis produced by the authorization to import foreign cloth, as a counterweight to the export of raw wool; the second, a stage of relative prosperity, coinciding with the early colonization of the Antilles (1505–1520). After that the Castilian cloth industry continued to grow, exporting its products not only to America and the traditional Portuguese market, but also to North Africa.

It would also seem possible to distinguish, as Klein does, between Ferdinand's policy and Isabella's. That is, after the death of the queen (who was the chief beneficiary of the Mesta's trade), the king effectively protected Castilian industry. But these are speculations which we have no time to look into. The incontrovertible fact is that after 1505 there was growing prosperity in Castilian industry, coinciding with the initial colonization of the Antilles and a favorable change in the direction of the long-term business cycle.

There is one other product which also underwent considerable development: the manufactured silk of Granada. (But only until 1503, the year in which the revolt of the *Moriscos* in Granada caused the silk industry to fall into a decline from which it did not emerge until the time of Charles V.)

The growing number of decrees regarding manufactures, which are so constantly mentioned in the texts, cannot hide the basic lack of coherence of Ferdinand and Isabella's industrial policy. For underneath them all, one fact sapped their effectiveness: the flight of the *conversos*. They had been the basic artisan class, and thus we can observe that soon after the Inquisition was established, Ferdinand and Isabella had to issue decrees calling for the presence in Spain of foreign artisans (1484). The lack of skilled manpower came to be felt even more strongly later, when America needed cloth and other products of the Spanish market.

EXPANSION OF THE CASTILIAN WOOL TRADE. It is in this area that Ferdinand and Isabella's favorable reputation among the historians of the past is fully justified. Their success derives not only from the fact that they carried out a mercantilist policy, but that they protected and favored the country's traditional wool trade.

Once Ferdinand and Isabella were seated on the throne, the wool trade was systematically organized. Thus, for example, they sent agents abroad who traveled to the various markets to find out about their needs, prices, and competition. The chief agents were permanent, residing in Bruges, La Rochelle, London, and Florence, from which cities they sent reports to the Court. Once they had collected the necessary information, they contacted the merchants of Burgos and the officials of the Mesta in order to organize exports.

In this regard we must point out the competition between the cities of Burgos and Bilbao, which had begun to appear during the previous reign. While Burgos controlled the wool market, Bilbao had control of shipping. The classic struggle between producer and carrier took place here, because Bilbao tried to carry out the transport of the raw product at high prices, counterbalancing Burgos' desire to control its rival's fleet in order to lower freight rates.

When Bruges gave the Biscayans great economic and commercial advantages in 1493, Burgos retaliated by obtaining from the sovereigns the famous privilege of 1494 creating the Consulate. This law granted Burgos *the monopoly of foreign trade in the Cantabrian Sea,* with the right to set freight rates on the coasts of Guipúzcoa, Biscay, and Santander, after informing the markets of the interior: Segovia, Vitoria, Logroño, Valladolid, Medina del Campo, and Medina de Ríoseco. This was a partial victory for Burgos, but, because it caused reprisals from Bilbao, one which resulted in the compromise agreement of 1499; Burgos obtained the exclusive right to authorize wool shipments to Flanders, Nantes, La Rochelle, and England, and permission to organize one annual fleet, while Bilbao retained the right to iron exports and one-third of the tonnage Burgos needed for wool shipment. In spite of this agreement, relations between Bilbao and Burgos continued to be strained, owing to the influence of citizens of Burgos at Isabella's court. Finally, Bilbao obtained from Ferdinand the privilege of 1511 creating the Consulate of that city, and then Burgos had to capitulate. This led to the agreement of 1513, which resembled that of 1499. But the merchant fleets of Santander and other Cantabrian ports lost their independence, and were not to recover it until 300 years later.

Let us mention at this point the internal wool markets. In accordance with the centralizing policy of Ferdinand and Isabella, they were reduced to three at this time: Medina del Campo, which was the queen's fair; Villalón, that of the Duke of Benavente; and Medina de Ríoseco.

Commercial life was given a strong stimulus because Ferdinand and Isabella made an effort to develop the technical instruments of trade. We cannot state unequivocally whether Isabella had a feel for commercial life or not. It is very possible that she did. On the other hand, we *can* make such a statement in regard to Ferdinand the Catholic, a great promoter of public works in the Crown of Aragon and in America. To demonstrate this we need only cite the fact that, when he got the news of the discovery of the Pacific by Vasco Núñez de Balboa, Ferdinand immediately ordered the creation of a port in Panama. In Spain itself too, the port of Bilbao dates from this period, as well as the paving of some highways and the organization of two important bodies, the *Brotherhood of Teamsters,* which in 1497 brought together the owners of oxcarts furnishing transport service within the country into the so-called *Royal Association of Teamsters;* and the great *Brotherhood of the Mails,* whose spiritual center was the chapel of Marcús in Barcelona. In the network of international communications of the period, Barcelona became the center of postal service for Italy, Germany, France, Aragon, Castile, and Portugal. In 1505 the monopoly of the Spanish postal service was granted to an Italian family named Tassis, and became the General Postal Service of Castile.

One fact should be pointed out concerning the technical organization of the merchant marine, apart from the laws on navigation which we shall discuss later. In 1498 an order was given by the terms of which the State paid a subsidy on the construction of ships of more than 600 tons. This measure has been very much argued over, for some historians accuse it of having been detrimental to merchant shipping in favor of a navy. At that time a ship of 200 tons could be sailed very satisfactorily; this was the size of the caravels which made the Atlantic crossing. Therefore, raising the tonnage limit to 600 in order to receive the subsidy meant favoring the construction of those enormous seagoing structures which were simply floating fortresses, rather than naval ships.

INSTITUTIONALIZATION OF THE CASTILIAN ECONOMY: GUILDS AND CONSULATES. The institutionalization of the Castilian economy is only one facet, in the economic sphere, of the transmission of administrative and technical information from the Crown of Aragon to Castile. Ferdinand the Catholic organized trade by setting up consulates and guilds copied from Catalonian models, just as he organized the chancellery, the administration of justice, and a number of other institutions imitating those of the Crown of Aragon.

As for the Consulates, their organization leaves no doubt that this was so. In the very document granting the Consulate of Burgos (1494), the statement is made that the merchants of the city ask for the same privileges as those enjoyed by the Consulate of the Sea in Barcelona. And when the Consulate of Bilbao was set up in 1511, it simply copied that of Burgos, which in fact meant returning to the original source, the Consulate of Barcelona.

The institutionalization of the guilds is no less obvious. Until 1475 the Castilian crown was opposed to guilds. Even in Henry IV's last Cortes "closed groups" (guild corporations) were banned once again, and the purpose of the brotherhoods was limited exclusively to pious concerns. This attitude changed radically after Ferdinand the Catholic came to the throne of Castile. Then guilds were set up with authorization from the State, which gave the cities power to grant ordinances concerning them. This was the case of Seville, Burgos, Segovia, and Valladolid after 1470, and especially after 1484.

It was also at this time that entrance examinations for trades, and the labor hierarchy of masters, journeymen, and apprentices, were introduced into Castile. The law-giving spirit which had characterized the last phase in the Catalonian guilds' evolution was also introduced. When Ferdinand dictated the Ordinances of Seville in 1511, which contained no less than 120 rules on the art of weaving cloth, he did no great favor to Castile, for its textile industry became influenced by the routine into which the Catalonian industry had fallen. At the end of the 15th and beginning of the 16th centuries, just at the moment when all Europe was starting to break loose from the guild, Ferdinand the Catholic put the corporative strait-jacket on the Castilians. If it had had more freedom of movement, perhaps the industrialization of Castile would have become a fact.

REFORM OF THE CURRENCY. Here also the Catholic Monarchs had a broad field of action for a positive policy, after the enormous dislocations brought about by the civil wars in Catalonia and Castile. They did not apply any exceptional ideas; what they did was to impose an honest and honorable administration on the minting and distribution of money.

Ferdinand and Isabella's system of monetary reform was very simple. Just as the Italian florin had been copied in the Peninsula in the 14th century, at the end of the 15th it was decided to imitate the medium of exchange which had the greatest acceptance in the international market: the *Venetian ducat*. In 1481 Ferdinand the Catholic created in Valencia the *excelente,* a coin which exactly corresponded in value to a Venetian ducat. It must be kept in mind that Valencia was the financial capital of Spain at the time, and this explains why the monetary reform stemmed from that city. The result was so propitious that in 1493 Ferdinand established a new monetary standard in Catalonia: the *principat,* equal to the Venetian ducat and to the Castilian excelente.

Reform was slower in Castile, for the war with Granada and the expulsion of the Jews did not permit the delicate operation of stabilizing the currency. Finally, on the fourteenth of June, 1497, Isabella and Ferdinand published the pragmatic decree or basic law of the Spanish monetary system that was to obtain for future centuries. The excelente of Granada was created as a *gold coin,* minted in $65\frac{1}{3}$ pieces from the mark of $22\frac{3}{4}$ carats, which had the same value—like the Valencian excelente and the Catalonian principat —as the Venetian ducat, and was often called so: *ducat.* The new *real* was introduced as a *silver coin,* minted in 66 pieces from the mark of 11 *dineros* and 4 grams (pure silver was considered to be divided into 12 dineros), as were its multiples (quadruples and octuples = the piece of 8 reales, issued especially by Charles V and equivalent to the Bohemian or Saxon "thaler") and subdivisions (half-, quarter-, and eighth-real coins). And finally, besides these gold and silver coins, a vellon coin was minted for small change, with a small quantity of silver. The coin called the *blanca* was minted of this metal, at the rate of 192 coins from the 6-gram mark. Ferdinand and Isabella, wishing to avoid inflation, had only 10 million blancas minted, an insufficient quantity that was to result in the influx of French vellon in exchange for American silver. To solve the problem, Charles V was obliged to lower the amount of silver in the blanca in 1552, and to mint 10 million more of these coins in 1558.

The coins we have just described were real ones. All of them were related among themselves by a money of account, the *maravedí,* to which they bore the following relationship: the excelente of Granada or ducat = 375 maravedís; the real = 34 maravedís; the blanca = one-half maravedí. A ducat, therefore, was worth 11 reales and 1 maravedí, or 750 blancas.

To sum up: for the first time, by about 1500, the three most important Spanish coins, the "excel·lent" of Valencia, the "principat" of Catalonia, and the excelente of Granada, or Castilian ducat, were all worth exactly the same. This was, in fact, *the only measure of economic unification* established by Ferdinand and Isabella. In regard to silver, on the other hand, since Castile kept receiving shipments from the Indies, little by little this metal began to spread from Castile into the kingdoms of the Crown of Aragon, devaluing the silver which circulated in Valencia and Catalonia; that is, the Valencian and Catalonian real. And this is why the Cortes of Valencia and Catalonia protested over and over in an attempt to avoid the influx of Castilian silver into their kingdoms, where it would produce loss in value and inflation. The Cortes of Monzón in 1511 succeeded in preventing this insofar as Valencia was concerned.

ORIGINS OF CASTILIAN MERCANTILISM: STATE MONOPOLIES. The origins of Castilian mercantilism have been studied by Hamilton. According to this author, its essential traits are as follows:

First, *imperialism,* brought about by the war with Granada and the military expansion into Italy and Africa. Second, the *prolonged drop in prices at the end of the 15th century;* the fall of prices favored mercantilism to the degree that it necessitated a measure of control over the money situation. Third, the *discovery of gold* in Hispaniola. Fourth, the *preponderance of the wool trade* and extractive industries, and the scarcity of manufactured goods. And fifth, the *need to develop the merchant marine in the Atlantic.*

Faced with these conditions, Ferdinand and Isabella took a number of measures to control the economy.

First, *the State undertook a monopoly of gold and silver.* This was a typically mercantilist measure, stemming from the belief that precious metals are the chief sources of well-being and universal wealth.

Second, *a system prohibiting the export of gold and silver* was established. There were already laws concerning this, but in 1480 Ferdinand and Isabella issued a famous pragmatic decree detailing the punishment, which even included the death penalty, for anyone who dared to take these metals out of Castile. This set a premium on smuggling, and consequently gold and silver went out of the country at a terrifying rate, so that in 1515 a new law on the subject had to be issued establishing an even more rigorous system of inspection.

Third, an attempt was made to maintain a *trade balance* which, if not favorable, would at least not be unfavorable. This is the sweet dream of mercantilism; so much bought, so much sold. The law was applied after 1491 in trade relations between Biscay, Navarre, and Castile, with the result that no merchant could cross a border unless he agreed to take out of the country as much merchandise as he brought in.

Fourth, *strict control of the metal coming from America* was decreed. When we speak of the Castilian monopoly in America, we are apt to forget that as far as metal was concerned, the monopoly was in the hands of the Castilian State. It was to the State's interest to control mines and ports of embarkation and disembarkation of the metal. The fewer people involved in the course of these operations, the smaller would be the leakage.

Other measures of a mercantilist type were the *navigation laws,* especially that of 1501 prohibiting the shipment of merchandise in foreign ships so long as there were Spanish ships in the ports (this measure was an imitation of the pragmatic decree issued by Alfonso V to Catalonia in 1451); and laws of *industrial protectionism,* such as the Ordinance of Seville of 1511.

FISCAL SYSTEM. Ferdinand and Isabella were certainly successful in their attempt to organize a State. In the administrative field their accomplishment was decisive, creating a number of organizations —the Councils—which centralized the work of government. Reform of the treasury was begun in 1480 by creating within the Royal Council the "Office of Chief Accountants of the Treasury Books and Royal Patrimony." This section was turned over to a hardworking Asturian, Alonso de Quintanilla. After that time royal revenues increased prodigiously, rising from some 800,000 maravedís in 1470 to the 22 million of 1504.

Although the administration functioned well and in consequence taxes were used more advantageously, there was no essential tax reform. The immunities of the nobles and clergy were maintained, while the poor commoner continued to be weighed down, as always, by the *alcabalas, sisas, tercias,* tithes, and the whole series of taxes which had come down from the Middle Ages. The only uniform contribution was the Bull of the Holy Crusade, obtained by Ferdinand and Isabella for use in the war with Granada. It produced a handsome sum of money for the Crown.

ECONOMIC LINKS AMONG THE KINGDOMS OF THE SPANISH MONARCHY. In 1479, just as Ferdinand and Isabella commenced to rule, the merchants of Catalonia felt that they had entered on a period of Hispanic "brotherhood"—according to words found in the documents. It is obvious that for the impoverished people and stagnant commerce of Catalonia, the idea of being able to count on markets such as Castile and Andalusia for their cloth, tools, coral, and spices was extremely attractive. They would also have been able to take part in the wool trade much more easily than other foreign intruders. However, these desires were frustrated, not because Castile had anything against the Catalans, but because its high financial circles were controlled by Genoese. Unfortunately, at that particular moment the Catholic Monarchs needed the Genoese more than the Catalans, and since the latter were in economic ruin, the sovereigns paid no attention to their insistent demands. The Cortes of Castile, for its part, shortsightedly refused to admit the Catalans to the fair of Medina del Campo on an equal footing, so that they continued to be regarded as foreigners. Thus the two sides of the Hispanic medieval economy, the Mediterranean and the Atlantic, lived separate lives throughout Ferdinand and Isabella's reign, establishing a fateful tradition which was not to be broken until the last third of the 18th century.

This fact is essential if we are to realize that Ferdinand and Isabella did not in fact aspire to the attainment of an effective unity in Spain; for the unity of a country, as we know all too well, begins with its economic infrastructure. The only link that existed among the kingdoms of the Hispanic monarchy was the monetary one. America could have been the decisive unifying force. Since in Castile the interests of the Genoese and the Mesta were so sacred that they could not permit an economic union between the Crowns of Aragon and Castile, America at least would have been an ideal field for a truly Hispanic common task.

Why, then—in practice, for there was no legal exclusion—was trade with America prohibited to the subjects of the Crown of Aragon? So many thousands of pages have been written about this problem that it would be a gigantic task even to try to sum it up. Let us point out, though, the conclusions to which the argument has led. The political version: Castilian-Catalan antagonism, and the desire of Ferdinand and Isabella to annihilate Catalonia. The legal version: America was the exclusive patrimony of Castile. As for the first point, there is nothing that proves such an assertion, and it is totally romantic; it will prove more useful to mention, later on, the opposition of the Sevillian monopolists to any kind of outside competition, including Catalan competition. As for the second point, the thesis of Ferdinand and Isabella's common property put forward by Professor Manzano undermines this solution and affirms Ferdinand's right and the right of his vassals to make use of half of the discoveries.

The controversy raised by these two points is outside the scope of this book. But we should like to point out three aspects of it which have not been adequately dealt with. First, the *mercantilist* aspect. From an economic point of view, it is obvious that the presence of non-Castilians in American trade was wholly disadvantageous to the Castilian State. Somebody had to carry on this trade, and it turned out to be the Castilians, for the Indies had been discovered by the Crown of Castile, though some Catalans and Aragonese took part in the discovery. This mercantilist position seems very justified to us, especially if we take into account the tradition created by the *Casa de Contratación de las Indias,* or House of Trade with the Indies, where this legislation was applied. Besides the mercantilist aspect, we must refer to what might be called *Catalonia's lack of interest.* This is an undeniable fact. The Catalans were not interested in America until well into the 16th century, when they took formal steps to engage in trade with the Indies. They were totally unconcerned during the reign of Ferdinand and Isabella. There was some question, as we have seen, of their taking part in Castilian trade, but of the Indies there is not a trace in the documents we have examined.

Last—the third aspect—this attitude of the Catalans was accompanied, on Ferdinand and Isabella's side, by a firm desire not to permit any Catalan, Aragonese, or Valencian noble or merchant to go to the Indies; they wished to avoid any application of the legalistic, pactist, and contractual spirit which had grown up in those regions during the Middle Ages. They had a hard enough time controlling the Castilians, in spite of the fact that the latter were accustomed to obeying an all-powerful monarchy. It is clear that the exclusion of the Catalans from America had something to do with the monarchs' desire *to rule the Indies without any sort of impediment.*

24 · Expansion of the Spanish Economy in America After the Discovery

GENERAL CHARACTERISTICS OF COLONIAL EXPANSION IN AMERICA IN THE FIRST HALF OF THE 16TH CENTURY. The first half of the 16th century witnessed one of the most impressive human accomplishments in history: Castile's expansion across the Atlantic and the discovery and colonization of America. At that moment Castile made history. And our thought is well summarized in the phrase "to make history," for making history is very difficult, and when a nation succeeds in inserting a wedge in the dense body of universal history and placing its name there, it can be then said that such a nation has fulfilled its destiny.

Perhaps no country but Castile, at the beginning of the 16th century, could have faced up to such an enormous task, and for the following reasons. First, the extraordinary vitality of the 15th-century Castilian; in spite of civil wars, of social disunity, of adverse circumstances, the Castilian of the period shows desires for greatness, perfection, and expansion which are obvious in his political and literary deeds. There was a consciousness of mission that was deeply felt, but whose final objective was unknown.

Second, the tension brought about by establishment of an authoritarian, administrative, and centralized government in the country. This abrupt restraint of the Castilian nobles, who had flown so high before Ferdinand and Isabella's reign, made them eager to take part in Spain's great task of discovery.

In the third place, the nomadic concept of life. The word nomadic is not used here in a pejorative sense, but reflects the continual desire for adventure. The nomadic shepherd, the *hidalgo* of the Reconquest, the man who yearned for new horizons, all went to America as a continuation of what they had been doing at home: constantly pressing forward, moving from one place to another. The conquest of America is not the accomplishment of a certain number of famous individuals who explored enormous tracts of land; it is the history of successive Castilian emigrations, of the men who first flocked to the Antilles, then the Isthmus, and then into Mexico and Peru.

A fourth factor was the strong craving for material wealth. It must not be believed that the Castilians went to America out of a pure missionary urge; the myth of gold shone in the minds of those valiant *hidalgos,* ruined by the great landowners. These people, who had a vital energy which they could not possibly put to work in large-scale business (for which they were not prepared in any case), found an escape valve in the gleam of gold and silver, in the dream of riches attained at one fell swoop, either by some lucky stroke or by the acquisition of lands and Indians.

Finally, there was the spirit of mission and of justice, for throughout the course of the 15th century there had arisen in Castile a select number of men who felt that their people were linked to an evangelizing mission. And further, they went to America with a tremendous desire for justice, for establishing a new order of things. However, in the economic aspect the Church was enormously conservative; and so, together with the spirit of justice, it established in America the same seigniorial system, the same latifundist and mortmain organization as in Spain.

These five factors trace a certain line on the graph of History. Castile, the conqueror of America, thought of the Indies as the exclusive patrimony of the country's collective wealth. It was a separate preserve in which, though a certain amount of collaboration was permitted, no interference could be countenanced. Thus America was set up to be a greater Castile, with all Castile's virtues and defects.

CONQUISTADORES AND COLONIZERS IN AMERICA. Once America was discovered in 1492, the years that followed the discovery were ones of tremendous disillusionment. Columbus had trumpeted propaganda about the supposed Indies he had found. The reality was very different. Absolutely nothing came from America. It was a fabulously rich continent, but it was underpopulated and had neither a social nor a political structure which could permit the utilization of its natural treasures. In consequence, the Castilians found at first that the efforts they had made to reach the Indies were fruitless. This great disillusionment was overcome by the desire to make use

316

of these lands for colonization. Therefore, after Columbus' third voyage in 1497, seeds and flocks, tools and utensils, were sent to America to form the basis for colonization of the Antilles.

This first period of colonization, stimulated by Ferdinand's order breaking Columbus' monopoly and opening the Caribbean to all Spanish discoverers, taught the Castilians much. Bartering for pearls and gold was begun on the continent, while the first plantations were developed in the Antilles. But in 1521 the discovery of Mexico took place, and in a short space of time Cortez shipped more gold to Spain than had been sent since 1492. At the same time, news of the existence of Peru was received, of temples covered with gold and the wealth amassed by the Incas. Once more, the discoverer won out over the colonizer. The Antilles were practically depopulated. Impelled by the same frenzy which brought people from all over the world to California in the 19th century, Castilians emigrated to the fabulous kingdoms of Mexico and Peru in such numbers that in the course of a single generation they settled all over the immense territory stretching from the Rio Grande to Tierra del Fuego.

By 1560 the era of discovery was over, and a phase of colonization was entered upon. Farmers and the industrial classes were now to dominate. The future of America was in the hands of these men, avid for adventure, land, and precious metals.

DEMOGRAPHY AND DISTRIBUTION OF PROPERTY. Until 1560 there were few Spaniards in America. By means of the permits granted after 1493, we can estimate that some 15,000 Spaniards arrived officially in the New World during the first half of the 16th century. But this figure is not statistically reliable, for the number of illicit emigrants was considerable. It is very possible that the number of Spaniards living in America was close to 120,000 by the middle of the century. Knowing that the native inhabitants totaled approximately 12 million (reduced to a little over 9 million in the course of fifty years), we can have some idea of the difficulty of organizing so vast a world with so few people, and furthermore, of having to use natives of such a low cultural and technological level. This explains the form which property took in America: on the one hand, continuation of the Castilian latifundia system, especially in New Spain; and on the other, the articulation of property into a system which, though it was neither feudal nor seigniorial, established a rigid social hierarchy.

If we keep in mind the basic principle that the soil and subsoil of the Indies were considered to belong to the Crown, there were two systems of distribution of land—by allotment and by grace or favor. *Allotment* was made by the king, giving the conquistadores, captains, and governors the privilege of distributing lands as they saw fit. These allotments were to respect what were called from the outset "Indian reserves"; that is, the territory left to the Indians for their own needs. Further, the beneficiary had to promise not to exercise any jurisdiction over the properties granted him, and to reside on them and cultivate them. This shows that the intention of the Castilian Crown was to grant the property to serve social and fiscal needs.

Grace or *favor* came later. The Council of the Indies granted this by patent. A person asked permission to go to the Indies and presented his titles or honors; then he was given a *peonía* or *caballería*. A *peonía* was exactly half of a *caballería,* equivalent respectively to 100,000 and 200,000 *montones,* a measurement derived from the earliest times of the colonization of the Antilles. A *peonía* property included: a lot on which to build a house, 100 *hanegas* of farm land, 10 *hanegas* for growing corn, two *huebras* (a measurement based on the amount of land one man could plow in a day with a yoke of oxen) for a vegetable garden, 8 for fruit, and enough land to pasture 10 sucking pigs, 20 cows, 5 mares, 100 sheep, and 20 goats. This was a good-sized property. The *caballería,* being twice as large, had the further advantage that it offered ownership of grazing land, while in the *peonías* pasture land was held in common.

Stated in this legal form, the history of property in America seems very clear. But examined in its real light it presents a very different picture. We can begin to understand the true situation when we realize that in certain American countries, at the beginning of our century, land was sold "by eye"; that is, taking in everything that could be seen from some hill or summit. Around 1560, it is doubtful whether anybody knew how much land he owned. And aside from the aforementioned procedures, it was enough for any person to cultivate land for forty years in order to make it his. This is why it became necessary, in the course of time, to confirm ownership of land. The bureaucrats came into this operation, wielding their pens to reshape the ownership of land to their own advantage.

THE NATIVE AND THE CONQUEST: ENCOMIENDA AND MITA. Tons of ink have been consumed over this issue, some authors attacking the Castilans (thus the origin of the "Black Legend"), and others defending them (hence the "White Legend"). In reality there were forces at work which we must attempt to understand. Modern studies are strongly rooted in this understanding, which is both impartial and humane. Such studies show that the juridical foresight of the Castilian Crown was deformed by the realities of economic life and the differing physical characteristics of conquerors and natives.

Jurists and theologians tried to resolve the problem presented by immediate relations between Castilians and Indians by asking two questions: To whom did the Indies belong? and, To whom did the Indians belong?

To whom *did* the Indies belong? After the period of Ferdinand and Isabella there was no uniformity of opinion about this question. There is an enormous body of literature concerning the so-called "just rights" of the possession of the Indies by Castile. Some said that Castile possessed them by right of conquest; others, by Papal donation. But neither side could deny the fact that certain politically organized groups neither dependent on the Holy See nor in open war with Spain existed in America. This is why Francisco de Vitoria expressed the opinion that neither the conquest nor the Papal donations could assure Spain's right to the Indies. Only their evangelization could justify a possession which was limited by the rights of the previous occupants of the country. However, the official theory continued to be that the Papal bulls of donation and the conquest confirmed Castile's right to hold the Indies.

Since we know the State's opinion, and since we can be sure that Castile did consider itself to be the owner of the Indies and that therefore it, and not the chiefs and headmen of the Indians, exercised supreme power there, we face the second question: To whom did the natives belong? The first conquistadores solved the problem by enslaving them. They adopted the procedure of all colonizing peoples when they face a strange environment, a difficult climate, and a race reduced to obedience by force of arms. However, the Crown forbade the enslavement of Indians, and so a new social category arose: the Indian who was *encomendado,* or "commended."

Encomienda was an intermediate system between European feudalism and native caciquism. When the distribution of lands was made, to which we have referred before, Indians were also distributed with the land to cultivate the soil, and were "commended" to the care of the person holding the land grant (*encomendero*). Theoretically, *encomienda* was based on principles which could not have been more humane: the grantee agreed to Christianize the Indian and not to treat him as a vassal; he further agreed to respect the Indian's personal property, and not to consider him as a chattel or subject him to personal abuse.

At least this was the contention of the Spanish Crown. Quite different procedures were used in the Indies. An incompatibility between theory and practice grew up, to the point that in 1526 a dangerous reversal favoring the grantee's jurisdiction was decreed; and in 1536, by means of trickery, hereditary *encomiendas* were established. From there, feudalism and serfdom to the land were only a step away. But that step was not taken because of the Crown's firmly ethical attitude.

There were individuals—there always are—who defended the practice of *encomienda* from a Thomistic point of view. They contended that Aristotle had established a category of inferior beings who served their superiors, and that the American Indian belonged to the first group. This was the thesis maintained by Ginés de Sepúlveda. But neither he nor his followers counted on the vehemence of Father Las Casas, nor with the spirit of justice which inflamed the theologians of the period, who never relaxed until they made the court admit the theory that the Indians were human beings like everyone else. From that instant, *encomienda* was doomed to extinction.

In 1542 the famous New Laws were published banning personal servitude by "commended" Indians and preparing for the abolition of the system by decreeing that no *encomienda* could be sold or inherited. This law provoked violent rebellions in New Spain and Peru. The Crown was forced to give ground, except in the matter of personal servitude (1546). But a mental climate was established which led to the inevitable decline of the *encomiendas.*

Another link between native and conqueror was *mita.* Since after

1542 the Crown regulated the expansion of the *encomienda* system, the Castilians found themselves without laborers to work the mines of Potosí, discovered in 1545. Then they resorted to the system already used by the Incas. To exploit the mines, build fortresses, and make roads, the Incas had established the *mita*. It consisted in requiring each tribe of Indians to supply annually, for a varying period of time, a contingent of men for forced, though paid, labor. The Indian spent two of the twelve months of the year working in his fields gathering corn and storing up food for his family. The other ten he worked as a laborer in the mines and on public works.

Officially, *mita* was established in 1575 by Viceroy Toledo in Peru. After that time it developed greatly and supplied a large part of the labor force in colonial Spanish America.

COLONIAL AGRICULTURE AND LIVESTOCK: INTRODUCTION OF THE NEGRO SLAVE. After 1497 the Crown's constant concern was to bring to America as many agricultural and animal resources as could foster development of the newly discovered countries. In the opinion of Gino Luzzato, the chief role carried out by Spain between 1490 and 1560 was precisely that of initiating agriculture in America, in order to convert the New World into a supply market for the overpopulated European continent.

The work accomplished was considerable: wheat, rye, and rice seeds were sent; also plants, such as sugar cane, orange and olive trees, vines; tools, such as plows and hoes; and livestock in quantity—horses, asses, oxen, goats, sheep, etc.

The State established prizes for agricultural production. But discovery of the treasures of Mexico and Peru paralyzed the development of farming in the Antilles. The only agricultural product that had any real weight in the early commercial economy of the Antilles was *sugar*. An account of the year 1550 states that New Spain had also made a certain amount of progress, for sugar, cochineal, and a little cotton could be exported; and the chronicler adds, "for nothing comes from Peru." That is, by about 1560 an initial period of colonization had been achieved, but decisive results had not been attained in agriculture.

The same can be said of livestock. There was a phase of slow development, assisted by the famous Mesta, which had passed from

Castile to New Spain. In 1529 it obtained the same privileges as the Castilian mother organization, and therefore it controlled the flocks and the wool trade, centralized the market, and brought about expansion of the agrarian latifundist economy.

The development of colonial agriculture, once it was realized that indigenous labor gave unsatisfactory results, fell on the shoulders of Negro slaves, whose introduction had been authorized by Isabella the Catholic in 1501. However, the slave trade did not become really active until 1518. It was in the hands of Portuguese, Dutch, and Germans. Fairly approximate figures indicate that in 1570 the Negro, mulatto, and mixed population of the New World was some 230,000 souls.

EXPLOITATION OF MINES: THEIR IMPORTANCE IN SPANISH AND WORLD ECONOMY. It was the myth of gold that attracted the Spanish colonizers. From the earliest times of the conquest, the old legend of El Dorado and the new legend of the Mountain of Silver were already located in American territory; the adventurers' imagination placed these in the region of Colombia and the interior of the continent. We should note that this fever for precious metals was due as much to the news brought by the earliest explorers as to the monetary contraction which Europe was undergoing. In this respect we must recall the rerouting of Sudanese gold by the Portuguese, and the fact that it became part of the trade with Far Eastern countries. Mintings of silver, and even of copper, became more and more numerous in order to make up for the scarcity of gold; these mintings utilized the products of the German mines, which reached their highest point of production between 1470 and 1540. But the lack of gold really ended only when, passing from myth to reality, exploitation of the treasures of America became an actual fact.

Let us take a look at the geography and chronology of mining, its yield and its effects.

GEOGRAPHY AND CHRONOLOGY. The following places and phases of exploitation should be pointed out:

Gold panning in the Antilles and the Caribbean. Includes the years 1503–1520.

Utilization of the *treasures of Mexico* (1521–1544). This industry, whose peak occurred from 1521 to 1537 and then fell off sharply after 1544, was concurrent with the exploitation of the gold deposits of *New Granada*.

First exploitation of the silver mines of the *Mountain of Potosí*. This revolutionized the world by producing the start of the great flow of silver to the European market (1545–1556).

Introduction of the *amalgamating technique* in the silver lodes, carried out by Bartolomé de Medina using German methods. This new procedure, applied to the extraction of silver in New Spain and Peru, required the shipment of quicksilver from Almadén during the first few years (1556–1564).

In 1564, the discovery of the *Huancavélica mine* furnished the greater part of the mercury needed for amalgamating silver. This marked the beginning of the most important phase of mining exploitation in the Spanish possessions.

YIELD. The treasure of the Indies was essentially composed of gold and silver, but Hamilton's figures, though they are unsatisfactory in absolute terms, confirm the great predominance of silver over gold. According to this scholar, who patiently examined the books of the House of Trade, 185,000 kilograms of gold arrived in Seville between 1503 and 1660, compared to 16,886,000 of silver. That is, in the 160 years he studied, the amount of silver imported was more than ninety times the amount of gold. This fact is very important, for it allows us to gauge the influence of both metals on the European economy: while American gold raised by only one-fifth the amount available in the Old World, imported silver tripled the amount in existence, and silver alone was responsible for the so-called price revolution.

Here is a summary of silver imports in three great periods:

1531–1580	2,628,000 kg. = 15%
1581–1630	11,362,000 kg. = 67%
1631–1660	2,896,000 kg. = 17%
1531–1660	16,886,000 kg.

This means that the greater part of the silver arrived in 1581–1630, with the largest amount reached in the years 1591–1600 (2,707,000 kilograms). After that time imports decreased considerably, but up to 1600—a fact which has often been forgotten—

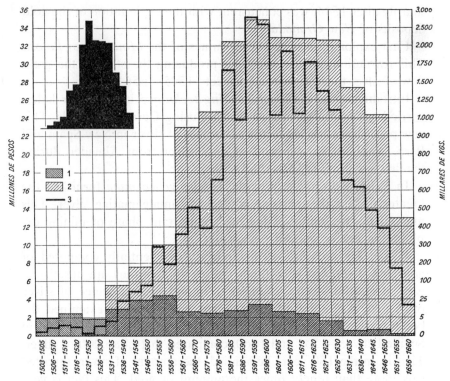

GRAPH OF IMPORTS OF AMERICAN METAL INTO SPAIN.—*Key:* 1, gold; 2, silver; 3, combined value of imports. Scale altered to show gold imports. At upper left, actual graph of silver imports in kilograms.

they maintained a level considerably higher than that of 1531–1580. We have no figures for the first years of the 16th century, but we know that exploitation of mines was in its infancy then. As for gold, the largest quantities came in from 1541–1560, some 70,500 kilograms and 38% of the total.

EFFECTS. The impact of silver on Spanish, and more importantly on European, prices will be studied later. Here we wish only to make clear that the figures cited above refer to controlled official shipments and not to the absolute yield of American mines. Illicit trade, outside the scope of official documents, was so brisk that we may agree, with Carande, that Hamilton's figures represent only about half of the production. This circumstance naturally invalidates the calculations of the silver and gold ratios made by Luzzato and other authors in reference to different times in the 16th and

17th centuries. We can only say, without going into more detail, that this ratio, maintained at 1:11 throughout the 15th century, changed enormously in favor of silver as a result of the colonization of America.

BEGINNINGS OF INDUSTRY IN AMERICA. In order to take up this subject, we must keep in mind the figures we quoted above in regard to the consumers' market which America represented at that time: 150,000 Spaniards and some 12 million Indians who, furthermore, did not have needs which implied large quantities of goods.

In spite of efforts both by the State and by private individuals, development of industry in the New World was hampered by three factors: Seville's monopoly, contraband trade, and absence of tradition. There were some industries, however, derived from agriculture, livestock, and mining, which gained a certain importance from the outset. Thus, for example, in the field of forestry the Spaniards took out of America Brazil wood, campeche wood, mahogany, and cedar; in agriculture, olive oil, used in the manufacture of soap; and especially, as has already been stated, sugar, first exported to Spain in 1522. As for livestock, this industry was particularly concerned with the obtention of hides and salted meat. In the area of minerals, apart from the precious metals we have already mentioned, there was mining of copper and iron, and exploitation of salt.

Attempts at starting a textile industry deserve special mention. In the early stages there was a certain amount of freedom in America regarding cloth manufacture. It seems that between 1548 and 1569 the difficulties which the Spanish industry was undergoing in supplying its domestic market were the occasion for granting a certain amount of liberty to establish textile industries in the American colonies. Thus workshops arose in New Spain, Quito, and Peru. But after 1569 a rigid monopoly was established in favor of the mother country, leading to exclusivism on the one hand and, on the other, to decline of the industries which had begun to arise in America.

THE INDIES TRADE. Much has been written about early trade in the Indies, and about commercial relations between the mother country and her colonies. The chief works date from 1917 and were written by Artiñano, a Spaniard, and Haring, an American. Although these works have contributed greatly toward clearing up certain problems regarding this trade, much exact data are still lacking which undoubtedly will be supplied by Chaunu's work on Seville and the Atlantic trade.

If we keep these studies in mind, we can say that from 1492 to 1560, the closing date of this period, trade does not appear to be a closed organization. We should also mention that it was not large-volume trade, for it was limited by what the colonies could consume and to such colonial products as could be absorbed by the home country. Generally speaking, exports from Spain included quicksilver, used, as we have said, in amalgamating silver; wine, especially from the Lower Andalusian area; cloth from the whole central part of the Peninsula; and luxury goods. Nor should we forget the export of men, for recent studies show that men crammed all the ships which left from Seville and Cádiz. The colonies exported to Spain, in the first place, gold and silver, so that for a long time the nickname of "silver fleet" describing the ships which traded between America and Spain was no misnomer. Aside from these precious metals we must include dye-producing woods, Brazil and campeche wood, which were very much in demand, wool from Mexico, and sugar from the Antilles.

THE HOUSE OF TRADE. In 1503 Ferdinand and Isabella created the House of Trade as a private office dependent on the Crown for business matters relating to the Indies trade and patterned on the Portuguese model. It was believed that the task of monopolizing trade between Spain and America would be easy, centralizing it by this means and making it circulate through the channels of this organization. But after the disillusionment suffered in the early years of the discovery, a new structure was given to the House of Trade in 1510. The decrees issued at that time established the administrative and bureaucratic nature of this center. It was a sort of trade ministry with special powers for guarding fleets, for colonial administration, for passage to America, and for enforcement of the commercial treaties in existence as a result of this economic movement. The House of Trade was also a mercantile tribunal. Later, in 1526, it became a dependency of the Council of the Indies

(*Consejo de Indias*), founded at that date; and therefore the House of Trade became subordinated to the central department of the Crown and lost a large part of its earlier importance, though of course it always maintained some prestige as Spain's chief economic instrument in America.

The Guild of the Merchants of Seville was closely related to the House of Trade. This consulate was founded in 1543 in imitation of those already existing in Bilbao and Burgos. The Merchant Guild of Seville represented the combined power of Genoese and Andalusians, which was so great that the Sevillian monopoly grew up as a result of it. This monopoly, which has been judged by historians as competent as Céspedes del Castillo to be clearly uneconomical, thus became definitively established.

THE INDIES FLEET. Mindful of the example established by the Venetians in the Mediterranean and imitated by the Portuguese in the Atlantic, that of sailing in convoys, the Spanish fleet adopted this system for American trade. It was successful at first because it utilized the experience gathered over a long period of time and permitted navigation under favorable conditions, and in particular offered protection from the pirates of all nationalities who menaced Spanish shipping at crucial points along the way: Cape St. Vincent, the Canaries, the Azores, and the Antilles.

In fact this system was not rigidly set up until 1563, so that the period we are now studying was one simply of gaining experience. Until 1560 the ships were of small tonnage, with a mean size which Chaunu places at around 100 tons. After that year an abrupt change can be observed: ships began to exceed 300 tons displacement, and this indicates a very important change in the general economic conditions in Spain, America, and Europe.

In 1521, as a result of the war with France, a coast guard fleet was organized to protect transatlantic ships from pirates; this was financed by a tax called the *derecho de averia,* or risk tax, paid by the merchants who traded with America. This coast guard grew in time until it became included in the flotilla system; so that in each flotilla there were two ships, the "capitana" and the "almiranta," which formed the vanguard and the rear guard of the convoy and kept a lookout for possible adversaries who might attack it.

We should keep one important fact in mind: the small number of ships making up these fleets which sailed between Spain and America up to the year 1560. Average figures show some 80 ships per year. When we compare this with traffic existing in the Sund, in the North Sea, at the same period, in excess of 500 ships per year, it seems almost incredible that there should have been so few. But their historical and economic interest is much greater. They really formed the umbilical cord between two continents, Europe and America. While the Sund engaged in mere coastwise trade, the Indies fleet, by contrast, represented the birth of a whole new world, into which all the material and spiritual resources of Spain were to be poured.

FLUCTUATIONS IN SPANISH ECONOMIC POLICY IN RELATION TO THE INDIES TRADE; THE MERCANTILIST SOLUTION. The Spanish State did not have a fixed policy in regard to trade with the Indies. After Columbus' monopoly, which was broken in 1497, the Crown entered upon a policy after 1503 which attempted to establish an absolute monopoly on trade between Castile and the New World. This was the origin of the House of Trade, imitated from the Agency for Negroes (Casa dos Negros) in Lisbon, whose sole purpose was to direct this monopoly. Its failure caused a shift in the direction of a more liberal policy (1510). It was then that a subsidiary branch of the House of Seville was founded in Cádiz, and greater facilities were given for trade with America. This liberal policy was reinforced during the period of Charles V by the Ordinance of 1529, by whose terms nine Castilian ports were opened to commerce with America (Corunna, Bayonne, Avilés, Laredo, Bilbao, and San Sebastián in the North; Cartagena, Málaga and Cádiz in the South), and a House of Trade was even established in Corunna. This arrangement declined when precious metals began to flow into Spain and strict control over their circulation became necessary. Then, the House of Trade and the Merchant Guild of Seville began to recover their old importance, and there was an attempt to set up a monopoly. This is why the Ordinance of 1529 was repealed in 1573, and Seville was given the exclusive monopoly of American trade.

This mercantilist solution of the problem of trade with America has been variously judged by historians. Carande defends the monopoly, believing that it was the only existing possibility for an integral colonization of America. Céspedes de Castillo, however, attacks it, holding that mercantilism benefited only Seville, and that Seville's selfishness choked off the possibilities for a more liberal experience of colonization and industrialization in America.

25 · Demographic and Social Structure
in the 16th Century

GENERAL DEMOGRAPHIC PROCESS. The Black Death, which rav-
aged the country about the middle of the 14th century, produced an
extremely serious drop in the population. Biological stagnation followed the extraordinary mortality of the period and lasted until the
end of the 15th century. After this time the population gradually
recovered, attaining a remarkable rate of increase—something like
40%—in the last two-thirds of the 16th century. This increase particularly affected the Castilian and Andalusian cities, which doubled
their population in the course of some sixty years.

In the Crown of Castile the period from 1530 to 1540, with a
mean increase of 65,000 persons annually, coincides with the
period of maximum recovery. Later, from 1540 to 1595, the annual rate of increase was only 40,000 inhabitants. At that time
many Castilian cities were already in a new phase of decline. This is
especially true of those which had benefited from the great commercial and financial axis of Medina-Bilbao-Antwerp, broken off in
1575. Thus, Medina's population fell from 20,000 inhabitants to
13,000, and Valladolid's from 38,000 to 33,000.

Catalonia's recovery came later. In 1553 the census of households gave figures lower by 40,000 inhabitants, that is, 10% less,
than those of 1359. However, and in response to a phenomenon
which was general all over the Mediterranean world, Catalonia
largely recovered during the second half of the century. The new
Barcelona-Genoa axis had something to do with this demographic
rise; it had taken the place of the old Medina-Bilbao-Antwerp axis
whose breakup, as we have mentioned, had spelled the ruin of a
number of cities in Old Castile and Cantabria. The demographic
surge in Catalonia lasted until approximately 1620.

Once into the 17th century Spain sank into a new demographic
depression (loss of some 25% of its population?) with the lowest

point around 1650 and the start of a reaction by the end of the century.

REGIONAL VARIATIONS. Data for the period are scarce and do not come from the same years in the different regions. Notwithstanding these difficulties, Ruiz Almansa has been able to reconstruct the population picture for about the year 1600.

POPULATION AND AREA OF THE PENINSULAR KINGDOMS

	Sq. km.	Per cent	Inhab- itants	Per cent	Inhab- itants per sq. km.
Crown of Castile	378,000	65.2	8,304,000	73.2	22.0
Crown of Aragon	100,000	17.2	1,358,000	12.0	13.6
Kingdom of Navarre	12,000	2.1	185,000	1.6	15.4
Kingdom of Portugal	90,000	15.5	1,500,000	13.2	16.7
Total for the Peninsula	580,000	100.0	11,347,000	100.0	19.6

Castile, then, accounted for two-thirds of the area of the Peninsula and three-quarters of the population. On its flanks the Crown of Aragon and Portugal, with a like area, had a similar population, although the Portuguese contingent was relatively greater. What stands out, therefore, is the *greater density in Castile*.

Regional differences within the Crowns of Castile and Aragon are given below:

CROWN OF CASTILE

	Sq. km.	Per cent	Inhab- itants	Per cent	Inhab- itants per sq. km.
NORTHERN ZONE (Basque country, Santander, Asturias and Galicia)	53,000	14.0	1,452,000	17.5	27.4

CROWN OF CASTILE (*Continued*)

	Sq. km.	Per cent	Inhab-itants	Per cent	Inhab-itants per sq. km.
CENTRAL ZONE (Pyrenees to Tagus; Castile and León, Guadalajara, Toledo and Madrid)	135,000	35.7	3,510,000	42.2	26.0
INTERMEDIATE ZONE (Tagus to Sierra Morena; La Mancha and Extremadura)	90,000	23.8	1,434,000	17.3	15.9
SOUTHERN ZONE (Andalusia and Murcia)	100,000	26.5	1,908,000	23.0	19.1
Total	378,000	100.0	8,304,000	100.0	22.0

CROWN OF ARAGON

	Sq. km.	Per cent	Inhab-itants	Per cent	Inhab-itants per sq. km.
Kingdom of Aragon	47,083	46.0	399,300	29.4	8
Principality of Catalonia	32,154	31.3	374,500	27.6	12
Kingdom of Valencia	23,222	22.6	583,800	42.9	30
Total	102,459	100.0	1,357,600	100.0	13

The precision of these figures leaves little room for comment. We need only sum up the essential conclusion reached from perusing them: "In the 16th century the population of the Peninsula had a markedly centripetal character, with a large central mass which acted like a center of gravity on the populations of less density or volume located in the peripheral zone."

MIGRATORY MOVEMENTS. *Internal migrations*. In chronological order, we may point out the following:

Displacement of *Castilians and Galicians toward the South,* caused by the Andalusian monopoly on trade with the Indies. Seville and Cádiz were the focal points of this movement, especially Seville, which in the course of only sixty years (1530 to 1590) doubled the number of its inhabitants, rising from 45,000 to 90,000.

Expulsion of the *Moriscos of Granada* after their revolt in 1568. This event affected some 70,000 to 80,000 families, the larger number of whom settled in Valencian territory. Castile also received an important contingent, however, and their presence has been observed as far north as Palencia. The departure of these New Christians was counterbalanced by the arrival in Granada of people from the North and center of the Peninsula.

Descent of the *Catalans of the Pyrenees* to the lowlands. This was a process which was to have important repercussions, becoming marked after the middle of the 16th century and continuing throughout the 17th and 18th. Barcelona, to give but one example, is a city almost wholly descended from people of the Pyrenees.

External migrations. Fundamentally this was a double-pronged movement, both of entrance and exit.

Departure of Spaniards for America. In what numbers? The answer to this question is still unknown. The official registers of the Archive of the Indies mention 15,480 emigrants from 1509 to 1558. But these figures must be considered as very far from the real ones because of the total lack of listings for twenty-one of the fifty years included between the two dates. And too, there is the question of the "llovidos," or those who embarked fraudulently. Andalusians and Extremadurans predominated among the emigrants. Aragonese and Navarrese were excluded by Queen Isabella from "the dealings and profits of the Indies"; the effectiveness of this order is doubtful, and certainly meant nothing at all after the queen's death (1504); non-Castilians were considered as foreigners only in the matter of obtaining public office in the Indies. This distinction lasted until 1581, when all citizens of the Peninsula were deemed to be equal, even for public office. To sum up, then: as we have said before, the most judicious estimates place at some 120,000 the number of Spaniards who emigrated to America up to the middle of the 16th century.

Related to this emigration to the Indies is the problem, likewise still unsolved, of Spanish soldiers and employees of the State, mostly Castilians, lost to the mother country in the service of her foreign enterprises.

In contrast to these figures is the arrival of foreign settlers in Spain. Two groups merit special attention: the Genoese and the French, to whom we shall refer in a later paragraph.

SOCIAL DISSIDENTS AND UNASSIMILATED CLASSES: CONVERSOS, MORISCOS, AND SLAVES. In spite of the expulsion of the Jews and the elimination of a goodly number of *conversos* and Moriscos at the time of Ferdinand and Isabella, the Spain of the 16th century was far from presenting the racial and spiritual homogeneity which those monarchs had tried to impose. The mingling of blood during the Late Middle Ages had been so prolonged, and private resistance to any creed imposed from without so tenacious, that the first two Hapsburg kings had very difficult problems to face. These problems stemmed from the presence of dissident elements, more or less concealed, and from the intransigent attitude of those who wished to defend at any price purity of blood and religion with no admixture of any kind. And to this circumstance we must add the rapid spread of slavery in the prosperous Castile of the 16th century.

We have just mentioned the *Moriscos* as a large group of people forced to emigrate to other parts of Spain. Though we lack wholly trustworthy figures, the most recent researches have helped to give us a fairly exact idea of their number. Some 200,000 Moriscos (former Mudéjares, forced to convert to Christianity in 1521), lived in the Crown of Aragon, while in the Crown of Castile, where conversion had been decreed as early as 1502, there were fewer than 100,000; the most important centers were in Valencia and the old kingdom of Granada, until the rebellion of the Alpujarras, when it became necessary to disperse them. The Moriscos were essentially peasants (tenant farmers, renters, and day laborers); but many were artisans in the cities, and some even managed to break into the preserve of the industrial bourgeoisie during the half-century of prosperity. The revolt in the Alpujarras, as well as the displacement of population which followed it, caused the Moriscos to adopt an attitude of resentment and suspicion toward the monarchy. The "uprooted Morisco" created the climate of social unrest which led to the dramatic general expulsion of 1613.

The *conversos,* both of old and recent origin, who lived within the Spanish State, continued to enjoy a good economic position and a bad social reputation. The problem of crypto-Judaism continued to exist throughout the 16th century and was damaging to those *conversos* who were really sincere. This problem gave rise to another which was no less serious: that of the definitive separation of Castilian society into two blocs, divided by the barrier of "proofs of purity of blood"—the Old Christians, with no stain of Jewish ancestry, and the New Christians, or *conversos,* who could not aspire to important bureaucratic or Church offices. They made up a total of some 300,000 individuals, the majority of them tradesmen and artisans, though there was a select minority who managed to blot out their racial or religious origins, became part of the Old Christian group, and exercised part of the governing power. In any case, the controversy over purity of blood stimulated the tendency of the Old Christian to take up the attitude of the *hidalgo* (which implied an aversion both to industrial work and to any form of trade).

As for slaves, their number grew rapidly in the 16th century. Domínguez Ortiz estimates their number as 100,000 individuals at the end of the 16th century, the high point of slavery in Spain. About half were in Andalusia. Seville was the chief slave market, and had connections with Russia and Guinea. Negro slaves were especially numerous.

FOREIGN COLONIES IN SPAIN: GENOESE AND FRENCH. *The Genoese.* The subjects of the Republic of Genoa had traditionally shown an interest in Spanish business dealings. From the times of Ferdinand III and Alfonso the Wise they had maintained a good-sized colony in Seville, while in the Mediterranean they not only kept up a fierce rivalry with the business community of Barcelona, but also became established in the mercantile cities of Catalonia and Valencia.

A spectacular decision by Andrea Doria renewed this tradition, and the Genoese received from Charles V a reconfirmation of all the privileges they had accumulated in the course of the Late Middle Ages up to 1500, the year in which these privileges had been revoked by Ferdinand the Catholic. After 1528, date of the new agreement, the Genoese played a principal role in Spanish finance, along with the German families of Welser and Fugger. Their enormous loans to the Crown made them arbiters of the most important political and military decisions, and of the most remunerative of tax-farming operations and the holding of *juros* (bonds on public revenue). This situation became even more favorable after the separation of Spain from the Empire; in this regard, the provisions of Charles V's will reinforced Genoese control of Spanish finance and commerce. We know, for example, that in 1575 Philip II granted them the monopoly on salt and of taxes on ecclesiastical property; and that in 1595 the Venetian ambassador, Vendramin, calculated that of the 80 million gold and silver ducats imported from America after 1530, some 24 million, or 30%, had gone into the pockets of the Genoese.

In another sphere, and taking constant advantage of the privileges granted to them by Charles V, the subjects of the Genoese Republic played in Spain the role of the Japanese in modern times; they flooded the country with cheap manufactured products, designed especially for the Indies, to the serious detriment of local industry. But Genoa's participation in the benefits of trade with America had other causes too, such as, for example, the slave trade, the monopoly of which was granted to them on several occasions.

In contrast to this information, we do not know very much about the actual number of Genoese in Spain. There were colonies of them in all the great mercantile centers, but their size is unknown. It has been estimated that by the beginning of the 17th century there were some 10,000 in the kingdom of Castile and perhaps a somewhat larger number in Aragon. At any rate, we can state that the Genoese merchants who had settled in Spain were more important for their influence than for their number.

THE FRENCH. The unity of the Pyrenean world, so real throughout the Middle Ages, had given rise to a permanent population exchange between the two sides of the mountains. The last medieval manifestations of this had been the contribution of Spanish mountain dwellers to the repopulation of Aquitaine, devastated by the Hundred Years' War, and the aid given by the French in overcoming the Catalonian population loss which had been aggravated by the politico-social struggles of John II's reign.

This latter current of migration was to reach extraordinary proportions in the Catalonia of the 16th and early 17th centuries. There were two kinds of causes for the great French cycle of emigration to Spain. Overpopulation of the French pre-Pyrenean zone, the ruin of the fields of Languedoc and Aquitaine by the wars of religion, and the traditional poverty of the highlands bordering the Massif Central led to emigration. Causes of attraction were underpopulation in Spain and the favorable economic conditions produced by the treasure flowing in from America. A large number of French merchants settled in Seville and Cádiz hoping to participate in the trade monopoly with the Indies. But we must point out, especially with relation to the Crown of Aragon, that French immigration was much more a demographic than an economic fact. In Catalonia, where close estimates of French emigration have been made, the *Gascons* constituted some 20% of the population at the end of the 16th century and formed the base of the rural, agricultural, and herding peasantry.

CONCENTRATION OF PROPERTY: MAYORAZGOS AND MORTMAIN. The economic situation in the 16th century, characterized by the price revolution, had profound repercussions on the economic equilibrium of the different social classes. In fact, once the brief phase favorable to production of manufactured goods had passed (owing to the higher price of Spanish products in comparison with foreign ones), the traditional forms of the Spanish economy, agriculture and herding, came to the fore again. And with this return, the ownership of land as the chief basis of wealth was reaffirmed.

In the legal sphere, the regulation of *mayorazgos* by the Laws of Toro in 1505 only facilitated this concentration of landholding wealth and caused the power of the noble class to grow even greater. *Mayorazgo* was an institution in civil law which tended to exclude part of the family patrimony from the normal order of succession and entail it in perpetuity to one family. An institution of medieval origin, the concentration of *mayorazgos* had resulted in the enormous fortunes of certain noble families. The Laws of Toro regulated this institution, converting *mayorazgo*, which up till then had been an exclusive privilege of the nobility, into an institution of common law. The bourgeoisie took advantage of this democratizing measure and used it to establish small *mayorazgos* on revenue from bonds or on small inheritances. Though this served in a certain sense to counterbalance the power of the nobles, it must not be forgotten that in the end the democratizing of the *mayorazgos* resulted in a growth of nonmarketable wealth and removed a large part of the Spanish patrimony from the laws of a healthy economy.

At the same time, another considerable part of the national patrimony was also entailed, for it went to swell the property of the Church. This *mortmain property,* whose origin was as old as the piety of the faithful, grew tremendously as a result of the religious fervor at the time of the Counter-Reformation. Since canon law did not permit this landed property to pass out of the hands of its owner under any circumstances, and since this owner was the Church and consequently imperishable, mortmain in fact implied perpetual entailment. It seems that in Castile the Hieronymites and Benedictines were the chief holders of mortmain properties. When Carande attempts to explain their growth in the 16th century, he cites as a possible cause, apart from the piety of the faithful, the donations made by the State and by city governments as rewards for the constant collaboration given them by the monasteries.

THE ARISTOCRATIC MIND AND ECONOMIC LIFE. The nobles of the Hapsburg period had fabulous economic power, inherited from medieval times. They owned most of the agricultural land and possessed a large number of jurisdictional rights in addition. There were 180 noble houses whose annual income ranged from 10,000 to 150,000 escudos.

It was with very bad grace that the nobles had consented to be deprived of their political power by Ferdinand and Isabella. Though it was impotent in the face of the Renaissance authoritarian monarchy, the Spanish nobility compromised by serving the Crown in its military or diplomatic undertakings, but only on condition that it could preserve and even extend its economic sway. The nobility gives the impression at this time of gathering its forces, biding its time till the first sign of weakness in the monarchy would permit it to regain its political position. And in fact this opportunity did arise after Philip III, when the system of royal favorites became an expression of the political triumph of Spain's great landowning nobility.

In addition, during the lull in the 16th century the evolution of the economy was entirely favorable to the noble class. A paradoxical situation existed in which the noble, who disdained labor and refused to lower himself by engaging in business, was the only one who did not lose money during the price revolution. To do this, he had only to redeem his lands—now much higher in value because of agricultural exports to the Indies—and return them to their former cultivators under the new lease law, which gave him an effective rate of interest instead of the ridiculously low tributes, taxes, and other levies of the feudal period. Thus, we can conclude with Braudel that it was these leased lands, or rather their increased value, which saved the great landholders' fortunes in the face of the price revolution.

METEORIC RISE AND FALL OF THE BOURGEOISIE IN THE 16TH CENTURY. Larraz distinguishes two great stages in the economic evolution of Castile between 1500 and 1700. The first, from 1500 to 1550, was the stage immediately following the discovery of the Indies. The influx of metal and the opening up of the American market combined to create a favorable economic situation, especially in the industrial sphere: during the first half of the 16th century the population of all the Meseta's manufacturing cities increased. For the country's bourgeoisie, the social class which supplied the motivating force behind this industry and dealt in its products, it was a period of splendor.

But things changed after 1550. The profits from trade with the Indies and the constant demand for products of all kinds meant that there was growing participation of foreign industry in this trade. No matter how hard Castile tried to retain the monopoly of the American treasure and the American market, it had to give in to the pressure of outside competition. This took place because foreign countries, less affected by the rise in prices, could produce at lower cost than Castilian manufacturers. Logically enough, they were ruined and trade was left in foreign hands.

Thus, the rise of the Spanish bourgeoisie in the 1500's took the form of a meteor, which was eclipsed after the middle of the century. After that the Castilian bourgeois, ruined and lacking incentive, would content himself with living modestly on the income he had accumulated in better times, and would subscribe to the ideas of the powerful aristocracy; he scorned business dealings, felt that "not to live off one's property is unworthy of nobles," and considered that to engage in agriculture, trade, or manual labor was a betrayal of the nobility to which he aspired.

The experience undergone by the bourgeoisie was so decisive, the fear of business dealings so deeply rooted, that we will not be surprised at the case of a merchant of the rank of Simón Ruiz, of Medina del Campo, who gradually relinquished his interests in the trading company of Nantes and Medina del Campo which he had formed with his cousin, Francisco de la Presa of Burgos, in order to concentrate all his attention on simple moneylending to the Crown of Philip II, with a profit agreed upon in advance.

MENTAL ATTITUDE OF THE RELIGIOUS CLASSES. In the 16th century the religious class was composed of some 160,000 persons (a proportion of 2%, in Catalonia as high as 6%) and monopolized half the national income (some 5 million ducats). These figures constitute the best proof of the Spanish clergy's economic potential.

Consequently, if we think of this clergy as a social class, we shall have to deduce that they were a rich class, the richest in the country, and that their interests were naturally concomitant with those of the noble class, which monopolized the rest of the real property. And in fact the government of the Church was in the hands of persons of ancient lineage, descended from the best families. But the spiritual factor was something apart from this concomitance and was a source of differentiation: although the religious class was as jealous of its privileged position as the nobility, it had, notwithstanding, a different idea of its employment. The ideal of religious renewal which had sprung up again with the Counter-Reformation led all the resources of the Church into helping the poor, who formed the great mass of population. Aside from this charitable activity the higher clergy was fully identified with official policy, especially in the time of Philip II. In Catalonia, for example, the promotion of a bishop to the position of viceroy was a normal occurrence.

As a special form of the aid given to the afflicted by the Spanish Church, we must point out the clergy's participation in the social conflicts which caused a confrontation between the aristocratic and the lower classes. Thus, in Catalonia, Dominicans and Franciscans actively supported the *nyerros* (plebeians) against the *cadells* (nobles). However, the latter could count on the favor of the Benedictines, who continued the tradition of ecclesiastical feudalism.

This difference in position between the mendicant orders and the Benedictines indicates to us how heterogeneous was the makeup of the ecclesiastical arm, and the necessity of distinguishing the different attitudes found within it. In fact, the difference between upper and lower clergy was very marked in all respects, especially in the cultural and economic spheres. In spite of the enormous revenues of the majority of Spanish dioceses, the lower clergy endured great privations, especially in Catalonia where they were so numerous. All in all, in a period when the social structure tended to polarization, the religious ideal which united all ecclesiastics no matter what their origin was the only crucible where heterogeneous individuals were fused into a common endeavor.

When symptoms of economic exhaustion became evident in the last third of the 16th century, the economic power of the clergy contributed toward increasing the number of ecclesiastics. To wear the habit was a guarantee of easy support. When the country's economic pulse faltered, many second sons realized this and went into the religious orders.

POPULAR MENTALITY. A bad example was offered to the working class of the 1500's; they saw how the nobles, with no effort on their part, became richer and richer by the simple mechanism of the rise in prices, and how the active and businesslike bourgeoisie went down to defeat. The rustic was told so many times that labor was degrading, and he had such an obvious example before his eyes, that he ended by believing it. On the social ladder, the middle rung which might have served as an incentive was disappearing, and the tenant farmer and laborer lost faith in their work. They worked because there was no alternative, because if they did not they would have nothing to eat. They had to work hard for mere subsistence: at any sort of activity they toiled from sunup to sundown, in exchange for a miserable wage that did not even cover vital necessities. A document of the tavern-keepers of Barcelona assures us, for example, that the workmen of the city in whatever trade had nothing to eat at midday but a chunk of bread, a herring, and a head of garlic.

And if by chance the worker had anything left over from his earnings, a taxation system which became ever more demanding was sure to take it away from him. In fact, the position of the laboring man was very similar to that at the end of the Roman Empire. There was only one social difference between the two: while the citizen of the later Roman Empire, hounded by taxation and tied to the *collegia,* could take refuge in the country, the mirage of industrial expansion in the 16th century attracted indigent rustics to the cities.

Once the industrial optimism had passed and the bourgeoisie was ruined, the harsh realities of urban life were not long in appearing. There was a constant increase in the number of unemployed who lived off the free soup offered by the convents, or who wandered all over the country in search of work or adventure. In such circumstances the only possible solutions were to enlist in the army, go into a monastery, or simply to exist on the fringes of society.

ORIGIN OF DESTITUTION AND BANDITRY. We have been putting great emphasis on one essential point: the increased power of the aristocracy and a parallel rise in the number of poor and the amount of destitution. Some evidence of this was the great increase of vagabonds, part of the army of unemployed who infested all the roads, especially those leading to Madrid.

The abundance of literary testimony makes it unnecessary for us to describe this world, allowing us to concentrate our attention on the Spanish Levant. As Braudel has made abundantly clear, at the end of the 16th century banditry was the most obvious social feature over all the Mediterranean world. Catalonia occupied a prominent position in this world. We shall point out the different manifestations of Catalan banditry in order to give some idea of its complexity.

In the repressive measures laid down by the viceroys of the Principality to the magistrates, one expression is repeated over and over; vagabondage must be closely watched because it is "the school of banditry." This expression shows the social character of the phenomenon, which must be related to the population increase coinciding with it. The Pyrenean region loosed a flow of excess population to the lowlands: because of this the shepherd traded his crook for the plow and became a peasant. The change was not always easy to make, and gave rise to a certain number of misfits who saw no other solution than to take to the hills and live outside the clutches of the law. This fact explains the great rise of banditry in the Guillerías, the intermediate zone between the mountains and lowlands of Catalonia. Also, the presence of Gascons among the Catalan bandits is related to the same phenomenon: these subversive Gascons were the French emigrants who had been rejected by the country where they had chosen to settle, because they had been unable to adapt themselves to it; this is a frequent phenomenon in all mass migrations.

Further, Catalonia is a frontier country. On the other side of the border France was controlled by Huguenots, who lost no opportunity to harass the domains of Ferdinand the Catholic. The bishopric of Urgel, especially, lived in a constant state of alert against the incursions of Calvinist bandits, who on occasion got far inside the territory of the Principality and subjected it to the danger of religious contamination.

Catalonian banditry probably had a political side. When bandits confronted the militia with the cry of "Death to the traitors!", was it not an expression of protest by one sector of the Principality against the ruinous imperialist ideals of the Crown of Spain?

And finally, there were clan rivalries among families who, divided into irreconcilable factions, hired outlaws to solve their quarrels. These extraordinary rivalries, corresponding to what has been called the passionate exaggeration of the Baroque period, also contributed in large measure to the development of banditry in Catalonia.

In consequence of all this, a number of separate social, demographic, geographic, religious, and economic factors combined to explain the special virulence of this phenomenon in Catalonia.

26 · Labor and Production in the 16th Century

THE NEW REGIME IN AGRICULTURAL LABOR. Although no study has been made on this subject, we do have clear indications that Spanish agriculture underwent a profound transformation during the first half of the 16th century, as a result of the opening of the American market and the increase in monetary circulation. America's great demand for agricultural products, and the profits to be gained from breaking new land or improving the yield of that already under cultivation, resulted in the extension of cultivated areas and an increase in harvests.

Theoretically this situation should have favored the farmer. But in fact, the deficiencies of the Castilian agrarian structure and the selfish intervention of other classes—nobility and bourgeoisie—had unfavorable repercussions on the interests of the peasant class. These repercussions occurred in the area of the legal system governing agricultural labor.

On the one hand, *leasing* of land took the place of the old feudal dues, by this time more theoretical than effective; on the other, investments were made in the form of *censos al quitar*. First step: the noble class, interested in obtaining better advantage from the country's land, which it owned in large part, made a double effort to create new agricultural properties in the wastelands of their ancient inheritances, and to recover those already in the hands of farmers. Then the nobles turned over, or returned, to those same peasants these colonized or simply recovered lands, but under different conditions than before. Instead of reserving the right, as heretofore, to certain often purely nominal dues, they instituted a rental contract issued for a limited time and involving a real profit. The second step was entry of bourgeois capital into agricultural dealings by way of the so-called *censos al quitar,* which were short-term, very high-interest loans secured by mortgages on the lessee's land. Thus rural land became an object of speculation, for the extremely high interest which was paid—sometimes as much as 50%—led many people to engage in this type of loan. That is, part of the middle class became a parasitic group. The text of one of the *arbitristas,* or panaceists, of the middle of the 16th century, Tomás de Mercado, gives us an exact description of this phenomenon: "As people saw that they could give some 2,000 ducats and receive 200 every year, and that after six or seven years they could get their 2,000 back, it seemed to them to be a profitable kind of loan." Valle de la Cerda also points out that in 1618 there were more than 100 million ducats invested in these *censos.*

CONSEQUENCES OF THIS PROCESS. So long as economic activity was expanding, leasing of land and the investment of capital which often went along with it favored the development of agriculture: high yields from the crops enabled the farmer to settle his accounts with the lord and the mortgage-holder. When the drop in agricultural prices occurred, however—because, among other reasons, the Indies now supplied their own needs—the farmer found that at the end of the year he did not have enough money to pay the interest he owed. Then the mortgages set up as a guarantee of payment came due, and a transfer of land took place which simply aggravated the process of concentration of property.

Only the Andalusian zone, living under the auspices of the great commerce of Seville, partially escaped the situation we have just described. Cultivation of the grape and the olive—both indications of capitalist agriculture—was gradually extended all over the Guadalquivir basin. The linkage of wine and olive oil to industrial prices, more remunerative than agricultural ones, resulted in the fact that in lower Andalusia, where capital was abundant, money was used not for simple land loans but in the direct stimulation of production. The prosperity of Ubeda and Baeza, for instance, stems from this period.

DROP IN PRODUCTION: PRICE-FIXING AND FAMINE. In contrast with the first phase of obvious prosperity, the second stage in Spanish agriculture in the 1500's is one of complete decline. This abrupt change, the exact date of which is impossible to pin down, was probably related to the self-sufficiency of America and especially to the rise in prices. Hamilton says in this regard that agricultural prices gradually rose throughout the 16th century as a result of the progressive drop in production. But was not the situation the reverse? Did not harvests fall off as a reflection of the effect of the general rise in prices on agricultural costs? We believe that this was the case. The flowering of the first half of the century must have been cut short at the moment when the price of seed, cost of tools, wages of farm laborers, etc., became exorbitant, raising the price of the product and placing it in an unfavorable position when it went to market.

Then came the finishing touch, the fixing of wheat prices. Price-fixing was the expression of an agrarian policy based on the principle of favoring the consumer to the detriment of the producer. When prices went up too much, the State simply chose to put a ceiling on them instead of helping production to fight the increase. Thus price-fixing, which had already been used by the Catholic Monarchs as an occasional measure, was restored as a permanent feature after 1539. This measure, called for by the Cortes (especially after 1535) and supported by the economists of the period, was a result of pressure by the urban proletariat beginning to grow up in the country's large cities. Its effects could not have been more lamentable. As a matter of fact:

The price ceiling placed the peasant in an unfavorable position compared with other branches of production where prices were left free. This situation became untenable with the *progressive unbalance between yield and costs* of agricultural production. Valle de la Cerda tells us, for example, that in 1611 lands which brought in a 5% net profit after labor, maintenance, and other costs were met, were considered to be very productive.

In consequence there was *absenteeism among the farmers,* who emigrated to the cities or the Indies, and *depreciation in the value of land,* which was taken over by the great landowners; the result was an increase in the urban masses who demanded "cheap bread," and a growth in latifundism.

Reduction of the cultivated area owing to lack of manpower. A survey made at the end of the 16th century gives reason to believe that one-third of the farm lands were no longer being cultivated.

Appearance of a black market and famine. The decline in production, coinciding with population growth, inevitably led to the appearance of these two plagues. Besides the legal price, regulated by the price ceiling, there was the market price, subject to the law of supply and demand and controlled by *regatones;* that is, the black marketeers of the period. As a symptom of the growing food shortage, we should keep in mind that after 1570 agricultural prices, which had always stayed far below industrial ones, became equally high and in many cases higher. Thus the specter of famine hovered over the whole Peninsula, cutting into demographic growth. After 1550 the terrible scourge of plague reappeared periodically, further damaging normal population development.

MEASURES FOR LAND IMPROVEMENT: IRRIGATED LANDS. It is a curious fact that the most important technical advances—among them improvement of land—were produced not during the period of prosperity under Charles V, but rather in the period of stagnation during Philip II's reign. Confronted with the necessity of producing more, Spanish agriculture in the first half of the 16th century almost always chose the method of breaking new land. At that time control of farming operations was still in the hands of the peasant class, who had little money—since they were the class least favored by the influx of American gold—and meager technical knowledge.

Obtaining a better yield from land already under cultivation was something which became possible only at a later date, when the bourgeoisie of the cities retired from industrial or mercantile affairs and applied their profits to agriculture. Their money made possible the drainage of swampy lands, which were the most productive ones. The new situation created in the Castilian cities at the beginning of the industrial crisis furnished the capital necessary to carry out a system which, though traditional throughout the Mediterranean world, had developed very slowly up to that time because of lack of money. Thus the countryside underwent an extraordinary change. At the same time as part of the farmlands were becoming depopulated and returning to wasteland, in the vicinity of the cities—where the former bourgeoisie, now engaged in agriculture, continued to live—splendid *vegas* and *huertos* grew up, made fertile by irrigation. Numerous foreign travelers of Philip II's time (among them the Venetian ambassadors, naturally), have left a record of this change when they observed that the countryside was cultivated only around the urban centers.

However, if in general this process of improvement was the work of the cities, the help given by the Crown on various occasions should not be forgotten. Colmeiro records, for example, that in 1529 Charles V began the great work of the Imperial Canal of Aragon, making use of the Ebro, though it was not finished until much later, during the reign of Charles III; that the same monarch aided in the irrigation of the Colmenar de la Oreja lowlands by using the waters of the Tagus; and that Philip II constructed the dam at Ecija, which watered many a garden and orchard.

There is one more aspect of this subject to be considered: the social side of measures for the improvement of the soil. Braudel sums it up by saying that the plains are the preserve of the rich. The elements of his theory are as follows: while in the north of Europe only a pick or an axe is needed to clear forests and put land under cultivation, in the south breaking new land is a slow process which begins to show results only after a number of years have passed. It requires, therefore, considerable capital, sufficient to pay the many persons who must work side by side in the process of drying up the marshes. Braudel recalls the use of urban wealth for this purpose, as we have already mentioned, and then emphasizes his idea by stating that in the case of 16th-century Spain, every time that the transition from dry farming to irrigation farming was made, there was likewise a transition from a relatively free peasantry to an enslaved one.

DEVELOPMENT OF HERDING: PEAK AND DECLINE OF THE MESTA. In previous chapters we have explained how Alfonso the Wise, in the 13th century, caused the almost total orientation of the Castilian economy to herding when he recognized the Honorable Assembly of the Mesta. After this recognition, migratory flocks gained the ascendancy over nonmigratory ones and also over agriculture. Later, Ferdinand and Isabella expressly proclaimed that "the breeding and preservation of sheep should be the chief support of these kingdoms." This was also the line of conduct followed by the early Hapsburg kings. Thus the privileged fortunes of the Mesta were assured.

Klein, the historian of this formidable livestock organization, affirms the perfect synchronization between the number of migratory flocks and the golden age of the Spanish Empire. And, conversely, he shows the parallelism between the collapse of the Mesta and the decline of the monarchy at the end of the 16th century. Carande goes still further and explains in his turn that the herding orientation of the Castilian economy facilitated the recruitment of soldiers for the continual political and military undertakings in which the House of Austria was embroiled. Since sheepherding is the form of economy which needs the smallest number of workers, it left a certain number of men free to swell the *tercios* of Flanders or Italy when it spread, to the detriment of agriculture. This could have been one of the reasons which moved Charles V to support the Assembly of the Mesta. However, we feel that a more important reason was the relationship of the predominance of migratory grazing to the political ideal of every Renaissance monarch: a form of authoritarianism which would permit him to recover the prerogatives wrested from him during the Middle Ages. Carande himself, who upholds this view, explains its results. On the one hand, there is no doubt that growth in the Mesta's privileges was made at the expense of the jurisdictional rights of the nobles, the religious communities, the cities, and the merchants' organizations. (Let us also add that Ambrosio de Morales, as early as Philip II's reign, had described the Assembly of the Mesta as a "political organization.") On the other hand, it is a known fact that the Mesta, though it had grown by means of such prerogatives, did not support royal authority as the monarchs had expected. Therefore, the monarchy's ideal was realized only in part, for the only aid it received in return for the privileges granted to the livestock breeders was the payment of *servicios;* that is, a compensation of a purely economic type.

So the Mesta's privileged position in the 16th century should be viewed in close relationship to the incessant demands for subsidies made upon it by Charles V, especially after 1525, when ratification of its privileges converted the aid the association gave the Crown into a sort of permanent open credit. Later, the abdication of the Emperor and especially the disparity between Castilian and European prices, which hampered Spanish exports, marked the beginning of the Mesta's decline. In fact, protected by royal support, flocks of sheep had been a good business operation so long as the wool they produced could leave the country without difficulty. But about 1550 the rise in prices became an impassable barrier; sales of wool decreased and so did Castile's migratory flocks. The reduction was so remarkable that in a period of only five years, from 1556 to

1561, the Mesta lost 15% of its animals, as attested by the following table:

FLOCKS OF THE MESTA
(*Median Annual Figures*)

Periods	Number of head
1512–1521	2,838,351
1522–1531	2,793,823
1532–1541	2,540,635
1542–1551	2,605,633
1552–1556	2,693,170
1557–1561	1,998,845

Now that we have described the peak and decline of the Assembly of the Mesta and of sheep flocks, we shall close this section by emphasizing once again that the predominance of herding was incompatible with other branches of the Castilian economy. In regard to agriculture, we have evidence of the farmers' terror in the face of the annual descent of the flocks, which often strayed outside the legal sheep paths and trampled their crops. Hence there was a constant struggle to reduce or widen—depending on whether the farmer or the shepherd was in control—the boundaries of the migratory routes. As for industry, the crux of the problem was the export of wool. While herders wished to export the maximum quantity, cloth manufacturers wanted to retain the amount needed for their manufactures. In the 15th century the latter had obtained the preemptive right for one-third of the wool produced. At the time of Charles V, coincident with growth in industrial volume, they made the necessary overtures to increase this third to a half. The failure of this attempt shows once again the State's protection of the Mesta.

INDUSTRIAL LABOR: ITS ORGANIZATION. Two essential points must be emphasized. The first is the extraordinary development achieved by the guilds in the 16th and 17th centuries. A visit to any guild archive shows that most of its documents refer to this period, more especially to the 17th century. This development produced most unhappy results, leading to fossilization of the professional structure. To demonstrate the point we can cite a very illuminating document of 1658. It deals with some ordinances regulating the pay which could be demanded by the stevedores of Barcelona, organized into the Confraternity of St. Peter. These were the folk who stood in the water and passed goods from ship to shore and vice versa. More than 200 possible cases are listed in the document, which gives evidence of a great deal of hairsplitting. Each piece of merchandise is listed separately, instead of giving a generic classification by weight, size, or shape of the objects to be unloaded. This means that the guilds' activities were regulated by the system of "numerus clausus," which became the source of innumerable obstructions and conflicts whenever an unforeseen case arose.

The other point which needs to be emphasized in guild organization of the 16th and 17th centuries is their protectionist role in regard to national production, especially the components of production. Guild documents become an interminable litany of protests against the intrusion of other sectors of local activity and the competition of foreign products. This attitude is a clear sign of the country's industrial decline. On the other hand, it exactly reflects the sterile mental outlook of a sector which, instead of undertaking the improvement of production through technical advances or the training of good apprentices, is solely and exclusively concerned with suppressing competition. In this respect, the protests of the confraternity of the "Julians" in Barcelona, a brotherhood of drapers and mercers, against the importation of French cloth and products, are very illuminating.

INDUSTRIAL PRODUCTION: TYPES AND GEOGRAPHIC CENTERS. The abundance of wool placed the cloth industry in first place within Castilian production. On the other hand, the monopoly of the American market opened up really unlimited possibilities to this industry.

Nevertheless, it appears that the progress achieved by Castile's textile industry was not commensurate with the possibilities offered by the favorable economic situation of the first half of the 16th century. We say "it appears" because we are aware that some scholars have found important documentation concerning the large amounts of cloth manufactured in some Castilian cities. But generally speaking the traditional herding and agrarian orientation of Castile's economy, ratified by the Catholic Monarchs and Charles V, was a hindrance to this progress. Another unfavorable factor was the support given by the Emperor to the manufactures of his native Flanders. And finally, the excessive regulation of industrial activity had an adverse influence. In this regard it would be well to mention the promulgation of the famous Ordinances of Seville by Ferdinand and Isabella; this was a collection of 119 laws which, though they did offer the advantage of unifying the techniques of cloth manufacture all over the kingdom of Castile, deprived the producer of any initiative. In contrast to this excessive regulation, Carande points out that these Ordinances paid virtually no attention to the training of workers, and believes that the ruinous state into which wool manufacture eventually fell can be traced to the weavers' lack of technical training. The same author states that Castilian woollens lost their market not only because they were more expensive than foreign ones, but also because of their inferior quality.

The wool industry, the most important in Castile, was concentrated in four main cities: Segovia, Toledo, Cordova, and Cuenca. Outside Castile, Aragon also had an important industry, regulated by the Ordinances of 1522, 1547, and 1550. In the kingdom of Aragon the dyes and woollens of Saragossa were famous, as were the cloth and baize of Huesca. Barcelona continued to export its *draps* and *cordellats,* famous all over the Mediterranean. Valencia and Perpignan were also important wool centers.

In contrast to the development of the woollen industry was the unsatisfactory condition of the spinning of vegetable fibers. Thus, in spite of the importance of *flax* production, Spain was a heavy importer of the linen of Brabant and Holland. Other fibers, processed only in small quantities, were hemp and esparto grass. Hemp was cultivated in Aragon and Valencia, though its manufacture was not even sufficient to supply the needs of the Spanish navy, which used it for sails and rigging. Esparto, heavily cultivated in the Levant, served for domestic uses as well as for navigation instruments and fishing; but it never achieved the level of a well-developed industry.

The production of silk fabrics, though, did reach a remarkable peak. This industry, which enjoyed a deeply rooted tradition in the old Moslem zone, with its chief centers in Toledo, Granada, and Valencia, gave rise to a great deal of export, especially to Italy. There was also an excessive urge to regulate the silk trade, but this responded more to fiscal than to strictly economic objectives. The greatest danger to which the silk industry was exposed in the 16th century came from the sumptuary laws, laid down by Ferdinand and Isabella in 1494 and reconfirmed in 1534 and 1586; their purpose was to reduce the living standard of the upper classes. Naturally, a lesser use of expensive materials in dress was an element in this reduction, and was unfavorable to Castilian silk production.

Another industry similar both in origin and growth to the preceding one was the leather industry, which had also developed as a result of Moslem influence. With the discovery of America came the famous Indies hides, the finishing of which gave new impetus to the medieval industry. American hides successfully took the place of those which formerly had come from the East, by now reduced to a few bundles bought by the Catalans not in their ports of origin but through intermediaries in Genoa and Marseilles. The most prized products of this industry were the *guadamecíes,* or leather embossed and decorated with pictures and drawings and used for ornamental purposes. Leather jackets were also worn and, very particularly, gloves from Ocaña and Ciudad Real were sold perfumed with ambergris in the main European markets, especially the Italian ones.

In another area we must cite the development of shipbuilding. Before the discovery of America, Castile had in general showed little interest in it. But after the discovery, and motivated by the need for a powerful fleet, Ferdinand and Isabella encouraged ship construction, using the system of bounties to shipbuilders and banning shipment of national goods in foreign vessels. There was, however, a good deal of confusion in this program, an example being vacillation over the size of ships; while large vessels offered greater resources in fighting off pirates, small ones had the advantage of easy management and could be loaded more quickly.

Aside from a long-standing tradition and an abundance of iron, one primary factor contributed toward establishing Biscay's supremacy in shipbuilding during the 16th century: its inclusion in the great Castile-Flanders economic axis. As long as this connection lasted, Biscayan shipyards worked at top speed (the first measures to replant the ruined forests were taken in 1547), and Biscay could even permit itself the luxury of exporting its shipwrights, who enjoyed a great reputation as extraordinarily skilled workmen, to other areas such as Barcelona, which was attempting to resuscitate its shipyards. But the same factor which had caused the prosperity of the Biscayan shipyards brought about their decline during Philip II's reign: the breaking off of the Medina-Antwerp axis, exacerbated by the disaster of the Invincible Armada (composed mainly of Basque ships), and the progressive conversion of Biscayan vessels for purposes of war (official measures of 1607, 1611, and 1613 lengthening the keel of the *naos*).

BEGINNING OF ECONOMIC STAGNATION: ITS CAUSES. At the time of the discovery of America, Castile did not have an export cloth industry; on the contrary, it sold only raw wool to foreign countries. But immediately after the discovery, the opening of the American market and the amount of available capital created a favorable situation for the wool-producing cities of the Meseta, especially Segovia, Toledo, Cordova, and Cuenca. The beginnings of this large export manufacture were difficult, due as much to the lack of industrial tradition as to the scarcity of skilled labor. But all obstacles were overcome, and Castilian woollens enjoyed an extraordinary prosperity from approximately 1540 to 1590. It was a fifty-year period during which the Meseta's woollen goods went out in large quantities to America, Portugal, and Italy.

Nevertheless, even at the start of this favorable phase, symptoms began to appear of the ruin which was to befall the industry at the end of the century. The difficulties arose from the excessive rise in prices, which gradually shut off both foreign and domestic markets to national products. In 1548 the Cortes of Valladolid, worried about the internal situation and convinced that excessive exports were the cause of the price rise, asked that entry of foreign cloth be authorized and export of native cloth prohibited, even to the Indies. The Cortes obtained this authorization in 1548 and the ban on export (not, however, extended to America) in 1552. Naturally the results of these measures were the opposite of what had been hoped for: the authorized import of foreign cloth merely revealed and emphasized the inferiority of national industry, which then faced competition from cheaper products on its own territory. In its zeal to favor the kingdom's consumers, the Cortes had forgotten that its concern would also have unfavorable repercussions on production, and in the last instance on prices inside Castile. Finally, in 1558, the monarchy repented of its error and lifted the export ban. But time had not passed in vain, for foreign products took advantage of the interval to gain positions in the traditional markets of the Spanish Crown.

Once this difficulty had been overcome, though, a few years of prosperity still lay ahead. However, competition continued to be so keen that in 1576 the Cortes acknowledged the decline of wool manufacture in Cuenca. The Cortes of 1588 and 1592 confirmed this, and though it reported that Segovian cloth was still on the market, it also disclosed the bankruptcy into which Castilian industry was slipping, for all the reasons we have set forth above.

When we try to summarize the history of this industry and establish the causes for its downfall, we must also take into account the change in attitude which had occurred among the country's bourgeoisie. As time went on and difficulties began to increase, industrialists preferred to invest the profits of their former activities in rural property, thus freezing available capital and swelling the ranks of the aristocratic class, which was socially more desirable. Once this rank was attained the bourgeois who might have been awake to business opportunities began to withdraw from them.

On the other hand, there were factors of a technical nature. The lack of concern showed by the Cortes and the governing class in general for technical improvements in production placed the native cloth industry in a position of inferiority not only in regard to prices but also to quality. Related to this negligence was the lack of orientation in economic policy, which showed in the crisis we mentioned before, in 1552–1558, and in the absence of any effort by industrial leaders to capture the national market. The ruling class, obsessed with preserving the American market, did nothing to make it possible for the working men of Castile itself to acquire the products of the country's industry.

To sum up: apart from the unfavorable situation created by the rise in Spanish prices compared to European ones, the very lack of a consistent policy contributed to the decline of Castilian industry.

FISHING. In this sector of 16th-century economy, what stands out particularly is the decline of the expeditions carried out by Basques who in previous centuries went to fish for cod in Newfoundland waters. The commercial prosperity of the early Hapsburg period had transferred Basque ships, which had previously engaged in this activity, to the new service of maritime transport. This change produced a gap in this Spanish market which was filled by Breton sailors. In the 16th century these took over the role previously played by Basques. They brought codfish, so necessary to the diet of the time, into Spain. Their ships arrived periodically on the Cantabrian coasts and occasionally entered the Mediterranean; shipments of deep-sea fish brought by Breton vessels were frequent in Barcelona.

In the Levant this Atlantic catch began to compete with the traditional fish which had formerly come from Sardinia; Sardinian tunny was famous. There is also evidence in Barcelona of frequent shipments of Portuguese fish: sardines or tunny shipped from the port of Lagos, which probably indicates a remote African origin.

MINING. The most notable fact in this branch of industry is the decline in Spanish metal production, especially of gold and silver, which could compete neither in price nor in quantity with American exports. It was at this time that many mines in the Peninsula were abandoned.

We should point out as an exception, however, the prosperity of the Biscayan iron mines. Somorrostro was at that time the chief area of exploitation. Part of this iron ore was exported to Great Britain and France, but part was manufactured within the country. The fame of Biscayan steel had its origins at this time. In contrast, we find the decline of the Pyrenean forges in Catalonia. The Catalonian Pyrenees region, especially the Conflent district on the French border, was very rich in iron deposits. The medieval forges were abandoned in the 16th century, following the industrial decline of Catalonia. The iron of the Conflent region continued to be extracted, but now for the benefit of the French, who established their forges in the neighboring county of Foix and obtained Spanish iron ore by contraband. On the other hand, the iron of the Roussillon was exported in large quantities to the Spanish domains in Italy, especially Sicily and Naples, to the point that at the beginning of the 16th century iron was the basic factor in the county of Roussillon's maritime trade.

27 · Trade and Currency in the 16th Century

STRUCTURE AND AREAS OF SPAIN'S EXTERNAL TRADE. Apart from traffic with America, which will be discussed in a later chapter, Castile's trade in the 16th century was based chiefly on export of raw materials and metals, and the regular import of manufactured products and occasional import of foodstuffs. So, on the credit side of the Castilian mercantile balance were shipments of wool, salt, olive oil, cochineal, iron, and hides; on the debit side, entry of woollen and linen cloth, dry goods, books and paper, and on occasion—frequent occasion—wheat and fish.

The structure of Spanish foreign trade during this period corresponds to the presence of four specialized trade areas. In the eastern part of the country the lands of the Crown of Aragon had an economic life which was both peculiar to them and independent; it was rooted in the Mediterranean economy, so different from that of the Atlantic. Its chief center was Valencia, the fourth largest city in Spain. In the southeast was the Alicante-Murcia area, where wool from Cuenca and Toledo had an outlet to the Mediterranean in the ports of Cartagena and Alicante, and where the products of Italian industry entered on their way to Madrid. In the southwest was the Andalusian area which, with Seville, Granada, Cádiz, and Málaga, was Castile's firm bastion on that side of the Atlantic and the anchor of trade with the Indies. And finally, in the north, was Old Castile's trade area in the Cantabrian Sea, with Valladolid, Burgos, and Bilbao as chief cities in the system.

EXPORT PRODUCTS. The most important export product was *wool*. Wool from Castilian merino sheep was famous all over Europe. When we discussed the Mesta we observed the privileged position enjoyed by the sheep population, and the connection between its development and wool exports. Shearing was done in May and June. The large proprietors waited until it was finished before they sold the product, while small owners were obliged to arrange for its sale in advance, at a lower price. The market was controlled by a very few: in the North, the great merchants of Burgos and Segovia; in the center of Castile, the Genoese; in Seville, Genoese and Spaniards in fierce competition. There were different grades of wool, depending on the place where the sheep had spent the winter. Thus, the preferred grade came from the flocks which had been in Andalusia and Extremadura, and was known under the name of *merina* or *extremeña.* The animals which had wintered in the chillier pastures of Castile produced a heavier wool of lower quality, called *churra.* Within these grades other qualities were recognized. Who were the chief customers for Castilian wool? The most important one was the Flemish wool industry; then, the Italian manufacturers who shipped it from Alicante—a wool port by definition—and the French. It should be noted that although Castile occupied first place in the export of wool, Aragonese wool was also exported in fairly considerable quantities by way of the Ebro and Tortosa.

Salt was one of the prime necessities of life at that time, as it was the only means of preserving meat and fish. The southern countries had a great advantage for obtaining it: the intense evaporation produced by heat. Thus Spanish salt deposits played a very important part in the European economy. In this regard, one author tells us that the beds of Puerto de Santa María produced more than 100,000 *cahices* of salt a year, and that on occasion as many as fifty or sixty foreign ships at a time were on hand to load it. Though the monarch did not own all of the salt beds, the entire production was concentrated in a few special storehouses called *alfolíes,* thus permitting strict control of sales.

The zone of olive cultivation was approximately the same as it is today. However, the precariousness of the transport system at the time reduced to two the number of Spanish regions which could find an outlet for their production. These regions were Andalusia and Majorca, and Dutch, English, and French merchants went to these places to buy it. This Spanish *oil* was not used exclusively for nutritional purposes; it was also utilized industrially, especially in textile manufacture.

In this same branch of industry *cochineal* was highly prized; it is a parasitic insect whose host is the nopal—a kind of cactus—and which gives a magnificent red dye. It was abundant in Mexico, and its commercial value explains the fact that cochineal production was under the strict control of a corps of inspectors, created in New Spain about 1572–1573. American cochineal arrived regularly in Seville with the fleet, and was then reshipped in large quantities to Flanders, Great Britain, and France. The peak of this trade came at the end of the 16th century.

The Indies produced other dyes besides cochineal, and these were also a Spanish monopoly. Chief among them was *indigo,* produced in Mexico and exported to the same countries which used cochineal, except for France, where the famous woad of Languedoc was preferred.

In addition, the home country itself produced some interesting dye products. Among them were the *alum* of Mazarrón, near Cartagena, a trade monopolized by the Genoese, and *scarlet,* an inferior type of cochineal cultivated in Andalusia.

To return to large-scale production; if wool was Castile's specialty, *iron* was the basis of Biscayan economy. In spite of repeated bans on export it was shipped in large quantities, especially to France. This contraband trade was necessary because it paid for purchases of wheat for the Basque Country, which was mountainous and produced very little; and also, because the country's metallurgical industry—which was considerable, for there were more than 300 forges—did not absorb all the ore that was mined. On the other hand, we have already spoken of the iron exports from the Conflent region, in the Roussillon, when we discussed the decline of the Catalan forge.

Now that we have enumerated the basic Spanish export products, we could spin out the tale with an interminable list of other less important ones. Among these were *Indies hides* and the goods manufactured from them (*guadamecí* work, Cordovan *leather,* the *gloves* of Ocaña and Toledo); *raw silk* and *silk hose,* sold in France and Italy, where they competed with those of Tours and Naples, respectively; Aragonese *saffron* for Flanders, Germany, and France; *sugar* from the Canaries and America; *Basque oranges* and *lemons,* inedible but used in pharmacy; *horses* from the Pyrenees, smuggled into France; and so on.

IMPORT PRODUCTS. Let us make a distinction between those which arrived regularly and those which were occasional.

The first group was composed of the *cloth* and *dry goods* of Flanders and France (Lyons-Arles), imported in quantity despite the constant protests of native manufacturers. Related to these was the *gold thread* of Milan, brought into Spain by the Milan-Lyons-Nantes-Bilbao-Castile route. Also included were *paper,* which occupied second place among the products acquired from France, and its by-products: *playing cards* and *liturgical books,* these last intended for the Indies market. This trade with America and the needs of the Spanish territory itself also brought about the establishment in Spain of numerous booksellers and printers, both French and German (the latter, about thirty of them at the beginning of the century, were referred to by Lope de Vega as "armorers of culture"); related to this same tendency, we should mention the project of Ruiz and La Presa, the great merchants of Medina, to become printers of liturgical books. *Small hardware,* such as scissors, combs, and the like, was sold by ambulant French vendors in every corner of Spain.

In the group of products imported only occasionally we find fish from Sardinia and Brittany (more precisely, deep-sea fish brought to Spain by Bretons), which can almost be considered a regular import product since it arrived with such regularity; and especially, *wheat.* Variation in harvests frequently confronted the Peninsula with shortages of grain. Then Hanseatic and French wheat were imported for the Meseta and Andalusia, and wheat from Sardinia and Sicily for the Levant. This distinction is valid for most of the 16th century. But after 1590 the Mediterranean wheat crisis also linked the supplying of Catalonia and Valencia to grain brought from the north of Europe by Dutch and English ships, or by the land route ending in the Italian port of Leghorn.

TRADE ROUTES. *Mediterranean area.* Within the Mediterranean, there is only one positive fact to be pointed out: the prosperity of the route which, setting out from Alicante, carried Castilian wool —wool from Villacastín in the province of Avila, as the documents usually specify—to Italy through the ports of Genoa-Leghorn or Venice.

In contrast to the supremacy of this route, the decline of most of the others stands out clearly. Thus Catalonia, the chief commercial center of the Levant zone, saw its trade area reduced to that of the Western Mediterranean, with its two extremes in Sicily—a way station on the Eastern route of former times—and in Cádiz-Seville, the terminus of the Flemish route, so traditional ever since the 14th century. And even within this nearby Mediterranean area there was a great diminution in trade. Its causes were many: first, the pact of 1528 between Charles V and Andrea Doria, which marked Barcelona's definitive defeat at the hands of Genoa. By taking advantage of the privileges they had obtained, the merchants of the Italian republic undertook massive import of their fabrics (which often were not Genoese but came from France) into Sicily and Naples, to the great detriment of Catalonian industry, which had always considered those places as private fiefs. In the second place were the difficulties placed in the path of Catalan merchants by royal officials in the Spanish-controlled markets of North Africa. And last, there were Papal interdictions on trade with the infidel. These obstacles, together with the decline of the Catalonian merchant marine, caused the ruin of that business spirit so often demonstrated by the Catalans in medieval times. On the other hand, Barcelona's trade with the large nearby ports of Marseilles, Genoa, and Leghorn was strengthened, for these cities became intermediaries for the exchange of Catalonian products and those of the remoter countries once related to Barcelona through direct trade. Thus, in the 16th century we could have observed the Catalans buying Barbary wheat and hides in Marseilles, Oriental spices and textiles in Genoa, and wheat from the Hanseatic League in Leghorn.

It is interesting to point out Catalonia's final reaction to this distressing situation. Since she had lost her traditional positions in Mediterranean trade, she tried to acquire others in the new Atlantic world through participation in Castile's trade with the Indies. Barcelona's first petition to trade with the New World dates from 1522. This application, which was rejected, coincided with another presented by Flemings and Germans and identical in terms. When they received a negative answer the Catalan merchants tried to put an alternative solution into practice; since direct communication was impossible, they tried to establish themselves in Seville, where contraband trade, indulged in even by the officials of the House of Trade, would serve to bridge the gap between them and the newly discovered lands. This was the sense of the petition to establish a Catalonian consul in Seville or Cádiz, presented to the Cortes of Monzón in 1534, and also denied.

When their second attempt failed the Catalans concentrated all their efforts on capturing the Castilian markets, the source and fountainhead of American trade. The same Cortes of 1534 has left evidence of the presence of Catalonian cloth in Medina del Campo, chief supply center for trade with the Indies. This fact proves the vitality of the country's industry, especially if we recall, with Carrera Pujal, the extremely stiff competition that the Catalonian *draps* and *corbellats* had to face from Flemish, English, and French stuffs, with which they often competed under unfavorable conditions; for while the Flemings, English, and French could place their merchandise directly in the ports of Seville or Cádiz by paying moderate customs duties, the export of Catalonian woollen or silk fabrics to Castile was subject to payment of a *Generalitat* tax in the customs houses of the Principality, transit fees to the *Generalitat* of Aragon, and then transit fees through the inland ports of Castile.

These efforts met with varying success. One result was the economic recovery of the interior of the country, of which the establishment of the *Taula de Canvi* of Lérida, created in 1585, is a symptom. On the other hand, they resulted in linking the Catalonian textile industry to the economic rhythm of Castile: the Castilian crisis of 1548–1558, for example, also had repercussions on the Principality's cloth industry, and the rise in prices, which grew sharper in the second half of the 16th century, also tended to displace Catalonia from supplying the American market.

ATLANTIC AREA. In this area the principal routes all turned on one essential axis, that which linked Flanders with Castile's two windows on the sea: the Cantabrian in the North, from Bermeo to San Vicente de la Barquera; and the Andalusian in the South, with its outposts in Seville and Cádiz.

The first segment, *Flanders to the Basque-Santander coast,* was the most heavily traveled in all Europe, with a constant coming and going of ships between Bilbao-Laredo-Santander and the North Sea ports. Besides Castilian wool and Biscayan iron the chief element in this trade was Castilian money, minted from American gold. Thanks to it Antwerp became a great financial capital, with a reputation as good or better than that of Seville or Lisbon. The city on the Scheldt—inheritor of the fortunes of Bruges, especially after the erection of its Stock Exchange in 1531—came to be the nerve center of a complicated system of exchange, circulation, and banking operations, which radiated from Flanders to upper Germany and England and reached as far as Lyons, for many years a dependency of the great banking center of the North.

This great route carried on normally until 1566. After that date, the revolt of the Low Countries and the Duke of Alba's intransigent policy (after 1568) marked the beginning of a period of brutal piracy, with no quarter given, against Biscayan ships carrying silver. In 1572 the Dutch took over the port of La Brielle and made it the cradle of their naval supremacy in the Atlantic. Shortly afterward, topping off the damaging action of the English corsairs, the bankruptcy decreed by Philip II in 1575 produced Antwerp's economic collapse, and with it the decisive rupture of the Castile-Flanders axis, to the serious detriment of the whole Spanish Cantabrian zone.

However, there was still a need to continue sending money from one country to the other. Hence the necessity of finding another route to take the place of the one that had disappeared. The route through France (1572–1578) having been abandoned because it was too expensive, reasons of security as well as economy finally dictated an itinerary by way of Castile, Barcelona, Genoa, the Franche Comté, and the Low Countries. This displacement of the economic axis gave new life to the Mediterranean world, and Spanish coins circulated throughout the area. Barcelona recovered part of her former commercial activity: her exchange fairs were reorganized, her ships sailed for the last time beyond the habitual limit of Sicily and went as far as Alexandria to buy spices from the Orient. Beyond Spanish territory itself, Genoa also gained greatly from the new route, and the famous fairs of Besançon were transferred to Piacenza, in her own territory.

Returning to the Atlantic area, we must point out a series of less important routes which fed into the main one between Flanders and Castile, and linked Peninsular ports with French ones. Particularly important was the route from *Rouen and the Breton ports to Lisbon, Sanlúcar, Seville, and Cádiz.* At that time Rouen was the most active French Atlantic port, for besides being an outlet for Breton products it supplied Antwerp when Dutch privateers made navigation in the English Channel and North Sea too risky. There was a large Spanish colony in Rouen, composed especially of citizens of Burgos. The *route from Breton ports to Spanish Cantabrian ports* carried less traffic than that of Rouen.

Two other routes originating in Nantes, at the mouth of the Loire, merged into the two routes mentioned above. One, based on the exchange of French wheat and Spanish salt, an irregular trade, led to the Andalusian ports. The other, much busier, merged with the great Flanders route and carried wheat from the Beauce and French fabrics and dry goods from Nantes to Bilbao and Santander, and on return, the gold and silver of the West Indies to France and Milan (through Bilbao, Nantes, and Lyons).

PORTS. In the 16th century the potentialities of a seaport were still determined by its natural configuration. Despite the fact that traffic had grown considerably in comparison with the previous period, few works of equipping and improvement were undertaken. In Barcelona, for example, in spite of the creation in 1435 of an anchorage tax intended for improvement of the port, the first stone in the breakwater was not laid until 1616. Given these circumstances, we are not surprised to learn that in the 16th century the principal Spanish seaports were on rivers: e.g., Seville and Bilbao, protected from the onslaughts of the sea and at the same time natural refuges from the attacks of pirates and privateers. Few improvements were made in either one, except for drainage of the Nervión to facilitate the entry of larger ships into the port of Bilbao and the beginning of the breakwater in Portugalete, the outer port of Bilbao, in 1530; this was paid for by the citizens of Biscay and Burgos.

Apart from this, the predominance of river ports of such limited capabilities was an exact reflection of the small volume of shipping at that period. It should be noted that this was not an exclusive characteristic of Spanish ports but was common to all countries: we need only recall the principal ports on the French Atlantic Coast—Rouen, Nantes, and Bordeaux—each located on a river estuary.

Besides the ports which carried regular traffic, there were any number of simple beaches and strands which served maritime trade. It was largely coastwise trade, and products were shipped from the nearest points on the shoreline. Catalonia can serve as an example of this assertion. According to Father Gil, the Jesuit from Reus who wrote about the year 1600, the coast of the Principality contained nine ports: from east to west, Colliure, Port-Vendres, Cadaqués, Rosas, Palamós, Barcelona, Salou, La Ampolla, and Los Alfaques. However, the documents scarcely mention any of these ports, while they continually refer to the multitude of beaches and natural harbors strung out all along the coast. Thus, grain shipped from the Ampurdán district to Barcelona was not usually embarked in Cadaqués or Rosas, the ports of the region, but on the beaches near the wheatfields: Graells, Molí de l'Ermentera, San Pedro Pescador, Ampurias, etc.

TRANSPORT OF MERCHANDISE. *Land transport.* In the 16th century transport by sea rather than by land was obviously superior for shipping merchandise. However, geographical conditions often necessitated land transport, while at other times the perils of navigation justified its temporary use on routes normally served by maritime transport.

In Spain the meager volume and irregular course of the rivers eliminated, then as now, transport by this means. Nevertheless, it is interesting to note that utilization of Spanish rivers was taken under consideration, and that in 1585 the Italian engineer Antonelli presented to the king and the Cortes a plan for making the Tagus navigable from Lisbon to Talavera.

Thus, transport in the interior of the country was limited to carts and pack animals. Carts were the traditional four-wheeled model, difficult to use in such hilly terrain as Spain's. On the other hand, the State concerned itself very little with the use and upkeep of highways, leaving their improvement to the merchants' guilds, who paid scant attention to them either. Under these conditions, in spite of the fact that in 1497 Ferdinand and Isabella had recognized the "Royal Society of Teamsters," transport by cart had little importance. Pack animals, though—especially horses and mules—were extraordinarily important. In the time of Charles V the agronomist Alfonso de Herrera estimated at 400,000 the number of mules engaged in transport. These convoys crossed the Peninsula in all directions. However, two chief itineraries stood out: the first went from Castile to the Mediterranean ports, especially Cartagena and

Alicante, shipping points for the wool exported to Italy; the second from the Meseta to Bilbao, passing through Burgos and the cities where fairs were held. This second route was the busier one, especially the portion from Medina del Campo to Bilbao.

SEA TRANSPORT. There is a good deal of published material on this subject, but not enough to give us a clear and exact picture. We shall try to summarize present information, concentrating on two essential points: tonnage and types of ships.

(1) *Tonnage.* During the period 1500–1700 we can easily distinguish three important stages:

From 1500 to approximately 1587: *gradual increase in ships' tonnage.* As examples we can give the following: Isabella's recommendation to the governor of Biscay (1502) to promote construction of ships of 1,500 tons, offering a subsidy of 50,000 maravedís, payment of freightage for six months, and the privilege of preference in the cargo; the Ordinances of 1552 excluding ships of less than 100 tons displacement and crews of thirty-two men from the convoys going to America; and the order issued by Philip II in 1587 raising the previous minimum to 300 tons.

From 1588 to the middle of the 17th century: return, though with many vacillations, to *small tonnage.* This change first took place in the navy, influenced by the success of the English and Dutch who, with their tiny but more maneuverable, faster, and better-armed ships very successfully harassed the Spanish and Portuguese monsters, until they caused the disaster of the Invincible Armada. The need for reducing the burden of merchant ships also became obvious. As early as 1579 the government of Biscay proclaimed the substitution of small ships for large ones as the only solution for a return to the shipping prosperity of former times; small ships, in fact, facilitated loading and could reach the river ports without difficulty in shallow waters.

After the middle of the 17th century: *definite triumph of large ships* of 500 to 1,500 tons, which, since they were unable to cross the Sanlúcar sandbar at the mouth of the Guadalquivir, spelled the triumph of the port of Cádiz.

Although the outline we have just given refers to the Atlantic, it is also applicable along general lines to the Mediterranean. The greater part of the 16th century was the golden age of large ships, symbolized in the victory of the *nave* over the *galera,* or galley.

After the end of the century came the drop in tonnage, following the example of Marseilles (very prosperous after 1570) and Genoa, favored by the defeat of Venice and Ragusa—first-rank naval powers up till then—at the hands of the Turks. Finally, the supremacy of the large Nordic (i.e., Dutch) ships after the middle of the 17th century.

(2) *Types.* There is great confusion on this point, arising especially from the fact that the same names were used for different types of ships (different in tonnage and even in shape) from one period to another and one place to another. But there is an essential point of difference. In general terms, the Mediterranean used *long* ships and the Atlantic *round* ones. In this second group we may mention the *nave* or *carraca* or *coca,* a short, round ship probably of Biscayan origin; the *carabelas,* of Portuguese origin, the type of vessel used in the great discoveries; the *galeones,* high-sided, round, and slow, with great fortifications on the prow to accommodate artillery. These ships evoke in our minds the treasures of the Indies and the defeat of the Armada. There were also Basque *zabras,* generally of less than 100 tons, very suitable for commercial traffic; *pataches,* used for coastwise trade in Galicia and Asturias; the *chalupas* and *pinazas* which abounded along the Cantabrian coast; the *venaqueros;* the *gabarras* of Seville; and so on.

As for the Mediterranean, we have already pointed out the decline of the *galera* ("queen" of the long ships) and the rise of the Atlantic ship; we need only mention the proliferation of small types—such as *barcas, tartanas,* and *saetías*—in the handling of which Provençal and Genoese sailors were particularly proficient, and, far behind these, the Catalans.

THE MAILS. Correspondence had a good deal of importance in the commercial system of the period. To give us an idea of its volume, Lapeyre tells us that the Ruiz Archive in Valladolid contains some 50,000 letters, averaging seven or eight a day for the years of heaviest correspondence. In contrast to the importance of letters was the unreliability of the mails, which obliged a writer to precede each letter with a résumé of the previous one in case of possible loss.

During the Hapsburg period the mails were not organized as a public service, nor were they a State monopoly. The governing power had instituted a postal service to take care of its own needs, but it was not the only one in existence; the merchants' guilds, the cities, and so on, also had their own private postal services. Nevertheless, during the 16th century the royal mail tended more and more to take over the others, and many private persons entrusted their correspondence to it.

At that time the official Spanish mail service was in the hands of the Tassis family, originally from Bergamo, an enclave of Venice in the Milanesate. One of the members of this family, Francesco, had obtained from Philip the Handsome the office of Postmaster of Castile. After that the post continued to be linked with the Tassis family, which gradually extended its field of operations. Thus, in 1556 Leonardo de Tassis lived in Brussels and had the title of Grand Master of Posts and Mails of the Royal Household and Court. The Tassis' monopoly gave rise to many disputes with the most important cities of the country.

At that time the Spanish postal network consisted of seven principal routes. All originated in Madrid and went to the following points: the French frontier, through Burgos and Irún; Barcelona, through Saragossa; the Portuguese frontier, by way of Toledo and Cáceres; Tarifa, by way of Cordova and Seville; Valencia; and Valladolid. Naturally, this does not include international mail, which had two chief destinations: France and Italy. Both these routes passed through France, the first crossing it completely from south to north and the second going by way of Irún-Lyons-Milan. Mail for Italy was a regular service; it left Madrid every two weeks and took either twenty-seven or twenty-four days to reach Rome, according to the season of the year.

COMMERCIAL TECHNIQUES. Lapeyre's important study of Castilian trade, based on material in the Ruiz Archive, states that the commercial techniques of the 16th century present nothing substantially new compared with those brought into Spain during the Middle Ages by Italian merchants. This conclusion is even more surprising when we realize that the Ruiz family, on whose business dealings the study is based, can be considered as prototypes of the most forward-looking businessmen of the period. However, Lapeyre's arguments are so convincing that we must accept this lack of modernity as the most outstanding characteristic of 16th-century commercial techniques.

As for method, all we can find is simple improvement of the old systems originally instituted by the Italians; nor is it possible to establish any fundamental difference between the commercial documents in the Datini Archive of the merchants of Prato, in Tuscany, who lived in the 14th century, and those belonging to the Ruiz Archive 200 years later. The 17th century was to be much more revolutionary in this respect, introducing among other novelties the development of the joint stock company and general acceptance of endorsements on bills of exchange, the beginnings of which we have examined in the Barcelona of the early 15th century. And insofar as his mental attitude was concerned, the merchant of the 1500's continued to be medieval. He was still afraid to break with the restrictive doctrines of the canonists. This fear of incurring ecclesiastical interdiction was shown especially in the matter of profits. Since the Church opposed the system of credits bearing interest, moneylenders had to hide behind a complicated system of contracts in which there was always an element of risk. No clearer example could be given of this system of indirect loans than the discretionary bills of exchange which were so popular at the time: the Church did permit charging interest in the case of a loan to be collected in another city, owing to the risks represented by the transfer of money and the expenses this incurred.

However, notwithstanding the sophistries engaged in by businessmen to flout the strictures of the Church, there is no hiding the fact that these still carried weight in the 16th century. Even at best, as in the case of discretionary bills, they complicated the operation. In other instances they caused serious damage to the country's economic interests: for example, the Catalans lost the North African market, among other reasons, because they were afraid of incurring the excommunication decreed by the Pope for merchants who traded with the infidel. We have already seen that merchants from Marseilles and Genoa, who ignored these spiritual penalties, took advantage of the Catalans' submissive attitude.

STOCK EXCHANGES (LONJAS) AND CONSULATES. The awakening of the Crown of Castile to seafaring and trading activity raised the problem of finding mercantile institutions which would channel and regulate this new activity. Confronted with such a need, Castile made use of an instrument offered by several centuries of Aragonese experience, and introduced *lonjas,* or stock exchanges, and consulates into its chief cities following the model adopted long before in the territories of the other great Spanish Crown. Of special importance was the transplanting of these institutions to the two main trade centers of Castile, Bilbao in the North and Seville in the South.

The monopoly of American trade bestowed on Seville by the State had necessitated the creation there of the organization called the House of Trade. Independently of the House, the Sevillian merchants very soon attempted to protect their private interests by forming a Consulate. And in fact, in 1525 they formulated the proposal (not, however, approved until August, 1543) which authorized them to band together and form the Consulate or Guild of Shippers to the Indies (*Consulado* or *Universidad de los Cargadores de Indias*).

In consequence, two organizations existed side by side in the Andalusian capital—one administered by the State, the other municipal and private—for the control of American trade. Both were bound together in a common cause: protectionism at any price, for the purpose of preventing any outside intrusion into dealings with America. Following this aim, in 1573 the Consulate obtained withdrawal of the privilege granted by Charles V in 1529, which had permitted the ports of Corunna, Bayonne, Avilés, Laredo, Bilbao, San Sebastián, Cartagena, Málaga, and Cádiz to send ships directly to America with the sole condition that they make Seville the first port of call on their return. After 1573, however, departures also had to take place from there. The series of privileges conceded to the Consulate of Seville aroused the rivalry of other, less favored cities. It is within the framework of this rivalry that we must place the establishment in Cádiz (1535) of the *Court of the Indies,* set up to authorize direct exports to America without having to pass through Sevillian control. The Canary Islands also carried on a fierce struggle with Seville; numerous foreigners became established in the Fortunate Isles and converted them into a warehouse for contraband goods.

The financial needs of the merchants' association (which was what the Consulate of Seville really was) were met by a certain number of taxes turned over to it by the State. Among these was the collection of a tax on trade called the *avería del Consulado*—modeled on one established in Burgos in 1514, which, as Céspedes del Castillo warns, must not be confused with the *avería* or risk tax collected to finance protection for the convoys to the Indies. The Ordinances of 1573 also gave the Consulate a certain amount of influence in the organization of these convoys, requiring its agreement in naming the officials put in charge of them, hitherto the exclusive right of the House of Trade. Also, Sevillian merchants were given an opportunity to channel their contracts through another organization of Mediterranean origin, the stock exchange. The Stock Exchange of Seville was created in 1582, and was patterned exactly after those of the Levant. To aid in the construction of its building—occupied today by the Archive of the Indies—the merchants were granted the right to collect one-third of 1% of the value of any articles entering or leaving the city. The Stock Exchange building was finished in 1598, but the tax continued to be collected until 1826.

At the other end of the Peninsula, the Consulate of Bilbao came into being in 1511 as a rival of that of Burgos, founded in 1494 by Ferdinand and Isabella. The hostility aroused by this Bilbao institution continued throughout the century. As has already been mentioned, the rivalry centered around the problem of control of Castilian exports: the rights claimed by Burgos as a wool market were disputed by Bilbao as the chief shipping port for wool. The agreement of 1513 establishing Burgos' right to dispatch wool shipments, on condition that at least half of them were made in ships from Bilbao, caused a great many irritations, but it was extended in 1553. Shortly afterward, disputes began to arise again, for the strong position of the Basque city made it feel disadvantaged by the agreement. Then Burgos responded with a mortal blow: the agreement reached with Portugalete in 1547, by the terms of which, in exchange for steering traffic toward the little port, the Consulate of Burgos would receive 1 maravedí for every sack of wool put on board ship and 1 ducat for every ship that landed there. It was an ideal solution for Burgos' interests. However, Burgos was not able to overcome Bilbao's supremacy, still less after Bilbao signed an agreement with Portugalete in 1573, thus resolving the somewhat annoying competition between the two ports.

In the end, the shrewd policies employed by her merchants placed Bilbao in a position to overcome Burgos' hostility and the rivalry of neighboring ports, and made her the most important commercial center on the Cantabrian coast. According to Lapeyre's figures, traffic in the port of Bilbao in 1564 was two and a half times greater than Laredo's and eight times that of Santander. Taking advantage of the natural excellence of their harbor, safer than the others because located inside a fjord and better situated for trade with France than any other, the Biscayan merchants succeeded in convincing those of Nantes and Flanders that their vessels should prefer Bilbao's roadstead to the other ports along the coast. In any case, it must be pointed out that after Bilbao had satisfactorily solved its traditional battle with Burgos, both cities were ruined by the breaking off of the Castile-Flanders economic axis, which took place between 1566 and 1575.

As for the internal organization and activities of the Consulate of Bilbao, we must mention the Ordinances of 1518, which allowed the city to charge half a maravedí per ton of burden on any ship entering or leaving the port, plus some specific taxes on iron, wool, and other import or export products, and the Ordinances of 1520 regulating marine insurance. These last were followed in Castile by the Ordinances of Seville (1522–1556) and Burgos (1538 and 1572).

MONETARY CIRCULATION: SYSTEM OF EXCHANGE. The monopoly exercised by the Spanish State over American treasure arriving in the Peninsula could not prevent a considerable fraction of it from spreading throughout Europe. The mechanisms which made this transfer possible were three:

The Ricardian mechanism of international movement of precious metals. The higher level of Spanish prices favored imports and worked against exports, so that the Spanish balance of payments could be settled only by sending currency abroad.

Divergence in bimetallic ratios. Undervaluation of metal within Spain, owing to its abundance, greatly favored remittances to other countries in which metal was overvalued. For example, Hamilton points out that a gross profit of 20.74% could be obtained on shipments of silver from Spain to Venice for the period 1609–1620, and one of 29.27% during the eight-year period after that.

Remittances made directly by the State to pay for its foreign policy. Financing the wars in Italy and Flanders, especially, meant an uninterrupted flow of money from Spain to other countries.

The use of the bill of exchange became general as an instrument of the important traffic we have just described. *Unconditional exchange,* obligatory either for the drawer or drawee of the bill, or for both, which is simply the result of a mercantile operation, had already been known in late medieval times. What was characteristic of the 16th century was the popularizing of a second type of exchange, the *cambio por arbitrio,* or discretionary bill, which was optional and not obligatory like the former one. This bill came into being solely out of a desire for profit, and was a stratagem adopted by the bankers of the period to flout the canonical interdiction on interest (*pecuniae pecunias non parent*).

The profit to be obtained from exchange was based on the differing monetary situation in the two places where the bill was drawn and where it was to be paid. Since a situation of abundance of currency (the prevailing case of the Spanish market) meant a fall in the exchange rate, and, conversely, a situation of scarcity (as in foreign centers) meant a rise, this type of business dealing or speculation consisted in being the *drawer* in places where money was dear and the *drawee* in others where it circulated at a low price.

The theologians tolerated such exchanges because the interest was masked in its current rate or quotation. A banker who bought a bill at the current rate did not know in advance what his profit would be, for this depended on the rate at the time of settlement. That is, he engaged in a speculation whose outcome was uncertain, for the interest earned depended on the price quoted at any given time. It was precisely this risk which, according to the theologians, justified exchange between two cities. Consequently, the canonical doctrine on exchange called for two indispensable conditions: transfer of funds from one place to another (*distantia loci*) and exchange of one currency for another (*permutatio pecuniae*).

Because it contravened this dual condition, the prodigious development of exchange within the country, especially between Seville and the Medina fairs, was stubbornly opposed in 16th-century Spain. The greater number of theologians opposed domestic exchange on the grounds that it was the same currency which was quoted both in the place of issue and the place of payment (that is, there was no *permutatio*) and that in consequence there could be no variation in price. This condemnation was made official in the *Edict of 1552* banning exchange within the kingdom at a rate different from parity. Thus the absurd situation came about that exchange between Seville and Valladolid was condemned as usury, while that carried out between Bologna and Florence was free from this stigma because there was a difference in the types of currency and a political boundary between the two cities (R. de Roover).

THE FAIRS: SUPREMACY AND DECLINE OF MEDINA DEL CAMPO. If exchange became the most widespread instrument of monetary circulation, the Castilian fairs of medieval origin became in the 16th century the typical terrain for negotiating bills of exchange. That is, the fairs, which before had been centers for mercantile relations, grew more and more into institutions of a marked financial character.

By the end of the Middle Ages there were three outstanding fairs in Castile: Villalón, fief of the Pimentels, counts of Benavente; Medina de Ríoseco, linked to the Enríquez family, admirals of Castile; and Medina del Campo, under the protection of Queen Isabella. Later, when the Crown's political and economic expansion showed up the inconveniences of dividing trade among several centers, Ferdinand and Isabella made a number of attempts to consolidate the three fairs in one, eliminating the other two. The Villalón fair in particular went through very hard times, and was saved only by the queen's death. And so, in spite of all efforts, all the fairs survived and became the regulating instrument of the country's finances during the reign of Charles V.

Hence the intimate connection between the fairs and the arrival of the Indies fleets; since the fairs were money markets, their opening had to depend on the arrival of the American metal which made their existence possible. But while the fairs took place at a fixed time, the galleons' arrival was irregular. The difficulty of synchronizing these two events occasioned serious difficulties for holding the fairs. These obstacles, always normal, grew worse with the passage of time, until in 1566 the delay of American silver with respect to payments to be made at the Medina fair became as much as a year, and the Council of Castile had to make up its mind to intervene.

374

Its first decision was to centralize all the fairs in Medina del Campo, which would at least bring more order into the situation and reduce expenses. Consequently, exchange operations were taken away from Villalón and that fair was reduced to its initial status of a simple economic market. Medina de Ríoseco's turn came in the next year, 1567; it was eliminated from the financial market in spite of the support given its resistance by the Bishop of Cuenca, confessor of Philip II.

In succeeding years the delay in payments became more acute, aggravating the problem and producing the bankruptcy of a number of merchants in the chief Spanish cities, and, as a result of this, a new delay in business transactions. The confusion created was so great that in 1571 the mayor of Medina del Campo decided on a forceful measure: that of expelling traders from the city and seizing the books of the money-changers. This operation was a harsh blow for Medina, since many merchants moved to Madrid, just then coming to life as a financial center owing to the disorder in the Castilian fairs. On the other hand, this lack of order gravely prejudiced the country's interests, for difficulties in liquidating bills of exchange progressively hampered the exchange contracted by foreign merchants for payment at the Medina fair. In 1567, for example, Genoa banned exchange on Spain.

In the face of this chaotic situation, the need arose for a new reform. The plan, set forth in 1574, called for suspension of all fair transactions pending from former years and a detailed series of regulations concerning payments to be made in the future. Nothing was accomplished, however, for disaster came the following year in the form of the bankruptcy of the monarchy decreed by Philip II, and a rise in the *alcabala* sales tax from 1.2% to 10%. Both measures meant the collapse of financial and economic activity. Medina del Campo felt the blow so sharply that its fair was suspended until 1578.

At that date the guarantees offered by the Crown to its creditors succeeded in bringing back the Genoese and Lyonese. Medina recovered some of its previous activity, though it could not prevent competition from Madrid and other centers. It progressively recovered, however, especially after 1590, a date which represented the high point in silver imports from America. But in 1594 came a definitive and unexpected crisis: just when the flood of silver was at its height, repeated delays in the return of the galleons gave rise to such serious difficulties that the fairs were interrupted for four years. They were resumed in 1598, though for only a short time, since the Castilian fairs were transferred to Burgos, coinciding with transfer of the Court there. Medina del Campo was still able to hold a fair in 1604, but in 1606 the definitive return of the Court to Madrid gave the kingdom's permanent financial leadership to its political capital.

BANKS. The banking system inherited from the Middle Ages rested on the distinction between two types of activities. The *cambium minutum* evolved very early into the *deposit bank,* probably introduced into Barcelona in the 13th century and certainly into Castile before 1348. This *cambium minutum* (exchange of large coins for small ones, national for foreign money and vice versa) was restricted to the *cambiadores* or money-changers (from Latin *campsores*). More precisely, they were called *canviadors de menuts* in Catalonia, where there also existed a specific term (*canviador público*) to distinguish the deposit banker. *Cambium per litteras,* or negotiation by bills of exchange, was accessible only to the great merchant-bankers, who dealt in merchandise as well as money.

This distinction continued to exist in the 16th century, although the old terms which expressed it became confused. Now the small money-changers of former times could also speculate on bills of exchange (some even began to call themselves bankers), while the old merchant-bankers could be called "cambiadores."

But apart from these fine points of language, what we must remember as characteristic of this period is the survival of the old system, with important modifications related to the extension of its different components. Development of *cambium minutum* declined, owing to the effects of Ferdinand and Isabella's monetary ordinances, and that of deposit banking increased, especially development of credit operations (camouflaged by discretionary bills) as a consequence of extraordinary financial and mercantile progress. When describing this situation we must emphasize the regulation of deposit banks (pragmatic decree of 1554, giving guarantees to depositors: obligation of all bankers to have the support of at least one other banker, and to furnish bond) and predominance of foreigners (Germans and Genoese) in large dealings involving public credit. Carande believes that Castilian merchants subscribed only one-fifth of these operations, and that of this fifth the better portion was held by Castilians living in Flanders (among them the Maluenda family of Burgos). As for operations carried out by the merchants who stayed in Castile, doing business at court and at the fairs, this same author attributes the following characteristics to them:

(1) The amount of their dealings in public credit—except for the cases mentioned in section (5)—was on a small scale.

(2) These were credits intended to cover the obligations of the kingdom, with no foreign payments made; and consequently they did not earn the profits which accrued in the conventional course of foreign exchange.

(3) Outstanding among their operations were contracts for lending money and supplying merchandise.

(4) The drafts which these merchants accepted to cover their credits were almost always assigned on ordinary and extraordinary sales made by the Crown, and could only be paid on receipt of remittances from the Indies.

(5) Among the contracts of this group of merchants the largest ones involved farming of collection of the revenues of the Crusade, while foreign bankers enjoyed almost without interruption the large profits brought in by masterships of the military orders.

One more class of Castilian bankers must be mentioned: the group of merchants resident in the country who worked in careful cooperation with the most active and powerful foreign bankers. This was the case, though it was seldom repeated, of one Rodrigo de Dueñas, Charles V's banker from 1529 to 1556, or one Simón Ruiz, Philip II's moneylender from 1576 to 1587. Both were natives of Medina.

THE PRICE REVOLUTION. In contrast to the regressive tendency of the 15th century, Spanish prices underwent a sharp rise in the 16th, with an index of 100 in 1501 climbing to 412 in 1600. That is, they quadrupled in the course of a century. This rise, well described as "revolutionary," is also perceptible in the other European countries, though in lesser degree. It deserves special attention, for it

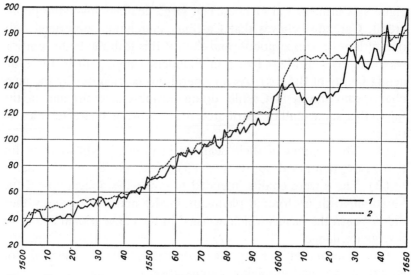

GRAPH SHOWING EVOLUTION OF PRICES AND WAGES (1 AND 2 RESPECTIVELY) AT THE DATES INDICATED (*after* HAMILTON). Figures at left have been estimated on the basis of index = 100 for the years 1570–1580.

comes within the area of the great debate over the origins of modern capitalism. Let us, therefore, analyze its chronology, its causes and effects.

CHRONOLOGY. After establishing annual indexes, Hamilton, the great specialist in the history of Spanish prices, proposed a division into three great stages: from 1501 to 1550, moderate rise (index going from 33.26 to 69.05); from 1551 to 1600 (index 137.23), climax of the rise; from 1601 to 1650 (index 143.22), no change.

There can be no doubt that throughout the course of the 16th century the secular trend of Spanish prices was upward. With few exceptions, the index numbers grow from year to year till they reach their highest point in 1600. In this sense it can be admitted that, as a consequence, the price revolution "culminated" at the end of the century. But the term is not so acceptable insofar as it suggests, by contrast, that the rise in the first half of the century was "moderate." We must establish as a point of departure that highest prices do not mean maximum rise, and that if we consult Hamilton's own figures, the *proportional* increase was higher in 1501–1550 (107%) than in 1551–1600 (98%). We must contrast the maximum *absolute increase* of the second phase with the greater

378

relative increase of the first. This is what is reflected in the semi-logarithmic scale of Hamilton's indexes (p. 380), and a fundamental truth can be deduced from it: in the evolution of Spanish prices *the year 1562 represents the point marking the transition from a clearly upward tendency (1501–1562, annual rate of increase 2.8%) to another, more moderate trend (1562–1600, annual rate of increase 1.3%).*

CAUSES. Hamilton's explanation comes fully within the area of the quantitative theory: according to him, inflation reached its peak in the second half of the 16th century, corresponding exactly to the massive receipts of precious metals from the Indies (see p. 324); in his words, "the abundant mines of America were the principal cause of the Price Revolution in Spain."

This argument could be discussed from two points of view, the theoretical and the real. As for the first, economists still cannot agree on the true relationship between the amount of money in circulation and the price level. We shall not go into a discussion of this, for it is very complex, though since we are dealing with the 16th century, a period of very rudimentary economies, Chabert's observation on present-day underdeveloped countries fits in very well here: "The quantitative theory gives a fairly clear explanation of the movement of prices in poor and underdeveloped countries where, since money is spent as soon as earned, volume of consumption is closely linked to the amount of currency. On the other hand, the theory loses value when applied to industrialized countries; since they have great currency resources at their disposal, these do not concretely and decisively influence overall consumption, and consequently the concept of speed of circulation loses much of its significance."

An analysis of Hamilton's thesis offers a great stumbling block if looked at from a real point of view. If it is indeed true that, in agreement with our analysis, the great rise in prices took place in the first half of the 16th century, it cannot very well be related to maximum imports of American metals, which took place in the second half of the century. Perhaps—as Elliott suggests—the objection could be resolved by considering that, in fact, American silver had the greatest influence on the Spanish situation during the first half of the century, when the proportion of genuinely Spanish products in shipments to the Indies was also greater. This sugges-

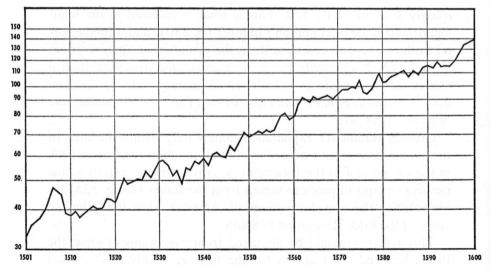

Semilogarithmic scale appled to HAMILTON's figures to show a *real* version of the expansion of prices and wages in the 16th century, as explained in the text. The evolution of the cyclical movement is more rapid early in the century than in its second half, in contrast to the impression given in the preceding graph.

tion, however, though it has the merit of putting us on our guard against the risk of falling into the opposite view (denial of any monetary influence on prices), does not give us sufficient grounds to speak of correlation.

Not forgetting the *monetary factor,* whose influence is certain though not fully determined, the acute inflationary process during Charles V's reign calls for other explanations. These might be, among others, the great increase in the national debt, and especially the tremendous increase in demand (creation of the new American market and growth in the Castilian market because of the larger number of inhabitants). The *demographic factor* deserves as much consideration as the monetary one.

EFFECTS. Exact knowledge of the effects of the price rise encounters an insuperable obstacle: the absence, up till now, of any statistical study of any aspect of production to compare with the unbroken succession of price indexes. This absence has made the argument center almost exclusively around the comparative progress of prices and wages, the only figures as yet available. The result has been a unilateral interpretation of the true facts.

The origin of this goes back to Hamilton himself; in 1929 he held that, in general terms, the gap between European prices and wages had favored accumulation of capital. The drop in cost of production, of which wages are the basic element, must have given businessmen the opportunity to realize exceptionally high profits. Hamilton presented the case of Spain as an exception to the general rule, for there "wages lagged behind prices, but not enough to afford extraordinary profits and thus to give a great impetus to capitalism." Immediately after this, in 1930, the authority of Keynes clothed and consecrated the previous thesis (theory of profit inflation) by again pointing out the excessive rise in Spanish wages (very close to the level of prices) as the largest contributing cause of the country's economic inferiority. And thus one of the "classic" explanations of Peninsular economic backwardness was formulated.

Objections, both theoretical and real, can also be raised to these theories. In regard to the first type of objection, it must be said that Keynes' and Hamilton's interpretation is excessively pessimistic, that it rests on a too absolute incompatibility of interest between capital and labor, between employers and employees, between accumulation of profits and real wages. Within the second type, we must point out the fact that apart from the Spanish wage indexes, which are an abstraction, the only Spanish wage actually comparable to foreign ones, that of the Valencian mason between 1520 and 1600, shows a loss in purchasing power (equal to the lag of wages behind prices) of about the same nature as that of European masons (around 40%). The conclusion to be drawn from this is not, then, the supposed lack of possibility for capitalization, but rather the absence of productive investments, or the predominance of unproductive ones, for the first capital sums amassed.

In any case, the problem has not been well stated. If it was improper to deduce the effects of the rise from the relation of prices to wages, it is still more so to restrict these last solely to industrial wages. The essentially agricultural character of these economies must not be forgotten, and then it will be understood that the effects of the inflationary phenomenon must be measured, particularly, in relation to the size and distribution of revenue from land. It is unfortunate that here we are confronted with a total lack of data.

THE MONARCHY'S FINANCIAL CRISES AND THEIR CONSEQUENCES.
The finances of the Spanish State in the 16th century were characterized by a headlong race between expenditures and income
which, when a balance between the two could not be achieved, implied the ever increasing intervention of businessmen as moneylenders to the Crown.

In *Castile* the chief sources of revenue were the *alcabala;* that is,
a use tax of 10%, and a *servicio* of 300 million maravedís, or
267,300 ducats yearly, granted every three years. To this were
added duties on imports and exports, other special taxes such as the
one on silk, the revenues of the three military orders (with a mean
of 50 million maravedís annually, or approximately 135,000
ducats), confiscations made by the Inquisition, the amount produced by sale of indulgences, and a special tax for the Crusade,
both these latter imposed by the Pope as a contribution to the
struggle with the Turks. *Aragon* paid an annual *servicio* of 200,000
ducats, granted by the Cortes of Monzón in 1533, but it could not
be obliged to make further payments. From the kingdom of *Sicily*
the Crown received an annual donation of 75,000 escudos and
duties on the export of wheat. *Naples,* apart from direct taxes collected from time to time, made a number of donations which between 1535 and 1552 amounted to 5,185,000 ducats, with an annual average of 290,000. In *Milan,* the salt monopoly brought in
the largest revenue; in addition, the territory paid an annual donation of some 300,000 ducats. The *Low Countries* brought in
3,500,000 ducats in some years, aside from the donation of
500,000. In comparison with these sums coming in from the Crown
countries, the amounts received from the "royal fifth" of remittances from the Indies were not very important: during the reign of
Charles V these amounts did not exceed 350,000 to 400,000
ducats; only at the time of Philip II did they increase considerably.

The sum of these revenues, which rose to fabulous totals for the
time, was still not sufficient to pay the heavy expenses of Spanish
policies. The State plugged up the holes as best it could, but was
unable to make regular payments, as the efficient working of Imperial policy demanded. For this purpose it was obliged to call for aid
from the bankers. Only the great moneylending merchants could
assure regular payments with their loans (for example, soldiers'
monthly pay). Thus, *asientos* or contracts became general; these

were loans which had to be paid in cash with absolute regularity, while their repayment was by its nature irregular. In fact, the king almost never paid at the time agreed upon, and hence the necessity arose of penalizing these arrears by a forfeit of 10% annually.

Asientos were guaranteed by revenues from public finances. Each of them was usually pledged against one of the State's sources of income: first, the Crusade, *alcabalas, servicio,* and later the *millones.* As a proof of this guarantee the moneylenders received so-called *juros de resguardo,* or income bonds, which had to come due, with accrued interest, at the time the credit was liquidated. These bonds were more substantial than a simple guarantee, however, for they were negotiable paper: the creditor had the right to give back different bonds from those he had obtained in deposit, so long as they yielded the same rate of interest (5 to 7%) and represented the same amount of capital. That is to say, the moneylender had the right to speculate with these collateral bonds, and along with this right the opportunity to recover the capital he had advanced, long before the time agreed on. When the moment came to liquidate the contract, he had only to buy some equivalent bonds on the market. This type of speculation was very frequent among Philip II's bankers.

Throughout the century, then, a constant increase in its financial needs led the State to an ever growing use of credit. But this recourse, which served to solve immediate difficulties, in fact only aggravated the problem, since it involved paying extremely high rates of interest. The budget of 1562, for example, assigned a total of 1,430,000 ducats to be paid simply as interest on *juros,* or fiduciary bonds. In the face of this onerous situation the State finally resorted to a number of unilateral measures. It extended the maturity of debts in 90% of all cases; reduced the rate of return, at least in 1563, 1608, and 1621; increased the value of gold in 1566 (the ducat raised from 350 to 400 maravedís); and, in particular, periodically declared itself bankrupt. Just when the time came to settle its debts, the Spanish State showed its inability to face up to its obligations by declaring itself in bankruptcy.

The first time it resorted to this radical measure was in 1557, when the Emperor Charles V was still alive. The decree in June of that year had attempted to fund a terribly burdensome floating debt of 7 million ducats, interest charges on the larger part of which had been in arrears since 1552. Eighteen years later, when the second bankruptcy was declared, the inadequacy of the method applied in 1577 became clear. In 1575, in fact, the official estimate raised the funded debt to 22 million ducats and the new floating debt to 15 million more. That is, a total of 37 million ducats, to which must be added the pledging of the royal treasury's total revenues, the refusal of the bankers to grant new credits, the economic prostration so clearly shown in the Castilian fairs, and the Cortes' bad temper about the magnitude of the usury problem and the unquenchable flow of precious metals out of the kingdom. This inescapable bankruptcy was well received by the people, who wanted to see the Crown's chief creditors, the Genoese, whom they accused of ruining the country, ruined as well. The only ones who escaped were the Fuggers and Lorenzo Spinola, owing to the numerous services they had bestowed on the Crown, and especially to the Crown's need to spare a couple of strong firms with which to do business in the future. It is hardly necessary to add that, contrary to popular opinion, the bankruptcy of 1575 had the most dismal consequences. It was a decisive landmark in Spain's economic prostration and marked a serious crisis in the international financial circuit, shaken to its foundations at the great junctions of Antwerp and Genoa.

After the bankruptcies of 1557 and 1575 the road ahead was all too clear. These unfortunate precedents and the ever growing difficulties of the Crown combined to place it on a sort of toboggan, in which every new suspension of payments—as happened in 1596, 1607, 1627, and 1647, showing an unusual periodicity of twenty years—only brought it closer to the indescribable chaos of the late 17th century. Thus foreign aid became more and more necessary. And so the vicious circle was complete: the larger the State's debts became, the harder it was to meet them; and, conversely, as collection became more difficult, higher and higher guarantees were demanded.

28 · American Colonial Economy from 1550 to 1700

The period of discovery and conquest of American soil by Spain came to an end about the year 1550, and the effective colonization of the New World began. This date represents the formation of the Hispano-American economic complex which for two and a half centuries was to determine, in large part, the destinies of world economy.

In the preceding pages we have examined some of the important repercussions, affecting both Spain and Europe, of the American territories' entrance into the economics of the 16th century, especially through exploitation of the mining wealth of those regions. In this chapter we shall attempt to sketch an overall picture of the American colonial economy from 1550 to 1700, in order to show how the recession which took place in the New World beginning with the second half of the 17th century served to aggravate the severe depression experienced by Spain during its second century of Hapsburg rule. As Pierre Chaunu, a recent and discerning historian of Hispano-American trade, has said: as soon as America, after the ten-year period from 1630 to 1640, ceased to flood Spain with its riches, a process of diminished trade and economic difficulties was ushered in, not only for Spain, but by recoil for the whole European area.

THE COURSE OF DEMOGRAPHY: DROP IN POPULATION. Up to the end of the 18th century we have no even approximately accurate figures for the population of the Indies. Therefore, whatever we say about American demography between 1550 and 1700 must be looked at with a critical eye.

One fact, however, seems to be certain: the steep drop in indigenous population throughout the 16th century. This vertical fall of the American Indian population appears to correspond with the figures given by the American writers Woodrow Borah and Shelburne Cook in regard to central Mexico: 25 million inhabitants in the pre-Cortez period; 16,800,000 in 1532; 6,300,000 in 1548; 2,650,000 in 1568; 1,900,000 in 1580; 1,375,000 in 1595; and 1,075,000 in 1605. According to these figures the population, notably dense before the conquest, diminished by more than 90% between 1519 and 1607 owing to the effects of war, economic and social upheavals, and new diseases. The demographic catastrophe which followed the conquest of Mexico can be described as one of the worst in the history of the human race.

What were its causes? The depopulation of the Indies has been attributed by some authors to the cruelty and frenzy of the conquistadores. However, the truth is more complex. The demographic drop was produced by some intrinsic causes, and by the lethal impact of a superior culture on an inferior one. As for the first-mentioned causes, Borah and Cook themselves have explained that during the 15th century the population of central Mexico had surpassed the number which the land would have been able to support in the long run, in relation to the existing technical level of agriculture. Their opinion is based on the fact that there were vast areas of land which had been destroyed or seriously eroded by the relatively harmless methods of cultivation with the *coa,* a sort of hoe. (The basic food crops were corn and beans.) This opinion is supported by the massacres practiced by the Aztecs, prevalent all over central Mexico. Even before the arrival of the Spaniards, the aboriginal population was headed for disaster.

And so, Hernán Cortez' landing merely quickened the process. To erosion of the soil was added the immense destructive force of European diseases (in a population which had little if any resistance to them), as well as very severe disturbances in the economic and social systems, among which were arrangements for distributing and storing food. Even the simple physical destruction caused by the conquest, in the face of the Indians' understandable resistance to it, was a contributing factor. On the other hand, the fact that many Indians retired into the jungle or into inaccessible mountain refuges must also have had a considerable effect.

Until 1650 the number of Indians continued to decrease, though more slowly than at first. The total population had risen, however, thanks to immigration of white Spaniards (along with Portuguese and Italian groups), imports of Negro slaves (which tripled in eighty years, from 1570 to 1650), and development of a *mestizo,* or mixed-blood class. The number of whites rose from 120,000 to 650,000; Negroes and *mestizos* from 230,000 to 1,300,000.

Depopulation resulted in one extraordinarily important fact of economic life: lack of manpower. This is the fundamental factor in America's decline during the 17th century.

STRATIFICATION OF AMERICAN SOCIAL STRUCTURE: THE RULING CLASS. During the second half of the 16th century there was a rapid stratification of America's population into social classes, called "colonial castes" in the official vocabulary. This process was carried out to the benefit of the white immigrant population.

It must be kept in mind, to begin with, that the Spanish population which emigrated to America throughout the course of the 16th century was even lower than that given by the least optimistic figures. Rosenblat has estimated it as some 120,000 souls. M. Hernández, basing his figures on the inventory of the *Catalogue of Passengers to the Indies,* and after correcting this number to include clandestine immigration and the possible offspring of marriages contracted in the Indies, establishes a figure of 69,000 by 1570. This represents less than 1% of the total population. The smallness of this figure, no matter what value can in fact be given to the data, explains the attention paid by the State to social hierarchy in the Indies: a white minority had to determine the development of the colonies.

The bases of power for this ruling minority—who very soon received the name of *criollos,* or Creoles—were control of property, concession of titles of nobility, connection with the upper bureaucracy, and the right to bear arms. In regard to the first point, suffice it to say that after 1560 all the factors tending to concentrate land in the hands of a few were developed in the widest possible manner. The history of property in America at this period coincides with the history of latifundism there, a subject which has been flawlessly studied for the 17th century in New Spain by the French historian François Chevalier. The distribution of *peonías* and *caballerías,* which had been carried out from the beginning (p. 318), in order to settle and cultivate the land, as we noted before, gradually lost its original character when a principle of qualification was introduced, giving preference in the distribution of land to the conquistadores and their descendants (ordinances of 1573). If we add to this the Crown's difficulties and economic straits, which led it to concede much unsettled and Crown land to those who had money—the great proprietors—and the depopulation of many Indian villages, we can understand that the large landowners were able to round out their possessions within a very few years. The royal cedula of 1591 recognized the failure of the Crown's policy when it ordered a review of all titles to land, confiscation of those which were not considered legitimate, and a demand for payment to legalize situations created outside the law. This order introduced the system called "composition of lands," so typical of the 17th century. Through abuses which are quite understandable, this order was equivalent to authorizing the usurpations carried out by the wealthy and powerful. And so latifundism was consolidated, and the State's successive bankruptcies during the 17th century only made it grow stronger. Nevertheless, official doctrine, revealed in the Laws of the Indies of 1680, continued to be based on the principle of avoiding the amortization and excessive concentration of property, a doctrine which conflicted with the daily practice of qualification and *mayorazgo,* the latter having been established in the Indies by the royal cedula of 1529.

The power of this landed aristocracy—called, as a class, *hacendados*—was further strengthened by the fact that the implementation of bureaucratic functions also devolved upon it; this came to be more and more true as the system of sale of public offices by the Crown became a general practice. The Crown fell into the trap which had been laid for it when it converted the bureaucracy of the Indies into a closed group, isolated from the people and surrounded by extraordinary privileges—apart from the fact that officials were allowed to perform their functions with impunity. Thus a bureaucratic and administrative class came into being which profited heavily from the American economy. Many members of this class succeeded in becoming large landowners.

The concession of a new type of gentry, "hombres hidalgos de solar conocido," or gentlemen of known landed origin, and the mania to acquire titles of nobility, which passed undiminished to the Indies, had the result of placing the Spanish element at a distance from the natives. After 1630 there were numerous cases of sale of *hidalgo* titles, but these were only the visible sign of a social situation that was already firmly established. Like the privilege of bearing arms, given exclusively to nobles and *encomenderos,* it served to emphasize their prestige and create a mental attitude which was both typical of their class and different from that of others.

Latifundists, bureaucrats, *encomenderos,* and *hidalgos* were the top rung of Creole society. They held the power and the agricultural wealth. Merchants and artisans were relegated to second place, since they were absolutely banned from public office. However, the Crown also intervened in the formation of a hierarchy, organizing "universities" of merchants and professional guilds, with all their privileges and disadvantages. Nevertheless, under the pretext of certain commercial activities, some merchants took advantage of the process of accumulating healthy sums of capital which permitted them to purchase urban real estate and acquire rural property by buying up mortgages. Thus, in the course of the 17th century an incipient moneyed bourgeoisie began to form, with business interests in the seaport cities and sugar and cocoa plantations or livestock ranches—according to the region—in the interior. This class was the one which gave form to the typical "Creolism" of the 18th century.

THE LABOR FORCE: INDIANS, MESTIZOS, AND NEGROES. The Spaniards, like other European colonial powers in the same period, found a large and cheap supply of manpower in America: the indigenous population. To tie this population to the soil and teach it labor discipline was an ungrateful task, during which many errors were committed. The selfishness of the proprietors was often corrected by the Crown, though the fact that the government was so far away meant that between legislation and practice there was a vast breach which made it easy to flout the laws. And thus the practices of *encomienda* and *mita,* forms of labor to which we have referred previously, became established in the Indies.

Not all of the indigenous peoples were incorporated into colonial society and economy. Rosenblat notes that in 1570 only 1,850,000 American Indians had entered the Spanish social orbit (18%). M. Hernández believes that the figure should be raised to 40% (he counts the population of villages and towns). In any case, the task of getting the American colonial economy under way fell upon a fairly small contingent, still further reduced in numbers at the end of the 16th century and the beginning of the 17th, under the direction of the civilized white minority. This obliged the Crown to make use of the Negro slave.

From the economic as well as the social point of view, the problem of the introduction of African slave labor into America offers considerations of enormous interest. It was a measure imposed by circumstances, essentially inhuman and further aggravated by the greed of slave buyers and traders; it inundated the New World with a foreign mass which strongly influenced its already divergent ethnic structure. The regions most affected were those in which the loss of indigenous population was most acute. This was precisely the case of the Antilles, where there is evidence of importation of slaves as early as Columbus' second voyage. The Crown's policy was vacillatory at first: it authorized the slave trade in 1510, banned it in 1516, and finally accepted it definitively—though always with repugnance—during the early years of Charles V's reign. In 1527 the contract system was established; earlier, a system of licenses had been used. The contract system meant that the Crown allowed a private individual to bring a quota of Negroes into the colonies in exchange for a fee. In the early stages it was German and Flemish traders who benefited from the contracting of slaves. Later, in the first half of the 17th century, it was the Portuguese who grew wealthy in the trade by exporting slaves from Angola. Once the political unity of the Peninsula was broken, they were succeeded by Andalusians (from Seville and Cádiz) until in 1696 the Portuguese again monopolized the Negro trade.

It is difficult to estimate the number of African slaves imported into America between 1560 and 1700 (by the end of the 17th century there were 800,000). For the year 1570, Rosenblat gives the figure of some 230,000 Negroes and *mestizos* (2.3% of the population). A prolific race, the Negro nevertheless was also subjected to the process of destruction by endemic diseases to which he had not previously been exposed. But he succeeded in overcoming the loss because of the constant renewal of his human material. And in the end he became completely acclimated. The revival of colonial agriculture after the middle of the 17th century was made possible by Negro peonage.

Crossbreeding of the three races which came together in America during this period resulted in the appearance of three chief mixed-blood types: *mestizo* (white-Indian), *mulatto* (white-Negro), and *zambo* (Indian-Negro). Mixed-breeds of all types, relegated to a subordinate position in colonial society, constituted, along with the Negroes, the manpower reserve, the colonial peonage.

EVOLUTION OF FORMS OF LABOR. The dramatic battle between the Crown and the *encomenderos* in regard to the New Laws of 1542 abolishing *encomienda* (p. 320) was ended during 1545–1546 because of suspension of the laws. Nevertheless, the action of the mother country had not been in vain. After the middle of the 16th century personal enslavement of the Indian, which had survived in some regions, was abolished; and, in the words of Ots Capdequí, "personal *encomienda*" (of a feudal type) was distinguished from "tax *encomienda*." This in theory at least. But in fact, social realities continued to impose, in New Spain as well as Peru, a labor system which strongly resembled medieval European serfdom. The Indian bound to the *encomendero* gave him part of his harvest and his domestic production (a portion which in certain regions later came to be paid in pesos), and the *encomendero,* besides fulfilling the obligations specified by the law, paid the Crown 1% of the income thus obtained. The bone of contenton continued to be securing *encomiendas* in perpetuity; this stemmed from the concession of *encomiendas* hereditary for two lifetimes, granted in 1536. In this regard there was a constant struggle between Crown and *encomenderos,* the latter profiting from the Crown's financial straits, especially during the reigns of Philip II and Philip III, to achieve their goals. As a matter of fact, these financial embarrassments were what brought about the extinction of the *encomiendas*. These had originally been a royal prerogative graciously granted to the conquistadores and their descendants, but eventually they became subject to taxation. This policy was begun in 1619 with a tax of one-third of their income placed on the *encomenderos* of Peru, and reached its peak after 1687, when a general tax of 50% was placed on all *encomenderos*. This lasted until 1695 and was a severe blow to the institution.

Besides the taxpaying Indians there were also those of the settlements, and the plantation Negroes. Settlement Indians, living on the periphery of the colonial world, preserved their old customs of communal labor and collective landholding under the direction of the religious orders. In this regard it is of interest to mention the Jesuit settlements in Paraguay, where the Guaraní tribes were slowly trained in up-to-date agricultural methods. A disciplined community of indigenous workers, such a settlement as this gave a new example of economic and cultural mingling between the world of the colonizers and the colonized. As for the plantation Negroes, especially those on the sugar plantations, their labor can only be described as slavery. In spite of this, however, once the Negro had reached America he was in a more favorable situation than the *encomendero's* Indian, for not only did he represent invested capital, but he was a precious work unit which could not be wasted or exhausted.

In the world of American labor the lowest rung of the ladder was occupied by those who worked for wages; that is, the miners, subject to the arbitrary transfer and forced labor of the *mita* system. Theoretically, the *mita* miner was a free laborer who received a wage for his work, agreed upon in advance. But in fact he was obliged to work in a specific place under very harsh conditions and away from his birthplace. As depopulation became more severe, measures were taken to fill the quotas of workers for the mines. The *comisario de alquileres,* or commissioner of hiring, whose task was to recruit a labor force and carry out the labor regulations, dates from the beginning of the 17th century. From the same period (1609) we find an order canceling the parceling out of Indians for agriculture and domestic service and obliging them to hire themselves out to private individuals in the public squares. None of these measures succeeded in overcoming the manpower crisis which existed in the mines after 1630. From that time onward there were frequent projects and counterprojects having to do with suppression or modification of the *mita* system. After a period of greater freedom in labor came the reestablishment of the pure *mita* system by the Marquis de la Palata (1681–1689), a viceroy of Charles II.

The *laborío* deserves a paragraph of its own. This was a means by which the Indian or *mestizo* might achieve a certain freedom of movement and even earn a good wage. *Laboríos* appeared in agriculture at the beginning of the 17th century and arose from the manpower shortage caused by Indian depopulation. To attract

Indians to their haciendas the owners had to offer higher wages, small plots of land, and advances of money. This system of *advances* on wages created a tie to the land on the part of the peon which he could not escape until he had paid his debt. And so these were fictitious wages.

AGRICULTURE: FOOD CROPS AND APPEARANCE OF INDUSTRIAL CROPS. The decline of Spain and her colonial empire in the 17th century stems from one decisive factor: the frustration of American agricultural life. This fact was much more noticeable in the New World because the State's mercantilist policy placed all its hopes on the development of mining, and the monopolistic goals of the mother country limited the expansion of agricultural products (vineyards and olive groves) which would have constituted a firm base for settlement, and the possibility of creating a consumer's market for Spanish industrial products.

As has been said before, in the initial stages of American colonization the State spared no efforts to convert America into a permanently settled colony, based on agriculture and livestock development. But just as the Antilles became almost depopulated and unproductive because of the lure of the treasures of the mainland, so the rest of the continent suffered during the entire colonial period from the oppressive weight of silver mining. In spite of this, however, the needs of the colonies themselves made it necessary for them to try to be self-supporting in the basic agricultural products, a stage which was attained about the year 1560 after a period of scarcity in foodstuffs that became very serious at times. After that date, coincident on the one hand with population loss and on the other with the extension of crop cultivation, agriculture in America went through a period of prosperity, as noticeable in New Spain as in Peru. Wheat was the basic crop everywhere, though the old native American plants such as the potato also flourished. The introduction of the plow and yoke of oxen was a considerable step forward, though it was not taken everywhere. On the other hand, it appears that in Peru the settlers scorned the use of guano, already known to the Incas, as fertilizer.

Besides these basic crops two others which were typically Mediterranean developed with equal success: the vine and the olive. Both spread out in all directions, beginning in small districts where they had become acclimated. They gained impetus because of the considerable profit earned by those who cultivated them, for wine and olive oil were products imported from the home country which commanded high prices. Harvests, more and more abundant, soon came to constitute a severe threat to the Andalusian producers and merchants, who obtained from Philip II and later from Philip III (1602) agreements banning the planting of olive trees and vines. Although these laws, compiled in 1680, were not universally obeyed, especially by ecclesiastics, who needed wine and olive oil for sacramental purposes, there is no doubt that they largely paralyzed the development of American agriculture. The home country's mercantilist principles won a Pyrrhic victory over the colonial producer.

Two products which underwent intensive cultivation, on the other hand, were sugar and cocoa. Sugar cane was the earliest crop to be developed. Established in the Antilles after 1506, it went over into New Spain (p. 321) and from there to Peru in 1561. This crop, produced by Negro labor, was of special interest to the Crown. Its prosperity was checked by the severe crisis of the 17th century. After 1618 rules were established to restrict its expansion.

As for cocoa, it began to be planted in Venezuela about the middle of the 17th century, in response to the economic stimulus of the European consumer's growing demands. Coffee and tobacco followed an identical path. However, the Crown found it difficult to harmonize the agricultural interests of the different colonial groups, evidenced by the fact that what was permitted in New Granada (Colombia)—coffee for instance—was banned in Peru.

LIVESTOCK: ITS DEVELOPMENT. The rapid spread of Spanish cattle in America brought about a revolution unprecedented in the history of that continent. For the first time the Indian had meat to eat, a horse to ride, and a draft animal to work for him. Many regions benefited from this situation, and even the poorest ones could count on the goat, which easily adapted itself to the Mexican and Andean slopes and was a great help in domestic economy on the lowest level.

Even if we take into account a certain amount of loss in native livestock, the Andean llama for example, the balance was enormously favorable for America and was a prelude to the future development of its prodigious possibilities. Horses, donkeys, oxen, sheep, goats, and pigs all contributed in different proportions, according to the region (in Peru, for example, raising of swine was very limited), to the self-sufficiency of the people. It is impossible to state which class of livestock gave the best economic results, since the ease of transport furnished by horses and the use of cattle in agriculture could not compete with hides from cattle and goats and the wool sheared from sheep.

Sheep flocks benefited from the extension of the Mesta's legislation to America (1529), though very soon the same conflicts arose between herding and agriculture as those which had affected and continued to affect the mother country. The livestock breeder soon became an *estanciero,* proprietor of a flock which required permanent *estancia,* or quarters, near pastures, even though he did not aspire to ownership of the land. The interests of *estancieros* and agricultural workers soon conflicted, with the result that in 1550 it was decreed that *estancias* could not be granted except in places remote from the *encomiendas,* and that the size of flocks should be reduced. The struggle between farmers and herders continued to grow, and sometimes was even fiercer than that between *encomenderos* and Indians. In spite of prohibitive legislation, what emerged from the dispute was the fenced-in, permanent *estancia,* or ranch, which would continue to develop throughout the 18th century in the places most favorable to it, such as the La Plata region.

MINING AND THE AMERICAN TREASURE. As we have already mentioned (pp. 322–323), by about 1560 the foundations of American mining had already been laid: great silver deposits in New Spain and Peru; the technique used to exploit them by mixing silver with mercury and salt; and the quota system for forced labor in the mines (*mita*). In the course of the next half-century, up to 1610, the yield of the silver mines continued to increase, owing to massive use of manpower and discovery of new seams by the so-called "mother lode" system. Also, the technique of "American amalgamation," used in Mexico after 1557, was soon brought to Peru. It became general there after 1571 and led to a high point in the exploitation of silver mines.

In New Spain the chief deposits were those of Pachuca, Sultepec, and Tlalpujahua; in Peru the gold mines of San Juan del Oro and Aporoma, and the silver deposits of Potosí, Pasco (discovered in

1630), and Tarapacá. The mountain of Potosí stood out over all the rest; its period of renown came between 1572 and the middle of the 17th century. The economy of Western Europe, by way of Spain, was fed by that "mountain of silver" for many long years.

We lack data which would permit us to evaluate the production of each of the mining zones and the American continent's total production. The only clue we have for estimating the real volume of American treasure is the metal actually received in Spain—an incomplete figure, for it omits the amount of gold and silver which remained in America, the amount shipped to the Far East, and the part which disappeared through the channels of fraud or contraband (as we have said, this may have amounted to double the known total). In any case, Hamilton's figures clearly show the worldwide importance of mining exploitation in America.

In the graph on p. 324 and the treatment of the price revolution on pp. 377–379, the volume and rhythm of gold and silver exports to Spain have been clearly shown. Let us recall the principal stages:

(1) *Predominance of gold exports (1503–1540)*. After the first shipments of gold from the Antilles in 1503, the export of this precious metal was predominant, and at times exclusive, until 1540.

(2) *Period of equilibrium in export of precious metals (1540–1560)*. The discovery of silver lodes in New Spain and Mexico began to counterbalance the predominance of gold. However, gold exports did not diminish but continued at a peak. In fact, the maximum figures for import of gold to Seville correspond to the ten-year period 1551–1560, with a total of forty-three tons.

(3) *Period of predominance of silver exports (1560–1630)*. Gold production remained stationary, with a drop during 1571 to 1580 and a recovery between 1581 and 1600 (nineteen tons). But the volume of gold imports became insignificant compared with silver. There were four periods in silver imports: a rise from 1560 to 1585 (beginning of the "patio" or amalgamation process); highest point between 1585 and 1630 (with the maximum between the years 1591–1600); slow decline between 1630 and 1650; distinct impoverishment after the latter date.

ROUTES OF AMERICAN TREASURE THROUGH SPAIN. Because of the concentration of American treasure in Spain, the country became converted into a distributing center for precious metals, especially silver, which up till then had been scarce in Europe. The emigration of this metal to Western Europe began—Spooner says—about 1551, or perhaps a little earlier, as a consequence of Charles V's imperialist policy. Remittances were made to Antwerp, with the result that a profound shock was felt in that key financial center. From Antwerp the silver went to England and especially to Italy, where it commanded a premium over gold.

The route established about the middle of the century was soon consolidated, as the needs of Philip II's policies continued to increase. As soon as the metal arrived from America it was sent, either by land or sea, to Laredo or Bilbao, whence it departed for Antwerp. This was the official route. The smuggling routes were less obvious and covered almost all the northern coast and the Pyrenees. After the beginning of the Anglo-Spanish conflict in 1568, the Atlantic route became less favorable; therefore, after 1572 Barcelona was chosen as a shipping point for the metal which, having crossed the entire Peninsula, ended its travels in Genoa. This route converted the Italian city into the chief European silver market, as Augsburg had formerly been for gold.

All along the precious metals route there were pirates and bandits. Gold and silver left a wake of insatiable appetites behind them, which shaped the Indies traffic for a very long time.

TEXTILE MANUFACTURE. American industry continued to move within the narrow limits set by Spain's monopolistic practices, illicit trade, and lack of tradition. Apart from the industries related to the use of vegetable products (precious woods), certain crops (sugar), or animals (hides), America knew no other types of manufacturing activity than artisan work (represented by the guilds). Although there were exquisite specialties in the working of precious metals, iron, and ceramics, though some few cities were outstanding in the production of cloth and blankets, in fact the stimulus of an industrial activity of international scope was lacking.

Only the textile industry seemed to attain this rank during the second half of the 16th century, when an attempt at self-sufficiency was made in the colonies because of shortages and the high cost of cloth in Spain. That was the time when the Peruvian *obrajes,* or mills, appeared; these developed rapidly to supply a growing demand, and were protected by the favorable legislation decreed by

Charles V in 1543. But after 1569 the attitude of the mother country changed and these mills began to be restricted; especially, there was a ban on the use of Indian labor in them under the *reparto* system. Pierre Chaunu believes that the decline of New Spain's looms was also due to the invasion of Oriental silks at reasonable prices, owing to Acapulco's smuggling trade (after 1571).

MONOPOLISTIC ORGANIZATION OF AMERICAN TRADE: ANDALUSIAN AND PERUVIAN MONOPOLIES. The establishment of trade between Spain and her American colonies as a monopolistic system favoring Seville (with an annex in the Canaries) was not achieved immediately. As has been pointed out before, the Crown vacillated—within the mercantilist orthodoxy of the period—between a system of private monopoly and one permitting a certain freedom of movement, a doctrine whose high point was reached in Charles V's Ordinance of 1529. This solution was thwarted after the middle of the 16th century, when it became necessary to defend the silver brought from America against the attacks of privateers. The process coincided with the development of a mercantile corporation strong enough to insure the defense of the Crown's interests, by subsidizing a fleet to protect the traffic of the galleons. This corporation received official sanction with the creation of the Guild of Shippers to the Indies in Seville (1543), the same year that the first step was taken to organize periodic fleets. Hence, it seems that there can be no doubt of the parallelism which existed between the idea of a single fleet and an Andalusian monopoly. The system received full confirmation after 1564–1566 (definitive organization of the fleet system) and 1573 (annulment of the Ordinance of 1529).

Seville's monopoly, confirmed in 1591 and 1626, slowly disappeared in favor of Cádiz during the course of the 17th century; but the idea of an Andalusian monopoly remained. This was due, first of all, to the financial resources of Andalusian businessmen, supported by foreign merchants (Genoese and Portuguese first, followed by French and Dutch); to the network of interests which had been created between the Guild of Shippers or Merchants on the one hand (now with their splendid Exchange building, inaugurated in 1583) and the officials of the House of Trade on the other; to another network, more obscure but no less powerful, between these same merchants and the great Andalusian latifundist magnates (like the Count-Duke of Olivares, as Pierre Chaunu tells us), who held the real power after 1598 and in general cooperated in monopolistic undertakings; and finally, to the routine procedures and lack of imagination of the Spanish administration, which, having prepared a system for transmitting merchandise to America and for receiving silver, allowed foreign interests to infiltrate it and take advantage of it for their own purposes.

In the New World, New Spain and Peru, especially the latter, whence came the largest amount of silver, possessed the counterpart of the Sevillian monopoly. Mexico and Lima were the places where all merchandise received from the mother country had to be sold, exclusively. The case of Lima represented a real obsession, for its monopolistic position is incomprehensible if we recall that Spain had an excellent port on the Atlantic seaboard of South America: Buenos Aires. But Lima's influence stifled the development of the La Plata estuary until well into the 18th century. Lima's monopoly was strengthened with the creation of a Consulate there in 1613. A few years before, a similar institution had been set up in New Spain (Consulate of Mexico, 1592).

THE FLEET SYSTEM: PORTS. The fleet system became established definitively after 1563–1566. All ships sent to the Indies had to travel in convoy, with the exception of those which were sufficiently well armed, slave trading vessels sailing from Angola, and the courier ships which were dispatched at top speed. The ships rendezvoused in Seville, Cádiz, or Sanlúcar de Barrameda, and were sent off in two relays. The *fleet,* going to Veracruz (New Spain), sailed in March or April; in July the *galleons* set sail, bound for Nombre de Dios (Isthmus of Panama). On their return the fleet and the galleons met in February in Havana, whence they returned to Spain about the middle of June.

This system worked without any serious breakdowns in spite of the fact that the escort ships carried merchandise even in the mouths of their cannons. Only on very rare occasions, such as the disastrous battle of Matanzas (1628), was a fleet totally annihilated. It was common to lose ships because their hulls were in bad condition, or because of navigational accidents. However, after the lifting of the tonnage limit in 1560 there was a period when Spain openly controlled the seas, and the important business of interimperial communication functioned at full efficiency. The galleon was the undisputed ruler of the sea, and could look with scorn on French and English intruders.

The situation changed after approximately 1620, the reason being a triple shortage of materiel, experienced crews, and tonnage. Holland's anti-Spanish policy included an embargo on high-quality rigging and mast wood, the lack of which soon became evident in vessels being outfitted for passage to the Indies. The critical shortage of experienced sailors and seamen coincided with the exhaustion of Cantabrian manpower reserves and the fact that Andalusian professional sailors were becoming city dwellers. The raising of the tonnage limit to 600, a more economical burden, meant a technical change in ships—suppression of useless parts, reduction in width—to which the Spaniards did not find it easy to adapt. By about 1630 the galleon was in full retreat before the new types of Atlantic vessels. Another consequence of the increase in tonnage was the inaccessibility of the port of Seville, because of the Sanlúcar sandbar.

After a three-week fair where both import and export merchandise were exchanged, a number of ships sailed from the Isthmus of Panama to Payta (light and valuable merchandise) and Callao (heavy cargo). In 1624, after the Dutch had entered the Pacific, there was a plan to create an Armada of the South Sea. The Sevillians even advanced the sum of 400,000 ducats to Philip IV to carry out this magnificent idea. However, the money was employed in the European theater of war. It was a bad investment, besides being a decision that was to have serious consequences for the future of the Spanish Empire. So an Armada of the South Sea never came into existence.

There was only one regular service on the vast expanse of the Pacific Ocean: the Manila galleon. Once Urdetana had discovered the western return route (Philippines to Mexico) and Manila was founded in 1571, two ships made the journey annually, one going and the other returning, between Manila and Acapulco. The economic importance of these two worlds linked by the Manila galleon, and their different products and needs (America, hungry for spices and silk; Asia, the greatest world consumer of silver), meant that this service, one of the great commercial routes for Imperial contraband, was vital.

In spite of the rigidity of the fleet system, American ports did not always experience the same mercantile prosperity. They rose or fell in importance as the development of the economic regions which they served waxed or waned. About 1560 the two great colonial ports were Veracruz, in New Spain, and Nombre de Dios in the Isthmus of Panama; after them, but much less important, was Santo Domingo. In 1600 the situation had changed in the sense that the first-named ports had progressed (Nombre de Dios was now called Portobello) while Santo Domingo had declined further and the importance of Havana, Cartagena, and San Juan in Puerto Rico had increased. This constellation of ports remained unchanged, within the depressive tendency of the 17th century.

MECHANICS OF AMERICAN TRADE. This subject is one of the most important, but relatively little-known, features of Chaunu's monumental contribution to the study of the Indies trade. We shall try to sketch the most substantial part of the documentation he has so far published. We will pass over the volume of traffic, which will be taken up later when we discuss the trade cycle.

American trade consisted in taking high-priced consumer products to America and bringing back cheap money. The idea that the Indies constituted a national patrimony and that their economy should merely be complementary to that of the mother country was strengthened by the presence of American treasure. Gold and silver would easily pay for the shipments made exclusively by Spain—or at least, that was the theory held at the time. Therefore, when the fleet was late in arriving or there was temporary abundance in the American market, a general outcry arose and drastic measures were adopted. There were frequent occasions when the merchants of Seville refused to load ships with their products, in order to cause shortages in the Indies which would result in fabulous profits the following year and make up for the immobilization of their capital. This was done in the case of Tierra Firme (in 1599) and also of New Spain (in 1629). The mistake made in both cases was the belief that the Indies were a true monopoly market, when in reality contraband and illicit trade made such an economic situation in America impossible.

Now that we have described the general orientation of American trade, its details are of considerable interest.

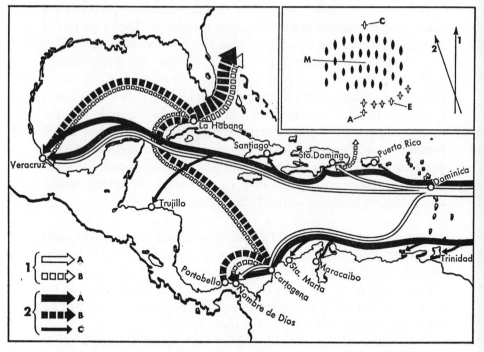

THE INDIES FLEETS IN THE CARIBBEAN.—*Key:* 1, route of the fleets between 1543–1564 (A, outward bound; B, homeward bound); 2, route of the fleets after 1564 (A, outward bound; B, homeward bound; C, route of the ships which separated from the fleet, rejoining it in Havana). INSERT: Composition of the fleet (1, direction of movement; 2, direction of the wind; A, *almiranta,* or flagship; C, *capitana,* or rearguard vessel; M, merchant ships; E, escort ships). *After* CÉSPEDES DEL CASTILLO.

Merchandise to be shipped to the Indies was collected in Seville (after about 1600 it was likely to consist of foreign-made goods), about the same time that the merchants began to worry about the return of the fleet and the ships which would have to be added to it (in cases of lack of cargo space or damage to some of the galleons). The House of Trade was the clearinghouse for claims and planning, which the Council of the Indies processed. All these matters were apt to drag on interminably, except for financial ones, because the Crown was usually in financial straits and the arrival of the fleet was one of its chief concerns, for payments were usually pledged long before its arrival. News of attack by a privateer or an enemy fleet (French, English, or Dutch) would put everyone in a depressed mood and in a frame of mind to make a contribution to the war chest. This was the origin of the "risk tax," one of the pivotal points in the close connection between the Crown and Seville.

Once the fleet had gathered in Cádiz and had been dispatched according to the "registries," which recorded ships, crews, and cargoes, it was under the orders of the captain-general, a very important personage in the American trade, for he was absolute master of the fleet not only during the crossing but also during its stay in the ports of embarkation and disembarkation. A growing number of privileges had placed him outside ordinary law. According to the merchants of Seville, his power was often used to detour American traffic from its normal course.

After the goods had been disembarked in the Indies and checked against the registry, they passed into the hands of merchants, correspondents, and agents; and meanwhile, in a similar manner, the embarkation of precious metals and export products took place: cochineal, indigo, leather, sugar, and medicinal plants. Sugar was very important in Hispaniola and Puerto Rico; cochineal and indigo along the Caribbean coast; leather in New Spain and Cuba.

INSURANCE AND PENSION SYSTEMS: RISK TAX. In the early years of American trade, its capitalist structure showed traces of the old medieval joint ventures: a number of persons would invest funds in the voyage of one or more ships and distribute the profits proportionally. After 1550, when the tempo of the Indies trade changed because of the surge of traffic and tonnage, and the establishment of the annual fleet system, it became necessary to invest large amounts of capital. From then on, as much to protect the ship as its cargo, the use of marine insurance began to develop. It was engaged in by powerful companies and is described in the Ordinances of 1556 of the Consulate of Seville (modelled on those of the Consulate of Burgos of 1537). Premiums were generally very high, as much as 30%; this resulted, as Carande and Céspedes del Castillo have pointed out, in an active campaign of speculation. There were subscriptions covering old ships and perishable cargoes, and there were even cases where nonexistent vessels and cargoes were insured. The profits from American trade permitted all this, even the existence of "betting insurance," which was finally declared illegal.

Another class of insurance affected seamen. It grew out of the atmosphere of brotherhoods and charitable funds so typical of the period, and in 1561 the Brotherhood of Santa María del Buen Aire was set up in Seville, insuring against accident, disability, old age, and orphanhood.

Still another type was risk or damage insurance (*avería*). After a large number of studies on the subject, the most important of which is that of Céspedes del Castillo, Pierre Chaunu has defined this as an *ad valorem* tax on merchandise, whose purpose was to insure it against enemy attacks through the creation of an escort squadron. This tax began to be collected in 1518 as a function of the House of Trade, fluctuated for some time in response to dangers and necessities, and finally became definitively established in 1562, when the Consulate of Seville leased the contract for the tax. It functioned regularly until the crisis of 1620–1630 (when traffic declined and foreign attacks increased), for by that time the tonnage of the escort fleet had become 37% of the total number of ships in the Indies trade (against 12% in 1601), and the cost of ship construction had doubled. In short, *avería* became a tax which devoured the trade it was trying to protect, all the more so because the rapid development of illegal traffic placed a great deal of merchandise outside the rates of such insurance. This is why it was suppressed in the end, together with *ad valorem* customs duties. The royal cedula of 1600 fixed an annual quota to support the so-called Armada of Tierra Firme (which observed the movements of privateers in the Caribbean). Its costs were divided among Peru (350,000 ducats), New Spain (200,000), New Granada (50,000), Cartagena (40,000), and the Spanish State (150,000).

ATTACKS ON AMERICAN TRADE: PRIVATEERS AND PIRATES. The history of foreign powers' aggressions against Spanish trade in the Indies is explained by the greed universally aroused by the silver fleet. Therefore, besides its political aspect, there is an economic one that is even more important: the struggle against Spain's monopoly of a number of colonies made immensely rich by silver.

In the first half of the 16th century privateers of every stripe swarmed over the triangle formed by the Canaries, the African coast, and Cape St. Vincent, lying in wait for ships returning from America. The French, Spain's chief adversaries at the time, were the protagonists at this stage. Later, the larger part of the action was performed by the English, who were the first, with Hawkins and Drake, to carry the struggle to American markets, even those on the Pacific coast. The first exploits were individual (1560–1580), but later they became joint operations stemming from the war unleashed by the defeat of the Armada. It was then that the English fleet tried to take Corunna and Cádiz by storm. After peace was achieved in 1605 the Dutch period followed the English, and was far more serious than its predecessors, for the United Provinces attempted to install themselves in the very heart of the Portuguese-Spanish empire. After 1620 the Dutch offensive began to take on serious proportions. On the one hand, Dutch forces established a foothold in Bahía (1624), whence they threatened Spanish commerce in the Antilles; on the other, they broke Spanish naval supremacy in the Caribbean with their sea power (Battle of Matanzas, 1628). After that time all the Antilles islands, an essential strategic area through which the Indies fleet had to pass, were exposed to foreign attack. Throughout the 17th century Dutch, English, and French installed themselves in the Lesser Antilles, where they encouraged attacks by privateers and buccaneers.

First established on Tortuga, an island off the northwest coast of Santo Domingo, then on different points along the Caribbean shore, supported by the English in Jamaica (after 1654) and the Dutch of Curaçao (after 1634), pirates were the nightmare of the rich Caribbean commercial centers (Portobello, Cartagena, and Maracaibo) and the unescorted ships which carried on intercolonial trade. As a reflection of the impotence which afflicted the Spanish Empire of the period, the fabulous increase in buccaneering demonstrated that Hapsburg economic incapacity had reached a lethal point.

ILLICIT TRADE. The presence of foreigners in the Caribbean raised to the infinite another evil which was gradually eating away the Indies trade: contraband.

Colonial exclusivism, by creating a strained situation in regard to the riches of America, led right from the beginning to a *system of fraud* in the very workings of the Indies trade. Chaunu has pointed out its main characteristics: fraud on the outward journey (false affidavits, unregistered cargo, waybills sent in later, etc.), and on the return trip (sending ships "unregistered" and "to be registered"); fraud outside the registry by means of "permits" given to the flagship and rearguard ship in the convoys.

Until the early years of the 17th century, fraud represented an important debilitating factor in the revenues of the monopoly. But after 1603 these were further weakened by contraband. At that date, in fact, as a measure against the Dutch, a cedula was issued banning import of most of the "rebel" articles intended for America. Not only was the measure flouted by the use of false certificates of origin, but the profit motive led the Dutch to trade directly with the colonies. The weakness of the Spanish fleet, incapable of covering the whole American coast, favored this traffic, and the Dutch were soon followed by the French and English. By the middle of the 17th century, according to Haring, contraband was universal, and governors, public officials, and colonial judges took part in it. Under the pretext of repairing some damage, a ship would get permission to tie up in a port; then it would proceed to unload the merchandise it carried "to lighten the cargo." The cargo was apparently guarded by a party of soldiers, but in fact it was being sold under the complaisant gaze of everyone.

To the scandal of contraband between the mother country and the colonies we must add that of such traffic among the colonies themselves, or between Mexico and the Philippines. Chaunu says that at the Acapulco fair, contraband goods were traded according to rites hallowed by tradition. The same thing happened in Portobello, key point of trade with Peru, and in Buenos Aires, center of contraband traffic in hides.

Illicit trade represented two-thirds of colonial commerce in the year 1686. Nevertheless, it was only beginning. It probably attained its maximum point in the 18th century, despite the Bourbons' administrative reforms. This indicates that its deepest cause was not corruption, but the economic tension caused by the policy of colonial exclusivism.

THE CANARIES IN AMERICAN TRADE. We have just mentioned one of the plagues which bedeviled commerce between Spain and her American colonies, and which in large measure made a laughing-stock of the mercantile monopoly exercised by Seville. Another of the vulnerable points in this monopoly was the Canary archipelago. But its peculiar characteristics merit special attention.

Because of the Canaries' favorable position on the route to the New World, the islands had played a role of primary importance from the very beginning of colonization. They were an obligatory stop on the outward voyage, frequented by all ships engaged in the Indies trade. And furthermore, the Canaries' grain and vineyards made them a valuable supply base. This explains why they received favored treatment. In fact, after 1509 the inhabitants of the islands were authorized to fit out vessels and send nonprohibited merchandise (slaves, among other things) to America. This favor, ratified in 1511 by Ferdinand the Catholic himself and in 1525 by Charles V, became regularized in the sense that the islanders had to give an annual guarantee and send a record of their exports to Seville within a period of six months.

In the first few years of his reign Philip II followed the policy of favoring Canaries trade, consisting especially of bread, flour, hardtack, and wine. But in 1558 this trade was prohibited because of the contraband traffic which centered on the archipelago. There were firm protests from authorities in the islands, met with no less firmness by the Council of the Indies and the House of Trade. These organizations appeared to win in 1566, when Seville's monopoly of the Indies trade was decreed and the fleet system imposed. But the resistance of the islanders was not overcome until 1572. In that year the king decreed that ships from the Canaries had to travel in convoy with the fleet, a severe measure, which affected the mainlanders, as we know, but which simply could not be carried out in the islands. Therefore, in 1582 the Canaries were authorized to send 1,500 pipes of wine annually to the Windward Islands without having to form part of the fleet. It was a narrow breach, but a breach after all, and one which made a mockery of Seville's monopoly.

The role played by the Canaries in illicit trade was more serious. In the first place, the archipelago served as a concentration point for anyone who wanted to go to America illegally. Then, a large number of ships, especially Portuguese, loaded merchandise in Canary ports which was then sold in the New World at lower prices than those of the fleets. But the most serious harm was done by deflecting traffic in precious metals. The system was triangular: vessels returning from America carried undeclared bars of silver or coined metal; they used these to pay for articles bought in foreign countries (France, Holland, and England), which they then sold to Atlantic smugglers. There are irrefutable proofs of this process. An inquiry at the end of the 16th century showed that the annual deficit in the Canaries' mercantile balance was on the order of 78,000 ducats, which, naturally, was covered by the silver brought in fraudulently.

Severe measures were adopted to stop contraband trade: the general regulation of 1591 was one of them. Another was the absolute ban on all commercial contact between the Canaries and America. This was imposed in 1611. The decision represented a mortal blow for the archipelago. The islanders insisted that the focal point of contraband was in the Philippines, which supplied the whole Pacific coast, especially Acapulco and Lima. They also accused the Portuguese in Brazil of flooding the interior of South America with contraband by way of the La Plata basin. They were right about both accusations. But they also were partly guilty; or rather, what was guilty was the fatal monopoly system, which necessarily converted the Canaries into a center for fraud. However, such complaints did accomplish something: the lifting of the ban (1613) and concession to the archipelago of an annual quota for export of wine and flour to the Indies. This quota fluctuated between 300 and 700 tons, until in 1649 a new ban was laid down: no ship could anchor in a Canary port without an official permit. This measure would have been fatal for the Canaries had they not been able to count on a very solid mercantile base: clandestine traffic. Finally, an agreement was reached with the Crown (1656) on the basis of a quota of 1,000 tons annually in five ships. This pattern was maintained, with slight variations, up to Bourbon times.

For the Canaries as for the rest of Spain, the second half of the 17th century was a period of severe economic depression. To the general contraction of the trade cycle was added the development of American self-sufficiency and the growing control of Cádiz, harsher than Seville in its monopolistic proclamations, for the inhabitants of Cádiz were direct competitors of the Canary Islanders in the export of wine. Only with the dawn of the 18th century and the resumption of traffic in precious metals from America was the economy of the Canaries rehabilitated; it had been a perfect example of fraudulent deformation by measures imposed from outside.

THE AMERICAN EMPIRE, COLONIAL PATRIMONY. From the first years of the American conquest, the problem had arisen as to who would be the beneficiaries of the discovery and colonization. As we have pointed out before (p. 313), a number of factors contributed toward excluding non-Castilian subjects of the Spanish Crown from America. However, the basic principle of the Papal donations was never successfully attacked: the Indies were the private patrimony of Ferdinand of Aragon and Isabella of Castile (as joint partners with Christopher Columbus), transmissible to their heirs through the half share each had held in the discovery, by virtue of the doctrine of community property under Castilian law.

From 1516 to 1700, the monarchy was inclined to reserve this patrimony for Castile, especially after 1560, when the pressure exercised by Seville and establishment of the fleet system forced a return to a trade monopoly. But in spite of the numerous cedulas issued in particular cases, a positive declaration about the matter was never achieved (it does not appear, for example, in the Codification of 1680). Even Solórzano, the most eminent 17th-century author of treatises on the Indies, begins with a doubtful "it seems that" the sentence in which he speaks of whether natives of other provinces than those forming the Crowns of Castile and León were foreigners or not.

In 1525 Charles V had authorized "all subjects and natives of the Empire" to go to America. This measure was obtained by the German merchants, and though it did not have a happy outcome, it did reveal the Crown's ability to dispose of its American patrimony. After 1560, however, Castilian monopolism was added to colonial monopolism. The other kingdoms in the monarchy protested this exclusion, their protests growing louder after the failure of this double system (1630–1660). First Navarre, then Aragon (1585–1646) and Catalonia (1689) claimed the right to be present in America, either through holding public office or through trade. Portugal obtained freedom of movement in 1598 and took advantage of it to establish very large colonies in the Antilles, to the point that Portuguese made up the majority of the poulation in San Juan, Puerto Rico, about 1630, and held an exclusive contract for the supplying of slaves. Later Catalonia and the Basque Provinces redoubled their efforts to obtain the establishment of companies for

American trade (attempts made in Bilbao in 1628, 1630, and 1668), but all these were frustrated not by the monarchy but by the cabal of officials and merchants in Seville. In 1701, on the eve of a new epoch, when Philip V granted the Catalans the right to send two ships annually to trade in the Indies with Barcelona as their home port, he explicitly stated that the monopolistic rights enjoyed by Seville were to be retained: a monopoly which was then transferred to Cádiz and which continued to stifle the Spanish economy until 1778.

29 · Demographic, Agricultural, and Industrial Decline of Spain in the 17th Century

THE PROBLEM OF SPAIN'S ECONOMIC DECLINE. The subject of Spanish economic decline has aroused debates of the most impassioned kind, from the time it was first broached by the *arbitristas* of the 17th century to the present. Legions of Spanish and foreign authors have dedicated themselves to studying it, often with open prejudice, as the American historian Hamilton has pointed out repeatedly. Thus, German writers have exaggerated the magnitude of the collapse, wishing to glorify by contrast the figure of Charles V, whose ancestry was partly German; the Italians have done the same out of a desire to put the blame for the downfall of their own country on someone else, a downfall which was coincident with and related to Spanish domination of Italy; French and Spanish authors have done so because they wanted to extol the Bourbons' economic policy; finally, the "liberals and Protestants of every country, to stigmatize the Inquisition and the persecution of racial minorities."

However, these exaggerations should not make us forget the coincidence of extremely abundant evidence pointing to a decline in herding, agriculture, industry, and trade in the Spain of the 17th century. "Aridity, deforestation, insufficient harvests, emigration, expulsions, spread of mortmain, alms-giving and ecclesiastical vocations, vagabondage, disdain for work, mania to acquire titles of nobility, *mayorazgos,* high prices, upward movement of wages, taxes, wars, weakness of royal favorites and of the sovereigns themselves . . ." are all terms used over and over to depict the country's disastrous economic situation. Nevertheless, we must point out with Pierre Vilar that "these causes of decadence" are too numerous for us not to suspect in them the presence of stronger reasons; that is, the general economic crisis of the 17th century, in which converged (in the case of Spain) political impotence, incapacity for production, and social disintegration. The origins of this crisis went back a long way, though it did not become clearly apparent until Philip II's death in 1589. As Hamilton writes: "In broad terms one can say that it took Spain only a century (from the union of Castile and Aragon in 1479, to the annexation of Portugal in 1580) to attain political pre-eminence and only a century (from the death of Philip II in 1598 to that of Charles II in 1700) to fall into the rank of a second-rate power."

DEMOGRAPHIC STAGNATION AND DEPOPULATION. We lack data which would permit us to draw up a general balance-sheet of Spanish demography at the end of the 17th century, like the one made by Ruiz Almansa for the last years of the 16th. In the case of Catalonia, for example, no census was taken during the entire century. Under such circumstances it is not surprising to observe the divergent figures given by different authors: while Ruiz Almansa holds that the population of Spain remained stationary throughout the 17th century, varying only slightly from the figure of 8 million inhabitants, Hamilton assigns to it a loss of about 25% of its total population and concludes with von Beloch that by 1700 Spain probably had only about 6 million people.

Stagnation or depopulation, the one certain fact is the break in the ascending curve of 16th-century Spanish demography. On the other hand, there was a growing tendency toward a new distribution of the country's human potential: the centripetal tendency of the previous period gave way in the 17th century to a relationship which placed the population of the Peninsula's periphery in an ever more favorable situation. This tendency was also apparent within the smaller area of Catalonia, where settlements along the coast grew with extraordinary rapidity at the expense of population centers in the interior.

Now that we have come down to the regional level, let us give a few cases in detail. As for Castile, Domínguez Ortiz points out as probably closest to the truth a number given in a memorial of 1623 which, basing its figures on the books of the Treasury of Papal Bulls, gives Castile some 6 million inhabitants. If we compare this figure with that of approximately 1600 (see p. 331), it would mean that in thirty years the kingdom had suffered a decline of 25%. But what happened during the seventy-seven years between 1623 and 1700? Domínguez Ortiz does not attempt to answer this, but describes the exodus from rural areas and the consequent "demographic concentration which, in certain extreme cases, reached the point in some parts of La Mancha or Andalusia where towns of many thousands of inhabitants were separated by 15 or 20 kilometers of desert," as the characteristic feature of Castilian demography in the 1600's. He finds specific causes for this phenomenon in the terrible tax demands which fell most heavily on the villages, levies of soldiers, absenteeism of rich landowners, and the oppression of hamlets and chief towns in certain districts. (For example, he says, the miserable state of the people of Las Hurdes is in large part a legacy of jurisdictional abuses originating in La Alberca.) And he points out as general factors in the population decline the decadence of the monarchy, sale of real property and of council positions, excessive number of clergy, attraction of the Indies, etc.

In the territories of the Crown of Aragon, the expulsion of the Moriscos, decreed by Philip III, occasioned the most spectacular drop in population. A memorial of 1638 states that of the 453 Valencian hamlets occupied by Moriscos up to 1609, 205 were still abandoned, while the resettlement of the remaining 248 had required the transfer of 13,000 households of Old Christians. In the Kingdom of Valencia the expulsion affected 23% of its inhabitants; in Aragon, 16%; and in Catalonia, where the Moriscos were concentrated along the course of the Ebro and Segre rivers, only a little over 1%. As for the Principality of Catalonia, recent studies have emphasized the influence of the same factors pointed out by Domínguez Ortiz for the Castilian rural exodus. Parish registers and much other subjective evidence coincide in placing the maximum population around 1615–1620; at that time, which coincides with the final stages in the great current of French immigration, the country probably had about half a million inhabitants. Later, especially from 1630 to 1660, the tendency was one of stagnation if not regression.

One more reference to the demographic trend in 17th-century Spain: in general, two great phases can be distinguished, one of depression during the first half of the century, and another of recuperation following the end of the great period of plague (1648–1654) which, concentrated in the Western Mediterranean area, affected not only the Levant—from the Roussillon to Andalusia—but also invaded the Meseta from the south and from Aragon. We must make perfectly clear, however, that our information is inconclusive, and consequently so are any generalizations we may necessarily have drawn. In the case of Galicia, for instance, a study by Ruiz Almansa, whom we have quoted so often, has revealed that population loss was moderate during the first few years of the 17th century and became progressively greater after the revolt in Portugal and subsequent war. In this area, therefore, we cannot speak of recuperation during the second half of the 17th century.

THE PLAGUES. Those specialists who have pointed out the demographic stagnation of the 17th century, while they have been concerned with its causes, have generally passed over the most important of them: incidence of the plague factor on population development. Contagious diseases, which periodically intervened in the demographic process (no generation in the 17th century escaped their impact), decisively influenced the tendency toward decline.

The survival of a medical system which still considered Galen the supreme authority, and the persistent state of undernutrition in most of the country, caused by economic decline in general and agricultural decline in particular, explain the extraordinary virulence of 17th-century plagues. At that time there was a very close relationship between harvests and population figures, and the inadequate system of land transport could not cope with large-scale shipment of grain. In a closed economy, as Hapsburg Spain still was, a district's food supply was reduced to what its agricultural resources could produce. Only the coastal towns could resort to importing grain in case of an insufficient harvest. Under these conditions mortality was closely linked to the ups and downs of local agricultural production. People made considerable efforts to soften the effects of these, such as storing the surplus harvest in good years, or simply resorting to biological measures. Nonetheless, a time would come when a series of bad harvests made all these efforts insufficient, and the specter of famine stalked the land. Then, when the disproportion between the number of men and the amount of available food became intolerable, the always latent factor of plague caused terrible ravages among the undernourished people. Jean Meuvret, in France, has demonstrated with statistics and graphs the exact coincidence in times of famine between the mortality curve and the price of wheat; when grain is lacking the curve shows a dizzying rise. There are no analogous studies for Spain, but we do have documents and proofs of the solid connection between demographic development and economic conditions.

As for the results of the plague itself, there is much evidence from persons and institutions of the period concerning the loss of one-third or one-fourth of the inhabitants of a given locality or region due to plague. That these figures are not so exaggerated as might be thought is proved from counts of deaths listed in parish records, or those which cities occasionally ordered made. Thus, the minute-book of the old Council of Barcelona permits us to follow very closely the impact of the epidemic on the Catalonian capital over a period of time. To sum up, and taking into account the fact that we do not have reliable figures for the whole country, we can at least state that the population loss in the Spanish Levant during the 17th century was due, more than anything else, to the constant incidence of contagious diseases, notwithstanding the counterfactor of a booming birthrate, on the order of 40 or 50 per 1,000.

Now that we have noted the importance of the plague factor in demographic development, we need to pinpoint its appearance in time and estimate its periodicity. As on so many other occasions, we find ourselves in an area where nothing has been published, where ground has not yet been cleared, insofar as the greater part of Spanish territory is concerned. On the other hand, studies made by Emilio Giralt and Jorge Nadal have succeeded in reconstructing the complete picture of the great plagues of the 1600's in Castile: 1589–1591, 1629–1631, 1650–1654, and 1694. That is, in the space of one century there were four appearances of plague, with a mean periodicity of twenty-five years; this was what we meant when we said that no generation could have escaped its effects. Generally speaking, these plagues affected the entire country, producing population losses that were difficult to overcome. The most serious of all was produced by the great epidemic we have mentioned before, that of 1648–1654, which came at the end of a series of catastrophic events and placed Spain in one of the most dangerous moments of her history. For the rest, the study of these plagues has corroborated the theory concerning a close relationship between undernourishment and rise in the mortality rate. When things were going badly in one region, the others, where circumstances were identical, soon saw themselves attacked as well. A good example of this is the path taken by the plague about the year 1650; it began in Andalusia in 1648, spread into Murcia and Valencia, spilled over into Catalonia and then Aragon through the passes of the Maestrazgo region, into France, and finally to Majorca, Sardinia, and Naples, where it still persisted in 1656.

Now that we have established the principle that plague depended on food supply, we would not be wrong in attributing the high incidence of plague to the long drought of the last few decades of the 16th century and the early years of the 17th. Aridity meant the failure of many harvests, hence undernourishment, triumph of plague, and depopulation. In this respect the 17th century, like the 14th, was a fateful one for Spanish demography.

THE SPANIARD AND LABOR: THE HIDALGO MENTALITY. We have already seen how, in the last years of the 16th century, the twin spectacle of a bourgeoisie ruined by its own enterprises and an inactive, though prosperous, aristocracy, had had a most unfortunate effect on the mental attitude of the Spanish working classes. Survival of the economic factors which caused this bitter paradox and the subsequent polarization of the country's social structure into two antagonistic groups—the active and the inactive—found confirmation in the 17th century by means of customs and laws which placed a stigma of social dishonor on the mechanical occupations, as they were called at the time.

Any number of examples, foreign as well as domestic, could be adduced to corroborate this thesis, and many authors have defined the attitude of the 17th-century *hidalgo* as the expression of a theory of leisure. In *Lazarillo de Tormes,* the 16th-century picaresque novel, just one step removed from the crisis that was to usher in the new century, we read that, "any no-good wretch would die of hunger before he would take up a trade." This aversion to work was accompanied by a puerile pride in indolence: "Let London manufacture those fine fabrics of hers to her heart's content; Holland her chambrays; Florence her cloth; the Indies their beaver and vicuña; Milan her brocades, Italy and Flanders their linens . . . so long as our capital can enjoy them; the only thing it proves is that all nations train journeymen for Madrid, and that Madrid is the queen of Parliaments, for all the world serves her and she serves nobody." This absurd defense came from the pen of

Alfonso Núñez de Castro during the dark days (1675) of Charles II's minority, on the eve of the financial disaster of 1680.

Groaning under the weight of all the disadvantages (direct taxes fell exclusively upon him) and none of the advantages, it is not surprising that the poor commoner of the 17th century should have pinned all his hopes on changing his status and going over to the other camp by purchasing a patent of *hidalguía,* or minor nobility. The consequences of the first step—changing his status—are well known: "People of the plebeian class disdain to work in factories, workshops, and manufactories, and steer their children into other careers in which, for one person who wins, a thousand lose"; and as a final result, "idleness, depopulation, and an increase in the crime and indigence which are found everywhere."

The second step was the acquisition of a patent of nobility. Literature is full of examples of the mania to attain the category of knight or *hidalgo* which obsessed the Spaniards of the 17th century. Let us take a look at the consequences of this mania. Traditionally the *hidalgos,* like the lesser nobility in general, had made up for the tax exemption they enjoyed by giving military service: while the plebeian paid taxes to the Crown, the *hidalgo* defended it by force of arms. However, the creation of professional armies and the discrediting of the military profession in the 17th century ("the people are so convinced that all those who exercise the soldier's profession are wicked, that there is no tailor or cobbler who would not consider it a great dishonor were his son to take it up") deprived the *hidalgo* of his function; and he often used his social position "not in order to go to war, but in order not to go." On the other hand, the Crown's financial needs, which required the collaboration of all citizens, leaped the barrier between commoner and noncommoner and extended taxation to those privileged persons who had not paid it previously.

Thus, though the 17th-century Spaniard's mania for nobility continued to gain ground, the boundaries between the status of commoner and *hidalgo* grew more and more imprecise. What difference could there be between a plebeian and a *hidalgo* if, as Prieto Bances assures us, the latter was hardly a noble (since he had no power), nor necessarily free (since it was possible to be one and yet be in a state of servitude), nor a soldier by obligation (*hidalgos* formed a large part of the knightly group, but could be

417

excused from all military service)? In reality the difference was purely formal. The *hidalgo* belonged to a higher estate in society and accepted everything on condition that his rank would not be affected. The example given by Domínguez Ortiz is significant: obliged to pay taxes by the Crown, the Castilian *hidalgo* defended his immunity as such with more fervor than he did his pocketbook, which in any case was slim. The medieval idea associating taxation with dishonor and servitude was still alive in Castile, and when the *hidalgos* of the 17th century were forced to pay taxes, they did not recognize the poll tax, which they felt to be an unworthy levy; they resigned themselves, however, to paying taxes of a general nature, "provided that, in defense of principle, a rebate or small quantity should be returned to them, given by the State or municipal government as indemnification for the part of the *sisa* corresponding to their personal consumption. Many paid taxes until they were ruined, but always insisted on observing the legal fiction that they need not be included in the list of taxpayers."

Conclusion: the Castilian *hidalgos* of the 17th century deprived the Spanish economy of an enormous human potential, which went into other, completely unproductive professions: "Church, royal household, or the sea."

DESTITUTION AND VAGRANCY: INDISCRIMINATE CHARITY. Though he did not entirely eschew work—as has been repeated so many times by those interested in presenting him as an archdrone—we will have to agree at least that the Spaniard of the Golden Century refused to put any effort into tasks which he considered plebeian (Carande). The same man who spared no effort to preserve his honor, win fame and achieve glory in Italy, Flanders, Germany, or the Indies, was quite willing to live, even under the best of circumstances, on some modest income from property, or, in the majority of cases, from some other form of parasitism, turning the country into "an idle and vicious republic," as Cellorigo puts it. This Spanish attitude toward life, which often displayed spectacular traits, coincides in any case with the development of the mania for nobility and the insufficient recompense given to sound work. This situation progressively decreased the needs of the poor and caused their stoicism to increase. In this respect, the literature of the period undertook to reflect faithfully the subterfuges of a society sunk in destitution and at the same time eager to hide its difficulties. On this point it is interesting to notice how closely the best literary witnesses to the crisis followed it: the two parts of *Guzmán de Alfarache,* the most important of the "black" novels, were published in 1599 and 1604, and the first part of *Don Quijote,* the liveliest satire on the society of the time, appeared in 1605.

Destitution reached a peak during Philip IV's reign. The king himself has left proof of his concern over general food supply in his letters to Sister María de Agreda, but he was as impotent to solve this problem as the others with which he was faced. There were moments when the situation became so desperate that it resulted in dangerous popular uprisings—for example, one in Seville in 1652, known under the name of the "Green Banner," a classic mutiny brought on by famine which kept the Feria quarter in a state of revolt for twenty-one days and had repercussions in Cordova and other Andalusian cities.

The cure proposed by the State to avoid similar movements was worse than the disease. Its supply policy was dictated by the simplistic mercantilist idea then in vogue (Viñas Mey): imposition of a price ceiling—"cheap bread"—on staple articles, without taking into consideration that a simple price war, ignoring any compensation to the poor laborer, would merely swell the army of unemployed who had had to abandon trades that did not give them a living wage. Nor did the attitude of the clergy, who stubbornly denounced the state of destitution, respond to a more intelligent view of the problem. The free soup of the convents, distributed indiscriminately to every sort of vagabond and needy person, raised begging to the status of a *modus vivendi,* was a contributing cause to "that sort of religious aura with which Spaniards invested the act of giving or receiving alms," and stripped beggars of "their shamefaced appearance, for they lived in a well-organized manner and turned begging into a lucrative business" (Pfandl).

FOREIGNERS IN THE SPANISH ECONOMY. Ever since the middle of the 16th century, in the wake of the discoveries and colonization of America, Spain had been the gathering place for many European businessmen. At the end of the century, to the influx of precious metals was added as a further inducement the industrial decline of the country, which made provisioning of the Indies fleet dependent on foreign imports.

During the 16th century the most favored merchants had been

natives of countries allied with the Crown: Genoese, Flemings, and Germans. We have already spoken of the advantages obtained by the former, beginning with the treaty of 1528. Their supremacy lasted exactly one century, for after 1629 they were dislodged from their Spanish positions by the Portuguese who, thanks to their African establishments, could open or close at will the supply of Negro slaves so necessary to the Indies. In fact, in 1640 there were 2,000 Portuguese traders—the majority of them Jews or *conversos*—in Seville, and to judge from the obituaries of the cathedral, their number was growing. The Portuguese *conversos*—or *marranos,* as they were called—could count on very favorable positions in the court itself and in the principal port cities on the Cantabrian Sea. Their central offices were in Hamburg, the city where they had taken refuge after the Spanish *tercios* captured Antwerp in 1585. Portugal's separation from the Spanish Crown put an end to Portuguese expansion in Spain and her colonies.

The Flemings, for their part, had relied upon the favor of Charles V. Export trade from the Low Countries to Spain was very active until the insurrection there. This event obstructed mercantile dealings. On the one hand, the Dutch became bitter enemies of Spanish shipping and commerce. Between the capture of La Brielle in 1571 and the Peace of Westphalia in 1648, Holland carved out a colonial empire at the expense of Spain and Portugal. On the other hand, the Walloons of the south, who were Catholics, and the Flemings remained loyal to Spain; but the war paralyzed industry and commerce in their country, with the natural repercussions on trade with Spain. It survived, however, and even experienced a period of considerable prosperity after 1621, when Holland again went to war with Spain after the Twelve Years' Truce. The Flemish colony in Andalusia was large. We need only recall that in 1596 whole companies of Flemings could be formed to defend the city of Cádiz against English attack.

Last, the Germans, the great bankers of the Crown during Charles V's reign, appeared on the Spanish coasts as merchants and sailors beginning in the last years of the 16th century. This was an action carried out by the Hanseatic cities (members of the medieval German Hanseatic League). These cities took advantage of the Dutch provinces' rebellion to bring to Spain wood, grain, tools, metals, and munitions supplied by the rebels. As neutrals, the

Hamburgers and other Hanseatic merchants were favored by the governments of Madrid and Brussels and made a great success of this trade, especially at moments when England and France found themselves at war with Spain. The great risks taken by Hanseatic shipping, which, pursued by the Dutch and other adversaries of the Hapsburgs, often had to sail around the north of Scotland and Ireland, were amply compensated by the large profits to be gained. During the truce of 1609–1621 Spanish-Hanseatic trade fell off considerably but later managed to recover, until recognition of the United Provinces in 1648 reestablished the former situation.

The lure of profits from the Indies trade was so great that even countries who were enemies of the Spanish Crown lost no opportunity to enter the country and swell the colonies of foreign merchants in every port. The French were prominent among them. Traders from Nantes appeared in Seville, Málaga, and the Canaries under the protection of those of Bilbao, whose privileges they shared because of the trade agreement existing between those two cities. Merchants from Vitré developed their contacts with Cádiz, Sanlúcar, and Puerto de Santa María after 1560. Finally, the Normans, who already thought of Seville and Cádiz as way stations on the Canaries route, stopped in those cities more frequently after the 16th century. We do not know the number of French citizens established in the Spanish seacoast cities, but the presence of French consuls in Cádiz (1575 or 1581), Seville (1578), Barcelona (1578), and Valencia (1593) attests their importance.

In regard to the French, we must mention the continuation of the great stream of peasants, herdsmen, and small artisans which had begun at the end of the 15th century. While immigration into Catalonia dropped sharply about 1620, it grew more intense in the rest of Spain. In Aragon and Valencia, French farmers assured continuation of the crops after the Morisco expulsion. In the Castilian cities, the French carried out the humblest trades, those which repelled the minds of the natives. By the end of the 17th century, French pressure in the large cities and towns of Spain was so considerable that there were even violent popular outbreaks against them.

The last to arrive in the deteriorating Spain of the 17th century were the English and Dutch. And this is understandable. Not only had they been the Spaniards' bitterest adversaries, but their Protestant status was also a barrier between them and Spain. It was necessary to seek a *modus vivendi,* however, for although the Spanish Crown owned the Indies, Amsterdam and London had the industries necessary to supply them. This fact was translated into a special regime enjoyed by Protestants in Seville, Cádiz, Málaga, and Puerto de Santa María. By the end of the century Santander also tried to obtain this same privileged situation. But the Crown did not give its authorization.

In the second half of the 17th century the enormous Dutch trade with Spain, in particular with Cádiz, changed Amsterdam into Europe's chief money market: the stock of currency concentrated in the city became so considerable that it permitted, against the rules of the mercantile system, export of precious metals and coins not only to India for its own trade, but even to a number of Western countries. Already active during the Thirty Years' War, this trade reached its apogee after the peace of 1648, when Hispano-French rivalry induced the Spaniards themselves to favor the business dealings of their late enemies, the Dutch. In the last decades of the 17th century Dutch and English merchants appeared in Catalonian ports as active buyers of the brandy made from Panedés and Maresme wines.

Owing to Spain's weakness in the 17th century, the activity of these foreigners was prejudicial to the country's interests. When we take up in detail the matter of trade we shall see how they monopolized almost all the great maritime traffic, especially that carried on with the Indies. Contemporary Spaniards were well aware of this process, and there were a great many complaints by *arbitristas* and even literary testimony to the situation. Both coincided in repeating *ad infinitum* the "desubstantization" of Spain through its effects. We shall conclude by quoting the opinion of Sancho de Moncada, who alleged that foreigners enjoyed the largest incomes in the nation: "more than a million in *juros* (bonds on public revenue), an infinite number of *censos* (bonds on private debts), all the funds of the Crusade, a great number of prebendaries, *encomiendas,* benefices, and annuities."

DECLINE OF AGRICULTURE: EXPULSION OF THE MORISCOS. Early in the 17th century the Spanish soil, always so neglected because of the traditional predominance of herding, received a rude blow. The expulsion of the Moriscos (former Mudéjares forced to convert in 1502 in the Crown of Castile and in 1525 in the Crown of Aragon), decreed in 1609–1611, deprived agriculture of the most skilled manpower it possessed. (Article 5 of the expulsion decree exempted 6% of the Moriscos "so that dwellings, sugar mills, rice harvests, and irrigation systems may be preserved, and so that they may give instruction to the new settlers.") How was such an unfair decision arrived at? We shall quote Pierre Vilar's reply to the question: "They (the Moriscos) were a residue of the conquered Moors, converted by force but not assimilated; sometimes shopkeepers, more often farmers, formed into closed communities at the service of the great lords of the Reconquest: a colonial problem on home soil which Spain had borne for two centuries without solving. About 1600, after so many revolts, repressions, expulsions, and mass displacements, the danger of a general uprising was probably only a myth. But suspicion toward the crypto-Christian, 'bad blood,' the spy, the marauder, the businessman who laid his hand on too many ducats, turned the Morisco into an all-too-obvious scapegoat in a moment of crisis. He was considered too prolific and too frugal: those were the real charges."

Let us examine the results of the expulsion. In the demographic sphere a new loss occurred which was difficult to recoup. The most reliable figures (Lapeyre's) give the following balance sheet of expelled persons:

CROWN OF CASTILE

	Absolute figures	Per cent of total population
Central and intermediate zone (Old and New Castile, León, La Mancha and Extremadura)	45,000	0.9
Southern zone (Murcia and Andalusia)	37,000	2.0
CROWN OF ARAGON		
Aragon	64,000	16.0
Catalonia	5,000	1.0
Valencia	135,000	23.0

In other words, the number of expelled persons came to nearly 300,000 persons altogether, equivalent to about 3% of all Spaniards. But the expulsion did not affect the different regions equally, so that those composing the Crown of Aragon, especially Valencia, were much more seriously damaged. In these regions the problem of resettlement became extremely urgent; but this does not mean that it was always solved. In Valencia, for example, almost half the Morisco villages abandoned in 1609 were still uninhabited in 1638. In Aragon, conversely, French immigration succeeded in "filling in," as the expression of the period was, the void left by the expelled Moriscos.

In the economic sphere the consequences were even more important. Essentially, disappearance of the agricultural *élite* (as early as May, 1610, the *Audiencia* of Valencia lamented the "scarcity of laborers caused by the expulsion of those very Moriscos who were so extremely hard-working") meant the disappearance of the *revenues* with which these vassals' lords paid their interest charges, or annuities obtained from mortgage loans (*censos* and *censales*), contracted with the speculators of the cities (*censalistas*). If we recall the extraordinary enthusiasm of moneyed people to invest their capital in *censos al quitar,* or annuities, we will easily understand the collapse produced in this parasitic society by the departure of the Moorish peasants who, in the last instance, supported it. Reglá, the first historian to bring this important question into focus, transcribes an essential document proving that contemporaries of the expulsion were well aware of its consequences in the economic sphere. The Archbishop of Valencia wrote to a minister of Philip III in 1608, "All those who are necessary to the Republic, for its government and spiritual and temporal adornment, depend on the services of the Moriscos and live from the mortgages with which they or their ancestors have burdened the Morisco towns; and thus, when they see that they are unable to live, they will have to make an appeal to their rights and call upon His Majesty, lamenting their indigence and destruction."

To prevent this "indigence and destruction" the landholding aristocracy, not content with seizing the property of the expelled Moriscos, finally obtained a reduction of the interest on *censales* to 5%. Thus the cycle was complete: the measure which began by affecting agricultural economy made its immediate effects felt on the feudal economy, and finally affected the bourgeois economy which was its creditor. We may therefore conclude that, despite

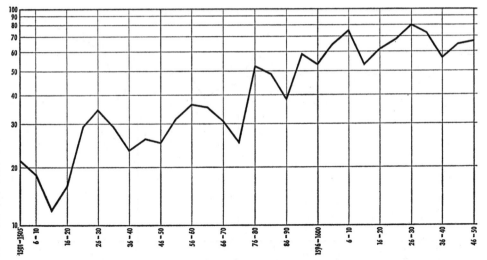

EVOLUTION OF WHEAT PRICES IN PALMA DE MALLORCA FROM 1501 TO 1782, EXPRESSED IN QUARTERLY WAGES AND FIVE-YEAR AVERAGES (*after* J. FONTANA, using documents of the Royal Majorcan Economic Society of Friends of the Country).

Hamilton's optimistic theory, the whole Spanish economic system suffered from the expulsion.

Along with the expulsion of the peasants who made a specialty of irrigation farming came the definitive victory of the old feudal concept that the basis of agrarian economy was cereals, olives, and vines. The only other crops that continued to be cultivated were sugar cane and cotton, in the southern part of Granada; silk in this same region, Valencia, and Murcia; linen and hemp in a number of regions in the North, and rice along the Mediterranean shore. No notable progress was made in a century which, to make matters worse, witnessed a constant drop in the price of agricultural products.

DECLINE OF HERDING AND OF THE MESTA. One of the incontrovertible facts of Spanish economy in the 17th century is the loss in livestock. Although continuous statistical series do not exist, we know through Klein that during the second half of the century the number of head of sheep controlled by the Mesta was less than 2 million, a fact which confirms the diminution in numbers which had begun a century before. There were many causes for this phenome-

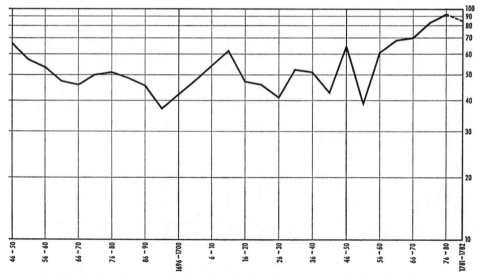

In this interesting graph, despite the insular nature of the place under observation, the great fluctuations of the international trade cycle can be observed, especially the two inclines of the 16th-century price revolution, the 17th-century decline, and 18th-century recovery.

non. Some authors attribute it to a period of drought undergone by the Mediterranean climate in the last decades of the 16th century and the early years of the 17th. Others add to this factor the disturbances which took place in the development of herding because of the wars in Catalonia and Portugal (1640–1641), interrupting use of the customary pastures and sheepwalks. And finally, we must not forget the attacks leveled against the Mesta, precursors of those which were to ruin it in the 18th century.

In the 17th century open warfare was declared on the Honorable Assembly of the Mesta. This powerful organization, so feared but at the same time so respected, became the target of every sort of criticism. Opposition to the privileged members of the Mesta arose from delegates to the Cortes, from the chanceries, the defenders of agriculture and enclosures, and from the great creditors of the Crown. The attacks converged particularly on the powers of the *Alcalde Entregador*, or President, who saw his powers limited on all sides and his jurisdiction questioned.

The Mesta gave way before these attacks inch by inch. Its chief support was its alliance with the monarchy, which, though in 1619,

426

in exchange for the *millones* tax, it had granted the Pragmatic of Belén declaring entrance into the stockbreeders' brotherhood a voluntary act and limiting the functions of the organization's judges, had compensated the Mesta in 1633 by reestablishing all its privileges and granting full protection to its grazing grounds. The royal cedula of 1633 prohibited plowing up new ground and ordered all arable land granted since 1590—private as well as municipal, public, common and uncultivated lands—to be turned back into pasture with or without permission, if the term of the concession had expired. "The carrying out of this decree of famine," says Colmeiro, "for it condemned men to suffer want so that the flocks could prosper," necessitated a demarcation and survey of such lands, thus originating an infinite number of lawsuits and litigations which aroused many passions and plunged agriculture and nonmigratory herding into a calamitous condition.

In spite of this monopolistic legislation it was no longer possible to change the course of events, for the herding crisis pushed the Mesta into a dead-end street. Klein observes that after 1685 the threat of imminent bankruptcy can be seen in the Mesta's account books. In this last phase the great livestock trust could count less and less on royal support: "The impecunious later Hapsburgs were quite as ready to dicker with the opponents of the Mesta for subsidies as they were to bargain for 'loans' from a scarcely solvent organization. . . ." Thus, throughout the 17th century the defeat of this formerly all-powerful herding organization was slowly being prepared.

COLLAPSE OF CASTILIAN INDUSTRY. "Even if we did not find convincing proof," wrote Colmeiro in 1863, "in the Parliamentary papers and the royal decrees, of the weakness and collapse of Spanish industry from the middle of the 16th century to the beginning of the 18th . . . we would be more than convinced of the sad truth by the inquiry of the Council of Castile in 1619, the very urgent *junta* of 1620 (though it bore no fruit because of Philip III's untimely death), and the efforts, pleas, and importunings of the impoverished and ruined cities, mainly Toledo, Cordova, Seville, Granada, and Valencia, which in 1655 were trying to bargain with the Court for a cure, or at least some relief from their troubles."

Though detailed studies are lacking, there are numerous memorials of the period (as for example Martínez de la Mata's, giving the list of seventeen guilds disbanded in 1655) which provide unequivocal evidence of this industrial decline. In particular, the table below, taken from Larraz, shows population decline in the old industrial and mercantile cities of Castile.

CITY	HEADS OF FAMILIES			
	1530	*1594*	*1646*	*1694*
Burgos	1,500	2,665	600	1,881
Valladolid	6,750	8,112	3,000	3,637
Palencia	1,364	3,063	800	972
Salamanca	2,459	4,953	2,965	2,416
Avila	1,523	2,826	1,123	965
Segovia	2,850	5,548	—	1,625
Toledo	5,898	10,933	5,000	5,000
Cuenca	—	3,095	800	1,641

The population loss for Toledo and Segovia is particularly significant as an index of Castilian industrial evolution. The recovery of Burgos and Cuenca at the end of the 17th century has a possible connection with renewed export of raw wool.

One of the few encouraging events in this moribund 17th century was the establishment of ironworks for casting cannon and munitions in Liérgana and La Cavada (Santander). Assisted by the policies of the Count-duke of Olivares, the Belgian Jean Curtius and the Luxembourger Georges Labande set up an excellent metallurgical works in those towns in the year 1622.

This seems the appropriate place to sum up, with Larraz, the different factors contributing to the decline of Castilian manufactures: (1) industrial superiority of the Low Countries, England, and France over Castile, (2) the deviation of Spanish prices from European ones as a consequence of the influx of American silver, (3) the lesser capitalistic spirit of Castile in the 16th and 17th centuries, (4) the unhappy results of the Hapsburgs' European intervention.

A realization of this process of decline was so widespread that by the end of the century, during the reign of Charles II, there was a general desire for recuperation, and many projects to attain it were devised. In Castile, among the excellent proposals of the Count of Oropesa one at least survived: the *Junta de Comercio y Moneda,* or

Board of Trade and Currency, created in 1679, which gave fruitful results in the following century. In 1674 thirty-two Aragonese deputies joined under the presidency of Don John of Austria to try to restore the kingdom's economic potential, but the committee was stalemated by a serious controversy over freedom versus limitation of trade. In Catalonia the efforts of a generation of men united around the doctrines of Narcis Feliu de la Penya obtained positive results with the aid of foreign technicians. Finally, in a general sense, the Royal Pragmatic of 1682 was—as Colmeiro says—the first step toward the rehabilitation of arts and trades, when it declared that possessing or having possessed factories for weaving silk, cloth, woollens, or other textiles was not unworthy of the nobility.

THE GUILDS AND INDUSTRIAL DECLINE. The guilds are usually blamed for the stagnation into which Spanish industrial production fell in the 17th century. Echoing the diatribes of the enlightened thinkers of the 18th, even apologists for the guilds attribute the stagnation of industry to them, because of the restrictions on entry into trades and the system of privileges enjoyed by the guilds.

The history of guilds under the Hapsburgs has not yet been written. The amount of material, both published and unpublished, is immense. But the published material is not very useful, for its authors based their studies on an idealistic view of the past and were unaware of even the rudiments of the economic life from which the guilds had sprung and out of which they developed. Just as they considered the institution to be very ancient—and we have already pointed out its relative modernity, even in Catalonia—they believed that its progress had been uniform, disregarding the tenacious opposition that had existed ever since the 16th century between the guilds of the old privileged cities and those which had arisen in the towns around them precisely to escape their monopolistic prerogatives. The relationship between the trade cycle and guild activity has also been forgotten, and, what is still more important, the State's tendency to submit guilds to uniform rules and strict control, not out of industrial policy but out of an obvious desire for tax revenue.

Now that we have cleared up these points, we can concentrate on guild history under the Hapsburgs and gauge its supposed responsibility for the country's industrial decline. After Ferdinand and

Isabella's measures, which gave form to guild life in Catalonia and Valencia and encouraged creation of guilds in the Crown of Castile, the 16th century was characterized by the appearance of a considerable number of guild corporations. The motive was Spain's industrial expansion in the wake of the expanding economy of the period. A simple examination of the known foundations shows us that most modern guilds were founded in the second half of the 16th century, especially after 1530, starting point of the upward trend. In Burgos, for example, the market gardeners received their charter in 1509; the tanners in 1512; cobblers, 1528; and masons, 1529; after 1540, embroiderers (1544), dealers in skins (1545), shoemakers (1552), thong-makers (1570), charcoal-burners (1574), hatters (1589), and gamekeepers (1591). In Toledo, to the guild of the wax workers, recognized in 1446, were added the dyers (1530), butchers (1560), pastrycooks (1580), locksmiths (1582), sieve-makers (1588), and straw workers (1598). The same phenomenon is found in Saragossa (1540, blacksmiths; 1550, wool-combers; 1556, harness-makers, mattress-makers, locksmiths, and hatters; 1565, linen-weavers; 1567, wool-weavers; 1584, glass-blowers; 1590, carters), and even in Barcelona and Valencia, where numerous similar lists could be made.

Simultaneously, the guilds appeared in towns of secondary importance. Economic prosperity caused journeymen to move from the cities, where a mastership was difficult to obtain, and set themselves up as masters in nearby towns and even villages. Little attention has been paid to this phenomenon in Spain. However, its strength is undeniable. There is evidence of it in Catalonia (for example, foundation of the wool-weavers' guild in Sabadell in 1558, competing with the powerful wool-dressers' association of Barcelona). More examples could no doubt be found in other regions.

During the prosperous phase of the trade cycle there was no guild problem. It arose when Spanish foreign trade began to decline, and with the decline came a reduction in labor activity. Then the guilds became organizations of resistance to the contraction of economic life. Such is their history—a very unflattering one—in the 17th century. Caught between the devil of business stagnation and the deep sea of the State's tax demands, the guild corporations lived miserably and poorly, generally speaking, with the all-too-predictable sequel of obstructionism, oppression, fraud, oligarchic monopolies, and so on. Gradually people began to think of them as a dead weight, especially in places where they had been established relatively recently. In 1678 voices were raised in the Cortes of Calatayud asking for their suppression. However, in places where money was abundant the guilds continued to prosper; this was the case of those in Madrid. It was, in fact, during the 17th century that the Five Greater Guilds of Madrid were established, whose importance in Spanish economic life will be taken up in the next chapter.

The Crown's interest in keeping the guilds under strict control became accentuated in this same century, as its fiscal needs continued to grow. It was essential to the plans of the reformers of the Spanish treasury at the time to have an assured tax base. Hence, when the Board of Trade and Currency was created in 1679 the guilds came under its jurisdiction in administrative and economic matters. With the exception of the Catalonian and Valencian guilds, which maintained their traditional independence, the life cycle of the guilds was over: they returned fully to the control of the State which had created them, and in the end the State itself decreed their elimination.

30 · Commercial Stagnation,
Tax Pressure, and Currency Inflation
in the 17th Century

STAGNATION OF COMMERCIAL LIFE. The view of mercantile law "as a statute . . . of persons who destroyed the harmony of medieval life and sowed restlessness in the human soul" is, according to Beneyto, what characterizes the abundant specialized literature of the Spanish Golden Age. Naturally there were some exceptions, especially in Catalonia and Valencia where, beginning with Eiximenis in the 14th century, a theological tradition more favorable to the world of business was kept alive. But the attack of the Dominicans, zealous continuers of Scholastic tradition against this Mediterranean type of deviationism, permits us to state in broad terms that in this area ethical prejudices reinforced those of the *hidalgo* mentality against economic activity in general. These several prejudices were linked to agricultural and industrial decline, and constituted the factors responsible for the downfall of Spanish commerce in the 1600's.

As for the interior of the Peninsula, Colmeiro points out "the thousand impediments derived from opinion and from laws" which hindered the development of trade: lack of roads and transport, the disdain with which the nobles treated merchants, the supply policy, monopolies, preemptive rights, intervention of *regatones* (the blackmarketeers of the period), internal customs duties (turnpike and municipal taxes, apart from those enjoyed by private persons by right of inheritance, and certain regional privileges designed to prevent the introduction of products and foodstuffs from neighboring regions), price-fixing, alterations in the currency, etc.

External trade did not cease, but it passed almost entirely into the hands of foreigners. We have already studied the settlement of foreign businessmen in Spain, and the results of the illicit traffic with America encouraged by them. But, as Larraz points out, foreigners also gained control of regular trade with the Indies, hampered as it was by strict laws and administrative regulations. The flow of legal trade, constantly dwindling as contraband grew in importance, fell almost totally under their influence. And here we notice the industrial and mercantile superiority of other countries, the bad effects of Spain's tax system, and its unsatisfactory customs organization. A memorial of French origin, quoted by Haring, See, and Larraz, sums up the consequences of this situation. According to it, in 1691 participation of the various countries in American trade, which officially continued to be Spain's exclusive monopoly, was distributed in the following manner: French, 25%; Genoese, 21%; Dutch, 19%; Flemings, 11%; English, 11%; Hamburgers, 7.6%; and Spaniards, 3.8%. We need not accept these figures as absolutely accurate, but if we recall that as early as 1619 Sancho de Moncada complained that "nine out of ten parts of the Indies trade are carried on by foreigners," we may conclude without fear of contradiction that Spain had lost by a very wide margin the game she was playing with other European nations for the possession of American riches.

Decline was equally noticeable on the other routes of Spanish trade. There are no detailed studies on the extent of this decline, but we can find symptoms of the phenomenon. Thus, we are told by Smith and Basas that in Burgos the number of marine insurance policies drawn up between 1594 and 1619 (that is, a period of twenty-five years) did not exceed 200, while the annual average in the middle of the 16th century had been more than 1,000; or, through mercantile records, we can see that maritime trade in Barcelona between 1630 and 1660 was largely in the hands of the French and Genoese, and that its radius was growing smaller and smaller, ending in Lisbon and Sicily.

DECLINE OF SHIPPING AND FAULTY COMMERCIAL POLICY. The situation we have just described is even less comprehensible when we recall that up to 1640 the united empire of Spain and Portugal was the center of world trade, and possessed, in Seville and Lisbon, the chief points of contact between the colonial world and continental Europe. Even after the political unity of the Peninsula was dissolved, the Spanish-American bloc continued to have a great deal of influence on the economies of all European nations.

We can realize this if we examine the centers of trade activity which were linked with the Peninsula. Indispensable colonial products converged on Seville and Lisbon: in the first place silver, and then sugar, cocoa, pepper, hides, and various dye plants. To these must be added the products of Spanish soil: silk, iron, and wool. And in the opposite direction, wheat and other foodstuffs, war and naval equipment, and a large number of manufactured products came into the Peninsula destined for use by Spaniards and by the colonies. From the Far East and the New World, an intense commercial life circulated along the chief maritime trade routes, which included the most important French, English, and Dutch ports, the Baltic trading posts, Central Europe by way of Hamburg, and even reached as far as Archangel in northern Russia. On the other hand, Spanish seaports controlled the best routes in the Western Mediterranean, especially that of Leghorn in Italy.

Certainly, and this was one of the fundamental causes of the Spanish economy's profound decline in the 17th century, maritime trade had fallen into the hands of foreigners. Chaunu has pointed out the tremendous difficulties undergone by the Spanish administration in order to organize the Indies trade within its own monopolistic area. After 1610 the number of ships in the Indies trade kept getting smaller and smaller, reaching its lowest tonnage in 1640. In fact, ever since 1590 the Portuguese fleet had helped to insure Atlantic service. The freight crisis brought on by the recession of 1640 could not be overcome, even though foreign ships were used for the first time. Perhaps this phenomenon had something to do with the change in navigation brought about by the disappearance of the galleon in favor of the lighter and more seaworthy *nave,* and the difficulties experienced by Spanish sailors in adapting themselves to the new type of ship, which the Dutch and English introduced everywhere. If this occurred in the Atlantic area, it is useless to ask what happened in places which were not closed to foreigners. The French controlled trade in the Levant; the British, trade between the North Sea and the Western Mediterranean; the Hanseatic League, in the Baltic Sea; and the Dutch everywhere, for Holland was the great sea power of the 17th century. To gain some idea of the decline of the Spanish merchant fleet during this period, suffice it to say that the Catalans, whose sea power in the later medieval centuries had been undisputed, now went to Marseilles to pick up Eastern goods and to Leghorn to buy Baltic wheat brought there by the English. The same thing happened in the Cantabrian ports, whose principal needs were served by foreign vessels.

Of course, Spain would have been able to defend herself against the danger which threatened her shipping if she had used heroic measures, such as a navigation act like the one promulgated by Cromwell in defense of English ports. But this would have forced the country first into a war with Holland, and then with England. In regard to Holland, Spain blundered at the Treaty of Münster in 1648, not only accepting Holland's *de jure* independence, which was already obvious, but also acceding to a disadvantageous commercial treaty by the terms of which Spain was left wide open to Dutch trade. At the same time, a tariff schedule susceptible to all kinds of illicit dealings was set up, based on weight of merchandise. Thanks to this policy of concession, the government of Philip IV obtained Holland's neutrality in the war it had undertaken with France and shortly afterward with England. The military defeat also carried with it a new economic recession. In 1659, by the terms of the Peace of the Pyrenees, France obtained the right to bring goods into Catalonia free of customs duty; and soon after, in 1667, by means of a commercial agreement with England (called Eminente's Agreement from the name of its negotiator), Spain opened her borders to British goods, with extremely unfavorable tariffs also based on weight.

The fatal result of these two tendencies—decline of the Spanish merchant fleet and opening of the internal market to foreign goods—could have been avoided only by a vigorous export policy. Unfortunately this did not take place. On the contrary, just at that time the traditional products sold abroad encountered brisk competition both in quantity and quality. About the middle of the 17th century Spanish wool was replaced by Irish wool in many Northern markets, at the same time as Swedish iron began to move out of the Baltic area into England and France. Silk also beat a retreat in the face of the ever increasing progress of the Piedmontese in this product.

In consequence, the tariff-free system set up by the Hapsburgs turned out to be of very little advantage to the country's interests.

TRADE MONOPOLIES: SEVILLE AND CÁDIZ. Another very serious drawback affecting 17th-century Spanish economy was the preservation intact of the monopoly system in American trade. We have already analyzed the causes which brought about the implanting of this monopoly, and the choice of Seville as the center of colonial economic activity. If we follow the Andalusian capital's development under the Hapsburgs, we shall see the best example of the virtues and defects of mercantilist economic policy in general.

In principle, monopoly of the Indies trade meant that, at a time when sea transport was extremely expensive, a premium was placed on the export of Sevillian products; this fact, and the abundance of available capital due to the presence of the monopoly itself, aided the industrial development of the city. Thus, 16th-century Seville, which had become the largest city in Spain (150,000 inhabitants), had the second largest shipbuilding industry in the country after Biscay, and was its chief manufacturer of silk: it had ships to supply the Indies trade and high-grade cloth for export. At the same time, since in spite of this development it was unable to supply the American market, the Andalusian capital also played the role of intermediary between the industrial powers of Northern Europe and the new lands which had been brought under exploitation. A great number of foreign vessels were constantly docking in the port of Seville, bringing in manufactured products and taking away gold and silver from Mexico and Peru: some figures from 1604, a period of maximum prosperity, tell us that imports were almost double exports. "This figure alone explains why silver became so scarce only a few weeks after the galleons' arrival; it took the route of merchandise in reverse, for the lack of equilibrium in the balance of trade could be resolved only by exporting precious metals."

This imbalance between incoming and outgoing trade grew ever larger as the rise in Spanish prices compared to foreign ones placed the industry of Seville in a position of obvious inferiority. Guilds of shipwrights, caulkers, and rope-makers (an Andalusian specialty) almost disappeared, and the number of silk looms decreased very noticeably (for the reasons described and also because of the sumptuary laws which limited industries producing luxury goods). Under these circumstances the Crown adopted the practice of sequestering the treasure of private individuals brought by the fleet (Charles V had already done this), of declaring itself bankrupt (beginning with Philip II), or simply of devaluing the currency (beginning with Philip III). These unilateral measures were especially damaging to Seville, the port where the galleons dropped anchor and where the chief bankers lived. Therefore the State's own mercantilist regulations, which had forged Seville's prosperity in the 16th century, also brought about its bankruptcy in the 17th.

Aside from the causes we have enumerated, there were others of a strictly local nature. In this area "the event which marked the irretrievable decline was the plague of 1649" (some 60,000 dead, almost half of the entire population), exhausting the city's demographic reserves. Cádiz took advantage of this misfortune to win the last attack in her fierce mercantile competition with the city on the Guadalquivir. Let us follow with Domínguez Ortiz the development of this struggle between the two great Southern commercial cities: Cádiz was one of the nine ports authorized in 1529 to send ships directly to the Indies; it is true that this arrangement had very unfavorable results and was finally abolished by another royal cedula in 1573, so that those ports, situated mostly in the North, never participated importantly in overseas trade. But Cádiz was more fortunate thanks to her geographical position: since it was absurd that merchandise loaded on the shores of the Bay of Cádiz (including most of the wine consumed in America) should have to be taken to Seville simply to fulfill administrative formalities there, measures of tolerance in this respect were soon taken; there were numerous ships which, with or without a license, sailed directly from Cádiz for the Atlantic crossing. In 1558 vessels coming from Hispaniola and Puerto Rico laden with hides and sugar were authorized to unload in Cádiz. Three years later this concession was amplified to include damaged ships which could not cross the Sanlúcar sandbar, provided that gold, silver, and pearls were taken to the House of Trade.

On the other hand, legal decrees could not alter the fact that the larger ships in the fleet came up the river with great difficulty, especially if they were heavily laden; and the practice grew up that large ones came no farther than Sanlúcar, or left Seville half-loaded and finished loading in Sanlúcar or Cádiz. From force of habit, this led to the practice of assigning to Cádiz a third of the fleet's total tonnage for its own merchandise. The diversion of sea traffic resulted in diversion of merchandise, and finally the transfer of the officials themselves. After 1547 there was a *Juzgado,* or magistracy, in Cádiz, a sort of branch of the House of Trade. By the middle of the 17th century Seville's monopoly was purely nominal, while Cádiz' volume of business increased for the following reasons: foreigners preferred it, for they wished to escape the vigilance of the Sevillian administrative bodies and found the Bay of Cádiz more convenient for contraband than the inland port of Seville; the difference in tariffs owing to the individual practices of those who farmed the customs, for they were interested in attracting the foreign merchants who came to Cádiz, and treated the obligatory and assured clientele of Seville more perfunctorily; and the demographic disaster of 1649, which stripped Seville of all her strength.

The rivalry between the two cities continued to be keen during the rest of the 17th and early 18th centuries, until in 1717 the activities of a well-known citizen of Cádiz, Andrés de Pez, governor of the Council of the Indies, assured the victory of his own city by obtaining from Patiño the decree transferring the House of Trade to Cádiz. In the end, Seville and Cádiz changed positions: now Seville retained only a judge delegated from the House, the "third of tonnage," and the right to appoint two consuls.

DECLINE OF BURGOS AND RISE OF MADRID. Another important phenomenon in Castilian economic life in the 17th century was the rapid decline of Burgos as Castile's coordinating center. We have spoken before of the pernicious effects of the 1575 financial crisis on life in Burgos. The disorganization of the Medina del Campo–Antwerp connection gravely affected all the cities which had formed part of the circuit, Burgos as well as Bilbao and Santander. Another factor was soon added to this: the decline in wool exports, to which we have also alluded. According to statistics of 1622, export through the port of Santander was not even a shadow of what it had been fifty years before: eleven ships and 605 sacks of wool annually compared to sixty-six and 17,000 respectively. Burgos suffered very severely from the consequences of contraction in the wool trade. This was why it sought so insistently the centralization of the Castilian wool market in the city (for example, during Charles II's reign), accusing the Cantabrian ports of fraud in trade with foreigners. This attitude stemmed from the great period of discord between Burgos and Bilbao, and therefore did not have great importance in a period of general decline.

Actually, Burgos had been reduced to the size of a large village in the course of the first forty years of the 17th century. From the 20,000 inhabitants it had possessed in 1575, the number had dropped successively to 13,000 in 1594, 7,600 in 1611, and 3,000 in 1646. Nazario González states the chief cause of this regressive phenomenon: the rise of Madrid as the economic capital of the Spanish State. Many natives of Burgos abandoned their trades and businesses to move to Madrid, where it was easy to do business and to prosper.

In fact, in the latter years of the 16th century Madrid had become an extraordinary human concentration by the standards of the time (14,000 inhabitants in 1570, 108,000 in 1617). When the crisis caused by the transfer of the Court to Valladolid (1603–1606) was over, Madrid continued to develop extraordinarily up till 1660 (340,000 inhabitants?), in response to the law of creation of huge urban centers in countries of low population density and impoverished agriculture. This accumulation in the city of revenues from the great latifundist aristocracy, especially the Andalusian aristocracy, the management of public finance, and the interests of the American empire, stimulated monetary circulation and commercial life. Hence important mercantile bodies arose which gained great strength from the proximity and needs of the administration. Such corporations demanded adoption of a free-trade policy, based especially on the import of luxury goods.

The basic pressure in this regard was not exercised by the Consulate of Madrid, installed in 1632 as one more organ of the State's bureaucratic machinery (it was, in fact, a dependency of the Royal Council, whose members were appointed by the king); the lever which really set the wheels in motion was the *Cinco Gremios Mayores,* or Five Greater Guilds. Their history is really the economic history of Madrid under the Hapsburgs and in the 18th century. Humbly born during the 15th century, by the middle of the 17th these guilds were powerful groups which stood out above the multitude of smaller ones. They were—it should be carefully noted—commercial rather than industrial corporations; the woollen merchants, the silk merchants of the Guadalajara Gate, the jewelers of the Calle Mayor, the spice merchants of the Calle de Las Postas, and the cloth merchants. Woollen merchants, silk merchants, jewelers, spice merchants, and drapers all benefited greatly from the installation of the capital in Madrid and slowly, separating themselves from the smaller guilds, joined forces in defense of their interests. With the exception of the woollen merchants, we find them acting together in a number of lawsuits after 1667; in 1679, year of the creation of the Board of Trade, they formed a compact group; on March 23, 1686, the ordinances were laid down which defined their particular field of action. They were well on the way, then, to becoming united in a single and powerful body, an aim not achieved legally until 1731 with the formation of the *Diputación de Rentas,* or Council on Revenues, of the Five Greater Guilds. But after the end of the 17th century the fiscal factor linked them more and more closely into a coherent whole from which each guild member gained new and fruitful advantages.

Thus Madrid, closely linked with Cádiz, was the new star which arose in Spanish commercial life during the 17th century. Firmly linked to latifundist economy and the free-trade tendencies of the Five Guilds, it foreshadowed through its bureaucracy the country's industrial rebirth by means of a controlled system. This was to be its great undertaking during the 18th century.

TAXES AND ECONOMIC LIFE. Following Sureda's example, we shall divide the Royal Treasury's revenues in the Crown of Castile into *ordinary revenues not deriving from taxation* and *tax revenues.* Among the first, the most outstanding were those coming from royal ownership of salt beds, mines, the tunny-fisheries of Cádiz, and revenues from masterships of military orders (incorporated into the Crown by Ferdinand and Isabella).

In the second group, revenue from taxes, we can point out:

TAXES LEVIED BY APPORTIONMENT and governed by the personal circumstances of the taxpayers. They were as follows: *servicio,* both ordinary and extraordinary; *moneda forera* (the tax paid by all vassals in recognition of the royal overlordship); *chapín de la reina* (150,000 maravedís on the occasion of the king's marriage). The so-called *vecinos pecheros,* or commoners, were obliged to pay these, the nobles and clergy being exempt. In compensation, the latter estate had to pay the *ecclesiastical subsidy.*

EXCISE TAXES, levied on the transport and production of goods. They included three subgroups:

(1) *Levies on transit of merchandise or customs duties:* sea tithes, revenue of inland ports, sale of provostships, revenues from wool, the export-import tax of Seville and of the Indies, a tax on sales of

coarse cloth, one on Málaga raisins, and 1% of the customs receipts in Málaga and Cádiz.

(2) *General sales taxes:* the *alcabala* and the *hundreds*. The *hundreds* were four charges of 1% on sales, created successively in 1626, 1639, 1656, and 1663. In 1686 they were reduced to four ½% payments. The *alcabala,* one part in ten "on everything sold," was the amplification of the 5% tax on the value of any transaction which had been conceded to the kings of Castile in the Middle Ages. The universal character of these taxes was not diminished by a few personal exemptions and a very few exceptions made on the transfer of certain articles.

(3) *Taxes on special articles of consumption.* Of these, some were set up in the form of a legal monopoly on the sale of certain articles (for example, those on salt, quicksilver, tobacco, playing cards, and chocolate were the ones which brought in the largest revenues), while others were *in the form of a levy.*

This usually took the form of the *sisa,* or excise (a sum reserved for the treasury out of merchandise fully paid for), in the places where the merchandise was sold, or by *fee* (payment of a certain percentage per unit of measure of the article taxed) in the places where it was produced or harvested.

The total of these taxes on consumption was very important, because together they brought in the majority of the revenues necessary to pay the *servicio de millones,* so-called because it was counted in millions of ducats instead of in maravedís, as was customary in all *servicios* requested by the king. The *servicio de millones* was granted by the Cortes after it had heard the royal proposal, in which the state of the treasury and its needs were explained. Once this proposal had been studied the Cortes agreed on the sum to be granted, indicating the taxes by means of which it was to be collected and imposing the condition that the *servicio* be used to meet the expenses for which it had been requested: hence, the official documents of the *servicio de millones* represented the beginnings of a budget system. The first *servicio* was granted to Philip II in 1590, for the sum of 8 million ducats to be paid within six years. In 1600 there was a new *servicio* of 18 million, also payable in six years. This was the largest of the *servicios* and was successively renewed throughout the 17th century with a number of variations (2,500,000 annually from 1608 to 1610, 2 million annually from

1612 to 1632, and 4 million annually after that date). But it was not the only one granted, for after 1632 the Cortes voted other *servicios de millones* which ran concurrently.

SUBROGATORY OR DIVERSIFICATORY TAXES on patrimonies or certain classes of revenue. In general these came from revenues belonging to the ecclesiastical class, exempt from all taxes except those on sales. In this group were: the *Bulls of the Holy Crusade*, granted by Julius II in 1500; the *subsidy on galleys* (420,000 ducats coming from ecclesiastical revenues), granted by Pius IV in 1561; and the *excusado* or tithe of the chief establishment of each parish, granted by Pius V in 1567. The *tercios reales*, or royal thirds, of medieval origin, still remained in force and consisted of two-ninths of the ecclesiastical tithes.

This is a general sketch of tax organization in the 16th and 17th centuries. Its main bases were the *servicios*, both ordinary and extraordinary, the *alcabalas*, and the *millones*. As the monarchy was plagued by constantly rising financial requirements, fiscal policy kept squeezing more and more taxes from the coffers of the taxpayers. The table below, taken from Larraz, refers to Philip II's tax policy regarding *alcabalas* and *millones*, the two great indirect taxes of the period:

INDEX NUMBERS

YEAR	Collected from alcabala and millones (1)	General price index (2)	Difference (1–2)
1504	100	100	0
1535	117	129	−12
1562	160	239	−79
1575	489	273	+216
1578	357	258	+99
1590	537	300	+237
1596	537	307	+230

The interpretation of these figures is quite clear: after 1575, the curve of the tax index is considerably higher than that of the general price index; after that year the treasury not only made up for the loss in purchasing power of money, but also greatly increased tax pressure. This increase becomes more significant if we keep in mind that Castilian industry and agriculture were less active in the last quarter of the 16th century. Hence, the treasury contributed toward aggravating the condition of national production.

Is it not clear that the burden of taxation on economic life in the 17th century became even more grievous when the *servicio de millones* reached its maximum?

STATE MERCANTILISM. Medieval economy, with its meager circulation of money, considered it axiomatic that an abundance of money intensified business, while restriction of currency depressed it. The maintenance of this principle at all costs by the Spanish State of the 16th and 17th centuries, completely inundated by American silver, was the initial cause of the country's ruin.

The identification of money with wealth established by Spanish mercantilists and statesmen of the period, dazzled by the abundance of American metal, could scarcely be equaled by any other nation. The measures taken with the prime objective of increasing and maintaining the stock of money can be classified into three groups:

Measures to stimulate discovery and exploitation of American gold and silver mines. Both natives and colonizers were guaranteed ownership in all claims involving personal property; tools and equipment could not be seized for private debts; royal officials took special care to supply mining districts, etc., so that 100% of the metal extracted would reach Castile; trade among the different colonies was restricted, and a rigid system of transport and monopolies established.

Stockpiling of metal in Spain by means of a ban on its export to other countries. With this object in mind, "Castile repeatedly altered the bimetallic ratio, the weight, fineness and tariff of gold and silver coins, deflated vellon; and prohibited imports of debased foreign money in an effort to curb the outflow of treasure. At least 75 per cent of the innumerable petitions in the Cortes and the pragmatics affecting money in the 16th and 17th centuries stated specifically that limitation of specie exports was a goal" (Hamilton). During the reigns of Philip III and Philip IV, the draining off of gold and silver, accelerated by uncontrolled inflation of vellon (bad money driving out good), and by the disparity between Spanish and foreign prices, brought the strictness of prohibitive measures to their maximum point: after 1624, the death penalty was applied as a punishment for exporting specie.

Notwithstanding these measures, currency always had a legal loophole through the numerous licenses for exporting money to settle the debts contracted by the Crown with foreign money-lenders.

Restrictions on export of raw materials through imposition of high customs duties. This measure was intended to favor national industry, whose development would have prevented the expenditure of part of the currency used in acquiring products from other countries. But it must be noted that these limitations were in the long run a financial maneuver rather than a protectionist measure properly speaking. Protective duties—says Hamilton—had little place either in the theory or practice of Castilian mercantilism, and the same could be said of the Crown of Aragon. On the other hand we should recall, with Larraz, that the circulation of Castilian currency and bullion to other countries, in spite of the prohibitions on exporting money, kept foreign exchange from fluctuating with sufficient elasticity to make up for the differences between internal and external price levels; so that imports into Castile were very much at a premium, and exports consequently at a disadvantage.

This observation brings us to a mention of the *results of Spanish mercantilism.* Hamilton emphasizes as the most important ones the sacrifice of general colonial interests in favor of the Sevillian monopoly system—created in large part to raise to a maximum and protect metal imports—and the sacrifice of some American territories (among them the La Plata region) because of Castile's gravitation toward the mining zones of America (Zacatecas-Potosí); the harmful rise in Spanish prices compared with foreign ones as a consequence of the artificial accumulation (that is, not produced by a favorable trade balance) of gold and silver; the illusion of prosperity created by an abundance of these metals, which gave fuel to the Hapsburgs' aggressive and ruinous foreign policy; disdain for work; and other phenomena which contributed to Spanish economic decline in the 17th century.

MONETARY INFLATION IN CASTILE: THE COPPER REVOLUTION. One of the culminating factors in the disintegration of 17th-century

Spanish economy, added to the many we have just described, was the monetary confusion produced by that international phenomenon which Spooner has recently baptized with the name of "the copper revolution." The end of the silver era began after 1621 with the first symptoms of exhaustion in American mines; twenty years later, the paralyzation of silver's influence on world monetary activity was a consummated fact. From that moment up till 1680, when the appearance of Brazilian gold reestablished the situation of the two great precious metals, there was a considerable drop in the circulation of specie and a throttling of exchange which surprised and disquieted all the financial centers. During these sixty years, that is, in the heart of the 17th century, the metal which saved the situation, in spite of its modest origin, was copper: no longer copper mixed with silver, like the medieval "dark" coins, but pure copper. Europe overcame the crisis by forcing into circulation the copious mintings of this metal, even though an inflationary process was instituted in the nations which used this instrument incautiously. One of these was, as a matter of fact, the Crown of Castile. There was a second price revolution within its borders during the 17th century, brought on this time by copper, now the credit weapon of an impoverished economy. The incapacity of the later Hapsburg governments to control the inflationary spiral, their lack of courage to resist the temptations of a monetary policy too easy not to be dangerous, explain the disastrous downfall into which the Castilian economy plunged during the last decades of the 17th century.

The stages in this process are known, thanks again to Hamilton's work. Putting his information together with Spooner's view, we shall now present the great phases of copper inflation in Castile. Let us first recall that the ordinance of Medina del Campo dictated by Ferdinand and Isabella in 1497 was the basis of a new monetary system which, along essential lines, remained in force until 1598. During the course of the intervening century only three reform measures were taken. Two of these affected gold currency. In 1537 Charles V heeded the Cortes' reiterated pleas that Spanish gold must be prevented from leaving,the country. He reduced the tale of the excelente of Granada (or ducat) from 24 to 22 carats, and its nominal value from 375 to 350 maravedís. With this measure, which made the fineness of Castilian gold money equal to

French, the profit obtained from exporting Spanish gold coins was wiped out. In 1566 Philip II proceeded to a new increase in gold prices, corresponding to the drop in the price of silver produced by the constant influx of American shipments of this metal. To adjust its nominal value to the market price, the tariff of the escudo (the name given to the devalued ducat of 1537) rose from 350 to 400 maravedís.

The third measure taken in the 16th century affected vellon. In 1552 there was an attempt to adjust the price of copper money to that of silver, which was falling as the stock of silver grew. Since the rise in copper prices compared with those of silver threatened to bring about the flight of the copper coinage minted in former times (when this metal was cheaper), the real value of vellon was lowered (leaving its weight and nominal value unchanged): the silver content in these coins dropped 21.43%.

BEGINNING OF THE INFLATIONARY PERIOD (*1599–1630*). Faced with a constant rise in expenditures, Philip II attempted all sorts of solutions, not even excluding a declaration of bankruptcy; but he always resisted debasing the currency. It must be said that he possessed an excellent asset with which to maneuver: American silver. When this began to dwindle, his successor, Philip III, had no recourse but to turn to copper. Thus the copper revolution of the 17th century began both for Castile and for Europe.

In fact, given the Crown's needs, there was no hesitation about resorting to successive mintings of copper. The era of vellon was unleashed in 1599. In a few years (1599–1606) 22 million ducats were minted. A decrease in the quality of vellon coincided with this process; thus, as early as 1599 the silver in this type of metal had been suppressed, and copper, which after that time was the exclusive substance used in vellon coinage, underwent a reduction in weight of 50% (140 former maravedís now rose to 280).

Public opinion was aroused and prevented any serious inflation from 1606 to 1617. On November 22, 1608, the Cortes extracted from Philip III the promise that he would not mint any more vellon for the next twenty years; in compensation, the delegates voted a *servicio* of 17,500,000 ducats requested by the king.

The Crown's difficulties after the expulsion of the Moriscos were so great that in 1617 there was a new coinage of vellon, this time by permission of the Cortes, which released the monarch from his promise of 1608 and allowed him to mint enough vellon to obtain a net profit of 600,000 ducats, on condition that the minting not exceed 800,000. That is, it was admitted *a priori* that the treasury would receive a profit of 75% from this minting. However, the total minted was far above the authorized figure. By 1619 some 5 million ducats had been produced. In the face of this situation there were new protests from the Cortes, which in June, 1619, wrested a new promise from the king (as in 1608) not to mint vellon coinage for twenty years. However, the Crown's needs were so pressing (imminent war with Holland) that by January, 1621, more vellon was being struck in the mint at Toledo. From 1621 to 1626 some 14 million ducats were placed in circulation.

DEFLATIONARY INTERVAL (*1627–1634*). This succession of inflationary measures resulted in placing the premium or overvaluation of silver in the 45% range, and vellon prices went up accordingly. The crisis came to a head in 1627, when a scarcity of wheat and of livestock, combined with inflation, resulted in extraordinarily high prices. This situation required a change in the monetary policy which had been followed until then. That same year, as a measure to contract circulation, a banking company directed by Italians was formed, with broad commercial privileges and the function of taking part of the vellon out of circulation by buying it up with silver at 80% of its nominal value, plus interest of 5%. But this project failed because the long-suffering Castilians had no confidence in it, and refused to part with their vellon.

Once this project had failed, the first effective deflationary measure since the days of Ferdinand and Isabella was passed in 1628: the nominal value of copper vellon currency was reduced by 50%. Holders of devalued vellon were not reimbursed.

GREAT INFLATIONARY PHASE (*1634–1656*); CRISIS OF *1641*. After all possible solutions had been exhausted, the return to inflation began in 1634, this time based not only on putting a larger quantity of money into circulation, but also on simple increase in the nominal value of coinage by means of the *resello* (or restamping a greater value on existing coins). The new inflationary race started in 1634 by means of a decree doubling the value of *calderilla* (vellon with an admixture of silver, and therefore minted before 1599), until then excluded from currency changes. Since profits from this restamping were divided between the Crown and the

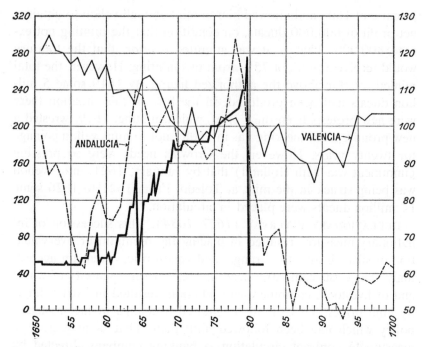

EVOLUTION OF PRICES IN THE SECOND HALF OF THE 17TH CENTURY.—
Heavy black line: curve of the silver premium over copper (index numbers
at left). The other lines represent price evolution in Andalusia and Valencia
(index numbers at right). Index, 100 = 1671–1680.

owners of the coins, the latter lost in this operation 25% of the
value of the coins delivered for restamping. Soon after, in 1636,
despite the royal promise "never to increase the tale of copper
vellon" made in 1628, a new restamping was decreed, tripling its
tariff. Later, following an unsuccessful attempt to withdraw vellon
from circulation completely, the revolutions in Catalonia and Portugal simply hastened the inflationary process. Then the inflationist
phenomenon of 1641 occurred. In February, restamping of the 4-
maravedí coin to double its nominal value was agreed upon: these
coins had been restamped once already in 1603. In October came
the restamping, at triple their nominal value, of all 2-maravedí
coins and those of 4 maravedís minted after 1603.

The prodigious increase in vellon prices and the fabulous rise in
the silver premium (190% by early August, 1642) which followed
the inflation of 1641, obliged the government to carry out a brutal

deflation. This was accomplished at the end of 1642: it reduced the 12- and 8-maravedí coins to 2, those of 6 and 4 maravedís to 1, and those of 1 maravedí to one-half.

Philip IV's promise to maintain the deflationary measure of 1642 was broken because of the expenditures necessary to reinforce his armies in Milan and Flanders. Forced to take action by extreme necessity, in 1651 Philip IV decreed the restamping, at four times its nominal value, of the 2-maravedí coin. This was accompanied by the minting of 100,000 ducats of pure copper in coins of 2 maravedís, weighing one-fourth as much as the old coins of this denomination which were now being restamped.

However, this bungling measure did not last long, and in 1652 there was a return to the line of 1642. The 8-maravedí pieces were again valued at 2, and the 2-maravedí coins minted in 1651 were tariffed at 1, as were 4-maravedí coins. On the other hand, and contrary to what had happened in 1628 and 1642, in 1652 holders of vellon were compensated for the reduction of its nominal value by means of bonds pledged by revenues from tobacco.

THE MONETARY CATASTROPHE (*1656–1680*); CRISIS OF *1680*. About the year 1650 a third phase in the depreciation of copper began throughout the world. This fact was what caused a change in monetary policy during the last years of Philip IV's reign and the early years of Charles II's. Castile's financial ship was adrift, lashed by the gales of inflation, foreign wars, governmental inefficiency, administrative corruption, and the collapse of agriculture, industry, and trade. This explains the crisis of 1680, when the economy of Castile foundered completely.

New currency disturbances had begun in 1654. That was the year in which *calderilla* regained its old value (it had been retired in 1653): it was restamped and its owners were given half its value, the other half being retained by the king. In 1658 restamping of the 1- and 2-maravedí pieces was decreed, giving them double value. In May, 1659, this measure was suspended and an effort was made to retire such coins from circulation. But this attempt at a radical contraction in the circulation of vellon failed, because people preferred the depreciated coins to the bonds offered in exchange by the monarchy. Finally, in October, 1660, there was a decree calling for turning in all *calderilla* and copper vellon which had not circulated at par for forty years, in order to melt it down and remint it in "rich" vellon. It was hoped that this would put an end to the monetary disorder. In spite of this measure, inflation continued its course, spurred by the government itself, which continued to issue new mintings of vellon currency. Hamilton says that there was a flood of bad money, with the result that the premium on silver went up to 150% (in 1650 it had still been 50%). It was the road to catastrophe. To avoid it, in 1664 the value of the coins minted only three years before was reduced by half. The premium on silver went down to 50%.

With Charles II's ascension to the throne the inflationary process knew no bounds, until the currency crisis of 1680 occurred. By 1665 the silver premium had gone up sharply to 120%, and about the middle of the year 1669 it rose to 180%. For the next six years the situation remained relatively stable; but from 1675 to 1680 abuses in mintings of low fineness, introduction of counterfeit money, and the need for making foreign payments produced a new rise, to 275%. The outcry was so great that in March, 1680, the government decreed devaluation of vellon coinage to half its nominal value; that is, one-fourth of its tale in 1664. This measure produced the collapse of wholesale prices, which dropped 45% in a few months. If we remember that in the great crash of 1929 American prices fell only 38%, we will have an idea of the magnitude of the disaster to which the monetary chaos had led.

It was a harsh but inevitable measure, followed by the order of May 22, 1680, strictly limiting mintings of vellon. Steps were taken at the same time to retire copper from circulation by using it to manufacture various articles and tools. In 1686 the situation could be considered stable. The revaluation of silver, aided by the appearance of Brazilian gold, contributed to the success of the operation. Vellon mintings ceased in 1693. The copper revolution was over.

THE ARBITRISTAS AND THE ECONOMY. Awareness of economic crisis, which spread over Spain at the moment of its greatest political splendor, was general around 1600. And with it came a proliferation of the literature of the *arbitristas,* who attempted to diagnose the country's ills and to propose suitable remedies for them. This abundant production, which shuffled "the prescriptions of the technician, the lament of the guild, and the thought of the patriot, worked out in the office of the jurist or the cell of the monk," has been satisfactorily summarized by Larraz. He divides these authors into two major groups according to whether or not they show themselves favorable to economic planning.

In the first group, those who along general lines were in accord with the economic policies of the time, Larraz points out the writers who called for adjustment of Spanish foreign policy to the demands of their economic planning. They were the heirs of the spirit of the 16th-century *comuneros,* defenders of the national interest as opposed to Castile's interference in European affairs. In their opinion, the restoration of the country required a change from offensive to defensive wars, from the policy of European expansion to one of preserving the American empire. With this change in attitude, they argued, would come realization of the supreme ideal inherited from the Middle Ages: to concentrate and retain in the mother country the enormous shipments of American precious metals. Most of the public shared this view, as was periodically demonstrated in the Cortes. Among the writings which favored this opinion we should recall those of Baltasar de Álamos y Barrientos (1598), Pedro López de Reino (1624), accountant of the Council of the Indies, and, to a degree, Fernández de Navarrete, chaplain and secretary to the royal family.

The conformist writers, who clung to the principles of the mercantilist theory, took issue with them. They formed the more numerous group and stoutly defended the growth and preservation within Spain of the stock of precious metals. *Memorial Against the Flight of Money From These Realms* (*Memorial para que no salgan dineros de estos Reinos,* 1558) was the title of a work by the first Spanish mercantilist, the accountant Luis Ortiz. In order to carry out his objective, he worked out a complete plan of development of all resources based on the following principle: a ban on export of raw materials and on import of manufactured products through establishment of the appropriate customs system. Ortiz is an isolated and forgotten author of the 16th century. It was in the following century that Spanish mercantilist literature reached its apogee. Doctor Sancho de Moncada, professor of Holy Writ in the University of Toledo, was its chief exponent. In his writings (1619), he developed a detailed economic plan based on the same principles as Ortiz'. Later, Martínez de la Mata (1659) proposed to raise public funds or banks to the category of the fundamental element in mercantilist policy, for the purpose of financing industrial and agricultural development.

It is not difficult to discover the contradiction in the Spanish mercantilists' noble proposals. The very historical reality of Spain was sufficient to demonstrate that when domestic prices climbed much higher than foreign ones, the monopoly of America metals was incompatible with the healthy progress of production of wealth.

Larraz singles out three central groups among the *arbitristas* opposing the economic policy practiced by the monarchy. In the first, we find the authors who attacked the accumulation of precious metals. They are the ones who, following the lead of the quantity school of Salamanca (which formulated for the first time the relationship between increase in the amount of currency in circulation and the rise in prices, as Larraz and Grice-Hutchinson indicate, demonstrating that they do not share the ignorance displayed by most foreign authors), reacted against the ideal of accumulation of money and campaigned for the reconsideration of productive labor as the basic element in wealth. On the other hand, these authors—Cellorigo (1600), Pedro de Valencia (1605), Fernández de Navarrete (1616), and Caxa de Leruela (1627)—who so skillfully described the effects of the discovery of America, were incapable of finding the formula that would solve the technical problems presented by exploitation of the Indies.

Another group is composed of authors who attacked the large profits earned by exporting to the Indies. When they confronted the problem which the previous group had been unable to solve, the members of the second—outstanding among whom was Father Tomás de Mercado—grasped the need for establishing a relationship between export to the colonies and import of metals from them. In fact, they realized that American gold and silver should be no more than a medium of payment, and the circulation of money an instrument for developing the economy of the home country.

Finally, there were some authors who attacked the whole theory of economic regulation. The thought of Alberto Struzzi, a foreign employee of the Spanish Crown writing in 1624, reflects this position. His doctrine has its origin in a doubly pessimistic assumption: Castile's incapacity to supply the American market herself or to prevent the disruption of economic planning based on a monopoly system. Taking as his point of departure the status quo of legal infraction so typical of Castile's economic policy, Struzzi defended freedom of trade with America.

GOVERNMENTAL APATHY AND BUREAUCRATIC IMMOBILITY. The transcendental fact of the beginning of American colonization took place at a moment when neither Castile nor the other European countries were prepared to cope with its vast economic repercussions. Consequently, the errors committed in the early years are excusable, even including the rigid monopoly on American metal which placed Spanish products in a position of inferiority. But by the end of the 16th century the Spanish ruling class was in the position of being able to make improvements: the immense possibilities of the Empire of the Indies had been recognized, and the quantity school of Salamanca had demonstrated its opposition to the simple identification of money with wealth.

At this crucial point, when Philip II might have acquired a sense of the need for changing his aims, the burden of his foreign policy prevented him from doing so. More and more involved in undertakings of war instead of putting his attention on intelligent exploitation of the Indies, the "Prudent King" walled himself up in the traditional system which at least would provide him with abundant and immediate supplies of silver. The country's interests were sacrificed to this need for money at a given moment—at an unbroken succession of given moments: in this regard let us remember that the tariff reform of 1566–1567 was of a fiscal rather than a protective nature. At the end of his reign Philip II made public the catastrophic result of his policies by declaring to the Cortes in 1592 that, after having gone through his own patrimony and his subjects' (remember the bankruptcies of 1557, 1575, and 1590), he owed more than 13 million ducats.

This inherently destructive economic regimen acquired its most dramatic traits during the course of the 17th century. The incapacity of the kings, the ruin of sources of production, and the constant increase in fiscal needs justified the most arbitrary unilateral measures. To the lamentable debasements of money we have mentioned, we must add, for example, the damage done to public credit: Colmeiro, with all the passion of a 19th-century liberal, points out the disorder, immorality, injustice, and scandal of an administration which betrayed its trust by arbitrarily altering the interest rate on *juros* (bonds on public debt).

And so it happened that the State argued in a vicious circle which made any solution impossible. This was clearly seen when in June, 1618, Philip III had his famous consultation with the Council of Castile. Six years of reforming effort (1618–1624) served only to see traditional regulation confirmed and even reinforced (Larraz). In the long run, the 17th-century Spanish State sacrificed the economy to the treasury, and the interests of its subjects to its own interests. Obsessed by the idea that each individual must give it more money (unbearable tax pressure) and keep less for himself (profusion of sumptuary laws fixing a limit on private expenditures), in the end the State neglected to develop the country's interests and trampled on the ethic which should have ruled its relations with its subjects.

If administrative inefficiency and immorality had taken control of the large cogs in the governmental machinery, we can imagine what happened to the smaller ones. The extremely bad example from above easily spread through a too numerous body of bureaucrats, imbued with all the prejudices of the *hidalgo* and obliged to too many expedients to subsist even from hand to mouth. On the other hand, the growing centralization of the State's machinery provided occasion for the worst of abuses. Some authors have given us ample description of the most outstanding of these. Thus, Uztáriz describes the extremely damaging practice of farming out the customs, which gave rise, among other anomalies, to the appearance on the scene of the famous Francisco Eminente who, together with his relatives, proceeded to exploit the revenues under his control from 1667 to 1717 "without feeling the slightest qualm over the public damage which resulted." Within this same area, Colmeiro points out the abuses and excesses of tax-farmers of all kinds who, since they had to give satisfaction to a treasury which grew ever more exigent, had no recourse but to compensate themselves as best they could, and "changed the lightest tax into an insupportable burden." In the last instance, the figure of 150,000 fiscal employees cited by Alcázar de Arriaza, giving as his authority the accountant Antolín de la Serna, or the figure of 9,000 persons employed solely in the administration and collection of the Bull of the Holy Crusade cited by Luis Valle de la Cerda, chief accountant of this section, are sufficiently eloquent for us to conclude that if the depreciation of productive work through the effects of the economic collapse produced the conversion of large sectors of Spanish society from activity to inactivity, the structure of the State assured the permanence of this process.

Only at the end of the century, when the feeling of disaster was inescapable, did the good faith of a few worthy members of the ruling class indicate a need for reform. The excellent plans of the Count of Oropesa were a failure, but one organization remained which in the following century was to give fruitful results: the Board of Trade and Currency, founded in 1679. Most important among its concepts were simplification of the working-class structure (the Cortes of Calatayud, in 1678, had requested abolition of the guilds) and the idea of bringing Spain more into line with other European countries.

31 · Study of the Trade Cycle
Under the Hapsburgs

EVOLUTION OF AGGREGATE ECONOMIC ACTIVITY IN THE 16TH AND 17TH CENTURIES. In the present state of research it is still too soon to give a final picture of the general economic conditions in the 16th and 17th centuries. Hamilton has attempted to give an overall view of Western Europe in his study entitled *American Treasure and the Flowering of Capitalism*. But some of his ideas have been contested by the American scholar Nef and the Italian Luzatto. On the other hand, several teams of researchers are now trying to pin down details of the evolution of the trade cycle. Chief among these are Braudel, Meuvret, and Lapeyre, in France; Cipolla and Romano, in Italy, and Verlinden in Belgium. As for Spain, a notable contribution has been made by Pierre Chaunu, who has studied trade between Seville and the Indies. Much data are also lacking about the fluctuations of the trade cycle in the Mediterranean area, in spite of the progress recently made by Nadal, Giralt, Fontana, and Castillo.

Along general lines, the European cycle in the 16th and 17th centuries can be divided into two stages, one of expansion in the 16th century and one of contraction in the 17th.

To examine this process more closely, we shall begin our study with England and France before taking up the case of Spain. In regard to England it has been possible, by collecting data about seventy-nine items of food and general consumption, to establish a graph of indexes showing an evolution in five stages. The price indexes are calculated on the base of 100 = mean of 1451–1500.

Period I. 1501 to 1550. Phase of stability; indexes for ten-year periods are: 95, 101, 113, 105, and 79. In 1550 there is a *sharp rise;* the index goes up from 79 to 132; that is, prices nearly double in one year. This was the moment when England received the impact of the price revolution, which had taken place in Spain some fifteen years before.

Period II. 1551 to 1602. The price rise in England is continuous, with progressively higher levels of 20 points for each decade: 132, 155, 171, and 198 for the years 1560, 1570, 1580, and 1590.

In the last period, the rise is on the order of 50 points.

Period III. 1602 to 1622. A stage of uncertainty is reached, with scarcely noticeable increases. The index rises from 248 to 257.

Period IV. 1623 to 1652. A new general increase is recorded: indexes rise from 287 to 331.

Period V. 1653 to 1702. In 1652 the change in economic activity is felt; there is a transition from the expansion phase, begun in 1550, to one of contraction. Here also, this change occurs with marked delay in comparison with Spain. The index falls from 331 to 308. From 1653 to 1702 we find a period of stagnation, as shown by the indexes: 308, 324, 348, 319, 339.

In regard to France the process is very remarkable. If we use the same index and the same items as a base, the results are as follows:

Period I. 1501 to 1550. Stability, with slight increase; indexes rise from 113 to 136.

Period II. 1551 to 1600. Sharp rise in prices culminating at the end of the period: indexes go from 174 to 248.

Period III. 1601 to 1625. Obvious contraction; prices fall to 189.

Period IV. 1626 to 1650. New increase; index at 243.

Period V. 1651 to 1700. Prolonged contraction, with a drop from 227 to 219.

The fluctuations of the business cycle in England and France are very similar, with two exceptions. First, the price rise was more noticeable in France than in England during the period 1525–1550. That is, in 1525 France reacted more rapidly than England to the price revolution. Second, cyclical contraction after the year 1600 is much more obvious in France than in England. What can be the cause of this phenomenon? Undoubtedly the principal one was the proximity of Spain, for that country was in fact the epicenter, the moving force of the price revolution, just as it was the first to suffer the disadvantages of an abundance of precious metals without the counterweight of strong industrial production and a favorable balance of trade.

PERIOD OF PROSPERITY UNDER CHARLES V. About 1516, coinciding with the death of Ferdinand the Catholic and Charles V's ascension to the throne, the prosperity phase of the 16th century was unleashed in Spain. Undoubtedly its causes were the early results of American colonization, especially the gold which flowed in from panning operations in Hispaniola, in uninterrupted though meager quantities, after 1505.

Very soon, in 1521, prices underwent a *sharp upward thrust,* almost equaling wages, which had been higher than prices ever since the wheat crisis of 1506. This jump in prices appears to be the result of the war of Castilian Communities, very shortly compounded by the effects of the arrival of Aztec treasure, as well as the demand for manufactured products in the internal market, development of naval construction, and the increase in orders of equipment and foodstuffs for the American settlers.

In 1530 there was a new and sudden escalation of economic activity. This was the moment when large sums of gold began to arrive in Spain from Mexico and New Granada (modern Colombia). The decade from 1530–1540, however, was one of relative contraction, with a low point about 1535; after that, and up till 1562, the evolution of prices was very rapid; the indexes rose from 58 to 91, taking 100 as the mean figure for the period 1570–1580.

This favorable moment in the business cycle was translated into general economic expansion in the country, especially in the Crown of Castile, where we may note the following facts: increase in the population; development of the Mesta, which in 1525 attained its peak number of sheep, some 3,500,000; self-sufficiency in grain, and balance between agriculture and industrial prices; development of industry, though with some rough spots produced by lack of technicians and organization, and the inadequacy of its equipment to cope with both internal and colonial demand; and monetary stability. The only mint operation of importance was the coinage of the *escudo* (1537), which instead of containing 24 carats like the ducat, had only 22, imitating the mintings of France and Italy. It was a prudent measure, for the new money conformed to the new bimetallic ratio imposed by the flow of gold into the market. Vellon currency was also strengthened, decreasing the fineness of silver by 23.43% (1552), the object being to avoid the flight of coined copper to other countries. In contrast to the Castilian Crown's prosperity we must point out, however, the lesser development of the Aragonese territories, now disadvantaged by their noncentral location and by the Spanish monarchy's alliance with the Republic of Genoa.

Therefore, the moment at which the price rise began to be noted in Spain was 1521, an important date because it marks the beginning of a change in the business cycle throughout Europe. After 1527 this movement became stronger and gave rise after 1535 to an extremely rapid evolution which is characteristic of the period of the price revolution.

THE FIRST CRISES UNDER PHILIP II. During Philip II's reign, that is, in the latter half of the 16th century, the wave of prosperity continued. In forty years the price-wage index rose from 80 to 120. Traffic between Seville and America showed a similar increase. Thus, at the midpoint of the century, still in Charles V's reign, the five-year average of traffic had been 30,000 tons; from 1561 to 1565 it rose to 67,000, or more than double; between 1586 and 1590, to 122,000, another doubling. From 1596 to 1600 it reached 120,000 tons, and then attained a high point for the cycle (127,000 tons in the years 1606–1610). These figures demonstrate that the rising trend was a tangible reality, monetarily as well as commercially.

Chaunu has used the relationship between prices and trade to deduce the evolution of the business cycle. He believes that two cycles existed, the first lasting twenty years, from 1561 to 1581, and the second lasting fifteen years, from 1581 to 1595. Two phases can be distinguished in the first cycle—initially, from 1561 to 1570, a ten-year period of unvarying and rapid increase, in which prices rise faster than trade with the Indies. In the second period, also of ten years (1571–1580), we find a cyclical descending phase which can be observed simultaneously in prices and in traffic of merchandise to the Indies. In the second cycle of fifteen years, from 1581 to 1595, two stages are also apparent; there is a spectacular rise from 1581 to 1590, with prices having a slight advantage over the volume of merchandise. In the second stage, from 1591 to 1595, an incipient decline is shown, all the more noticeable because it is found within a general rising tendency.

But we need other indispensable data to establish correctly the progress of the cycle, such as information concerning yield of the chief productive sectors of the economy and the respective participation of Spanish and foreign goods in trade with the Indies. Only when these data are known will we be able to judge Hamilton's theories correctly, and to learn whether the development of the price curve corresponds exactly to that of the general level of economic activity as established by Chaunu.

Meanwhile, we believe that the views of these two authors err on the side of optimism. In any case we cannot ignore the presence of certain signs which reveal serious difficulties. Among such signs are, in the first place, the *State's financial bankruptcies*. Since late in the Emperor Charles' lifetime, the State's expenditures had been much higher than its income: the former reached the figure of 3 million ducats while the latter totaled only half that amount. The floating debt was 7 million ducats. The religious wars and the expansion of Philip II's imperialist policy raised these figures very rapidly, so that by 1573 the State's debt had risen to 37 million ducats.

Philip II had two choices. The first was inflation; that is, trying to find a method of payment by minting vellon currency. But as Hamilton says, the "Prudent King" feared inflation even more than the Devil, and therefore he inclined toward the second choice: to declare the bankruptcy of the State. And in fact, this was done on three occasions during Philip II's reign: the first in 1557, the second in 1575, and the third in 1597.

If there is one important single date in the history of the Spanish 16th century, it is November 1, 1575, when Philip II published for the second time a decree of bankruptcy for the State; this not only destroyed the credit of the Spanish Crown but also ruined the merchants of Antwerp and Medina del Campo and brought about the downfall of the famous Medina del Campo–Antwerp financial axis, which had been the central pivot of world economy for a hundred years.

The second sign of latent crisis in the bosom of the Spanish economy during Philip II's reign was the *appearance of famine* in Castile. Until 1550, with the exception of a few periods of scarcity (1521–1522, 1525–1527, 1539), the price of wheat had coincided with the average of agricultural and industrial prices; that is, Spanish agrarian economy was in tune with the general development of the country. But after 1550 the price of wheat began to fluctuate sharply, exceeding the average price of other food products. If we take a closer look at the price curve for wheat, we will be able to divide it into three periods: from 1555 to 1565, an initial sharp rise, a serious warning for the future; from 1565 to 1575, a period of relative normality; and from 1575 onward very sharp fluctuations, as a result of lack of supplies from Sicily (which had ceased to be the granary of the Mediterranean) and insufficient production within Spain. Famine appeared in Castile, and conditioned Philip II's external policy to such an extent that he even had to apply to his chief enemies—the English and Dutch—to transport "bread from oversea," grain which came from Sweden and Poland after a roundabout route through hostile seas. An economic prisoner of his adversaries, the statesman responsible for the Invincible Armada was doomed to disaster.

A third sector of the economy which underwent difficulties during this reign was *livestock:* after 1588 the Mesta declined to such a degree that the wool trade, formerly so productive, became depressed as a result of the drop in production. If to this we add the first symptoms of industrial crisis (complaints by the cities to the Cortes, unemployment, depopulation) and the commercial crisis (ruin of Medina del Campo, 1575, and Burgos, 1585), we will become convinced that underneath the apparent atmosphere of prosperity indicated by the price and trade curves, the most dire foreshadowings of the near future can be discerned in the depths of Spanish economic structure during Philip II's reign.

BREAKDOWN OF THE ECONOMY UNDER PHILIP III AND PHILIP IV; THE MOMENT OF CRISIS. According to Chaunu, the evolution of the trade cycle under Philip III and Philip IV occurred in six ten-year phases, with a five-year period of increase and another of contraction.

The first phase, from 1595 to 1600, was an ascending one, representing the high point of the general revolution in prices; the curve rose from 110 to 141, and traffic with America from 97,000 to 120,000 tons in the five-year period. From 1600 to 1610 there was a tendency toward stability: the change in the cyclical pattern is obvious; there was to be a shift from phase A to phase B. The first inflationary tendencies can be observed in the currency; prices show slight losses and traffic also tends to fall off, although in 1608 the record figure for volume of merchandise sent to America was reached with 45,000 tons in a single year, and total exports for the five-year period reached 127,000 tons.

In 1610 the economic conditions changed in Spain, twenty or thirty years earlier than elsewhere in the West. Prices underwent two or three notable drops and traffic diminished, falling to 114,000 tons for the following five-year period. Between 1621 and 1630 the crisis developed in giant strides: though prices rose, this was due to monetary inflation. Real prices actually fell (90% in 1622 compared to 1600; 88% in 1624; 113% in 1627; 99% in 1630), and the contraction in American trade also continued, with a total of 103,000 tons per five-year period.

In 1630, an extremely important date, imports of American precious metals fell off sharply. The massive stream of silver which had flowed into Spain ever since 1530, with a maximum amount after 1560, decreased in 1630 and dramatically endangered the country's European ventures. In spite of constant inflation real prices tended to drop, while commercial traffic with the Indies experienced a new decline: 82,000 tons per five-year period.

From 1641 to 1650 American traffic suffered a prodigious loss, dropping to 57,000 tons for each five-year period, or a little less than the figure for the single year of 1608. Inflation knew no bounds: in a few years the price index rose from 116 to 143.

The causes of this change in the trade cycle which we have just sketched were widespread: quantitative insofar as they had to do with the exhaustion of the American mines; technical and economic insofar as they included a readjustment of the European market after a period of incessant rise in prices. However, for Spain the change represented a fateful crisis, for it befell the country at a moment of absolute spiritual and political confusion. Following the tradition established by Philip II, his two successors Philip III and Philip IV did not hesitate to resort to periodic declarations of bankruptcy of the public treasury. In 1607, 1627, 1647, and 1656, or approximately every twenty years, the Spanish State declared itself insolvent, which meant that the bankers either would not lend it money or, if they did, it was under such onerous conditions that instead of favoring the recovery of public credit, they destroyed it again, with no hope of recuperation. But though Philip II had clung to the principle of sound currency, as soon as Philip III came to the throne his councilors led him down the dangerous path of inflation.

And not only did they do this, but they conditioned the monarchy's economic policy to a rhythm of alternate inflation and deflation. This process began by ruining consumers and ended by devouring producers, and with them *rentiers,* holders of public funds, landowners, etc. Hamilton harshly accuses this incompetent and frivolous government, which was unable to cope with the circumstances and mark out a path for the future. Constantly wavering between its imperial ambitions and the impoverished reality of the country, it lived swayed by circumstances, until the final disaster of the great monetary crisis in 1680.

During the reigns of Philip III and Philip IV, as we noted in the preceding chapter, there was uninterrupted inflation which, beginning in 1599, reached high points in 1617 and 1621, until the crisis of 1627 took place. In that year violent deflation succeeded in counteracting the anomalous trend of the currency for about seven years. But the requirements of the monarchy's foreign policy, the decline in American trade, and the exhaustion of American mines gave new impetus to inflation. The second inflationary wave began in 1634 and lasted until 1641; debased money invaded the market and wiped out property values and fortunes. It was necessary to apply a brake for a ten-year period (1642–1652). But inflation was inevitable given the characteristics of the country's financial and economic situation, and again the monarchy abused this recourse. After that, a stage of successive inflation and deflation began which reveals the death-throes of the Hapsburg State.

How can we satisfactorily explain this mismanagement of the State and the country, this incapacity for facing up to the change in economic conditions and taking measures to counteract the phase of cyclical contraction which occurred in the 17th century? The economists of the period had already pointed out the evils of the situation.

Let us examine the causes which they believed were responsible for the Spanish economy's lack of resistance, even more apparent because Portugal, which shared the same experience, was able to save herself from disaster and orient her colonial economy anew. Here are some of the factors: entailment of property; increase in mortmain; vagrancy; deforestation; an excessive number of ecclesiastics; scorn for work and for the liberal arts; indiscriminate charity; monetary chaos; and oppressive taxation.

To these points made by the economists of the period, we must add other factors which have been made clear by historical research: budgetary imbalance; expulsion of the Moriscos; emigration of the country's youth; industrial competition from Northern Europe (Dutch, French, English); stagnation of agriculture and industry; and the vice and corruption of public administration.

Recapitulating what we have discussed previously, we must refer to the *crisis of the Spanish economy between 1599 and 1620*. The collapse of the currency in 1627, the dissolution of Iberian unity in 1640, and the military defeat at Rocroi in 1643 are remote consequences of that cataclysm. Its first shocks were felt at the turn of the century, shortly after Philip II's death. Between 1599 and 1601 Castile suffered the effects of famine, which spread north from Andalusia, and of a devouring plague. Prices of staple goods rose at a dizzying rate and wages followed suit. Many measures to stabilize prices and wages were taken at this time by municipal councils, such as the ordinances of the district of Trasmiera (Santander), approved in 1603. But worst of all was the fact that workers were not to be found. Manpower had disappeared from the market, giving a clear field for the invasion of foreign merchandise. Paralyzation of colonial expansion in America, expulsion of the Moriscos, inflation, all were concomitant causes which aggravated the ills of Spain's social and economic structure. Long before the reduction in shipments of precious metals, during those crucial years separating one century from another, Spanish society was sick unto death. Cellorigo wrote in his *Memorial,* in 1600: "Truly, it seems that this Republic has become a republic of men who are bewitched, living outside the natural order of things." This "bewitchment" was, Pierre Vilar believes, the fundamental cause of the Spanish economy's lack of resistance in the face of economic contraction; it was an anguished rejection of reality which developed as soon as the first symptoms of unease began to appear (in literature, Cervantes and *Lazarillo de Tormes*), and which eventually led to the total pessimism of a Saavedra Fajardo. Between one set of factors and the other, the feudal type of society—a survival of Ferdinand and Isabella's efforts—had collapsed and with it the Hapsburg State (rumblings of revolt in Catalonia in 1639, a year before the break with Portugal).

DISORDER UNDER CHARLES II. In the last five decades of the 17th century the Spanish economy felt the full weight of the depression. The case is particularly clear if we examine Valencia's economy; in Castile, by contrast, the process was masked by monetary inflation.

We can establish the following ten-year phases for Valencia: first, from 1650 to 1660, a slight drop in prices; the index falls from 121 to 116. Second, from 1660 to 1670, a new descent; index falling from 116 to 106. Third, from 1670 to 1680, tending downwards, but with a slight tendency toward recovery; index 100. Fourth, from 1680 to 1690, nadir of the depression; index, from 100 to 90. Fifth, from 1690 to 1700, the first sharp rising tendency; index rising from 90 to 103.

In regard to Castile, the cyclical pattern was masked by spiraling inflation, beginning in 1655, and the sharp deflations of 1659, 1664, and 1680. By studying the premium of silver over vellon during this period, Hamilton obtained the following results: about 1650 it was 50%; from 1657 to 1659 it went up to 80%; in 1659 down to 50% again; in 1664, in the wake of a new wave of inflation, it was 150%. That was the moment when there was an unsuccessful attempt to check inflation. It explains why, after 1665, the premium on silver went up to 180% (1669), 190% (1675), and 275% (1680). In the last-named year the crisis was so serious that the inevitable deflation which followed prolonged the destitution of the kingdoms of Castile. Strict regulations governing prices and wages were set everywhere, in accordance with Charles II's ordinance of 1680. Some of these regulations, such as those pertaining to Santander and Laredo, have been published.

This was why, while the Valencian economy followed the European process of contraction in business and then slowly recovered, Castilian economy followed the sharp changes in monetary inflation, with the price curve almost corresponding to them. The table below shows the evolution of these last ten-year periods:

		Indexes
1651–1660	Limited contraction	74 to 69
1661–1670	General inflation	69 to 98
1671–1680	Inflationary peak	98 to 103
1681–1690	Economic collapse	103 to 59
1691–1700	Stagnation	59 to 65

ATTEMPTS AT ECONOMIC RENEWAL AT THE END OF THE 17TH CENTURY. The violent deflation of 1664, followed by the inflation of the 1670's and the crisis of 1680, ruined what little was left of the Spanish economy. All the great cities cried havoc: Toledo, Cordova, Seville, and Granada sent memorials to Madrid saying that the old artisan classes were abandoning the cities and that their population had fallen off very greatly. During this period Madrid lost almost half of its inhabitants; in thirty years it declined from 340,000 to 170,000. Guilds were dissolved everywhere. The situation became so serious that even the traditional Toledan steel industry was in danger of disappearing from a lack of skilled workers and had to request the government to bring in specialized foreign workers.

The Crown simply drifted in the face of this situation, and "the Crown" means of course the circle of courtiers who worried only about finding out whether Charles II would leave the inheritance of the Spanish Empire to France or to Austria. There were, of course, some exceptions, such as the Count of Oropesa, promoter of the first treasury and trade reforms. But the impulse toward renewal was felt especially in the periphery. In Saragossa, Dormer brought together an economic council (1674) to discuss means of restoring the Aragonese economy, laid low by the intrusion of foreign professional workers. The attempt failed, but it was a sign that the country's pulse had not stopped completely.

On the other hand, the Mediterranean periphery gave signs of surprising activity after two centuries of prostration. The causes of this were very complex. But there is one which leaps to the eye. The monetary autonomy of Valencia and Catalonia saved them from alternate inflation and deflation, and consequently from ruin. In the Principality, after the deflation of 1654, imposed by the necessity for ending the War of Secession, any inflationary tendency was carefully resisted. New mintings obeyed only the needs of an expanding market. The Catalan monetary authorities flatly refused to follow the lead of Madrid, in the belief that an excess of currency would be injurious to international trade.

There is a further important phenomenon in the case of Catalonia, as J. Fontana has pointed out: renewal of the textile industry as a result of the freedom of trade established by the Treaty of the Pyrenees (1659). While the neighboring kingdom of Aragon was being stifled by protectionism, which favored only the producers of low-quality products, the Catalonian textile industry was going through a phase of renewal during which many ancient privileges were lost, but from which many leaders of the future textile industry of the 18th century were to emerge. To compete with French, English, and Dutch fabrics (on which a duty of only 11% of their value was charged), it was necessary, though with difficulty and reluctance, to rise to the level of foreign competition. This and other phenomena are reflected in the vitality achieved by Catalonia in the course of a few years.

The Catalans began to work. Bandits gradually disappeared and tillers of the soil appeared in their place. Brandy, sold to the English and Dutch, began to be profitable, and vineyards and rural industries grew up under the aegis of this trade. At the same time, loss of the Sicilian market spurred the activity of merchants and shipbuilders. Catalonian vessels began to frequent the port of Cádiz, and went to Lisbon for colonial products: sugar, cocoa, and tobacco. In 1680, the same year that witnessed the economic collapse of Castile, Catalonia's resurgence was clearly visible. There was a whole generation of Catalans, with Feliu de la Penya at their head, who extolled labor and trade, even trade with America. All this was a foreshadowing of what was to take place in the 18th century.

Statistics confirm this divergence in the development of Castile's and Catalonia's trade cycle. The table below, taken from Robert Smith, shows movement in the ports of Barcelona and Seville at the beginning and end of the 17th century.

BARCELONA			SEVILLE	
Years	Per cent		Years	Per cent
1605–1606	100		1605–1606	100
1693–1694	132		1621–1625	45
1694–1695	121		1641–1645	27
1695–1696	137		1661–1665	17
1696–1697	172		1681–1685	13
1697–1698	131		1691–1695	23
1698–1699	189		1695–1700	10

That is, while in Barcelona at the end of the century traffic in merchandise was almost double what it had been at the beginning, in Seville, by contrast, it had dropped to 10%.

V · ECONOMIC TRANSFORMATION IN THE 18TH CENTURY

32 · Bourbon Reform Policies

TRADITIONALISM AND PROGRESSIVISM. In 1700 the House of Bourbon ascended the throne of Spain. This event has significance not only in the dynastic and political sphere; its meaning is much broader, for with the establishment of the Bourbons in Spain came the culmination of a period of French influence which had begun about the middle of the 17th century.

French influence, evident in intellectual activity, fashion, taste, technology, and economy, tended to fill the vacuum left in Spain by the failure of Hapsburg policies. And this vacuum was filled not only by French solutions, but by the European ones which inevitably accompanied them into Spain. In short, a European concept of life now attempted to modify and even supplant the Spanish mentality which had been molded by the Counter-Reformation. This was a moment, then, when two strong currents were apparent within the country, breaking the mental conformity which had characterized Spain ever since the early decades of Philip II's reign.

On the one hand there were those who, recognizing the nation's backwardness, wished to raise it to a European level at whatever cost, sometimes without paying due attention to geographic factors and historical precedents. We shall call this group the reformers. From it were to arise the "afrancesados," or French sympathizers, of the War of Independence and the liberals of the 19th century.

In opposition to this group were those who viewed any novelty with suspicion, and who felt that Spain's possibilities had been defined by her glorious past, from which it would be hazardous and possibly fatal to depart. This group, deeply rooted in history and society, was more conscious of the Spanish social reality than the reformers. But the fact that they relied on routine and inertia made them less capable of replying to the reformers' attacks.

471

This difference of opinion brings up the so-called problem of the two Spains, a problem which has been the center of both political and spiritual concern from the 17th century to the present. But do two Spains really exist, as proclaimed in the refrain repeated by so many generations of Spaniards?

In the first place, it seems obvious that no such difference exists from the material and economic point of view. What we find is the spectacle of a single country which, within the framework of Western civilization, has been endeavoring since the middle of the 17th century to raise its living standards: endeavoring to do this, as has been shown, sometimes under adverse circumstances and sometimes under more favorable ones. The tensions resulting from this expansion—class tensions—are similar to those experienced by the world at large.

In the second place, as Américo Castro has observed, the problem of the two Spains does not exist in terms of a position between two differing human groups. It really begins spontaneously inside each individual Spaniard and spills over into the outside world by a vital contradiction which constantly leads us to act as though we were two persons, blaming all that is bad within us not on ourselves, but on our fellow man. That is, the Spaniard does not assume responsibility for his acts; he discharges his guilt onto "the other fellow," on his neighbor; and this stimulates, in his intimate personal life, a profound social maladjustment which is sometimes resolved by a systematic coercion from above and at other times breaks out into wildfire anarchy, also systematic, arising from below.

In the third place, the two Spains of the traditional political game disappear if we consider the ruling minority which has governed the country during most of the years from Charles III's day to the present. This minority, sometimes mediocre, but at others made up of eminent personalities, has attempted to accomplish a practical synthesis between reformism and tradition. Thanks to it, the economic, social, and cultural betterment of the country has been made possible. This minority's sole creed has been to realize the ideal of Jovellanos, the great Spanish thinker of the end of the 18th century, who succeeded in reconciling the maintenance of the country's traditional spirit with one of the noblest and deepest of reform campaigns.

COMPOSITION OF THE REFORMIST MINORITY: IDEALS AND STAGES BY GENERATIONS. It is a proven fact that Spanish progressivism in the 18th century was characterized by its desire for reforms which would liberate the country from its self-evident evils: superstition, easy belief in the miraculous, ignorance, a conformist attitude, and a tendency towards inertia. But this reformist urge was shared only by a minority which, during the course of 200 years, was some-times—not often—in power but more frequently ostracized; how-ever, it did influence society, and gradually pushed Spain in the direction of the modern world.

This minority formed slowly and gradually. There was no col-lege, no university institution, from which such impulses could arise. It was formed by reading, by travel, by informal conversa-tions, by intellectual affinities. Its members were politicians, like Campomanes, Floridablanca, Aranda, and Cabarrús; writers, like Feijoo, Jovellanos, Cadalso, and Meléndez Valdés; economists, such as Istúriz, Assó (an Aragonese), Capmany (a Catalan), and Alavide (a Peruvian); doctors, like Virgili, Gimbernat, and Casal, all Catalans; naturalists, such as Cavanilles, a Valencian; mathema-ticians such as Jorge Juan, a native of Cádiz; scholars, like Pons and Villanueva. Everywhere there was a great desire to mark out a path which would restore Spain's greatness and her role in the polit-ical and spiritual community of nations.

In reality each of them aspired to a Utopian city, where the rem-nants of medieval barbarism would disappear in the melting pot of a higher culture molded by progress and tolerance. This is the dream of the "enlightened" Spaniards of the 18th century, as it was that of all superior human beings of the period.

They had an unshakable belief in a number of basic ideas for building this Utopian city. First, the *efficacy of culture,* for they felt that, once ignorance was dissipated, man would not only be better but more capable of practicing the arts which would raise his stan-dard of living. Second, in the *effective guidance of this culture,* which could not with impunity be turned over to just anyone, but must be planned for concrete ends—happiness for all men—by the State and the philosophers who supported the State's authority; this was precisely the origin of the dramatic battle between the "enlight-ened" group and the Society of Jesus. Third, *direct knowledge of the outside world:* to travel, to know the world, to see how other people differ from us, what beliefs they hold, how the arts prosper among them. Fourth, the *implantation of scientific knowledge,* based on mathematics and physics. Fifth, an *economic ideal;* that is, the application of those material and even mechanical principles which make nations prosperous, through agriculture, trade, and industry. And finally, the summit of their desires, the reformers believed in a *State which would implement these ideas:* not a liberal State necessarily, but one in which political power would be at the service of reformist thought.

What generations make up this movement? As many as four can be distinguished, within the limits proper to this summary. First, the *generation of 1714.* The War of the Spanish Succession was over, and victors as well as vanquished believed that the time had come for a change of direction. And no solution was closer to hand than applying the technical structure of another State, France, to Spanish social reality. The men of 1714, such as Patiño, believed that applying a brace to the body politic would suffice to set it in motion; but though appearances changed and administration was slightly improved, the social structure remained inert and unaltered.

Second, the *generation of Father Feijoo* (middle of the 18th century). In the face of proof that the French technical superstructure was not galvanizing the country into action, that it continued to be ignorant, superstitious, and idle, criticism of the real state of affairs arose. And this criticism was initiated by Father Feijoo through a number of writings, in particular a work entitled *Teatro crítico universal,* which first appeared in 1726 and continued until 1760, the closing date of this period.

Third, the *generation of Campomanes.* Many persons of influence and talent had now joined in the criticism. This group, encouraged by Charles III, a king who was more or less carried away by the new ideas, was raised to power; its members occupied ministerial posts, the presidency of the Council of Castile, intendancies and magistracies, and from these posts they systematically applied the plan for renewal which we mentioned before: reform of the country's culture, education, economy, and mental attitudes.

Fourth, in 1790 the *generation of Jovellanos* appears, composed of intelligent but skeptical men who believed neither in imported structures nor in a reform dictated from above. They believed that Spain needed to evolve gradually, and that the cure (like the French Revolution) might be worse than the disease. It was a disillusioned and moderate generation, though a liberal one at bottom, which prepared the way for the Spanish 19th century.

MODIFICATION OF THE POLITICAL AND TECHNICAL STRUCTURE OF THE STATE: ITS CONSEQUENCES. These four generations all accepted a postulate established by the generation of 1714. Since the reign of Charles II had been characterized by the resurgence of regional powers, the basic assumption after the War of Succession was that it had become absolutely necessary to centralize the country's government. French precedents and the importation of French rationalism served to strengthen this tendency, but another cause must also be mentioned: in 1714 there existed a general atmosphere favorable to the abolition of special regional regimes. According to this idea, Spain ought to form a single monarchy, with single codes of law and a single administration.

This concept has had extraordinary importance in Spain's history; it has forced a country of widely divergent elements into the channel of elementary simplification. From the economic point of view some authors, such as Viñas Mey, have held that centralization was equivalent to economic progress. It is obvious that the disappearance of internal customs barriers favored the development of a common market, and that in consequence manufacturers and businessmen, landowners and farmers, could sell more. This is logical and self-evident and requires no comment. But to say that the miracle of Catalonian recovery was due to the mere fact of centralization is to assert an arbitrary conclusion with neither empirical nor rational justification. The economic rebirth of Catalonia dates from 1680 and is more closely tied to Venezuelan cocoa and Cuban sugar than to the ink on decrees issuing from Madrid.

As for technical changes in the State's machinery, the monarchy of Philip V, simply because it was victorious, was able to impose an effective bureaucracy on the country, for it was not restricted by local charters or constitutions. It is difficult to create a bureaucracy, however, and though the Bourbons achieved a certain degree of success in this regard, it was not sufficient to meet all the country's needs. On the other hand, as soon as favoritism was introduced in high places (reign of Charles IV), the serious errors of the past were repeated.

ADMINISTRATIVE, FINANCIAL, AND INSTITUTIONAL REFORMS: RE-PERCUSSIONS IN THE ECONOMIC FIELD. The basis of administrative reform during the Bourbon period was monarchical absolutism. In the same fashion as an authoritarian monarchy had developed in the 15th century, the absolute monarchy of the House of Austria had flourished in the 16th and 17th. It differed, however, from the subsequent Bourbon monarchy in the sense that it had to conform to the country's constitutional tradition. Once this was eliminated—theoretically at least—by the omnipotence of the monarch, the Bourbons acquired extraordinary freedom of movement. Their will was law—residents of the Court called the king "the master"—in spite of the fact that Spanish traditionalism managed to survive through innumerable and invisible barriers. On balance, however, the administrative reforms were both profound and tenacious.

The principal measures adopted had to do with *political uniformity*. As a consequence of the War of Succession, the political privileges and ancient charters of the Mediterranean regions were suppressed one after another: Valencia in 1707; Aragon in 1711; Catalonia in 1716 by the "Nueva Planta" decree; Majorca in 1715; and Minorca in 1782 after it was wrested from English hands by Spanish troops. That is, along general lines the State imposed equal laws, and all subjects of the monarchy were subjected to a common system, though in fact great discrepancies, many of which have survived to the present day, existed in the systems of private law. The only regions not subjected to this unification were the Basque Provinces and Navarre. Both retained a very important privilege, that of being isolated bodies in the financial bosom of the monarchy (Exempted Provinces).

Other measures centered on *administrative uniformity*. The Hapsburgs had ruled through a system of councils, a method of government known as "polysynodism." After 1714 ministries were set up (State, Church Affairs and Justice, War and Navy, plus an office for general supervision of the Treasury and a Superintendency for settlement of disputed claims). The Council of the Cabinet dates from the same year, but was changed into the *Junta de Estado,* or Committee of the State, in 1783. What were the advantages of the ministries? For the first time in the history of Spanish administration there were specialized persons held directly responsible to the king.

The central power mechanism of the Crown's policies was the Council of Castile, which after 1707 stood out above the other councils when that of Aragon was incorporated into it by virtue of the centralizing doctrine put into practice by the Bourbons. From that time onward, the Council of Castile represented the moving force behind the country's renewal. Its president was the first magistrate of the realm after the king, and at the same time president of the Council of Military Orders and the Cortes.

The Council of Castile acted through numerous committees, whose creation it encouraged. Of these the Board of Trade was outstanding, owing to its importance in the development of 18th-century Spanish economy; it had been founded by the last of the Hapsburgs and reached its maturity under Charles III. Within its own jurisdiction the Council of Castile had charge of everything relating to the State's legislation: approval of bulls and Papal briefs; development of economic interests; cultural progress of the country; and nomination of administration officials.

As for *regional administration,* there was also an attempt to make it uniform, conforming to the precedents existing in France and in the development of colonial administration in America. Along general lines, there were two stages in this process. During the first, the country was divided into kingdoms administered by a captain-general and an *audiencia,* or magistracy. The captain-general carried out the government's administrative functions and the *audiencia* was his consultative organ. In 1749 another more flexible and modern structure was established at a lower level, that of *intendentes,* or intendants, copied from France. This system was first applied in Catalonia (1718), but did not become widespread until 1749. The intendants' main function was to develop the economy of their respective territorial jurisdictions. From this point of view, the actions of these agencies were most important in the 18th-century Spanish economy's effort toward renewal.

STIMULUS OF THE ARISTOCRATIC MINORITY AND PERIPHERAL BOURGEOISIE. Apart from this administrative reform, there were also certain social groups within the country who concerned themselves with economic progress and gave tremendous impetus to technical, agricultural, commercial, and industrial activities. We shall not refer here to the social structure, leaving it for a later chapter, but will merely allude to the ideological stimulus of these social groups.

One of them was the nobility. As a social body, it obviously represented a conservative drag on Spanish reform efforts in the 18th century. But some of the protagonists in that century's economic reform in Spain were recruited from the aristocracy, not only among the grandees and upper nobility (like the Duke of Alba, a fervent Encyclopedist, or the Duke of the Infantado, who instituted an irrigation scheme on his lands, or the Count of Peñaflorida, founder of the Basque Society of Friends of the Country), but especially among the vast legion of knights and *hidalgos* from the north of Spain (Capmany in Catalonia, Assó in Aragon, Campomanes and Jovellanos in Asturias, and Floridablanca in the Rioja), highly cultured individuals who enjoyed a certain economic position and were open to the ideas of material, spiritual, and technological progress reaching them through France and England.

But in general the largest numbers came from the bourgeoisie of the peripheral regions. We still are not certain about the stages in the growth of this social class (except perhaps, in general terms, for Barcelona); but we do know that throughout the 18th century it achieved an increasingly favorable economic position which permitted it to demand from the State a number of laws beneficial both to it and to the country. This conclusion is important, for the Bourbons' labor of economic reform did not arise simply as the abstraction of a few theorizing aristocrats, but from the constant pressure of the nation's controlling economic media: businessmen from Cádiz, Málaga, and Corunna, merchants and manufacturers from Barcelona, Valencia, Gijón, and Bilbao.

INSTRUMENTS OF REFORM: ECONOMIC SOCIETIES OF FRIENDS OF THE COUNTRY AND BOARDS OF TRADE. This was the period when a number of local groups arose in Western Europe, united into academies, societies, or committees, whose purpose was to foment progress in the specific activities of the region or city where they lived. Some received the support of the State from the very first; others were private foundations which developed in proportion to the vitality of the social milieu within which they grew. The Spanish Bourbons profited from this atmosphere and established official

Academies in imitation of France. But after the middle of the century, regular meetings were held in private circles which brought together persons concerned with the development of the country's activities. These groups discussed matters of interest to the inhabitants, commented on some foreign book, and suggested topics of study.

In 1748 in Azcoitia (Guipúzcoa), *hidalgos* and priests held evening meetings and laid down rules suggesting the topics to be discussed. This group of gentlemen from Azcoitia is important because the Basque Society of Friends of the Country arose from it in 1765.

Its founder was the Count of Peñaflorida, a man who had traveled widely in Europe and was in contact with the principal European scholars. The Society, authorized by the monarchy in 1765, began to concern itself systematically with national and domestic economy and the technological preparation of the country's youth. According to Shafer its program may be summarized in the following points: precise and detailed information on the condition and needs of the Spanish economy; studies of the principles governing economic policy; technological improvement, applied to all branches of production; amplification and better utilization of the labor force; governmental action; and exclusion of foreign goods. As concrete achievements of this program, the following, among others, are worthy of mention; the memorials drawn up periodically, containing large amounts of information; the Royal Basque Patriotic Seminary, established in Vergara (1776), where courses in chemistry and metallurgy were given; the Royal School of Metallurgy, with a separate administration until 1783, after which it was included in the other seminaries supported by the Society; and campaigns in favor of vaccination against smallpox (after 1771), which created a number of enemies for the Society. In spite of this, however, the Basque Society forged ahead and in a very short time managed to attract the best people in the country. In fact, the number of its members rose from 41 in 1766 to 143 in 1771 (of whom 92 lived in other Spanish regions, 9 in other European countries, and 6 in Spanish America), 400 in 1773 (47 in the Basque Provinces, 159 in the rest of Spain, and the remainder in the colonies and other countries), and 1,000 in 1776. It is also noteworthy that for the first time in Basque history, the Society succeeded in incorporating an important sector of the region's upper nobility into active life.

The labors of the Basque Society of Friends of the Country were so well thought of by the State that ten years after the Society's foundation, in 1774, Campomanes, then attorney-general of the Council of Castile, ordered the foundation of local societies of the same type everywhere in Spain. As Carande points out, Campomanes must have had in mind the program formulated by Bernard Ward, an Irishman in the employ of the Spanish State, in his *Economic Project* (*Proyecto económico*) (1762). Ward suggested as a remedy for the ills of Spain an imitation of the Dublin Society. In any case, the attorney-general of the Council of Castile was well informed on the subject, and the definition of the aims of the Society of Friends of the Country is very evident in Chapter X of his *Discourse on Popular Industry* (*Discurso sobre la industria popular*) (1774). With his support, various Societies were founded—Carande has counted about sixty—some of which had been established prior to the circular of 1774: those of Cádiz and Baeza (1774). In 1775 five were set up: Madrid, Soria, Seville, Granada, and Vera, in the province of Almería; in 1776 two, Saragossa and Valencia; one in Tárrega in 1777; four in 1778, in Talavera de la Reina, Tudela, Almuñécar, and Palma de Mallorca; one in Lucena in 1779; three in 1780, Segovia, Osuna, and Sanlúcar de Barrameda; two in 1781, Oviedo and Cuidad Rodrigo; in 1782 two, Jaca and Vélez Málaga; one in 1783 in Valladolid; one in 1787, Motril; and another in 1798 (Santander). There was a Society in operation in Zamora in 1785 and another in Tarazona de la Mancha in 1794. By 1804 there were seventy-three Societies of Friends of the Country in Spain, many of which had declined as a result of the shocks produced in conservative spirits by the French Revolution. Others, those of a more local type, had disappeared, having foundered under the weight of routine or scarcity of funds. Among the Societies we have just listed, the most outstanding were those of Madrid, Seville, Saragossa, Valencia, Segovia, and Palma, besides the Basque one; this because of their publications, of great interest as sources for the study of 18th-century economy. The Society of Saragossa has the honor of having founded the first Chair of Economics, inaugurated on October 24, 1784.

As we can see, in this roster (which should be completed by the list of overseas Societies, beginning with that of Manila, founded in 1781) there is one notable omission: Barcelona. Barcelona did not have a Society of Friends until 1835. This was due to the fact that after 1758 it possessed a magnificent instrument: the Board of Trade, derived from the *Junta Central,* in which the bourgeoisie of Barcelona had concentrated not only their economic, but also their social awakening. This Board, whose funds stemmed from the "periaje" tax collected by the port of the city, encouraged nautical, mathematical, and technical studies, gave scholarships to the most brilliant students, and very early in the 19th century founded chairs to teach the most modern studies, such as chemistry, stenography, botany, and mechanics. Its activities were supremely important for Barcelona's economic and cultural future.

Other institutions were created following its example, such as the Consulate of Málaga, founded in 1785, whose purpose was to encourage the development of the merchant marine, trade, industry, and agriculture in the region, plus founding—in imitation of the Board in Barcelona—chairs of commerce, pilotage, agriculture, and drafting, later superseded by the magnificent donation given to the famous College of San Telmo (1787). This was also the case of the Consulate of Santander, created in 1796, which, beginning in 1790, sponsored schools of navigation and drafting. In other areas the reformist movement which affected all the institutions we have described was the originator of other bodies of a different type, but of no less interest: for example, the Academy of Agriculture of the kingdom of Galicia, established in Corunna in 1765; and the Royal Cantabrian Society, created in Santander in 1791 after seventeen years of vain petitions, which gained fame through its support of agriculture and trade in the Montaña region and by the foundation of the Cantabrian Seminary in Comillas, specializing in natural sciences.

POPULAR AND TECHNICAL EDUCATION. We know very little about the development of popular and technical instruction in 18th-century Spain. Apart from the programs of the Societies of Friends of the Country and the Boards of Trade, which constitute convincing proof of the ruling classes' interest in providing broader horizons for the more capable segment of society, we do not have enough material at hand to sketch an adequate picture of popular and technical education in the Spain of the period.

There is, however, one undeniable fact. After 1750 the outlook changed in regard to studies in secondary schools and centers of higher education. It was not an abrupt transformation, but one which gradually achieved ever more meaningful results. We need only note what instruction in Spain was like in the middle of the century, as the studies of Sarrailh, Soldevila, and Galí have presented it, and then compare it with the programs and progress made by 1800, to realize that much ground had been gained during that half-century. Declamation and bombastic oratory, the absurdity of disputations and public exercises, were supplanted by a desire to work for tangible results, especially in the field of so-called natural philosophy (natural sciences). Cultural battles are not won in hours, however, but in decades, so it is no wonder that the net results were not wholly favorable.

The defects of the old system were blamed on the Jesuits. Augustinians and Dominicans were far from being the last to criticize. The fact that, after the Jesuits were expelled in 1767, the mathematician Jorge Juan was put at the head of their Madrid stronghold—the Seminary of Nobles—is very symbolic. But the truth was that the real effort to spread popular and technical culture did not arise from the old teaching centers which survived the Society of Jesus, but from the endeavors of the new social and economic organs of Enlightened Despotism, spurred in their efforts by official stimuli such as Campomanes' famous work, *Treatise on the Popular Education of Artisans (Tratado de la educación popular de los artesanos)*.

Nevertheless, the two greatest successes of this period were owed to private foundations: the Royal Seminary of Vergara, created by the Basque Society of Friends of the Country, and the Institute of Gijón, sponsored by Jovellanos. Of the two, the Seminary of Vergara was better balanced, combining a classic scientific education with a practical course of study. In the Institute of Gijón, on the other hand, Jovellanos adopted the program of a specialized technical school, for it combined mineralogical prospecting, essential if we keep in mind the growing development of coal mining in Asturias, with advanced mechanical studies.

33 · Population and Labor

DEMOGRAPHIC RECOVERY IN SPAIN: SPECIFIC AND REGIONAL CHARACTERISTICS. The 18th century marks the transition from a "demographically primitive" to a modern population. This phenomenon, common to all the European countries, was the combined result of economic progress, the beginning of better hygienic conditions, and the end of the disastrous wars of the Hapsburg period. These factors helped to limit great famines and pestilences like the medieval ones; that is, to reduce the extraordinary mortality rate which periodically wiped out the normal surplus of births over deaths.

Spain, which underwent its last great visitation of plague in 1649, shared in this progress. The fact is proved by the first general censuses (indispensable for the new regime, whose administrative centralization made them possible), which in fact date from this period.

The first approximate idea of Spanish population is given us by the economist Jerónimo de Uztáriz in his *Theory and Practice of Trade and Shipping* (*Teórica Práctica de Comercio y de Marina,* 1724). His data are drawn from various military and tax statistics for the years 1710 to 1717, corrected for possible errors of misrepresentation. His total gives 1,140,013 heads of families, or some 7,500,000 inhabitants. This figure is, of course, lower than that of the period of Ferdinand and Isabella, and confirms the belief that Spain's population declined throughout the 17th century.

An increase in population took place during the reign of Ferdinand VI. Campomanes, in his *Fiscal Allegations* (*Alegaciones fiscales*), asserts that in Castile alone there were 6,700,000 inhabitants, a figure in line with Ward's statement in his *Economic Project* that Spain's population was then approaching 8 million.

The first official census on an individual basis dates from 1768–1769 and is known as Count Aranda's census. It gives us a figure of 9,300,000 inhabitants. The progress here had been considerable. Not long afterward, at the end of the 18th century, two other population censuses were made, that of 1787, called Floridablanca's census, and Godoy's in 1797. The first gave a total of 10,400,000 inhabitants, with a population increase of a million souls over the previous one; however, the second resulted in a total of 10,500,000, a very slight increase of 100,000, not easily reconciled with the result obtained previously. Most writers agree, therefore, that there was some misrepresentation in reporting census figures.

In 1808, in the so-called Antillón enumeration, Spanish population approached 12 million souls, a figure which corresponds to the normal curve displayed throughout the 18th century. In short, from 1708 to 1808 the country's population increase was nearly 4 million persons, obviously a considerable growth, though less than that of other European countries. The conclusion is clear: after a bottleneck of more than a thousand years which, though with slight normal variations, had remained fixed since Roman times with a maximum of some 6 or 7 million inhabitants, the 18th century shows that the Spanish demographic vehicle was once more on the move.

At what precise moment did this important change occur? Current investigations seem to place the acceleration of the process at about 1770. In any case, it is a proven fact that after 1770 the rhythm of growth in Spain was similar to that of Europe (6.3 and 6.8 per 1,000 per year, respectively).

However, the statesmen of the period considered that the country was underpopulated compared with others on the continent. The disadvantage was attributed to the following causes: wars; too widespread celibacy (related to an excessive number of religious vocations); entailments; *mayorazgos;* the privileges of the Mesta, which worked against agricultural development and in consequence the possibilities for food production; and lack of industrial progress.

As for its geographical distribution, the population increase in the 18th century was not uniform, benefiting the peripheral provinces more than those of the interior. This inequality, which replaced a centripetal demographic tendency by a centrifugal one, finds eloquent proof in the distribution of Spanish *depopulated areas* according to the census of 1797; of a total of 932, there were 739 in León and the two Castiles and 61 in the arid lands of Aragon. Other figures will give us demographic details for other regions:

Asturias rose from 150,000 to 360,000 inhabitants in the course of the 18th century, and Galicia from 600,000 to 1,140,000. In both these cases the population doubled, as it did in the Basque Country, where the increase was from 175,00 to 334,000 inhabitants. In Catalonia the censuses give the figure of 406,000 in 1720 and 899,000 in 1787, implying an increase of 121% in the course of seventy years; it is probable, however, that the earlier figure is somewhat low, which would mean that the rise is exaggerated. It is also certain, though, that there was a considerable dispersal of Catalans outside the region, which would more or less compensate for the exaggeration. In Valencia the population tripled, jumping from 300,000 to 915,000 inhabitants. It also doubled in Murcia and Andalusia. In Aragon the increase was similar; from 375,000 to 657,000 souls. In Extremadura and Castile the figures stayed on a much lower level. Both regions were underpopulated. At the end of the 18th century there were 25,000 more Extremadurans than at its beginning, an insignificant gain in a total of 400,000.

As for the relationship between country and city, Spain continued to be a nation of country dwellers. We need only observe the scanty population increase in the cities during this period. Only two attained more than 100,000 inhabitants, Madrid and Barcelona. The former rose from 130,000 in 1723 to 167,000 in 1797. Between the same two dates Barcelona tripled the number of its inhabitants (from 35,000 in 1717 to 111,100 in 1787). Following these were three cities whose population approached the 100,000 mark: Seville, Valencia, and Granada. Cádiz, with 70,000, was in a period of apogee, followed by Málaga and Saragossa with 50,000. In the cities of the North the population was still extremely sparse: Bilbao had 12,000 inhabitants, Gijón and Vigo 6,000, and Santander 2,000 (650 heads of households, triple those of the municipal census of 1712 with 225). However, these cities gave an impression of great vitality, in contrast to those of the interior (Burgos, Salamanca, Toledo, Segovia, and Avila), which were mere shadows of their former splendor.

INTERNAL AND EXTERNAL MIGRATIONS. The rapid population increase in the periphery of the Peninsula gave rise to a sizable migratory movement about which we do not have much information even at the present time. Along general lines, it can be said that Spain continued to move *southward;* that is, people from the overpopulated Cantabrian and Pyrenean regions spread toward the south (when they did not solve their problems by emigrating to America). Galicians, Asturians, and Basques, but especially Santanderians and Catalans, took part in this movement, so totally dissimilar to that of our own day. Men from Galicia and Santander moved to Castile and Andalusia, the former as day laborers, the latter as artisans and tradesmen. The Catalans became established in most parts of Spain and, as we shall see, stimulated general economic activity.

As for emigration to America, we have no exact figures. Isolated letters in the archives of the House of Trade reveal that in 1729, 1749, and 1780 respectively 416, 287, and 347 Spaniards went to America. This leads us to suppose that in the course of the century some 35,000 persons emigrated officially from Spain to America; adding 50% to this figure to allow for illicit emigration, we obtain the figure of 52,000 emigrants for the entire century, not a particularly high number.

By using the same procedure we can estimate the social distribution of the emigrants: merchants, 13%; ecclesiastics, 5.8%; soldiers, 3%; administrators, 8%; artisans, 1.6%; stevedores and laborers, 33%; family members, 6.2%; and the rest, servants, 30%. As can be observed, the number of specialized persons going to America was very small; most of the emigrants belonged to the servant or unskilled worker classes.

One obvious fact is the participation of Catalans, Valencians, and Aragonese in this migratory movement, once the obstacles set up by administrative routine and Sevillian monopolistic interests were removed.

In regard to immigration, an increase was observed early in the 18th century, especially of Frenchmen, who believed that the change of dynasty would favor them. Uztáriz counted some 8,000 families settled in Spain at the beginning of the 18th century; the Marquis of Villars estimated at 60,000 the French who moved in and out along the Pyrenees. Temporary French immigration, a habit left over from Hapsburg times, fell off slowly. It is possible that as many as 100,000 Frenchmen were established in Spain by mid-century, a figure we offer with considerable hesitation.

There were permanent colonies of foreigners in the cities, especially Madrid, Cádiz, Seville, and the Mediterranean ports (Barcelona, Cartagena, Alicante, and Málaga). Cádiz had the largest number of foreigners; in 1797 nearly 12% of her population (some 8,700 persons) was of foreign extraction, among them 2,700 French, 5,000 Genoese, 350 Portuguese, 270 English, 270 Germans, and 100 of other nationalities.

German immigration—mainly farmers and skilled artisans, experts in the manufacture of glassware, textiles, toys, and porcelain—was very important during this period. Most of the Germans were Catholics from the Sudetenland, but there were also some from Hamburg and the Hanseatic cities, businessmen who settled in the port cities to carry on large-scale operations.

The Italians continued to be active in many branches of politics and economics, for we must not forget that ties between the two peninsulas continued to be close in spite of the breakup of Spain's Mediterranean empire. Neapolitans and Sicilians on the one hand, Genoese on the other, were still deeply involved in the economic, political, and spiritual life of the country.

Repressive measures were taken against random and impermanent migrations. During the 18th century the most important of these were the expulsion of the Armenians from Madrid (1753), of the Greek colony in Minorca (1782), and the ban on popular pilgrimages to Santiago (1778). Pilgrimages brought in a large number of vagabonds and petty criminals, and so there was an order to draft into the army any pilgrims who had strayed from the road to Santiago.

FOREIGNERS IN 18TH-CENTURY ECONOMIC LIFE. Throughout the century, the number of foreigners involved in Spanish economic life diminished, as much because of growth in the country's active population as from the equalization of prices and wages with the rest of Europe, making it less attractive for foreigners to come to Spain in search of coveted silver. Thus, the hordes of day laborers and unskilled workmen from southern France disappeared.

Immigrants of higher caliber increased, however, especially technicians, merchants, and skilled workers. The theoreticians and statesmen of the period expressed two different opinions on this matter. Some considered foreigners indispensable to national economic life, while others thought them harmful. The latter opinion was shared by Antonio de Capmany, the Catalan economist, whose ideas undoubtedly responded to the anti-French feeling which existed in Catalonia after the Peace of the Pyrenees.

The State adopted a vacillating policy on the question of admitting foreigners, though in general it favored them. In 1714 the Agency for Foreigners (*Junta de Dependencias de Extranjeros*) was created in Madrid for the purpose of taxing their activities in Spain. Later, in 1726, a royal cedula was issued granting citizenship rights to any foreigner engaged in trade or industry. Two years after this, in 1728, during a period of open protection to foreign merchants, they were exempted from certain taxes. In Ferdinand VI's reign, plans to establish Catholic settlers in Spain were advanced; but it was not until Charles III that these attempts at mass importation of foreigners became an actuality. Apart from the process of repopulating certain localities, which we shall discuss later, various important steps were taken. In 1765 consulates and viceconsulates for foreign traders were established in the chief Spanish seaports, and in 1773 a registration of resident foreigners was undertaken: this separated useful foreigners, worthy of the State's protection, from idlers, who were to be deported. In Charles IV's reign the policy favorable to foreigners was interrupted by the French Revolution. Between 1791 and 1794 there were a number of decrees attempting to control not only political emigrés from France but also those individuals who might endanger Spain's political stability. An order laying down rules for naturalization of foreigners as subjects of the king dates from 1791, and in 1792 and 1793 there are any number of decrees taxing the activities of foreigners, even foreign priests. The wave of anti-French sentiment reached its peak in 1793 and 1794. Many establishments and business firms belonging to Frenchmen were attacked in various parts of the country, including Valencia, where the wave of xenophobia was especially strong (1794). Anti-French sentiment in Catalonia was fanned by the war against the Convention; but in fact quite a number of families who had taken refuge from revolutionary terrorism settled there.

There was a sharp change of attitude in 1797, when, by an order of September 8, Godoy authorized the establishment in Spain of any foreign manufacturer or capitalist, even a Protestant, if he agreed to respect the country's religion. This edict of tolerance, the first since the Counter-Reformation, had great repercussions, for it permitted the establishment in Spain of persons whose religion was not in accord with official orthodoxy.

REPOPULATION ATTEMPTS. The governing class in the Spain of the early Bourbon kings often complained of the country's depopulated condition and blamed its weakness—compared to the chief European powers of the time, England and France—on this factor. Since it was known that Prussia, ever since the 17th century and especially after the early part of the 18th, had obtained excellent results from internal colonization of her most arid provinces, a similar ambition was aroused in Spain after the time of Ferdinand VI: that of repopulating vast zones of the country in order to foster international political and economic competition.

When the Marquis de la Ensenada was Prime Minister, the first projects to establish settlers in Spain—Catholic peasants of Dutch, German, Irish, and even French origin—were set in motion. These attempts were made in 1749 and involved the Sierra Morena region. The mission of the minister Bernard Ward to Ireland in 1752 is of interest in connection with this idea. The Irish, oppressed by heavy taxation and the spiritual tyranny of the English, were looking at that time for a place to emigrate, and Ward urged them to move to Spain. However, lack of capital and Ensenada's dismissal forced the suspension of these projects.

Under Charles III a second and more decisive phase was initiated, characterized by the colonization of Sierra Morena. This extremely important experiment should, we feel, be considered as one of the principal chapters in 18th-century Spanish economic history. If we keep in mind conditions in Andalusian rural areas, characterized by latifundism and low agricultural yield, biological underdevelopment and technical incompetence, we will realize that nothing less than the transformation of the agrarian social structure in southern Spain depended on the success of the Sierra Morena experiment. The attempt at colonization failed, not only in the districts where it was carried out, but on a broader scale as a decisive reality for the nation's future. We regret that there has been no thorough study of the progress of this colonization which would permit us to analyze the causes of its failure, very possibly not only local but regional and even national in scope.

Colonization of Sierra Morena was proposed by the Bavarian colonel Thürriegel, recommended by the Spanish ambassador in Vienna in 1766. His project was to send 6,000 German and Flemish Catholic settlers to America. After the proposal had been studied by Pablo de Olavide, an expert in this field, the Council of Castile reacted unfavorably to the idea; but it did favor the prospect of the settlers' going to Sierra Morena. With an enthusiasm which was quite extraordinary at the beginning of Charles III's reign, all arrangements were made for the success of the project. Pablo de Olavide was named intendant for Andalusia and superintendent of the colonizing venture. Campomanes personally drew up the Population Code (1767) and determined the district where the settlers were to locate, situated between the towns of Baeza, Santa Cruz de Mudela, and Bailén, at the foot of the Despeñaperros pass, though there was also to be an attempt to extend the zone of colonization along the Guadalquivir valley toward Cordova and Carmona.

The economic basis of repopulation consisted in the concession of individual tracts of land, exemption from taxes, and the offer of aid in foodstuffs and cash until the first harvests were brought in. The plantings selected were wheat, olives, grapevines, and fig trees, crops which were to be complemented by the establishment of a small local textile industry (linen, silk, and wool). Under Olavide the colonization had a certain amount of success; but in 1773 he was relieved of his post because of the Encyclopedist ideas he had imposed on the governing of the territory, and which had not been well received by the Capuchin monks who were his assistants. During the six years of his governorship the State spent some 40 million reales on the project. By 1775 fifteen towns and twenty-six villages had been founded, with 1,900 peasant and 150 artisan families: a total of 10,300 individuals, plus 3,000 day laborers and servants. The number of Spanish colonists, especially Catalans, exceeded that of foreigners; and the Englishman Dalrymple said in 1774 that the success of the project was owed to Spaniards. Many Germans returned home, others died because of the harshness of the climate and illnesses suffered in the ground-breaking stage; the rest quickly became Hispanized. There was also an unsuccessful attempt to settle 10,000 Galicians in the area.

The crisis in the undertaking came about because of the leaders' deficient technical preparation, difficulties of organization, lack of capital at the peak period of development, resistance to the reformist spirit which inspired the project, and opposition from natives of the region. We do not know whether this last factor was motivated by racial disagreements or by vested interests. In any case, Olavide's departure spelled the end of the attempt to colonize southern Spain, the great project so cherished by the reformers of Madrid. La Carolina and a few other centers survived the wreck, as did Las Navas de Tolosa, Carboneros, Santa Elena, Miranda del Rey, La Carlota, etc., whose development was due to other causes; but all zeal for attacking the problem of the Andalusian countryside at its roots was lost.

Other resettlement projects include one also proposed by Thürriegel in 1785, that of settling 500 Scottish families on a farming colony in Sacedón, near Madrid. It was unsuccessful. Cardinal Belluga was more fortunate in Orihuela, near which the towns of Dolores, San Felipe Neri, and San Fulgencio were founded.

A final type of colonization, spontaneous but very important, was the resettlement of the Catalonian coast, thanks to the vitality of the country's interior (twin towns of the Maresme) and the cessation of piracy.

POPULATION AND SOCIAL STRUCTURE: ACTIVE AND DEPENDENT POPULATIONS. We have said before that the chief demographic phenomenon in 18th-century Spain was population increase in peripheral areas. We shall now examine population distribution in relation to economic life and social structure.

The censuses of 1787 and 1797 disagree on the point of the different social classes' occupations. However, if we compare both censuses and analyze other characteristics of the population of the time, we can state that the following social groups emerge from the 10 million inhabitants of Spain at the end of the 18th century: aristocrats, some 400,000 individuals; ecclesiastics, about 170,000; bureaucrats and military personnel, about 110,000; peasants and agricultural laborers, some 1,800,000; industrial workers and artisans, 310,000; tradesmen, 25,000; and servants, 280,000.

As can be seen, the economically active population was meager (about 25% of the total). The dependent population was burdened with a considerable number of idlers and beggars, though we do not know exactly how many. Campomanes says that there were some 140,000 of them.

NOBILITY AND CLERGY IN 18TH-CENTURY ECONOMIC LIFE. The social status of the *nobility* continued without change. However, though the noble class can be considered as a single body from the legal and even ideological point of view, its economic state was extremely varied, according to the various groups which can be distinguished within it.

In 1797 the nobles comprised some 400,000, or 4% of the population. This figure indicates that there had been a century-long tendency towards reduction of the aristocracy; it will suffice to compare this number with that of 1768, when the roster of nobles was 722,000, to see that there had been a decrease of some 300,000 individuals. This was due especially to the restrictive measures taken against the *hidalgos;* so far as the upper nobility was concerned, in spite of Ferdinand VI's cautious policy (he created only two titles of Castile), Philip V as well as Charles III and Charles IV felt no hesitation about granting a large number of high ranks.

The restraining policy with regard to the *hidalgos* began with the royal cedula of 1703 laying down the conditions of blood and wealth necessary for those aspiring to acquire or preserve such rank. In 1758 Ferdinand VI decreed that any aspirant to this title would have to make a payment to the Crown of 15,000 to 30,000 reales. Some years later, in 1785, Charles III imposed an even more restrictive measure, for he ordered that those who obtained such a title had to exhibit extraordinary merit. Under Charles IV there was a return to the fiscal practice begun under Ferdinand VI; the royal cedula of 1800 stipulated a payment of 50,000 reales by aspirants to *hidalgo* rank.

In spite of these economic conditions, we must not fail to note that nobility was a privilege of blood, as is shown in the proofs demanded by the Council of Military Orders of aspirants to its offices or prebends. Any person of base ancestry, doubtful blood (Moorish or Jewish), or manual occupation was excluded from them.

As Domínguez Ortiz has pointed out, the geographic distribution of the Spanish aristocracy is very instructive. This author has been able to distinguish three zones. The first, comprising the Cantabrian area, together with some adjacent provinces (Navarre, Álava,

Burgos, and León), had the largest number of aristocrats (more than 10% of the total). This was because of the considerable number of *hidalgos* (some 120,000) residing there; suffice it to say that *all* the inhabitants of Guipúzcoa had this rank. The second zone, one of transition, takes in all of Aragon, Soria, and Valladolid. Here the proportion of nobles varied from 1 to 5%. The third zone includes all of the South and the Levant. Except for Madrid and Murcia, it contained less than 1% of the total number of nobles. It was in these last-named places that the grandees of Spain and holders of titles of Castile were concentrated.

If we analyze the noble hierarchy vertically, we first encounter the upper nobility. This group was made up of some 600 persons, of whom 100 were grandees of Spain and 500 were titled persons of Castile. Among them they controlled a considerable percentage of rural and urban property, commanderies, municipal offices, and revenues and rights on jurisdictional seigniories. They supported a horde of servants, divided within themselves into "abovestairs" (gentlemen and pages), and "belowstairs" (valets, jesters, and slaves). They amassed enormous quantities of unproductive, uninvested, and idle wealth in the form of chaplaincies, seigniorial properties, silver plate, and buildings. Owing to lack of issue and successive entailments of *mayorazgos,* very powerful castes were created which gained possession of a large part of the agricultural land. We can point out as an example the dukes of Medinaceli, who also held title to the dukedoms of Segorbe, Cardona, Alcalá, and Feria, the marquisates of Denia, Pallars, and Priego, the countships of Ampurias, Prades, etc. There were other families of the same type, such as the dukes of Frías, Infantado, and Alba.

The middle nobility was represented chiefly by the knights of the South, who controlled a number of offices as well as their rural and urban revenues: commanders of the orders, familiars of the Holy Office, and governors. The *hidalgos* of the North did not usually own much rural property. Some engaged in business.

Less numerous than the nobles were the *clergy* (some 170,000 persons, or 2% of the total population); but they were of equal or greater importance because they were recruited from the whole country, had cultural prestige and especially wealth, which had come down to them from previous centuries. There is no systematic study of the wealth represented by ecclesiastical property at the end of the 18th century. According to Ensenada's census, the most accurate of all, Church properties accounted for one-seventh of the grazing and farm land in Castile (equivalent to one-fourth of the total agricultural revenues), and one-tenth of the country's sheep (2 million head out of 20 million). But this was not all, for the Church held 135 million reales, as opposed to 170 million for all lay persons, in houses, artifacts, revenues, and rights. In short, out of Castile's national income of 2,650,000,000 reales, almost one-eighth (346 million) belonged to the clergy. These figures, however, may mask undeclared amounts, for neither tithes nor firstfruits were included in them. In Castile (1750) tithes amounted to some 600 million reales, of which two-thirds passed into the hands of the Church. There is no way of estimating firstfruits taxes. But all this channeled an enormous mass of capital into the Church's coffers, a large part of which was invested in real estate mortgages. It has been stated that three-fourths of the mortgages in Castile were held by ecclesiastics, and hence many properties passed over to the Church because of foreclosures or failure to fulfill obligations connected with agricultural rents. And we must add to these the income from much urban property.

Agricultural land, accumulations of cash, investment in mortgages, interest in the form of tithes and firstfruits, all made the Church a powerful force in Spanish economy. It is true that part of this wealth went into social service and public charity; but the capital remained immobilized, hampered by an ideology which conceived of life as something austere, from which everything that was superficial, comfortable, and attractive should be eliminated.

Now that we have examined the total wealth of the Spanish clergy of the period, we shall study briefly its distribution in the hierarchy. Three chief groups can be distinguished. The first was made up of bishoprics and archbishoprics, generally held by persons of the *hidalgo* class. Some dioceses were extremely rich. Most of them had annual incomes of over 100,000 reales, varying between this sum and the million reales enjoyed by the great dioceses of Valencia, Seville, Santiago, and Saragossa. The richest of all was Toledo, with annual revenues of 3,500,000 reales. The second layer was that of the cathedral chapters; their wealth depended on that of their respective bishoprics. The third was composed of the lower clergy, both urban and rural. At that time the parish priest was a pillar of society and fared quite well, though with a good many exceptions (16,000 priests for 19,000 parishes). Besides these there was a horde of benefice-holders and ordained persons depending on private funds, some 35,000 individuals in all, who usually led a frivolous, irregular, and disorganized existence, especially because of the disproportion between their expenditures and the benefices they enjoyed.

As for the regular clergy, there were some 2,000 monasteries in Spain with a population of 60,000, of whom 37,000 were ordained; the others were servants, unprofessed and lay brothers. Convents numbered more than 1,100, with 24,000 professed nuns. The Benedictines, Hieronymites, Carthusians, and monks of St. Basil were particularly outstanding because of their wealth in rural property. The mendicant friars continued to enjoy great popularity. They were concentrated in the rich cities (Madrid, Seville, Cádiz, and Barcelona), where there were large numbers of Carmelite, Franciscan, Augustine, and Dominican foundations.

THE AGRICULTURAL WORKER; REGIONAL DIFFERENTIATION. There is a certain amount of confusion about the numbers and social status of country dwellers, for the censuses do not distinguish between nobles, *hidalgos,* and peasants residing in rural areas, and urban and absentee proprietors employing day laborers for the actual work. Thus, in the census of 1787 the figure of 1,860,000 is given. To establish a criterion we shall define a farmer as one who directly cultivates the soil, either for himself or for a third person, not someone whose cash income is derived from rural property. Used in this sense, the census of 1797 gives us three types of peasants: 364,000 owning their own land; 507,000 renters, among whom are included those renting land both on long- and short-term leases; and some 800,000 day laborers.

Antonio Domínguez Ortiz has studied the geographic distribution of this last group. As in the case of the aristocracy, he has distinguished three zones. The first is made up of Galicia, Asturias, Santander, and the Basque region—the Cantabrian area, in a word—in which less than 25% of rural workers were day laborers; this figure coincides with the maximum number in the distribution of rural property, although in the case of Galicia there were no fewer than 31,500 day laborers. In the second zone the proportion rises from 25 to 50%. It takes in the provinces of Castile and León, and also Navarre, Aragon, Guadalajara, Cuenca, and Valencia, except for Palencia (with more) and Soria (with less). In the third zone day laborers predominate; it is the area of the great latifundia of the South. The maximum inequality occurs in the province of Seville, where the number of proprietors is 5,300 and of renters 14,000. One curious case: Catalonia and Majorca must be included in this third zone; even though they are regions of medium-sized property holdings, there is a large number of day laborers. This exception can be attributed to factors arising from booming demographic development and to these areas' special laws of succession, based on inheritance by the eldest son (*hereu*).

Regional differences in agriculture were due not only to variation in types of property and the traditional agricultural evolution of each region, but also to the different seigniorial systems. This has barely been studied, in spite of the fact that it has great interest for a basic understanding of the progress of Spanish agriculture. The latest studies referring to the 18th century show that, out of 22,000 towns existing in Spain, 10,600 belonged to secular seigniories and 2,200 to ecclesiastical ones. The others were royal property. The towns subject to seigniorial jurisdiction showed extremely varied characteristics, the result both of history and legislation. Four chief groups can be distinguished, however: towns in which the lord had jurisdiction but not ownership; those in which the lord had both jurisdiction and ownership; those in which he did not exercise jurisdiction but did own the property and have certain rights; and finally, towns in which a few private persons had certain rights in connection with public offices. All this, according to figures of the early 19th century, represented some 82 million reales of revenue annually.

SOCIAL TRANSFORMATION; FORMATION OF THE PERIPHERAL BOURGEOISIE. One of the characteristics of 18th-century European society was the formation of the bourgeoisie, owing to economic expansion, accumulation of capital, use of manpower in factories and workshops, and the technical transformation of industry, all of which produced the so-called Industrial Revolution during this period.

Some authors have spoken of the formation of a bourgeoisie in

Spain, as well as its role in the development and triumph of the policies of Enlightened Despotism; but in fact, a bourgeois class similar to that of the rest of Europe was formed only in a few coastal cities, and slowly even there. In the rest of the country what actually existed was a middle class, or rather, several middle class layers, which appear once we have eliminated from the urban population the nobility, the clergy, and the lower classes. We may define them as self-supporting classes not engaged in manual labor: tradesmen, masters in the guilds, liberal professions (doctors, professors, and lawyers), military officers, and civil servants. Their economic situation was widely divergent and so was their place in the social hierarchy.

The bourgeoisie, properly speaking, made up of businessmen engaged in wholesale trade without retail outlets (that is, eliminating simple shopkeepers), and especially of manufacturers, appeared only in a few characteristic places. One of these was Cádiz, a center for the great native and foreign businessmen; another was Barcelona, the only city where the development of a specifically industrial bourgeoisie can be observed. Far behind these cities was Valencia, with a combination of guild masters and businessmen; Madrid, whose role as capital meant the presence of a social stratum composed of *asentistas,* or holders of leases on public services, wholesale merchants, and guild masters; and the seaport cities of the North (Bilbao, Gijón), where there were only rudimentary signs of the new social tendency.

Leaving for a later section a discussion of guild life, which accounts for a large part of 18th-century industrial activity, we shall pause for a moment to examine the process of development of the Barcelona bourgeoisie, the most important and best-known of the bourgeois groups. Trade in Barcelona underwent a severe crisis after the War of Succession; only about 1730, when demographic improvement began to be felt and prices rose in the international market, did the cycle of prosperity which had begun in 1680 really get under way. Profits from international trade, especially in dried fish, wine, brandy, and colonial products, were translated into the formation of a *social class of great merchants,* among whom were nobles and knights, patricians of ancient lineage, and shipowners. This group found expression in the Royal Company of Barcelona, founded in 1756, and the Assembly of Merchants, established in

1758. This first generation of bourgeois had forty-one members, some of whom owed their inclusion to the "factories" for calicoes established some ten years before. But they were in a minority.

The appearance on the economic scene of manufacturers of *indianas* (calico or print cloth) produced some priceless statements by the bureaucrats charged with classifying their activities. Since they did not fit into any of the established guilds, the census put them down as "idlers," that is, unclassifiable. These "idlers" were to make the country's future. In fact, in 1772 they founded the Cotton-yarn Company, representative of the second bourgeois generation in Catalonia, the one which was, properly speaking, industrial. There were twenty-five individuals in this group, though the majority represented joint stock companies.

So by 1775 Barcelona possessed a bourgeois *élite* composed of two branches, the overseas merchants and the calico manufacturers. This second branch received a strong stimulus from the great wave of prosperity enjoyed by the country after 1783. It created the third bourgeois generation in Barcelona, that of *manufacturers of cotton yarn and cloth,* which like its predecessors had a representative organization: the Association of Cotton Cloth and Yarn Factories, created in 1799. Its fifty members formed the nucleus of the powerful organism formed by the 19th-century Catalan textile industry. Its symbol was the factory, and the factory summed up its social and economic concerns.

By the end of the 18th century the bourgeoisie of Barcelona was made up of overseas merchants, large calico manufacturers, and small textile manufacturers; further, there was a bourgeoisie of guild masters, whose capital was small and who were fated either to develop into a manufacturing bourgeoisie, properly speaking, or to sink into the lower bourgeoisie or artisan class.

The growing prosperity of the bourgeois world in the chief Spanish cities resulted in a solemn royal declaration concerning the legal incompatibilities which had existed up till then between noble status and industrial activity. Charles IV declared in a royal cedula of March 18, 1783—as a result of pressure by the Madrid Society of Friends of the Country—that no trade was an obstacle to attaining *hidalgo* status, and that the honorable practice of a trade for three generations could lead to noble rank.

DECLINE OF GUILD LIFE. Some authors, seconded by Professor Antonio Rumeu de Armas, a specialist in these matters, hold that the 18th-century guilds still represented an important reality in the country's social and economic life, and that their extinction was not due to a "slow process throughout the nation, but was produced by foreign influences and took place very rapidly."

Before we go into this argument, let us look at the true state of affairs. It is clear that guild structure was still evolving in the 18th century; the number of guilds increased throughout the course of the century (for example, by the end of the 18th century Barcelona had ninety guilds and Madrid some seventy). Not all had the same characteristics, however. There were guilds set up as labor corporations, with rules approved by the Council of Castile, a municipal government, or royal authority; uniform guilds with a national charter, a type which became widespread at the end of the 18th century; confraternity-guilds, religious brotherhoods with charitable aims, among whose rules some article of guild policy was inserted; and finally, the guild only in appearance, free crafts banded together under one heading for tax purposes.

According to the classic writers on the subject, the guilds' chief vices were the obstacles they placed in the way of apprentices and examinations, the caste privileges they maintained against outsiders, and the establishment of a *numerus clausus* system to avoid competition; nepotism, favoritism on the part of fathers toward their sons or relatives; fragmentation within a trade owing to an overspecialization which could only be harmful; and finally, fossilization brought about by clinging to technical traditionalism.

To these causes we must add one more general consideration. If we examine in detail the relationship between masters and workmen at the end of the 18th century, we will find that in general the former were more numerous than the latter. In the silk industry there were 8,800 masters and 5,200 workers; in the wool trade, 35,000 and 21,000; among blacksmiths, 9,100 and 2,400; among carpenters, 25,000 and 5,000; tailors, 27,000 and 6,000. These figures reveal one obvious fact: the guilds defended a closed type of artisan life which was very far from filling the needs of modern industry. Security, of more importance than business spirit, and the principle of social respectability made the whole system move within ever narrower limits which became less and less favorable to the progress of industry. Consequently, as soon as free and profitable work appeared, that represented by modern industry, journeymen and masters without shops of their own, and even masters who did have them, flocked toward the new horizon offered by the factory. This seems to have been the case in Barcelona, so conservative in guild matters, where the establishment of the cotton mills produced a disbanding of guild members in the direction of the new industrial installations.

But what essentially damaged the development of guild life was lack of capital. This was responsible for the fact that many artisans fell little by little under the influence of merchants and powerful manufacturing groups.

If we keep this in mind we can now examine the attitude of economists and politicians toward the guilds. Dispensing with minor differences, we can distinguish three groups: reformers, innovators, and revolutionaries. Among the first group were those who, recognizing the abuses of guild organization, hoped to preserve their essential services through reform: defense of quality and good taste, technical training in the workshop, and security within a given trade. Chief among these reformers was the Catalan Antonio de Capmany, in his book *Economic and Political Discourse in Defense of the Mechanical Work of Journeymen* (*Discurso económico-político en defenso del trabaio mecánico de las menestrales*, 1778). Among the second group, that of the innovators, is Campomanes. His ideas are expressed in his famous *Discourse on the Education of Artisans, and Its Development* (*Discurso sobre la educación popular de los artesanos y su fomento*, 1775). According to Campomanes, whose ideas are derived from the work of the French author Bigot de Sainte-Croix, entitled *Report on Guild Communities in France,* the guild ought to survive in certain cases; not for the merchants' sake, since trade should be absolutely free, but for the workers', in its double role as training school and political organization for the profession. In any case, he believed, technical obstacles and monopolistic practices should be suppressed, and all trades united in large affiliated guilds, thus avoiding fragmentation. And lastly, the principal figure among the revolutionaries is Jovellanos, in his famous *Report on the Free Exercise of the Arts,* published in 1785. Jovellanos' essential thesis, a metaphysical one, is that man is condemned to labor; and that in consequence of this condemnation he merits the absolute right to engage in any useful occupation, unshackled by society. "Let us break the chains," was the phrase he used in his book, and which throughout the 19th century was to be the battle cry of economic liberalism.

The result of these three tendencies within the State's general policies can be observed in the series of governmental measures adopted after 1772. In that year foreigners were permitted to establish themselves without examination; between 1787 and 1789 various decrees were laid down authorizing cloth manufacturers to own an unlimited number of looms. In 1790 freedom to exercise any trade without examination was proclaimed, on condition that the candidate demonstrate ability. And finally, in 1798 the possibility of passing an examination without having undergone apprenticeship or journeymanship was made legal.

CHARITABLE AND SOCIAL SERVICE ACTIVITIES. Under the Hapsburgs the organization of charity was left to the Church, with the results we have discussed previously. In the 18th century, however, thought began to be given to a lay structure of charity and social assistance. The Irishman Bernard Ward fired the first gun against the systems represented by brotherhoods and confraternities in his *Good Works* (*Obra pía*), written in 1750. Its fundamental thesis is that vagabondage and idleness deprive the real poor of a livelihood, and that in order to avoid indiscriminate charity a beneficent organization should be formed which would put the idler to work, aid the poor and disabled, and retrain the unemployed. His idea was to plan industries which could absorb unskilled labor. In Capmany, as in the case of the guild, we find a defense of brotherhoods and confraternities, which he praises as an expression of social brotherhood in no way replaceable by a simple mechanical distribution of State aid. Campomanes draws a distinction between the religious confraternity, which he attacks on the grounds of its general ideology, and the brotherhood, which he proposes converting into a lay mutual aid society, making it possible to insure against old age, disability, widowhood, and orphanhood. On the other hand, he attacks relief payments in cases of illness or death, so common at that time. The bases of the policies proclaimed by Campomanes were savings funds, loans, and public hospitals. As was to be expected, in Jovellanos we find an impassioned defense of absolute freedom, with suppression of brotherhoods and confraternities. According to him the State should supervise the hospital system, where the unfortunate would find shelter and aid.

As a consequence of these ideas the government's general policy throughout the 18th century tended toward limiting vagabondage and confraternities. As for the former, we should mention the ordinances of 1749 decreeing that beggars unfit for work or military service should be put in charity hostels, those of 1778 decreeing the return of vagabonds either to their native town or the capital of the diocese, and those of 1798 on applying the funds of purely beneficent societies to payment of the public debt. As for the confraternities (19,000 in Castile and 6,500 in the Crown of Aragon), they were reviled by all the liberals and innovators, who accused them of excessive spending and of constituting a heavy burden on their members without those members obtaining positive benefits from them. The attack on the confraternities became sharply focused during Charles III's reign. After 1767 rules were laid down suppressing confraternities and the guild type of brotherhood. In 1783, after the archbishops' report criticizing the abuses of popular confraternities, especially fiestas, banquets, and the like, their suppression was decreed. This spelled the extinction of guild confraternities set up without civil and ecclesiastical approval, and those which did not receive a new charter from the Crown. All the religious confraternities had necessarily to be approved by the government. As for those with purely sacramental functions, they were to be absolutely respected, but incurred the obligation of transferring their headquarters to the parish churches.

The social-aid brotherhoods, which had had an extraordinary development in the 18th century, after 1760 turned more and more into loan associations affiliated with the guilds. These were of many types, some of which had social significance, like the *Monte de Piedad* of Madrid founded by Piquer in 1702. The majority were associations insuring against illness and death, and developed within the bureaucratic atmosphere of Madrid or among the middle, liberal, and artisan classes. Their peak came between 1761 and 1783; their decline, after the latter date, was due to overenthusiasm in recruiting members and failure of the State to protect them.

APPEARANCE OF THE MODERN WORKER AND THE FIRST SOCIAL CONFLICTS. There is a theory that the truly modern worker—that is, the proletarian living on his wages—did not exist in 18th-century Spain. This doctrine may be valid for a large part of the country, but not for the industrial centers, especially Barcelona, where we can confirm the fact that the modern workers' movement had indeed appeared, as well as the first sparks of class conflict.

In Barcelona, after 1716 the construction guilds were split into two groups, that of the master builders and that of the masons. The same thing happened in other sectors which had evolved out of guild activity (carpentry, shoemaking, etc.). But the essential impact arose from development of the textile industry and the concentration of considerable numbers of workers in large shops and factories. Though they are probably exaggerated, there are some significant memorials of the period which inform us that there were 30,000 workers in Barcelona employed in nonguild industries (1779); of these, 18,000 were employed in twenty-five calico and cotton factories. This would give the fabulous figure of 720 workers per factory, an excessive concentration judging by trustworthy data from another source: the factories themselves. The factory of Juan Ponçgem, with seventy-five looms and eleven coloring tables, employed 127 workers (95 men and 32 women). In the woollens branch we find the factory of Jaime Ordeig, with ten looms and one warping frame, 57 workers in the factory and 174 working at home. These figures correspond to a scale which fits in well with what we know about the 18th century. However, by the end of the century the concentration of workers in Barcelona reached considerable numbers. The spinning and weaving factory of Erasmo de Gónima employed 800 to 1,000 workers.

Worker agitation had made an appearance in public industries before it showed up in Barcelona, especially in the factories controlled by the State. Protests were particularly noticeable in these because of the barracks-like regime under which the workers lived. The harshness of the working day, cuts in wages, and suppression of holidays, combined with the rigidity of bureaucratic control, led to a profound sense of social unrest. In 1730 there was a strike in the Guadalajara cloth factory, the first organized strike in 18th-century Spanish history. We also know of strikes in Avila about

1790. However, true social conflict on a large scale did not occur in Barcelona until 1789, when the so-called "bread riots" broke out, coinciding with the high cost of living and the political crisis of the moment. It was the prelude to a social debate destined to dominate all of the century which followed.

CHARACTERISTICS OF 18TH-CENTURY SPANISH AGRICULTURAL PRODUCTION: THE PRICE REVOLUTION. At first sight, the traits of Spanish agriculture in the 18th century are not essentially different from those of the preceding one. When we read travelers' descriptions and the narratives, either one-sided or impartial, of national authors, certain words are repeated with monotonous regularity: "depopulation," "poverty," and "routine." The Spanish countryside is presented as unproductive, famine-stricken, almost without tools, totally lacking in the progress achieved in Europe since the beginning of the 18th century, first by the Flemish, then the Dutch, and finally the English, who were the teachers of the Continental nations in this field as well as in political life and industrial activity.

Depopulation, an inheritance from the 17th century, was the great calamity afflicting rural Spain. Mediterranean geography entails a constant struggle between man and steppe; once the equilibrium had tipped in favor of the steppe, man found it difficult to restore these areas to cultivation. The uncultivated lands not only produced no harvests but were the center of epidemic diseases and the nucleus of devastating plagues. Among them was a plague of locusts, that Biblical calamity, which extended from the wastelands of New Castile and Extremadura and spread in all directions, in search of the crops of the only really well-cultivated fields, those on the edges of towns. There are records of the terrible ravages caused by the plague of locusts in 1755–1756. Others were less serious.

The cause of depopulation is to be found in the harshness of the peasant's life. It gave much labor and little return, and was always at the mercy of a poor harvest or an unfavorable cycle of plantings which would put his fields in the hands of moneylenders. Anomalies of climate, lack of food reserves, difficulties of transport, and pestilences kept the agricultural worker in a state of exhaustion. A good harvest might mean ruin for him, while only a few leagues away others got rich on the grain shortage. And thus the Spanish peasant sank into apathy and undernourishment, his only alternative being flight to the cities, where begging for free soup or toil at the most backbreaking jobs awaited him.

Nevertheless, there were some seeds of hope within the century, and these germinated slowly but surely. Plague had ceased to be a grave threat to the peasant, and the sharp claws of famine were slowly being clipped. Up to mid-century there were a few sporadic years of famine (1709, 1723, 1734, 1752); then a more regular cycle became established, of two or more bad years followed by a longer, more favorable period: 1763–1765, 1770, 1784–1793, 1800–1804 were years of scarcity, separated by intervening periods of abundance. Society had more resources to combat famine. Peripheral regions became free of it thanks to the steady increase in coastwise trade and the development of new grain-producing countries such as the United States; but even interior regions benefited from development of the national transport system. Catalan and Valencian muleteers solved the serious supply crisis in Madrid in 1752–1753 by bringing in grain from Alicante and Albacete.

The essential problem continued to be yield of the agricultural soil. We do not possess accurate statistical data, but everything seems to indicate a very low level, owing to technical backwardness and the pressure put on the peasants by the proprietor or overlord. Plowing was still done with the Roman plow, and land was left fallow in alternate years. The farmer had little capital with which to improve his equipment, and few work animals to help him. In the last third of the century, livestock censuses tell us of the existence of 214,000 mules, 139,000 horses, and 237,000 asses, extremely low numbers for a population of some 2 million peasants. These were the reasons why the harvest was scarcely triple the amount of seed used. A year which yielded four times the amount was considered to be abundant; very good if it gave five times; extraordinary if six to seven times were harvested. If the figures we possess are accurate, 12 million *fanegas* of wheat and 1,600,000 of barley were imported from 1756 to 1773. Such numbers are truly indicative, for there is no way of extracting the truth by consulting the figures of the Census of Foodstuffs and Manufactures (1797); some authors find in it a deficit of 22 million *fanegas* and others a

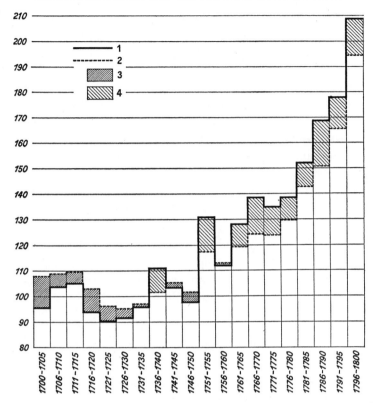

AGRICULTURAL AND INDUSTRIAL PRICES IN NEW CASTILE IN THE 18TH CENTURY.—*Key:* 1, five-year mean of index number of agricultural prices; base = 1726–1750 = 100; 2, same for prices of nonagricultural products; 3, difference in favor of mean index numbers of nonagricultural prices over agricultural ones; 4, same for agricultural products.

surplus of 66 million, a completely unjustified figure by any standards.

But what is perfectly clear, and we do not need figures to emphasize the point, is the expansion of Spanish agriculture after 1763–1765.

We should not seek the cause in the measures adopted by Charles III's ministers, such as the extremely important royal cedula of 1763 providing for freedom in the grain trade, but in the leap forward made by the international trade cycle, which was clearly on a rising trend from 1755 to the early years of the 19th century. After the serious setback from contraction of farm prices following the crisis of 1630, Castilian agricultural products began to regain their value. Not only this, but very soon, keeping pace with imperial wars and industrial concentrations, they came to represent much more than the money invested in industrial projects. The agricultural price revolution is the dominant fact in Castile's economic history during the 18th century. We need only cite the figures below to demonstrate this.

As a consequence of the recovery of farm prices, rural property acquired an interest which it had lost over the course of the preceding century. *Agrarian income rose even faster than prices.* This fact is fundamental. It has been proved by Labrousse in regard to France and by Vilar for Catalonia, and explains how the enrichment of rural property especially benefited the proprietors, and that these had a special stake in bringing new ground under cultivation, limiting the Mesta's privileges and attacking mortmain. This was the origin of the policy of disentailment to which we will refer later.

BASE: 1726–1750 = 100

Years	Agricultural products	Nonagricultural products	Differences
1700	103.1	107.4	−4.3
1720	83.2	96.9	−16.7
1740	114.4	104.8	+9.6
1760	110.0	111.8	−1.8
1765	149.9	125.7	+24.2
1780	144.4	135.5	+8.9
1790	181.2	157.1	+24.1
1800	200.0	187.6	+12.4

TYPES AND DISTRIBUTION OF AGRARIAN PROPERTY. After recovery of the land occurred about the middle of the 18th century, in the wake of demographic improvement and the new rising trend in the economy, the anachronism represented by the distribution of rural property, as it had been inherited from the latter days of the Reconquest, became painfully obvious. Plans for agrarian reform were all aimed at a necessary readjustment, as we shall soon see. But before we take up the study of agricultural life in general, we think it indispensable to review the situation of this property at the end of a process as long as it was harmful. For this purpose we shall adopt the latest results of historical research (Herr and Domínguez Ortiz, among others).

TYPES OF PROPERTY. There were five different classes of proprietors:

(1) *The Crown.* The royal patrimony retained a large part of its private domains; but, conversely, it had ceded to the aristocratic class many of its old jurisdictional rights over privately owned lands. That is, part of the royal lands had become either lay or ecclesiastical seigniories. The transfer is important because it indicated an obvious weakening of monarchical power: in fact, in the royal patrimony unproductive mountain areas and infertile fields predominated.

(2) *The Church.* Like the Crown, the Church was the owner of great tracts of land, and in addition exercised jurisdictional rights over many others. But the ecclesiastical patrimony was much more extensive in both respects. Thus, an official inquiry reveals that in 1760 one-sixth (according to Carrera Pujal) or one-seventh (according to Domínguez Ortiz) of Castilian-Leonese territory belonged outright to the Church, while it exercised jurisdiction (ecclesiastical seigniory) over 2,592 localities (census of 1797, which excluded Aragon). This last figure represents one-twelfth of the national territory, a proportion which in some places, such as Galicia (1,423 localities under ecclesiastical jurisdiction) and La Mancha (61), rose to more than half.

(3) *Municipalities.* Even more extensive than the two previously mentioned classes were *common* or *council lands.* These lands, which had originated as royal concessions during the Reconquest, were usually woods or arid tracts (*montes* and *baldíos*), located beyond the private holdings of the inhabitants of a town. Their use took two forms; there were *lands of common utilization* by the whole community, thus responding to the interests of the group, and lands called *propios* which, though belonging to the community, were rented out to individuals. Together with *arbitrios* (income from local taxes), the *propios* in the 18th century represented the chief revenues of most towns. At this time council lands formed the largest percentage of amortized Spanish property.

(4) *The nobility.* Nobles were owners of private patrimonies,

usually entailed to their families in the form of *mayorazgos,* and had jurisdictional rights over others (*lay seigniories*). We have already mentioned the enlargement of these at the expense of the Crown. The result was that in 1797 a total of seventeen cities and one-third of all the villages and hamlets in Spain (5,300 in absolute numbers, without counting Aragon) were part of lay seigniories. Like the ecclesiastical lord, the noble-owner intervened in the appointment of local authorities, collected a small part of the harvests (tithes and firstfruits), as well as some taxes in cash, enjoyed a number of monopolies (hunting and fishing, milling and baking, etc.), and in short, received his best revenues out of these feudal rights.

(5) *Small private owners.* The census of 1797 tells us that peasant proprietors numbered 364,000 and represented 22% of all tillers of the soil. (See pp. 495–496 for their regional distribution.) If this figure seems small in itself, we shall have to add that many of these peasant proprietors were attached to a lay or ecclesiastical seigniory, with all the restrictions this implied.

SYSTEM OF RENTALS. The fact that the majority of Spanish peasants did not own the land they cultivated brings up the problem of the legal conditions under which they worked. In the previous chapter we analyzed the two possible positions (the peasant might be a renter or simply a day laborer), and the proportion represented by each in different areas of Peninsular geography.

Now we shall describe in detail some of the features of rental practice. In the first place, it can be said that the contractual conditions under which a peasant worked were favorable to him in the North and unfavorable in the South. And even in the North, Catalonia and Galicia offer different extremes. In Catalonia the typical rental contract was the *censo enfiteútico,* of practically indefinite duration except in the vineyards, which came under the *rabassa morta* contract lasting for the life of the vines. The peasant paid a moderate rental and was free to improve, bequeath, or mortgage the property on payment of a small extra sum to the proprietor. This system, which in fact converted the renter into a real owner, had contributed so much toward the formation of a progressive peasant class that the ministers of Enlightened Despotism (Campomanes and Jovellanos) foresaw the extension of this system to the rest of Spain.

In Galicia and Asturias the situation was originally quite similar to that of Catalonia (rental for three generations, called *foro,* with a tendency to become perpetual), until the agricultural recovery of the later 18th century, combined with population increase, undermined the system. The process developed as follows: rise in agricultural prices, request for an increase in rent on the part of proprietors, and denial of this by the Council of Castile in 1763. After that, assured of the possession of their land by virtue of a very low rental, the holders of *foros* speculated by subleasing it for a higher rate than they paid themselves. In a short time the practice of *subforo,* already in existence, became general and attained unbelieveable extremes. The same land was rented over and over, with the result that the farmer found himself owing rent not to one person but to three or four. The consequences could not have been more unfortunate: at Charles III's death, land in Galicia and part of Asturias was so divided, and the income from it grasped by so many parasitic hands, that the farmer could not even make a living. This was one of the main causes for the stream of Galician emigration.

This same abuse of subleasing was practiced in the Andalusian areas not cultivated by day laborers. As there were fewer of these lands than in Galicia, the number of persons affected was also less considerable. In the places where it was practiced, however, Andalusian subleasing involved even more abuses than in Galicia, for since contracts were of very short duration (customarily six years), the successive leasers tried to exploit their lessees as much as possible.

AGRICULTURAL PRODUCTION. During the 18th century Spain continued to be a grain-producing country. But although heretofore it had been one almost exclusively, after the 18th century other vegetable crops began to compete with cereals both in geographic distribution and volume. Some of them—and this was the novelty—appear for the first time in lists of cultivated plants.

Wheat, barley, and *rye* occupied three-fourths of the Spanish lands under a one-crop system. It appears that the area of cultivation was expanding; but unfortunately we do not have exact data on this important point. Cultivation of *rice* also continued to spread, in spite of its mortal dangers (fever, malaria, etc.). The fertile Valencian plain alone produced 420,000 *fanegas.* But the prime cereal crop at this time was *corn*. Known in Spain since the beginning of the 17th century (it had been introduced into Asturias in 1604 by Gonzalo Méndez de Cancio, governor of Florida), it made very little progress for the rest of that century but triumphed about the middle of the 18th. Used for fodder and for bread, it transformed the Cantabrian coastal region, permitting it to maintain a much larger population than formerly and making it possible for the area to sustain a vigorous economic life.

Along with cereals, another Spanish culinary *pièce de résistance* was *vegetables*. Though statistics indicate a total production of 16 million *fanegas,* this figure can only be approximate. Chickpeas, Lima beans, peas, and French beans, in that order, occupied a prominent place among the products of national food supply. However, they were gradually pushed into third place by an American tuber, the *potato*. As everywhere, this plant was received with suspicion and distrust. Its systematic cultivation in Spain was begun in the Galician district of Mondoñedo (1768) and slowly spread from there in all directions. By the end of the century we find it introduced into the Montaña region (thanks to the efforts of the Cantabrian Society, 1799–1800), and in 1795 it appeared in the Sierra de Aracena, an area between Extremadura and western Andalusia. The triumph of the potato came after 1812, when that year's terrible famine caused the starving peasants to eat the vegetable which up till then they had used only for animal fodder.

Chief among *tree crops* continued to be the olive, which covered large areas in Andalusia, Aragon, and Catalonia. The chief national crop in real value was olive oil, with a production of 6 million *arrobas* per year. Wine competed with olive oil in the export field; not only the fine Andalusian wines (the international fame of the "olorosos" of Jerez and the sweet wines of Málaga dates from this period), but also the Catalonian wines with high alcoholic content. First place among regional exports in 1758 was held by Catalonian vintages, largely in the form of brandy, which the English sold to Northern Europe and the North American colonists. Pierre Vilar has done a splendid job of documenting the great period of the Principality's wines after 1680 and their extraordinary importance as a source of capital during a period of economic depression: until the decade 1730–1740, in fact, the high prices of grape products were an exception to the slump in other rural products.

As for *fruit trees,* at this time two of them began to acquire a wider value than a merely local one: the apple tree, which had a privileged position in the North, and the orange tree, planted on a large scale in Valencia. It appears that the prosperity of the Valencian orange groves dates from the end of the 17th century, when the secession of Portugal left the Spanish market in the hands of Valencian farmers.

Industrial crops, with some exceptions, were in a depressed phase during the 18th century. The cause was stiff competition from more privileged countries, which could offer a better product at lower prices. Sugar cane and cotton could not compete with their American counterparts, nor, in the case of cotton, with European ones (Malta, for example); and thus they were cultivated only in small areas of Andalusia. The hemp and linen of Galicia and León suffered from competition with France, Flanders, and Holland. Cultivation of saffron was also in a state of decline. Silk, however, continued to prosper, and production of saltwort and madder was rising.

Silk, a trade monopoly of the State, flourished in the Levant region of the Peninsula, from Granada to Catalonia. Although it is impossible to obtain exact production figures, since fraud was common owing to the monopoly and the volume of demand, the following figures will give us an approximate idea: total annual production was 1,150,000 pounds, more than half of which was supplied by Valencia (650,000), followed by Murcia (300,000) and, at some distance behind these, Granada, Aragon, and Catalonia.

The incipient development of industry was also responsible for the rise in production of *granza,* a dye plant from which madder was extracted. Catalan businessmen promoted plantings of it in Valladolid and its vicinity, after the middle of the century. The first ordinances concerning cultivation and processing of madder date from 1747. By the end of the century 24,000 *arrobas* annually were being produced in Castile, in large part for Catalonian consumption. As for saltwort, it was used to produce soda ash for soap and similar detergents. Its annual production amounted to 320,000 *arrobas.*

IMPROVEMENTS IN CULTIVATION: AGRICULTURAL SOCIETIES. In spite of the profound impact of technology on the industrial world of the 18th century, what was really in vogue during this period was agriculture. Both doctrinaire and sentimental writers joined in singing the praises of the farmer and the good earth, the source of true wealth according to the physiocrats.

This spirit crossed the Pyrenees and, like so many other new ideas of the Century of Enlightenment, soon gained many supporters in Spain. The informal meetings which gave rise to the Societies of Friends of the Country had a special fondness for agricultural topics. Some of these groups were even specifically founded as agricultural societies, such as the Academies of Agriculture which appeared in Lérida and Corunna in 1764 and 1765. Their contribution to the progress of agricultural operations has not yet been studied, but it must have been considerable. In any case, these societies contained a number of enthusiasts (scientists, poets, journalists, and amateurs), who used newspapers and books to spread modern technical ideas on agriculture as expressed in the works of Necker, Rozier, and the Count of Guillemberg.

The influence of the agricultural societies made itself felt in many directions: by attracting the sympathies of powerful persons (the brothers of Charles III as well as Godoy, who founded the "Seminary of Agriculture"), by giving demonstrations of new agrarian practices (in 1807 the Economic Society of Valladolid established a model farm, the Huerta del Rey), and so on. However, the innovators' main objective was to control the levers of power. By manipulating them, they were sure that the agrarian renaissance they desired would be accomplished.

ENCOURAGEMENT OF AGRICULTURE BY THE STATE. After the fifteen-year period 1760–1775, when the revolution in agricultural prices became apparent, the Spanish State found itself subjected to pressure from various groups requesting its intervention in agriculture and demanding an agrarian policy. It was not only the Encyclopedist intellectuals who, nourished by their reading of the works of the physiocrats, called for such a decision; in reality there was a powerful trend combining lust for money on the part of the wealthy class and the vital and urgent needs of the country's new demographic strata. Thus, the State had to attend to several fronts at once: improvement of crops for large-scale public works; freedom in the grain trade; competition among farmers; agrarian reform and disentailment.

It is evident that the monarchy paid an extraordinary amount of attention to rural problems, within the limitations of its resources, through a suitable policy of public works. For the first time in two centuries the State invested the country's revenues in something positive. Though its first concern was communications, it never lost sight of the serious problem of irrigation, intimately linked with that of cheap transport by means of canals. As soon as Ferdinand VI's ministers could consider the country's financial future reasonably secure, a plan of hydraulic works was begun. In 1746 Carvajal planned the Madrid-Tagus and Guadalquivir canals; three years later some ordinances on irrigation were issued, and in 1753 work on the Canal of Castile was resumed, though it was suspended in 1779. Also, the firm which in 1770 had begun the Tagus-Manzanares canal went bankrupt. But, as evidence of the desire of Charles III's government to overcome technical and financial obstacles, we have the completion of the Imperial Canal of Aragon (1768–1778), continuation of work on the Canal of Tauste (1775), prolongation of the Royal Canal system of the Júcar and construction of the Lorca dam (1785–1791), without counting the studies it stimulated (for canals in Amposta, Urgel, Albolote, and Ujíjar) and the private ventures it encouraged (canal of Alcira). Good results, on balance, though they did not merit the euphoric words of the Count of Floridablanca's report in 1783: that works of irrigation had been undertaken which would leave distant posterity astounded.

FREEDOM OF TRADE IN CEREALS. The ideal of the physiocratic theorist was *freedom of trade in cereals,* which would assure the foundations of a healthy economy. Ever since the great famines of the early 16th century, a whole series of precise regulations had confined cereals within the district where they were produced by subjecting them to price ceilings, licenses, and monopolies. But this did not succeed in conquering the specters of hunger and high prices, nor did it convince those who were demanding a free grain market. Therefore, following the example of other countries, freedom of internal and external trade in wheat was decreed in 1756.

This was only a paper measure, however, for it dealt with a very delicate problem which included supplying cereals to the cities, as well as prices, storage, and marketing—all matters upon which very differing opinions existed. Therefore the Marquis of Esquilache, a minister of Charles III, brought up these matters in the Board of Trade in 1763. In spite of food shortages in 1763–1765 the Board's report, with an assist from Campomanes' *Fiscal Reply* (*Respuesta fiscal*)—in it he said, "Any law which infringes the freedom of either buyer or seller is not just, nor will it ever be fully observed"—favored abolition of the price ceiling and freedom in the buying and selling of grain. And this was decreed by the law of July 11, 1765, one of the fundamental pieces of legislation in contemporary Castile's early economic expansion.

Many factors worked against the law: insufficient harvests, lack of storage facilities, the traditionalism of the experts, and absence in Castile of a nonmonopolistic commercial network like the one that supplied Portugal and Catalonia with wheat. It was especially opposed by those who complained on the grounds of high prices. And certainly, after 1765 wheat and other cereals began an uninterrupted price rise, reflecting the economy's upward trend. The royal governor of Salamanca did not know this in 1769, but stated that high prices made the peasants happy. In 1775, ten years after the law was promulgated, Campomanes looked back and observed that cultivation as well as the breaking of new ground had increased. Both he and Cabarrús attacked the complainers. Who were they? "A troop of idle and ignorant courtiers who [according to Cabarrús himself in 1778] in their campaigns against the law were ruled only by their selfish interests."

However, it would be untrue to suggest that with the law of 1765 absolute freedom of internal trade was achieved (external trade always had to count on a ceiling price). Free trade was hampered by transport difficulties and the inefficiency of the commercial wheat network. The period of greatest balance was attained between 1783 and 1787. After 1789, a critical year, with popular riots stemming from the high cost of foodstuffs, cereal prices went up constantly, while the fluctuations produced in the market by the revolutionary situation in France and the subsequent wars interfered with any sort of advance planning. This is why Charles IV's reign was characterized by series of contradictory pieces of legislation, though the royal cedula of 1790 ratifying the principle of free internal trade in cereals was never abrogated.

RISE OF STOCKBREEDING AND DECLINE OF THE MESTA. The expansion of agriculture in the 18th century again brought to the fore, as we have just mentioned, the problem of competition between farmer and shepherd which Ferdinand and Isabella had solved in favor of the latter, through their policy of protection to the Mesta. The obstacles which migratory herding had placed in the path of agricultural development in a large part of New Castile and Extremadura had the primary result of ruining those who, by exercising this favored monopoly, paid no attention to improving the breed or to marketing their products. This was the lesson learned by the Spain of the last Hapsburgs, which saw its national flock decrease and the export of its chief product, wool, greatly reduced. Livestock breeding and the Mesta entered the 18th century already defeated, while other countries (England, France, the Piedmont, Sweden, Prussia, and Saxony) were using new methods of fattening cattle and producing wool, and were making use of breeding animals (Andalusian horses and merino sheep) imported from Spain.

For half a century the Bourbons continued to favor the Mesta, whose widespread network of interests included ministers, civil servants, and members of the Court. As late as 1726 it extended its system and jurisdiction into the Crown of Aragon, especially to the shepherds' brotherhoods of Daroca, Albarracín, and Teruel. About the middle of the century Ferdinand VI's government renewed the ancient laws perpetuating the predominance of grazing over agriculture, thus upholding the right of possession (royal cedula of 1753, fixing the rental of pasture lands at the price paid in 1692) and a ban on breaking new ground (royal cedula of 1749). But shortly before this monarch's death the situation had completely changed. The royal cedula of 1758 canceling the *servicio y montazgo* tax, which the Mesta collected and paid through a duty on wool exports, was the hardest blow suffered by that institution, for it severed the financial connection with the State which had been essential to its prosperity. That was also the time agricultural production began its upward trend; it began to gain ground over herding, as did the advantages of sedentary over migratory flocks, and native commercial organization over foreign. After 1750 a new consumers' market had opened up for Castilian wool: the Catalonian textile industry.

Twenty years later, at the peak of the boom in agricultural products, paralleled by a rise in the value of nonmigratory livestock (a pound of beef was worth 32 maravedís in 1700; 28 in 1750; 38 in 1756; 40 in 1765; 51 in 1776; 57 in 1785; and 79.9 in 1798), it was evident that the Mesta's monopolistic hold over grazers in particular and farmers in general was doomed to extinction, even without taking theoretical considerations into account. In 1764 Vicente Paynó, a deputy of the Extremaduran cities with voting rights in the Cortes, first pronounced the judgment of history on the Mesta when he placed the blame for the indigence of that region on the privileges enjoyed by herdsmen. This debate, which constituted the basis of one that was to be even more sensational (that on agrarian reform), resulted in various reports from the Council of Castile (1771 and 1783, the latter Campomanes') and the signing of four important pieces of legislation: one authorizing enclosure of vineyard and olive groves (1779); another abolishing the very important rights of possession and rental ceilings on pasture lands established by Ferdinand and Isabella (1786); the third (June 15, 1788) making universal an authorization to enclose any rural property; and finally, elimination of the office of *alcalde entregador,* the official specifically charged with defending the Mesta's interests in opposition to the farmers (1796). However, the Crown's financial straits just at this time caused Charles IV to accept a petition from the Mesta (preceded by a grant of a million reales) by whose terms the choice of new lands to be brought under cultivation was put within the jurisdiction of the Mesta's president and his delegates.

It cannot be said, therefore, that the policies of Enlightened Despotism were really in opposition to herding. As the result of general economic conditions enormously favorable to agriculture, the fossilized structure of the Mesta simply broke down, without damaging the development of national livestock. According to the census of 1797, this was distributed in the following manner: sheep, 11,700,000; goats, 2,500,000; swine, 1,200,000; oxen, 1,650,000; horses, 230,000. These figures reveal that in a very short time the liberal policy had increased fourfold the number of animals in the country. It was the period when Galicia began to stand out as a privileged livestock region.

PLANS FOR AGRARIAN REFORM. During the last third of the 18th century a debate began which is still the center of the Spanish economy's problems: the debate over agrarian reform. Philosophers and rulers, professors and poets, bureaucrats and economists, all who considered themselves chosen spirits, lent their pens to the treatment of this transcendental question. In the literature of the period, as yet not thoroughly studied, the names of Floridablanca, Campomanes, Jovellanos, Cabarrús, Sisternes Feliu, Sempere Guarinos, Foronda, and others, figure prominently. All of them had a real problem to work on, owing to the lamentable situation of certain Castilian regions; and they made this question a matter of public interest and official concern, paralleling the new philanthropic currents and the country's strong demographic development.

Two inquiries or investigations had been opened in regard to poverty in Extremadura, one by the Central Board of Trade and one by the Council of Castile. Information was given by governors and deputies—among them Payno, whom we have mentioned before, in 1764—as well as ministers and economists. In 1766, while the matter was still being examined in the ministers' offices, Esquilache's mutiny demonstrated that it had an eminently popular foundation. There were pseudo-socialist outbreaks in a large part of Spain, especially in Castile, Extremadura, and Catalonia. On May 2 of that same year Charles III, advised by Aranda, who had been raised to the presidency of the Council of Castile, decreed that "all cultivable lands (in Extremadura) belonging to the towns, as well as wastelands and those belonging to municipal councils, shall be plowed and cultivated, appraised by experts, and distributed by lot to the neediest inhabitants." The royal cedula in question also set the order of preference (day laborers and *senareros,* or servants who received use of land as part of their wages, were given priority, followed by farmers owning two yoke of oxen, then those owning three) and the conditions for exploitation (prohibition of subleasing, punctual payment of charges, and two or more years of uninterrupted cultivation). Other royal decrees extended this system

to Andalusia, La Mancha, and the rest of the country (1767–
1768), and reserved plots of land for poor and middle-income
farmers owning a yoke of oxen (1770). Neither then nor previously did it occur to anyone that the municipal councils, controlled
by powerful landowners, were going to twist the law in their own
favor and that, even in the most favorable cases, the peasants would
not have sufficient capital to carry out their attempts at settlement.
Thus, much of the income derived from the land brought under cultivation through these procedures only swelled the coffers of the
landowners.

Application of an individualistic criterion marking this first attempt at agrarian reform can also be observed in the laws through
which Charles III tried to regulate rural leases. The Pragmatic of
1765 established the principle that any proprietor could draw up
any sort of contract concerning rental of his properties. We do not
know how this order was applied, but we have proof of some of its
effects through a royal cedula of 1768 which forbade depriving
"renters" (leaseholders) of their lands without just cause. Thus, the
conflict between individualists and collectivists came up in its
crudest form within the very bosom of the group of innovators.

This was, in fact, the sense of the acrimonious debate over the
Proceedings on the Agrarian Law, in which the two reports mentioned above were combined (1771). A year previously the Count
of Floridablanca, in his *Fiscal Reply to the Investigation of the
Province of Extremadura,* had established the bases of an agrarian
reform which, by attacking the Mesta's privileges, had put at the
disposal of all farmers *propios,* pastures already allocated, unused
and common lands, as well as grazing grounds both common and
private. Floridablanca, in a strong position because of the experience gained since 1766, advised in a later confidential memoran-
dum that a reserve fund should be established with moneys derived
from expropriations and vacated Church offices, one-third of which
should be devoted to the encouragement of agriculture and resettlement of rural areas (buildings, irrigation projects, fertilization,
acquisition of machinery). Thus he placed his finger on one of the
sore spots of the Spanish tragedy.

Campomanes studied the Proceedings for six years and came up
with an important solution, which figures in his *Revised Report* of
1771. The famous economist considered it necessary to work for

the formation of "fenced-off, indivisible and inalienable plots" which would constitute the basis of a family patrimony. Every peasant family should have a "congruous grant," which he thought should consist of fifty *fanegas* of land, suitable for cultivation in alternate years, a yoke of oxen, and sufficient grazing land for necessary animals. Later, in his *Report* of 1784, he again emphasized the same theme, pointing out still more clearly the object of his reform: to transform the renter into a long-term lessee, an idea deeply rooted in his mind because of his excellent impression of the progress of quasi-ownership in the Catalonian rural economy.

Neither Floridablanca nor Campomanes spurned the tenets of tradition when they confronted the serious problem of land hunger in Spain. Jovellanos, faithful to his liberal and individualist doctrine, showed himself to be more radical than either in his famous *Report on the Agrarian Law* (*Informe sobre la ley agraria,* 1795), one of the cardinal pieces of writing in the Spanish economic debate. Starting from the principle that property is a natural right, explicit in the labor of those who cultivate the soil, Jovellanos judged that the law should protect the land but not interfere with it, much less remove it from the common weal by accumulations of any type: uncultivated or communal lands, entailments, inheritances, etc. All of this wealth should be put into circulation immediately: sold, distributed, or offered in the form of long-term leases. In this way the path would be opened to the perfecting of private property, constantly improved through labor.

Jovellanos' program must have had a strong effect on the minds of the legislators of the first national Cortes, that of Cádiz in 1812. All during Charles IV's reign there continued to be hesitation about practical measures of land reform. The position of the leaseholder grew ever more solid, for the royal cedula of December 6, 1785, had forbidden expulsion from his lands of anyone who resided in the parish, possessed farming tools, and cultivated the land himself; the Pragmatic of 1793 provided for the distribution of eight *fanegas* of common land (pastures, grazing grounds, *propios,* and woodland) per yoke of oxen. This was something at least, but its scope was small after the laws of 1766–1768 and successive reports on the need for a reform that would lay new foundations for Spanish agriculture. The only positive measure was that which obtained permission from Rome (1805) to disentail up to 6,400,000 reales of revenues in ecclesiastical properties, by delivering a like sum in royal notes. Some 8 million pesetas' worth of these were sold, but with little profit to the State, which carried out the operation under the worst possible psychological and credit conditions.

FISHING. Fishing activity had fallen off considerably under the later Hapsburgs. Not only had the whaling and codfishing tradition been lost—a practice which had received its death blow with the Treaties of Utrecht in 1713—but the most rudimentary fishing activity had been neglected even along the coasts of the Peninsula. With the exception of Catalonia, the only fishing done merely served to meet the needs of the coastal communities. Any commercial fishing—or salted or smoked fish—was left to foreign importers.

The Bourbon ministers took a number of steps to end this situation. The most important of these was the setting up of the Registry of the Sea (*Matrícula de Mar*) in 1737 (Patiño's Ordinances). Revised by the Marquis de la Ensenada in 1748, they had the virtue of grouping seafaring folk together and giving them a monopoly on maritime activities: fishing, loading and unloading, and navigation, with the complementary factor of service in the navy. Some authors believe that these ordinances were the basis of the fishing prosperity of the latter half of the 18th century. But this is far from true. Catalan fishermen, who by the end of the 16th century had learned from the Provençals the technique of fishing-barges or trawling, slowly perfected the system until they achieved the *bous* method (two boats dragging the net between them). In spite of the attitude of more traditional fishermen, who insisted that the new technique would fish out the sea, it spread successfully all along the Mediterranean coast, matching the commercial expansion of wine and brandy. In 1750 we find these fishermen in Almería, in 1766 in the vicinity of Málaga, and shortly afterward they were successful in the fisheries of Ayamonte.

However, Galicia was the locality where the Catalans achieved their greatest success. They certainly demonstrated the new *bous* technique as far away as Santander and Guipúzcoa; but in the Galician fjords they challenged those who controlled the market and set up a modern industry: the salting of fish. They were the outfitters of the ships which brought wines, brandy, wheat, and colonial products to the Cantabrian Sea; and then, wishing to take home salted fish, they taught the arts of their homeland to the Galician fishermen. After 1762, thanks to the Catalans, the ports of Guardia and Muros began to have importance. Later, naturally, there was heated debate over the suitability or unsuitability of Catalan expansion into Galicia. The chief opponents were José Córnide (1774) and Francisco Somoza de Monsorín (1775). But the plan of a mutual-aid society for fishermen suggested by the former, with initial funds of 750,000 reales, ended in total failure. After that, and solely from "the sweat of their brows," the Catalans succeeded in converting Galicia into Spain's chief producer of salt fish.

35 · Industrial Revival

THE INDUSTRIAL REVOLUTION OF THE 18TH CENTURY. A new epoch opened in the economic life of Western Europe during the last third of the 18th century. Of course, as Professor Nef has observed, it cannot be called a revolution in the political sense of the term, that is, an abrupt change. Rather it was a quickening of evolution which rapidly transformed the factors of industrial production. Even if we keep in mind the deep roots of this change, all of which really sprang from the Renaissance mind, a whole series of circumstances aided the unfolding of the European world of machines: demographic growth, higher revenues from agriculture, scientific and technical advances, the demands of the colonies, the avalanche-like rush of commerce, and finally, a sensational advance in the amount of currency in circulation as a result of Brazilian gold-mining operations and the recovery of the Spanish-American silver mines. This combination of factors made possible the triumph of the machine, first in England and then, gradually, in the rest of Western Europe.

The launching of the machine era depended on a mass of population which it was necessary to clothe and shelter. This is why the Industrial Revolution is essentially one of textile machinery, closely linked to the spinning and weaving of cotton and the employment of manpower. In this last respect the role of the mine was extremely important, for out of it were to come the steam engine and the railway; in other words, the coal and iron industries so characteristic of the 19th century.

THE MACHINE AGE: ITS SPREAD INTO SPAIN. Spain's contribution to the movement we have just described was almost nil. Technically and economically, the Spain of the first half of the 18th century was too backward to have any important role in the circles which were rushing headlong toward the establishment of machinery as the basic means of production. Later, after the sensational successes registered by the Industrial Revolution in England, Spain became an importer of new things, though not always with the speed and enthusiasm which the circumstances warranted. Sometimes by official means, sometimes through private initiative, winding a tortuous path through invention, contraband, and plagiarism, Spain succeeded in bridging the ever-widening gap between one side of the Pyrenees and the other.

Until the last quarter of the 18th century the chief manifestation of the development of the machine age in Spain was the search for, at times almost the pursuit of, foreign technicians. French, Flemish, and Swedish engineers swarmed about the factories established by the Crown, or in the cotton-cloth factories created by the efforts of businessmen. Recent studies reveal that foreign technicians were the victims of real persecution, subject to contracts which on the one hand were favorable and on the other unfair—some even called for life imprisonment for quitting one's job. Other better-known studies give us the names of foreign technicians and artisans who offered their services to Spanish corporations in order to teach them how to manage the machines or carry on certain trades. The archives of the Board of Trade of Barcelona brim with such offers between 1768 and 1789.

Besides these imported technicians, members of a trade rather than real inventors, there were Spanish businessmen who crossed the Pyrenees to observe the novelties of the moment and to work on the new machines, returning with apparatuses and sketches. It is difficult to give even an approximate description of this interesting process, buried under the heavy weight of professional secrecy. But there can be no doubt that it contributed greatly to the industrial advance of certain regions, especially Catalonia. This is demonstrated by the fact of the rapid acceptance there of Highs' spinning frames (1780), which were transformed by the natives' ingenuity into the so-called "berganadas" (Berga machines), and by the no less curious fact brought out in the course of our own researches relative to the concession of a twenty-year patent for a "double-injection fire engine, to Simón Plá and Co. of Barcelona" in 1790. This engine could only have been the steam engine perfected by Watt some years previously and patented in 1768.

By the end of the century, in Catalonia and other regions of

Spain, especially the Basque Country, various scientific and technical groups had formed which kept in close contact with the most progressive circles abroad. Industry, however, continued to be supplied by foreign machines. The massive importation of textile machinery in 1804—an operation directed by Cabarrús—gave Catalonia really modern machinery, which then could not be improved until the great industrial push of 1830 to 1850.

THE STATE AND INDUSTRIAL EVOLUTION: ROYAL MANUFACTORIES. In France the deep depression of the second half of the 17th century had resulted in adoption of an economic system in which the State played the dual role of protector and participator. French Colbertism, resting as it did on a firm mercantile and industrial foundation, was able to weather with considerable success—for its inseparable companions were military expansion and tariff war—the worst depths of the depression. This was enough to cause it to have imitators in secondary European countries, where French mercantilism and the absolutism of Versailles had caused an equally profound impression. But in all these countries the bourgeois base was lacking, so that it was the State which took over entirely the direction of the economic process, in capital investment as well as in the creation and administration of factories.

Establishment of the line of Bourbon second sons in Spain led to the adoption of measures based on French precedents. To overcome the country's industrial decline, Philip V's ministers included Spain in the area of Colbertism, adding to the old goal of medieval monopoly the new one of State intervention. The development of this tendency constitutes one of the most interesting chapters in the economic policy of Enlightened Despotism, and we shall refer to it later. Here we shall merely analyze the industrial results of this tendency, in the shape of the foundation of the so-called Royal Manufactories.

With help from the Royal Treasury and capital contributed by the Castilian nobility, Philip V and his successors founded a number of factories. The only function of some of these was to maintain a tradition of high-grade artisanship or to furnish the material necessary for the monarch's great construction projects: the Royal Palace in Madrid and those of La Granja, Aranjuez, and elsewhere. This is the category into which we must place the factories of Madrid (tapestries) and San Ildefonso (glassware). Other projects attempted to save from ruin private manufactures considered to be vital, such as the silk factory of Murcia and the woollen factory of Ezcaray. In another group were factories linked to the State's military power, such as the artillery arsenals, of which we shall speak later, or to the needs of the fiscal monopolies, like the tobacco factory in Seville. Finally—and this is the most interesting group—other establishments attempted to fill some industrial vacuum, or rather, to encourage techniques which had declined, by setting up pilot projects. Among these we should mention the silk-weaving industry of Talavera de la Reina and the cloth factories of Guadalajara, San Fernando, Brihuega, and La Granja.

The history of the Guadalajara factory serves as a perfect example. It had been suggested by Cardinal Alberoni, and the man who built it was the Baron of Riperdá, who in 1718 brought in fifty Dutch weavers. First installed in Santander and then in El Escorial, they were eventually sent to Guadalajara. In six years the fabulous sum of 12 million reales was invested in the factory, and all the while production declined both in quality and quantity because of exceedingly bad administration and the dissatisfaction of the foreign technicians. A commission appointed in 1724 decided that the king should protect the Guadalajara factory, but not operate it as a royal enterprise. But already it was difficult to turn back. The factory was a heavy burden on public funds, and its workers protested against their low wages and the iron discipline to which they were subjected. For years only half of the hundred looms originally installed were in use, for the warehouses created in Madrid to sell Guadalajara stuffs were overflowing with cloth: there was no market for them either within the kingdom or in the colonies. In 1740 there was a proposal, never carried out, to decree that merchants inside the country be obliged to buy it. Four years later the Madrid warehouses were closed. The whole problem passed over to the ministers of Ferdinand VI, who granted the factory an annual subsidy of 2 million reales—the sum it was losing in its operations—and a free supply of wool. Neither these measures, nor the tariff exemption on Guadalajara cloth production, served to remedy the situation. The plan of one adventurer also failed: in 1756 he bought the factory's surplus cloth, together with that of San Fernando, Brihuega, and La Granja, to sell in America in exchange for the privilege of returning with gold and silver by way of Cape Horn. This deception induced the Crown to accept a compromise solution: in 1757 the powerful Five Greater Guilds of Madrid leased all the royal cloth factories for ten years. But they did not make a profit, and consequently the contract was broken in 1767. Charles III's ministers decided to make a new effort, and poured money into the cloth factories we have mentioned (7 million reales a year). Losses continued, obliging the Crown to close the factories of San Fernando and Brihuega and to concentrate production in Guadalajara (1784), which was provided with new machinery. But with all this, production was inferior to the low-quality woollen cloth of Barcelona (according to Larruga) and much more expensive than any high-grade Abbeville product (according to Bourgoing). Foolish pride in maintaining a model industry and in avoiding harm to the interests of the Alcarria region and its capital carried more weight than common sense, so that Charles IV continued to carry the burden of this unfortunate affair, whose final liquidation coincided with the fall of the old regime in 1808.

Another no less instructive example is that of the factory of printed cotton goods established in Avila, in spite of the fact that the original plan had been to locate it somewhere in Catalonia or Galicia. After five years, when the enterprise had begun to falter, the Catalan Ramón Igual was appointed inspector. He pointed out the defects in its organization, production, and sales, the ineptitude of the technicians, and the drawbacks inherent in Avila's great distance from seaports. Igual's suggestions did serve to institute a change in management, but not the necessary readjustment in the factory, whose losses were so heavy that within a few years it passed into the hands of a private company and then disappeared in 1807.

The history of the royal manufactories is in sharp contrast to the success of private textile enterprise in Catalonia; they were two worlds in opposition, and the second of them represented the immediate future. It also contained a lesson in regard to investment policy when the industrial plan is not solidly based, and which therefore becomes unprofitable from the very beginning (largely because of the high cost of transport and a limited consumers' market).

MINING AND METALLURGICAL INDUSTRIES. Mining production in Spain, and heavy industry in general, did not emerge from their previous state of stagnation during the 18th century. In some fundamental sectors, such as the extraction of iron ore, there was even retrogression. In other sectors some small progress can be noted by the end of the century. But taken all together, the period left much to be desired in this fundamental aspect of economic structure.

There was no systematic exploitation of minerals, except in the construction branch (*marble*) and the exploitation of *salt,* a State monopoly. The mines of Navarre, Aragon, and Catalonia, as well as the coastal salt beds, continued to supply an abundant and deservedly famous export product for the markets of Northern Europe, in competition with French and Portuguese salt. Exploitation of the *mercury* of Almadén also continued to be a monopoly of the State. These mines were worked at a much slower pace than their productive capacity: some 38,000 *arrobas* annually compared with a potential output of 80,000. Perhaps the fire which occurred in these mines at the end of the 18th century had something to do with this.

In the *metals* group, the most profitable was copper (Ríotinto mines), while the lead workings of Linares and iron mines of Biscay declined. This drop in Basque ore production went along with the decline in the regional iron industry, to which we shall refer later on. *Silver* mines were also in a depressed condition, for they could not compete with those of Mexico. The mining company of Guadalcanal went bankrupt in 1805.

The coal industry began in Asturias in response to the needs of the State-owned arsenals or arms factories, especially those in nearby El Ferrol. Greed for profit led to inconsistent legislation until the Royal Order of 1792, which prescribed that free ownership of mines resided in the owners of the land and not in its renters or lessees (as the royal cedula of 1789 had stated), and also declared freedom of trade and transit for coal. After this ordinance, and keeping pace with industrial development, Asturian mines gained a privileged position within the Spanish economic framework.

The program of naval and land armament undertaken by Ferdinand VI's ministers, especially the Marquis de la Ensenada, and later continued by Charles III's government, favored the development of a *State metallurgical industry.* Since the reign of Philip V everything having to do with military matériel had received great protection. But, as we said before, it was not until Ferdinand VI's reign that we find full development of the arsenals of Barcelona, Ripoll, Seville, Liérganes (cannon and musketry), La Cavada (bombs), Toledo (swords, bayonets), and Oviedo, all using Biscayan iron, Asturian coal, and copper from Ríotinto, Peru, or Mexico; the royal arsenals of Cádiz, El Ferrol, and Cartagena; and the anchor factories of Ampuero (Santander), and Tolosa (Guipúzcoa). Under Charles III the stimulus of war speeded up this process, which came to an abnormal end at the time of the War of Independence.

On the other hand, it does not appear that *private metallurgical industry* followed this path, though we do not possess accurate figures on the subject. The one concrete fact is that this industrial activity was concentrated in northern regions. Biscay and Guipúzcoa were in the forefront, the former with 178 forges and 12 drop-hammers, the latter with 80 and 33. Valladolid had 122 forges and Santander 25, with 4 drop-hammers. As for the number of metalworkers, we know that Guipúzcoa had 3,500; Catalonia, 1,752; Galicia, 919; and Navarre, 680. These figures do not permit more than a superficial analysis. But the only published statistical series relating to Biscayan ironworks reveals a gradual contraction of their activity after the golden age of the early Hapsburgs (16th century, 300; 1796, 152; 1800, 117).

According to F. Sánchez Ramos, the cause of this decline was the mistaken policy followed when an attempt was made to transport Asturian coal to the sea (giving preference to the river system of the Nalón rather than to construction of a Suero-Gijón highway as proposed by Jovellanos), raising the price of the product and preventing it from being linked up with the Basque iron industry. Among the figures cited by this author confirming the decline we mentioned before, one is worth noting: in 1794, export of Basque iron ore to England ceased altogether. From 1711 to 1718 it had reached an average of 1,500 tons yearly; from 1729 to 1735, 1,700; from 1786 to 1794 it was never more than 275 tons. This circumstance is explained by the triumph of the vastly superior Swedish ore over the Basque product in all the European markets. Swedish ore would even have gained the upper hand in Spain had it not been for the protectionist tariff policy which favored the Basque iron industry. This measure was adopted by Charles III's government in 1775, in an attempt to prevent collapse of the Basque industry. It seems that this arrangement did have some favorable influence. But by the end of the century the final result, in spite of Herr's statement to the contrary, was unfavorable to the Basque iron industry.

AGRICULTURAL AND FORESTRY INDUSTRIES; NAVAL STORES. The appearance of industrial activity related to vegetable products, either wild or cultivated, is one of the characteristics of the 18th-century spirit of recovery. Naturally, a large part of the agricultural transformation took place on a small household scale and can scarcely be said even to have approached the level of a workshop. But there were certain sectors where the infiltration of the new spirit was felt: sugar refineries, *pasta* factories on the Italian model, cheese-making, etc. In some special cases industrialization clearly took place.

Let us begin with the *flour-milling industry*. Milling was done all over the country for local consumption. But after 1786 a real flour industry, for export purposes, was established in Santander. This was possible thanks to the ease of communication with the wheat-growing regions of Old Castile following the opening of the Escudo pass and inauguration of the Reinosa-Santander road (1753). It was the constant concern of the authorities of this latter city—and after 1786 of its Consulate—to improve this important route. Castilian wheat supplied, first, the mill established by Antonio de Zuloaga in Campuzano, and then others modeled on it. It is estimated that by the end of the century some 50,000 barrels, of eight *arrobas* each, were being sent to America annually.

The distillation of *brandy* also merits special attention; it was one of the chief instruments of Spanish international trade during this period. It is hard to establish figures and comparative percentages. But there is no doubt that Catalonia, followed at a considerable distance by Valencia, occupied a privileged place in this branch of the wine trade. Emilio Giralt has studied the development of brandy production in Catalonia, its main centers (Reus and Villafranca del Panadés), the activity created in the ports of embarkation, the impetus given to shipping, and finally the export markets: England (accounting for one-fifth), the Baltic countries, and the New World, from New Orleans to Buenos Aires. Freedom of American

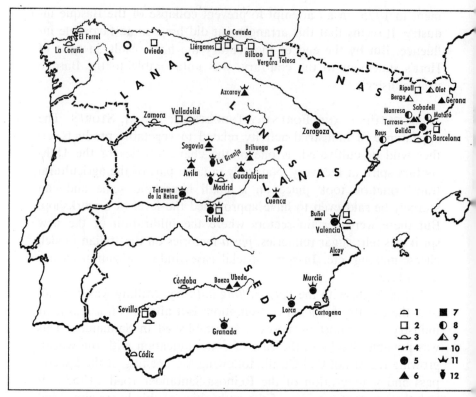

SPANISH INDUSTRIAL ACTIVITY IN THE 18TH CENTURY (*after* HERR, with modifications).—*Key:* 1, arsenals; 2, iron and steel centers; 3, hats; 4, shoes; 5, silk; 6, wool; 7, linen-weaving; 8, cotton cloth manufactures; 9, cotton; 10, paper; 11, royal manufacturing companies; 12, luxury articles. Notable in this map are the royal manufacturing companies and the nucleus of industrial activity created in Catalonia by development of the cotton-cloth or "indianas" industry.

trade (1778) and the French vineyard crisis of 1768 to 1772 fostered the development of brandy production on the Spanish Mediterranean coast. By the end of the century Catalonia was exporting some 50,000 pipes annually, and Valencia some 20,000 jugs.

Production of high-grade wine was being fostered along the Andalusian littoral. We have already mentioned the role played by Jerez and Málaga. Exports of fine wine, increasing daily with the opening of new markets in Northern Europe (Ireland, Germany, and Holland, in addition to England), brought up two thorny questions: the battle between processors and growers (especially acute in Málaga), and the infiltration of low-quality wines (especially Catalonian) into Andalusian regions, for mixing and sale at a lower price. Nevertheless, the authority of the Consulates was invoked, and they were able to overcome these difficulties and definitely accredit Andalusian wines.

Beer also became a widely used beverage at this time. The first brewery was established in Santander in 1787, making use of the hops which grew in the region. The promoters of this activity were José de Zuloaga and Antonio del Campo. Bottles were imported from Bristol and the brew was exported to the American colonies (60,000 bottles in 1803, more than half to Mexico).

A forestry product that was to give rise to a very prosperous industry in the 19th century, related to the wine industry, was *cork*. The great cork-oak woods on Spanish territory began to be of value when the recently popularized glass bottles called for corks. Cork-making techniques were taught to the Catalans by the French of the Roussillon. The industry's progress began at the end of the 18th century in the Pyrenees towns (Agullana), but very quickly spread to the Costa Brava (San Feliu de Guixols, Palamós, Palafrugell), well located for large-scale trade. In these towns a type of artisan arose who gave well-merited renown to the industry. From the earliest years of this activity there were conflicting interests between owners of forests (who favored export of cork in sheets, before it was manufactured) and the manufacturers (who were in favor of a ban on such exports).

Shipbuilding still depended on forest resources, though other important industrial factors were also involved (textiles for rigging, cables and cordage; tar and pitch; metallurgy, etc.). Beginning in Philip V's reign the felling of trees in the Pyrenees was of the greatest importance; the trunks were floated to the seacoast by way of the Ebro tributaries and the Ebro itself. Other special wood-producing areas were Galicia and Asturias. The pine forests of the Peninsula's interior were too far from the coast to be usable. The only important utilization made of them was for turpentine and resin.

CLASSIC TEXTILE INDUSTRIES. Throughout the 18th century there existed a decided inclination on the part of the State to protect the textile industries which had formed the axis of Spanish industrial life ever since the 13th century; manufacture of woollens, the hemp industry, silk production. Some private persons also bent every effort in this direction, though it was impossible to overcome the general inertia, or to convince factory owners that the world of artisan textile work was outmoded and that it was the factory, with its mechanized and rational organization of labor, that was going to prevail. Though the example of the pilot factory in Guadalajara was not attractive, though attempts to revive the woollen industry in Segovia and Valladolid were unsuccessful (both projects failed, in 1733 and 1737), something was gained by a trial of the new system, such as the rise of the woollen factories of Béjar where, thanks to the protection given to the Flemings by the Duke of Béjar, 145 working looms were soon installed (1744).

The overall picture in the classic Spanish *woollen industry* by the end of the 18th century was certainly not brilliant: scanty production (3,500,000 yards) and poor quality. There were many workshops scattered all over the country, but most of them had antiquated looms and very little skilled personnel; the common thing was the individual weaver working for a promoter. The most important woollen-producing centers were Aragon (Saragossa, Teruel), Castile (Béjar and Segovia), and Andalusia. In all of them industrial concentration was very light and techniques very backward. At that time Catalonia occupied a very secondary place. In 1789 Sabadell produced 45,000 yards of cloth, mostly for export (*bayetones*). To remedy the decline of this industry the Crown set up, as we have mentioned, high-grade cloth factories in Guadalajara and Brihuega. Other mercantile corporations concerned themselves with encouraging cloth production. First and most important were the Five Greater Guilds of Madrid, which owned the woollen-goods factories of Cuenca and Ezcaray (Logroño). They took over these factories in 1787, after both had undergone a number of vicissitudes which eventually brought them into the orbit of manufactures subsidized by the State. Neither of these two experiments was successful.

A similar phenomenon occurred in the *hemp* and *linen industry*. Although again we have few exact statistics, we do know that Aragon and Valencia, followed by Galicia, Catalonia, and Granada, occupied first place in a production which was still insufficient for the needs of the national and American markets.

534

As for the *silk industry,* the 18th century witnessed a fabulous development in Valencia. While Toledo, Barcelona, and Granada were declining, and plans to establish large factories in Talavera de la Reina and Madrid (1719–1735) failed, 600,000 pounds of silk per year were being woven in the city on the Turia. Valencia had 2,500 silk looms in 1724 (according to Uztáriz), 3,400 in 1750, and 5,000 in 1787, when the English traveler Townsend visited there (possibly an exaggerated figure). The American historian Herr says that the creator of this industrial recovery was the silk dealer Joaquín Manuel Fos, a technician who first worked in a number of English and French factories. Granada, however, had taken the opposite path: 1,000 and 200 looms in 1724 and 1750 respectively. Murcia was also declining little by little. One of the factories founded there in 1770, which spun and twisted silk by the Piedmontese method, had to be sold to the Five Greater Guilds of Madrid in 1787, but this did not turn out to be beneficial to the industry. And the Catalonian and Sevillian silk industries were simply vegetating. With a total of 4,450 looms in operation, 2,500 more would have been needed in 1750 to absorb annual silk production: 1,150,000 pounds. Businessmen of all kinds made rich profits by exporting Levantine raw silk to France and Northern Italy.

ORIGINS OF THE COTTON INDUSTRY. Though by modern standards this subject has not been studied scientifically, it is one of the best known in Spanish economic history. Cotton, in fact, gave rise to a revolutionary industry, and was the cause of Catalonia's economic predominance in 19th-century Spain. Both these aspects have interested many capable scholars, among whom we may name Lucas Beltrán, Durán Sampere, Ruiz y Pablo, P. Romeva, Carrera Pujal, and above all, Pierre Vilar.

In the development of the cotton industry there has generally been an attempt to show the action of the Bourbon governments who, through a series of prohibitive measures, created the necessary opportunities for the formation of a domestic and colonial market for such products. But this alone is not sufficient, for it neither clarifies the rhythm of development of Catalonia's cotton-cloth production nor the enviable commercial and technical level which it quickly attained throughout the world.

Other circumstances must be kept in mind: in the first place, formation of a large amount of commercial capital out of profits from maritime trade, and especially the commercialization of rural products, particularly those of the vine; in the second place, the enterprising spirit shown by the Catalans of the period who, when at mid-century they saw that profits from the wine trade were declining, had the good sense to transform this commercial capital into industrial capital by investing it in the manufacture of cotton (P. Vilar).

It is well known that Philip V, by a Royal Decree of October 25, 1717, corroborated by another of July 20 of the following year, banned the introduction and sale in Spain of silks and other fabrics imported from China and Asia. This measure, possibly requested by the Andalusian silk trade in an attempt to shut off contraband trade originating with the Manila galleon, was renewed in 1728, and printed linens and cotton goods originating in Asia or imitated in Europe were also banned. As in the rest of the Continent, in spite of these measures Spaniards—or rather, Spanish women—continued to give preference to the novelty fabrics, both comfortable and inexpensive, elegant and varied, represented by "indianas," or cotton cloth printed in various colors. The margin of profit made possible by closing the market not only encouraged contraband trade along the Pyrenean frontier and the Mediterranean coast, but caused some French manufacturers to establish the first looms and printing tables in Barcelona. It is possible that at first their intent was to mask a profitable contraband venture. But this establishment became the key to the spread of the Catalonian cotton-goods industry. Its development was not spectacular, for it required technicians, machines, designers, chemists, a sense of organization, and market possibilities, etc., and these were things which could not be improvised. Only after many difficulties were these considerable obstacles overcome.

Before 1738, and perhaps as the heir of the French establishment to which we have referred, Esteban Canals' calico factory was in operation in Barcelona. It was undoubtedly the first modern industrial center in Spain. In the subsequent ten-year period other factories came into being, some of them located outside Barcelona. They did not always turn a profit, and some went bankrupt through lack of technicians or financial acumen, such as the factory of Campins and Company in Mataró. But this was the end of the stagnant phase, thanks to the first pull of a favorable movement in the trade cycle and an increase in American trade; for Catalonian fabrics broke into the Caribbean market through the outlet opened by the Company of Barcelona, founded in 1756. Four years later, in 1760, when the budding Catalonian cotton industry ran afoul of the Royal Decree of May 15 of that year, signed by Charles III and wiping out the protectionist legislation of 1718 and 1728, the manufacturers of "calicoes, printed linens, dimities, and *blavetes*" of the Principality stated that there were 10,000 workers in the industry and that capital investment in it amounted to 200,000 pesos.

This critical phase in relations between the government and the cotton manufacturers ended with the publication of the famous protectionist Pragmatic of September 14, 1771, banning the importation into Spain of all types of cotton cloth and products. At that time the king was concerned with consolidating the American economy by cultivating cotton, and the Catalan manufacturers, following in the footsteps of one of their most prominent members, Bernardo Gloria, undertook to spin and weave American fibers in their factories. This was the origin of the Catalonian Cotton-Yarn Company, founded in 1772 with a capital of 30,000 *libras,* whose purpose was to absorb and distribute American cotton. Unfortunately, the cotton reached Spain in small quantities and was of poor quality, and consequently the operation was unsuccessful in spite of the advice and reiterated complaints of the manufacturers concerned.

The Company's statutes reveal that in 1772 there were twenty-five cotton-yarn mills in Catalonia. These had arisen in response to the needs of the calico industry. At about the same time as in England, and probably on the same level of importance as the discoveries being made there, cotton spinning became highly successful in Catalonia. Though the precedent of Gloria's yarn mill probably existed (1752), it seems more likely that spinning-works began to develop in 1765 with the factories of Canals and Magarola, and that they were very soon able to supply great quantities of yarn to a textile industry which was growing more and more active. The cotton came from the island of Malta. In the space of thirty years this industry progressed tremendously and earned enormous profits.

A decisive step was taken along the way when the problem of

dyes began to be solved. For a long time this was the Achilles heel of the Catalonian cotton industry. The dyes used were corrosive, and either ran or caused deterioration in the material. Great progress in the solution of this problem was made, as we shall soon see, by Juan Canals, son of the first manufacturer of calicoes, who earned the well-deserved title of Baron of Vall Roja for his studies on the production of madder. This serious problem was solved between the years 1760 and 1779.

Finally, after 1780 mechanical looms were introduced into Catalonia, first from England and later from France. To these must be added the native enthusiasm for perfecting machinery. Practical inventors, and others who were more or less imitators, gave really adequate machinery to the Catalonian cotton-cloth industry, which by the end of the 18th century totaled more than 3,000 establishments and some 100,000 workers (of whom two-thirds were women).

WEARING-APPAREL INDUSTRIES. Within the industrial activity of 18th-century Spain the factories which turned out wearing apparel represented an important chapter. *Hat* factories were particularly prominent among them; hats were exported to America in fabulous quantities after the royal cedula of March 26, 1758, decreed that in shipments to the colonies half the supplies of hats had to be of Spanish make. This type of manufacture flourished in Madrid, some cities in Old Castile (Valladolid, Zamora), and in the coastal regions, especially Barcelona, Valencia, Seville, Sanlúcar de Barrameda, and Corunna. An important factory was established in San Fernando, near Madrid, and was one of the royal manufactories. In 1758 it came under the control of one of the Five Greater Guilds —that of the jewelers; in 1786 the ruling body of the Five Guilds took it over. In spite of the success of this enterprise (it produced some 20,000 hats a year), poor administration, losses, and embezzlements gradually ruined the business, while private hat factories continued to prosper.

Hatters used Peruvian vicuña wool. American hides supplied a large industry in Barcelona, preponderant in the 18th century; it was that of the *shoemakers,* about which we know nothing except that it developed without interruption and expanded its market throughout Spain.

Finally, a few words about the *hosiers.* This was one of the industrial activities which contributed most toward destroying the guilds in Barcelona and Valencia. Based on a solid artisan tradition of knitted wear, an industry developed along the Catalonian coast which quickly grew very profitable, requiring only technical skill and inexpensive machines. Many cotton manufacturers began their careers as hosiers.

Along these same lines we may mention the prosperity attained by the ribbon and handkerchief makers in Barcelona and Valencia.

DYE AND PAPER INDUSTRIES. If we except soap production, which had been a traditional industry with well-established centers in Andalusia, Valencia, and Aragon, the modern chemical industry really began in Spain with the development of dyes. As manufacture of cotton cloth progressed in Catalonia, the demand for dyestuffs became more pressing. Some of these had to be imported from outside the country, while others could be obtained within Spain. Juan Canals, whom we have mentioned before, bent his activities to the latter possibility. He encouraged the cultivation of madder, or *rubia tinctorum,* in fields near Valladolid (1760–1779), especially in Mojados, and taught the process for distilling the characteristic red color given by the plant. Canals was appointed inspector-general of madder and general director of the kingdom's dye industry.

The paper industry was a subsidiary of the textile industry in the 18th century. Rags and scrapings from the flesh side of hides, which formerly had been exported, were the raw materials. In 1737 their export was banned. This measure came in response to pressure from the revitalized paper industry, whose center once again became Catalonia. The Catalonian paper mills grew in response to the demand for high-grade papers for interior decoration, books, and cigarettes. Thus the Catalonian mills perfected their techniques, which by mid-century were spread over the rest of Spain by Pedro Cornet. In 1787 more than eighty-six paper mills were in operation in Catalonia.

BOURBON REFORMS IN AMERICA. The 18th century was a period in which the Spanish government was much concerned about America. From the moment the first Bourbon came to the throne, a great deal of attention and care was lavished on the region. This stemmed from one primary cause. After France and Spain had been defeated by England in the War of the Spanish Succession, Spain had the feeling that her American empire was going to be wrested from her. Later, after the Peace of Utrecht, this foreboding constantly hovered over Madrid and dictated a large part of the domestic and foreign policy of the Bourbons and their ministers. To prevent the loss of America was the general watchword, all the more so because England's example emphasized the tremendous importance that could be achieved by a power backed by colonies which had made effective progress.

A series of reforms was instituted—especially during Charles III's reign—designed to pull the Empire out of the morass of Hapsburg bureaucracy: viceregal and local administration, defense of the La Plata and Pacific coastlines, stimulation of colonial production, freedom of trade, etc. All of this was well received on the other side of the Atlantic and served to make the colonial world prosper, and in particular made it more attractive to those who thought of it as a colossal market for raw materials and manufactured goods. Thus were planted the seeds of the crisis which broke out at the end of the century as a consequence of the wars against the French Revolution, and which was resolved after 1808–1810 by Spanish America's political independence.

AMERICAN POPULATION. The most essential fact in American history during the 18th century is the considerable increase in its population, very much greater than that of metropolitan Spain and independent of the mother country's emigration potential. It has already been mentioned that the number of immigrant Spaniards was small: some 50,000 throughout the course of the century. Owing to purely natural growth, the Hispanic population in America jumped from 10,300,000 inhabitants in the middle of the 17th century (Rosenblat's figures) to some 14,600,000 (Baron Humboldt's figures).

This growth was extremely lopsided, not only in relation to density but also in effectiveness. There were colonies in which only an enormous fertility rate overcame the terrible factor of plagues, famine, and lack of hygiene. In general, the high-altitude countries—Mexico and the Andean nations—continued to have the highest population (Mexico, 5,800,000; Colombia, Peru, and Bolivia, 5,300,000). Other regions, destined to have a prosperous future, were practically deserted. Chile and Argentina had 500,000 inhabitants each. Neither Paraguay nor Uruguay had as many as 100,000.

The principal beneficiaries of the population increase were the native races. The Indians constituted some 7 million inhabitants, or 46% of the total population, an extraordinary figure considering the fact that in North America the Anglo-Saxons represented some 80%. Of this number, Mexico, Central America, Peru, and Bolivia had the highest percentage, with proportions up to 60%.

There were some 3 million whites. They represented the economic and social reality of America: large landowners, businessmen, intellectuals. Numerous in Mexico (1,200,000), they were particularly scarce in Peru. The fact of having been born in Spain or in America divided this racial element into Metropolitans and Creoles. The former were very few at the end of the 18th century (150,000) and in general represented the colonial bureaucracy.

In addition to the whites, and making up an intermediate world of artisans, stewards, peons, and vagabonds, there were the *mestizos,* numbering some 4,100,000. Their world was restless, unstable, of debatable economic value; but it constituted an undeniable human reality.

Finally, there were the Negroes. The development throughout the 18th century of tropical agriculture in the Antilles and Caribbean littoral flooded these regions with swarms of African slaves. It is estimated that some 70,000 Negroes were brought in yearly. By the end of the century there were 400,000 Negroes in the Antilles and 800,000 in the rest of the continent—a total of 1,200,000 souls, laborers in the cocoa, sugar, and tobacco plantations, porters in the cities, and servants of the white men.

NATIVE LABOR. As in previous centuries, the manpower problem continued to be the chief obstacle to the American economy's development. Men were neeeded for agricultural and mining work and they were not easy to find, owing to the natives' resistance to labor discipline. Many of the Indians continued to be isolated from the economic world of the colonies, living in closed, self-ruling agricultural groups. The majority of these slowly became integrated into colonial life, partly because of pressure applied by the *caciques,* or native bosses, whose brilliant career began at this time, and partly by capture at the hands of colonizers of new land (as late as 1772 the colonists of Nueva Santander captured Indians to sell them). The missionaries also carried out part of this assimilation of the Indians, though by less brutal methods (colonization of California by the Franciscans, etc.).

But in spite of all this, numbers were always insufficient. Hence the necessity for slave labor, which grew in proportion to the agricultural needs of the so-called colonial products, of which we shall speak a little later. It also resulted in the establishment of a labor hierarchy in which the Indian found himelf enmeshed and obliged to perform a certain kind of labor. This was the specific case we find in the 18th-century Mexican *hacienda:* an estate, focal point of the latifundia system, harshly ruled by *mestizo* foremen and forced upon the mass of native peons. The situation was the same in the Venezuelan *hato,* though there the owner himself took over the role of foreman, and thus had first-hand knowledge of his employees' work. On the Argentine *estancia* the gaucho represented a sort of peonage on horseback, in a pastoral type of economy.

This labor structure made the *encomienda* system unnecessary, and in consequence this semifeudal organization did not survive the 18th century. The Bourbon monarchs applied tax pressure on owners and decreed that vacant *encomiendas* were illegal; these became the property of the Crown by the Royal Decree of November 23, 1718. Both measures combined to eliminate from the labor picture the *encomendero,* "a man who possessed neither theoretical problems nor distinction," as Silvio Zavala writes. However, *en-*

comienda persisted in a more or less bastardized form in some American regions up to the period of independence.

The *mita* system in the mining regions of Peru suffered the same fate. The Spanish governments of Enlightened Despotism, their envoys, and higher authorities were bitterly opposed to this form of forced labor. But the tyranny of *caciques* and local governors, mine owners and leaseholders, kept it functioning up to 1808. At the end of the 18th century a controversy was still going on between those who considered the *mita* system to be an evil and those who defended the theory of the Indians' natural subservience.

SLAVERY AND THE SLAVE TRADE. The conversion of American colonial crops into a commercial type of agriculture was made possible, in the semitropical zones, only by the massive introduction of African labor. Three crops were particularly influential in this development: sugar, cotton, and cocoa, which required heavy capital investment, the continuous work of many hands, and cheap unskilled manpower.

From the very beginning of the dynastic change in Spain, the great powers vied for the right of contracting for slaves. France was the first beneficiary; but the fortunes of war tipped the scale in favor of an English monopoly. By the terms of the Treaty of Utrecht (1713), England obtained the monopoly of the slave trade for a period of thirty years (4,800 slaves a year could be brought to America). Together with the famous clause pertaining to the "permission ship," this contract was one of the instruments of the British commercial offensive in Spanish America. In spite of the Bourbons' attempts to recapture the freedom of action they had so unfortunately lost, the British retained control of the slave trade until 1750. At that time they were replaced by Spanish contractors, generally companies already doing business with America. The Havana Company was particularly outstanding among them. Finally, in 1789, full freedom in the Negro trade was decreed; this benefited Negroes not at all, but resulted in a considerable increase in the opportunities available to Spaniards interested in this lucrative and abominable traffic.

As has been said, the Antilles and the Caribbean littoral received the largest number of Negroes. It would be interesting to chart exactly the rhythm of slave imports. As for Cuba, we know that

80,000 were brought in between 1763 and 1800, or one and one-third times the estimated number for the whole preceding colonial period. This implied fabulous profits for slave owners; but it resulted in social and economic backwardness in those countries, which were unable to absorb the human wave, of a low mental level, poured into them by the slave trade.

Even if we ignore the slave's pitiable social condition (branding, legalized beatings, etc.), which legislative measures in Spain did nothing to correct, his working life was usually terribly hard, especially if he was employed in a hacienda or sugar mill and was subject to a *mestizo* foreman. The day laborer, hired out by his master to anyone who needed him, was a little better off, and the domestic slave best of all, within the limits of the system. As for the freed Negro, his lot was always hard, for he had no social base from which to launch himself in an economically free profession. Nevertheless, many slaves managed to free themselves from the sugar mills and achieve artisan rank. By the middle of the 18th century Negroes and *pardos* (mulattoes) were engaged in almost all crafts in Havana. The same occurred in other port cities: Veracruz, Portobello, Cartagena.

MODIFICATIONS IN COLONIAL AGRICULTURE. As we have said before, the 18th century was the golden age of latifundia owned by native-born colonials. Beginning with the huge accumulations of real estate of the preceding century, the proprietors combined their power over men and things with the favorable turn of agricultural prices in the world market and the ever growing demand for colonial products by a teeming and prosperous Europe. These facts explain the success of colonial agriculture during this period, especially in the case of products destined for European markets.

The bases of native subsistence continued to be corn and rice, the banana, manioc flour, and the potato. Each of these crops expanded outside its original areas during the course of the 18th century. The potato reached Mexico, and the banana began to be grown all along the tropical coasts. As for wheat, the grain preferred by the Creole class, it had considerable success, especially in its expansion, together with corn, into the pampas. After 1780 wheat began to establish, in the La Plata region, the most brilliant record of any cereal plant in America.

Among commercial or potentially commercial products, *sugar* was especially important. As we have said before, to follow the trail of this crop means to become involved with the slave problem and with the great fortunes invested in America; it also involves deciphering the secret of Atlantic trade. Sugar was cultivated especially in the Antilles and along the coast of the Gulf of Mexico. During the 18th century's period of economic contraction, Cuban production suffered because of competition from Jamaican and Haitian sugars; but after 1765 there was no obstacle in its way, except for brief cyclical fluctuations. By the middle of the 18th century the average annual production was 50,000 *quintales;* in about 1800 it was 650,000, thirteen times greater. Cuban sugar flooded Europe by way of the Mediterranean and made Barcelona wealthy.

Cocoa followed an almost identical path and resulted, during the period of the Royal Company of Caracas, in the prosperity of Venezuela and the Creole *hatos.* Coffee, also established in Venezuela and in Cuba (after 1769), grew alongside cocoa. Tobacco, however, did not have such good luck as the other crops because of the monopoly decreed by the Spanish State in 1764. An obvious decline can be noted in all the zones which produced this plant, in quantity though not in quality.

To this list, significant in itself, must be added the cultivation of dye plants such as indigo (from Guatemala and Venezuela), the cutting of Campeche wood on the Honduran coast, and exploitation of high-grade tropical woods such as mahogany.

DEVELOPMENT OF LIVESTOCK. The recovery of economic momentum was also shown in the matter of livestock breeding. Herds increased everywhere in the colonies, but nowhere was this so evident as in the La Plata region. The stock called *cimarrón,* that is, descended from animals which had gone wild after their original importation by the Spaniards, became so numerous at the beginning of the 18th century that herds were found all over the pampas from Buenos Aires to the Negro River, and spread out in the direction of Chile, Mendoza, and Rosario. It was only necessary to provide Buenos Aires with export facilities (permission ships after 1735) for the future Argentina to become the chief producer of leather. Within a few years the slaughter of wild stock threatened to make cows and horses extinct, but after the serious crisis of

1770–1775, when an organized system of herding was established and many *estancias* came into operation, the production of leather rose sharply: 150,000 hides were exported annually by 1778, and 1,400,000 fifteen years later.

The dizzying success of the leather trade also involved the development of a salted meat industry. This important food resource began to be exploited after 1776, when the first warehouses were constructed in Buenos Aires. Specialized workers were brought from Spain to carry out the various processes, which were also stimulated by the discovery of salt mines (Salinas Grandes). The dried product was exported to Spain and particularly to the Antilles.

The interior provinces of Mexico also experienced a considerable increase in livestock, though not in the fabulous degree of La Plata, a region which had an exceptional port in Buenos Aires.

DEEPSEA FISHING. Apart from inshore fishing activity for supply of coastal localities, two other types of fishing came to the fore in the 18th century: the Chilean fish-preserving factories and the whale-processing stations of Patagonia. Both developed greatly at the end of the 18th century as a result of the greater demands of the continental market and increased activity in trade with Spain, carried out by Catalans.

All along the Chilean littoral, especially the island of Chiloé and its immediate surroundings, there were fabulous quantities of fish. In some port towns it was salted down to supply the Andean regions of the interior (Potosí). The preferred species were conger-eel and bream. In the La Plata region there was less interest in fishing. But on the southern shores of Patagonia the presence of whales gave rise to the establishment of colonies of harpooners, especially after French ships began to appear in those waters. These colonies—San José, Río Negro, Puerto Deseado (1779–1780) —languished until they were reorganized by the Royal Maritime Fishing Company of Barcelona. Over a period of several years this company founded new processing stations and carried on active fishing campaigns.

REVIVAL OF MINING PRODUCTION. The decline in American silver production about the middle of the 17th century was one of the causes of the period of contraction in the European trade cycle, and one of the elements most deeply involved in the combination of factors which brought about the Spanish financial collapse. For nearly a century the situation scarcely changed. But beginning in 1740 Spanish America again became the inexhaustible source of world silver production. This time, however, Mexico was in the forefront of production, as is shown by the following table, taken from Soetbeer:

SILVER PRODUCTION: 1721–1810

	Mexico	Spanish America	Percentage
1721–1740	230,000 kg.	431,000 kg.	53
1741–1760	301,000 kg.	533,000 kg.	56
1761–1780	366,400 kg.	652,000 kg.	56
1781–1800	562,000 kg.	879,000 kg.	64
1801–1810	553,800 kg.	894,000 kg.	61

After the middle of the century, therefore, a new stream of silver entered world economy, adding to the previous stimulus given it by the appearance of Brazilian gold on the market twenty years earlier. Discovery of new lodes, greater availability of labor, and the use of better techniques all contributed to this new flood of silver. Unfortunately we lack exact data on annual production, which would permit us to compare it with the evolution of prices and wages. But in several places in his work Professor Hamilton states that the effects of this new wave of precious metal were even more important than in the 16th century. Those who support the quantity theory find it easy to relate this second phase of prosperity in American silver production to the Industrial Revolution and the formation of a modern manufacturing bourgeoisie.

In any case, American silver again flooded Spanish soil and permitted the brilliant recovery of the reigns of Ferdinand VI and Charles III; it contributed to the flowering of Cádiz and Barcelona and resulted in a powerful commercial intercourse which on the one hand reached China—that great country greedy for silver—by way of Acapulco and the Philippines, and on the other arrived in that same Celestial Empire after having revived Mediterranean commerce and given wings to the British conquest of India.

The discovery of a new precious metal—platinum—in Nueva

Granada (Colombia) also came at this time, though it had little importance at first.

LOCAL INDUSTRIES. Urban crafts continued to be the industrial pattern of the Spanish colonies in America during the 18th century. To be sure, part of the responsibility for this must be assigned to the colonial "pact" system, which integrated the colonies with metropolitan Spain as producers of raw materials and buyers of manufactured products. It is even possible that in some cases Madrid may have sacrificed industrial projects to the interests of port cities in the Spanish periphery. However, the main cause of America's lack of initiative in achieving a modern industrial structure had its origin in the economic and mental makeup of the Creole class. We must remember that the 18th century was the golden age of latifundism in America, and that profits from the ever-increasing prices of agricultural products were channeled into new acquisitions or more extensive cultivation of land, or into lucrative commercial ventures. Agriculture paid for commerce and commerce stimulated agriculture. In this closed circle the role of modern industry was nonexistent. And so we find the survival of an economy based on artisan industry.

It had a period of great prosperity. A larger population and increased wealth served as incentives to labor. The artisans of the time achieved a very high quality of work, especially in silversmithing. The cloth industry also enjoyed a period of expansion, though always in lesser degree because of foreign competition and the invasion of silks, printed linens, and cotton prints from the Far East or from Spain and England. Peru was especially hard hit by this competition. Because she could count on an old textile tradition and an ample supply of cotton fiber, she was able to establish the first modern industrial center in Spanish America. In fact, textiles were exported to Chile, Buenos Aires, Tierra Firme, and even the Philippines. But the separation of the viceroyalty of La Plata and inability to develop a good yarn out of the local cotton were factors which destroyed the future of this industry. By 1790 it was showing signs of decay.

Specialized industries were the cigar factories (Mexico, Cuba, and Peru), which enjoyed a period of prosperity at the beginning of the century, later cut short by establishment of the tobacco monopoly (1764); the sugar industry, closely related to development of the sugar cane plantations; distilling, which utilized fermentation of this same plant to obtain liquor with a high alcohol content (rum, cane brandy, etc.). The distilleries carried on an active trade which was often highly remunerative.

INTERAMERICAN TRADE: STRUGGLE BETWEEN PERU AND LA PLATA. It is very difficult to separate the study of American trade from that of the Spanish commercial network. Therefore we shall leave discussion of this important point until later. At the moment we shall limit ourselves to an analysis of intercolonial trade as it developed in response to the New World's demographic and economic growth during the century with which we are concerned.

Three special facts governed the internal dynamics of inter-American trade: (1) Spain's determination to maintain the monopolies granted to Mexico and Peru within the framework of the Empire, (2) inability of Spanish industry to supply its colonial markets, and (3) continued pressure of foreign products in the seaports through the "permission ship" system and contraband. These factors were responsible for the effort made by the Spanish governments, especially after Ferdinand VI, to give the colonies adequate means of communication which would make commerce possible and avoid economic collapse in case of interrupted Atlantic communications due to deployment of the English fleet, mistress of the seas. In spite of this prudent policy land communications remained few and poor, while the limiting of colonial shipping to mere coastwise trade delayed lasting prosperity.

However, improvement was considerable. In New Spain as well as in the viceroyalties of Peru, Nueva Granada, and La Plata, there did exist a communications network, somewhat precarious but effective. The principal land route in South America was the road from Buenos Aires to Lima and Quito, which could be used by carts from Buenos Aires to Tucumán, by mules from Tucumán to Potosí, by llamas to Cuzco and Lima, by carts again to Payta, and finally by mules to Quito. It was a difficult road, but it formed an indispensable spinal column which united the opposite poles of the Spanish American viceregal economy: Lima and Buenos Aires.

The struggle between these two cities is symbolic of the battle between monopoly and freedom of trade, a battle which was also

joined in Spain at the time. Buenos Aires' growth was directly related to its leather export trade and its imports of merchandise, either controlled or contraband. The La Plata estuary was a center
for illicit trade from 1713 to 1739. Buenos Aires grew by sending
its products to Chile across the Andes and to Paraguay by way of
the river and the Rosario highway. Lima managed to take care of
itself until the serious imperial crisis of 1763. Then Havana and
Manila fell to the English, and Buenos Aires was seriously threatened. The constant menace of the Sacramento colony in the La
Plata estuary, and the infiltration of contraband through this enormous opening, could have been sufficient to bring about the political and economic downfall of the Spanish empire in South America. Therefore strong measures were taken: some were political,
such as creation of the viceroyalty of La Plata and its separation
from that of Peru; others were economic, such as the first measures
establishing freedom of trade between Spain and the colonies; and,
in particular, a series of licenses governing trade in commodities
among the colonies themselves. The first of these was granted to the
two viceroyalties of Peru and Nueva Granada (1768); six years
later permission was extended to those of New Spain and the
captain-generalcy of Guatemala, and in 1776 the viceroyalty of La
Plata became included in reciprocal trade. This gave greater flexibility to the American economy, but without bringing it into balance,
for unfortunately the colonies' products were not complementary.
Therefore other measures became necessary, such as the freedom
of trade decree of 1778 and the Royal Order of 1797 concerning trade with neutrals, which really spelled the end of the Spanish
monopoly in America and the beginning of the colonies' era of
independence.

THE "PERMISSION SHIP" AND ILLICIT TRADE. We have already
gone into some detail about contraband trade in the America of the
Hapsburg kings. After the Treaty of Utrecht in 1713 illegal trade
expanded enormously. This treaty authorized England, besides giving her a monopoly of the slave trade for thirty years, to send one
ship of 500 tons burden to the Indies annually. This ship, called a
"permission" or "registered" ship, was the basis for official organization of contraband trade. England appointed consuls in the main

American commercial towns; their sole job was to protect the illicit trade carried on by the slave and permission ships.

After this time a serious danger threatened the American economy: that of having to count almost necessarily on effective cooperation with the contraband trade. It was impossible to supply the colonies without illicit traffic, as was demonstrated in 1763 and again in 1796. The inadequacy of Spanish production explains this seemingly paradoxical situation, created by monopolistic principles which the Bourbons gave up only in the measure that they could count on Spanish products to take the place of those which arrived by illegal means.

As in the 17th century, the main centers of this traffic were Acapulco and the Canary Islands—in the former place merchandise from the Far East, in the latter that from Europe, all set in motion by American silver. In the case of the Canary Islands a few concrete examples will suffice to show the extent of the fraud. In 1755 one ship declared 4,717 silver pesos; actually it had illegally unloaded 62,203. A year later 33,788 pesos were seized from another ship. These were private fortunes, which served to swell England's coffers during the fierce hunger for silver that she experienced during the 18th century.

The ailment went back a long way, no less than two centuries. There could be only one solution: the English contraband organization would put an end to the Spanish monopoly structure, thus anticipating the moment of American independence.

37 · Commercial Development

COMMERCIAL MENTALITY OF THE 18TH CENTURY: LIBERALISM AND COLONIAL PACT. The 18th century, inheritor of the tendency toward depression of the 17th, dawned still under the influence of mercantilist monopoly. But the expansion unleashed by new American supplies of precious metals (1720–1750), demographic growth, and industrial initiative changed the mental outlook both of the statesman and the businessman, corresponding to the change which had taken place in the cultural and spiritual fields. After the middle of the century the word "freedom" was heard everywhere, and in the economic field it soon found brilliant expression in the mouths of the physiocrats: "Laissez faire, laissez passer, le monde va de lui-même," and an explicit theoretical expression in Adam Smith's *The Wealth of Nations*.

In the second half of the 18th century economic freedom did not yet mean total withdrawal of the State and predominance of the law of supply and demand in a free market; but it did stand for doing away with monopoly and privilege. No matter how many restraints the State had placed on economic life, no matter how many channels it had opened to make industrial and commercial energies circulate in a particular manner, no matter how many barriers it had erected to compartmentalize or limit, all must be lifted, rechanneled, or torn down. And this not only in the name of theory, but by virtue of the fact proved in those places where the system had been applied; that economic freedom brought in its wake a colossal increase in all types of wealth. In this as in other aspects of 18th-century life, England was a powerful light and guide. Her astounding private and collective wealth was obviously owed to the fact of the great autonomy enjoyed by any given cell in her economic structure.

England's example involved a paradoxical corollary. The economic freedom of which she boasted rested on a division of labor within her vast Empire: the mother country supplied the colonies with manufactured goods, which she transported in her own ships, and the colonies sold her raw materials both for food and for industry. This was the colonial pact. Theoretically, it was at odds with the freedom of movement so much praised in the mother country, for it subjugated the colonies to the home country's interests through a system of commercial and industrial prohibitions. In fact, however, it responded to the differing level of economic development between Europe and the virgin continents. This did not prevent its being a contradiction, nor did it fail to arouse lively protests in the more advanced colonial societies.

Destruction of monopolies and the colonial pact, a definite tendency toward imperial liberalism: this was the keynote of Spanish trade following the initial period of mercantilist survival.

SPANISH DOMESTIC TRADE: PROGRESSIVE INTEGRATION OF REGIONAL ECONOMIES. One of the difficulties experienced by the Spanish monarchy in its attempt to develop true solidarity among the kingdoms of which it was composed was the lack of a cohesive economic policy. Limitation of the American area for the benefit of Castilians solidly sealed off the regions of the Crown of Aragon, which, though they were excluded from profiting from the colonies, were at least insulated from catastrophe during the periods of terrible crisis in the 17th century. The economic contraction which followed did not foster *rapprochement* among the regional economies. Thus, after the War of Succession, Philip V found himself in a juridical and actual situation similar to that of medieval Spain.

The juridical situation could be solved immediately. Once the local statutes of Aragon and Valencia were annulled and Catalonia was conquered, the royal cedula of November 19, 1714, wiped out the inland ports (customs houses) between Castile and the various regions of the Crown of Aragon and declared them United Provinces. Shortly after this the Royal Instruction of August 31, 1717, announced the suppression of all internal customs offices and their removal to frontiers or seaports. Thus internal freedom from customs duties was established (though not freedom of traffic, for many products needed transit permits).

It is easy to abolish systems and proclaim solutions on paper. The reform of 1717 raised such a storm in Navarre and the Basque

Provinces that Philip V's government had no choice but to surrender and restore customs, creating a tariff barrier along the line
of the Ebro, whose basic points were in Vitoria, Orduña, and
Valmaseda. On the other side of this line were what were called in
18th-century financial jargon the "Exempted Provinces," to distinguish them from the so-called "United Provinces" (Castile and
Aragon). This situation was legalized in 1727, and in that same
year Santander was granted customs exemption for articles brought
in under the registry. According to very reliable sources, this permitted development of contraband along the Cantabrian coast and
the beginning of the Basque regional economy's prosperity. Men
from Santander, the Montaña, and the Basque Country feathered
their nests very successfully by smuggling unauthorized merchandise through the Cantabrian mountains into Castile.

As for Catalonia, the elimination of frontiers with Castile meant
a stimulus for her trade. But before this could be possible the country had to recover from the terrible ravages of the War of Succession and the repression that followed it. By 1740 Catalan trade,
greatly benefited by low tariffs (which were lower than the revenue
from tithes), had made great inroads in Castile, smothering the
competition from Levantines, Aragonese, and Castilians. A number of ports and cities complained, and on August 8, 1742, the
cabinet minister Campillo established two customs stations for
Catalonia, one at Fraga and the other at Tortosa, to collect a percentage on the merchandise coming from Catalonia and intended
for the interior of the nation.

A similar measure, though of lesser scope, had to be adopted in
Cartagena in that same year, for serious damage had been done to
Alicante's trade because of subsidies granted by the government for
construction of an arsenal in the former city.

As can be seen, suppression of internal customs was neither so
clear nor so complete as is usually supposed. Nor did plans for
unifying weights and measures according to the Castilian standard
make much progress, though this was proposed a number of times
after 1758. Regional authorities resisted the move and stated, with
perfect truth, that no one was ready to undertake this important
reform.

In fact, if internal economic integration progressed at all it was due to the energy of the Catalans, to which we have referred before. Thanks to this expansion Catalonia created the economic foundations of modern Spain. Beginning between 1720 and 1730, and certainly as a result of difficult living conditions in the Principality, this energy took the form of a wave of emigration in the twenty years which followed: the first to leave were artisans, then technicians, later muleteers and industrialists. The names of Pedro Sit (1728, employed in the royal glass factory in San Ildefonso), Durán (1732, who had plans to replace England as a supplier of salt fish), and Pedro Cornet (1737, the paper expert) were simply precursors of the human wave which was shortly to deluge the coasts and the interior of Castile. This phenomenon is obvious after 1768, when Francisco Romá drew attention to it in his book *Signs of Felicity in Spain* (*Las señales de la felicidad en España*). Later it increased more and more. The dispute between the Five Greater Guilds of Madrid and the Catalan merchants in 1783 merely emphasizes the large number of the latter in the capital: they paid 20,000 reales to enter the General Company of Trade and obtained from the government the privilege of selling their manufactured products freely at retail. There were Catalans in Valladolid, Galicia (17,000 in coastal areas), Andalusia, etc., and even in Soria, where Larruga found them in every village, engaged in the sale of cotton goods, hosiery, and shoes. And in another area, Catalan muleteers (especially those from Copóns) had what amounted to a monopoly of transport between Galicia, Portugal, Andalusia, and Catalonia.

The impact of this group of Catalans on the interior of the Peninsula was obvious. It aroused resentment. "Those who love idleness, those who content themselves with indolence and want to gain easy riches at the expense of their neighbors' lack of concern," wrote Larruga in 1792, "are not in favor of the establishments made by the Catalans outside their Principality; but sensible people appreciate these men, whom they look upon as brothers and good Spaniards."

DYNAMICS AND GENERAL STRUCTURE OF SPANISH FOREIGN TRADE. Available information on Spanish trade during the 18th century is not very satisfactory, nor is it even very close to the truth. There is a need for studies which will fill this obvious gap in our economic history. Nevertheless, we shall try to give an overall view based on some recent researches.

First of all, we must mention a notable fact in Spanish foreign trade during this century: wars. Unlike the character previously assumed by conflicts among the great European powers, after the second half of the 18th century wars were waged on a worldwide scale and for colonial economic interests. In most cases blockade fleets were much more important than the land battles which figure in the history books, for they paralyzed the adversary, harried and ruined his commerce, and obliged him to sue for peace. In this sense, Spain's great rival in the 18th century was England. When England and Spain were at war, the superiority of the enemy's fleet was such that Spanish-American trade was for all practical purposes blockaded. When peace was signed, on the other hand, interimperial mercantile activities quickly recovered their prosperity. Hence we would do well to recall the high points of English-Spanish hostility: 1761–1763, the Seven Years' War; 1778–1783, the American Revolution; 1796–1803, war of alliance with revolutionary France.

These events were not necessarily reflected in trade relations between France and Spain, in regard to which we possess a statistical series covering more than sixty years, published by R. Romano. The development of Hispano-French trade from 1716 to 1780 reveals a number of curious facts: in the first place, a trend contrary to that of the trade cycle. While this was still in a period of contraction during the first half of the century and was to enter a phase of expansion during its last decades, the curve of trade relations we are considering shows a continuous expansion from 1716 to 1755 (with two peaks, 1716–1720 and 1742–1750), and a noticeable period of stagnation, almost of regression, from 1755 onward. This fact is at variance with the real situation of Spanish trade in general, which, as we shall see, received decisive forward momentum after the declaration of "free trade" with America in 1778.

The second fact is the permanent deficit in Spain's trade balance with regard to France. Spain does not show a surplus in a single one of those sixty years. In fact, there are long periods of brutal deficit, such as that from 1749 to 1756, or in 1720, 1723, and 1756. This confirms the unfortunate direction, begun in the pre-

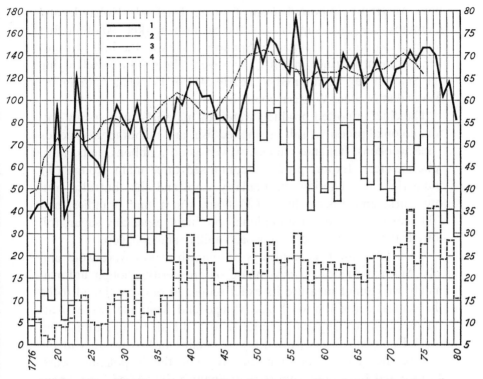

HISPANO-FRENCH TRADE IN THE 18TH CENTURY.—*Key:* 1, total exports and imports; 2, six-year moving average of same; 3, movement of imports; 4, movement of exports. At left, index numbers (base, 100 = mean for 1737–1750); at right, value in millions of francs. White area represents the deficit in Spain's balance of trade with France.

vious century, taken in Spanish trade policy. Though we do not possess continuous statistical data, it will suffice to observe the following figures taken from Canga Argüelles:

Year	Exports	Imports
1789	289,000,000	717,000,000 reales
1792	396,000,000	714,000,000 reales

The negative balance was compensated for, as in Hapsburg times, by selling American silver. As we have mentioned, Western Europe was experiencing a silver famine in order to fill the Chinese vacuum (bimetallic ratio in China, 1:12), and this could only be satisfied by American metal coming in through Spain. Here silver arrived cheap (bimetallic ratio in America, 1:37) and was used to buy everything imported from France, England, Holland, and Germany, the chief suppliers of the Spanish market. Another fact unfavorable to development of Spanish trade was the inferiority of her merchant marine: in 1801 there were about 930 vessels flying the Spanish flag (compared to nearly 500 in 1778), a number far below that of other Western countries.

The chief imported products were raw materials such as raw cotton, colonial products, salt or smoked fish, and manufactured goods (fine woollens, hollands, linens, woven goods, ribbons, hats, fans, jewelry, etc.). Export products comprised three main groups (1) industrial raw materials, particularly wool and silk, but also iron ore, cork, and esparto fiber, (2) flour, wines, and brandies, and (3) reexports of American colonial products, especially sugar, followed at some distance by cocoa, vanilla, and tobacco.

Until 1765 the two mainstays of Spanish export were wool and silk. Silk experienced a new phase of prosperity, though unfortunately we cannot measure its exact scope. Burgos continued to be the central depot for wool, and Bilbao and Santander were rivals for its export to England, France, and Holland. Competition from other European flocks caused a new decline in this product at the end of the century, but particularly after the Napoleonic wars. France and Italy were importers of Spanish silk. After 1765 Spanish sugar and brandy gained control of the Mediterranean, displacing Marseilles from her traditional markets. By 1778 the battle was won.

TRADE WITH THE MEDITERRANEAN WORLD OF THE LEVANT. By the middle of the 17th century Sicily had ceased to be the golden goal for Catalonia and Valencia's Mediterranean trade. For a hundred years this region's trade was restricted to coastwise vessels, which trailed far behind the French merchant marine. This was a period of splendor for Marseilles, undisputed mistress of the Mediterranean, which she dominated thanks to her trade with the countries of the Sublime Porte, especially Syria and Egypt. Meanwhile the ships of the Mediterranean littoral were making their first advances into the Atlantic, in preparation for the great flowering which began in the last third of the 18th century.

The development of the Catalonian cotton industry gave birth to a new Mediterranean center of interest: the island of Malta. After

1740 Maltese cotton came regularly and in quantity to Catalonian shores, thus stimulating shipping in this area. Very soon the sugar trade routes were added, although we know very little about them. They were, however, of vital interest to the Spanish economy at the end of the 1700's. Many of these routes must have ended in Italy.

The French Revolution brought up the problem of trade with the Levant. Since communications between France and the Ottoman Empire were interrupted and this market was being neglected by its usual suppliers, it seemed that the time had come to try to dislodge them from their entrenched positions. This was the project presented by Juan Soler, the consul at Smyrna, to the Board of Trade of Barcelona in 1793. An ambitious project, it was postponed again and again for lack of ships, and especially for lack of experts in navigation to Greece and Egypt. Seamen cannot be produced out of a hat, nor can a trade organization. Finally, in 1797, the expedition of the *Firme* and the *Experiencia* left for the Levant with a cargo of capers, almonds, cork, iron, woollens, and anise—too late, for Napoleon Bonaparte's expedition to Egypt was destined to put Levantine trade on a new basis. The attempt was not successful. In spite of this it was repeated in 1802 and 1803, until the outbreak of war with England closed the matter for good.

It is possible that during this period there was some development of trade with Morocco, which consisted essentially in taking cheap silver there and acquiring in exchange grain and livestock for Spain, or for supply of the military posts and Spanish army in Morocco. It was a profitable business operation. French competition and the cutthroat rivalry among the Spanish merchants themselves cut down on its possibilities. In 1796 this trade was granted as a ten-year monopoly to the Greater Guilds of Madrid, who exploited it to the hilt.

TRADE WITH THE EUROPEAN ATLANTIC WORLD. Within the general lines we have drawn for Spanish commercial structure, the Atlantic European zone occupies a privileged place. France, England, Holland, Belgium, and Germany (Hamburg) were Spain's great customers in the 18th century. The United Kingdom of Great Britain and Ireland stood out especially, as a rival fearsome in war and still more fearsome in commerce, especially after its interference in American trade as a result of the agreements of Utrecht.

England continued to acquire wool, salt, wine, brandy, iron, and dried produce (almonds), and to sell textiles, salt fish, and high-grade manufactured products. Under the protection of a one-sided commercial treaty—that of 1667—renewed in 1713 and 1750, the English had both Spanish agriculture and industry at their mercy. The Dutch were in the same position, for they profited from identical customs privileges. Holland was the great purchaser of wool, produce, oil, wine, and iron, which she then redistributed throughout the Rhineland; she sold to Spain silks and muslins imported from the Orient, as well as hardware, fabrics of Dutch manufacture, and luxury goods. Belgium presented the same picture (the Low Countries were under control of Austria after 1714), for she had never interrupted the prosperous trade she had maintained with Spain ever since the wool revolution of 1300. She exported fine cloth (Brabant linen) to Spain, as well as hides, porcelain, and small hardware; and she imported wool, salt, and dried fruits. Hamburg specialized in the purchase of colonial agricultural products.

Though of lesser volume than trade with England, that with France was very considerable in Spanish economic life during the 18th century. The center of attraction, as has been demonstrated by many studies, was Cádiz, at least as long as it maintained the monopoly of American trade. Many French manufacturers had branches and trading establishments there, and shipped to Cádiz for the American market cloth, silks, laces, plush, and various products of the incipient luxury industry (furniture, jewelry, perfumes, etc.).

One curious statistic relating to Hispano-Flemish trade in Ostende shows us, in the absence of more complete figures, both growth and change in the Spanish Atlantic trade structure. In 1766 thirty-three Spanish vessels visited that port, of which about 33% came from Cádiz, 20% from Bilbao, and the rest from Alicante, Málaga, and Seville. In 1780 the traffic had doubled (seventy ships); Barcelona now held first place with nineteen vessels and 27%; second place, Málaga with 20%; third and fourth, Seville and Bilbao with 15%. Cádiz had 7% and the rest was shared by Alicante, Valencia, and Villaviciosa.

We know of Spanish commercial establishments all over Europe. The Greater Guilds of Madrid had them in London (1787), Hamburg (1790), and Paris (1797). Antonio del Río and Marcos

Fonegra of Santander traded with Danzig (1752) and Riga (1753).

TRADE WITH AMERICA. Population and production increases in America stimulated the development of trade within the Empire, later assisted by the government of Charles III, which practiced an extremely liberal economic policy. Later we shall treat this subject with the attention it deserves.

Trade currents between the mother country and the colonies consisted, on the outward voyage, of traditional products (wine and olive oil, mercury, and foreign manufactured goods), as well as products supplied by Spanish industrial activity, such as raw iron and steel from the Cantabrian ironworks, Catalan calicoes and muslins, Guadalajara woollens, paper, books, and hats, of various kinds. The slave trade also moved in this direction.

On their return, ships brought a variety of products. Among textile fibers were cotton and vicuña wool; among woods and dye products, Campeche wood, Brazil wood, rubber products, indigo, cochineal, and cinchona bark; among specifically agricultural products, cocoa, sugar, coffee, tobacco, and vanilla; among minerals, Mexican and Peruvian silver, and copper and tin; among animal products, leather and hides from the La Plata region.

We must keep another fact in mind: wheat supplied by the United States of America after 1783, shipped to Spanish ports in the Mediterranean. These vessels helped to increase traffic between the two sides of the Atlantic.

ROADS, PORTS, AND TRANSPORT; POSTAL SERVICE AND ECONOMIC JOURNALISM. The mobilization of economic life, starting from a situation of collapse, was made possible only by refurbishing communications, an area where practically nothing had been done since the days of Ferdinand and Isabella and Charles V. The installation of French ministers and civil servants in the Spanish government helped to arouse interest in public works, for they were imbued with an admirable engineering tradition in the construction of good highways, roads, and canals.

This explains the fact that as early as the reign of Philip V, in 1718, a long ordinance was drawn up concerning road construction. It was the origin of the radial arrangement of the Spanish highway network, with Madrid as its center. It was a centralization molded to the Peninsula's economic geography. But it is undeniable that this was the beginning of a fruitful era. The pace of construction speeded up after 1749 (ordinances to royal governors concerning roads and bridges), and especially after Charles III's famous ordinance of June 10, 1767, prescribing improvement of the highway system between Madrid and Catalonia, Valencia, Andalusia, and Galicia, which gave rise to the appearance of the famous "royal roads," the first paved highways since Roman times. The ordinance in question prescribed a monthly budget of 250,000 reales, a modest sum but one which gave good results when wisely administered. But these good results required the supervision of an efficient administrator, Floridablanca, who carried out an important campaign as superintendent of roads from 1777 to 1788. According to his own figures, in those eleven years 200 leagues of highways were repaired, 195 constructed, and 322 bridges built. It was not much, but something had been accomplished: inertia was overcome and some goals defined.

The new layout of the highway network meant slow replacement of muleteers and heavy carts, equally suited to mountain trails and level roads. After the middle of the 18th century Spain could count on a regular fleet of carts and other light vehicles. The coach became a popular means of locomotion at this time; it possessed the feature of a body suspended by a system of springs which softened the bumpiness of the journey. Eighteenth-century variations of the coach were the chaise and the landau. The stagecoach also put in an appearance. In February, 1763, a radial passenger service was put into operation between Madrid and the provinces, under the supervision of the General Coach Service (*Diligencia general de coches*). Between Madrid and Barcelona or Puerto de Santa María service was biweekly. The trip lasted six days, six hours a day. By the end of the 18th century the highway network totaled some 10,000 kilometers, somewhat more than in the Roman period. Though still insufficient to integrate the regional economies, it did represent notable progress. The road over the Guadarrama pass connecting the two Castiles was inaugurated in 1749. For five centuries the pass of Aguardenterías had been used, but it was so steep that it was almost impossible to negotiate with horse-drawn vehicles. We should also recall the opening of the Escudo pass (1753), which had such favorable results for Santander's economy.

Maritime transport, of course, was the most widely used because of its cheapness, speed, and relative comfort in comparison with land travel. Suffice it to say that the Cantabrian port cities drank Catalan and Andalusian wines since these reached them more easily than those of the Castilian hinterland, separated from them by the barrier of a mountain range almost inaccessible to commercial traffic. Technical innovations in high seas and coastwise shipping, in particular the appearance of jib sails, contributed toward making the sailing ship more maneuverable, and this period was its golden age. At the same time, the seaports began to receive due attention. In the last third of the 18th century works were completed in all the great Spanish seaports, and they were given the necessary technical equipment (signal lights, beacons, etc.). Barcelona, Tarragona, Valencia, Corunna, Gijón, and Bilbao received special attention. Early in the following century a great lighthouse was erected in Tarifa, making passage through the Strait of Gibraltar much easier.

The intensification of economic life and the noticeable improvement in communications contributed toward development of the postal service, a most useful trade instrument now that commerce could count on reliable and regular information. Documents from business firms of the period show the increasing importance of correspondence, which permitted establishment of complicated networks of affiliated branches. The State recognized these needs and gradually transformed the postal service, an inheritance from the Hapsburgs; this, as we know, consisted of an administration leased to a Chief Postal Officer. In 1706 this office was incorporated into the Crown; but until 1720, when the ordinances of the Master of Posts were laid down, there was no direct official organization (up to 1716 postal service was leased to an individual or individuals). As in other sectors of Spanish life, the men of Charles III's reign gave considerable momentum to this branch of administration: in 1756 the office of Postmaster General was created, and in 1776 the Superintendency of Mails and Posts, where Floridablanca also gave evidence of his intelligence and capability. The Postal Ordinances worked out by Campomanes in 1776 and the General Postal Ordinance of 1794 drew up rules for the functioning of one of the most flexible and competent bodies in the central administration and established postage rates for letters, parcel post, printed matter, and newspapers.

Journalism, in fact, was beginning to assuage the curiosity of a growing number of readers, among whom must be numbered, of course, landowners, manufacturers, and businessmen. Thus the first newspapers either gave a great deal of space to news of an economic nature or were subtitled, eloquently, mouthpieces for agriculture, industry, and trade. This fact makes them precious sources of information about 18th-century economic life, for not only do they list the market price of products, but also give arrivals and departures of vessels in the seaports. The newspapers also issued weekly handbills (called *mercuriales*) and annual almanacs with statistical résumés, which have not been properly studied as yet. Some of the journalists who engaged in these economic campaigns, such as the Aragonese Nipho, deserve a place of honor in the 18th-century cultural picture.

MERCANTILE PRACTICE: DEVELOPMENT OF SOCIETIES AND STOCK COMPANIES. During the 18th century, the practical and juridical innovations which turned the 19th-century business world upside down did not yet exist. At least in Spain, people continued to rely on the experiences of the past in the matter of societies, freight rates, insurance, transfer of funds, exchange operations, etc. The country's financial and industrial media were too weak for the same evolution to take place as in France or England, where at the beginning of the century the experiments of Law or the South Seas Company boom had brought incorporated companies into being, together with stock-exchange operations, credit systems, and fiduciary mechanisms. In Spain, we repeat, if we rely on what modern sources of information tell us, mercantile practice progressed only slowly.

One fact is immediately evident: the different strata of mercantile sophistication. Just as the illiterate laborer coexisted in rural life with the Voltairean aristocrat, so did the shopkeeper who kept no accounts and the wholesale merchant who was obliged by the pragmatic of 1737 to keep four kinds of books: copy books, ledgers, invoices, and copies of letters. (After 1783, with the appearance of the journal, there were to be five obligatory ones.) And in the same fashion, there could coexist the *mota* company (a simple share in a marine venture characteristic of multiple small investments of a popular type) with the privileged joint-stock company. Between these two types was the partnership, mostly of a family type, which at this time became the most widespread in the country (especially in Catalonia and Biscay). A good part of the cotton industry was born under the sign of the partnership.

The history of the joint-stock company is not altogether clear. Closely linked to the idea of the success of the great English and Dutch companies, this type of firm obtained a foothold in Spain not from the bottom up, in response to a mercantile base which made it necessary, but from the top down, put in motion by an act of public power which gave it the necessary assets to fulfill a specific economic need. This process, copied from France, produced results in Spain which were opposite to those expected, for since the stockholders—most of them landowning aristocrats—were unwilling to risk their capital funds in mercantile investments showing a profit only after a long interval, they had to be guaranteed a satisfactory income through the concession of monopolies, exemptions, and privileges to the companies which were founded. Thus the joint-stock company did not increase risk, and with it the possibility of large profits, but led rather to a pernicious stagnation of certain industrial activities and even to their artificial preservation. The example of the Company of Zarza el Mayor gives a clear example of this. And so does the company formed by the Five Greater Guilds of Madrid. We shall refer to these in a later chapter.

Stock companies of a colonial type deserve special mention. Although they enjoyed a monopoly—that is, monopoly of an area reserved for a special economic activity—they were able to carry out their role and reap considerable public gain and private profit. Their capital was largely peripheral, coming from businessmen and shipowners. We should introduce a division in these companies, separating the private ones (such as the Companies of Caracas and Barcelona) from those which received State subsidies, like the Company of the Philippines. We shall also speak of these in the next chapter.

EVOLUTION OF THE ECONOMIC MENTALITY. The economic mentality of the 18th century manifested itself in Spain as a conflict between protectionism and economic liberalism. However, the debate between the partisans of the two positions was conducted quietly; for not in vain was it recognized that the country was underdeveloped, and that it depended on the European economic complex to take care of its own needs and especially those of the American colonies. This was why the government's attitude was influenced less by the economists (none of whom was of sufficient stature to impose a personal criterion) than by the contingent factors of commercial treaties or international wars.

When the century began, economic policy was still of a mercantilist type, not only in its preservation of the Hapsburg customs and monopoly structure but also in its admiration for Colbertism, which was reinforced by Philip V's French ministers. The chief exponent of this postmercantilism was Jerónimo de Uztáriz, a Navarrese, author of a private report, *The Theory and Practice of Commerce and Maritime Affairs* (*Teoría y práctica de comercio y marina,* 1724) which, after having been widely read and commented upon, was published in 1742. Like a good mercantilist, Uztáriz identified wealth with precious metals. His great design was to retain American metals for Spain. For this purpose he proposed a customs discrimination based principally on the payment of fees *ad valorem* and not by weight, as had been done since 1648. He thought it necessary to ban the export of industrial raw materials (wool and silk, soda ash and potash) and to reduce import and export duties on products of national interest (textile machinery, industrial raw materials, dyes, glass, hides, fabrics, paper, and soap, respectively). Further, strong encouragement should be given to the industrialization of Spain, protecting it even at the risk of damaging agricultural interests; for this purpose he proposed a radical reduction of taxes and levies on manufactured products, tax concessions to newly established industries, and imposition of maximum taxes on olive oil and agricultural products. Internal customs should be abolished, the monopoly of Cádiz maintained (though preventing at all costs contraband trade in America, through a policy of cheap prices), and the creation of privileged companies avoided.

During the reign of Ferdinand VI, Uztáriz's ideas clashed with those of economists formed in the English or French schools. From Ward to Jovellanos, the same theory was held. In his *Economic Project* (1779) the Irish economist stated that "freedom is the soul of trade, and monopoly its worst enemy," and that "neither prohibition nor price-fixing create abundance, but rather freedom in business dealings." These basic ideas led him to call for freedom of trade with America, the suppression of Cádiz's monopoly in favor of Catalans, Valencians, Galicians, *Montañeses,* and Basques, and an end to the fleet system. All the Encyclopedists were in agreement with these ideas. Capmany stated that gold and silver mines were not as useful as trade in the enrichment of the State, an idea opposed to that of doctrinaire mercantilism.

After 1795 Adam Smith's ideas on free trade and economic liberalism became widespread. The Spanish public could read of them in the English original and in two French translations (one by Roucher and the other anonymous). It was from this time that Jovellanos' liberal writings gained such fame; they were filled with resounding statements about the importance of trade and industry as the only supports of a State's power, and the decisive role of production in determining the true wealth of a country. All this can be summed up in one formula: "The political principle of first importance is that of leaving men in the greatest possible freedom, in whose wake trade, population, and wealth will flourish."

Closer to the outlook of the industrial bourgeoisie, the newspaper *El Diario de Barcelona* advised its readers in 1792, "Wealth should not be confused with its visible sign." Spain had come a long way since Uztáriz.

INTERNATIONAL TREATIES AND TRADE TARIFFS IN THE 18TH CENTURY. The Bourbons inherited a disastrous trade policy from the Hapsburgs. As we said before, Charles II had signed an unfavorable commercial treaty with England in 1667. This was renewed by the Treaty of Utrecht (1713), which also introduced the onerous clauses pertaining to permission ships and contracting of slaves. When he comments on this, Ward says he cannot understand how there can still be any economic activity in Spain. The *arbitrista* Aguirre wrote in his *Abuses of Royal Revenues* (*Abusos de las Rentas Reales,* 1759) that, thanks to such pacts, other nations treated Spain "like the Indies of Europe."

In 1748 and 1750 (Treaty of Aachen and the Carvajal-Keene agreement) the situation did not change much. Certainly England gave up, for a payment of 10,000 pounds, her slave contract and permission ship rights, but on the other hand she and France succeeded in maintaining the principle of evaluation of goods according to the tariffs of the preceding century. The result of this was that English products, whose price had doubled, paid the same duties as in 1667, even without counting the 25% reduction known as "tabla y pie de fardo," a concession made by the customs farmer Eminente. In short, it is estimated that England paid only one-third of the royal customs duties.

On their side, England as well as France maintained a policy of restrictions in regard to Spanish trade, England prohibiting Spanish ships from carrying produce and goods there, and France imposing heavy tariffs on the import of Spanish wool. All of this revealed the absence of commercial reciprocity. Aguirre requested equality of duties on foodstuffs and other goods, equality of admission of cargo in ships, and equality in mercantile dealings. But for the moment it was impossible to attain these elementary demands.

With Ferdinand VI's reign a number of battles were won, though slowly. The Marquis de la Ensenada made the king sign a royal cedula in 1745 establishing the principle of "intrinsic value" and not "appraisal" for evaluating merchandise in customs. Also, the protectionist tariffs of 1744 (for silk) and 1747 (for wool) were promulgated. But positive results were achieved only during the reign of Charles III. During this period seventy-four protectionist tariff lists were published (a larger number than in the reigns of all the other Bourbons), and periodic revision of the schedule was provided for, as well as imposition of a 15% tax on any new merchandise until the office of Superintendent of Customs should decree what duty was to be assessed. These measures culminated in the tariff schedules of 1778, prepared by Miguel Gálvez, one of the most intelligent men in the Enlightened government. Forming part of the ordinance for freedom of trade with America, these schedules were drawn up with the triple goal of preventing export of *simples* (raw materials, in modern language), and facilitating the entry and exit of manufactured goods. On the other hand, Charles III's tariff policy rested on the principle of winning the economic battle by basing it on the mass of mineral or agricultural products (Spaniards bought at twenty-two reales the same *fanega* of salt which foreigners bought for five). This was a new aspect of the sacrifice of individuals on the altar of the country's potentialities.

In spite of this criterion, the struggle for commercial and manufacturing freedom in Spain underwent many fluctuations. Let us examine the policy in regard to the two chief branches of export, silk and wool. In 1744 Ensenada established three storehouses for Levantine silk (Alicante, Cartagena, and Denia) and authorized only three seaports to export it (Valencia, Alicante, and Gandía): the ministry authorized the quotas to be exported. In 1761 Granada and Málaga were also included in the system. In 1778 the export of silk was banned in order to stimulate Spanish manufactures for the benefit of the American market, open at last to trade with all nations. However, the wars with England paralyzed this industrial activity and obliged Charles IV to revoke the ban.

The same thing happened with wool. The struggle between exporters and manufacturers, already traditional, was aggravated by the presence in the internal market of a powerful buyer: Catalonia. In 1746 the suppression of interior customs houses was confirmed in the wool trade, and "tornaguías," or permits, were instituted to prove that shipments were indeed intended for Barcelona. The principal ports qualified were Puerto de Santa María, Málaga, Cartagena, Alicante, and Valencia. This measure had repercussions on external wool trade, for in 1747 a protectionist tariff schedule was published. It seems that this schedule was in force for some time and that there was even a period of restriction in exports (1779–1789). But with the reign of Charles IV and its financial difficulties there was some relaxation. Hence numerous seaports and inland ports of entry received authorization to export wool.

Coinciding with the period of strong protectionism of Charles III's reign, a wave of contraband was unleashed on the frontiers. Muñoz Pérez has described its main geographic areas: the frontiers of the Exempted Provinces and Mediterranean Andalusia (from Algeciras to Málaga). Secondary places were the Portuguese border and the Canaries. The difficulty of controlling such open frontiers as Spain's explains the rival trends toward protectionism and toward smuggling which, beginning at this time, came to a peak in the 19th century.

STAGES OF PROTECTIONISM IN THE TEXTILE INDUSTRY. In addition to tariff policy, the Bourbons' protectionist ideas affected the textile industry, especially that of cotton. Even at the risk of repeating data already given when studying the development of this industry, we shall try to give a sketch that will sum up what is known about the matter today, and correct a good many errors which have appeared in print.

The first group of protectionist measures was handed down in 1717–1719. Among them are not only the royal cedulas of 1717 and 1718 prohibiting the sale of silks and other fabrics from China and Asia, but also two cedulas of 1719 banning the entry into Spain of ready-to-wear garments, and decreeing the use of national fabrics for army uniforms. This combination of measures tended to encourage production of woollens and linens in Spanish factories.

At the end of the third decade of the 18th century, new protectionist measures were decreed. Chief among these was undoubtedly that of 1728 renewing the royal cedulas of 1717 and 1718, which many authorities consider to have been the foundation stone of the Catalan calico industry. But we must also remember that two years previously, in 1726, a royal cedula had decreed that Spaniards could dress only in silks and woollens of national manufacture. It is through this legal text that we know that silk factories were located at the time in Valencia, Granada, Toledo, and Saragossa, and woollen factories in Segovia, Guadalajara, Valldemosa, Saragossa, Teruel, and Béjar.

There was no noticeable change until 1742. The protectionist attitude toward the textile industry can be seen very clearly in the royal cedulas of April 6 and August 30, 1734. But in 1742, on October 19 to be precise, the ban on importing cotton cloth was lifted, contrary to the text of the cedula of 1728. This measure was corrected a year later (December 16, 1743) at the insistence of the Barcelona manufacturers, on the grounds that it was causing damage to their industries. These had come into being under the shelter of the tariff, but were now strong enough to nullify a governmental decree prejudicial to them.

Ferdinand VI inherited this situation and left it unchanged. Indeed, in April, 1751, he renewed the 1728 prohibition in regard to cotton fabrics and printed linens coming from China, Asia, and the Levant, except for the simple printed cotton cloth of Malta and muslins, which were subjected to a surcharge of 35%. The monarch and his government now cooperated with the Catalan cotton manufacturers because they used American raw cotton.

When Charles III ascended the throne an unexpected shift occurred. In fact, the royal decree of May 15, 1760, authorized the importation of cotton goods, with a customs surcharge of 25%. This free trade measure aroused violent campaigns on the part of the cotton manufacturers, and through their influence on those of wool and silk, for they too suffered from the avalanche of inexpensive materials coming in through the Cantabrian ports and Andalusia. A report of the General Office of Revenues estimated that 25,000 yards of materials had been imported, with a total value of 50 million reales. The ruin of national industry was clear, especially in the cotton-goods branch. In 1768 the calico manufacturers had 78,000 pieces of unsold cloth on hand, 58,000 in their warehouses and 20,000 scattered throughout Spain. Some factories had closed and others had dismissed most of their workers. The realization that to maintain a free trade policy was to inflict serious damage not only on a group of bourgeois beneficiaries of protectionism, but on the nation itself, caused Charles III's government to return to a protectionist system through the royal cedulas of July 8, 1769, and January 19, 1770, prohibiting the importation of cotton goods. This legislation was incorporated into the Pragmatic of June 20, 1770, making textile protectionism permanent. It was incorporated as a fundamental policy of the State in the *Novísima Recopilación,* or new compilation of laws. This was a rude blow for the English businessmen established in Cádiz.

In spite of some limited and occasional changes in policy, such as that of 1789 regarding muslin, the Pragmatic of 1770 was responsible for the development of the textile industry up to the War of Independence. The fact that it benefited the cotton industry most of all, while it did not mean a great deal to the woollen and silk industries, is an example of one postulate of economic history: the unprotectable cannot be protected.

PRIVILEGED COMPANIES AND AMERICAN TRADE. In Spain as in the rest of the Western world in imitation of Holland and England, the 18th century was the period of privileged companies. An expression of State mercantilism and the bourgeois monopolistic ideal, they arose in Spain as an inevitable result of meager concentration of capital and a legitimate desire to encourage the economic development of the colonial empire. However, it is not possible to sketch a joint history of these companies, for we must distinguish the purely mercantile society more or less protected by the State from the State foundation with vague financial aims. There is a whole gamut of intermediary types. The factor holding them all together was American trade.

The reign of Philip V was the golden age for the foundation of privileged companies. The constant desire to imitate French mercantilism and offset the irresistible rise of English trade encouraged the State's activities in this field. Uztáriz says that as early as 1714, the year after the Peace of Utrecht, Philip V had authorized formation of the *Company of Honduras,* giving it control of Central American trade and the monopoly of traffic in mahogany and logwood. The date appears to be much too early. True privileged trade companies did not exist in Spain until about 1730: in 1728 the Company of Caracas was founded, that of the Philippines in 1733, and that of Galicia in 1734. These last two never emerged from an embryonic stage. The *Philippines Company,* carefully planned by Patiño, was frustrated by opposing interests in Manila. In the organization plan a capital of 4 million escudos was envisaged, plus a tax-free warehouse in Cádiz, the privilege of trading with Africa, India, and the Philippines for twenty years, authorization to ship national and foreign products, to carry up to 500,000 reales in silver (this was the heart of the matter), and to import spices, miscellaneous goods, and fifty tons of silk cloth for Europe and America. The *Company of Galicia* was intended for trade in Campeche wood.

On the other hand, the *Caracas Trading Company* achieved sensational success, to the point that it can be considered as the starting point of modern Venezuela. It was founded in 1728 by a group of Basque businessmen, for the purpose of encouraging the cultivation of cocoa in that captaincy-general. Its headquarters was San Sebastián and its capital 2,250,000 reales (300 shares of 7,500 reales each, of which 200 were held by the king). Its plan was to send two naval and merchant vessels annually to supply Cumaná, Margarita, and Trinidad and to guard the coasts between the mouth of the Orinoco and the river Hacha to pursue smugglers. These ships were to sail from Pasajes and San Sebastián, paying the same duties as those of Cádiz and stopping there on the homeward journey for registry; but merchandise was to be unloaded in their home port. Outward bound, they carried all sorts of manufactured goods; on the return trip, cocoa, gold, silver, tobacco, and hides. In a very few years the company earned enormous profits, so that in 1734 it received unlimited authorization to increase the number of its ships. According to Larruga, it gave Philip V an annual grant of 100,000 pesos and owned thirteen ships. Its holdings in Venezuela were enormous. After 1742 it exercised a trade monopoly in Caracas, and ten years later it annexed that of Maracaibo. Thanks to a rigid system it succeeded in greatly increasing cocoa production, raising it from 643,000 *fanegas* (1700–1730) to 1,450,000 (1730–1748). But the expansion of its economic and political power aroused opposition from the Creole proprietors. After 1750 its privileges were gradually cut down (revolt of Juan Francisco de León); it suffered a harsh blow in 1778 with Charles III's "free trade" regulation, and by the end of the century it was almost extinct.

The Caracas Company's success stimulated the formation of similar societies. Some never emerged from the planning stage, like the one proposed by the Merchants' Committee of Bilbao in 1736 (and again in 1739 and 1745) for trade with Buenos Aires, Tucumán, and Paraguay. The plan was magnificent, but it interested neither the businessmen of Lima nor those of Cádiz, so it died in the ministries. Others had considerable success. Outstanding among them was the *Royal Trading Company of Havana,* which exercised a monopoly of Cuban trade from 1740 to 1765, importing cloth, canvas, flour, and particularly slaves, and selling sugar and tobacco. It carried on excellent business, in which the Crown had a share: its largest profits came from contraband.

An important group was that of companies whose purpose was

to encourage a specific industrial activity in Spain with a view to possible marketing of its products in America. In 1746 the *Company of Zarza la Mayor* was founded, with a capital of 2 million reales, for the purpose of manufacturing woollen and silk fabrics in Extremadura, Valencia, and Toledo for export to Portugal; it was granted a 75% reduction in customs duties. Shortly after this the *Companies of Granada and Seville* were established (1747). Both were founded for the purpose of manufacturing silk cloth and exporting it to the Indies, with a similar customs reduction. The Granada company very soon got into difficulties and merged with that of Zarza la Mayor in the so-called *Company of Extremadura,* which shortly absorbed the *Trading and Manufacturing Company of Toledo* founded in 1748. At the time of the merger the society's capital was 5 million reales. In 1754 the company had lost so much money that an inevitable split took place. The companies were generally considered to be prejudicial to the public interest, and they did not survive the Marquis de la Ensenada's famous decree (May 18, 1756) declaring an end to the favors and privileges granted to them and to private persons, in detriment to the common good. This decree marks an important moment in the government's commercial orientation. The era of the great privileged companies ended, leaving open the way to free trade with America.

However, one new experiment did take place: the *Royal Trading Company of Barcelona,* approved in 1755 (its charter was authorized in 1756), which for twenty years carried out profitable dealings in the Antilles and Central America, for it was granted the trade monopoly with the islands of Santo Domingo, Puerto Rico, and Margarita, plus ten registry ships for Honduras and freight rights in the port of Havana. It had a capital of 1 million pesos and realized profits—distributed—of 30%, and accomplished the revaluation of the whole Antilles area. This was the opening through which, after 1778, the influence of Catalan trade and products entered America.

THE GENERAL TRADING COMPANY AND ITS UNDERTAKINGS IN COLONIAL TRADE. The most powerful trading company of the 18th century in Spain was the one founded by the Five Greater Guilds of Madrid. We have already mentioned the origin of these corporations, which received legal confirmation as associated bodies by means of the ordinances of 1731 and 1741. The monopoly they exercised over the capital's chief mercantile activities permitted the Five Guilds to achieve considerable financial power, which they employed to open new and profitable horizons, including that of aspiring to control American trade. This venture began in 1734 when the Five Guilds formed themselves into a company at the time they were granted the lease for collecting royal revenues (a year before, they had made a gift to the Crown of 150,000 doubloons). In 1748 the members of the woollen-merchants' guild, in an attempt to extend their influence, formed a private company to encourage production of woollens in Spain. It was a new step. Arising out of both these events, and with the silk merchants taking the initiative, the first company of the Five Guilds arose (December 4, 1752), with a share capital of 1 million reales and the objective of trading freely with Europe and America. The new society immediately contacted the Uztáriz brothers, rich businessmen in Cádiz, and simultaneously formed another company with them, with a capital of 15 million reales. Thus, after January 1, 1753, the Five Guilds had a foothold in Cádiz, the door to American trade. The company formed with the Uztáriz brothers, established for six years, was extended for six more. But after 1761 the Five Guilds felt they were capable of carrying on by themselves. Thus, on December 6, 1763, they founded the *General and Trading Company of the Five Greater Guilds of Madrid,* with a capital of 15 million reales, two branches (Cádiz and Valencia), and various agencies. The profits were fabulous, to the point that while the initial paid-in capital was 5 million, the remaining 10 million reales were paid in in 1768 out of realized earnings. Spicers and mercers were those most involved in the company's affairs, and more than once attempted to organize it by individuals and not by guilds, something which the Crown never permitted. In 1777, says Larruga, the 375 guild members, of whom 90 were spice merchants and 40 wool merchants, represented a capital of 210 million reales.

Cabarrús' grandiose plans in connection with the issue of royal promissory notes and the foundation of the Bank of San Carlos, to which we shall refer later (pp. 596–597), were aimed, according to Hamilton, at breaking the financial supremacy of the Five Guilds as great tax-farmers and moneylenders to the Crown. In the mercantile aspect his policy centered on the reform of December 20, 1785, by means of which the State, conceding to the General Trading Company a capital increase of up to 30 million reales and intervention in various royal factories (Ezcaray and Talavera), obliged it to make its profits public. Yet at that time the company was experiencing its last period of splendor, with silk factories in Talavera, Valencia, and Murcia, or woollens in Ezcaray and Cuenca, hats in San Fernando, and cotton prints in Barcelona; with headquarters in Barcelona and Cádiz and agencies in London, Paris, Hamburg, Mexico City, Veracruz, Guatemala, Arequipa, Lima, and Manila.

Direct trade with the Philippines, in which the company had engaged since 1777 with large profits, gave rise to the foundation of the *Philippines Company*. In view of the decline of the Caracas and Havana Companies and the anachronistic tendencies of many of the Five Guilds' operations, Cabarrús obtained permission from Charles III to found the new firm, with a capital of 160 million reales and the privilege of exclusive trade with the Philippines. Shares were bought by the king (60 million), the Bank of San Carlos (21 million), and other corporations, among them the General Trading Company (13 million). As in the plan of 1753, the basis of trade was export of Mexican silver to China and sale of Oriental muslins in America. The venture was not badly planned, but its downfall was due to the wars of the Napoleonic era as well as to the prodigality with which the State had determined the company's fixed expenses.

As for the General Company, the support given it by the State in 1785 turned out to have disastrous results during the reign of Charles IV, the revolutionary wars, and inflation. The constant demand for funds (for public works, military needs, scientific advances, popular celebrations, etc.) broke down the institution's solid prestige. In an official report it was recognized that supplying the army had caused the company to lose 140 million reales; 50 million had been spent to aid work on the canal of Aragon; 115 million on the government's effort to hold down the cost of provisions for Madrid, "to preserve an illusory tranquillity, bought at the expense of other peoples' pockets." Up to 1808 the company had borrowed 397 million reales, which, combined with a heavy load of interest, made its normal functioning impossible. Napoleon's army delivered the death blow by confiscating its assets and burning its factories.

FREEDOM OF TRADE WITH AMERICA: FACTORS AND STAGES; LAWS OF 1765 AND 1778. From the moment that the Bourbon dynasty, recently installed in Spain, had had to concede the permission ship to England, the problem of trade relations between Spain and her colonies became linked with that of freedom of trade. Nevertheless, when the House of Trade moved from Seville to Cádiz in 1717, the monopoly system was still being proclaimed.

There were innovators, and precedents as well, and even some official acts, such as in the case of the Canaries. For it was, in fact, in 1718 that those islands received a permit to export 1,000 tons annually to seven American ports: Havana, Campeche, Caracas, Trinidad, Cumaná, Puerto Rico, and Santo Domingo. In April, 1720, Philip V's government proposed to Spanish businessmen a "Project for Registry and Dispatch Ships," whose immediate actions found an echo in the far-off La Plata estuary. In December, 1721, imports up to a value of 700,000 pesos were authorized in the port of Buenos Aires. The colonial monopoly was beginning to break up, in this case at one of its poles: Lima.

The registry system continued to make progress, although very slowly. In 1733, in the famous *Secret Information from America* (*Noticias secretas de América*), a report presented to the Marquis de la Ensenada by two naval officers, Antonio de Ulloa and Jorge Juan, it was stated that the only way of preventing illicit trade was to keep American markets supplied with inexpensive goods, through suppression of monopolies and the fleet system. Of course the menacing problem of Asian silks still existed, for they were of such good quality and so cheap that they made competition impossible. They easily gave profits of a hundred to one.

This report eventually had its effect. There was a ten-year period of vacillation (in 1740 the fleet and galleon system was suppressed; in 1754 it was reestablished for New Spain), proving the reluctance of the organizations profiting from the monopoly to give in on any point. However, after an unsuccessful attempt to qualify certain ports for American trade (1748), it was decided to make the single ship system general (same year). In 1754 an ordinance was proclaimed opening the Pacific Ocean to Spanish ships sailing through the Strait of Magellan or around Cape Horn.

At about that time the monopoly of Cádiz was breaking up, owing to the astounding financial and colonial success of the Company of Caracas. Freedom of trade, the only formality being registry in Cádiz, had given new life to the colony. It represented the triumph of cocoa, shortly followed by brandy and sugar. In August, 1756, free export of Spanish wines and brandies was decreed, with exemption from all duties if they were carried in vessels flying the Spanish flag. A large part of this trade went to America, which responded with the fabulous expansion of the Cuban sugar industry. Sugar gave such obvious flexibility to the fossilized Hapsburg monopoly system that it simply could not survive. In 1765 the way was opened for a widespread trial of commercial freedom. In fact, the Royal Decree of October 16, 1765, put an end to the one-port policy and authorized dispatch of ships from nine Spanish ports (Santander, Gijón, Corunna, Seville, Cádiz, Málaga, Cartagena, Alicante, and Barcelona) and five American islands (Cuba, Santo Domingo, Puerto Rico, Margarita, and Trinidad). When we realize that this was the Antillean area where the Company of Barcelona had a monopoly, it is perfectly clear that this order had been obtained by the Catalan sugar traders. In the texts of the period we read, "authorization to the Catalans for *trade in the Windward Islands*." A few years later this trade was extended to Louisiana (1768), Campeche and Yucatán (1770) and Santa Marta (Colombia, 1776) in America, and also to the Canaries (1772).

The impetus of Catalan trade, allied to the cotton industry, made itself felt in governmental circles in Madrid. The Royal Decree of July 5, 1772, gave complete freedom of entry in any Spanish port to any Spanish ship loaded with cotton fiber. Several years later (February 2, 1778), free shipping to the viceroyalties of Peru, Chile, and Buenos Aires was authorized. This measure has been overshadowed by the Pragmatic of October 12, 1778, laying down regulations and establishing customs schedules for *Free Trade of Spain and the Indies,* which is its corollary. These regulations qualified thirteen Spanish ports, the ones mentioned above plus Almería, Los Alfaques, Palma de Mallorca, and Santa Cruz de Tenerife; and twenty-two in the colonies—nine major ports: Havana, Cartagena, Buenos Aires, Montevideo, Valparaíso, Concepción, Arica, Callao, and Guayaquil; and thirteen minor ones: Puerto Rico, Santo Domingo, Montecristo (Hispaniola), Santiago de Cuba, Trinidad, Margarita, Campeche, Santo Tomás de Castilla, and Omoa (the latter two in Guatemala), Santa Marta, Río de la

Hacha, Portobello, and Chagres. To encourage traffic between Spain and America, duties were lowered in the sugar trade, on cloth, and on other less important national manufactures.

It is obvious that only the Basque Provinces in Spain, and Venezuela and New Spain in America, were for the time being excluded from the benefits of free trade. But its advantages were so evident from the outset that the Crown could not refuse to qualify San Sebastián (1788) nor to include Mexico and Venezuela in 1789.

DEVELOPMENT OF SPANISH-AMERICAN TRADE ACTIVITY AT THE END OF THE 18TH CENTURY. It has been stated again and again that as a result of the freedom of trade granted in 1778, volume of traffic between the two shores of the Atlantic increased enormously and rapidly. We cannot measure it scientifically, however, for we lack adequate statistical data; and they in turn would be affected by the rising trend of the business cycle and the effects of the end of the war with England, which had lasted from 1779 to 1783, permitting the release of considerable quantities of merchandise in 1783–1795.

However, the pulse of Spanish-American trade relations during these latter years shows a strength and velocity unknown before. All writers, both contemporary and modern, agree on this point. Abbot Pradt stated in 1816 that the volume of business between America and Spain had totaled 37 million francs in 1778 and 277 million in 1788. The figures given by Canga Argüelles are less optimistic, for they indicate only half of the increase noted by Pradt: four times instead of eight (75 million reales of imports into America in 1778 and 300 million in 1788), but this can be explained by the factor of illicit trade. In any case, we feel that when full statistical series are available they will merely confirm the strength of the thrust given the economy by the law of 1778.

Territorially, some regions benefited more than others from this measure. In Spain, for example, Catalonia was extraordinarily favored, since she controlled two important elements of American trade: printed cottons and sugar, to which she very soon added shipping, under the clause in the Regulation which obliged American trade to sail under the Spanish flag. But not even Cádiz, which had felt herself so gravely threatened by the end of the monopoly—the House of Trade was abolished in 1790—could complain, for until 1796 her port was the richest and busiest in Spain. As for the colonies, all had the same feeling of enrichment, but the viceroyalty of La Plata, the captaincy-general of Chile, and the island of Cuba stood out especially. In Buenos Aires the increase was 2 million pesos in the single period 1792–1796, to a total of 7,200,000.

Unfortunately, the war between England and Spain which broke out in 1796 as the result of Charles IV's alliance with the French Republic interrupted this brilliant development. For seven years, until after the Peace of Amiens in 1802, Spanish shipping, confined in the Mediterranean, disappeared from the Atlantic. They were years of great economic and financial upheavals. We are told that Cádiz's trade suffered losses of 2,700,000,000 reales. Those of Barcelona, while not so heavy, were nonetheless large, and many workers lost their jobs. American ports, on the other hand, were not closed, for the Crown decreed on December 18, 1797, that they would be allowed to trade—while the war lasted—with neutral countries, either from national or foreign ports, on condition that they did not carry prohibited goods (that is, Negroes, currency, and produce) and that they necessarily returned to Spain. These regulations were not observed, and both licit and illicit trade developed greatly.

Pierre Chaunu says that the decree of 1797 concerning permission to trade with neutral ships was the prelude to the Spanish-American colonies' independence. And this was not only because it implied a declaration of Spain's obvious incapacity to maintain the vital ocean link, but also because it permitted the entrance upon the scene of shipping and trade from the United States in the southern part of the continent. Twenty-six ships from Boston visited Chilean ports from 1788 to 1796; 226 from 1797 to 1809. Veracruz, Callao, Havana, Buenos Aires, La Guaira: no port was overlooked by the enterprising Yankee traders. In 1795 the volume of United States exports to Spanish America was $1,389,219; imports were $1,739,138. Six years later the figures had multiplied by six and seven respectively: $8,437,659 and $12,799,888. Truly, once the colonial pact had been broken, the trade structure of the Spanish-American world changed completely.

39 · Money and Finance

CURRENCY AND ECONOMIC RECOVERY. One of the fundamental causes of the collapse of Spanish economic life during the Hapsburg period had been monetary disorder, the alternating inflations and deflations which culminated in the chaos of the first years of Charles II's reign. The new dynasty had to start from this position, and go against the tide to organize a stable monetary system. This was the task to which the ministers of Philip V, Ferdinand VI, and Charles III were dedicated. The main lines of their policies were to unify currency in the entire Spanish territory, to create flexible monetary units, and to fight against export of coined metal.

The hardest part of this plan was to get through its early stages, for to the confusion arising from the previous period was added, during the initial years of Philip V's reign, the disorder brought about by the War of Succession (military expenses, invasion of foreign troops, etc.). The greatest evil was not the minting of debased currency in the dependent territories of the Archduke Charles of Austria, but the permission given to introduce French money (louises and crowns), recognized as legal tender. Philip V's government, however, instead of allowing itself to be led by circumstances, did its best to overcome them. Thus, as soon as military events permitted, it gradually took monetary policy in hand: 1709, devaluation of the French reales minted in Bayonne and the end of importation of foreign coins; 1711, a ban on circulation of the coins minted by Archduke Charles; 1707–1715, progressive extension of Castilian coinage to the territories of the Crown of Aragon.

Such measures improved the situation somewhat. However, at that time a solution for the silver problem had not been found. In fact, the mintings of 1716–1717 in Segovia, Seville, Cuenca, and Madrid placed the so-called *real provincial* on the market, representing a devaluation of about 1.50% compared with the old real, or *real nacional*. This dual standard produced an unhealthy state of confusion for a whole century. In regard to vellon, on the other hand, the government's efforts to avoid the multiplicity and falsity of many of the mintings had some success. On September 24, 1718, a royal cedula decreed the minting of pure copper coins in 1-, 2-, and 4-maravedí denominations, with an intrinsic value equal to that of legal coinage, and very difficult to imitate; these would be legal tender in Catalonia, Aragon, and Valencia. This order marked the opening of the period of monetary uniformity, which was not fully achieved until the middle of the 19th century. The royal cedula of January 26, 1718, completed the cycle of monetary reform by reorganizing the mint and regulating the functions of its superintendents. Hamilton says that by 1725 Spain had recovered the monetary stability she had lost a century earlier.

In spite of the disturbances produced by these measures, such as the disappearance of fractional coins in Catalonia because of the fact that the Catalan *real de ardite* was worth more than the Castilian *real,* the policy of stabilization prevailed for fifty years, interrupted only by inevitable readjustments of the bimetallic ratio. By 1742 Mexican silver production was giving a noticeable boost to that metal, at the same time as it conferred an international prestige on Spanish coinage—it was, in fact, accepted from London to Canton, from St. Petersburg to Buenos Aires—which made it very much sought after in other countries. Hence the constant flight of coined silver, made inevitable by the government's inability to resolve the dual system of *pesos* and *reales* and reduce the mass of vellon in circulation. Nevertheless, some progress was made with the royal cedula of 1726, which raised the value of gold coinage (the *escudo* rose from 16 to 18 *reales provinciales*) and American silver (the *real de a ocho,* or *peso,* from 9.5 to 10 *reales provinciales*). This succeeded in fixing the bimetallic ratio at 1:16, favorable to silver; it was done by taking the international market, deeply influenced by the cascade of Brazilian gold, into account. Thus, within a few years silver disappeared from the Spanish market, later returning to the country in search of cheap gold in the form of Portuguese gold coins. To counteract this phenomenon, which was hindering the country's commercial development, Philip V had recourse to a thorough monetary reform, characterized by a rise in the price of silver and a reduction in that of vellon.

In the table below we can observe the main features of the Pragmatic of May 16, 1737.

Silver coins	Value in *reales de vellón*	Value in maravedís	
		Old	In 1737
Peso, escudo grueso, or real de a ocho	20	—	—
Half-peso or *escudo*	10	—	—
Real de a dos (struck in Spanish America)	5	—	—
Real	2.5	—	—
Real de a dos, provincial (peseta)	4	—	—
Real (struck in Spanish America)	1	80	85
Real provincial	1	64	68

The *real de a dos* in the provincial silver coinage began to be called *peseta,* almost certainly influenced by the name given it in Catalonia, although not all philologists admit this etymology. Corominas believes, in fact, that the word "peseta" is inseparable from "peso," and that only the suffix "-eta" is a Catalanism. Moll, on the other hand, reminds us that silver "pecetes" existed in Catalonia as early as the beginning of the 15th century.

As a corollary to this measure Philip V authorized the minting of 300,000 pesos of pure copper, in coins of 2 (one-eighth) and 4 (one-fourth) maravedís (1739–1741). The excess of vellon put on the market, especially in Castile, which could not absorb it, was on the point of producing one of those inflationary outbursts so typical of 17th-century monetary history in Castile. However, experts became aware of the danger and it was prevented in time. Once monetary normality was established, Ferdinand VI ordered another minting of copper coins in 1747 (20,000 pesos). A rising economic trend, already under way, necessitated putting this mass of currency into circulation.

INFLATION DURING CHARLES III's REIGN. After the middle of the 18th century, the abundance of Mexican silver in Spain produced an inflationary process very similar to that of the 16th. But the currency held firm, thanks to the interplay of commercial or illicit withdrawal of silver and an acceleration in the country's economic rhythm. There were even times when the situation came close to the opposite phenomenon, deflation. But when, at the end of the century, a dizzying rise in prices coincided with a succession of wars arising from the French Revolution, inflation broke the barrier of metal currency and spread into the area of paper money.

Charles III's reign represented the watershed of the two tendencies of monetary evolution during this period—stability and inflation. The crucial date is 1772. During the course of that year a series of pragmatics was issued (the chief one on May 29) on gold, silver, and vellon coinage. Essentially the tendency was toward absolute uniformity, taking previous types out of circulation and ordering the minting of new coins, with exterior details changed (figure, edges, etc.). Neither fineness nor weight was to be altered. However, a confidential Royal Order to the mint decreed the contrary: gold content was reduced from 22 to 21 carats 2.5 grains, and that of national silver from 11 dineros to 10 dineros 20 grains. As Sardá says, it was a surreptitious currency devaluation. The declared objective was to keep in circulation a coinage of less metallic content, thus preventing its exportation; in fact, fiscal objectives (seigniorage) figured in it. The same explanation must be given to the group of pragmatics of 1786 intended to prevent the export of gold coins to England. There was also a confidential Order among these, reducing gold content to 21 carats and raising the seigniorage tax. This surreptitious curtailment was a secret devaluation. There was never open devaluation, which would have attracted gold and silver to the mints and stimulated the Empire's total economy with cheaper money.

The inflationary process had as an additional objective the stabilization of the bimetallic ratio, which fluctuated in times of great affluence of precious metals into the market (and also in times of their flight in quantity toward other countries). Therefore it was necessary to readjust the value of gold (1779), giving the doubloon the value of 16 pesos (before, it had been 15 pesos 10 maravedís). In this way the ratio of 1:16 was established. By the laws of 1786, the ratio varied to the detriment of silver: 1:16.5.

As for vellon coinage, it was overproduced after 1772; but the risk of inflation was overcome by population increase and the development of economic life. The case of provincial coinage was more damaging; it was exported to America to acquire silver minted there. The entry of these mintings into the market produced commercial disturbances and fiscal fraud.

Charles IV's reign did not present any changes in the picture we have just described. The weight of inflation, as we shall soon see, fell on paper money. But before we continue, we shall present a table of the actual coins which circulated in Spain about 1808.

	Castilian coins	Catalan-Valencian coins
GOLD		
8 escudos	320 reales vellón	
4 escudos	160 reales vellón	Onça
2 escudos	80 reales vellón	Mitja onça
1 escudo	40 reales vellón	Dobleta
½ escudo	20 reales vellón	Doblonet
SILVER		
1 peso	20 reales	Duro
½ peso	10 reales	Mig duro
1 peseta	4 reales	Pesseta
½ peseta	2 reales	Ral
½ real	1 real vellón	Quinzet
COPPER		
8 maravedís	—	Diner
4 maravedís	1 cuarto (¼)	Dos diners
2 maravedís	1 ochavo (⅛)	Xavo

INFLATIONARY PRESSURE OF PAPER MONEY: ROYAL PROMISSORY NOTES. The Crown's financial necessities, which became apparent during the war declared by Charles III on England in 1779 in support of England's American colonies and in alliance with France, led Floridablanca's government to take a transcendental step in the history of Spanish currency: the creation of paper money. In fact, accepting the plans of a Franco-Spanish-Dutch banking syndicate directed by Francisco Cabarrús, Charles III decreed (royal cedula of September 20, 1780) the emission of royal promissory notes totaling 9,900,000 pesos (the remaining 100,000 were the share retained by subscribers to the operation).

According to the terms of this decree, Charles III's government assigned a dual role to these paper notes. On the one hand they were income bonds, amortizable in twenty years and yielding 4% annual interest. On the other, they were credit media, which could be transferred by endorsement and used to pay taxes and levies. Further, they could be used in commerce as "effective money";

however, we cannot speak of true fiduciary money in connection with them, for salaries and pensions could not be paid with them, and workmen, artisans, and shopkeepers were not obliged to accept them. Another notable peculiarity: to avoid the danger of their putting gold and silver out of circulation, the notes were issued with a nominal value of 600 pesos and notes of lesser denomination were not legal tender.

The requirements of the war, centered on a campaign to take Gibraltar, brought about new issues of these royal notes: 5,300,000 pesos during 1781 and 14,799,900 in 1782. This produced a rapid depreciation of paper money, which eventually sold at a discount of 25%. But when peace was signed in 1783, the firm policy of payment of interest and renewal and amortization of the notes produced a noticeable readjustment, to the point that in 1784 they were quoted at a premium of 2.5% over metallic money. During the years that followed they never dropped below par. This success made it possible for the State to apply the royal note system to the financing both of public works and those of commercial interest: 6,600,000 pesos (1785 and 1788) for the Canal of Aragon and Tauste; 3,900,000 (1790) for the Philippines Company. Altogether, during Charles III's reign 540,900,000 pesos in royal notes were issued, a sum which the market was easily able to absorb.

The war against the French Revolution changed this picture. Although patriotism or fear of disorder paid for military expenses through donations and subscriptions of all kinds during the first year of hostilities, after 1794 the State had to resort to the easy remedy of inflation by means of royal notes. In a few years a considerable amount of paper money was put into circulation, with the inevitable result of depreciation. Here are some pertinent figures:

Issues	Amount	Quotation (Per cent discount)
1794 (January)	16,000,000 pesos	
1794 (August)	18,000,000 pesos	From ¼ to 9
1795	80,000,000 pesos	From 9 to 14
1799	53,100,000 pesos	From 29 to 47

In 1799, when royal notes were completely discredited, the government decreed their obligatory circulation, wiping out the limita-

tions of the 1780 decree and stipulating that the discount would be
6% of their nominal value. This measure was unwise and soon had
to be corrected by giving guarantees to commerce that it would not
have to accept notes and setting up a system for redeeming them;
to do this the State resorted to money from various sources, even
from the Church. But all promises, even the one drawn up in 1800
stating that the government considered as sacred the debt resulting
from its seven note issues, did not suffice to improve the situation.
Holders of notes, in view of the political, military, and financial
failure of Godoy's government, got rid of them at large discounts,
up to 75%. In fact, their average value in 1808 varied between 51
and 66%. This was the end of the first Spanish experience with
paper money, leaving a good deal of misery and considerable ruin
in its wake, especially in the bourgeois and worker classes. The
absolutist State's credit collapse preceded the collapse of its political
structure in 1808.

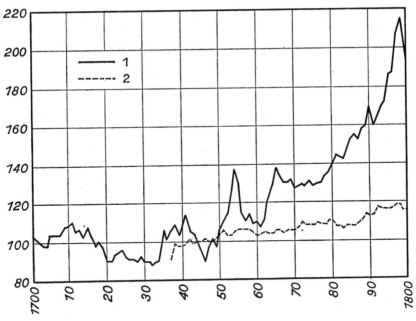

PRICES AND WAGES IN CASTILE (*after* HAMILTON).—*Key:* 1, prices; 2 wages.
Base for prices, 100 = mean for 1726–1750; for wages, 100 = mean for 1737–
1750.

PRICE AND WAGE EVOLUTION IN CASTILE: STABILITY AND FINAL
INCREASE. The history of 18th-century prices and wages in Castile
conforms, along general lines, to the same pattern we have just observed in the evolution of currency: a long preliminary period of
stability, followed by one of rapid and continuous rise. The analysis
of this interesting process is as follows:

The first two decades of the 18th century belong to a stage of deflation, with one minimum in 1705–1706 and another in 1720–
1721, separated by a crest whose maximum occurs in 1711. The
corresponding index numbers ($100 =$ the 1726–1750 mean) are
99-111-90. After 1726 and until 1731 there is a ten-year period of
little change, with the lowest indexes of the century (90-93-95-93-
92-94-92). Then there is a movement of recovery which shows
sudden strength in 1735 (index 106; 1734, 93). This was the turning point in the business cycle.

After 1735 the ascending portion of the long secular trend
begins to develop; its peak comes about the year 1808. In the portion falling within the 18th century we can distinguish two well-
defined phases, separated by the year 1775. In the first phase, prices
rise in four sharp and well-differentiated cycles; in the second, the
increment is almost constant, without any meaningful descents.
Here is the process in figures:

Cycles	Years	Type	Indexes (maxima and minima)
1. Ten-year	1736–1745	1st upward thrust	$101 < 114 > 96$
2. Intermediate	1746–1749	depression plateau	$90 < 101 > 97$
3. Ten-year	1749–1761	2nd definite upward thrust	$97 < 137 > 107$
4. Ten-year	1761–1771	upward continuation	$107 < 137 > 127$
5. Five-year	1771–1775	depression plateau	$128 < 131 > 128$

1775. A situation of high prices becomes established. Prices
now rise without interruption. The strongest upward thrusts take
place in 1785 (indexes $148 < 153$), 1790 ($160 < 169$), and
1795 ($173 > 186$). There is a sensational boom in 1795–1800
($186 < 187 < 206 < 224 > 204 > 193$). The previous minimum occurs in 1791 ($169 > 160 < 164$).

Study of the five-year index numbers of wheat prices in Castile,

Andalusia, and Valencia, as well as analysis of the curve of cereal prices in Majorca, confirms the general tendency toward high prices which we have just described. In this area also, the period of depression stability ends during the five-year period 1731–1735, and then assumes a sharp rising tendency following the slight dip of 1746–1750. The culmination of the rising trend is to be found in the last ten years of the century, after the strong upward movements of 1766–1770 and 1781–1785. However, because of the system of price ceilings and the war at the end of the century, cereal indexes do not correspond exactly to general evolution.

As for wages, the tendency is also an ascending one, though they still lag far behind prices. This is why the turning point in 1775 does not appear so clearly in the area of wages. Workers and artisans slowly improved their earnings, so that indexes rise from 96 in 1737 (base = mean of 1737–1750) to 100 in 1745, 106 in 1755, 105 in 1765, 108 in 1785, 116 in 1795. By studying these figures and comparing them with prices, Hamilton—whom we have been following in these paragraphs—was able to show that real wages fell after the moment when the price rise began. He says that the reduction must have been about 40% in New Castile and 30% in Valencia. Here are some figures:

| Period | Real Wages | |
	Valencia	Madrid
1741–1745	100.0	96.1
1771–1775	77.2	84.4
1786–1790	71.7	69.5
1796–1800	—	59.0

DISCREPANCY IN THE EVOLUTION OF WAGES IN CATALONIA: ITS SIGNIFICANCE. The general features of price and wage movements which we have just sketched do not correspond to the particular characteristics these assumed in Catalonia. Such is Pierre Vilar's conclusion after a systematic study of wages in Barcelona throughout the 18th century (as for prices, an analysis of industrial prices is yet to be made). This fact is of supreme importance because it reveals not only a difference in the rhythm of economic events but a total change of structure, and further, the transference of economic supremacy from the center of the Peninsula to its periphery.

Along general lines, the phenomenon is parallel: after a long stage of stability in wages, an upward movement takes place both in Madrid and Barcelona. But while in the capital of Spain this process does not show up in basic wages until 1781, in the Catalonian capital the sharp rise had taken place twenty years previously, in 1761. The spread of variation is also different. Here are some of Vilar's figures:

	1738–1742	1794–1798	Difference
Day laborers (Madrid	100.0	121.2	+21
and Barcelona)	100.0	210.0	+110
Masons (Madrid	243.6	317.7	+34
and Barcelona)	157.1	321.5	+104
Masters (Madrid	262.0	299.9	+14
and Barcelona)	200.0	390.0	+95

This author eliminates all monetary or fortuitous influence (political, or caused by war) on this process. He points out as decisive the change in the trade cycle, which Barcelona turned to advantage in the double fields of commerce and industrial progress; by the end of the century this resulted in a manpower shortage, translated into a dizzying rise in wages. After 1775, that is, at the very moment the continuous price rise begins, the wage curve of Barcelona is higher than that of Madrid (see graph on p. 601). After that moment the transfer of economic power from the country's center to its periphery became a fact. Its consequences will be seen when we discuss the evolution of the business cycle.

THE STATE AND FINANCIAL ORGANIZATION: MINISTRY OF FINANCE. During the 18th century there was a considerable effort to simplify the State's treasury organization. But, as in other fields of activity of the governments of the Enlightenment, the energies put into the task were not always translated into tangible realities, to the point that at the end of the period modern uniformist practices were superimposed on old traditionalist ones, creating the confusion so characteristic of Charles IV's reign.

Philip V had inherited a federal financial structure from the Hapsburgs. The monarch administered Castile's resources through a Council of the Treasury (*Consejo de Hacienda*), founded in 1593 as an outgrowth of the accounting division created by Ferdinand and Isabella. Besides, there was a Deputation of the Kingdom (*Diputación del Reino*), an organization created in 1515 to administer *servicio* and *alcabala* taxes, and the *Comisión de Millones,* a commission which since 1601 had administered the post of the same name. Outside Castile (but still within the Crown of Castile itself, as in the case of Navarre, the Basque Provinces, and Galicia) there were autonomous administrations, which operated, however, on the principle that only the national Cortes could grant subsidies to the monarch and had the power to collect them. On the other hand, in these same territories municipal financial autonomy was great, and neither the monarch nor his officials could meddle in these matters.

Throughout the 17th century there had been certain tendencies toward financial unification, both administrative and territorial. In the administrative aspect, let us recall the creation of the General Superintendency of Finance (*Superintendencia general de Hacienda*) in 1687, followed by that of provincial superintendents (1691), which superseded the local hierarchy of royal governors; and also the integration of the Commission of Millones into the Council of the Treasury (1658). In 1694 this commission absorbed the functions and name of the Deputation of the Kingdom. In the territorial aspect, we need only remember the policy of the Count-Duke of Olivares in regard to the Crown's financial centralization, and the extremely grave consequences of that policy.

Philip V, the heir of this tradition, proceeded to attain his goal as soon as the fortunes of war gave him an opportunity to do so. In 1707 and 1716, after resistance had been overcome in Valencia, Aragon, and Catalonia and the local authorities suppressed, all matters relating to the Spanish Treasury passed directly under control of the Crown. This fact gave great importance to the Council of the Treasury, within which was the Deputation of the Kingdom, the name assumed by the *Cámara* (Chamber) *de Millones* after 1694. Through the Deputation, Aragon and Valencia (1712), Galicia (1752), and Catalonia and Majorca (1767) were brought into the common system. The Council, however, had to struggle with the growing influence of the *Veeduría general de Hacienda* (the overseeing office of the Treasury), and later with the Superintendency of the Treasury (1709), institutions which were a prelude to the creation of the Secretariat of State and Superintendency of

Finance (1724), and finally the Ministry or Secretariat of Finance, founded in 1754. This last agency gradually took upon itself the functions of the Council of the Treasury, until the latter was reduced to the role of a consultative or appeal body.

At the end of the 18th century the uniform organization of the Treasury was completed with the *Direcciones generales de Renta* and the *Tesorería General* (general administration of revenue, general treasury) with headquarters in Madrid; the intendants, who were counseled by two administrators of sales (*administradores de ventas*), in charge of the provincial exchequer; and the *subdelegados de ventas,* or subdelegates of sales, a function very often carried out by municipal governors. The office of Inspection of Finance also appeared at this time, in the form of *visitadores* who traveled through the provinces.

THE STATE'S ECONOMIC RESOURCES. In spite of the evident simplification of the Spanish treasury's administrative structure in the 18th century, confusion continued to be the principal motif in collection of the State's revenues. It is very possible that not even the officials themselves had a clear idea of their distribution and the financial mechanism they represented. The most elementary clarification was made difficult by the multitude of taxes and levies, the diversity of systems of collection, regional variations, new collection methods, and transfer of revenues from one group to another.

By custom, revenues were divided into two great groups, general and provincial, the former being those which had to do with foreign trade (customs and *almojarifazgos,* tithes from internal ports of entry and the wool branch) and the latter those arising from domestic trade (*servicios, alcabalas, millones,* etc.). This is the classification established by Aguirre, the accountant of the office of revenue from lead mines (*Renta de Plomos*), in 1759. Its technical base is very deficient; therefore we shall follow the same standards used in the analysis of taxes relating to the 17th century as we study those of the 18th.

THE CATASTRO. The most important novelty in 18th-century tax history is the introduction of the *catastro* in Catalonia. Drawn up by Patiño, it was established on October 16, 1716. It consisted of dividing a total annual sum "proportionately and fairly" among the taxpayers. For this purpose the *catastro* was divided into two great branches, the royal and the personal.

Royal *catastro* was levied on income from rural and urban property. Patiño especially calculated the revenue it would draw from agricultural lands, and divided properties into thirty-two different types for the purpose, according to their location and size. But rural and urban buildings were also affected by the *catastro,* as well as dwellings, factories, mills, etc., and leases and tithes. No one was exempt from paying this tax.

Personal *catastro* was a tax on wages, commercial profits, and merchandise, and only nobles, *hidalgos,* ecclesiastics, and civil servants or persons of like status were exempt. The appropriate authorities set up personal quotas through the municipalities and guilds.

In general, the *catastro* tax represented the timid implantation of a principle of social justice in Catalonia. At first there were protests against it on the grounds that it was very onerous, and undoubtedly it could not have been imposed had it not been for the circumstances accompanying its introduction. But later, once it was wisely adjusted to the country's potentialities, it turned out to be a useful and flexible system, and its very modernity made it one of the causes of the Catalan economy's success in the 18th century.

During Ferdinand VI's reign the Marquis de la Ensenada tried to apply the *catastro* system to Castile. The Royal Decree of October 10, 1749, was prepared for the purpose, establishing the *single tax* into which all the Provincial Revenues were to be merged (*millones, alcabalas, cientos,* and the ordinary *servicio*). However, preparatory operations for the *catastro* began only in 1770, at the request of Charles III; but in the end the bureaucracy was unable to overcome the numerous signs of social resistance. The project remained as an ideal to be realized, and as a social and historical document of the greatest importance.

GENERAL REVENUES. As we have said, this class of taxes was levied on foreign trade. The State regained administration of these in 1716, but it was not until 1740 that a fixed and coherent system was applied to them, reflected in the Superintendency of General Revenues created in that year. The men who embodied this policy were Campillo (1740–1743) and the Marquis de la Ensenada, superintendent from 1743 to 1754. Under Charles III the customs organization reached a point of perfection with the creation of general and subordinate administrations, principal customs houses, and a body of guards both on foot and on horseback. The aims of the system were to obtain uniformity in collection, supervision of local administrations, and a smoothly interlocking customs procedure.

PROVINCIAL REVENUES. These were exacted only in the kingdoms of the Crown of Castile and went back to Hapsburg times. If we recall the summary we made of that period (pp. 440–442), we need merely say that as late as the mid-18th century the *alcabala* (plus the four 1% taxes comprising the so-called *cientos*), the *servicio de millones* (imposed on consumption of meat, wine, sugar, soap, and brandy), the *sisa,* and *personal taxes* (like the *lanzas,* a duty paid by the nobility in lieu of military service, or the *medias anatas,* a tax paid on entry into a benefice or secular employment, or revenues from bulls of the Crusade, etc.), continued to make up the Castilian treasury's tax structure. To these must be added the *ordinary and extraordinary servicios,* taxes levied by apportionment.

But throughout the 18th century, and especially after the failure of Ensenada's single tax plan, the State decreed new taxes, a prelude to the great reforms of the 19th century. One of them was the direct tax on industry and trade, which at the beginning took the form of *patents,* as in France. Another was the *paja y utensilios,* or straw and equipment tax (a provincial levy for supply of troops), *cuarteles* and *frutos civiles* (established in 1785 on income from the rental of lands and property), and royal and jurisdictional taxes, which foreshadowed the appearance of territorial ones. And finally, the *succession tax,* created in 1798 to supply the Fund for Amortization of the Public Debt, introduced the principle of taxation on inheritances between spouses and those of collateral or unrelated heirs.

MONOPOLIES AND MONOPOLY GOODS. Various types of public revenue increased during the 18th century, for example the revenue from stamped paper, which doubled between 1707 and 1794. The monopolies or *exclusive outlets* taxing different products such as salt, tobacco, playing cards, and so on, were no less productive. The most remunerative of these was the tobacco monopoly, which brought in almost double the amount provided by salt (82 million reales in 1797 compared with salt's 43 million).

REGIONAL SYSTEMS. Apart from the Catalan *catastro* system, the kingdoms of the old Crown of Aragon were also exceptions to Castilian tax structure. In Aragon the *Real contribución única,* in Valencia the *equivalente,* and in Majorca the *talla* were introduced. These systems were based on global apportionment of fixed sums, but without direct knowledge of the individual taxpayers' ability to pay, as in Catalonia. In Navarre and the Basque Country statutory tax structures persisted, connected with the general system by means of the Navarrese *servicio* and the Basque *donativo.*

SUPPRESSION OF THE "BOLLA" TAX. The persistence of the ancient taxes is illustrated by the case of the "bolla" tax in Catalonia. Of venerable medieval origin (p. 236), like the Castilian *alcabala,* it severely hampered Catalan commerce, for it was still in existence as a tax on mercantile transactions in 1716, when the *catastro* was established. At that time it represented 15% of the retail value of all merchandise sold in Catalonia. As long as economic conditions were good there were no complaints about the "bolla." But when the old and powerful guild industries saw themselves threatened by the new silk ribbon, calico, and hosiery industries, they put the blame for their own backwardness and decline on this tax. Between 1750 and 1760 they began, therefore, to stir up public opinion until the Board of Trade authorized the Committee and Consulate of Barcelona (November 1, 1760) to meet to find a substitute for the "bolla" tax. They proposed a 15% levy on foreign goods. But this and other suggestions were vetoed by the Accounting Office of Barcelona, which for ten years firmly opposed any change. Finally, after a favorable report from the Board of Trade, Charles III decreed the suppression of the "bolla" beginning in January, 1770. This tax reform helped to make Catalan commerce more flexible at that moment of expansion in its industrial activities.

DEVELOPMENT OF BANKING: THE BANK OF SAN CARLOS AND PRIVATE BANKING. The history of Spanish money in the 18th century is not complete without an examination of the role played by banks during this period. After the War of Succession traditional institutions, such as the *Taules* of Barcelona, Gerona, Lérida, and

Valencia, were dead. It can be said that banking was entirely in the hands of private persons of foreign extraction, especially Genoese and French. Their operations were minimal: they lent money to those engaging in agriculture and exporters. And all this in addition to a widespread system of loans at usurious rates of interest.

Once the period of contraction during Philip V's reign was overcome and the flow of money into the market coincided with development of industry in the periphery of Spain, this system gradually changed and developed. In the first place there appeared, about 1751, the so-called Royal Remittance Office (*Oficina del Real Giro*), which was in charge of remitting funds to foreign countries. It had branches in Paris, Rome, Amsterdam, Naples, and Lisbon. Its main function was to take the place of the money-changers, who charged discounts of 20% on exchange transactions, and to curb the flight of currency. Once this aim was accomplished, its function was slowly absorbed by the bankers.

In Barcelona two notable banking bodies developed at the end of the century: the so-called Company for Annuities (*Compañía de Fondos Perdidos*), whose director was a Fleming, Tibelein, and the Foreign Exchange Banking Company (*Compañía de Banco en Cambios*) founded by a Frenchman, Larrard, and a Dane, Herrier. This last had a subscribed capital of 400,000 pesos. Both companies suffered from the inflation of Charles IV's reign.

The spectacular Bank of San Carlos also came to grief at that time. It had been founded in 1782 by Charles III at the moment of the Treasury's greatest difficulties, owing to the requirements of the war against England (siege of Gibraltar). This new institution's principal purpose was to underwrite the royal promissory notes which had become depreciated following the huge circulation of 1781–1782. For this purpose the bank could acquire royal notes by paying for them in gold, or even with its own banknotes, for which it was specifically authorized. Furthermore, as a private institution it received certain privileges, among them that of participating in monopolistic companies such as the Philippines Company. The plan was developed by Francisco Cabarrús. The subscribed capital was 30 million reales, contributed by the king, the nobles, the brotherhoods, and the municipalities, though more slowly than had been anticipated. Nevertheless, when the bank opened its doors in June, 1783, the happy coincidence of the end of the war seemed to augur a very rosy future. Cabarrús got credit for the recuperation of the royal notes; but Hamilton has recently demonstrated that he withdrew from circulation only 7¾ % of the existing paper money, which scarcely justifies the pretensions of the bank's directors.

Until 1785 it operated with the acquiescence of international finance and the confidence of the ruling class in Spain. But its intervention in risky operations, such as the purchase of French funds in 1788, soon placed it in a compromising situation. In 1790 Cabarrús resigned, severely criticized by the Minister of Finance, the Count of Serena. Shortly afterward came the outbreak of the Franco-Spanish war (1792–1795), followed by the Anglo-Spanish war (1796–1802 and 1805–1808). This produced inflation. After 1796 the bank could not cope with the torrent of paper money and had to ask for protection from the State. Three years later it entered a very serious crisis, due to the paralyzation of trade and the arrival of American silver. At that time it had in its possession only 0.05% of the notes which had been issued, a fact that reveals its failure as an instrument for balancing the means of payment. From then on until 1808 it slipped farther and farther along the path of hand-to-mouth solutions, the same solutions that produced the collapse of the Old Regime in Spain.

40 · The Business Cycle in the 18th Century

INITIAL STAGE OF RECONSTRUCTION. After 1680 there was a change in world economy. The reappearance of gold in the market, thanks to the discoveries made in Brazil, put an end to the depression which had lasted since 1630, and everywhere there were signs of stabilization in economic life. The wars of the early 18th century had the effect of mobilizing Western Europe's resources, resulting in a rising trend in the business cycle. Though brief, it served to counterbalance the effects of the century-long contraction and to prepare men's spirits for the great change of the 1730's. The new Bourbon dynasty was favored by this process, which gave impetus to peripheral regional centers that had already showed signs of recuperation in the latter years of Charles II's reign.

Hamilton points out that the technical structure was provided by the Colbertism—an economy of resistance in the phase of cyclical contraction—introduced by Philip V and his ministers Amelot and Orry, and which, thanks to new administrative principles worked out by men of the stature of José Patiño, José Campillo, and the Marquis de la Ensenada, made it possible to put an end to the country's decline. Hamilton particularly emphasizes the end of the alternating inflation and deflation which had been so fatal for Spain ever since the reign of Philip III. Treasury reforms, establishment of pilot factories, protection of national industry within the limits of the Treaty of Utrecht, suppression of internal customs, bans on the export of raw materials, all were effective weapons with which to consolidate the country's economic and financial position.

We must also keep in mind the circumstances produced by the War of Succession, which was waged in the Peninsula for ten years (from 1704 to 1714). Apart from the invasion of French currency, soon checked, the supply needs of the armies in a war in which there was a great deal of movement but little destruction kept prices and wages at a high level. This phase appeared in Castile as well as in Catalonia. Pierre Vilar has defined it as a definite point of departure, with stability of wages. In Castile the average index of prices from 1701 to 1716 is 104.50; that is, very much higher than in the rest of the century's first fifty years (index 100 in the period 1726–1750).

After this plateau, two decades of contraction followed. They mark a period of modest activity and great stability. Labor sources were organized and structured in a slow and elementary process which was not to bear fruit until later. It is possible that during this period there was a reconstitution of the Spanish demographic base, and it is clear that agriculture was reorganized, the rise of commerce was foreshadowed, and the first industrial activities were beginning to flower. But there is no detailed study on this slow development.

ABRUPT RISES DURING THE REIGNS OF PHILIP V AND FERDINAND VI. The last decade of Philip V's reign (1736–1746) and the entire reign of Ferdinand VI (1746–1759) bear witness to a reversal in the business cycle, which took the form of two sharp rises separated by a five-year period of stability. The more intense of these was the second, caused, Hamilton says, by the flow of Mexican silver into the European market.

These rises were felt in all fields of economic activity, but were especially noticeable in agriculture and trade. The decisive five-year periods in agriculture were 1736–1740 and 1751–1755, when the increase in agricultural prices was substantially greater than in industrial ones. This was the golden age of 18th-century *latifundist agriculture,* with fabulous profits for the owner of rural properties. It was one source of capital accumulation. The other was *colonial trade.* This period saw the expansion of monopolistic trading companies, supplanting the cramped pattern of State monopoly. In America, especially in the Caribbean (Venezuela, the Antilles) and the La Plata region, sugar, cocoa, and hides made the fortunes of a number of Spaniards.

In industry we find, as Vilar writes, a period of preparation. The accumulation of capital by means of colonial trade and agricultural income affected only one region: Catalonia. This was due to previous Catalan momentum and also to the facilities inherent in the Principality's new financial organization. But in any case there was also an element of spiritual decision, of a desire to triumph in life, of profound biological expansion. Simultaneously with the establishment of the calico industry (1739–1742), the Catalans forced the introduction of their merchant fleet into the Antilles and the Western Mediterranean (sugar revolution), and found northern markets for their wines and brandies. And in addition, Catalan fishermen, demonstrating new techniques, appeared as far away as the Atlantic.

EVOLUTION OF THE TRADE CYCLE UNDER CHARLES III: PRICE RISE AND PREDOMINANCE OF THE SPANISH PERIPHERY. Except for a brief five-year period (1771–1775), Charles III's reign (1759–1789) evolved under the protection of a highly favorable rising trend. Prices and wages were in a state of frank prosperity—prices more than wages—and this coincided with the country's demographic, agricultural, commercial, and industrial expansion; increasing quantities of American precious metals were arriving in the country almost without interruption. This is a summary of the 18th century's golden phase, which, along with the general prosperity, witnessed the breakdown of the feudal regime in rural areas and the guild regime in the cities. The bourgeoisie was formed at this time, not only in the great mercantile and industrial centers of Cádiz and Barcelona but to some degree all over the country, though outside these two cities it took the form of an influential middle class rather than a true bourgeoisie.

The five-year period of contraction we mentioned before divides these thirty years into two periods of differing rising trends. During the first, initial steps were taken toward liberalizing the Peninsula's economy, such as the law concerning freedom of trade in cereals (1765) and the free trade decree on imports of cotton cloth (1760). The first ordinances on distribution of *propios* and uncultivated lands also belong to this period, as well as the beginnings of the colonization of Sierra Morena, measures which seem somewhat contradictory in years of such hopeful development.

During the second stage the price rise was really unleashed. In the two-year period 1774–1775 the people themselves could feel the sharp inflationary burst. Wages went up everywhere in the wake of prices, but even more intensively, as we know, in Barcelona than in Madrid, in the periphery than in the center. This was the decisive

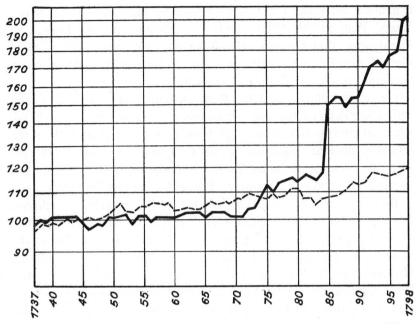

Evolution of wages in Madrid (broken line) and Barcelona (solid line) between 1737 and 1798. Indexes are taken from HAMILTON and VILAR, respectively. Base, 100 = mean for 1737–1750.

moment of transference of the economic center of gravity in modern Spain. As if to confirm it came the publication of the decree relating to freedom of trade with America (1778). In a few years the triumph of the peripheral regions would become a fact. Cádiz was bursting with riches, and Barcelona increased her profits tenfold and tripled the volume of her trade, while in the interior of Catalonia the new cotton spinning and weaving industry was founded. The Industrial Revolution began in this portion of the Spanish soil.

CHARLES III'S WARS AND ECONOMIC LIFE. From 1779 to 1783 Charles III carried on a tremendous war effort, in alliance with France, to recover the Spanish possessions held by England in the Mediterranean (Minorca and Gibraltar) and at the same time to push England out of America, where her colonies were in open rebellion. The plan rested on obvious strategic and political considerations, but economics also entered the picture. Great Britain's expansion after the great victory won by her fleet in the Seven Years' War (1756–1763) had been so gigantic, its impact so threatening, that Charles III felt he had no choice but to align himself with France and try to ward off the inevitable blow which very soon would break up the Spanish-American empire.

Currency inflation and the Bank of San Carlos arose from the war. The price rise became irresistible, especially after 1785–1786, when an enormous postwar expansion took place as a result of the return to normal conditions. From then until the end of the century, the cycle never halted its rising tendency, in one of the most spectacular trends the history of world economy has ever seen.

But the war with England, in spite of its favorable conclusion (the American colonies had obtained their freedom under the name of the United States of America in 1783), had not resulted in the recovery of Gibraltar or Canada or the Antilles. Above all, the Hispano-French allies had not succeeded in destroying the British fleet. Atlantic communications continued to be controlled by London, and this meant that a serious threat was still hanging over the Spanish Empire and the mother country's domestic economy.

This had been clearly shown during the war. The English blockade had paralyzed traffic in Spanish ports, delayed the installation of factories in Barcelona, and resulted in unemployment and destitution in workers' homes. After the victory the Spanish-American empire was more menaced than ever.

EFFECTS OF THE PRICE RISE AND THE REVOLUTIONARY WARS UNDER CHARLES IV. The Spain of Charles IV was characterized by two facts, revolutionary wars in Europe and general inflationary conditions within the country. While his predecessor had been able to absorb the price rise with the aid of demographic, commercial, and industrial expansion, Charles IV was obliged to feed inflation by putting paper money into circulation, spending beyond budgetary limits, and resorting to loans. French pressure in the Pyrenees and the requirements of the kind of modern warfare represented by the irregulars of the Convention broke up the inner workings of the lethargic Bourbon administration. Only a policy of firm tax demands, imposed especially on the powerful classes—nobles and clergy—could have restored the balance. But instead of this the monarchy resorted to sale of ecclesiastical properties without any valid guarantees. After 1794–1795, a two-year period of sharp wage and price increases, the Spanish Revolution took place in the depths of the social structure, though it was not to break out until twelve years later in the upheaval of May, 1808.

The inflationary spiral had two periods of steep rise, one lasting till 1804, another from 1806 to 1812. The peak of the intersecular cyclical boom occurred in 1804. Though we have no specific studies on Spain, we know that the crisis of overproduction took place in 1805 in Portugal and in 1807 in France. In Portugal the succession of events was as follows:

1804: production peak
1805: beginning of collapse
1806: decrease in imports
1807: decrease in exports

It is possible that the Spanish picture was altered by the wars of the French Revolution. Until 1795 Spain was allied with England against the French Republic; after 1796 it was always on France's side against England. It was a natural alliance, but an unfortunate one. Without England, the Spanish colonies in America could not develop (as the law on Trade of Neutrals demonstrated in 1797); with England they rushed toward independence. Hence the supreme effort to eliminate the British from the seas, which cost Spain the serious and decisive defeats of Cape St. Vincent (1797) and Trafalgar (1805). In consequence, the inflation at the end of the century was so severe because it was not accompanied by an increase in the volume of trade; rather, after a period of splendid commercial and industrial achievement (1796–1798), the most buoyant in Spain's 18th-century economic history, prosperity crumbled and Spain entered a bitter phase of unemployment, destitution, and economic contraction brought on by the British blockade of the Atlantic.

As proof of this we cite the revenues of the Customs Service at the end of the 18th century:

1772	53,000,000 reales
1789	159,000,000 reales
1792	182,000,000 reales
1798	47,000,000 reales
1799	59,000,000 reales

603

The country, which considered itself reborn about 1802 (Peace of Amiens), knew a few years of prosperity, characterized by importation of producers' goods and attempts to absorb paper money. But the defeat of 1805 was to put an end to these hopes, to Charles IV's reign, and to the monarchy of the Old Regime.

VI · THE IMPACT OF THE INDUSTRIAL REVOLUTION

41 · 19th-Century Spirit of Reform

GENERAL CHARACTERISTICS OF THE SPANISH 19TH CENTURY. The period in Spanish life from 1808 to 1898, that is, from the start of the War of Independence to the loss of the last overseas colonial possessions, is customarily reviled by most of our contemporaries. The traditionalists accuse the 19th century of having broken the backbone of Spanish glories with its liberalism, of having disfigured the essence of Spain with its oppressive centralism and unrestrained language. For their part, the liberals insist that they were in power only for short periods of time, and that the country's misfortunes were based on the constant frustration of political and ideological progress by the action of a backward mass which found its main support among the great feudal forces. If we move from the ideological to the social point of view, workers' movements have inveighed against the injustices which the 19th century brought to peasants and workers, condemned to helplessness before the crushing advance of the wealth of latifundists and manufacturers. The bourgeoisie have objected, however, that in spite of their wishes they could not give direction to their longing for economic and political reform, that they were paralyzed by an ignorant and chaotic administration and the country's colossal technical and educational backwardness.

Recent historiography, however, has proved that none of these positions is well founded. All respond to the desire to interpret facts from one's own point of view. But in this case there is yet another factor, for our ignorance of the 19th century is almost total. We know something of its political surface, what its rulers, soldiers, and intellectuals did, but we are almost completely unaware of the true nature of events. In particular, we know little about the century's social dynamic and its formation in successive economic strata. We cannot, then, make accusations against our 19th-century forebears unless our charges are based on irrefutable documentary proofs.

To judge from the discoveries being made by the new historiography, the tribunal of history will largely absolve our forebears. The Spanish 19th century is characterized by the constant effort of a minority to attain a progressively higher technological level and greater wealth, and this not only in the economic field, but also in cultural and scientific areas. For the first time in centuries it became commonplace for Spaniards to go abroad. This fact is of supreme importance, for Spain began to realize that she belonged to Europe. This was a new, though timid, realization, and marked an indispensable change of attitude.

On the other hand, the history of the Spanish 19th century offers one trait which we cannot help finding attractive: its absolute authenticity. Without the aid of artificial supports based on the romantic vision of life, Spain was more truly Spain than ever before, at least since the 15th century. This authenticity of the 19th century is what gives us a certain feeling of timidity as we observe it, for its sincerity is positively brutal, in its passions and its conflicts. Intolerance and dogmatism, pride and sectarian spirit, resulted in a constant atmosphere of civil war, which engulfed the country from 1808 to 1876 and paralyzed its economic development. It is clear that Spain would have been something quite different within world structure if during those seventy years she had been able to work instead of fight.

The struggle among the different interest groups was, furthermore, inevitable, as it was everywhere in Europe owing to the change in economic structure caused by the impact of the Industrial Revolution. Feudal and seigniorial Europe was supplanted by the Europe of the factory; bourgeois and worker took the place of princes and hierarchs. This shift in the social body's center of gravity was translated into a political phenomenon: the bourgeois revolution. But in Spain the weakness of the structural change resulted in the failure of this bourgeois revolution. The Spanish bourgeoisie had neither numerical density, nor wealth, nor a firm and clear ideology sufficient to spell its triumph. Established in the periphery of the country, this class lived in a permanent state of contradiction: it wanted to impose on the center a political and economic solution which inevitably resulted in the threat of social unrest. It progressed with enthusiasm, only to retreat before the first sparks of public disorder; and once these were forgotten, it took up anew the argument for spiritual and economic conversion of the interior. But in spite of all this, it was the only social class that tried to swing the helm of Spain in the direction of progress, and on balance it was responsible for all—and it was a great deal—that was achieved in the course of the century.

Another circumstance which we must keep in mind is the constant interference from abroad in Spanish economic life. Ever since medieval times Catalonia as well as Castile had been economic areas profoundly influenced by the economies of other nations; in the 19th century this influence was so overwhelming that at times it almost seemed like a case of financial colonialism. As a reaction to this, the 19th century as a whole is often thought of as a period of prostration, during which foreign interests completely destroyed the national economy. But this statement is not confirmed by the facts. What happened was that Europe, the Europe of England, France, Germany, Belgium, and Holland, experienced a period of unprecedented prosperity at that time. The coffers of these nations were overflowing with money which had to be put to work somewhere. Spain became included in a circuit of Western foreign investments covering the whole world, even the United States of America, which owed its transcontinental railroads to France and England. Therefore, only a narrow and anachronistic nationalistic view could find fault with this fact. The truth is that these investments, administered and directed by foreign technicians and managers, contributed on a large scale to Spanish economic progress in the 19th century. The sad fact was that the country was incapable of taking full advantage of the possibilities offered it after the middle of the 19th century, and that, burdened by an agriculture which was insufficient, underdeveloped, and feudal in type, it was not able to make an economic conversion to industry in time. And then it had to pay the price of its inevitable industrial equipment (railways, machinery, raw materials) by sending abroad at very unfavorable prices mineral products which, if used in other ways, would have contributed enormously to Spain's economic independence and helped her to overcome her general underdevelopment.

BREAKDOWN OF THE OLD REGIME AND REVOLUTIONARY MOVEMENT OF 1808. After this survey we can proceed to an analysis of Spanish 19th-century structure. But first we have felt it necessary to establish a correlation between the chief historical periods and the different phases of economic life. We are not making a study of economic fluctuations here—that will be done later—but merely sketching the general configuration of the economic process.

One major fact must be established: the 19th century began with a profound revolutionary upheaval, unleashed in connection with the events of May, 1808. Generally, in these events we think only of the patriotic factor; but apart from the heroism of those days of May 2 and 3 in Madrid, the fact of real importance is the breakdown of the Old Regime which took place in every part of the country at the end of May, 1808. The shock was particularly intense in the periphery, where the bourgeoisie and enlightened classes seized power.

Is this an anomalous event? No indeed. It was shaped by a confluence of factors, among which we may mention: (1) the ideological influence of the French Revolution. It had broken out in 1789, and during the twenty years which had passed between that date and 1808 many Spaniards had become accustomed to the mental attitude implied by revolutionary dialectic, which from the economic point of view proclaimed freedom of trade, freedom of industry, and destruction of the guilds. (2) The growing opposition of the nobles and the Church to ministerial despotism. After Charles III's death, both nobles and Church had complained of the oppressive dictatorial system employed by Charles IV's ministers. (3) Onset of the secular economic depression. It started in 1804–1806, resulting in a series of fluctuations which seriously unbalanced Spanish society and gave rise to a profound sense of unease. (4) Criticism of Charles IV's foreign policy, which was blamed for the ruin of trade resulting from the war with England and the bankruptcy of private fortunes through inflation of royal promissory notes.

Consequently, in May, 1808, popular pressure was exerted as much against the Old Regime as against the invaders whom that regime had made inevitable.

ECONOMIC EFFECTS OF THE WAR OF INDEPENDENCE. From the economic point of view, the War of Independence was a calamity. For six years there was a bitter struggle. The country was occupied and overrun by foreign troops who lived off the land. Spain was plundered time and again, and part of her wealth was carried off to France.

Agriculture lost the forward thrust which had been characteristic of it in the last decades of the 18th century, and declined terribly. There were widespread famines. This coincided with the great drop in prices after 1814. It was literally a disaster, from which the country did not recover until much later.

Businessmen also experienced terrible losses in the course of the War of Independence. Paralyzation of commerce, both foreign and domestic, and the burdens placed on loyalists by the occupying troops, resulted in a paralysis of the bourgeoisie's ascending rhythm. This does not mean that there were not persons who made money: contract-holders, for example, who organized contact (contraband contact, of course) between the opposing armies and carried out a number of very satisfactory operations.

As for the politico-economic effects, they were of great importance, though without immediate results. The Cortes of Cádiz (convoked in 1810) drew up a series of magnificent plans regarding ownership of land, trade policy, and organization of national industry. It was this Cortes which timidly initiated the bourgeois ideal: elimination of legal feudalism in rural areas, ecclesiastical disentailment, and suppression of the guilds.

ECONOMIC EFFECTS OF AMERICAN SECESSION: COLONIAL SURVIVALS AND THEIR IMPORTANCE. Simultaneously with the War of Independence, Spain was faced with another no less frightening problem: the emancipation of the American colonies. The phenomenon was the same: breakdown of the Old Regime in Spain, breakdown of the Old Regime in America; in Spain it meant the downfall of the absolutist monarchy, in America the secession of the American colonies.

In fact it was a very grave setback for a country like Spain, which was laboriously beginning its reconstruction after the War of Independence. If Spain had been able to maintain a satisfactory flow of American metals for twenty more years, it is clear that she would have recovered much more rapidly and fully. But the *criollos,* or colonial bourgeoisie, refused to grant Spain's requests for aid. That was the real American secession: America's *non volumus,* the *criollos'* lack of cooperation. And so, after 1810 Spain

611

lost the La Plata market and with it the vantage point for controlling illicit trade in South America. In 1818–1820, after Bolivar's campaigns, she gave up her great cocoa interests in Venezuela and Colombia; and in 1825, in Ayacucho, she lost the Peruvian mines. Those of Mexico had been abandoned two years before, so that all she had left was the sugar of the Antilles.

The shock of these events was overwhelming, to the point that it is fair to state that the Carlist civil war broke out as a result of American secession. If Ferdinand VII had been able to retain the American possessions, their shipments of metal and their enormous commercial possibilities would have mitigated the contraction produced in the Spanish economy by the War of Independence and the depression phase of the trade cycle. The civil war was, from its first outbreak in 1834, a war born of famine and indigence, not a war of the rich and powerful.

There was something left of the old Spanish colonial empire, though—the Antilles and the Philippines. And this was no mean portion. In fact, it was a great deal. In 1835 Moreau de Jonnès could still compare the Spanish colonial empire with those of Britain and France. The Philippines were the great marketplace, the open door from Europe to Oriental trade; the Antilles were the center of the sugar and tobacco economy, and further, a strategic place from which to trade with the old Spanish colonial area. Consequently, so long as the Antilles stayed loyal Spain could count on their wealth as much as on that of the Philippines. But when this situation ended in 1898, Spain found herself restricted to her own efforts. This is why the crisis of 1898 was so important: for the first time in their history since the beginning of the Reconquest, Spaniards had to fall back on their own resources. And with those resources a new era was begun in the country's political, ideological, and economic life.

POLITICAL LIBERALISM AND ITS PART IN SPANISH ECONOMIC LIFE. Political liberalism triumphed in 1834 after a short period of ascendancy in 1820–1823. Some authors discuss this change from the simple point of view of internal and dynastic conflicts. But the matter is more important, more widespread, and more complex than this. In fact, after 1827 Ferdinand VII and the liberal bourgeoisie were in agreement on establishing in Spain what was called at that time "freedom properly understood." The bourgeoisie showed their satisfaction by supporting the change of regime through the Stock Exchange of Madrid: a change resulting in the crowning of Isabella II and the exile of Prince Charles.

The formula of "freedom properly understood" is bourgeois *par excellence*. The bourgeoisie wanted a bloodless revolution, with freedom given to all those who deserved it. Since they thought of themselves as the hub of society, this freedom was first and foremost for the bourgeoisie: ideological and political freedoms certainly, but especially fiscal and economic ones.

Spanish liberalism had notable theoreticians (Flórez Estrada, Canga Argüelles) and mediocre practitioners. Thus it existed in a perpetual state of paradox. Each new liberal victory was followed by a new protectionist shackle. It was a paradox finally solved by the fact of the support given by the industrial bourgeoisie (protectionist by definition) to the liberal movement of lawyers and poets, grandees of Spain, latifundists, and generals.

In spite of this, once liberalism was in the saddle it undertook important transformations in the Spanish economy. Let us take a rapid look at them.

Mobilization of agricultural property. It was badly mobilized—there is no doubt of that—but it was jerked out of the paralysis which had stifled it up to 1814. Uncultivated and crown lands, entailed and mortmain properties, all were put on the public market and into economic circulation. This shock permitted a recovery of the national economy which after 1855 was translated into tangible benefits.

Freedom of labor was legally established for all; a revolutionary principle, for it did away with the age-old work of the guild institutions. It was, however, indispensable if technicians and manpower were to be found for the country's budding industry.

Finally, liberalism introduced into the administration a certain amount of *interest in economic and statistical matters*. Suffice it to say that it was the liberals who created the *Ministerio de Fomento*, or Ministry of Development, whose purpose was to stimulate the country's progress, and that after 1827 they organized expositions, encouraged statistical studies, and concerned themselves with the progress of the national economy. The great sources for studying the economy of this period are all liberal ones.

THE GREAT MODERATE PHASE. From 1843 to 1868, a period of twenty-five years, Spain was going through what has been called the "great moderate phase." This does not mean that all the governments belonged to the political party specifically called "moderate," but that a ruling class of a moderate type existed which combined principles of relative freedom with those of relative authority, and kept at a distance from the impassioned extremism of either Carlism or progressivism.

This "great moderate phase" has decisive importance in 19th-century Spanish economic life. Almost all the century's institutions—and even some present-day ones—arose out of those years: reform of the Treasury and tax structure, establishment of the Bank of Spain, creation of the Civil Guard, definite establishment of provincial administration, law of Public Instruction, etc. In the economy itself, the moderates began the country's modern industrial equipping, favored construction of railways, supported the textile industry, and developed financial capitalism.

Further, this period forged the triangle which, up to 1931 at least, was to govern the country's financial activities, both economic and political. One vertex of this triangle was the Catalonian textile industry, another was Castilian (and therefore Andalusian) agriculture, and the third was the Basque iron industry. Those who controlled iron and steel, wheat, and cotton formed a solid triangle, much more effective than any ministerial, political, or military combination. They were the real rulers. They were to hold sway during the moderate period and actually to be masters of the country during the Restoration.

THE REVOLUTION OF 1868 AND THE FREE TRADE ATTEMPT. The economic order established by the moderates, very beneficial to the liberal latifundist aristocracy and the industrialists and financiers, was too limited in its national aspirations. Great masses of population were left outside it: peasants and workers (restless after 1821 and 1828, respectively), not to mention civil servants, retail merchants, and artisans. This was why the moderates fell from power when they could not cope with the economic crisis of 1866.

Out of this crisis arose the revolution of 1868, which was to last until 1876, through the reign of Amadeus of Savoy and the First

Republic. From the political point of view it was a manifestation of all the problems afflicting the country. Economically it was a systematic attempt—the only one ever made—to establish free trade as a normal form of Spanish foreign trade. On the other hand, it led to new departures in such fundamental aspects as the monetary system and fiduciary circulation.

The representatives of the revolution, most of whom were theorists, succeeded in saving the Spanish economy, so hopelessly bogged down in the morass of the 1866 crisis, though at the cost of sacrificing some national resources, especially mining products, to foreign interests.

THE RESTORATION AND NATIONAL ECONOMIC CONSTRUCTION. The final period in 19th-century history is called the Restoration (because the Bourbon dynasty was restored to the throne), and lasted from 1876 to 1898. It was an important period in 19th-century Spanish life, based on the principle of the State's neutrality in regard to the individuals who made up the country. Ever since 1808 the State had been belligerent toward Spaniards as individuals, who had been successively purified, purged, confiscated, etc., no matter whether they called themselves Carlists or Liberals, Progressives or Socialists. But in 1876 the men of the Restoration agreed that this must stop, and it did. The State founded at that time was a neutral one, governed by men belonging to political parties, but the country was ruled by law. This fact permitted not only a stable peace, without excessive waste in the ministries, but also a forward thrust without precedent in Spanish economic life. Between 1878 and 1898 extremely powerful economic energies were developed and accumulated, for now no one feared the future.

The Restoration also favored investment of foreign capital, which was now applied to private industrial enterprises or municipal public services. The country's prosperity was obvious, at least in the early years of the new regime, in spite of the fact that the administration faltered more than once in the face of corruption and wasteful spending. The agrarian economy took a great leap forward, while the textile economy experienced a golden age and the powerful Basque metallurgical industry began to take shape.

Therefore, when the Restoration reached the colonial, economic, and political drama of 1898, it cannot be said that the country was dead. On the contrary, it possessed notable energies, so notable that they helped Spain live through the disaster and give birth to a new and powerful Spanish economic generation.

DEVELOPMENT OF SPANISH POPULATION IN THE 19TH CENTURY: STAGES. After the victory which had been won over abnormal mortality in the 18th century, the 19th was to mark the first assaults on normal causes of death, especially in the early years of life. This fight, begun in 1801 with the introduction in Barcelona of the smallpox vaccine recently discovered by the Englishman, Jenner (1796), was to end with a still more important victory. Thanks to it Spain became part of the great demographic revolution which was to revive the whole social and economic problem everywhere in Europe.

The statistics we possess (reliable after 1857) permit us to measure the tremendous scope of the progress achieved:

1797	10,541,000 inhabitants
1822	11,661,865 inhabitants
1833	11,962,767 inhabitants
1857	15,454,000 inhabitants
1860	15,645,000 inhabitants
1877	16,622,000 inhabitants
1887	17,549,600 inhabitants
1897	18,108,610 inhabitants
1900	18,594,000 inhabitants

That is, in the 19th century Spain's population increased by 8 million inhabitants, equal to more than three-fourths of those she had had before. It was an increase without precedent in the country's history. It alone was to break down administrative and social structures, and from 1821 to the present was responsible for five civil wars. Or, stated in a different way, the rapid demographic development destroyed the structures which had existed till then, and hastened economic and political changes in an atmosphere of great tension, owing to the poverty of the working classes—proletarians in the cities and day laborers in rural areas.

There are three quite clear stages in this process: (1) from 1797 to 1833, a period of some thirty years, the population increased by 1,800,000 inhabitants, at the rate of approximately 60,000 a year, (2) from 1833 to 1860, thirty more years, it increased by 3,300,000 inhabitants, at the rate of 110,000 per year, more than double the rate of the previous period, and (3) from 1860 to 1900, forty years, the increase was 3,300,000 inhabitants, at a rate of 76,000 per year.

These stages have reference to a factual situation, without taking into consideration important phenomena such as emigration. Consequently, we had better go into a little more detail as to what they actually represented.

The *first period* (1800 to 1833) is one of moderate demographic progress; it even represents a relative slowdown. Why? The most direct explanation can be found if we consider the effects of the War of Independence and the early struggles between absolutists and liberals. Fermín Caballero states that Spain lost 1,500,000 souls between 1808 and 1823. This estimate seems exaggerated. However, it is possible that in the War of Independence some 300,000 persons in the flower of youth perished. To this figure we must add, as the last medieval survivals, extraordinary outbreaks of epidemic diseases and famines. Yellow fever made its appearance in 1821, representing destruction and horror for many cities. Later, in 1833, it was succeeded by cholera, with even more deaths resulting. As for famine, let us recall that in 1812 it caused the same ravages as its medieval predecessors.

The *second period* (1833–1860), one of rapid increase, shows that the loss caused in the early years of the century by the War of Independence had been made up. And in addition, the new demographic thrust was also aided by improvement in the economic situation. New lands brought under cultivation by the laws of disentailment, the onset of industrialization, and great public works (highways and railways), offered means of livelihood for a larger population.

For the *third period,* after 1860, statistics show a slowdown in the ascending tendency. This does not imply, however, a worsening of the Spanish demographic situation, but only that a new factor had come into play. This was a wave of emigration which sent abroad a large part of the country's surplus human resources. We

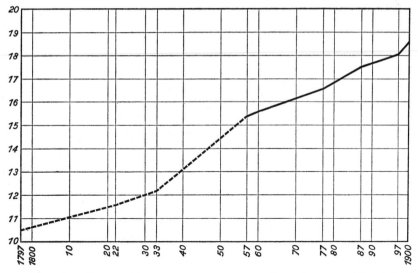

EVOLUTION OF SPANISH POPULATION DURING THE 19TH CENTURY. The dotted portion indicates doubtful census figures.

should also keep in mind the third Carlist war (not because of the number of victims it produced, but because it was the source of one of the first decreases in the Spanish birthrate), the colonial wars in Cuba and the Philippines, episodes of great epidemic violence such as cholera morbus (which in 1885 killed 120,000 persons), and finally, a number of periods of famine, such as that undergone by Andalusia as late as 1881–1882.

What value shall we assign, then, to the figures we have just stated? To have a clear idea we shall have to compare the demographic progress made in 19th-century Spain with that of other countries. The result is as follows: the Spanish rate of growth was somewhat less than that of Western Europe (77% compared to 91%), especially during the last period.

REGIONAL POPULATION PROGRESS. The 18th-century reversal of demographic values—that is, predominance of the periphery over the center—was consolidated and accentuated. The loss in specific weight of the block formed by the two Castiles, León, Extremadura, Navarre, and Aragon can be clearly seen in this statistic:

1797	1857	1910
41.57	37.4	36.0

The point is obvious: the center, already in a disadvantageous position, lost 11% of its demographic mass within the Spanish whole during the first sixty years of the century, and another 4% during the remainder of it.

Let us point out, however, that the rhythm of loss was very unequal during the two periods we have mentioned. The tendency toward stabilization observable after 1860 was due to initial loss of fertility in the periphery; to extension of the fight against mortality to the whole country; to concentration of the great current of emigration in the littoral zone; and to the birth of "greater Madrid," resulting in an important center of immigration which kept the inhabitants of the Meseta in the center of the country.

Let us pause for a moment on the first two factors we have mentioned. The Spanish birthrate, more or less stable up to the middle of the 19th century, began to decline after that time. Following the European tendency, the phenomenon first appeared in the more advanced coastal regions, where the fight against mortality had also progressed more rapidly. Thus, by 1900 the map of Spanish natality already showed profound changes, ranging from the figure of 41.6 per 1,000 in the province of Cuenca, the highest, to the figure for the province of Barcelona of 27.8 per 1,000, the lowest. Outside the provincial boundary two high birthrate zones stand out clearly, Old Castile-León-Extremadura and La Mancha–Eastern Andalusia. Spreading out from these two centers, which formed a great inner arc, there was a progression from north to southeast in a number of concentric circles, each representing a descent from the previous one, down to the epicenter of low birthrate located in Catalonia, the Balearic Islands, and the northern part of the province of Valencia. The problem was especially serious in Catalonia (27.8 births per 1,000 inhabitants in 1896–1905, compared to 36.3 in 1861–1865), where the industrial effort required an abundance of manpower. After that time immigration was the only possible solution.

As for mortality, the differences were as remarkable as in the previous case, though of an opposite kind: in general terms, the most fertile provinces were also those whose sanitary conditions were the worst. But here the differences tended to level out more quickly, for we have already said that the second half of the 19th century is precisely the time when the fight against the death rate spread throughout the country. In spite of this, even in 1900 Spain's backwardness was perfectly obvious. In that year 30 Spaniards per 1,000 died, compared to only 18 Europeans per 1,000. And since, on the other hand, our birthrate advantage was only 0.50%, Spain's passive growth was 0.70% less, by virtue of her unusually high death rate, than that of the other Western countries as the 20th century dawned.

INTERNAL MIGRATORY MOVEMENTS. Until 1880 the Spanish peasant had few prospects of solving his two great problems, work and food. Sometimes he fled his native district, forming part of the pitiful army of beggars who were one of the great national shames up to the end of the century. But it was a desperate, degrading type of emigration. At other times he took up arms in defense of political causes he was unable to grasp, but which he considered good since his leaders were fighting the government he hated—any government, in principle—and furnished him with food and clothing. Occasionally he emigrated, attracted by the prospect of good wages. Only after formation of the first industrial complex in Spain—that of Catalonia—can we observe regional migratory movements of any consequence: that of Valencians and Aragonese to Barcelona, Tarrasa, and Sabadell (about 1850). This process took on greater intensity during the Restoration. After 1880 the railway network was finished and ease of movement was greatly increased. This coincided with the demand for manpower in the manufacturing centers. The great Basque iron and steel industry came into being; in Catalonia, the textile industry was in its golden age; chemical and mechanical industries went along with them, demanding and absorbing manpower. In consequence, after 1890 internal migration grew in intensity. This time its general direction was from the south and center of the country to the north, a change from the tendency of the previous century.

Such migrations benefited the cities first of all; but, contrary to what happened in other European countries, urban concentration in Spain continued to be low. Thus, in 1900 50.92% of Spaniards lived in centers of less than 5,000 population, 40.06% in those of 5,000 to 100,000, and only 9.01% in cities larger than 100,000. At that same date there were only two cities with a population of over half a million, Madrid and Barcelona. In 1800 both had had not much over 100,000 inhabitants. Therefore, they had increased their population more than fourfold, which was not excessive by any means. The competition between Madrid and Barcelona is a curious one, as can be seen in the following table:

Years	Inhabitants	
	Barcelona	*Madrid*
1800	115,000	160,000
1850	175,000	281,000
1880	346,000	398,000
1900	533,000	540,000

Population increase in the capital is noticeably similar to that of Barcelona up to 1880. After that, Barcelona's rhythm of growth is faster, corresponding to her most prosperous period, which was just beginning in 1880 and is shown in the extent to which Barcelona overflowed its medieval walls after 1870.

The cities with a certain demographic importance were located in the periphery: Valencia, Seville, Cádiz, Málaga, Bilbao, Oviedo, and Vigo.

EMIGRATION. As a consequence of increase in the Spanish population, and the scanty resources with which State and nation were able to satisfy it, the problem of emigration became a serious one. At the beginning of the 19th century, when the effects of population increase began to be felt, a number of restrictive measures were applied. Thus, in 1822–1823 the Cortes agreed to ban emigration, for it was believed to be of the greatest importance for a healthy State to retain its younger citizens. But between 1834 and 1874 the demographic tide was so considerable, the symptoms of social discontent so profound, that the government had to give in. Even during the First Republic provincial governments were authorized to issue passports to emigrants, and the deposit of 320 reales demanded by the law was waived. Later this measure was canceled (1876). But the favorable attitude of several South American countries, anxious for new infusions of European blood (Argentine law of 1876, for example), opened the gates of the New World to a new and second great phase of emigration. We have statistical evidence of this after 1882. At that time the number of emigrants to Spanish America was about 11,000 annually. The number continued to increase until it reached a maximum of 133,994 in 1917 (slightly higher than the total population increase in Spain). From this figure we must deduct the return of those who had been successful as well as those who came back to Spain totally defeated.

The chief nuclei of emigration were in the periphery: the Canary Islands, Pontevedra and Corunna, Asturias and Santander, Barcelona and the Basque region. Of these four nuclei, while the Canaries and Galicia represented unskilled labor exclusively, the latter two also sent technicians and even factory-owners and businessmen.

Another important source of emigration was southeastern Spain (Alicante, Murcia, and Almería) in the direction of Algeria, especially to Oran and its hinterland. It was a directed emigration, of a capitalist type, and involved shocking exploitation of laboring people by unscrupulous persons. These emigrants were subjected to innumerable privations, sometimes to the point of being annihilated by bands of Algerian outlaws. Many of them returned to Spain in 1891 and 1895. But by the end of the century there was a considerable residue of people from Alicante and Murcia in those African localities.

SOCIAL STRUCTURE OF THE POPULATION. It is very difficult to present a true picture of the social structure of the population, especially because the century tended to be democratic, and titles and honors were usually not listed in the statistics. The nobility and clergy, of course, slipped into second place in economic life, but not in as clearly defined a fashion as many scholars, influenced by the French experience, believe.

In 1787 the nobility was composed of 480,000 individuals. Four years later, says Moreau de Jonnès, it was still 430,000, one-tenth of the European total. It does not, however, appear in the census of 1860. But, contrary to the opinion of Professor Sánchez Agesta, who believes that this is a sign of growing democracy, we believe that the apparent disappearance of the nobility in 1860 was a mere trick of statistics. The nobility was still in existence, with all its titles and a good share of its arrogance, and was even adding members as a result of the civil wars. Even many financiers and industrialists attained noble rank. This does not mean, though, that the hereditary nobility maintained the same economic power it had held before, for, as a result of the disentailment law of 1822, all the ruined nobles, who lived miserably burdened with heavy mortgages, sold off their properties. At that time a large number of aristocrats gave up their last possessions to the bourgeoisie. But the nobles who were able to survive the drop in agricultural prices became stronger and more powerful than ever.

The clergy diminished with lightning rapidity. Figures do not lie. In 1797 the census gave some 200,000 individuals; in 1803 there were 203,000; in 1826, 150,000; and in 1860, 56,000—that is, a 75% decrease. It is fair to suppose that this was the lowest point for religious vocations. Not for nothing had the Church undergone secularization, the War of Independence, and the religious persecutions of 1834–1835, which affected the regular clergy in particular. In 1851, Article 29 of the Concordat authorized the existence of only three monastic congregations: two explicitly stated (St. Vincent de Paul and St. Philip Neri) and one unspecified. As for congregations of nuns, their number was not stated. After 1860, and especially after the Law of Associations of the Restoration (1886), the clergy was to recover. But we possess no trustworthy figures on this point until the early 20th century.

As for peasants, laborers, industrial workers, and wage earners of all kinds, we do possess a reliable document: the occupational census of 1900. At that time the economically active population of Spain—taking into account necessary rectifications—was approximately as follows: those engaged in agriculture, 4,500,000 (68% of the active population); industrial workers, 1 million (16%); service workers, another million and another 16%. Certainly these figures conceal basic data of social structure, for they do not distinguish between the agricultural middle class and rural day laborers, nor between bourgeoisie and proletarians.

To get closer to the truth we shall have to take the indirect path of the electoral census. According to the laws of 1858 and 1865, persons paying more than 400 and 200 reales in direct taxes, respectively, had the right to vote. These were the ones who really held economic power and political influence. So, in 1858 the number of recognized voters was 157,931, which in a population of 15,400,000 inhabitants represented exactly 1%. In 1865, when the vote was given to those paying more than 200 reales, the number of electors rose to 418,271, which, for a population of 16,600,000 inhabitants, was something under 3%. The truth is that in the middle of the 19th century, as at the beginning of the 16th, from 1 to 3% of the Spanish population, whether it went under the name of duke, general, or bourgeois, proprietor or civil servant, controlled the remaining 99–97% by means of the electoral vote or the exercise of power.

DISTRIBUTION OF AGRARIAN PROPERTY; CIVIL AND ECCLESIASTICAL DISENTAILMENT. Ever since Spain had experienced the first biological thrust in the middle of the 18th century, the division of rural property had been anachronistic, for it had been inherited from the latter days of the Reconquest. It became necessary to think of agrarian reform, and this was done by jurists, politicians, and intellectuals, and initiated by the governments, as we saw on pp. 519–522. We should particularly remember the royal cedula of 1766 on the plowing and distribution of new lands, the Royal Pragmatic of 1793 on division of communal lands, and the Papal authorization of 1805 on disentailment of some ecclesiastical properties.

The downfall of the Old Regime, brought about by the Spanish revolution of May, 1808, favored these desires for agrarian reform. The invading Napoleonic government as well as the patriots who were fighting it took important measures. In 1808 and 1809 Joseph I decreed the suppression of religious orders, confiscation of their properties, and the conversion of these into national assets. The Cortes of Cádiz, for its part, voted a number of laws in 1810–1814 favoring the modification of rural property. However, the War of Independence which was being fiercely fought throughout this period made it impossible to put this reform into effect, so that when the Restoration took place under Ferdinand VII, the revolution had not been carried out in regard to agrarian property. Thus the doctrines upheld by the Cortes of Cádiz were not applied for thirty years, in some cases fifty years. This delay was exceedingly harmful, since agrarian reform, intended primarily for the peasants, in the end benefited only the rich; that is, those who had money to buy the lands which were being disentailed. Instead of providing, as in France, a medium-sized agrarian property of an individual type, Spanish reform resulted in a latifundism which was much more extensive territorially, much more selfish economically, and socially a great deal more sterile than its predecessor.

DISENTAILMENT OF PATRIMONIES. The history of the disentailments (not simply ecclesiastical disentailment) should begin with a study of the elimination of the seigniorial power exercised by nobles over their peasant vassals. The Cortes of Cádiz approved the law of August 6, 1811, abolishing survivals of the feudal system in rural areas. These were vassalage, jurisdictional and personal service, and the exclusive, private, and prohibitive privileges having to do with economic and labor monopolies. This law was abrogated by Ferdinand VII in 1814. The 1813 law abolishing *mayorazgos* of less than 3,000 ducats of annual income and banning entailment to private persons, titles of Castile, and grandees beyond certain monetary limits (3,000, 10,000 and 80,000 ducats of income respectively), suffered the same fate. But when liberalism came into power in 1820 it again took up the work begun by the Cortes of Cádiz. The law of December 11, 1820, called the Law of Disentailment, totally suppressed *mayorazgos* and entailments, making it possible for *hidalgos* and nobles to sell their lands. This law was suspended in 1823 as a result of the restoration of absolutism, but was confirmed and reestablished by another law enacted on August 30, 1836. After that moment there was a quiet and uninterrupted transfer of property which had formerly been held as *mayorazgos* and civil entailments. Salvador Millet gives the following figures: in 1845 the number of transactions of disentailed prop-

OUTLINE OF THE MOBILIZATION OF SPANISH AGRARIAN PROPERTY
IN THE FIRST HALF OF THE NINETEENTH CENTURY

Civil Disentailment		Ecclesiastical Disentailment
Seigniorial Lands	*Municipal Properties*	
CORTES OF CÁDIZ (1810–1814)		
August 6, 1811.—Law abolishing jurisdictional rights	January 4, 1813.—Law distributing *propios* and common lands	June 17, 1812.—Law incorporating into the State the assets of religious orders dissolved by the invader
	June 8, 1813.—Enclosure of farms	

	Civil Disentailment		Ecclesiastical Disentailment
	Seigniorial Lands	*Municipal Properties*	
LIBERAL TRIENNIUM (1820–1823)			
	December 11, 1820.—Law of disentailment	June 29, 1822.—Decree converting uncultivated and crown lands into private property	October 25, 1820.—Law incorporating into the State the assets of monasteries and convents dissolved by the Cortes
PROGRESSIVE PERIOD (1835–1843)			
	August 30, 1836.—Reestablishment of Law of 1820	March 6, 1834.—Royal Order legalizing sales and possession	October 11, 1835.—Dissolution of religious orders
		May 18, 1837.—Royal Order repeating previous one	July 29, 1837.—Law of National Assets
			September 2, 1841.—Law restating previous ones
MODERATE DECADE (1843–1854)			
			April 9, 1845.—Law restricting sale of National Assets (Concordat of March 16, 1851)
PROGRESSIVE BIENNIUM (1854–1856)			
		May 1, 1855.—General law of disentailment (suspended September 14, 1856)	
MODERATE GOVERNMENTS (1856–1860)			
	October 2, 1858.—Law putting into effect the provisions of the law of May 1, 1855 regarding disentailment of municipal assets	August 24, 1860.—End of the extensions of time granted to legalize occupations of the land	April 4, 1860.—Renewal of sales with the consent of the Church

erty was 63,000, with a value of 190 million reales, while in 1854 there were 273,000 transactions with a total value of 1,007,-000,000. These figures indicate not only a quickening in the tempo of buying and selling, but also the total number of transfers of property, which were greater, taken all together, than the sum of those freed by civil and ecclesiastical disentailment, as can be seen by comparing them with other figures we shall shortly cite.

Placing the aristocracy's real estate on the market had indubitable consequences in the economic and social spheres. But we do not possess enough information to reach a precise judgement. It is to be supposed that this disentailment resulted in better exploitation of the properties, although their regional and agricultural diversity left room for a great number of specific results. We should also keep in mind the fact that the most powerful families managed to keep their possessions intact. This was the case of the counts of Sobradiel, as we are told in a study made by Father Juan Fernández Marco: the latifundist estate of the same name (1,200 hectares of land irrigated by the Canal of Aragon) emerged unscathed from the hazards of the 19th century. Precisely the same thing occurred with other patrimonies of the great Castilian and Andalusian nobility, though there were exceptions, like the case of the dukes of Frías, constables of Castile, who disposed of a great many pieces of real estate because of their political activity in the service of liberal ideals. On the other hand, it is probable that the properties of the middle and lower nobility, who suffered the consequences of the country's economic transformation and emerged the losers, went into the hands of the newly rich bourgeoisie. We do not know the rhythm of this economic and social process, and therefore any hypothesis we might form today would be rash. Only a minute analysis of legal documents would enable us to form a clear idea of a process which depended so heavily on the progress of economic fluctuations and the vicissitudes of industrial expansion. This is the case, for example, of the increase in value of the Castilian, Extremaduran, and Andalusian cork forests, largely owned by the aristocracy, which came about as a result of the development of cork-manufacturing activity in Catalonia.

CIVIL DISENTAILMENT. Simultaneously with this process of breaking down property entailed to the nobility, the sale and use of uncultivated lands, *propios,* and common lands took place; this was one of the fundamental problems of the 19th century. We have spoken earlier of the magnitude of municipal possessions in Spain, in terms of *propios,* communal lands, and Crown or uncultivated lands. Collective use of these resources, even disregarding the unfortunate system by which the Mesta prevented their use, did not respond either to the requirements of the increased population or to the high prices paid for private property which came on the market. Thus there were two kinds of people who cast envious eyes on such properties; the dispossessed laborer, hungry for land, and the wealthy farmer who wished to round out his fortune by taking advantage of the rise in the prices of agricultural products, beginning in 1765 and even more noticeable after 1789. Hence too the dual attitude reflected in the texts of economists who studied the question: those who approved of collective use of land based on the establishment of family holdings and cooperative work, and those who, headed by Jovellanos, were in favor of a radically individualist solution. The latter doctrine won the day in the Cortes of Cádiz. The decree of January 4, 1813, provided for splitting up *propios* and uncultivated lands into lots, under a system of full proprietorship. But, taking into account the social situation created by the war, it was decreed that only half of these were to be put on sale, while the other half was to be divided among combatants and landless heads of families, in exchange for an annual fee to be applied to the purchase price. This was a clearly democratic measure, for it gave to the soldiers the same land they had defended with their blood on the field of battle.

This measure, like the law of July 8, 1813, concerning enclosure of farms, which accentuated the private and individualistic nature of property, was annulled by Ferdinand VII. However, the problem continued to be a very real one. The Restoration was faced with the necessity of giving land to the poorer classes and legalizing the occupations made during the War of Independence, especially in Andalusia where before 1813, according to Francisco Gómez Fernández, deputy for Seville, "with the pretext of aiding the poor, the rich succeeded in carrying out a distribution of land in such a way that they soon became the owners of all of it." Therefore, it is not surprising that in 1818 Ferdinand VII's government decreed the sale of uncultivated and Crown lands, with the proceeds from their sale to be applied to amortization of the national debt. The royal cedula of July 22, 1819, providing for the sale of uncultivated lands to peasants, followed the same lines. These measures, basically very cautious ones, were extended by the constitutional ministries in the three-year period 1820–1823. The Royal Order of November 28, 1820, and the Royal Decree of June 29, 1822, ratified and completed the 1813 law; one-half the uncultivated and Crown land was to be turned over to free buyers for payment on the national debt, and the other half was to be distributed, in plots sufficient to maintain a family of five persons, among officers and veterans of the War of Independence, or destitute heads of families. There was an explosion of claims from the Andalusian day laborers, as we know from a number of contemporary pamphlets such as *Discourse on the Manner of Increasing Public Wealth, the Merchant Marine and Civil Virtues* (*Discurso sobre la manera de aumentar la riqueza pública, la marina y las virtudes civiles*), published in Cordova in 1820, and *Distribution of Uncultivated Royal Lands and Crown Lands* (*Repartimiento de baldíos realengos y realengos*), in 1821. The first of these demanded distribution of the land among its cultivators, and drew a comparison between 4,500,000 peasants and the 1,350 illustrious houses "useless for the service of arms and incapable of carrying on agriculture, trade, and the arts." In the same demagogic vein, the anonymous author of the second pamphlet attacked those landowners who had "taken over" the lands given by God for the enjoyment of all, leaving nothing to the poor but the soil of their graves.

But these laws were not carried out either, and as Costa, the common source for all authors who refer to the matter, writes, "The revolution passed without the people's having acquired a handsbreadth more of land"—an opinion which is not entirely true, for after 1808 and 1823 there were illegal occupations of farms by people who had no land on which to work. To legalize these acts the liberals dictated the Royal Order of March 6, 1834, admitting the inscription of properties acquired by the terms of the law of 1813 and the decree of 1822, giving possession of them to those who, though unable to demonstrate their right of possession, would agree to pay a perpetual rental equal to the average annual rent of the five years previous to its occupation.

This almost forgotten measure was more revolutionary than

many decrees of disentailment, for it established a legal precedent, and many persons took advantage of it to "bring under the plow" uncultivated lands. Thus, the decree of May 18, 1837, confirmed possession of lands to those who had improved them with plantings of trees and vines and promised to pay an annual rental equivalent to 2% of the value of the land before its improvement. The problem of breaking new ground even appeared as late as August 24, 1865, in a law providing for a final and unrenewable limit on legalizing occupation of land.

As for the *propios* and communal lands, they were incorporated into the general law of disentailment of May 1, 1855, drawn up by Pascual Madoz. After that moment, municipal governments could convert them to private property. Receipts from the sale (minus one-fifth) were to be used to buy untransferable bonds on the public debt. Thus the municipalities would continue to receive revenues similar to those formerly provided. It was a question, therefore, of changing the form of property and not the property itself. But the ensuing trading in public debt bonds, with open scandal in some provinces, ruined municipal finance in many Spanish towns, to the detriment of the functioning of municipal councils in general and the possibilities of their citizens' earning a living. However, a number of municipalities managed to escape the terms of this law, kept alive by another of October 2, 1858, so that in certain regions collective patrimonies were triumphant.

It is very difficult to estimate the volume of transfer of municipal agrarian property, both in the form of uncultivated and Crown lands and *propios* and council lands. According to an official declaration by the Ministry of Finance, in 1896 the common woodlands and grazing grounds belonging to municipal governments totaled 4,100,000 hectares. This figure would almost coincide with that of the end of the 18th century, which is absolutely impossible, for reliable estimates set at 16,859 the number of municipally-owned rural properties disentailed during the single period 1834–1856. We must, therefore, wait until new research clears up the area of these sales, whose value can be set at almost one-third of the total of ecclesiastical disentailment (some 43 million reales). We must also keep in mind the discrepancies existing between official measurements and private declarations. In 1885 it was estimated that concealment existed in regard to almost half of rural properties in general. These discrepancies contributed toward masking the truth of the events we have been examining.

ECCLESIASTICAL DISENTAILMENT. The sale of municipal lands is somewhat clouded by the process of ecclesiastical disentailment. As we have seen, this had its roots in the ideology of the Enlightenment and in the financial difficulties of the Old Regime monarchy. The measures taken by the alien government of Joseph I (August 17, 1809) suppressing the monastic and mendicant orders and those of the regular clergy, and confiscating their property as national resources, found an echo in the Cortes of Cádiz, especially in the decree of June 17, 1812, providing for seizure of the assets of ecclesiastical communities dissolved or reorganized by the decrees of the invaders. Other, later measures required declarations of their properties and income by the monastic houses and convents not included in previous legislation, using these as the basis of an extraordinary war tax.

The restoration of Ferdinand VII demolished the work of the Cortes of Cádiz. But it was necessary to recognize the true situation: the straits of the Treasury, the decline of religious communities after the War of Independence, and the financial burden felt even by those which had managed to survive in the face of tax demands. For these reasons, when the liberals regained power in 1820 they not only revived the decree of 1812 (October 1, 1820), but included in it, by the law of October 25, the property of monastic orders containing fewer than twenty-four members, those of various congregations, and the monasteries and schools of the military orders. In addition, ecclesiastical communities were forbidden to acquire any revenue-producing property, so as to prevent establishment of new mortmain holdings within the bosom of the Church. A still more radical measure was the seizure by the State of ecclesiastical tithes, even though their amount was reduced by half. Many of the surviving monasteries and communities were obliged to sell part of their lands, for which they received legal approval from the Cortes.

This first wave of disentailment had practically no effect. The downfall of constitutionalism in 1823 created a new parenthesis in this dramatic process, in which both anticlerical ideas and the country's vital economic needs entered into play. With the definitive return of the liberal regime, legislation concerning disentailment came to a logical climax under the minister Mendizábal. By the terms of the law of July 29, 1837, the real estate, revenues, rights, and shares of religious communities and orders of either sex were declared national property, and their sale at public auction was provided for. According to the preamble of the law, this transfer of property was to be carried out for the benefit of the peasants and was not to damage the regular clergy, for the latter group would keep the revenue it obtained from its former properties, for which the State made itself responsible. These were principles typical of every bourgeois revolution, and must be understood within the atmosphere of the period and the Spanish government's constant financial straits, aggravated by the Carlist war then in progress.

Mendizábal had foreseen that land would go into the hands of middle-income farmers, as had happened in France during the 1789 revolution. To this end, the law of 1837 provided that there were to be two types of buyers, those who paid in cash and those who would do so in State scrip. The first group was given a period of sixteen years to pay off the purchase, at 5% interest; the second, eight years at 10%. Both were to make a down payment of one-fifth of the sale price at the time of purchase. As for owners of public securities, they could make payment under the following conditions: one-third in the consolidated 5% debt; another one-third in the 4% debt; and the rest in a nonconsolidated 5% debt. This arrangement favored the bourgeoisie because the majority of the bonds were quoted at considerably under par, especially those of the last group, for they were accepted for exchange at their nominal value.

In 1843 the progressive party, which had supported ecclesiastical disentailment, fell. The moderates came to power and restricted the sale of national assets by the law of April 9, 1845. It was the first step toward achieving an agreement with the Holy See. Once the Concordat was arranged on March 16, 1851, the Papacy accepted the *fait accompli* and the State agreed to recognize the Church's right to acquisition of property by any legal means, to return the assets not yet alienated, and to give the Church certain annual sums for support of religion and the clergy. The return of properties was accomplished on condition that they be put up for public auction, with the sale price converted into nontransferable State bonds at 3%, to be administered by diocesan authorities.

Scarcely had this Concordat been published than the progressives gained power again as a result of the coup of Vicálvaro (1854). The General Law of Disentailment of 1855 was then passed, combining all the existing laws relating to both civil and ecclesiastical disentailment, and further, as we have already mentioned, including council-owned lands under civil assets. Pascual Madoz was the force behind this piece of legislation, which aroused the opposition of the collectivists, such as the Extremaduran deputy Bueno, and the Catholics, who appealed to the text of the 1851 Concordat. The law was in force for only fourteen months, for in a new political twist the progressives were forced out of power. Their opponents suspended the law in September, 1856. A large number of transfers of ecclesiastical property were made during that short period of time, however, and so it was necessary to reach a new agreement with the Holy See. This was the nature of the law of April 4, 1860, an addition to the Concordat of 1851. Taking into account the deteriorated condition of most of the properties that had not yet been taken over, the difficulty of administering them, and the inaccuracy of the computation of their income, the Holy See accepted their total exchange for bonds on the Spanish consolidated debt at 3%, excepting from this arrangement the buildings and structures of the regular clergy of both sexes and other properties intended for the use and disposal of bishops and parish priests. Bonds worth 1,200,000,000 reales were turned over to the Church for this purpose, with an annual income of 36 million reales. But interest payments on this debt were suppressed after 1862 and not renewed until 1948.

NATURE AND CONSEQUENCES OF THE DISENTAILMENTS. The disentailment process which we have just studied has aroused reactions of very different kinds, though in general they have been adverse. Catholic historians and politicians have considered the disentailment as an enormous act of pillage revealing the impiety and injustice of the 19th century. Collectivist and socialist-minded authors are of the same opinion. According to them, the bourgeoisie took over the assets of the Church and the municipalities by manipulating the individualist theory of property and reducing the peasants to destitution. They believe that contemporary neo-latifundism arose out of this process, and that it resulted in an army of 2 or 3 million "desperate" landless peasants.

The truth is that we do not possess the systematic study which this delicate question requires. The polemical material accumulated in the course of a century does us no good, for emotion is predominant in it, not a scientific attitude. Therefore we shall have to wait until scholars interested in this subject can give us exact data before we can comprehend the material and spiritual motives ruling the disentailments.

At present there is one working hypothesis which seems promising: the administration and use of mortmain properties, civil as well as ecclesiastical, responded to anachronistic formulas. They were a burden on the growth of national income and consequently on just distribution for the common good. When this factor came into play as a result of the War of Independence, and the country had to make a tremendous effort, the problem of entailed properties began to occupy first place among public concerns. Even the religious communities themselves were aware of the situation, for they recognized the country's economic and tax problems. We have proof of the sales made voluntarily by monasteries and convents in 1820–1823.

This would have been a good way to solve the problem of mortmain; in the ecclesiastical field, a progressive disentailment (similar to that of the *mayorazgos*); on the civil side, a reform of communal and Crown properties, *propios* and *arbitrios,* in the spirit of effective social collaboration. Political debates, rendered more acute by the restorations of 1814 and 1823, made this slower and surer path impossible to follow. And when the crisis of 1835 occurred, after twenty years of unavailing efforts to contain a process that was unavoidable both from a demographic and an economic point of view, the inevitable happened: a political program was put into operation, in which the financial concerns of a State on the verge of bankruptcy entered into play.

Therefore, disentailment did not live up to its chief objectives: to give land to poor peasants under a system of collective municipal use or indefinite private utilization (as in the case of emphyteutic, or long-term, leases); and to break up the latifundia which had accrued as a result of historical and geographical processes. Nor did disentailment represent the manna from Heaven expected by the liberal Treasury ministers. Revenue from it was diluted in the course of the different bureaucratic processes, especially when property was converted into bonds, which were very easy to use fraudulently.

Nevertheless, for the bourgeoisie disentailment was a battle flag, and this feeling was shared by both progressives and moderates. The bourgeoisie profited from the process, and supported it one hundred per cent. They bought disentailed lands from the nobles, flocked to auctions, and put under cultivation the farmlands abandoned by monasteries and convents. Catholics were the great buyers of these national assets; moderates and conservatives were those who, in 1833 and 1868, publicly supported the necessity of disentailment.

The figures in Pascual Madoz's *Dictionary* (revised by J. Fontana) give us some curious information about ecclesiastical disentailment. In the first place, they present the disentailment picture about 1845, the year in which the data later published in his book were collected:

SITUATION OF RURAL PROPERTIES RESULTING FROM ECCLESIASTICAL
DISENTAILMENT IN JULY, 1845

Total assessed value of the properties	1,866,226,000 reales
Assessed value of unsold properties	723,166,000 reales
Assessed value of properties already sold	1,061,893,000 reales
Amount realized from public sale of properties	2,454,053,000 reales
Percentage of properties sold	57.9%
Percentage of increase over assessed value in amount realized from properties sold	131.1%

If we consider the provincial distribution of the figures we have just presented, a number of interesting features can be observed. The first is concentration of the most valuable rural properties belonging to the Spanish Church into three groups: the old kingdom of León (with maximum concentration in Salamanca); Andalusia (maximum in Seville); and the Castilian-Extremaduran area (maximum in Toledo). On the Mediterranean coast there is one atypical maximum: Valencia. In general, therefore, we find a reflection of the process of the Slow Reconquest (a war of recovery, united with herding activity).

The largest buyers of ecclesiastical properties correspond exactly to these areas of greatest density: Seville, Cordova, Salamanca, Toledo, and Valencia produced the largest number of purchases up to 1845; in the other provinces the process corresponded almost exactly to the value of the former ecclesiastical possessions. However, the real proportion of sales by disentailment reveals certain peculiar facts. The first is the increase in sales: the majority of Spanish provinces had sold more than 60% of clerical properties before 1845, and six of them (Valladolid, Huesca, Guadalajara, Teruel, Albacete, and the Balearic Islands) more than 80%. The second fact is the increase in purchases in relation to the economic potential of certain regions or provinces: on the Catalonian coast and in Madrid, in the Balearics and the Andalusian littoral, in the Canary Islands, the rhythm of disentailment was more rapid than in other parts of Spain.

All this gives us a great deal to think about. Ecclesiastical disentailment probably did not present a problem of conscience. It was a political measure imposed by the bourgeois revolution, and responded particularly to the problem of the country's economic expansion. But in every part of the nation it took place in the light of very special local conditions, so that it is impossible to generalize about its development and consequences province by province. It would seem erroneous to believe that ecclesiastical properties lost value when they were put up for public auction, though we do not know how they were paid for and whether depreciation of State bonds involved an unprofitable piece of business for the State. On the other hand, the traditional version of the facts which attributes most of the gains to the richer classes, especially aristocrats and capitalists, seems incontrovertible to us.

In 1855–1856 acquisitions of disentailed properties received, as we know, a further impetus. According to the figures of the Ministry of Finance, the result of civil and ecclesiastical disentailment was that reflected in the following table:

Clergy	Properties Rural	Urban	Censos and foros	Value in reales
ECCLESIASTICAL DISENTAILMENT				
1836–1844 Secular	44,852	5,901	5,312	399,258,967
Regular	66,093	7,212	73,308	503,571,422
1845–1854 Secular	2,350	1,030	2,393	45,380,906
Regular	1,381	299	13,689	22,465,745
1854–1856 Secular	22,351	4,576	46,946	354,912,492
Regular	2,494	629	15,468	80,593,951
Totals	143,526	10,645	92,688	1,406,183,483
CIVIL DISENTAILMENT				
1834–1856 Corporations	16,859	3,327	24,434	431,451,459
State	5,074	661	5,803	87,717,269
Totals	21,933	3,988	30,237	519,168,728
COMBINED TOTALS	165,459	23,633	122,295	1,925,352,211

The above figures can be relied upon in general terms. Madoz estimated that, in 1844, 54% of all rural ecclesiastical properties had been sold, and valued them at 1,872,782,420 reales (and this 54% is not far from the figure of 900 million in the preceding table, representing sales for the period 1836–1844). If the figures are correct, the fact would be that no more than 1,400,000,000 reales of ecclesiastical properties were sold, out of an estimated total of 1,900,000,000. On the other hand, in the area of civil disentailment, property previously valued at 329,500,000 reales was sold for 520 million, with a profit to the Treasury of some 200 million. This increase is in agreement with the one obtained by the auction of ecclesiastical properties, as we have just established.

LATIFUNDIA AND MINIFUNDIA. The present structure of agrarian property derives from the colossal transfer of real estate which took place between 1833 and 1876 as a result of municipal and ecclesiastical disentailment and the breaking up of *mayorazgos*. As we said before and must repeat, this transfer of real estate did not benefit the peasants or give rise to the appearance of peasant owners, the goal of the reformers ever since the middle of the 18th century. On the contrary, it strengthened latifundism to a degree dangerous for the country's economy and its social well-being.

Nineteenth-century latifundism gained ground in parts of the country where great agricultural and herding domains were already traditional, held by a single owner and cultivated by a legion of wage earners, day laborers, or plowboys: Andalusia (especially in the western zone), Extremadura, the southern part of New Castile, and León. These lands had known the Reconquest, the flocks and officials of the Mesta, the military orders and the great nobles. A large part of them wound up in the hands of the upper aristocracy, while the bourgeoisie, especially the bourgeois financiers, took a huge bite out of the former Church possessions, communal lands, and the properties of bankrupt *hidalgos*. Thus patrimonies were rounded out and swelled to unseemly size, while the number of landless laborers increased and unrest in rural areas grew, as we shall soon see.

By the end of the 19th century and the beginning of the present one, according to the official tax surveys of 1930, the land of central and southern Spain was concentrated into a small number of great estates or dispersed in myriad small properties of no practical agricultural use. Here are the figures:

	Number	Area	Average area per unit	Per cent of Total In no.	In area
Latifundia (larger than 250 ha.)	12,488	7,468,629	598.0	0.1	33.28
Large holdings (100 to 250 ha.)	16,305	2,339,957	143.0	0.1	10.42
Medium holdings (10 to 100 ha.)	169,472	24,611,789	27.0	1.6	20.55
Small holdings (5 to 10 ha.)	205,784	1,379,416	6.0	2.0	6.14
Minifundia (up to 5 ha.)	9,810,331	6,635,299	0.6	96.0	29.57
Totals	10,214,380	22,435,090		99.8	99.96

The figures in this table are extremely significant. One-third of the real estate in 1930 belonged to great latifundia, with an average area of 600 hectares per unit, while another third was composed of small properties of less than 10 hectares; altogether these totaled more than 10 million parcels of land with an overall average size of less than 1 hectare (0.6, in fact). These data are of even more interest if we relate them to the figures concerning proprietors. Pascual Carrión, using the tax figures available to him in 1930, established the following table in regard to 22,500,000 hectares of land:

Proprietors	Hectares	Respective Percentage	
12,721	11,068,700	0.8	49.4
1,774,104	11,366,390	99.2	50.6
1,786,825	22,435,090	100.0	100.0

The accuracy of this anomalous distribution of property is proved by turning to the distribution of rural wealth among proprietors. Here are two series of figures, published by Pascual Carrión and Fernando Martín-Sánchez Juliá, one referring to the tax rolls of 1930 and the second to those of 1945.

Martín-Sánchez Juliá points out that, out of 2,500,000 small proprietors, almost 2 million (1,993,951 to be exact) were considered to be poor and were exempt from rural taxes in 1949.

	1930	1945
Large proprietors (paying more than 5,000 pts. in taxes)	17,349	5,817
Medium proprietors (1,000 to 5,000 pts.)	73,029	35,515
Small proprietors (up to 1,000 pts.)	1,699,585	2,651,644
Totals	1,790,026	2,692,976

Thanks to Carrión's detailed study, we have been able to construct the map of Spanish latifundism which accompanies these pages. As can be observed, there is a clear latifundist grouping which takes in the provinces of Cáceres and Badajoz, Toledo and Ciudad Real, Albacete and Murcia, and Huelva, Cádiz, Seville, Cordova, Granada, Málaga, and Jaén. In each of these provinces there are more than 750 pieces of property larger than 500 hectares. If we look at the proportion of properties larger than 250 hectares in each province, the grouping mentioned above contracts slightly, excluding Albacete and Murcia. In three provinces (Cádiz, Seville, and Ciudad Real), the proportion of holdings of over 250 hectares rises to more than 50%. This is the heart of latifundist Spain. The situation is even more glaring if we examine the municipal districts

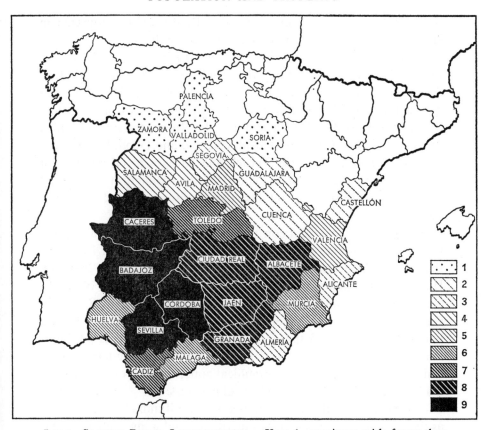

LARGE SPANISH RURAL LANDHOLDINGS.—*Key:* 1, provinces with fewer than 50 holdings of 250 ha.; 2, from 50 to 100; 3, from 100 to 200; 4, from 200 to 300; 5, from 300 to 400; 6, from 400 to 500; 7, from 500 to 750; 8, from 750 to 1,000; 9, more than 1,000. The provinces left blank are those for which no tax survey was made in 1930.

within each province. In the province of Cádiz, the municipality of Jerez de la Frontera is characterized by very widespread lati-fundism: 73% of the properties are of more than 250 hectares. But even this does not equal the dramatic proportion in the municipality of Castellar de la Frontera, where properties of more than 250 hectares occupy 96% of the land. A similar case is that of Horna-chuelos (Cordova), with 93%.

This explains the existence of holdings larger than 5,000 hectares (50 sq. km.; equivalent, that is, to a zone 10 km. in length and 5 in width), of which there were seventy-four in Spain at the beginning of the 20th century: twenty in Ciudad Real province, fourteen in Huelva, ten in Granada, six in Toledo and Seville, etc.

To the north and east of this great latifundist zone there is a region of medium-sized properties (and even with some "minifundia" in the valleys) and land leased on a short-term basis. We can consider as included in this group the two provinces of León and Zamora; those of Old Castile south of the Duero; the nonlatifundist provinces of New Castile (Madrid, Cuenca, and Guadalajara); and those of Almería, Alicante, Teruel, and Saragossa. Of course, not all districts in the provinces named fit this configuration of land ownership, but in their totality they conform to these general outlines.

From the uplands of León to the Mediterranean, all along the Cantabrian mountains and on the southern slopes of the Pyrenees; that is, in Asturias, Santander, the Basque Provinces, Navarre, Huesca, and Catalonia (and furthermore, as a reflection of juridical institutions and methods of settlement in medieval Spain, in Castellón de la Plana, Valencia, the Balearics, and a considerable part of Old Castile to the north of the Duero), there is predominantly a system of medium-sized holdings with long-term leases. This is the best-balanced geographical zone, and the one which has made the most agricultural and social progress.

And finally, in the Galician region "minifundia" predominate, as the result of a free system of inheritance and a high rate of population increase. We need to keep in mind that the minifundia of wet regions and irrigated areas represent an economic reality very different from that of the dry farming regions of Spain. This consideration makes it necessary to proceed with caution when we speak of the evils of minifundism, which are evils only in the dry provinces of Spain where irrigation is not employed.

The polarization of rural property into latifundia and minifundia after the disentailments responds to the law of concentration of capital. While large landowners could survive occasional bad harvests, small ones had to bow to them, sometimes by direct sale and sometimes through usurious loans which eventually deprived them of their holdings. Doctrinaire liberalism, on the other hand, reflected in the provisions of the Civil Code, aided the progressive subdivision of Castilian property by means of inheritance. Hence the legion of owners of tiny parcels which, as we have said, predominate in a large part of Spain. There are landowners in Cáceres, in Palencia, in Soria, and in many other Spanish provinces, but they are destitute landowners.

43 · Agricultural and Livestock Production

STAGES IN SPANISH AGRICULTURAL DEVELOPMENT DURING THE 19TH CENTURY. At the beginning of the 19th century, says Salvador Millet, Spanish agriculture was hampered by three obstacles: the ban on cultivation of idle lands, the ban on enclosing arable land (with the sole exception, decreed in 1778, of market gardens and vineyards), and the removal of much land from cultivation because of a number of laws enacted in favor of the Mesta. These three obstacles, together with the effects of entailment, produced a dizzying rise in the price of real estate and the progressive diminution of rural income, which in turn meant the flight of capital from agriculture, abandonment of arable land, the impossibility of introducing improvements, and separation between the proprietor and the farm worker.

By 1837 the situation had changed radically, to the point that we may even speak of an *agrarian revolution*. This received considerable momentum, as we have seen, from the basic demographic thrust. But the Spanish liberals' political ideas also contributed to it. As early as 1813 the views of the Cortes of Cádiz were obvious, when it issued the decrees of June 8 ordering enclosure of farms in perpetuity, abolition of price-fixing, and full freedom of internal trade for agricultural products. This transcendental measure was not ratified until the decrees of January 20 and 29, 1834, which further declared freedom of trade in all articles of food, drink, and fuel, and suppression of any obstacle to their circulation. Thus the free-market system was established for agriculture. No less stimulating were the disentailment measures adopted almost simultaneously, as well as abolition of the ecclesiastical tithe, which represented a burden of 854 million reales on rural producers (law of July 29, 1837).

As a consequence of these measures there was a considerable

process of agricultural expansion, as can be seen in the following figures:

	Crop area in thousands of ha.		Production in millions		Annual yield per ha.		Production per inhabitant	
	1800	1860	1800	1860	1800	1860	1800	1860
Wheat	2,900	5,100	18.30 qm.	29.60	6.31 qm.	5.80	174 kg.	188
Cereals	6,100	9,000	39.50 qm.	55.75	6.47 qm.	6.20	371 kg.	355
Vines	400	1,200	3.85 hl.	10.30	9.62 hl.	9.00	36 l.	68
Olives	—	859	0.69 hl.	1.44	— hl.	1.67	6 l.	9

In fact, between 1818 and 1860 some 4 million hectares had been brought under cultivation, a really sensational figure. The larger part of these did not proceed, as we have already noted, from the sale of ecclesiastical properties, but from the entry into the market of real estate formerly entailed in *mayorazgos*. Millet estimates that these last totaled 3 million hectares, while property stemming from uncultivated lands and *propios* was about 600,000, with only 500,000 coming from the Church. These figures are subject to correction, for they do not agree with those we have noted in the previous pages.

A decrease in yield contrasts with the expansion in crop area. Wheat production per hectare went down from 6.31 metric quintals in 1800 to 5.8 in 1860, cereals from 6.47 to 6.20, and grape products from 9.62 hectoliters to 9. This decrease was not general. There were lands where, by contrast, yield increased thanks to the interest of their owners, who had bought them at good prices from the nobles offering them for sale. We should also keep in mind that, with disentailment, inferior land not suitable for constant and efficient production was put under cultivation. Probably these lands would have been better used under the traditional system of woodland or grazing ground. And also, with few exceptions, there was a dearth of capital to invest in agricultural exploitation. Agrarian credit was an empty concept in the middle of the 19th century, for the public granaries were ruined and discredited. There were 3,410 of these altogether, with some 100 million reales of capital, a very scanty figure and one with little liquidity.

In short, this was the period of inordinate expansion of wheat cultivation. Salvador Millet defines the consequences of this process as follows: "The extensive cultivation of wheat made Spain temporarily independent of other countries, but it also made us permanently dependent on our own poverty."

In 1860 came the beginning of a second phase, which we might call *readjustment of agricultural production*. The area under cultivation diminished (perhaps by as much as 500,000 hectares), but yield increased. Here are some figures showing the process:

	Crop area in thousands of ha.		Production in millions		Annual yield per ha.		Production per inhabitant	
	1860	1900	1860	1900	1800	1900	1860	1900
Wheat	5,100	3,700	29.60 qm.	25.70	5.80 qm.	6.92	188 kg.	138
Cereals	9,000	7,000	55.75 qm.	51.54	6.20 qm.	7.06	355 kg.	336
Vines	1,200	1,450	10.80 hl.	21.60	9.00 hl.	14.88	68 l.	116
Olives	859	1,360	1.44 hl.	2.09	1.67 hl.	1.80	9 l.	11

This phenomenon is explained by the drop in cereal production compared with more specialized crops such as the vine, the olive, and fruit trees. Expansion of the railway system had a decisive effect on the process of selection of cultivated areas, so that the great contemporary Spanish agricultural regions became clearly marked at this time.

After a hundred years of total indifference, the State began to take an interest in agriculture. There were men in the government whose outlook was more modern. However, the country gave them little support. This was shown in the teaching of agriculture. The first school was founded in Aranjuez by the progressive government of Espartero (1855). Reorganized in 1869 under the name of General School of Agriculture, the idea was picked up by the Restoration, which in 1876 and 1881 began to take an interest in this important subject. In 1881 the provincial agricultural schools of Valencia, Saragossa, Seville, Granada, Cordova, and Valladolid were founded; but none of them succeeded in arousing much interest in their respective districts. Also, the decree of 1887 creating farm schools never emerged from the planning stage. However, the invasion of phylloxera was of great interest to agrarian opinion. In 1893 vitilogical stations were established to introduce American vines.

In the area of rural credit, the governments of the Restoration tried to modernize the machinery of the public granaries. Romero Robledo's law of June 26, 1877, was enacted for the purpose of giving new life to these institutions. But this excellent idea was frustrated by the facts of political life, and in practice the law became the financial basis of *caciquismo,* or local bossism. On the other hand, although the Commercial Code (1885) authorized establishment of agrarian banks, these were very slow in entering the area of credit to farmers. Their real development took place at a later period.

The fundamental reform in Spanish agriculture was really the result of private effort and was connected with the development of fertilizer techniques. These began to be used in Valencia and Catalonia about 1860, but they did not become widespread until early in the 20th century. In any case, it was during the last third of the 19th century that the country received the strongest push toward serious consideration of agriculture. Here we are referring to Joaquín Costa's scientific work of propaganda. His campaigns in defense of the countryside and its problems are at the very foundation of the new official orientation, which became clear after Gasset's plan for hydraulic improvement in 1903.

EVOLUTION OF WHEAT PRODUCTION IN THE 19TH CENTURY. As we have said, wheat cultivation experienced a considerable expansion in the first half of the 19th century: so much so that of the approximately 4 million hectares added to the area of cultivation, 2,200,000 went into wheat production. On this subject I am following the opinion of Professor Larraz, who, by examining the 19th-century Spanish economy's lines of expansion, establishes that the first forward thrust was made by agriculture, more precisely by the cultivation of wheat. He bases his conclusions on the report of Moreau de Jonnès (1835) concerning the increase in area of wheat cultivation (70%) and harvests (that of 1833 doubled the 1800 figure), and on other information gathered by Muchada in 1847. Larraz's working hypothesis encounters two difficulties— first, that it is hard to imagine an important agrarian expansion at a time when agricultural prices were collapsing, as in the years from

1812 to 1843, and second, that the expansion of the export trade in wheat which had begun with such vigor in 1786 declined after the War of Independence, and became active again only about 1840. Thus, we would find a number of phases: great agricultural expansion at the end of the 18th century and beginning of the 19th, a decline or period of stagnation between 1814 and 1835, and slow improvement after that date. The effects of the protectionist decrees of 1820 may come into this picture, for they prevented the Spanish peripheral regions from buying foreign wheat and reserved for Spain the supplying of flour to Cuba and Puerto Rico. These measures, adopted to support wheat prices in the cereal-growing regions of the interior, mark an important point in the aggregate economic history of the Spanish 19th century.

As a result of the monopoly granted to Castilian wheat after 1820, there was an inevitable expansion in the area of the traditional wheat-growing regions. Early in the 19th century the Castilian grain-producing area formed a sort of ring, taking in the provinces of Burgos, Valladolid, Salamanca, Toledo, Cuenca, and Soria. After 1834 the wheat area spread both inward and outward from this ring; that is, from the most favorable zones into less favorable ones. In 1860 a movement of regression began which continued without interruption until the end of the century. This phenomenon had many causes. In the first place, the Spanish peasant's lack of technical knowledge; wheat is a difficult grain to raise, giving a high yield if it is cultivated with technical perfection, backbreaking and unprofitable if not well cared for or if old-fashioned methods are used. That is what happened in Castile, and yield dropped so severely that it became an obsession for the most enlightened men in Spain, who even said that wheat cultivation was one of the causes for Spain's economic backwardness. It was during this period that many landowners either gave up wheat cultivation, leaving the land fallow, or used it for other types of production such as vineyards. Wheat lost an area of 1,400,000 hectares in forty years. The sharpest drop took place between 1860 and 1880; during that period no less than 1,100,000 hectares were taken out of cultivation.

Result: a Mediterranean country, particularly fitted for grain production, again had to import wheat from abroad. After 1877

Spain imported from 100,000 to 200,000 metric tons of wheat annually. The years 1882 and 1883 exceeded this average (275,000 and 238,000), as did 1887 and 1888 (314,000 and 243,000), 1893 and 1894 (418,000 and 424,000), and 1898–1899 (314,000 and 222,000). The only good years were 1880, 1881, and 1898, in which imports did not exceed 69,000 metric tons. It was a harsh lesson indeed, and a very severe experience. As we have seen in the table, wheat production, which in 1800 was 174 kilograms per person, gave only 138 in 1900. These figures require no comment. Only with the introduction of chemical fertilizers was it possible to improve this tendency.

THE VINE IN 19TH-CENTURY SPANISH ECONOMY. Professor Larraz singles out the vine as one of the agricultural products which, besides the olive, the almond, the orange, and other fruits, contributed toward making possible the so-called "fourth expansion" of 19th-century Spanish economy (1870–1890). Salvador Millet's studies confirm, as had been suspected, that the vine had much greater importance than this. In fact, its products (wine, grapes, raisins) form the basic support of the entire Spanish economy in the 19th century, along with minerals. There were two reasons for this—first, a traditional dedication which gave Spanish wines and brandies an aureole of prestige throughout the world, and second, because it was the most capable farmers who raised vines. Between 1800 and 1860 the vine was the prestige crop, giving successful results with the new spirit of selection, improvement, and enterprise.

The vine was the catalyst, therefore, in the revolution of Spanish agrarian techniques in the 19th century. Enormous fortunes were made in wine, permitting the introduction of improvements hitherto unknown in agricultural practice. These methods were costly, but very profitable. The first Spanish agricultural experts did not arise in the cultivation of wheat, which is a cheap product and one requiring no irrigation, but in the cultivation of the vine, a high-quality and expensive crop which, therefore, permitted the luxury of being worth the cost of training.

We need only present the figures below to illustrate what we have been saying.

AGRICULTURAL AND LIVESTOCK PRODUCTION

EXPORT OF SPANISH AGRICULTURAL PRODUCTS

Year	Wheat *R.	Wheat V.	Wine R.	Wine V.	Raisins R.	Oil R.	Oil V.	Olives R.	Oranges R.	Oranges V.
1851	19	1.0	1	33.5	4	8	4.5	—	23	0.75
1860	5	12.5	1	81.0	3	11	5.0	—	9	0.30
1870	25	2.0	1	115.0	3	14	6.0	—	20	3.00
1880	—	—	1	249.0	5	7	13.0	—	8	12.00
1890	—	—	1	310.0	6	12	13.0	—	9	18.00
1900	—	—	2	82.0	10	8	31.0	24	5	39.00

* (R. = rank, among the 25 principal export products; V. = value, in millions of pesetas)

As for figures on area of cultivation, yield, and production, which have appeared in previous tables, we need only recall the constantly expanding character of vine cultivation: in area, 400,-000 hectares in 1800, 1,200,000 in 1860, and 1,450,000 in 1900; in yield, 9.62 hectoliters per hectare in 1800, and 17.34 in 1860; and production, 3,850,000 hectoliters in 1800, 10,800,000 in 1860, and 21,600,000 in 1890–1900 (mean annual value).

This increase was due to the constant progress of exports. Vine cultivation, unlike that of wheat, was a "peripheral" crop which spread from the borders to the interior of the country as its prosperity increased. At the beginning of the 19th century there were three chief areas: the Galician, the Mediterranean (with its main centers in Barcelona, Tarragona, Valencia, Alicante, and Murcia) and the southern (with Badajoz, Huelva, Cordova, Seville, Cádiz, and Málaga). These were export markets, some for America and others for Europe. This is the period of the union of British financing and Andalusian wines, giving rise to the famous brands which invaded the international market and gave an openly free-trade character to the market of Cádiz, in contrast to Castilian grain protectionism and the industrial protectionism of Catalonia.

Later, the vine moved into the interior provinces. The competition between vines and wheat began between 1860 and 1865, and the result was total victory for the former. The expansion of the vine into León, the Rioja, and La Mancha dates from this time.

An important event altered the normal process of the Spanish wine economy. This was the invasion of phylloxera, which when it destroyed the French vineyards brought a sensational increase in

650

the sales of Spanish wines, and then resulted in a very serious drop in yield and production as the plague progressed through Spanish vineyards. Phylloxera was recognized in France in 1868, and within ten years the plague had wiped out the vines. This had an immediate effect on export of Spanish wines. Here are some significant figures:

EXPORT OF ORDINARY SPANISH WINES
(in millions of liters)

1865	62	1877	187	1889	919
1866	70	1878	254	1890	1,108
1867	115	1879	345	1891	654
1868	113	1880	580	1892	501
1869	92	1881	723	1893	397
1870	95	1882	725	1894	520
1871	103	1883	615	1895	655
1872	106	1884	680	1896	525
1873	174	1885	697	1897	630
1874	114	1886	797	1898	479
1875	53	1887	872	1899	382
1876	143	1888	840		

At that time Spanish vineyards experienced a period of truly exceptional profits, especially after the commercial treaty with France in 1882. It can be said that between 1882 and 1892 Spain monopolized the world wine trade. But this period of splendor, during which there was wild optimism and not the slightest attempt to plan for the future, naturally ended when phylloxera appeared in the Peninsula. From 1878 to 1893 the disease made constant progress, from north to south, destroying in its path vineyards which were two and three centuries old, and which would never be replanted. In 1892, when phylloxera had attained maximum destruction and the treaty with France had been carried through, Spanish wine underwent a profound crisis from which it was not to recover for a long time. We need only point out that by 1893 the rural component of the emigratory group, which had risen from 11,173 in 1892 to 20,791 individuals, had increased from 54.4% to 73.6%.

OLIVE PRODUCTION. The progress of the olive tree in the 19th century is also impressive. A traditional crop, it increased tremendously and attained maximum production about the middle of the 19th century, according to Larraz, and between 1880 and 1900 if we are to give credence to Millet's figures. It is possible that a study based on longer statistical series will cast light on this process by showing that there were two periods of rising tendency. In any case, in the development of this crop, the requirements of the international market and the freedom of trade enjoyed after 1837 were influential. It is possible that during the last expansion of the area of olive cultivation, between 1880 and 1900, the country's two great production zones were formed—the Andalusian, with centers in Jaén and Cordova, and the Iberian, with important centers in Lower Aragon and Catalonia.

Spanish olive production developed in relation to the needs of the American market and still more in response to the increase in Spanish and Italian emigrants to the Latin-American countries, for they were great consumers of olive oil and olives. Lack of industrial and commercial skill caused a large part of this trade to be diverted to Italy, where Spanish oil was refined and bottled for South America.

The following figures show by five-year periods the progress of olive oil exports after 1868:

Five-year periods	Thousands of metric tons	Five-year periods	Thousands of metric tons
1866–1870	7.5	1886–1890	8.2
1871–1875	11.5	1891–1895	8.0
1876–1880	12.6	1896–1900	13.0
1881–1885	12.6	1901–1905	21.4

The years from 1875 to 1877 produced extremely scanty harvests. Export peaks occurred in 1873 (5,200 metric tons), 1885 (4,200 metric tons), and 1898 (5,400 metric tons).

FRUIT AND IRRIGATION CROPS. In the last three decades of the 19th century, signs began to appear of a great transformation in Spanish agriculture that was to have considerable effect in the future. Instead of the trilogy of cereals, vines, and olives, an agricultural economy based on fruit trees and irrigated crops began to develop. The areas benefiting most from this tendency were those of the Mediterranean littoral, those known from time immemorial for their skillful and industrious farming population and their market-garden crops located near the cities which consumed them. And furthermore, in these zones the early development of industry served as a stimulus for using modern methods and securing the capital necessary to carry out works of irrigation and fertilization. This is what happened, for example, in the construction of the Canal of Urgel, which after 1860 changed the district around Lérida into one of the most fertile agricultural regions in Spain.

Therefore, Larraz quite accurately points out the influence of food products in the Spanish economy's upward swing after 1870. The export curves of such products begin to go up after that date: in 1871, those of almonds and preserves; 1887, fruits and vegetables; 1890, oranges; 1899, sugar beets. Almonds were preceded in the international market by the filberts of Tarragona and Reus. In Logroño preserves were developed thanks to application of the Appert process by the Marquis of La Habana, Espartero's brother-in-law. As for the orange, its process of expansion began only in 1894–1895, rising from exports of 90,000 metric tons annually to 230,000, a level it maintained until the second sharp rise in 1907. Here is an interesting set of figures:

Five-year periods	Orange exports in thousands of metric tons
1886–1890	91.6
1891–1895	127.8
1896–1900	259.6
1901–1905	354.2

The *sugar beet industry* began in Cordova and Granada in 1882 (sugarmills of Santa Isabel and San Juan, respectively). In spite of the restrictions placed in its path by Cuban sugar cane, ten years later we find it established in Aranjuez and in Aragon. Cuban independence led to freedom in sugar beet production, and its cultivation increased noticeably in the Ebro and Genil basins and the warm valleys along the southern Mediterranean shore. This fact explains why sugar beet production jumped from zero to 140,000 tons (more than national consumption, estimated at 90,000 metric tons).

EVOLUTION OF LIVESTOCK. We do not know as much as we would like to about the development of Spanish livestock in the 19th century, in spite of the fact that we possess apparently complete official statistics, such as the Statistical Annual of 1859, the Livestock Census of 1865, and the Geographical and Statistical Review of 1888. But discrepancies in the data are so great that we cannot establish a logical relationship between estimates previous to the Restoration and those following it, which lead normally into those of the 20th century. Here are the figures in question:

	Livestock censuses up to 1865				Livestock censuses after 1888	
	(in thousands of head)					
	1797	1803	1859	1865	1888	1910
Sheep	11,700	12,000	18,687	22,468	13,773	15,117
Goats	2,500	—	3,145	4,531	2,650	3,216
Cattle	1,650	2,680	1,869	2,967	1,460	2,369
Swine	1,200	2,100	1,608	4,351	1,162	2,424
Horses	230	140	382	680	310	520
Asses	—	236	750	1,298	537	868
Mules	—	214	665	1,021	458	886

If we accept as valid the figures of the Livestock Census of 1865, which are based on detailed provincial statistics, we would have to believe that in the following twenty years Spanish livestock suffered a real disaster. Though one factor, as we shall soon see, was the displacement of animals from the old livestock areas, to be killed in the slaughterhouses of the peripheral cities (a development made possible by establishment of the railway network), the discrepancy between figures of the two censuses of 1865 and 1888 is so great in every category that we can only attribute it to an error in computation or statistical method. It seems more logical to relate the figures of the census of 1803 to those of 1888 and admit a progressive development of Spanish livestock in the 19th century, with an increasing rhythm in its last decades.

This fact must be related to a number of different circumstances, whose influence cannot be evaluated at the present time. Among them, the development of the woollen industry in Catalonia and the efforts of Catalan manufacturers to improve the quality of merino wool undoubtedly occupy an important place. We have precise

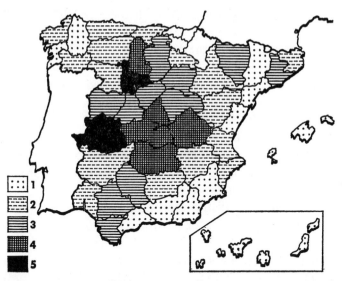

MEAT CONSUMPTION PER INHABITANT IN SPAIN DURING THE THREE-YEAR PERIOD 1865–1867 (excluding the Basque Provinces and Navarre, all provincial capitals, and the ports of Cartagena, Gijón, and Vigo). *Key:* 1, up to 10 lbs.; 2, from 10 to 20; 3, from 20 to 30; 4, from 30 to 40; 5, more than 40.

information about these activities after the middle years of Isabella II's reign. We must also take into account the increase in value of Spanish agricultural and livestock resources as a result of the Crimean War. And finally, successive railway connections helped to move livestock from the places where it was raised to those where it was consumed. As we shall see later on, the national railway network did not really begin to function until the early years of the Bourbon restoration under Alfonso XII.

This explains why, until very late in the 19th century, the map of meat consumption in Spain responded to the following fact: more slaughtering of animals in livestock-raising regions, generally quite poor ones, than in the peripheral provinces; they were richer, but meat was a luxury article there. About 1866 both Castiles, Salamanca and Cáceres, Cordova, Seville, and Cádiz were consumers of their own flocks, while the Cantabrian and Mediterranean areas, though overpopulated, had to content themselves with a fourth or a fifth of the Meseta's meat diet.

In spite of the suspicion with which we must view early livestock censuses in Spain, it is easy to observe that they indicate the same great stockbreeding regions as those of the late 19th century. One of these corresponds to the great zone of migratory sheepherding between Extremadura and the Leonese mountains, which is as old as the natural geography of Spain. In 1888 Extremaduran-Leonese flocks totaled more than 3 million head (Badajoz alone: 1,250,-000) or almost one-fourth of the national flock. Another region was composed of the Castilian and Aragonese mountain systems, from the Moncayo to the Montes Universales and from there to the Sierra de Gredos. We can estimate its animal population at another 3 million head (of which there were 2,100,000 in the provinces of Teruel, Soria, and Saragossa alone).

In contrast to this distribution, cattle became established in humid Spain. The provinces of Asturias, Corunna, and Lugo occupied first place with some 310,000 head, more than one-fifth of the total, followed by the Leonese herd (160,000) and the important Andalusian nucleus (Cádiz: 96,000 head), as well as one in Extremadura (130,000). These were the territories where raising of swine had also flourished since early in the century: Cádiz (190,000 head), Badajoz and Cáceres (278,000), Salamanca (99,000), Cordova (67,000), and Oviedo (62,000).

Two great problems for Spanish livestock in the 19th century were the extraordinary increase in the number of goats, "scourge of the highlands," especially on the slopes of the Mediterranean and Andalusian hills, and in the number of mules. Once the mid-century crisis was over, the same economists who had criticized cereal agriculture and considered it the cause of agricultural decline now complained bitterly over the progress of the mule. There were even some who proposed cutting the throats of all such hybrids. Others, less extreme, sharply attacked what they called "the capricious demands of foolish farmers." As a result of these campaigns the idea gained ground that there was a need to exchange the mule, a sterile animal after all, for the placid and powerful ox. Nevertheless, the muleteer with his team and the peasant with his mule continued to be a familiar sight in the Castilian and Andalusian countryside.

CHARACTERISTICS AND STAGES OF MINING EXPLOITATION DURING THE 19TH CENTURY. In the course of the 19th century Spain became one of the most valuable mining zones on the European continent. The great mineral deposits outside Europe had not yet been discovered, or, as in the case of the United States, they were being used in the industrialization of the country. At the same time, England, France, Belgium, and Germany, which were expanding in an ever increasing rhythm, required and absorbed ever larger amounts of industrial raw materials. And the country which furnished them with the most important minerals, at low prices and in considerable quantity, was Spain.

Aside from mercury, which had an old tradition already, there were three metals which contributed to the rise of Spanish mining: copper, lead, and iron. Copper was obtained in the Ríotinto deposits, which were the center of world copper production during the 19th century before the discovery of the Malaysian and Rhodesian fields. Lead was extracted all along the line formed by the Baetic seam, from Huelva to Jaén, and in the mountain ranges of Cartagena; finally, iron was widely mined in Biscay after 1865, immediately following discovery of the Bessemer process (1856). In 1877 Spain was the chief country in Europe in production of lead, copper, and iron ore. But its iron and steel production was only 10% of Belgian and 0.70% of British production.

Owing to the great foreign demand for these minerals, private persons responded by restoring old mines or seeking new ones. They frequently appealed to the government, asking for this or that mining policy. In this interplay of interests we can distinguish the following stages:

AFTER THE WAR OF INDEPENDENCE AND UNTIL THE MINING LAW OF 1839. This was a period of serious economic contraction, with few possibilities for mining. Interest in mining production was revived only after 1826, thanks to the efforts of a group of business-men who united around the Minister of Finance, López Balles-teros. This group was responsible, in the first place, for the scientific study of the Asturian soft coal mines by Elhuyart, a Franco-Spaniard, and later for putting abandoned mines and those of low yield into production. The most prominent of these men was a Catalan, Gaspar Remisa, who took over exploitation of the silver mines of Guadalcanal in the province of Seville and the copper mines of Ríotinto.

MINING RECOVERY FROM 1839 TO 1868. The law of October 25, 1839, ushered in full recovery of mining activity by establishing broad regulation of mineral deposits throughout Spain. It also re-sulted in the founding of a large number of mining companies. This impetus was especially intense in Catalonia, so much so that in the period 1841–1851 no fewer than fifty-six companies were founded; these were of the most varied types, but mostly companies for soft coal, copper, and lead. The total capital of twenty of these companies was more than 27 million reales. These figures demon-strate the Catalans' propensity for mining investments and for incor-porated capitalistic companies (such as the one called "El Veterano Cabeza de Hierro," which exploited the soft-coal deposits of San Juan de las Abadesas). Only the absence of large seams of iron and soft coal prevented a persistent and well-directed effort to establish heavy industry in Catalonia.

MINING EXPANSION THROUGH FOREIGN MONOPOLIES (1869 TO 1880). The third period began with the basic law of 1868, coincid-ing with the dethronement of the Bourbons, the triumph of demo-cratic ideals, and the predominance of free-trade doctrines in gov-ernmental circles. This law ceded mines in perpetuity, either to nationals or to foreigners, on condition that they paid a royalty to the State. The application of this law, which coincided with ap-proval of the free-trade tariff schedules of 1869 prepared by Laureano Figuerola, placed Spanish mineral wealth in the hands of England and France. It is true that the Spanish treasury was in a state of collapse, and further, that a political ideology existed which demanded liberalization of foreign trade. When a deputy to the Cortes questioned the minister Echegaray in 1874, saying that "all we have left to hand over is the air we breathe," that philosopher, man of letters, and politician answered him disdainfully, "That is a concern unworthy of the times we live in." This remark demonstrates a combination of the ingenuous idealism and the acute financial straits which characterized the period, during which Spain was stripped of her mineral resources by foreign business.

ESTABLISHMENT OF NATIONAL MINING PRODUCTION (1880 TO 1900). The fourth stage was characterized by establishment of a national mining production, thanks to the appearance of a relatively vigorous iron and steel industry and progressive development of the country's industrial equipment. It was made possible by capitalization of sales of Basque iron ore and the modernization of soft-coal mining techniques in Asturias.

THE SOFT COAL INDUSTRY. By the end of the 18th century a certain interest had been awakened in some Spanish circles concerning the soft coal mines of Asturias. The problem was a dual one—how to exploit them, in the first place; next, how to transport their production to the coast. In the middle of the 19th century the problem became pressing because of the incipient development of the iron and steel industry and the growing use of the steam engine in railways and ships.

About 1827, coinciding with formation of the ministerial team headed by López Ballesteros, there was an attempt to concentrate on the coal problem. This desire of the government's was stimulated by a memorial presented to the ministry in 1828 by the intendant of Asturias. López Ballesteros turned the matter over for study to Elhuyart and a group of experts, and they presented a report on a system of transporting coal to the sea. Rejecting the idea of opening a canal to harness the waters of the Nalón, they accepted Jovellanos' plan for a Langreo-Gijón highway, whose cost was estimated at 2,500,000 reales.

In 1833 this measure was seconded by a very favorable law under whose terms Spanish coal exploitation was declared free of any tax or price restriction; ships flying foreign flags could be used to transport coal by paying a tax of 3 reales per quintal, and a duty of 3 reales per quintal was levied on foreign coal if imported under the Spanish flag and 4 reales if under a foreign flag.

In spite of these measures, the soft coal industry continued to stagnate because the iron and steel works did not use coke until 1848. Until that time they had preferred to use charcoal in spite of the fact that it cost more and gave off less heat. According to Sánchez-Ramos, this involved a psychological problem which merits thorough study.

Up to 1860, the date when the Spanish railways began to be fairly complete, and even up to 1880, when the Basque iron and steel industry entered a period of youthful expansion, soft coal mining did not attain the stature of a national industry. Asturian production figures (taken from Adaro) reveal this state of affairs. (See Table A below.)

A. ASTURIAN SOFT COAL PRODUCTION

	Tons	Increase	Percentage
1860	278,400		
1870	447,000	168,600	60.7
1880	428,500	−18,500	−4.2
1890	597,700	169,200	39.7
1900	1,360,000	762,900	127.8

That is, the most notable progress was made between 1860 and 1870 and again between 1890 and 1900. The same increase can be seen in the other Spanish soft coal centers (Aragon, Andalusia, Catalonia, León). Total national soft coal production between 1865 and 1900 is given in Table B:

B. SPANISH SOFT COAL PRODUCTION

	Tons	Increase	Percentage
1865	450,000		
1870	660,000	210,000	46.6
1875	610,000	−50,000	−7.5
1880	847,000	237,000	38.8
1885	946,000	99,000	11.7
1890	1,187,000	241,000	25.58
1895	1,784,000	597,000	30.30
1900	2,674,000	890,000	49.38

To the increasing rhythm of production we must add that of imports of foreign coal, especially from England. In 1900, 1,992,-000 tons were imported, almost as much as national production.

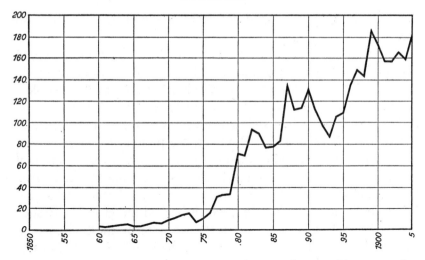

DEVELOPMENT OF EXTRACTION OF IRON ORE IN SPAIN. 100 = mean for 1866–1876.

This was made necessary by the progress of the Basque iron and steel industry.

IRON MINING. The 19th century, besides being the century of coal, is essentially that of iron and steel. Without iron there can be no machines in which to use coal and steam, and without steel the 19th-century industrial machinery is inconceivable.

Spain had iron ore everywhere: in the North (Biscay and Santander), the South (Almería), the center (Guadalajara and Teruel), and in Catalonia.

During the first half of the 19th century the type of ore called "vena" (red hematites) continued to be used. It had an iron content of up to 61%.

When the Bessemer process was discovered in 1856, permitting the rapid production of steel by the use of an ore low in phosphorus content, a number of Spanish fields became important sources of iron exports. This launched the career of the "campanil" type of ore (anhydrous ferric oxide), with an average of 52 to 58% of iron. The years 1860 to 1880 saw the best development of exports of this grade, whose iron content was richer than that of foreign ores. Later, the new Thomas process (after 1879), this time usable for phosphoric ores, which were much more abundant, canceled out this advantage, though it did not decrease the demand for Spanish ore.

Export of Biscayan iron ore had been banned for a long time, in conformity with local legislation. Inclusion of the Basque region in the Spanish customs system (law of July 21, 1876) made possible a wider distribution of ore. The inauguration of the Triano railway (8 km.) took place in 1865, and erection of the first aerial tramways on the fjord in 1875. However, the period of real expansion began only after the end of the third Carlist war. Several important foreign companies took part in this enterprise—the Orconera Iron Ore Company, Ltd. (1874) and the Societé Franco-Belge des Mines de Somorrostro (1876), which backed the group of Basque mine owners headed by Ybarra. Between them these companies possessed the greatest sum of capital in the iron and steel industry: the Geuschin and Krupp companies, which were German; Consett, English; Cockerill, a Belgian firm; and Denain, a French one. Large foreign capital investments were involved in the export of iron ore. Under such conditions Spanish mining production increased rapidly after 1875, keeping pace with the rhythm of foreign demand. Here are some figures:

Year	Production	Export
	(in thousands of metric tons)	
1856	69	—
1860	173	—
1865	191	—
1870	436	253
1875	520	336
1880	3,565	2,932
1885	3,933	3,311
1890	6,546	4,795
1895	5,514	5,100
1900	8,675	7,800

The real peak occurred in 1877, after pacification of the Basque Country by Alfonso XII's troops. Production doubled in that year: Basque Country, in 1876, 432,000 metric tons, 1,040,000 in 1877; Spain, in 1876, 884,000, 1,578,000 in 1877. Maximum exports were attained in the period from 1895 to 1903, with a peak in 1899. In that year 9,500,000 metric tons were exported.

Lequerica states that 225,000,000 tons of iron ore were extracted in the Basque region after 1865. What positive advantage did these exports represent? Not a very large one so far as the whole of Spain was concerned. But for the Basque Country, on the other hand, its position as a leading financial center was established. Not for nothing did an average annual sum of 100 million pesetas flow into the region. Lequerica calls it "a real financial shot in the arm," and says that it created Basque capitalism. Sánchez-Ramos concurs with this opinion. Capital formation from the iron sold abroad made possible the creation of Basque industry and banking, such admirable institutions from so many points of view.

OTHER MINING INDUSTRIES: LEAD AND COPPER. There are no reliable monographs which study Spanish lead and copper mining in detail. However, we must emphasize the fact that these were the chief metals exploited throughout the 19th century. Moreau de Jonnès says that they predominated in his time, and this predominance lasted throughout the century, even in its last two decades, when the expansion of iron seemed irresistible. In fact, in the early years of the 20th century iron occupied second place among Spanish export products (first place was held by the vine and its by-products) and first place among minerals (15.90% of the total; copper, 10.78%; and lead, 9.26%). But up till then lead had occupied first place, followed by copper and then by iron. Here are the figures:

EXPORT OF MINERALS

	R.*	lead	R.	copper	R.	iron
1883	2	8.47%	3	5.99%	4	5.96%
1893	3	10.76%	4	9.00%	5	8.50%
1903	4	9.26%	3	10.78%	2	15.90%

* (R. = Rank)

Lead production in 1864 was 275,000 metric tons annually; 382,000 metric tons in 1900. There was no dazzling increase, as with iron. Copper, however, followed the same path as iron, especially after its production came to be controlled by English capital. In 1864, 213,000 metric tons were produced; 237,000 in 1868; in 1885, ten years after they were taken over by the Ríotinto Company, the mines of the same name increased production to more than a million metric tons; in 1900, 2,706,000 metric tons of copper pyrites were extracted.

THE IRON AND STEEL INDUSTRY. For the study of the 19th-century iron and steel industry we possess, besides several excellent monographs, a solid piece of guidance in the work of Francisco Sánchez-Ramos, *Economy of the Iron and Steel Industry in Spain* (*La economía siderúrgica española*). This author divides its evolution into four great stages: *from the early part of the century to 1832,* in which practically nothing was done; *from 1832 to 1855,* characterized by construction of blast furnaces, predominance of the puddling method in the industry and of Asturias among the Spanish iron and steel provinces; *from 1855 to 1880,* slow reversal of economic factors in favor of iron ore over soft coal, thanks to the discovery of the Bessemer process; and finally, *from 1880 to 1900,* predominance of the Basque industry and the effective and systematic use of the Bessemer, Siemens, and Thomas processes.

(1) If we study these four periods more closely we find that during the first, in the early part of the century, open hearth furnaces and a primitive type of forge predominate. Precise information is difficult to obtain, but along general lines we can say that the decline observed in the 18th century continued, characterized by a reduction in the number of iron-working establishments everywhere in Spain. The industry was still scattered, so that about 1815 there were sixteen ironworks in Biscay, fifteen in Guipúzcoa, twenty-two in Santander, thirteen in Catalonia, eleven in Asturias, and six in Aragon. Except for those of Biscay, which annually produced some 5,000 tons of iron, one-fourth of the total, the others yielded very little.

(2) The second period began (1832) with construction of a blast furnace (using charcoal) in Marbella, province of Málaga, by the Heredia Company. For thirty years this was the most important furnace in Spain. Other blast furnaces in Huelva and Seville followed it. Later, blast furnaces began to be built in the North. The first was in the Trubia works (1840). Those of Bilbao followed. After 1827 the Ybarra family exploited the Poval ironworks; after the first Carlist war ended, it reorganized exploitation and acquired the factory at Guriezo, which some Frenchmen had bought from

the Count of Miravalles. This was the foundation of the "Fábrica de Hierro de Nuestra Señora de la Merced," in Guriezo, with a blast furnace (1848) using charcoal and a cold blast. Seven years earlier, in 1841, a group of mine owners and bankers from Bilbao, headed by a Navarrese, Romualdo Arellano, had founded the "Santa Ana de Bolueta" company, which also built a blast furnace in 1848 to manufacture iron from Mount Ollargán. This was the origin of the Basque iron and steel industry. In that same year, 1848, a notable step forward was taken by this branch of industry when the first blast furnace for soft coal was inaugurated in Mieres. Asturias was still in competition with Biscay.

Important metallurgical works also became established at about this time. Barcelona was at the head of this movement. In 1833 the Bonaplata brothers' "El Vapor" factory began to function, for the production of textile machinery. It was destroyed during the popular uprising of 1835. In spite of this, the progress of metallurgy in Barcelona continued. In 1836 the "Nuevo Vulcano," a works for the construction of steamships, made its appearance; in 1838 the Pablo Llobera company was founded, whose chief technician was Nicolás Tous, while Valentín Esparó bought out the Bonaplata factory's installations. The Bonaplata brothers continued along the same lines with the "Santa Bárbara" works. Later, in 1841, Nicolás Tous established the "Compañía de Fundición y Construcción de Máquinas," popularly called "La Barcelonesa." From the merger of this last with the Esparó factory was to come, in 1855, the "Maquinista Terrestre y Marítima," a firm which became the dean of Spanish metallurgy.

Madrid also experienced a certain amount of metallurgical prosperity during those years. Thus it is understandable that by 1848 Spain consumed 43,000 metric tons of iron, or double the amount of 1828. There were 30 blast furnaces, 366 ironworks, and 98 roasting furnaces. These may seem like respectable numbers, but we must keep in mind that at that time world production of iron and steel was 4,400,000 metric tons, representing 100 times the Spanish production.

(3) Two important events mark the opening of the third phase in 1859—construction of the blast furnace in the Ybarras' "Carmen" factory in the Desierto de Baracaldo, and inauguration of the first true blast furnace in Pedro Duró's factory in La Felguera.

After that point the iron and steel industry continued to develop and become concentrated, especially in Asturias and Biscay, though at a rate very much lower than that of the rest of Europe. In 1865 production was only slightly over 54,000 tons, of which 15,000 were produced by Asturias and 10,000 by Biscay; that is, these two regions accounted for 45% of national production. In the following decade (1870–1880) progress was constant, in spite of the Carlist civil war. Here are the figures:

	Ingots	Wrought iron	Steel
		(in metric tons)	
1870	54,007	36,112	231
1875	36,900	20,056	148
1880	85,939	49,021	445

This was the period of greatest railway construction. From 1860 to 1880, 5,500 km. of railway lines were laid.

(4) In the fourth period, from 1880 to 1890, the Asturian-Biscayan iron and steel industry triumphed, not only because of the capital invested in it but also because of the stature of the firms founded by businessmen of the region. Production increased notably; in Asturias, for example, the Duró company in La Felguera produced 30,000 metric tons of ingots annually. In 1900 this represented one-twentieth of the national total (594,000 metric tons, of which 328,000 were in iron ingots and 166,000 in steel). But if we compare this figure with total iron ore production, it will be observed that by the end of the century the Spanish iron and steel industry used only about 10% of the ore extracted from her soil. This is explained by the small consumption of industry in the interior of the country, as can be seen in the per capita distribution of iron and steel production: while the United States used 230 kg. per person; England, 207; Belgium, 168; Germany, 146; and France, 62; in Spain the figure was only 20 kg. per person.

Let us dwell for a moment on the process of concentration of the Basque industry. As we have said, the two oldest works were those directed by the Bolueta and Guriezo companies. The latter was the one which founded the factory of Nuestra Señora del Carmen in Baracaldo. It was a limited company (Ybarra Hermanos and Co.) which was enlarged in 1860 with the participation of various stockholders (the Villalongas, Murietas, and Uribarrens). The business, a family one, evolved in the direction of the new capitalist type of companies, along with the development of mining and connections with England. In December, 1882, the corporation called "Altos Hornos y Fábrica de Hierro y Acero de Bilbao" was founded, with a capital of 12,500,000 pesetas, the factories in Guriezo and Baracaldo, and six mines in Saltacaballo. Three months previously the corporation of Metalurgia y Construcción, "La Vizcaya," had been founded. It was created by the Chavarris, one of the most prominent families in Basque mining, which had close relations with the firm of Olano, Larrinaga and Co. of Liverpool. It was founded with a capital of 12,500,000 pesetas. Eight years later, at the height of ironworking prosperity, the "Iberia" corporation appeared. The Goitias and Echevarrías, prestigious names in the annals of Basque business firms, were among its directors. These three great firms were merged in April, 1902, resulting in establishment of the "Altos Hornos de Vizcaya," a joint-stock company with a capital of 32 million pesetas. Catalan money also participated in the venture, especially through Manuel de Girona, one of the magnates of the industry and of Catalan finance.

This process of capitalist concentration was made possible by exports of iron ore and the abundance of English soft coal. In fact, English merchant ships going to Biscay for iron ore paid for their voyage by transporting coal. This movement of coal toward iron is the same one expressed in the construction of the La Robla railway, which after 1894 transported soft coal from the León coalfields to Bilbao.

NAVAL INDUSTRIES. The crisis of the War of Independence and the break with the independent American nations had left Spanish trade in a very weakened condition; naval construction, therefore, was in the same plight. Only after 1827 do we find symptoms of recovery in some shipyards and dockyards. The first to show signs of life were those of Catalonia, which experienced a first period of splendor from 1828 to 1835. The law of November 1, 1837, prohibiting the importation of all kinds of ships, either navy or merchant, stimulated naval construction into new activity and ushered in the golden age of Spanish shipping in the 19th century. Shipyards on the Catalonian coast worked constantly, especially during the periods 1838–1841, 1845–1852, and 1853–1857. It is estimated that 732 vessels were constructed between 1790 and 1870, with a total displacement of 128,000 tons, representing an annual average of twelve ships and 2,100 tons.

However, after 1848 the Basque shipping industry drew ahead. The figures collected by the Basque office of Lloyd's show the great prosperity of Basque shipbuilding from that date until 1859, with peaks of thirty-two and thirty-three vessels per year and 6,700 tons total burden. From 1841 to 1859 the shipyards of the river Nervión launched some twelve ships per year, while from 1855 to 1870 the average number in other Spanish shipyards was only 4.44.

The introduction of steamships and vessels with iron hulls meant a difficult process of adaptation, during the course of which many Catalan shipyards underwent serious difficulties or perished, and the Biscayan yards declined greatly. The law of November 22, 1868, suppressing the differential duty on foreign flags and admitting foreign ships carrying national cargoes into Spanish ports, marked a new crisis for naval construction. Under these catastrophic circumstances, Basque tenacity managed to find a satisfactory solution: large naval construction companies were formed, assisted by the State and dependent on the growing regional iron and steel industry. The Nervión shipyards arose in this way, in Sestao; a company was founded in 1888 by the Martínez de Rivas family to supply the Spanish government's order for construction of three warships. Later, in 1900, the "Euskalduna" Ship Construction and Repair Company appeared, equipped with fine technical resources.

In spite of this activity a good number of the steamships in the Spanish merchant marine continued to be acquired abroad. With these and with national ships, by the end of the century the Spanish merchant marine figured among the most important in the world. In 1886 it was composed of 1,800 units (430 steam, 1,370 sail), with a total of 610,000 metric tons (390,000 and 220,000 respectively). The largest number were registered in Barcelona (167,000 metric tons and 77 steamships), with Bilbao next (151,000 and 101, respectively).

COTTON AND WOOL TEXTILE INDUSTRIES. Throughout the 19th century the textile industry was the most important Spanish industrial activity, not only through tradition but also because of the amount of capital involved and the extent of its trade outside the frontiers of the Peninsula. Furthermore, it was the industry with the greatest business spirit, and the one most influential in the inner circle of national policy.

(1) In the preliminary period, which, as in the case of the iron and steel industry, lasted until 1832, the Spanish textile industry was very scattered, at least to judge from the figures published by Canga Argüelles. Since they are the only point of departure we have, they are presented here:

	Linen		Wool		Silk		Cotton	
	Work-shops	Workers	Work-shops	Workers	Work-shops	Workers	Work-shops	Workers
Aragon	7,793	22,693	5,350	14,869	162	843	—	—
Catalonia	4,610	7,612	680	3,545	1,859	3,211	3,470	6,321
Valencia	7,049	9,920	2,093	11,101	2,168	4,202	622	693
Seville	208	688	797	7,722	5,231	5,471	10	150

We can deduce from these figures that the textile industry had a predominantly artisan character, that it was scattered throughout Spanish territory, and that in certain branches there were regions which surpassed Catalonia.

(2) In the second phase, which takes in the years from 1832 to 1869, the textile industry had a remarkable development. This high point was due to the presence of two factors which gave it great impetus after 1832, the mechanical loom and the steam engine. Both inventions went to work for the first time in Barcelona, in the factory of Bonaplata and Company, which was destroyed in the uprising of 1835. After 1832 we find a remarkable group of businessmen who were to shape the Catalan textile industry, bringing to it their fortunes (sometimes earned in the Atlantic trade or the Cuban sugar plantations), their appreciation of hard work, and their assiduous use of foreign technical innovations. They were the ones who, about 1844, introduced the "self-acting," or automatic spinning frame; who developed water and steam power; who succeeded in raising their industry to fourth rank in the world, after the English, French, and North American ones. Their names are linked to true dynasties of Catalan industrialists: the Güells, the Muntadas, founders of *La España Industrial* in 1848, and the families of Battló, Fabra, Serra, Sert, Valls, etc.

The process of industrial concentration is revealed in two circumstances—geographic grouping of factories, and reduction in the number of firms and increase in that of workers. The first phenomenon is the disappearance of all competition in the Peninsular market in the face of the Catalan textile avalanche; in the second place, typical establishment of the textile industry in Catalonia. As for cotton, it became rooted in Barcelona, a receiving port for the raw product, and in the so-called river corridors (Fluviá, Ter, Llobregat, and Cardoner) where the convenience of water power was added to a fairly humid climate and a supply of labor which was abundant, resourceful, and expert. In 1842, according to Sayró's figures, which have been accused of exaggeration in demonstrating the Catalan textile industry's potentialities, there were a total of 4,583 mills and 97,346 workers in Catalonia, distributed as follows:

	Mills	Workers	Spindles	Looms
Cotton yarn	1,763	31,284	1,298,391	—
Cotton textiles	2,117	38,659	—	25,111
Cotton mixtures	397	5,745	—	2,093
Printed cottons	62	3,663	—	—
Utility cottons	62	2,765	—	~~
Small factories	—	15,670	—	—
Totals	4,583	97,786		27,204

Furthermore, the industry used 2,095 HP, of which 301 were steam, 565 water, and 1,227 horse. The capital invested in the industry was 414 million reales. In 1860 the number of factories had decreased; instead of 4,500 there were 3,600. The number of workers had increased, for instead of 97,000 there were now 125,000; the number of looms had increased to 37,640; of spindles, to 1,075,000; of horsepower used, to 7,800, and the invested capital to 1 billion reales. No figures could show more clearly the process of concentration, expansion, and progress of the Catalonian cotton industry.

(3) The third stage began in 1869 and ended in 1898. It started well, with a high state of prosperity, for the Civil War in the United States was over, manufacturers could supply themselves with cotton, and since 1864 the Spanish textile industry had been granted the monopoly of textile sales in Cuba and Puerto Rico. Certainly

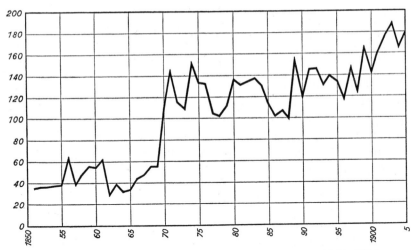

DEVELOPMENT OF COTTON IMPORTS. 100 = mean for 1866–1876.

Figuerola's free-trade tariff schedules (1869) were prejudicial to high-quality cotton cloth production; but the industry managed to get along and to prosper, thanks to increased consumption in the internal market, as is shown in the figures revealing growth in cotton imports. Finally, in 1891 a protectionist tariff was obtained, and from then until the end of the century there was a tremendous wave of prosperity in the industry, which at that time experienced one of the most splendid periods in its history, as can be seen in the statistics. In 1883, 1,100 tons of fabrics were exported; in 1898, on the other hand, 10,297 tons were sent abroad. That is, the total increased tenfold during this period.

In the wake of this prosperity the figures for cotton imports increased sharply: 22,000 metric tons were imported in 1868; 35,000 in 1871; 54,000 in 1883; 63,000 in 1889; 75,000 in 1897. The graph illustrates this process, in which the drops correspond to cyclical crises which we shall examine later.

Another important fact during this period is the triumph of the Catalonian woollen industry. The cotton industry had arisen within the region, and its progress had been achieved with no other competition than that of foreign cloth. But the woollen industry had to compete with other Spanish centers which controlled it early in the century. The battle was joined in the middle years of the century when the woollen manufacturers of Sabadell and Tarrasa, follow-

671

ing the cotton manufacturers' lead, introduced steam power and modern machinery into their factories. Little by little they succeeded in concentrating production in their hands, especially after they gained control over the national wool market and improved the quality of fleece. The decisive opportunity was given them by the free-trade tariff of 1869, which permitted imports of high-quality German and Australian wools. Within ten years the woollen industry of Tarrasa and Sabadell was at the forefront of national production. The handicraft type of workshop disappeared, and only a few such firms in Alcoy and Béjar remained. By the end of the century, out of 226,000 spindles for carded wool in operation in Spain, 130,000 were located in Catalonia, which furthermore monopolized the 120,000 spindles for combed wool.

At the end of the 19th century the Catalonian textile industry continued to be the most highly developed technical and commercial complex in Spain.

THE SILK TEXTILE INDUSTRY. The silk industry deserves separate treatment, for it developed in a direction opposite to that of cotton and wool textiles. At the beginning of the 19th century its decline had already begun. This process appeared to have halted between 1835 and 1852, as a result of a series of protectionist measures dictated by the favorable attitude of the governments in power. This was so much the case that in 1852 the province of Valencia alone produced 800,000 kg. of silk cocoons. But a few years later, after 1856 in fact, a serious epidemic occurred among the worms. They were saved thanks to a serum invented by Pasteur, which was cultivated and used in sericulture stations established for the purpose; but the cocoon harvest never recovered its old splendor. By 1900 it had fallen to 620 tons, fewer than that produced by the single province of Valencia in 1852.

What were the causes of this constant decrease in the production of cocoons, and consequently of the decline of the Spanish silk industry which depended on them? It seems that the cause of this decline was failure to modernize the industry between 1830 and 1850, and its inability to compete with that of Lyons. After 1840, not only did this city absorb Spain's silk production but also that of Lombardy, at the same time that it gained acceptance in the Western world for its technical excellence, its spirit of inventiveness and good taste, and finally, its policy of widespread diffusion of credit, which meant that the silk harvests fell in advance into the hands of Lyons' representatives abroad. All this caused the ruin of many small silk manufacturers, who disappeared mostly around the middle of the century. The Spanish harvest also declined in quantity and quality, and no group except the Catalans was disposed to defend it. Barcelona, which before had been a secondary center within the national silk industry, became the chief market for silk production by the end of the 19th century, especially in the important hosiery and handkerchief branch.

INDUSTRIES RELATED TO FOODSTUFFS. The Spanish agrarian economy did not give rise to great processing industries in the 19th century. The majority of rural products were consumed in nearby areas, and their importance was limited to the peculiarities of strictly local demand.

Of course this general estimate must make an exception of the wine industries, which defended certain interests and brands in their traditional centers in Andalusia and Catalonia. The close relationship between Spanish products and consumer markets in England, France, and Germany had the result of attracting foreign capital toward this branch of national production. Hence mixed companies arose, which in the course of time became consolidated through matrimonial connections. This phenomenon occurred most frequently in the Andalusian wine centers of Huelva, Puerto de Santa María, Cádiz, and Málaga.

Another important industry was that of flour. In spite of the fact that grain production was localized in the interior regions of the Peninsula, modern wheat milling developed in the periphery, especially in Santander. The reason is obvious: the 18th-century process of supplying flour to the Antilles continued, under protective tariffs, and Santander was the ideal port of embarkation for the flour milled in the province. With the growing prosperity of this type of business, many old ironworks were converted into flour mills. When the Canal of Castile was finished and barges could go as far as Alar del Rey (1840) at the foot of the Cantabrian mountains, a new step was taken in the development of this industry. Modern flour mills appeared at that time. In 1854 the Campogiro flour mill was started, using steam power, and others soon followed.

In 1866 the railway crossed the mountains and linked Alar del Rey with Santander. Ox carts gave way to railway cars, and with this development production and export increased. In that year more than forty flour mills processed 35,000 tons of wheat; and a number of merchants handled 90,000 tons of flour for export. The ships that went to Cuba laden with flour returned with sugar, and there was speculation in Santander in both articles. This industry suffered from the effects of the insurrection in Cuba, and failed with the loss of the Antilles. Spanish flour exports, which had known brilliant periods between 1875 and 1881 (from 37,000 to 90,000 metric tons), gradually declined in the years which followed, revived again at the time of the last separatist struggle (1895–1898) with exports on the order of 50,000 metric tons, and almost disappeared after the Peace of Paris (600 metric tons in 1902).

Another important milling center was located in Catalonia, linked to imports of Castilian grain by railway, and imports of American or Australian wheat by sea.

The loss of Cuba, which represented such a serious setback for the milling industry, saved the sugar beet industry, allowing it to live up to its promising beginnings. After 1897 imports of Cuban sugar practically ceased (8,000 metric tons compared to 76,000 in 1890 and 1892); in 1900 only 500 metric tons of Cuban sugar arrived in Spain. This opportunity was seized by the sugar beet growers, whose activity had begun about 1880 in different places in Catalonia, Aragon, and Granada. In the last decade of the 19th century forty-nine factories were built in Spain, of which fifteen were in the province of Granada. In three years, from 1899 to 1902, the number doubled. The production capacity of these establishments rose to 140,000 metric tons of sugar per year, a figure exceeding Spanish consumption, which was estimated at 90,000. Thus the sugar beet industry began with the troublesome problem of overproduction.

ELECTRICAL AND CHEMICAL INDUSTRIES. The last third of the 19th century marks the timid development in the world of two industries destined to capture positions of primary importance in this century. We refer to electricity and chemistry. Spain followed this process very closely, stimulated by foreign experts and foreign capital.

Catalonia was in the forefront of this progress. In 1873, three years after its invention, a Gramme machine was in operation in Barcelona. It had been imported by Ramón Majarrés, of the School of Industrial Engineers of that city. In 1875 the firm of Dalmau y Xifré installed the first Spanish electrical plant, which operated with great success. After the invention of Edison's incandescent lamp was applied to public illumination, it was used in Madrid in 1881 and Barcelona in 1882. Three years later Gerona was using alternating current for lighting purposes; it was one of the first cities in the world to do so. The success of this new energy source led to creation of the Sociedad Española de Electricidad (1881) by Dalmau y Xifré. Within a few years the Compañía General de Electridad in Madrid, the Barcelonesa and Sevillana de Electricidad, the Eléctrica de San Sebastián (1893), and the Eléctrica del Nervión (1894) all appeared. These are only a few names among the mass of 861 electric stations (480 of them thermal) with a capacity of 128,000 HP, established all over Spain by 1900. Very soon, in 1901, another name was to come forward: the Hidroeléctrica Ibérica, founded by Juan Urrutia with an initial capital of 20 million pesetas, a fabulous sum at that time. Basques were also leaders in the field of electricity.

The chemical industry was the last-born in 19th-century Spanish production. However, it had a long tradition, related to the chairs established by the Societies of Friends of the Country. As the textile industry developed and needed detergents and dyes, chemical activities increased in Catalonia. Catalan chemists had shown samples of their products as early as 1827, in the Exposition of Spanish Industry in Madrid: Prussian blue, muratic acid, tin salts, vitriol, etc. Francisco Cros, a Frenchman turned Catalan, was prominent among the manufacturers. Thirty years later the manufacture of basic industrial acids (sulfuric, nitric) and copper and iron sulfates was commonplace in Barcelona. About 1880 the progress of the Basque iron and steel industry helped to increase the range of chemical products. The explosives industry was born in Bilbao (S.A. de la Dinamita, 1872). The first factory for making sulfuric acid on an industrial scale also developed there: it was founded by the Sociedad Española de Explosivos (1896), though in competition with one owned by the Cros firm in Badalona (Barcelona). The appearance of the Electroquímica de Flix (1897), the Sociedad Española de Carburos Metálicos (1897), and the Industrial Química de Zaragoza (1899) complete the roster of the leading companies in the national chemical industry.

FORESTRY INDUSTRIES: THE BOTTLE CORK INDUSTRY. During the 19th century deforestation continued in Spain. This fact demonstrates that, when the liberals came to power, they were unable to overcome the obstacles which their Encyclopedist ancestors had long ago denounced. Yet more: enslaved by their doctrinaire beliefs, they simply looked on as the country's forest patrimony finally perished. The Mesta came to an end, of course, and legislation on the enclosure of property was approved; but no limits were set on the selfishness of the privileged persons who bought up national resources, nor was the administration able to put an end to the ravages caused by herds of goats in the greater part of the national territory, especially in the Mediterranean area. In consequence, owing to the depredations of goats, the abusive freedom of purchasers of ecclesiastical properties and *propios* and common lands, and the defects of a chaotic administration, irremediable damage was done to Spanish forests. In 1932, Antonio de Miguel estimated that, between 1850 and 1900, 2,700,000 hectares of forest were felled in publicly owned lands alone, including 1 million hectares in pines, 1,200,000 in oak forest, and 500,000 in beech. As for privately owned property, the estimated figure is enormous: 7 million hectares.

The irresponsibility with which this suicide was carried out in the middle years of the 19th century is terrifying. It was only in its last two decades that there was a firm reaction, one proof of which is the protest made in 1886 by the Madrid Economic Society of Friends of the Country against this barbarous destruction. The leader of the campaign in favor of forests was the Aragonese Joaquín Costa, who denounced deforestation as symptomatic of a lack of culture and of economic destitution.

As a counterweight to this destruction, and as a unique case in the 19th-century history of Spanish forests, there was one type of forest which was very well cared for, perfectly developed, and which gave the country both resources and jobs. It was the cork forest, in spite of the fact that this tree is a slow-developing one whose utilization can only be anticipated fifty to seventy years after it has been planted. How can we explain this paradox?

The cork forest was the basis of one of the most important industries of the Spanish 19th century, as regards commercial and technical organization and results of a social and human kind: the bottle cork industry. The industry as such began in the 18th century (p. 533). First established in Catalonia because of its proximity to France, the industry found first-class material there: an odorless cork, soft and highly pliable, perfect for bottling wines of high quality such as champagne and the sparkling Rhine wines. Keeping pace with the development of the bourgeoisie in the West, the cork business grew rapidly. Between 1860 and 1870 its exports doubled (from 500 million to 1 billion corks); between 1890 and 1900, coinciding with the golden *fin de siècle* and the depreciation of the peseta, it gave another leap forward, from 1 to 3 billion—a decade of fabulous business, which made the fortunes of the three centers of Catalonian cork manufacture: San Feliu de Guixols, Palamós, and Palafrugell. French, Germans, and Americans settled in the region, bringing in their experience, customers, and capital, which greatly influenced the development of this important industry.

When the cork industry expanded about 1840, it became necessary to seek other forest reserves. There were cork trees in the rest of Spain, and though none of them could compare with Catalonian trees except those in a few small areas, it was necessary to make use of them. Extremadura supplied corks for sparkling wines, but they were not as reliable as the Catalonian corks, for they disintegrated after a few years. Andalusian cork was only mediocre, except for the Motril variety, and served for bottling wine, beer, and mineral water. The cork of Salamanca turned out to be no better. But as a result of their commercial interest, Catalan buyers taught owners how to take care of the forests and get the best results from them. It is obvious that at first they took advantage of the situation and extracted handsome profits. But after a few years a well-organized and well-cared-for cork forest earned enormous profits for its owners, to the point that it can be stated that cork woods were the salvation of not a few remnants of the Spanish landowning aristocracy.

This prosperity gave the cork industry a character unique in the annals of 19th-century Spanish labor: optimistic, gay, democratic, without class distinctions. From the purchase of the bark to the delivery of the finished corks for export, through a series of delicate operations in which manual dexterity was paramount, a great community of bosses and workers, of large and small manufacturers, maintained a constant activity along the Catalan Costa Brava. It is a spectacle which shows us what Spanish industry might have been if it had not always followed in the wake of an eternally deficient agriculture, an absolutely nonexistent technical training, and an infinitely low consumer potential.

45 · Transport and Trade

THE REVOLUTION IN TRANSPORT SYSTEMS. THE HIGHWAY NET-
WORK. The possibility of an organic system of internal Spanish
trade was realized after the middle of the 19th century because of
the technical revolution in the means of transportation which involved expansion of the highway network and the introduction of
the railroad. Procedures invented in England, John McAdam's
smooth roadbeds for highway construction and George Stephenson's steam locomotive, were applied in Spain following the first
wave of peace and prosperity during the five-year period
1843–1848.

Early in the 19th century, and under the direction of Agustín de
Bethancourt, inspector-general for highways, Charles IV's government took the first steps toward solving the road problem. The
Corps of Engineers of Highways and Canals was created in 1799,
and all public works undertaken were turned over to it. Four years
later Bethancourt, taking advantage of the truce in international
politics represented by the Peace of Amiens between England and
Napoleon's France, gained approval for a practical plan of highway
construction and maintenance. Although our information is not entirely trustworthy, it appears that during Bethancourt's term as inspector some 2,000 km. of new highways were constructed.

The War of Independence and the great depression of the 1820's
meant that public works were in a state of paralysis, and that the
highway network deteriorated. In 1835 Madoz speaks of the ruinous state of the bridge over the Guadiana at Mérida, the result of
two of its arches having been blown up by the English in 1812.
Twenty-three years later there had not even been an attempt to
repair the damage. The struggle between liberals and Carlists was
also of no help to this type of activity. It may fairly be said that for
thirty years the State hardly concerned itself with this vital struc-

tural element in the country's economy. Authoritative estimates fix at 144 million reales the amount spent on highways during the entire reign of Ferdinand VII; new kilometers of highway opened for travel totaled 914, or 45 per year. These figures are laughable and reveal the negligence and poverty of those years.

Meanwhile, the wealth of some peripheral centers was developing, and these required intensification of commercial relations with the center of Spain. Cádiz as well as Barcelona, followed at some distance by Valencia, and at a still greater distance by Bilbao and Gijón, called for better roads. In 1815 the "Company of Royal Diligences" was founded in Catalonia, which within a short time extended its regular services to Valencia, then to Madrid and later to the rest of Spain, with weekly service from Madrid to Cádiz, Bayonne, Saragossa, and Burgos. In 1825 came the founding of two other stagecoach companies, linking Barcelona with Madrid and Perpignan. Both had a franchise for ten years. Later, when road transport was in full flower, and on the threshold of the railway revolution, two societies were founded, also in the capital of Catalonia. These were the "Company of Diligences and Messages of Catalonia" (1840), which monopolized the Barcelona-Madrid service, and the Company of Diligences called "Crown of Aragon" (1843), responsible for connections with Saragossa and Valencia. After 1827 other services of the same type had appeared in the rest of Spain, especially between the French frontier at Irún and Madrid, and between Madrid and Cádiz.

This spirit of progress was taken up by the government as soon as administration and public finance were reorganized in the Moderate Decade (1843–1853). After 1840 about 100 km. of new highways were constructed annually; after 1856, some 600 km. In 1868, at the time Isabella II was dethroned, the Spanish highway network totaled 18,000 km., of which 9,500 had been entirely constructed during her reign. This figure is even more significant if we add to it the use of techniques formerly either unknown or neglected: roadbeds, cuttings, embankments, and especially bridges and viaducts. Isabella's reign was the great moment for construction of "stone bridges" throughout Spain. Thanks to all this, the problem of getting from place to place was largely solved, though Spanish highways could never compete with French ones.

Effective period of construction	Kilometers constructed	
	Total	*Annual*
1800–1808	2,850	320
1843–1856	1,737	124
1856–1868	7,822	651

Highway construction activity was not interrupted during the Restoration period. In fact, it was then that the plan dividing national highways into first, second, and third class, plus provincial and neighborhood roads, was worked out. In 1884 national highways measured as follows, compared with the figures for 1908:

	1884	1908
First-class highways	6,491 km.	7,171 km.
Second-class highways	7,777 km.	9,975 km.
Third-class highways	8,947 km.	24,319 km.
Totals	23,215 km.	41,465 km.

Study of these figures reveals that the efforts made had been concentrated on construction of connecting highways, whose length tripled in the period we have indicated. Some progress had been made, though it was still insufficient. Highways carrying heavy traffic, on the other hand, increased hardly at all, for first-class roads added only 27 km. per year and second-class ones 88 km.

With all its gaps and technical deficiencies, this was the condition of the Spanish highway network at the beginning of the 20th century, at the time the automobile made its sensational appearance in the history of transport. An unimaginative administration had been miserly with money and effort in adapting Spain to the needs of modern traffic. And in addition, the public works plan did not take regional situations into account. The budget was parceled out at the pleasure of politicians who pulled the strings of the local "boss" systems. Thus, distribution of the national road network per kilometer and per inhabitant, with the exception of Navarre and the Basque Country (autonomous in this respect) was as follows in 1900:

Regions arranged according to no. of km. per inhabitant	No. of inhabitants per km. of highway	Regional total, in km., of State highways
Old Castile	254	5,037
Aragon	297	4,168
New Castile	321	5,531
León	346	4,168
Extremadura	378	2,137
Murcia	454	1,585
Asturias	476	1,290
Andalusia	593	5,716
Galicia	694	2,832
Catalonia	726	2,752
Valencia	792	1,843
Canary Islands	893	338
Balearic Islands	903	347

The law of the greater the wealth, the greater the traffic, was not followed, therefore, but instead the simple and ineffectual rule of relating highway construction to the inverse ratio of the provinces' distance from the center. The rich and heavily populated periphery had 5,000 km. less than the agrarian center, where traffic consisted mainly in transporting the grain harvest.

THE RAILWAY NETWORK. Introduction of the railway system in Spain was of more importance than highway development. In 1825, as soon as the railway from Stockton to Darlington began to function in England, a few Spaniards whose businesses kept pace with the times began to show an interest in bringing this novelty to Spain. On September 23, 1829, José Díaz Imbretchts obtained a concession from Ferdinand VII's government to install and exploit an "iron rail" from Jerez to the wharf of Portal, on the Guadalete; on March 28, 1830, Manuel Cabero obtained royal permission for his railway project from Jerez to Puerto de Santa María and San-lúcar; in 1833 Francisco Fassio obtained one for the Reus-Tarragona project. These were premature concessions, linked to wine and almond exports, which did not find support from the corporations who were supposed to underwrite them. They expired in 1838. To counterbalance this, however, we find the protection granted by the local Deputation of Biscay for the plan of a commission charged with taking over the province's highways—a project entitled "Plan for improvement and construction of roads" (1832)—which mentioned "an iron rail for the Valmaseda route." But the Carlist war paralyzed all plans and projects.

After about 1835, groups of industrialists and businessmen began to make efforts to construct two railways, from Barcelona to Mataró and from Madrid to Aranjuez. But official concessions did not come until the end of the civil war and the ministry of Espartero. The first was granted to J. Roca y Roca (though the prime mover was not Roca but Miguel de Viada, a Catalan who had made his fortune in America) on August 23, 1843, and the second to Pedro de Lara in April, 1844. This last project became linked with the banker, Salamanca, a great though shadowy figure in the early period of Spanish railway construction. A short time later, on May 2, 1845, authorization was granted for construction of the railway of Langreo (Sama or Gijón). These three plans turned out to be viable, for the Barcelona-Mataró railway was inaugurated on October 28, 1848, that of Aranjuez in 1851, and that of Langreo in 1855.

Meanwhile the government had adopted the necessary legislative measures. After the report submitted by two engineers, Subercase and Santa Cruz, the Royal Order of December 31, 1844 was published. It established three fundamental principles: the expected expiration of concessions, periodic revision of fares to prevent immoderate profits (until then some foreign companies had distributed dividends of 15% and more), and establishment of the gauge at six Castilian feet (1.67 meters). It must be stated that the only calculation which entered into this last decision, so prejudicial to future railway connections with foreign countries, was that of offering users of the Spanish railways the greatest possible comfort and security.

The law's stipulations did not please the railway companies, for they preferred a system of perpetual concession and freedom in fixing fares, on the English model. However, they did profit from one article in the Royal Order just referred to, establishing a system of *provisional concessions* which could be enjoyed by "persons of known antecedents." This article resulted in wild speculation in railway concessions—more than twenty-five were granted in two years—which paralyzed the work of those who were really trying to build railways in Spain, and who were obliged to pay a premium to the concessionaire. But what really checked this first railway effort in Spain was the economic crisis of 1847–1848 and the scandals resulting from the unholy financial alliance of government ministers and the builders of certain railways. A star of the first magnitude in this sorry affair was José Salamanca, who as minister granted enormous subsidies to the Madrid-Aranjuez company, which he himself then received in his capacity as manager and director of the company. This ministerial policy, also seconded by the Court, was one of the reasons behind the *pronunciamiento* of 1854 (dubbed "La Vicalvarada"), which had an important influence on railway legislation. The new Cortes, in fact, approved the law of 1855. This law corrected the spirit of the Royal Order of 1844 and gave the railway companies all sorts of facilities for construction of their lines: subsidies from the State, province, or municipality; free importation of railway construction material during the construction period and for ten additional years; concession of ninety-nine-year leases and readjustment of fares every five years, by means of a law which would have to be approved in the Cortes. Abuses of every kind had justified the policy proclaimed by Bravo Murillo in 1851, calling for creation of a national railway network by the State.

Under the new system of broad protection to national and foreign capital, and favored by highly stimulating international economic conditions, a colossal thrust was given to railway construction. At the time the law of 1855 was passed, the three railways we mentioned before were in operation, plus the Barcelona–Molins de Rey, Jerez–Puerto de Santa María, and Játiva–Valencia–El Grao lines. Their total length was 305 km.; that is, since the inauguration of the Barcelona–Mataró line some 40 km. had been constructed annually. The picture changed after 1855. From that year till 1868 some 5,000 km. were built (4,803, to be exact), or 340 km. annually. There were years, such as 1859, in which 800 km. were built. A statistical study published in 1864 placed Spain after England and France and ahead of Prussia and Austria in annual railway construction.

This was the decade of great accomplishments. Between 1858 and 1860 the Spanish railway system became defined, with its great companies: Northern, Madrid-Zaragoza-Alicante (M.Z.A.), Catalan Network, Andalusian, and Western. The first came into being as a result of French capital invested in Spain by the Pereire brothers, who in 1856 won the bidding for the Madrid-Irún line. Six years before work was completed—in August, 1864—Spanish Northern Railways Company was set up (December 29, 1858), with a capital of 380 million reales. The Railway Company of Madrid to Saragossa and Alicante had been founded two years before, in January of 1857, with a capital of 456 million reales. Its stockholders were José Salamanca, the House of Rothschild, a group from the French Grand Central Company, and the Spanish Mercantile and Industrial Company. It took advantage of the Madrid-Aranjuez-Alicante line (completed in 1858) and concession of the Madrid-Saragossa line which led to France by way of the central Pyrenees. The railway reached Saragossa in 1864. But three years before, in September, 1861, a train had linked Saragossa with Barcelona. It belonged to the Saragossa-Barcelona Railway Company (by way of Lérida). In fact, the Catalan capital controlled railway investments, not only those of the Ebro basin but those of the rest of Spain (Cordova-Málaga-Granada, Saragossa-Pamplona, Medina del Campo–Salamanca, Orense-Vigo, Almansa-Valencia, Valencia-Barcelona). By 1862 the Barcelona Stock Exchange had absorbed 445,000 shares of railway stock with a nominal value of 61,600,000 duros and an effective value of 35,872,000. Also, a large company had been set up which controlled the Catalan Network: the T.B.F. (Tarragona to Barcelona and France). The stock market crash of 1866 was a hard blow to the Catalonian railways, and this permitted the expansion of the Northern and M.Z.A. companies in their own domains. The former bought considerable stretches of roadbed which had been controlled by the Catalonian companies (Pamplona-Saragossa-Barcelona, in 1878) and the latter eventually absorbed the T.B.F. (1898), after its financial collapse as a result of the construction of the very difficult portion from Barcelona to Saragossa by way of Caspe (1881–1891).

Meanwhile, the Barcelona-France railway had reached the frontier at Port-Bou in 1878, fourteen years after inauguration of the Madrid-Paris line by way of Irún (1864). It was during these same years that the chief railway connections were constructed. Bilbao was linked to the main line in 1857 (Tudela-Bilbao railway), Santander to Valladolid in 1866 (Alar de Rey–Santander), and Seville to Madrid after the conquest of the difficult Despeñaperros pass in 1861. Two companies date from the end of this period, that of

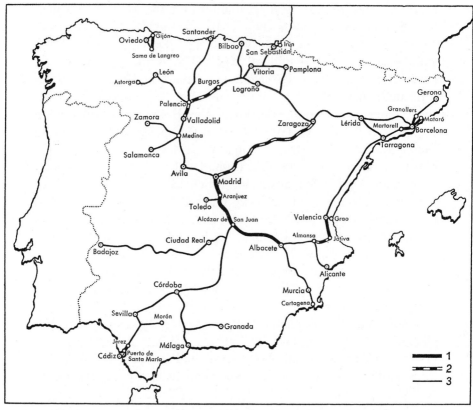

CONSTRUCTION OF THE SPANISH RAILWAY NETWORK.—*Key:* 1, railways constructed between 1848 and 1855; 2, between 1855 and 1860; 3, between 1860 and 1868.

Madrid-Cáceres-Portugal, nucleus of what would later be the Western Company, and the Andalusian Company, for which a concession was granted in 1869 but which was not legally set up until 1877.

That was the year of the general railway law of November 23, which echoed the spirit of the law of 1855. After it there were no important changes, though there was an open battle among the various companies to finish lines and fill out networks. In fact, the M.Z.A. Company monopolized service in the Levant and Andalusia, and the Northern that between Madrid and the Cantabrian regions. The kilometers constructed during this half-century are given in the table below.

To sum up, and this can easily be seen in the table, there were three periods: (1) from 1848 to 1865, in which the bases of the Spanish railway network were laid, with some six years of maximum activity (1860 to 1865, with more than 3,600 km. of track laid, one-fourth of the total up to 1900, and one record year: 1865, with 929 km. constructed), (2) from 1865 to 1875, a period of stagnation owing to the financial, political, and military crises of the time, and (3) from 1876 to 1900, a period of extension of the railway network at a steady and sustained pace, permitting doubling of existing trackage. During this last period the best years were 1878, 1882–1884, 1891, 1893, 1896, and 1899, all years in which more than 400 km. were constructed.

5-year periods	Km. of track in operation	Km. of track built	Average annual km. built
1848–1850	28	28	—
1851–1855	477	449	89.8
1856–1860	1,918	1,441	288.2
1861–1865	4,826	2,912	582.4
1866–1870	5,478	652	130.4
1871–1875	6,124	746	149.2
1876–1880	7,478	1,354	270.8
1881–1885	8,931	1,453	290.6
1886–1890	10,021	1,090	218.0
1891–1895	11,314	1,293	258.6
1895–1901	13,168 *	1,854	370.8

* of which 10,989 were wide-gauge

This last period marked the moment when Spanish railways began to be viable from an economic point of view. This phenomenon took place during the five-year period 1880–1884, as is shown in the following table:

Year	Km. traveled by trains	Year	Km. traveled by trains
1867	1,025,934	1881	9,378,848
1873	915,968	1882	11,609,593
1875	1,053,902	1883	18,551,424
1878	1,431,866	1884	25,089,295
1880	2,709,144		

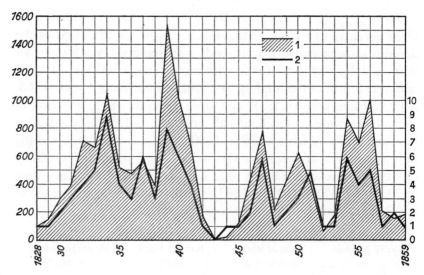

DEVELOPMENT OF SHIP CONSTRUCTION IN THE LLORET DE MAR (GERONA) SHIPYARDS FROM 1828 TO 1859.—*Key:* 1, tonnage (figures on left); 2, number of sailing vessels (figures on right).

In the last year shown, cost per kilometer traveled was 2.98 pesetas. Twenty years before, it had been 40.93 pesetas. The railway had become profitable, and the companies began to distribute excellent dividends.

MERCHANT MARINE AND PORTS. After the War of Independence, followed by that of the American secession, the Spanish merchant marine underwent a period of severe prostration. In spite of the optimism with which Moreau de Jonnès tries to present Spanish affairs, he himself recognizes the disappearance of naval prosperity as a result of these reverses. Though 600 foreign ships had, in about 1780, passed through the port of Cádiz, 350 through Barcelona, and 300 through Málaga, fifty years later (in 1828) Cádiz had only 385 and Barcelona 269, mostly Sardinian and French vessels of small tonnage.

In 1832 the seaports experienced certain symptoms of recovery, especially Cádiz, which had benefited from having been declared a free port (1829). But the onerous conditions she had to accept in order to obtain this privilege rapidly destroyed her deceptive prosperity (from 1828 to 1832 exports from Cádiz had risen from 21 million to 202 million reales). The recovery of the port of Barcelona was slower but more solid. It was owed to the prosperity achieved by the Catalan merchant marine after Joan Mirambell, captain of the schooner *Constancia,* successfully restored trade relations between Spain and the republics of the La Plata region in 1834. After that year individual initiative replaced the feeble efforts of a government that was in constant financial and political difficulties. The golden age of Catalan and Levantine sailing ships began. Shipyards, especially those of Blanes, Arenys de Mar, and Lloret, worked unceasingly, constructing a great variety of sailing ships, mainly brigantines and schooners of 100 to 150 metric tons burden. With such vessels daring captains undertook voyages of three and four years, carrying wine, almonds, olive oil, salt, and construction materials to Río de la Plata, taking on jerked beef for Havana there, and returning to Spain with wood, sugar, molasses, cotton, petroleum, hides, and other colonial products. Sometimes these ships made a second and third sally out of Havana to Argentina. This was the famous *jerked-beef route,* often involved in the slave trade between Guinea and Cuba and contraband trade between Cuba and Spain.

About 1858 the Catalan merchant fleet on the Levantine coast suffered an eclipse. Studies carried out among shipyard records show us the date with absolute precision. Consequently the crisis of the merchant marine (we are now also speaking of the Spanish merchant marine as a whole) took place before the decree wiping out the differential duty on foreign shipping (1868). This is certainly related to the competition offered to sailing ships by a powerful rival: the steamship. At least this was the case of the Biscayan merchant marine which, aroused from its torpor about 1848, with a registry of 410 ships in 1854 (two-thirds of the number registered in the Cantabrian region), went into total decline between 1859 and 1864. It became necessary to make some effort to adapt to the new type of navigation.

Spain had not lagged behind in accepting this new type of progress. The first steamship service was inaugurated in 1817 between Seville, Sanlúcar, and Cádiz with the vessel *Real Fernando,* replaced two years later by the *Neptuno.* Ships of the paddle-wheel type, unsuitable for open-sea navigation, such steam vessels did not compete seriously with sailing ships until after invention of the screw propeller by the Swedish inventor Ericsson, and its application in the *Archimedes* (1836). After that time, naval construction was taken over by the great steel tycoons: namely, the English. The modest beginnings made in Spain did not succeed in filling the existing vacuum, and in 1853 the government had to authorize purchase of steamships abroad.

It must be remembered that in 1852 the firm of A. López and Co. was founded in Santiago, Cuba, by Antonio López and Patricio de Satrústegui. This company ordered construction of the *General Armero,* the first screw-propelled vessel in the Spanish fleet, of 716 tons burden. This was the embryo of the powerful Transatlantic Company, founded in Barcelona in 1881. At the time it possessed twelve ships, with a total displacement of 27,000 tons, and lines to Cuba, Central America, the Mediterranean, and the Philippines (after 1884). Beginning in 1861 the López firm had obtained the mail contract between Spain and the Antilles, which helped it to survive the crisis of 1868–1873.

With the Restoration the Spanish merchant marine very definitely entered a new phase. Ports were considerably improved, thanks to the efforts of the commissions for public works. The first work of this sort was done in the port of Barcelona (1869); that of Bilbao followed (1872). In a short period of years the commissions modernized and enlarged the seaports, making them suitable for steam traffic. These ships exercised growing control over maritime transport, though in brisk competition with sailing vessels. At least, this is the impression we gain from the figures involved in a study of traffic in the port of Barcelona from 1870 to 1900; though the number of sailing ships decreased, their total tonnage increased:

Year	Units	Thousands of tons
1869	3,540	380
1870	2,855	311
1875	5,732	720
1880	3,101	869
1885	1,645	701
1890	1,840	692
1895	2,007	1,221
1899	1,962	1,481

The percentage increase in sail tonnage follows a rhythm similar to that of steam, and even to the total amount of imported merchandise in the port of Barcelona itself (which rose from 1,077,000 tons in 1869 to 5,300,000 in 1895). It may be a purely Catalonian anachronism and may explain the future success of the Basque merchant marine.

The Basques, in any case, identified themselves with the steamship. In the figures we quoted above, their superiority over Barcelona in the matter of steamships in 1885 is clear. This advantage increased thanks to the capital funds available to the Basques at the end of the 19th century. From 1896 to 1902, citizens of Bilbao alone spent 130 million pesetas buying foreign vessels. This explains the fact that by the end of the century 39% of the national total of 786,355 tons was registered in Bilbao.

The steamship required concentration of capital, regular lines, and a rational business organization. These factors also favored the development of Basque activities in this field. Small shipping lines, such as the Ybarra Company, founded in 1823, extended their activity toward the south. In 1860 José María Ybarra created the Basque-Andalusian company, located in Seville but with main offices in Bilbao. The founder's sons changed the name of the company, calling it Ybarra and Company, extended its activities to Mediterranean ports (1885) and made it the most important coastwise shipping company in the country. Another Basque company, the firm of Sota and Aznar, specialized in navigation on the high seas and very soon dominated this area. In 1890 Eduardo Aznar de la Sota and Ramón de la Sota y Llano had four steamships: in 1901 they owned sixty-seven vessels with a total tonnage of 216,000. In 1906 the Sota and Aznar Shipping Company was founded.

As for regular transatlantic service, in addition to the Transatlantic Company there was the firm of Pinillos, Sáez and Company, founded in 1884 with headquarters in Cádiz and a heavy volume of business in the Antilles. Both the Transatlantic Company and the Pinillos firm suffered serious losses when the Spanish colonial empire was liquidated in 1898.

MODIFICATIONS IN BUSINESS PRACTICE. The history of Spanish commerce in the 19th century has not yet been written. This is true not only in regard to domestic and foreign trade but, even more importantly, in regard to the history of commerce in itself, its techniques and procedures, its developments and setbacks.

Up to the middle of the 19th century commerce moved within

the limits reached at the end of the 18th; there were no profound changes or radical transformations. Large-scale mercantile operations usually consisted of a central house in Cádiz or Barcelona which maintained two or three branches in America, often directed by members of the family, and correspondents in London or Paris. Recent studies show that exchange of funds was accomplished by exporting merchandise to America, importing precious metals from there, and applying the rich profits earned to the purchase of French or English government bonds; that is, by establishing funds abroad. Thus a pernicious custom was established, made necessary by the political ups and downs within Spain.

About the middle of the century this system underwent a number of shocks which eventually resulted in its becoming a more rational, modern type of commerce. The battle was long and slow. But the revolution in transport and news transmission systems helped to overcome routine methods. Of all these, the most important was the inauguration and development of rail locomotion (1848), which coincided with establishment of the first telegraph systems (also in 1848) and the use of the postage stamp in correspondence (after 1850). Thus commerce could count on very effective instruments of communication.

Commerce also experienced a revolution in its own methods. After the turn of the century the medieval practice of haggling over prices was supplanted by a fixed-price system in the large cities. The new norm was to sell in volume to earn in volume. This explains the appearance of two essential elements of mercantile business, advertising and the traveling salesman. Advertising began about 1830, and its chief instrument was the newspaper. Thus the public could be offered merchandise which grew steadily more inexpensive and larger in volume. But the newspaper could not take the place of the direct contact established at regular intervals by the salesman. The development of the railway, the telegraph, and the postage stamp paralleled this increase in the activity of traveling salesmen.

Let us add two events which contributed to this mercantile flowering—in the first place, establishment of the *decimal metric system,* which after 1858 started Spain on the long road of unification of weights, measures, and currency; then there was the visual as well as commercial tool represented by the spread of expositions.

In the 19th century these were the common meeting ground of businessmen, and served as a very effective method of publicizing industrial techniques and manufactured goods. Spanish businessmen flocked to the great international expositions held abroad (Paris, London, Philadelphia, Chicago) and returned home with new ideas. National expositions, on the other hand, held since 1827, and regional ones (the first being the Barcelona exposition of 1841) also contributed toward opening new horizons for industry and commerce. The International Exposition of Barcelona in 1888 crowned the golden decade of 1876–1886 and signalized the consolidation of Catalan capital as a star of the first magnitude in the European economic firmament.

In spite of its great advantages, the new commercial system took hold very slowly. Only a minority, almost exclusively rooted in Catalonia, followed the new path with real vigor. The rest of the country continued to cling to its fairs and traditional markets, unaware of the most rudimentary elements of credit (such as the bill of exchange) and mercantile negotiation (such as sales on commission). The stagnant condition of the mass of consumers in Spain explains this weakness in the country's economic development.

DYNAMICS OF SPANISH FOREIGN TRADE. Two great stages can be distinguished in the development of Spanish foreign trade throughout the course of the 19th century. There was a stage of contraction from 1814 to 1854, and one of expansion from 1854 to 1900. We have only fragmentary information about the first stage, so that there is no coherent statistical series on which to base its process. After 1850, however, the figures, though not absolutely trustworthy (Professor V. Andrés Alvarez has pointed out the falsification inherent in the confusion between "tariff value" and "'statistical value" of merchandise which characterizes all Spanish customs legislation from 1869 to 1930), do furnish us with a very important element of continuity.

The period of contraction in world trade following the Napoleonic wars was aggravated, in the case of Spain, by the loss of the American colonies. We have already alluded to what this represented for the Spanish economy as a whole. In order to give precise statistical details, we shall present the figures collected by Moreau de Jonnès at the moment of rupture between Spain and her former colonies.

In 1789 the structure of Spanish foreign trade could be summarized in the following manner (figures are in *reales de vellón*):

	Foreign	Colonies	Totals
IMPORTS			
Goods	520,000,000	216,000,000	736,000,000
Specie	—	488,000,000	488,000,000
	520,000,000	704,000,000	1,224,000,000
EXPORTS			
Goods	172,000,000	564,000,000	736,000,000
Specie	348,000,000	—	348,000,000
	520,000,000	564,000,000	1,084,000,000
Combined Totals	1,040,000,000	1,268,000,000	2,308,000,000

From these figures we deduce that the real deficit (some 100 million *reales de vellón* in goods) was more than compensated for by the favorable balance in precious metals (some 140 million).

In 1829 the structure was as follows:

	Foreign	Colonies	Totals
Imports	380,800,000	77,200,000	458,000,000
Exports	204,400,000	56,000,000	260,400,000
Totals	585,200,000	133,200,000	718,400,000

The decline in foreign trade over a forty-year period is indubitable and represents losses on the order of 75–80%, even without counting contraband trade. The country was indeed passing through one of the most dramatic economic crises in its history. But it gradually recovered between 1830 and 1850. After that time, statistical series permit us to reconstruct the dynamics of Spanish trade up to 1899, in the following five stages:

An abrupt rise between 1850 and 1859, starting in 1852–1853 but developing rapidly because of the Crimean War. The annual average of total trade in the period 1850–1855 was 352 million pesetas; in the following period it was 606 million. If we take 100 as the mean figure for the decade 1866–1876, the ascending

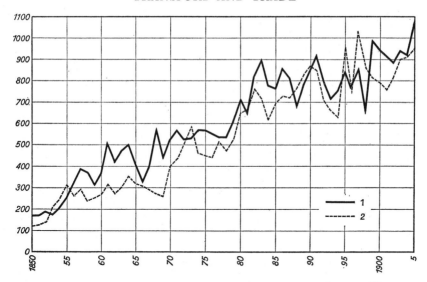

FLUCTUATIONS OF THE SPANISH TRADE BALANCE IN THE SECOND HALF OF THE 19TH CENTURY.—*Key:* 1, imports; 2, exports. Figures at left, in millions of pesetas.

curve of the figures is very clearly shown—36 in 1852, rising until 1857: 43, 49, 62, 64, and 74. Then there is a short readjustment (1854, > 67 <).

The *second phase* corresponds to the period 1860–1869 and is characterized by relative stability, with a second five-year period of contraction. The figures are as follows: For the first five-year period, an annual average of 759 million pesetas, and for the second, 724 million. There are two high points within the ten-year period: 1861, index 90; and 1868, index 93. Between these two high points there is a notably low one, culminating in the crisis of 1866 (79 > 69 < 76).

The *third phase* in foreign trade takes in the ten-year period from 1870 to 1879 and reveals an obvious state of euphoria. The commercial expansion of this period was largely due to the fact that it coincided with the peak of the century's rising cycle. Spain had instituted a moderate free-trade policy after approval of the tariff schedule of 1869. The characteristics of this phase are as follows: during the first five-year period, an annual average of 1,025,-000,000 pesetas, and for the second, 1,045,000,000. The index figures reveal a certain instability (1873, 122; 1874, 113; 1876,

695

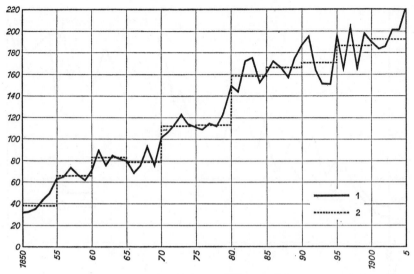

DEVELOPMENT OF SPANISH TRADE IN THE SECOND HALF OF THE 19TH CENTURY, ESTIMATED IN ITS NOMINAL MONETARY VALUE (uncorrected).—*Key:* 1, annual indexes; 2, five-year averages. 100 = mean of 1866–1876.

109), but with a frankly rising trend after the restoration of the monarchy in Spain (1877, 115; 1879, 124).

The *fourth phase* is one of tremendous expansion and takes in the period from 1880 to 1889. In the Catalan phrase, which we can extend to describe the whole country, this period receives a typical name: "gold fever." A great volume of business was carried on in the export of wine, sale of minerals abroad, the great surge in textile exports, and industrialization of the country. For all these reasons this decade represents the peak of the effective economic progress made during the Spanish 19th century. Its first half showed an annual average of 1,455,000,000 pesetas; that is, in the space of thirty years (one generation) the volume of Spanish external trade had increased fivefold. In the second half of the decade (1885–1889) this progress became stabilized (annual average index, 167, compared to the previous one of 59), which becomes more obvious if we correct the figures for depreciation of the peseta abroad.

The *fifth phase,* from 1890 to 1899, is one of contraction, similar to that throughout the West, though in the case of Spain it is significantly marked by obvious irregularity, with peaks of 195 (1891)

696

and 206 (1897) and lows of 150–151 (1893–1894) and 166 (1896). This can be explained by the war in Cuba and the depreciation of the peseta, whose decline after 1895 falsifies indexes and figures on production and trade.

BALANCE OF TRADE. Thanks to statistical series, we are aware of a characteristic phenomenon of the 19th-century trade balance: its constant deficit. Foreign trade almost always shows a loss. Spain imported more than she exported. From 1850 to 1900 only eleven years, or one-fifth of the total, were favorable. Professor Sardá has pointed out the ways in which this deficit was made up: foreign loans, loss of metallic currency, investments of foreign capital, remittances of funds from Spanish emigrants in America. However, it was a heavy burden, and explains one of the causes of the Restoration's failure in the economic and financial spheres.

From 1850 to 1900 there were four favorable occasions in the Spanish trade balance: (1) a three-year period, 1853–1855, at the time of the Crimean War, (2) two widely separated years, one at the time of the First Republic (1873) and the other a momentary peak in 1881, (3) the years of the French phylloxera crisis, 1888, 1889, and 1890, and (4) the period of the Cuban and Spanish-American wars, 1895, 1897, and 1898, when goods were being shipped to the Spanish armies operating in the Antilles and the Philippines.

As is shown in the graph on p. 695, there were two periods in which the deficit was most pronounced; the one lasting from 1861 to 1871 (the era of great industrial equipping), with a maximum deficit of 296 million in 1868, the year Isabella II was dethroned, and that of 1883–1887, with deficits which were less pronounced but still on the order of 127 million in 1886.

STRUCTURE OF FOREIGN TRADE. We have little data for the first half of the century. It is almost useless to attempt a reconstruction, for the presence of a given item on import or export lists may be fortuitous or occasional. We believe this to have been the case of wheat, as it appears in Moreau de Jonnès' figures for the year 1829.

In accordance with these figures, Spain imported, in the first place, colonial products (sugar, coffee, and cocoa) for 25% of the total; textiles (cotton, wool, linen, and silk) for 23%; tobacco and salt fish, 8% each; the rest was miscellaneous. Imports of a modern industrial type, such as iron and steel, represented only 0.25% of the total. On the export side, first place was occupied in 1829 by wheat, wool, and wine, with 20, 15, and 14% of the total respectively, followed at a considerable distance by fruit, lead, and brandy (from 8 to 4%). Except for the appearance of lead and the fortuitous first place held by wheat, the export picture (which also included cork, iron, mercury, skins, and colonial products) was a survival from the 18th century. In 1830 the coal and steel revolution had not yet come to Spain.

Now let us look at the structure of foreign trade at about the middle of the century. The figures are given in the table below.

IMPORTS 1857			EXPORTS 1857		
(in millions of reales)					
	1851	*1857*		*1851*	*1857*
Sugar	87.50	118.83	Tobacco	—	29.81
Cotton	83.48	93.97	Machines	13.10	27.98
Cocoa	41.78	48.43	Wines	133.91	379.93
Wool textiles	37.52	62.36	Lead	50.65	92.79
Codfish	37.36	59.85	Wool	37.55	40.52
Cotton textiles	32.90	33.46	Raisins	33.44	59.66
Silk textiles	27.99	31.15	Flours	29.44	71.26
Thread	18.39	—	Cork	19.80	38.98
Hides	18.23	16.51	Olive oil	17.66	62.12
Coal	17.53	23.25	Silver	15.64	117.61
Linen textiles	16.70	15.34	Soap	10.77	12.97
Wheat and flour	—	370.16	Salt	9.88	—
Corn	—	46.19	Oranges	—	10.01
Iron	7.09	74.90			

We do not find many changes in the picture since the beginning of the century. The most startling is the appearance of wheat, flour, and corn in the import figures of 1857. But, contrary to what might be supposed, they are not of consistent importance. We know that the three-year period 1856–1858 was one of terrible scarcity in cereals. Therefore, it was necessary to import them. But the figure is deceptive, for, as we know (pp. 647–648), the period of export of wheat and flour did not coincide with the early years of the restoration of Ferdinand VII, but rather with the period 1853–1878, following disentailment. Once this factor is eliminated the most notable changes are, in imports, the increase in the area of iron and machinery, and in exports the increase in volume of sales for each specialized sector.

The figures for foreign trade in 1877 reveal a rapidly changing structure of imports, as a result of the industrialization of the country. In exports, the items scarcely vary. Here are the figures:

(in millions of pesetas)

Textile fibers	87.94	Wines	129.92
Machinery and construction materials	70.34	Lead	59.98
		Flour and wheat	43.10
Food products	52.79	Raisins	26.42
Fuel	37.16	Oranges	10.83
Textiles	34.51	Mercury	10.65
Tobaccos	27.58	Cork	8.83
Brandy	14.28	Olive oil	8.62
Hides and skins	13.85	Footwear	8.43

This structure was to change greatly in the last two decades of the 19th century. The statistics look like this:

IMPORTS FOR 1883, 1893, 1903
(per cent of total)

	1883	1893	1903
Food products	31.38	26.13	17.88
Fuel and lubricants	5.64	9.78	11.65
Textile fibers	18.72	19.82	23.27
Chemical products	2.30	3.15	9.10
Textiles	7.98	5.26	6.49
Machinery and construction materials	24.33	26.57	22.73
Miscellaneous	9.65	9.29	8.88

As we can see, in 1883 Spain had to resort to foreign countries to aid her in her food supply problems. The deficit in wheat is particularly serious, not only because of the expenditure of foreign exchange it involved (9%) but because it reveals the failure of Spanish agricultural methods in the 19th century. Besides wheat there are other important and traditional articles: salt fish, sugar, coffee, and cocoa.

In the area of textile fibers cotton was particularly important. In 1883 it represented 12.5% of the total, a truly considerable figure. But the proportion represented by textiles was no less considerable. As for machinery and construction materials, the size of this percentage reveals the intensity of the industrialization process. At this time railway construction material was still being imported (5.35%).

EXPORTS FOR 1883, 1893, 1903
(*in percentages*)

	1883		1893		1903	
Wines	48.35		18.74		11.34	
Grapes } Raisins }	4.39	52.74	4.80	23.54	4.56	15.90
Olive oil	3.66	3.66	5.50	5.50	6.67	6.67
Oranges	3.29		2.88		8.15	
Almonds	0.70	3.99	2.03	4.91	0.46	8.61
Wool	1.25		1.08		1.93	
Animals	3.45	4.70	2.09	3.17	3.18	5.11
Lead	8.47		10.76		9.26	
Copper	5.99		9.00		10.78	
Iron	5.96	20.42	8.50	28.26	15.90	35.94
Textiles	1.46		10.88		4.42	
Footwear	1.41	2.87	5.20	16.08	2.35	6.77
Cork	2.04	2.04	4.57	4.57	4.97	4.97
Miscellaneous		9.58		13.97		15.03

In 1893, ten years later, the structure of imports has become slightly modified, for food products have gone down to 26.13%, textile fibers have risen to 19.82%, and machinery and construction materials also rise to 26.57%, though following a normal process of expansion. On the other hand, we can find a sharp rise in the group of fuels and lubricants, which rise from 5.64% to 9.78%. And conversely, cloth imports diminish.

In 1903, that is, already within the 20th century, the process of readjustment of imports is much better developed. Imports of foodstuffs diminish greatly (from 31% in 1883 to 18%), for the Spanish soil has become more productive thanks to the introduction of fertilizers (as will be noted in the column of chemical products, which have risen from 2.30 to 5.10%. The amount of hard and soft coal needed by industry has also risen, climbing from 5.64 to 11.65%. Purchases of textile fibers continue to rise, but imports of machinery and construction materials have dropped, indicating the continuing progress of the textile industry and the growing surge of Basque iron and steel activity.

Any comment on this table is obvious. In 1883, 52.74% of exports had to do with the vine and its products. To this figure we must add 12% more for agricultural and livestock products. In second place, with 20.42%, are mineral products: lead, copper, and iron, exported in similar proportions. The other classifications are unimportant. None of them, not even cork, represents more than 3%.

In 1893, as a result of the effort toward industrial equipping, export structure has changed. Wine has fallen to 23.54% of the total. A tremendous loss has taken place in this area, corresponding to the spread of phylloxera through Spain and the defense put up by the French market. Export of minerals, on the other hand, continues to increase and represents almost 30% of the total. At that time there was a real hope that Spain would be able to count on an export industry based on fabrics, footwear, and cork. These three products together make up more than 20% of the total.

In 1903, on the threshold of the present century, export of viticulture products has decreased again, falling to 16.90% of the total. That of minerals, on the other hand, has risen to 35.94%. It is the moment when Spain is running out of copper, lead, and iron; the best veins were in the process of exhaustion between 1890 and 1910. The export industry still maintains a total of 11%, but it has lost 9%, and except for cork, which is increasing, all the other areas are in a state of crisis. Here the loss of the colonies is deeply felt. In other agricultural products there are two notable changes, which foreshadow the Spanish export structure during the 20th century—olive oil increases to 6.77%, and oranges already comprise 9% of total exports.

INTEGRATION OF THE SPANISH ECONOMY. The integration of the Spanish economy initiated during the preceding century became a fact in the course of the 19th, and this was thanks to two essential factors—the development of communications systems, permitting an increasing exchange of goods, expecially after 1880, and the expansionist zeal of certain industrial groups which were very active in the country's economic life. The latter, who controlled considerable amounts of capital and were responsible for the labor of their workers and, in the last instance, for their own selfish interests, applied pressure until they were able to achieve an integrated Spanish economy. The bourgeoisie triumphed where the Hapsburgs and early Bourbons had failed.

The groups to which we refer were: (1) the Catalan cotton manufacturers, on the scene after 1827 through their characteristic institutions, first the Factories Commisssion, then the Industrial Institute of Catalonia, and finally, the Council on Development of National Labor, (2) the grain growers of Castile and Andalusia, who exercised maximum political influence through the government and the Cortes, and (3) the Basque metallurgists, present in the last and definitive phase of economic integration, that is, after 1880.

These groups worked in a protectionist direction, raising obstacles to freedom of foreign trade in the products in which they were interested (cereals, fabrics, and iron). However, none of these three protectionist possibilities would have been viable if they had not been able to count, as Flores de Lemus so accurately stated, on the trading counterbalance of export products: olive oil, wines, and mineral ores.

PROTECTIONISM AND FREE TRADE. The 19th century was marked by harsh and stubborn struggles between the exponents of free trade and the protectionists. To explain this seems in the nature of a historical exercise; but it is also a necessity, for there have been many arguments on the subject, which continue today and will undoubtedly do so in the future.

Let us examine the main positions. Apologists for free trade insisted that protectionism responded to a unilateral cause: the bourgeoisie's desire to make money at the expense of the consumer. They were convinced that instead of accepting "educative" tariffs, the industrial groups defended a position of monopoly. This word was not new, for it had already figured in the debates of the 19th century. Ensconced behind the highest tariff walls in the world, the protectionists succeeded in sacrificing any possibility of industrial expansion, reduction in the cost of products and improvement in technical quality, so that Spain constantly lagged behind world progress.

To this argument a second and no less significant one is commonly added. Since it was the Catalan manufacturing bourgeoisie which largely carried out the protectionist campaign, it has been argued that Catalonia sacrificed the interests of other Spanish regions to her own, demanding a protectionism which was only a ruse to accumulate capital. The argument has often been used that Catalan protectionism created political regionalism as a weapon which it could brandish at will in order to attain its ends. The accusation of this school of thought is that, with the cost of the shirts Castilians bought at high prices, Spain would have been able to pay for more than the railway system and dress herself at reasonable cost to boot.

The protectionists' position during the 19th century, on the other hand, was that without the State's intervention in matters of foreign trade (tariffs and commercial treaties) and in the suppression of contraband (which was vast and widespread), it would have been impossible even to dream of maintaining existing industry in Catalonia or in any other part of Spain.

The protectionists' ideological point of departure was very diverse, and this shows that it responded, not to a political argument, but to convictions linked with industrial development. Nurtured in the bosom of the progressive party, its great initial defenders were Jaumeandreu, Borrego, and Madoz. The protectionist theory was later shared by both political liberals and conservatives, by democrats and federalists.

The basic doctrine of the protectionists was that Spain could not be compared with England because of the differences between her domestic and foreign markets. If Spain's doors were opened to foreign trade, all possibilities for a national economy would be wiped out. The protectionists looked for, and found, arguments in the current situation. The decline of the silk industry after the tariff laws of 1841, and the drop in naval construction after abolition of the differential flag duty in 1868, were powerful arguments which they used boldly and effectively. In a word, they defended, with romantic enthusiasm, national labor as the source of wealth, and answered the free-traders by saying that without its hard work Spain would have had neither clothing nor railways.

Between these two schools of thought, the protectionist and the free-trade, the modern historian must find a scientific position, and the way he can do this is to link protectionism with the business cycle. In fact, protectionism was inevitable from 1815 to 1841, not only as a governmental tradition stemming from the 18th century, but as the only solution for overcoming the catastrophe of the War of Independence and especially the secession of the American possessions. From 1841 to 1848, coinciding with the first sharp upward movement in the long wave of the business cycle, customs barriers began to crumble. No doubt this would have been the most favorable period to put an end to protectonism if the industrial groups, overdeveloped in comparison with the meagerness of the country's economic resources, had been able to find a consumers' market to sell high-grade products; but the lack of industrial experts, as well as the low living standard of the Spanish rural population, led to the survival of a concealed protectionism. However, from 1869 to 1891, when Europe was breathing deep draughts of the air of free trade and experiencing the full force of a favorable business cycle, Spain found it necessary to open her doors to foreign trade in order to complete the country's technical and industrial equipping, and especially to overcome the losses caused by the crisis of 1866, for which protectionism was blamed. Trade took on an extraordinary vigor at that time, and basic industries such as iron and steel also experienced improvement. However, two decades later the international crisis of 1886 gave the Catalan protectionists a chance to bring the Basque metallurgists and the Castilian cerealists over to their side. Thus the tariff battle of 1891 was won, and the bases of the Spanish economy's protectionist structure were laid. The loss of the colonies in 1898 finished the job and prepared the way for adoption of the tariffs of 1906. There was no solution but to put a protectionist stamp on the colonial disaster.

MAINTENANCE OF THE PRINCIPLES OF A PROTECTED MARKET: TARIFFS OF 1825. At the beginning of the 19th century the State's position, still based on the mercantilist principles proclaimed in the tariff schedule of 1778, ratified by the Royal Tariffs compiled in 1785, was beginning to change, at least in a technical sense. This was shown in Charles IV's tariff schedule issued on April 14, 1802, which according to some authors marks the change from a mercantilist system to one of protectionism of a 19th-century type.

This progress was halted by the War of Independence. The upheaval of 1808–1814 threatened to bring down the tightly protectionist edifice of the 18th century, on the one hand by the development of an economic philosophy of a free-trade type, represented in the universities and the ministries by figures of the intellectual stature of Canga Argüelles and Flórez Estrada; and on the other, because of the extraordinary development of contraband, practiced not only by English and French troops but also by the Spaniards themselves, who took advantage of the unhappy circumstances to engage in profitable dealings. The paralyzation of the Spanish economy explains why even the liberals adopted an openly protectionist policy during the three-year period of constitutional rule. This was the tendency of the so-called Tariff Schedule of the Cortes, voted in by the law of October 6, 1820, and completed by the customs organization of November 11 and the General Tariff Schedule of October 20 of that year. The modernity of the liberals' views on tariffs and techniques puts their tariff achievements at the base of Spanish tariff development during the 19th century.

But theory was one thing and reality another. The disorders produced on the frontiers by the royalists' rebellion in 1821–1822, and later by the intervention in Spain of the army of the Hundred Thousands Sons of St. Louis (1823–1827), increased contraband trade and again endangered Spanish economic life. But in 1825 the group made up of the minister López Ballesteros and his collaborators gave signs of an inflexible attitude which was in accord with the country's interests. Therefore, the tariff schedule of October 19,

1825, approved by a Royal Order of March 8, 1826, was frankly protectionist. It permitted the remaking and reordering of the Spanish economy and brought Ferdinand VII closer to the bourgeois point of view and the protectionist groups closer to each other. Sánchez Ramos has described it as a protectionist tariff system with great "educative significance," though he laments the fact that this attitude led to an absolutely protectionist policy and prevented the idea of a lowering of industrial costs.

The 1825 schedule was based on application of a single *ad valorem* duty, in reales and maravedís, on a differential flag fee, imposing duties 50 to 300% higher on foreign ships than those levied on national ones. It also included a list of tonnage and port duties, often very heavy, and another list of banned products. This list was composed of 657 articles, thus defining the system of a protected market.

Nevertheless, no active group in Spain's economic life found the 1825 schedule sufficiently protectionist. This is shown in a memorial published in 1827 by the Deputation of Biscay, asking for more vigorous measures to prevent competition and give special privileges to iron production. The same thing happened in Catalonia, as is shown in the history of the Board of Trade and the Factories Commission, made up of cotton manufacturers. These two institutions showed themselves to be extremely jealous of their rights, as can be seen in the complaints they made against the permission given in 1827 to an Austrian, Heinrich Dolfuss, to bring in 30,000 pieces of percale and muslin under the pretext of establishing a textile and cotton factory in San Fernando, and against the concession received by Bonaplata in 1832 to bring in merchandise valued at 1 million reales in exchange for setting up looms and steam engines in Barcelona. This argument, though, was ended by the Royal Decree of April 30, 1832, establishing the principle that no licenses were to be granted for bringing cotton manufactures into Spain.

This decree did not correct the situation, for in the following year the civil war between Carlists and Liberals broke out, and this increased contraband trade in the country. The Carlists, who controlled the frontiers, took advantage of their position to flood Spain with foreign goods (iron and textiles) which were cheaper than national products. This was a system that had certain advantages in collecting funds and disorganizing the economy of the liberal side, upheld by industrialists.

CHANGE IN TARIFF POLICY; MODERATE TARIFFS OF 1841 AND 1849. Once the civil war had ended in 1839, reorganization of the country became necessary. Among many other matters to which the government had to attend, the most important was certainly the chaotic and involved tariff legislation. Complaints against it were constant, especially from the free-trade groups who at that time controlled the government, and whose outcries against the protectionists had stirred up the intellectuals and newspapers in Madrid. We must keep in mind that the government was particularly concerned with the consumers' point of view and that, although it did consider the industrialists' interests, it also had to heed public opinion in Madrid. Thus, in 1841, the government presented to the Cortes a piece of legislation establishing four types of tariffs: one for import of foreign goods, another for American goods, a third for those imported from Asia, and the fourth for products exported from the kingdom. Approved by the law of July 9, 1841, this schedule aided greatly in the classification of goods. It consisted of 1,506 items, of which 807 were subject to a duty of 15%; 247, to 20%; 94, to 25%; and some few to 30 or 50% of their value. The following manufactured goods continued to be banned: cotton, footwear, ready-to-wear clothing, furniture, ships of less than 400 tons, firearms, wrought iron, tinplate, and certain agricultural products (wheat, cereals, wool).

These prohibitions, which made up a group of eighty-three items in the 1841 schedules, represented an important victory for the groups to whom we have referred before: Catalan textile manufacturers, Castilian grain-growers, and Basque iron merchants. The leader of the protectionist campaign, who fought the hardest battles with the progressivists determined to obtain a free-trade tariff schedule, was Juan Güell. Working from the Industrial Institute of Catalonia, he succeeded in galvanizing energies and gathering the necessary forces, in Barcelona as well as Madrid, to impose a tone of moderation in the renewal of the 1841 tariff schedule. Obviously it was a schedule of transition. Once the progressive regime had fallen and the government was in the hands of the moderates (the

more conservative liberals), the reorganization of the State undertaken by these men made it clear that they would not neglect so important an aspect of national economy as the tariff issue. As early as
1845 Alejandro Mon, who was responsible for the reform of the
Spanish Treasury, had concerned himself with the tariff question.
After that time the debate was omnipresent in the press and the Parliamentary cliques; even in governmental centers the Catalan industrialists were accused of keeping up the civil war and the country's
internal struggles simply to foment protectionism, a charge which
was far from being the truth. It was in the heat of this debate that
Juan Güell, Yllas y Vidal, and Manuel Durán y Blas, through newspaper columns and the Industrial Institute of Catalonia founded in
1848, undertook a new campaign and answered the accusations
leveled against the cotton industry.

The debate was finally closed by the law of July 17, 1849, authorizing reform of the tariff schedule. Great pressure was put on
General Narváez, who was at that time president of the Council of
Ministers and exercised a kind of dictatorship. A royal commission
went to Barcelona to ascertain the truth of the information offered
by the Catalan industrialists. While this commission was sitting, a
number of changes took place in the Ministry of Finance (Bertrán
de Lis, Orlando, Mon). Finally, Mon succeeded in getting the new
law passed. It provided for the following: machinery for agriculture, mining, and factories would pay an import duty of 1 to 14%
of its value; raw materials similar to those found in Spain, foreign
soft coal, and manufactured goods, 25 to 50%; foreign articles not
manufactured by Spanish industry, 15% in general, and in some
cases up to 25%. And finally, a differential flag duty of up to 20%
was to be established on merchandise exported.

The schedule published (October 5, 1849) as a result of this law
contained 1,410 items, and only 14 articles were banned: therefore
we can say that the principle of a protected market had passed out
of existence. All types of privileges to industries or companies were
wiped out, tariffs for America disappeared, and commercial depots
were authorized (these were considered by industrialists to be
sources of contraband). Technically, the system of specific tariffs
was adopted. In the metallurgical field the only prohibition was that
on the importation of firearms, but articles made of iron could enter
the country with heavy duties. As for the textile industry, No. 60 or

finer yarn could come in, and fabrics, muslins, and handkerchiefs with thread counts of 26, 15, and 20, and up, respectively. The fact that these limits were established saved the Catalan industry, for it worked almost entirely in counts lower than those we have mentioned; in general, the Spanish market used yarn with a count of 18 to 22.

The 1849 tariff schedule was in force for a long time, since those published later (September 29, 1855; October 6, 1856; October 2, 1857; October 28, 1858; November 29, 1862; and November 25, 1865) were customs rules adjusted to accommodate the new principles of the decimal metric system or the new currency units, reales and escudos, to the basic schedule of 1849. Sánchez Ramos says, in connection with its survival, that it prevented the destruction of Spanish mining resources, a statement with which we would hesitate to agree completely.

THE FREE-TRADE PERIOD; SCHEDULE OF 1869 AND THE FIFTH BASE. After 1859, coinciding with progressivist opposition to Isabella II's government, an association for reform of the tariff laws had been formed in Madrid. This society gained importance as a result of the cycle of lectures which it organized in 1862–1863. In this course of lectures the politicians who were to be the stars of the 1868 revolution all appeared: Echegaray, the Duke of Almodóvar del Río, Moret, Castelar, Figuerola, Azcárate, Pedregal, and Pastor. Their insistent campaigns on behalf of important Madrid mercantile associations are reflected in the law of July 21, 1865, which authorized the government to suppress the differential flag duty for articles coming from Europe and to decrease tariff rates in certain cases.

Under these circumstances, it is easy to understand that once Isabella II was dethroned and the liberal elements of the September Revolution were victorious, the provisional government took under consideration a proposal formulated by Laureano Figuerola, the Minister of Finance, to accept a tariff schedule of a free-trade type. The atmosphere in Madrid, in the Stock Exchange as well as in commerce (represented by the Mercantile Circle), was frankly favorable to such ideas, which were opposed only in Catalonia. Figuerola put through the abolition of the differential flag duty (November, 1868) and prepared a free-trade schedule, based on the need to set in motion an economic mechanism which had been throttled by protectionism.

On this occasion the protectionist leader was Bosch y Labrús, who found an echo for his words in the Society for the Development of National Production, founded on March 8, 1869, with the express purpose of opposing Figuerola's plans. A few days later, on March 21, there was a protectionist demonstration in Barcelona in which not only the bourgeoisie took part, but also workers from the Circle of Employees of Trade, during the course of which it was decided to create the Spanish Protectionist League. In spite of this, Figuerola obtained approval, after a number of maneuvers, for the principles of the future tariff law (July 1, 1869), published on July 12, 1869.

This legislation did away with all restrictions, on exports as well as imports, and also with the differential flag duties, putting Spanish ships on an equal footing with foreign ones for trade among the various Spanish ports and those of America. The so-called customs duties, established for imported merchandise, were of three classes: the first included the so-called "extraordinary duties," which were as high as 30 and 35%; the second, items of "fiscal duty," with a maximum of 15%; and lastly, those called "balance-of-trade duties," modest fees per unit of number, weight, or measure.

The Fifth Base of the Basic Law provided that for six years (that is, until 1875) the duties classified as extraordinary would remain unchanged, but that after that date they would be reduced gradually until by the twelfth year (1881) they would be equal to the fiscal duties. Consequently, Article 4 of the schedule established that duties between 15 and 20% would be cut to 15% in 1875; and those of more than 20% would be reduced by thirds (1875, 1878, and 1881) until they were brought down to 15% in the last-named year.

The tariff schedules of 1869 governed the long free-trade period which lasted until 1891. The diffusion of the United States' example, which had changed its tariffs to a protectionist type in 1861, and especially the doctrines of List, which had triumphed in Germany, aroused the enthusiasm of the Catalan bourgeoisie and was one of the essential factors in Alfonso XII's restoration. It explains why one of the first measures taken by the Restoration government was the decree of July 27, 1875, followed by the law of July 17,

1876, suspending application of Article 4 and the Fifth Base of the 1869 tariff schedule until new reports were prepared. These measures succeeded in stopping the reduction threatened by the Fifth Base and in halting the development of the free-trade policy; but they did not change matters in the direction of protectionism, as was shown in the schedule approved on July 17, 1877, introducing the system of differential tariffs derived from commercial treaties. In fact, from then on the schedule contained three columns: first, normal tariffs; second, reduced tariffs; and third, extraordinary ones. Because of this distinction, commercial treaties were able to inflict serious damage on certain Spanish agricultural and industrial products.

The position of some industrial sectors was seriously affected by these schedules. For fourteen years the Catalan cotton manufacturers carried on the fight alone; the Basques and even other industrial groups in Catalonia, such as woollen manufacturers, were favored by the 1869 law. And the same advantages were enjoyed by the businessmen and farmers who cultivated export products, such as grape growers. Later the protectionists' positions were gravely threatened by the rise to power of Sagasta's liberal governments. In 1882, through a proposal by a minister, Camacho, the Hispano-French commercial treaty was approved. For a period of ten years, and on behalf of Spanish wine, this treaty provided for an essential lowering of import tariffs on French products in Spain. Soon after this, on July 6, 1882, and through the efforts of the same minister, the Cortes put through a law revoking the suspension of the Fifth Base. The new legal text prescribed that duties between 15% and 20% would be reduced to 15% on August 1, 1882, and that those in excess of 20% would be reduced by thirds to 15% in 1887 and 1892. The schedules of 1886 were drawn up in accordance with the terms of this law.

RESTORATION OF PROTECTIONISM: SCHEDULES OF 1891 AND 1906. Renewal of the free-trade policy had been possible because it coincided with a period of great prosperity, that stage in the business cycle which we have called "gold fever." But as a result of the first downward movements felt in Spain, the economic conflicts which they aroused in Catalonia as well as Castile, Asturias, and Biscay resulted in close cooperation among the Castilian grain growers,

Asturian ironworkers and miners, and Basque metallurgists, who all flocked to the aid of Catalonia. In 1892 a meeting was held in Bilbao with Catalan industrialists in attendance, and another in Madrid ending with a huge demonstration in favor of the restoration of protectionism. The leaders of the movement were Adaro, an Asturian, Zaracondegui, a Basque, and the Catalan Bosch y Labrús. Even the president of the Council of Ministers, Antonio Cánovas del Castillo, published a pamphlet at the end of 1890 entitled "Why I Have Come to Believe in Protectionist Doctrines" (*De cómo he venido yo a ser doctrinalmente proteccionista*). It is not surprising, then, that in this atmosphere the decree of December 24, 1890, was published, suspending the Fifth Base of the law of 1869 and the law of 1882, and that it was followed by the decree of December 31, 1891, approving the new tariff schedules which, according to Gual Villalbí, stood for progress toward "healthy protectionism."

The schedule of 1891 (or 1892, if we count from the date on which it went into effect) was based on the same tariffs as those approved in 1877. All trade exemptions granted since 1882 were canceled. The Spanish iron and steel industry developed under this protectionist system, and the textile industry achieved its greatest prosperity. However, politics entered the picture and precipitated an even more protectionist solution: loss of the colonies forced Spain to defend herself, and there is nothing strange in the fact that on March 3, 1906, a decidedly protectionist tariff was enacted, which has continued to guide Spanish commercial policy to the present day.

47 · Money, Credit, and Banking

THE SPANISH MONETARY SYSTEM IN THE 19TH CENTURY. During this century the Spanish monetary system was characterized by an urge toward unification and simplification, culminating in adoption of the decimal system already in use outside Spain's frontiers.

The monetary history of the 19th century can be divided into three great periods:

FROM *1808* TO *1848*. Monetary regulations at the beginning of the century continued to be those established by Charles III's royal cedula of 1772. This meant that confusion reigned, for to the confusion left by Charles IV's reign was added that produced by the War of Independence, with the appearance of regional or local mints and the circulation of a great deal of English and French coinage. The monetary bases established by the Constitution of 1812 were never implemented. Among the great variety of coins in circulation, the fundamental one was the *peso* or silver duro, 900/1000 fine, weighing 26.291 grams, but the effective coin was the silver *real de vellón* weighing 1.319 grams. The *medio real,* in copper, was of 19.170 grams. Intermediate types were the *peseta* and the *escudo,* both of silver; at the top of the system was the gold *onza.* We should recall that there also existed a type of coin called *columnaria* (struck in the Indies). These coins were worth more than the ordinary coinage, as we have already remarked (p. 583), so that the *peseta columnaria* was equal to 5 *reales de vellón* and the *peseta provincial* to 4.

FROM *1848* TO *1868*. This monetary system was reformed on April 15, 1848, by the minister Bertrán de Lis, thus inaugurating the second period in the history of 19th-century currency.

During the preceding period monetary circulation had reached the point that in 1842 foreign coins made up half of the total money in circulation. The effective unit of payment, instead of being the peseta or real, was the *napoleon,* a French coin with a value of about 20 Spanish *reales.*

Various solutions were tried in an attempt to solve this problem. When Salamanca was minister in 1847 the government put forward a piece of legislation establishing the *real de vellón* as the monetary unit, but instituting the decimal system. The real was reduced to 25 grams; that is, 900/1000 fine. This plan was rejected but was later applied as a decree issued by Bertrán de Lis (minister in Narváez's cabinet) on April 15, 1848. The units of currency were as follows; the *doblón,* or *centén isabelino,* a gold coin, was to be worth 100 reales or 10 silver escudos; the *medio duro,* equivalent to 10 reales or 1 escudo. In addition there were the *duro,* the *peseta,* the *media peseta,* and the *real.*

This system underwent some changes by the terms of the law of February 3, 1854, which, although it confirmed the previous system, decreed that silver *reales* should have less weight. Sardá says that the reform of 1854 introduced a bimetallic system based on gold.

When the revolution of 1854 (known as "La Vicalvarada") took place, the minister Juan Bruil, in a decree of December 30, 1855, dispensed with the *maravedí,* which up till then had been the money of account in the Spanish economy. The *real* was fixed upon as the effective unit, divided into one hundred parts or *céntimos,* a word which from that time onward has stood for the minimum accounting unit in Spain. It was decreed that 3 céntimos were equivalent to a maravedí and that 50 céntimos equaled 17 maravedís.

These reforms were purely superficial. The important change took place in 1861–1864, and for two reasons. The first was the rise in the price of silver, which ever since the 16th century had constituted the chief basis for monetary systems throughout Europe. And the second was the change from the metallist to the nominalist system; that is, people had become accustomed to thinking of money not as an instrument of exchange for its intrinsic value alone, but for the credit deposited in it by the public or by the State. These two changes in attitude are reflected in the opinion drawn up in 1861 by a technical commission which, in giving its report on the budgetary law of that year, decided that "it was essential to create a silver standard, with gold circulation to be reviewed periodically, or a fractional silver coinage redeemable on demand, subject to a seigniorage of 30%." These ideas were taken up by the minister Pedro Salaverría, who established a new monetary system by the law of June 26, 1864. Its basic unit was the silver *escudo*, weighing 12.98 grams and 90/1000 fine, equivalent to 10 *reales*. In gold coinage, the *doblón* or *centén isabelino* was retained, equivalent to 100 reales or 10 escudos, and the duro (equal to 2 escudos) was kept as a fractional silver coin along with the peseta, half peseta, and real, the latter to be 800/1000 fine. The half real, fourth real, tenth real, and half-tenth real were placed in circulation as bronze, tin, and zinc coins.

FROM *1868* TO *1898*: SYSTEM BASED ON THE PESETA. These reforms crystallized in the decree of October 19, 1868, dictated by the minister Figuerola as soon as Isabella II was dethroned and the triumphant revolutionaries seized power. Certainly Figuerola had a number of notable precedents in mind, first and foremost the establishment of the Latin Monetary Convention (December 23, 1865). Its terms were as follows: (1) limitation of bimetallic mintings, at the ratio of 1:15.5, (2) limitation of silver mintings by the State, so that no more than 6 francs per person would be in circulation, (3) coins equivalent to or of lesser value than 1 franc could not be used except in the internal system of payment in each country, while the 5-franc coin or its equivalents would be redeemable on demand internationally, and (4) gold minting would be unrestricted.

Spain had not signed the Latin Monetary Convention, but the Revolution of 1868 accepted the system proclaimed by this body, so that in Figuerola's decree the monetary unit designated was the peseta of 100 céntimos and 835/1000 fine. Higher in the scale than the peseta were various gold coins (100, 50, 20, 10, and 5 pesetas), and in silver a 5-peseta coin (900/1000 fine) and another of 2 pesetas. One-half and one-fifth peseta coins in silver were also authorized. In bronze, the fractional coins were of 10, 5, 2, and 1 céntimos.

All this was based on one assumption: the overvaluing of silver in terms of gold. But the shift in this relationship after the beginning of the century's final decade caused the ruin of the system, owing to the flight of gold to other countries and the multiplication of silver mintings. The government did not decide to adopt the gold standard in 1876, when it would have been opportune, and after that a truly anomalous situation grew up. It could be described as that of a silver standard, with fluctuating quotations and fiduciary money, based on the law passed by the minister Echegaray in 1874 granting the Bank of Spain the monopoly on note issues.

FLUCTUATIONS OF MONETARY POLICY IN THE 19TH CENTURY. This last consideration leads us to speak of the fluctuations of Spanish monetary policy in the 19th century, a subject related to the preceding one; that is, to the reorganization of monetary systems, but one which has a total economic foundation in the Spanish economy. The great scholar of these fluctuations is Professor Sardá.

This author considers that Spanish policy underwent four phases during the 19th century. The first, extending from 1814 to 1834, he calls the *anachronistic period*. In fact, except for the intervention of the liberal Cortes during the years 1821–1823, this period is characterized by a do-nothing policy and persistent adoption of anachronistic measures. Thus the country had a "heavy" currency which escaped abroad, while the "light" French money invaded Spain. Spain acted as though the colonial empire were still in existence and able to supply indefinite amounts of silver; but since this empire had disappeared, what happened was that a huge breach was opened through which the silver still retained by Spain flowed abroad. The government defended this heavy coinage with bans on export and duties on import of metal. Both policies were completely erroneous, as was shown in practice. The only possible remedies would have been either devaluation of the peseta or foreign loans. Since Spain did not have the courage to adopt the first measure—the only proper one—she resorted to the second, so that Spain, the monarchy, and absolutism fell into the hands of international credit.

The second period, from 1834 to 1848, can be described as *deflationary*. It began with the plan of the finance minister, Toreno (1834), to devalue the real, making it worth 32 maravedís, and to reduce its fineness. This project met with opposition from the Cortes, so the country went on living under the previous system; that is, resorting to foreign loans and allowing coins of other countries to circulate, such as the napoleon, the English sovereign, the Portuguese crown, and even the Mexican peso. In spite of this iniquitous policy, there were some examples of proper procedures to stem the invasion of

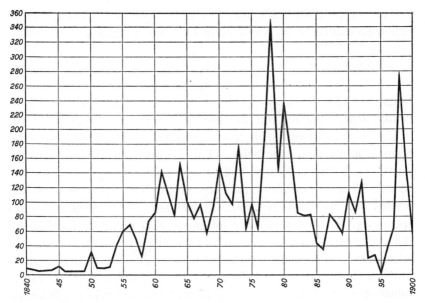

EFFECTIVE VALUE OF SILVER AND GOLD MINTINGS, IN MILLIONS OF PESETAS, BETWEEN 1840 AND 1900 (*after* SARDÁ).

short-weight foreign currency. The mint in Barcelona, which had resumed production in 1834, bought silver in 1836 at 23 reales 15 maravedís per ounce instead of the 22 reales 15 maravedís prescribed by the law; as for seigniorage, it was fundamentally lowered, placing it at 1.5 instead of 2.2 and at 2 instead of 3.8. Thus the mint was able to attract precious metals, mint up to 130 million reales both in gold and silver (half of those in circulation in Spain), and to drive out of Barcelona the French currency, especially that of Marseilles, which had dominated until then.

The third period, from 1848 to 1873, is characterized by an important phenomenon: the *rise in the price of silver*. There was a transitional stage marked by plans for monetary reform in 1846–1847. Through these reforms the country accepted the idea of devaluation as a last resort; it was all the more necessary in view of the fact that the rise in the price of silver, owing to the gold discoveries in California, was daily aggravating the problem. This was the spirit behind Bertrán de Lis's decree of April 15, 1848, whose purpose in relation to monetary policy was as follows: to expel foreign money from the country and to devalue coinage with a high silver content.

For this purpose the mark fine, which had been worth 181 *reales de vellón* ever since 1824, was fixed at 182, thus placing the bimetallic ratio at 1:15.77.

This reform, which could have meant the country's salvation, arrived too late, and it was soon necessary to resort to new devaluations. In 1854 the mark 24 carats fine was set at 194.1 *reales de vellón,* which meant that the bimetallic ratio was now 1:15.40.

Under these conditions, more precious metals flowed into the Spanish mints than ever before. This is shown in the pertinent reports. For instance, though in 1841 the gold coming into the mints totaled 17 million reales, and silver 5,800,000 reales, in 1850 the figures had risen sharply: 64,800,000 and 27,700,000 reales respectively. In 1854–1857 the inflow of gold was considerable, on the order of 84, 146, 179, and 123 million reales, while that of silver stayed at an almost constant level of 32, 36, 41, 30, and 25 million. However, in 1857 there was a considerable decrease in the influx of silver to the mints (only 13 million came in), which forced a change in the general orientation of the Spanish system. In 1864 the minister Salaverría adopted the nominalist criterion, discarding the idea of intrinsic value of money. This involved suppression of the seigniorage and minting charges, with an immediate profit for the Treasury estimated at 2,140,000 reales. The value of the silver mark was set at 196.8 *reales de vellón,* and the bimetallic ratio became 1:15.74.

More gold than silver continued to be minted during this whole period, in response to the stocks in the market. Thus, in 1860, 228 million reales were minted in gold and only 36 million in silver, and in 1866–1867 197 million and 88 million respectively. It was this tendency which caused application of the currency reform of 1868, introducing into Spain the bimetallism of the Latin Union; but the sudden rise in gold prices frustrated this arrangement and led to other measures which characterize the fourth period of monetary policy in 19th-century Spain.

This fourth period, lasting from 1873 to 1902, is characterized by the *predominance of gold* and the *collapse of Spanish currency.* The report of the consultative Commission on Currency in 1876 stated that silver money was worth less than its legal value, that it was devalued in fact, and that the base of an effective Spanish monetary system ought to be gold currency. In fact there was an inclination toward establishment of the gold standard, as is shown by the minister García Barzanallana's decree of August 20, 1876. However, the gold crisis to which we have just referred destroyed these plans. Gold now went abroad in such quantities that although in 1881 Spanish mints had coined 127 million pesetas in gold, in 1883 they produced only 36 million.

Lack of gold at the mints coincided with a decrease in the Bank of Spain's gold reserves (brought about by interest payments on public and private debt). The situation had become dangerous, and in 1883 suspension of convertibility was decreed for gold notes. An economy of a fiduciary type was entered upon, lasting until the end of the period.

During the long era of the "sick" peseta, fiduciary circulation acquired considerable volume. Up to 1891 the figures doubled: 364 million in 1833 and 734 million in 1891. At that moment the following were in circulation in Spain: 300 million pesetas in gold and 800 million in silver; in banknotes, 811 million. Instead of proceeding to a readjustment of the Treasury, the government authorized, by the terms of the Cos Gayón law of 1891, a fiduciary circulation of 1,500,000,000 pesetas. This explains why the peseta began to have a fluctuating quotation in the foreign market, especially because it was not supported by a favorable trade balance or by adequate gold reserves. Depreciation of the peseta began about 1881, that is, at the very time when the decision to suspend the convertibility of gold notes was taken, and continued to increase until it assumed alarming proportions in the decade from 1890–1900. In 1881 the premium of gold over paper was 0.46%; in 1885, 2.07%, and in 1889, 3.18%.

The increase in fiduciary circulation in the last years of the 19th century was literally overwhelming, for as a result of the colonial wars and the Treasury's difficulties it rose from 884 million pesetas in 1892 to 1,600,000,000 in 1900. In international markets the quotation of the peseta fell correspondingly (the pound was worth 26.21 pesetas in 1890, and 39.24 in 1898). We must keep in mind that these figures correspond to average annual values, so that if partial quotations are examined there were moments at which the pound was worth 54.15 pesetas. In other words, in ten years the peseta had lost half of its buying power. The country was on the verge of ruin, as in the worst times of the inflations under Charles II or Charles IV.

EVOLUTION OF THE EXTERNAL DEBT. The debasement of the Spanish monetary standard during the 19th century had multiple causes. We have already mentioned the most important: the loss of American metal and inability to create a favorable trade balance. To these two factors we must add others even more deeply rooted in the Spanish historical process during the preceding 100 years: civil wars, administrative confusion, the poverty of the internal market. The Spanish State very often had to resort to foreign credit in order to survive. The history of this process is, as we shall see, complementary to that of currency movements during the same period.

The War of Independence was waged by means of national contributions—the lesser proportion—and foreign loans. But when Ferdinand VII returned from his French captivity, he refused to recognize a debt that had been largely responsible for the establishment of a constitutional regime which he detested. In consequence, the foreign loans recognized in 1821 totaled only 291,700,000 reales. The politicians of the Constitutional Triennium recognized old debts and converted them into new obligations, so that by the end of the period, in 1823, the Spanish external debt had gone up to 3,125,400,000 reales (nominal value), or 2,500,000,000 reales (effective value). This was approximately what the War of Independence had cost in foreign credits.

During the following decade, while the country was in the midst of the crisis of recovery, the Spanish economy was unable to furnish the government with the financial aid it required as a result of the collapse of the American empire. Thus, the finance ministers of the period, like López Ballesteros, had no choice but to ask the help of wealthy, liberal Spanish *emigrés* such as the banker Aguado. In all, the money loaned to Spain between 1823 and 1833 was 1,825,-000,000 reales, which we must add to the debt previously contracted, giving an effective total of some 4,400,000,000 reales.

When the liberals took over the government in 1834, the Minister of Finance, the Count of Toreno, reduced the nominal value of the Spanish external debt by two-thirds. This measure—the law of November 16, 1834—*ruined Spanish credit* in Europe and did not help the Spanish State, which was embroiled in a bitter civil war. In order to fight the Carlists the liberal governments accepted operations that were very onerous, such as the Ardoin loan of 1834 with a nominal value of 700 million reales (45%). Therefore it is not

720

surprising that by the end of the civil war the foreign debt was up to 5,875,000,000 reales.

Reorganization of the Treasury under the minister Mon, and the first cyclical phase of prosperity, permitted a certain amount of progress. But the dawn of industrialization very soon raised the external debt to some 6,500,000,000 reales, of which nearly 4 billion were in a consolidated external debt at 5%.

Once the crisis of 1847–1848 had ended and the rising trend was in full swing, aided by favorable Spanish trade operations during the Crimean War, Bravo Murillo decided on an important operation: *that of consolidating the external debt*. Consolidated bonds at 5 and 4% were transformed into deferred perpetual debt at 3%. The system was truly drastic: interest would not be paid for four years, and in the fifth payments would begin at 1%, going up to the 3% provided for. The nominal value of the external debt was fixed at 5,016,000,000 reales. Fortunately, the Crimean War permitted excellent profits, customs duties brought in funds, and both the government and Spanish society as a whole could breathe easier. To cap the climax, the Pereires and Rothschilds were channeling foreign currency into Spain for railway construction. By 1867 the Spanish debt was down to 4,100,000,000 reales (1,025,000,-000 pesetas). It is true that the credit of the public treasury had not improved; in 1863 the perpetual debt of 1851 was quoted at 52%.

The crisis of 1866, coinciding with a period of unfavorable trade balances and imminent changes of regime, inaugurated a period of *accumulation of new debts*. From the 1,025,000,000 pesetas of 1867, they rose to 2,444,000,000 in 1869 and 3,889,000,000 in 1873. The total debt almost quadrupled, therefore, in the space of six years. This was the price Spain paid for the civil war, the revolutionary outbreaks, and, above all, the war in Cuba. We must also keep in mind that interest on the external debt was paid in gold, which meant annual sacrifices from the public treasury and the almost inevitable appeal to foreign capital.

The Restoration found, therefore, that its external credit had greatly deteriorated (the perpetual debt of 1851 was quoted at 10.07% in 1881) and that its debt was on the order of 4,400,-000,000 pesetas (nominal value). Sardá believes that its effective value was only half this figure, for in the debt conversion undertaken by Cos Gayón in 1876 the old debt was exchanged at the rate of 43.74%. In any case, the task of the first governments of that period was to stabilize the external debt. We have just spoken of the conversion carried out by Cos Gayón in 1876; the most important conversion of all was that of the minister Camacho in May, 1882. At that time the perpetual external debt at 4% amounted to 1,930,000,000 pesetas.

The fluctuation of the peseta led many Spanish capitalists to acquire bonds of this type, for interest payments were made in gold. This represented a beginning—an involuntary one—toward the retirement of the external debt. This came to pass in 1898 when the bonds were restamped for ownership by Spaniards. However, it was not definitively retired until the war of 1914.

BALANCE OF PAYMENTS AND FOREIGN INVESTMENTS. To complete our study of Spanish money movements in the 19th century it is necessary to keep in mind the very important area of private debt; that is, the amounts spent abroad for purchase of production and consumption goods, and interest on capital loans. This factor, added to the trade balance and the State debt, permits us to trace with precision the ups and downs of the Spanish indebtedness, as well as the fluctuations of currency.

Sardá, whom we have been following in these two sections, estimated that the mean annual deficit in the trade balance between 1814 and 1848 was 31 million pesetas. This means that in the latter year total balance of trade loss was 1,075,000,000 pesetas (4,300,-000,000 reales). This last figure can be broken down as follows:

External debt	3,000,000,000 reales
Currency loss	1,300,000,000 reales
	4,300,000,000 reales

After 1848 there was a period of large foreign investments in the building up of Spanish industry. This fact, together with the successive calls made by the State on foreign credit, caused the trade balance to become a heavy burden. Up to 1881, a date corresponding to the peak of the Spanish debt, capital funds owed by the country increased in the following manner:

External debt	1,400,000,000 pesetas
Private debt	2,000,000,000 pesetas
Total increase	3,400,000,000 pesetas

Keeping the previous balance in mind, we see that the total debt had risen by 1881 to 4,200,000,000 pesetas. From this figure we must subtract existing stocks of silver and gold, which in their turn had increased by 1,250,000,000 pesetas. In fact, the definitive loss for the period 1848–1881 is 2,150,000,000 pesetas, which approximately agrees with the net deficit in the trade balance, totaling 2,400,000,000. Where does the difference of 250 million come from? It may have stemmed equally from exported silver, following a long tradition, or from overseas revenues.

In the last twenty years of the 19th century the deficit in the trade balance was covered by export of currency, revenues from foreign investments, and the abundant remittances of income and capital from Spanish emigrants in America. This aspect has been examined only lightly, but it is of fundamental importance if we are to understand the endurance of the Spanish economy after 1898. It is estimated that in 1899 Spain received 235 million pesetas, of which 180 million came from Argentina, 25 million from other Spanish American republics, 10 million from Algeria, and 20 million from repatriation of Cuban capital. In 1902 the amount of repatriated capital rose to the considerable sum of 1,200,000,000 pesetas. In 1904 the external debt had decreased by 1,200,000,000 pesetas, and private debt had increased by 1,500,000,000, with an increment in capital owed of 300 million pesetas.

All that we have been saying is summed up in the table below:

EXTERNAL DEBT		PRIVATE DEBT			
(in millions of pesetas)					
Year				Total	Remarks
1823	500		—	500	{ Export of currency and foreign loans
1848	800		—	800	
		+1,400	+2,000		{ Foreign investments in: (1) railways, (2) mines
1881	2,200		2,000	4,200	
		−1,200	+1,500		{ Foreign investment in public utilities and remittances of capital and interest by emigrants
1904	1,000		3,500	4,500	

MOVEMENT OF FOREIGN INVESTMENT: STAGES AND OBJECTIVES.
Fundamentally, we deduce from study of the Spanish trade balance
that the country's industrial equipping would not have been possible without the aid of foreign capital. But of course a high price had
to be paid for this, not only in interest payments but in concessions
of monopolies on national resources.

Up to the time of the price rise in the decade from 1850 to 1860,
we do not find much interest on the part of foreign capital in Spanish industrial affairs. In financial matters, as we have already stated,
the connection between French banking and the Spanish Ministry
of Finance had been close ever since 1827. After 1856 the Pereire
brothers, creators of the "Crédit Mobilier" in France, attempted to
extend their activities into Spain. They were the ones who, taking
advantage of the railway law of 1855, underwrote one of the most
active Spanish groups in railway construction. This inaugurated a
period of great activity, characterized by the opening of the market
in Spanish railway shares in the principal Western European stock
exchanges. After 1859 small French, Belgian, and English share-
holders invested their savings in Spanish railway bonds. This flow of
money lasted some twenty years, approximately until 1882, as
trade and exchange statistics show. The main Spanish railway lines
were now complete and had begun to show a profit. Investments of
this type are difficult to estimate, because of the fragmentation of
the capital invested. Estimates range from 1,500,000,000 to
2,500,000,000 pesetas.

Simultaneously, and this time in the shape of large companies,
non-nationals took over the Spanish mining industry. The Royal
Asturian Mining Company appeared in 1853: 36 million pesetas of
capital, Belgian in origin. In 1866 the Tarsis Sulphur Company
(English), with a capital of 78,500,000 pesetas, began its exploitation of the Huelva pyrite deposits. Seven years later the Ríotinto
Company bought for 93 million pesetas the extremely rich copper
deposits in the same district. The same year (1873) saw foundation
of the Orconera Iron Company in Bilbao, with a capital of 30 million pesetas. In the decade which followed there was a real
avalanche of foreign companies interested in mines and real estate.
The Mortgage Bank of Spain was founded in 1875 with French
capital; the Peñarroya Company in 1881, with 87 million pesetas,

to exploit the mines of Bélmez and Puertollano. All this represented another billion pesetas, perhaps more.

In a second period, from 1881 to the end of the century, foreign capital was invested in public utility companies (water, gas, electricity, streetcars, etc.) or in banking and insurance companies. Spain was a fertile field for capital investments: she possessed abundant manpower, strong authority, corrupt administration, little money, and a lack of great financial initiative. Foreign enterprises flourished everywhere: in Seville, with the Water Works (1883), Valencia with the Compagnie de Tramways et Chemins de Fer; in Barcelona with Lebon et Cie, Aguas de Barcelona and Barcelona Traction (from 1882 to 1911); in Bilbao, the Compañía de Tramways y Electricidad, etc.

In 1916 an Englishman, Arthur N. Young, stated that foreign capital investment in Spain totaled 4 billion pesetas: 1,500,000,000 in mining, industrial, or financial companies; 2 billion in railway bonds; and 500 million in non-nationalized external debt. These figures are subject to revision.

SPANISH BANKING AT THE BEGINNING OF THE 19TH CENTURY. During the first half of the 19th century banking continued along the same path which had characterized its activities at the end of the preceding century, in the official as well as in the private field. The National Bank of San Carlos, created in 1782, continued to function until 1827, a survival of the reigns of Charles III and Charles IV. Its credit had fallen very low, for it engaged in extremely dubious activities such as speculation on its own shares and distribution of high dividends in order to maintain the level of its quotations. All this meant that it existed at the State's expense. The War of Independence and especially the Liberal Triennium (1820–1823) caused it to lose even more prestige. Once this dangerous period was over, Ferdinand VII decided, on the advice of the minister López Ballesteros, to transform the National Bank of San Carlos into the Spanish Bank of San Fernando. This was done by means of the Royal Decree of June 9, 1829. The statutes of the new institution were drawn up by Don Pedro Sainz de Andino, author of the 1831 law on the Madrid Stock Exchange and the Commercial Code. The Spanish Bank of San Fernando had a capital of 60 million reales and the privilege of issuing banknotes for thirty years. Its function was limited to that of an amortization fund. In 1833 it received authorization to broaden its activities, thus falling into the error which had caused the decline of its prede- cessor, the National Bank of San Carlos. In 1838, while Mon was Minister of Finance, the Spanish Bank of San Fernando and the State signed a fiscal contract by whose terms the State centralized its credit operations in the Bank. The Bank gave an advance of 20 million reales and 48 million more in acceptances; the State, for its part, promised to put in 10 million within four months and give a guarantee of 50 million reales in forced loans. The country's posi- tion improved considerably after the end of the Carlist war, and the Spanish Bank of San Fernando enjoyed a brilliant period as a result of this prosperity. In 1844 it paid dividends of 22% to its share- holders.

In that same year competition appeared in the form of the Bank of Isabella II, founded on January 25. It had been created by José de Salamanca and the Count of Santa Olalla, who represented a new mental attitude, a new banking spirit, combined with the financing of railway construction and concession of credits to industry and trade. The initial capital was 100 million reales in shares and twice that amount in certificates of indebtedness. It issued banknotes be- ginning on October 1, 1844. Its existence was truly precarious. At first, coinciding with the euphoria of the first cyclical upturn, it earned sensational profits, to the point that in October, 1846, its shares went up to 230. The crash soon occurred, and in 1847 they were quoted at 170. At that moment the Bank of Isabella II was on the point of suspending payments and declaring itself bankrupt. But the danger passed thanks to Salamanca's influence, for he suc- ceeded in solving the banking crisis by merging the Bank of Isabella II with that of San Fernando (February 25, 1847) and forming out of the two an institution which has presided over recent Spanish economic life under the name of Nuevo Banco Español de San Fer- nando, or Banco de España: the Bank of Spain.

As for private banking, its development was minimal in the first half of the 19th century. It continued to be the traditional type, that of the banker who held deposits for his clients and gave a few ad- vances, generally more in the nature of simple money-lending than commercial credit. What was more characteristic of banking during this period was the growing use of drafts, running parallel to the increase in international mercantile relations. One of the most typical bankers of the period was the Catalan Gaspar Remisa. After having managed to accumulate a fortune as a contractor to the army and as an undertaker of public works, he founded the firm of "Casals and Remisa." In 1827 he moved to Madrid, where he founded the firm of "Marqués de Remisa," an institution which played an important role in Spanish finance. Its capital was truly impressive: 50 million reales of its own and 9 million in customer deposits. These figures give us an idea of what the structure of a bank was at that time. As for the mechanics of its operation, the bank in Barcelona bought bills of exchange on Madrid and other centers; everything was sent to the capital. There, Remisa covered these with payments from Madrid on Barcelona or with remittances from the provinces on Madrid. Barcelona also operated through Paris. Remisa was a correspondent of the Banque Lafitte and placed funds on England and Gibraltar at the request of his clients. The rate of discount was 6%. Loans to private persons carried interest of up to 14%.

By the end of this period the Bank of Barcelona was founded in that city, with a capital of 5 million pesetas. We shall discuss this institution more fully a little later.

THE BANK OF SPAIN AND PRIVATE LOCAL BANKS IN THE MIDDLE OF THE 19TH CENTURY. The second period of Spanish banking includes the years 1847 to 1874. As we have said, the Bank of Isabella II was incorporated into the San Fernando bank by the Royal Order of February 25, 1847. Salamanca's operation amalgamating the capital of the two banks made the Nuevo Banco Español de San Fernando the most powerful institution in Spanish financial circles. Nine years later, on January 28, 1856, it received the name of Banco de España: the Bank of Spain. Its stipulated capital was 400 million reales, and it was given the privilege of issuing banknotes for Madrid and the right to create branches, called "auxiliary deposits," in Barcelona and Cádiz.

The first years were very difficult, for they coincided with the crisis of 1847–1848. Nevertheless, it was during this period that the Bank received its definitive stamp. The law issued by Mon on April 4, 1849, started it off in a modern direction. This law established control of the Bank of Spain by the State, through appointment of a governor and two subgovernors. In February, 1851, Bravo Murillo took a further step, requiring the Bank to reduce its capital and eliminate doubtful credits; but at the same time he granted it the privilege of issuing notes for all of Spain. Both these legal texts were precedents for the law of January 28, 1856, which really created the Bank of Spain. Besides creation of the bank, the law recognized its right to issue notes of a local character. This right was extended not only to the branches in Barcelona and Cádiz, which already had it, but to those of other centers which requested it within a period of three months.

If the Bank of Spain did not exercise this right, it had the obligation of establishing branches in Valencia, Seville, Saragossa, Bilbao, Málaga, Alicante, Valladolid, and Santander. The abovementioned banks could issue bearer banknotes up to a limit of three times the capital paid in. The following operations were authorized: deposits, current accounts, discounts and remittances (at 6%), and advances. They could not trade in public securities nor pledge their own shares as security.

Besides the Bank of Spain, whose prosperity was tremendous after 1854, coinciding with the upward trend in general economic conditions, private banking enjoyed a period of splendor. In Madrid, besides the central institution, there appeared important branches of foreign banks, such as the House of Rothschild, the House of Lafitte, and also those of Manzanedo, Girona Sainz, Miqueloterena Brothers, etc. In 1857 the "merchant capitalists," as the bankers' guild of Madrid was referred to at that time, numbered fifty-two. The chief operations of this type of banking had to do with Treasury operations, especially the purchase of drafts on the provinces geared to the collection of taxes. They also operated in the area of subscriptions on the public debt, arbitrage in securities, orders on the Paris and London Stock Exchanges, foreign payments, and finally, remittances to Cuba. All these operations, clearly, were of a semiofficial nature.

Barcelona had a very different sort of orientation. There, the leader in banking was the Bank of Barcelona, created by Girona, Serra and Co. on May 1, 1844. Its capital was 20 million reales, with permission to establish branches and to issue banknotes up to the limit of its capital, with a guarantee of one-third in cash reserves. It could make discounts, advances, deposits, and so on. It was wisely administered, and managed discounting and note issue operations with extraordinary skill. Thus the Bank of Barcelona was able to overcome the crises of the time and emerge victorious. It was the institution that gave the banking business in Barcelona its chief orientation: investment in railway enterprises and municipal loans. Other banking houses made their appearance at about the same time, and were the germ of future great business enterprises. For example, the House of Evaristo Arnús, founded in 1852 and specializing in stock-exchange operations, which established the system of the free market in securities; and the Caja Vilumara, whose founder, Domingo Taberner y Tintorer, established a credit system for the textile industry.

This was also the moment when the Bank of Bilbao made its appearance, created in November, 1855, by a commission from the local Board of Trade, and authorized by the Royal Decree of May 19, 1857, in accordance with the terms of the law of 1856. Its initial capital was 8 million reales. From its earliest days it was connected with commercial and mining operations. During the crisis of 1866 it showed tremendous soundness, foreshadowing the prestige which Biscayan banking was soon to acquire everywhere in Spain.

The Bank of Santander was authorized on May 15, 1857, to fill the needs of economic development in the Montaña region.

It is also of interest to point out how finance companies developed during this period, under the protection of the law we mentioned before, that of January 1856, which regulated them. The object of these companies was to invest money in industrial and commercial operations. They represented a great novelty compared with the banking methods of the previous period. Taking as their model the French "Crédit Mobilier," many finance companies began to make their appearance, such as the Catalana Comercial de Crédito, the Crédito Mobiliario Barcelonés, the Sociedad Española Mercantil e Industrial, the Sociedad General de Crédito Mobiliario Español, etc.

THE BANK OF SPAIN, PRIVATE AND LOCAL BANKS AT THE END OF THE 19TH CENTURY. As a result of the Revolution of 1868 and the somewhat chaotic situation produced by the economic crisis of 1866 and the years which followed it, Spanish banking life changed direction. In fact, under the terms of the law signed by the minister

José Echegaray on March 19, 1874, the monopoly on issuance of banknotes was given to the Bank of Spain for thirty years. Its capital was set at 100 million pesetas and the limit of issue at five times that amount, or 500 million pesetas, backed by one-fourth of the latter sum in coins or bar silver and gold. The Bank of Spain granted the Treasury a minimum advance of 125 million pesetas. Thus the banking business was centralized and the Bank officially linked to the State, to the point that their mutual histories became inseparable.

Echegaray's law provided for suspension of local banks of issue if they did not affiliate with the Bank of Spain. Eleven accepted this condition and four refused; among the latter were the banks of Bilbao and Barcelona.

As for private banking, this third period was one of expansion and concentration. Thus, where there had been thirty-nine banks in Madrid in 1874, only twenty-seven were left by 1892.

New banking activities were also developing at this time, such as those of the Bank of Castile, controlled by the Girona-Vinent group, or the General Bank of Madrid directed by a German named Gwinner. He started the custom of placing political figures of first rank on the bank's Board of Directors. Another was the Spanish Credit Bank, founded by the Marquis of Cortina, which triumphed in the field of mortgage credit after a number of unsuccessful experiences.

However, the highest level of banking activity during this period was to be found in Barcelona, and not only by the discount type of bank, but especially by commercial banks and those providing mercantile credit. The Spanish Colonial Bank, founded in 1876 by Girona and López y López with a capital of 15 million duros, is of the first type. The government was in serious straits, and the Spanish Colonial Bank lent it 25 million pesos to carry on the war in Cuba and the pacification of the Philippines. The bank's guarantees were provided by Cuban customs receipts. As a commercial bank the Spanish Colonial was responsible for the foundation of the General Philippines Tobacco Company, the General Railways Credit Company, the Northern Railways Company of Spain, the Asturias-Galicia-León Railway Company, and numerous agricultural and industrial undertakings in Cuba and the Philippines. As for the mercantile credit bank, the company known as Crédito y

Docks, founded in 1882, carried out this type of operation. It discounted warrants on goods deposited in the port of Barcelona.

THE STOCK EXCHANGE AND STOCK OPERATIONS. The Madrid Stock Exchange was created by Royal Decree on September 10, 1831. The date is significant. It was the moment of Ferdinand VII's great foreign loans, and also the time when the capitalists—both those who had left the country and those who had not—achieved a position of influence in the orientation of the monarchy. It was essential for the government to be able to count on a suitable organ to handle bonds on the national debt, and, following the examples of London and Paris, the Madrid Stock Exchange came into existence as the favored instrument. After 1831, then, different kinds of securities were negotiated there, all of them State obligations.

During the first few years of its life the Madrid Stock Exchange was very prudent in its speculations, though it did reflect the capital's reaction to political events with rapid changes in its pulse rate. But at the time of the century's first rising trend (1845–1846) a real frenzy of speculation was unleashed, with transactions running as much as sixty days late. As more and more capital came into the market the Exchange went up and up, until the crisis of 1846 arrived with a crash in February of that year. Following it, a number of restrictive measures were adopted which gradually became more liberal, until the law of February 8, 1854, was passed in a climate of euphoria and optimism.

After that date a second period began in the Spanish Stock Exchange. Railway construction and foreign investments, the development of corporations in imitation of foreign ones, caused the arrival in the stock market of nongovernment securities, particularly industrial stocks and bonds. Barcelona was the center *par excellence* for the absorption of these last. However, there was no official Exchange in Barcelona, though there was a powerful private group, a sort of syndicate which operated under the name of "Salón de revendedores," or sellers' association. This group was undoubtedly connected with the buying and selling of stocks in Madrid. In 1860 it adopted the name of "Casino Mercantil." It lasted until the financial crisis of 1915, when the minister Burgallal took advantage of the situation to install an official Stock Exchange in Barcelona.

In addition to the Casino Mercantil there was the so-called

"Bolsín Catalán," a purely speculative nerve center which was very sensitive to telegraphed news concerning political and economic matters. However, large-scale speculation was reserved for the cliques in the Lonja, the merchants' exchange of medieval origin, where the brokers of the Board of Trade operated, many of them members of the Mercantil as well. The closing of deals took place in the Café del Liceo, a hangout for the powerful businessmen of the period.

The Exchange of Barcelona, with its polymorphous constitution, gave flexibility and a speculative cast to the stock market, according to Ramón de San Pedro. Through it, Catalan savings poured into industrial and railway stocks at a time when the Madrid Exchange was "still living in the era of State securities." However, the predominant orientation was toward bonds and the safe "coupon clipping" of the 19th-century bourgeoisie. In this as in other aspects of Catalonian finance, Evaristo Arnús was a virtual dictator. And this was the origin of one of the chief defects of Catalan finance; that it did not know how to encourage the financing of business enterprises when it possessed two bodies as powerful as the Bank of Barcelona and the Bolsín Catalán.

Many stock operations which had their origin in Barcelona spread to the Exchanges of Madrid and Bilbao (founded toward the end of the century, on July 21, 1890). Introduction of the current account in securities was particularly fruitful, and gave great activity to the market for mortgage bonds during the Restoration period.

48 · Survey of the 19th-Century Business Cycle

GENERAL CHARACTERISTICS OF STUDY: FLUCTUATIONS AND WORLD CRISES. Even among the most recent authors there has been a strange ignorance concerning the evolution of the business cycle in 19th-century Spain. Many prominent economists have foundered on this particular reef, among them Professor Tallada, who in his *History of Spanish Finance in the 19th Century* (*Historia de las finanzas españolas del siglo XIX*), published in 1946, continues to attribute the crisis of 1848 to the influence of the revolution which took place in France in that year. We need hardly say that political historians seem unaware of even the broad outlines of this important chapter in economic dynamics, despite the fact that J. Sardá presented it very effectively in his outstanding work *Monetary Policy and the Fluctuations of the Spanish Economy in the 19th Century* (*La política monetaria y las fluctuaciones de la economía española en el siglo XIX,* Madrid, 1948).

Obviously, Spanish research has not yet attained the level of the masterly studies of a Simiand or a Labrousse, in France; an Ayres, in the United States; or a Rostow, in England. As we know, the study of economic fluctuation is measured in terms of population development, agricultural yields and land area cultivated, the production of consumer goods, the evolution of prices and wages, the volume of domestic and foreign trade, the bank discount rate, and the amount of per capita income, among other secondary factors. In all these areas we possess only rudimentary, regional, or partial statistical series. Sardá has published the longest series of all: prices in Barcelona from 1812 to 1914. To this we can add, from 1850 onward, the figures on foreign trade, production of certain crops, volume of mining exploitation, quotation of the public debt, cotton imports, the rhythm of railway construction, and little more. By following this path, however, we shall proceed to a study of the business cycle in Spain during the last century. But before we go on, it

733

is essential to emphasize the intimate connection between the Spanish cycle and the world one, which is particularly evident in a century with a tendency toward free trade. Modern studies of the regional trade cycle have proved the thesis of Nikolai Kondratiev, according to which there were three great cycles in the 19th century:

First cycle	1789–1844	with a boom period from 1810 to 1817
Second cycle	1844–1890	with a boom period from 1870 to 1875
Third cycle	1890–(1929)	with a boom period from 1914 to 1920

From this table we can deduce three periods of expansion (1789–1810, 1844–1870, and 1890–1914); and three depressed periods (1817–1844, 1875–1890, and 1920–1929), separated by the following crucial dates: 1789, 1844, and 1890.

Each of these three dates stands in itself for a serious crisis. But in a free market system and a *laissez-faire* economy such as the 19th century's, besides these long cycles there were short ten-year cycles (according to Juglar) with deep intercyclical depressions, the famous crises of production, sales, and unemployment which industrialists of the period attributed to murky machinations on the part of revolutionary elements, or to the negligence of governments. In 19th-century world economic history these crises have a number which corresponds approximately to the fifth or sixth year of each decade. Here they are (the asterisk denotes a world crisis of more importance than the others):

*1816	*1846	1879
1825	1854	*1886
1836	*1866	1894

In Spain, we may as well say at once, the same thing happened, with a variation of a year or two on either side. The century's worst crises are connected with the years 1827, 1847, 1866, 1876, 1886, and 1892.

FLUCTUATION OF PRICES. The parallelism between the world economic forces and Spanish ones can be observed in the only long series we possess for the 19th century: that of prices. We refer to prices in Barcelona between 1812 and 1914, published, as we have said, by Sardá.

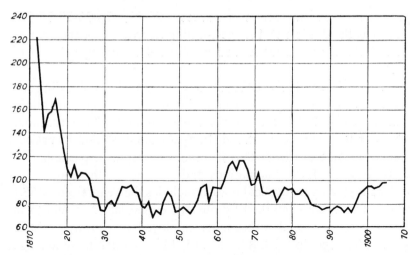

PRICE CURVE IN BARCELONA. 100 = mean 1866–1876.

If we analyze it we shall discover the following phases:

COLLAPSE OF PRICES BY STEEP STAGES FROM 1812 TO 1843, with three holding stages in 1817, 1822, and 1837. In the first cycle (1812–1821), the high prices which had prevailed during the Napoleonic period plummeted, so that from 1812 to 1814 the index falls by the fabulous figure of 80 points (from 224 to 142). The next few years, coinciding with the return of political normality, appear to be years of recovery; in 1817 the index has regained 30 points. But the cyclical phenomenon shows itself as tending downward: in 1821 the index has fallen almost to 100 (103).

The second cycle (1821–1830), though it tends downward, is less catastrophic. A recovery ceiling is maintained until 1826, with figures on the order of 113-108-107. But in 1827 the curve becomes sharply depressive, breaks the 100-point barrier, and falls to a very low series of figures: 81-80.

The third cycle (1830–1843) offers similar characteristics. However, between 1835 and 1839 there is a slight improvement (index: 96-95-97) which does not have sufficient energy to assert itself for long. The descending phase of the cycle brings us to the lowest point in the century (1843: 70).

BOTTOM OF DEPRESSION (1843–1853). While in France and England this decade is one of recovery, in Spain it is characterized, despite the peak achieved in 1846–1848 (83 < 91 > 88), by a

735

persistent drop in prices (indexes: 76-73, 74-76-79-77-73). This was the deepest and longest-lasting depression of the century, though the nadir we mentioned announced a turning point in the cycle.

BOOM PERIOD (1853–1886). The Crimean War, coinciding with the success attained by industrialization in the West and the mining discoveries in California, marks the beginning of the ascending phase of the long secular trend. In Spain the evolution of prices is somewhat different from that in other countries, in particular because it shows fewer fluctuations and is firmer at the end.

The first ten-year cyclical upturn includes the years from 1853 to 1865. This cycle is marked by obvious euphoria, often due to the heavy foreign capital investments employed in railway construction. Indexes go up—79, 89, 95, 115, 119—though there are some sharp oscillations like that of 1857 (index: 83) and 1865 (119 > 111 < 119), indicating interference of other economic processes on prices.

In the second ten-year period (1865–1876) there is an obvious downturn, though the level of prices stays high, with points reaching as much as 109. This is the moment when the curve of Spanish prices begins to differ from that of international prices, though without departing from its general characteristics.

The third cycle (1876–1886) shows this contrast clearly. While international prices are in a frankly descending curve, Spanish prices show signs of steadiness, especially during the period 1877–1883 (indexes in the 90–94 range). The restoration of the monarchy and renewal of the process of Spain's industrial equipping can explain these differences.

DESCENDING PHASE (1886–1896). The theoretical clarity of the long cycle is masked in Spain by many factors: suspension of convertibility of banknotes (1881), inflation (1891), protectionism (1891). Thus the movement of prices gives a sensation of greater strength than in other countries, in spite of the fact that the depression which ends the rising cyclical movement of the 19th century is evident.

RECOVERY OF PRICES (AFTER 1896). Internationally, recovery of the price index becomes a fact after 1896. In Spain it is strongly felt: the index rises from 75 in 1896 to 90 in 1898 and 96 in 1900.

DEPRESSION AND ECONOMIC ANACHRONISM UNDER FERDINAND VII: THE CRISIS OF 1827. The War of Independence brought the country to ruin, and it was unable to emerge from its economic torpor during the first decade of restoration of the absolute monarchy. Certainly this was a moment at which world prices were falling rapidly, and a phase of stagnation began. Contraction in the price indexes is on the order of 50%, involving the ruin of commercial and agricultural activities. Lack of capital increases lack of resistance to the downward course of general economic conditions. And so we come to 1821, in a cul-de-sac where adverse political, economic, and social factors are combined: suspension of Mexican and Peruvian silver shipments, the separatist war in America, internal political unrest, disparity of economic opinion between conservatives and liberals.

With the Hundred Thousand Sons of St. Louis, the army which restored Ferdinand VII's absolute power in 1823, there was a short period of price recovery. But the rising impulse evaporated with the extremely grave crisis of 1827, which in Spain was a two-years-delayed echo of the crisis of 1825. In that year the price index fell below the 100-point barrier and stabilized at about 80. This collapse was decisive, for it represented the political and financial failure of the absolutist governments. An attempt had been made to govern with aristocrats and great landowners, contrary to the interests of bourgeoisie and peasants. The results were obvious. The restless peasant joined the first, genuine Carlist movement, while the monarchy allied itself with the industrial bourgeoisie (Ferdinand VII's trip to Catalonia, 1827).

After that time, the governmental team formed by López Ballesteros, the Minister of Finance, received firm support. Contractors, *emigré* bankers, businessmen, etc., became associated with it. This group was the one which promulgated the mining law of 1825 and the tariff of 1826. In the years which followed they prepared the fundamental financial and commercial machinery: Commercial Code, 1829; Madrid Stock Exchange, 1831. Three men—Aguado, an *emigré,* the Catalan Gaspar Remisa, and the Castilian Javier Burgos—set important projects in motion: mines, canals, blast furnaces. Meanwhile, the first great 19th-century fortunes were being made in the Antilles, those of the Güells and the Xifrés. Altogether, underneath the depression the first signs of a brighter future could be observed.

The key problem during this period was that of agricultural expansion. Larraz believes that the first stimulus received by the 19th-century Spanish economy came from agriculture. He thinks that the arguments of Moreau de Jonnès are sound when he states that the Napoleonic invasion and the civil war had renewed the spirits of Spaniards, changed their interests, and given rise in the countryside to "the love of work." Moreau's figures are worthy of mention also: in 1833 the wheat-growing area had increased by 70% and the harvest had doubled in thirty years. In the livestock branch the increase had been on the order of 50%. Madoz accepts Moreau's figures. In 1847 Muchada also confirmed this agricultural expansion, relating it to the loss of the colonies and the need to take advantage of home soil; but he believed that this movement had begun only about 1830.

As we have said before, Salvador Millet attributes agrarian expansion to the group of legislative measures on property and free trade in agricultural products enacted between 1833 and 1836, after two decades of harsh political struggle and economic depression. We think it very possible that, after the flowering of Spanish agriculture at the end of the 18th century and beginning of the 19th, there was a period of paralysis brought on by wars (the War of Independence, civil war of 1822, French war of 1823) and the worldwide depression. Spain emerged from this period during the decade from 1830 to 1840, coinciding with the first crest of rising prices and demographic development. The only study that has been made on this matter, based on documents in the monastery of Montserrat, shows how between 1827 and 1828 the agricultural recovery of Catalonia had become a fact. And further, output showed a sharp upward trend within a few years, not only in wheat but in other cereals, in olive oil, and in wine.

BEGINNINGS OF INDUSTRIAL AND AGRICULTURAL EXPANSION: THE CRISES OF 1843 AND 1847. From 1833 to 1853, or from the death of Ferdinand VII to the Crimean War, there were two ten-year cycles which, from the point of view of price fluctuations, correspond to the lowest levels of the 19th century. However, in both cycles there is a tendency toward favorable reaction, with high points which show that the country's economic pulse was recovering.

The first cycle is the dawn of the Industrial Revolution in Spain. To be sure, the factory-building process of the previous century did exist in Catalonia. But even in that region the War of Independence and the subsequent depression had in large part paralyzed the factories' activity. Only after 1827, when the Factories Commission was revived in Barcelona, do we find indications of new momentum which, as in agriculture, would begin to develop after the depression of 1829–1831. After 1832 the cotton industry prospered, though the first Carlist war obscures this fact on the graphs. A wave of ironworking activity also appeared, rising from its own ashes in Barcelona, on the Andalusian coast, and especially in the North (Asturias and Biscay). After 1840 the population increase and expansion in cereals acted together to form a consumers' market, still somewhat weak but forming a fundamental base for industry. Cotton imports show this rhythm: 74,362 metric quintals in 1834; 184,094 in 1840; and 183,675 in 1841. The figures speak for themselves.

This cycle ended in 1843 with a spectacular crisis. It was the time when one of the lowest price levels of the whole 19th century was reached. It was an international phenomenon which showed up very clearly in Spain: cotton imports dropped 70% (from 183,000 metric quintals to 58,000 in 1843) and lead exports underwent a similar reduction (the mines at Adra exported 475,000 metric quintals in 1841 and 341,408 in 1843). The social unrest which accompanied the economic upheavals made itself felt in Spanish cities, spreading through groups of unemployed workers. The crisis of 1843 brought down the progressivist regime, just as that of 1827 had caused absolutism to disintegrate. The bourgeoisie inclined toward more conservative modes, such as those which the French minister Guizot was proclaiming about that time: "Enrichissez-vous."

In the second cycle of this phase, from 1843 to 1853, the bourgeoisie did in fact grow rich. The cyclical pattern is uncertain, for while prices sank to a deflationary low, a few preliminary movements of the incipient rising trend began to appear in commerce, industry, and finance: hence, the margin of profit available to audacious managers; the difference between wages and prices, be-

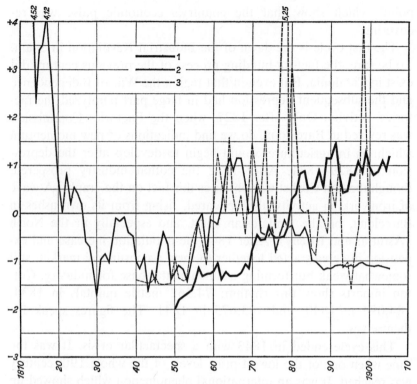

EVOLUTION OF THE BUSINESS CYCLE IN SPAIN IN THE SECOND HALF OF THE 19TH CENTURY.—*Key:* 1, average of the mean deviation in indexes of the chief industrial products and the trade balance; 2, ditto for the general price index; 3, ditto for value of issues.

tween internal and external prices, and especially between real and speculative prices. It was the golden era of the banker José Salamanca, of the first railway undertakings, of the mining rush and the establishment of modern banking firms—Bank of Isabella II, Bank of Barcelona. It was also the era of Mon's reorganization of the Treasury and establishment of a more or less efficient State administration.

These factors, added to the international feeling of euphoria, resulted in the *boom of 1846,* the first wave of optimism in the history of Spanish finance. As though it were the password of the moment, people felt carried away by a desire to invest their savings, and many brought out of hiding the coins they had hidden during the War of Independence or the Carlist war. Nearly 8,800,000 pesetas flowed toward the mints (3,600,000 in 1843 alone), most of this sum (7,600,000) in gold. In the cotton industry some enormous figures were reached, in the use of manpower (54,000 workers in 1846 compared to 34,000 in 1841) as well as in capital investment (649 million compared to 152 million, respectively). There was an air of optimism in the iron and steel industry—it was the period of development of the first blast furnaces in Biscay and Asturias. These were also the golden years of sailing ships in the American trade (especially Catalan and Basque ships). However, the place where the inflationary climate found its truest expression was in the Stock Exchange. Stocks such as those of the Bank of Isabella II rose like an arrow in 1846 (166 > 227 < 230), only to plummet to 170 in April, 1847.

This phenomenon ushered in the great Spanish crisis of 1847, a reflection of the international crisis which, unleashed the previous year, was to bring about the first violent convulsion in the structure of the capitalist world, and with it the socialist-democratic revolution of 1848. For five or six years the economy was in a state of collapse from which it seemed impossible to emerge. In Barcelona the paper money put into circulation by the Bank of Barcelona kept contracting, falling from 5 million pesetas in 1848 to 2,400,000 in 1850 and 1,200,000 in 1853. Cotton imports and export of metals, cereals, and wines fell to minimal levels. But the rising reaction was not far off.

CYCLES OF INDUSTRIAL OUTFITTING: CRISIS OF 1866. The decisive cycles in the structural change in 19th-century Spanish economy, and, consequently, in contemporary economy, are those which took place from 1854 to 1876. After the outbreak of the Crimean War, with the exception of a few unfavorable fluctuations, the international business cycle was persistently a rising one, delighting the capital market and encouraging it to make profitable investments everywhere. Spain benefited from this favorable cyclical movement, especially in the establishment of her railway network and the beginning of intensive exploitation of her mining deposits. The serious crisis of 1866 separates this movement into two very different cycles, even from a political point of view—the first rising cycle, 1854 to 1866; the second cycle, from 1866 to 1876.

The first cycle opened with the stimulus given to business by the

Crimean War. For several years the Spanish trade balance was favorable, and in any case, after that point Spanish external trade began to acquire an expanding rhythm (volume index 38.61, average of the five-year period 1850–1855; 66.54 for 1855–1860; 83.63 for 1860–1865). Imports of naval and railway material contributed to this, as well as exports of lead, copper, and iron. To the arrival of foreign capital, channeled into Spain by the Pereire-Rothschilds and other tycoons, all interested in the railway business through their connections with the two great companies (M.Z.A., 1856, and Northern, 1858), was added the development of an interregional consumers' market and the maximum point in expansion of cereal crops. Certain governmental measures, such as the practice of a correct policy of monetary deflation and ample guarantees to foreign capital (railway law of 1855) kept the pace of business brisk. In 1863 Spain was approaching a boom period. Fiduciary circulation in the form of Bank of Spain notes had increased from 39 million pesetas in 1856 to 66 million in 1859 and 71 million in 1864, and in notes on the Bank of Barcelona from 2,600,000 in 1855 to 15 million in 1861 and 21 million in 1866. The euphoria was general. In 1863 seven great credit companies were formed in Madrid alone, with a total capital of more than 170 million pesetas: the Bank of Madrid, Compañía General de Crédito Iberia, Sociedad Española General de Crédito, Compañía General de Crédito, Bank of Madrid and London, Sociedad Central Española de Crédito, Depósitos y Fomentos and Sociedad Española de Crédito Comercial. All were in imitation of the Pereires' company, whose Spanish counterpart—the Sociedad General de Crédito Mobiliario Español—had been founded in 1856.

In 1864 the symptoms of imminent crisis began to darken the horizons of the business world. The American Civil War had paralyzed cotton imports, which in 1862 reached the absolute minimum level for the period from 1850 to 1900 (index: 29.35). This process created a persistent feeling of uneasiness in Catalonian textile circles, which was very soon felt by the other industrial groups: iron and steel, railways, etc. In fact, the crisis made its appearance in international circles late in 1865 and became acute in 1866. It had immediate repercussions in Spain. A number of credit institutions failed in Madrid and Barcelona in May. In the Catalonian capital, 55 million duros were lost in a few days, a fabulous sum for the period, from whose loss Catalonia was not to recover until much later. The crisis was also felt in all its gravity in Bilbao. The Bank of Bilbao had to reduce its portfolio and restrict credits. This resulted, as in Catalonia, in unemployment and industrial and mercantile stagnation. In 1867 the directors of the large firm "La Maquinista Terrestre y Marítima" were convinced that the company could not survive for more than a year. Precious metals, which during the boom period (1864) had flowed into the public mints at the rate of 116 million pesetas, dropped to the figure of 57 million in 1866–1867.

These economic circumstances explain the success of the *pronunciamiento* against Isabella II in 1868. The country needed a new ministerial team to pull it out of its difficulties, and found one in the provisional government of 1868. Its measures—we must recall—were dramatic: monetary and tariff reforms, liberalization of the economy, generous recourse to foreign capital. The measures of a Figuerola or an Echegaray had a good deal of the Utopian and the doctrinaire about them, but basically they responded to the nation's needs. It was essential to open up Spain to outside influences, to bring fresh air into the rarefied atmosphere of protectionism and excessive speculation. For this reason, and also because of favorable international economic conditions, the cycle which centered on the Revolution of 1868 (1866–1876) was decidedly helpful for the Spanish economy. And this in spite of the colonial, military, social, and political upheavals of the period.

The figures could not be more eloquent. In cotton imports—an unequivocal sign of greater demand from the rural market—the index rose from 48.13 in 1867 to 143.71 in 1871 and 135.51 in 1875. In foreign trade, the figures show a reaction after the low point of the crisis of 1866 and quickly rise to 106 (76.19 in 1867) and 122 (1871 and 1873). Extraction of iron ore decreased (because of the Carlist war), but banking held firm and aided the liberal cause with its funds (the Bank of Bilbao loaned 16,695,583 reales without interest to the military authorities defending the city). Copper and lead prospered. However, the most noticeable feature of the period is the fact that the price curve dipped below that of the country's economic expansion. This happened in 1874 and foreshadowed the great period of social peace represented by the Restoration.

"GOLD FEVER" AND THE CRISIS OF 1886. In 1876 there was an intercyclical crisis, especially noticeable in trade, prices, and monetary circulation. It was an international crisis which indicated a cyclical decline, but one which for Spain inaugurated the most brilliant period in the 19th century: the decade from 1876 to 1886, on whose golden crest the Restoration was firmly established. We call it "gold fever," for this was the name it received in Catalonia at the time.

In fact, a second wave of economic dynamism swept over the country. A number of causes combined to produce this phenomenon: in the first place, renewal of activity in railway construction; then, the investment of foreign capital and founding of the mining companies (Orconera, 1874; Ríotinto, 1875; Somorrostro, 1876; Peñarroya, 1881). The capitalist countries of Western Europe, especially England, France, and Belgium, which were bursting with wealth, kept widening the scope of their investments. A consequence of this activity was the flood of industrial metals exported from Spain, especially iron, copper, and lead. Iron exports increased fourfold, rising from 1,578 metric tons in 1877 to 6,796 in 1887. Simultaneously there was a great wave of exports of agricultural products, with wine leading the list. These exports—keeping pace with the phylloxera crisis on the other side of the Pyrenees—increased almost six times in a ten-year period (from 143 million hectoliters to 797 million). Nor is it necessary to say that these figures and others like them were reflected in the commercial index (which rose from 115 to 168, a formidable upward surge) and in the business cycle index, which shows mean positive deviations on the order of +0.95.

The gold fever, described by Ramón de San Pedro, had its epicenter in Barcelona. Operating on a peaceful social base—prices were still very low (general index 90)—the Catalan bourgeoisie accomplished its most positive actions during this period: industries such as the woollen industry of Tarrasa and Sabadell, banks like the Hispano-Colonial (1876), companies such as the Philippines Company (1881), shipping companies like the Transatlantic Company (1881). The families of Güell, López, Arnús, Valls, Taberner, Bertrand, Battló, etc. created an important industrial and financial complex, reflected in the stock market in Barcelona. The study of this market permits us to fix exactly the development of the "gold fever." After a few moments of vacillation, the rising movement began in 1877 in railway and banking shares. State bonds followed their lead, but with a twelve-month lag. The rise was constant and rapid and reached its zenith in 1881. Many securities doubled their original value at the time; some, such as stocks of the M.Z.A., tripled. The situation remained steady until 1882. From then until 1884 there was a sharp drop, which restored the exchanges to a reasonable level (30 to 40 points profit, in general), and slowly sank into the trough of the intercyclical crisis culminating in 1886.

END OF THE RESTORATION: INFLATIONARY COLLAPSE. After the euphoria represented by the heavy investment of foreign capital between 1875 and 1881, the Spanish economy adjusted itself to the tone of the international economic cycle, which had meanwhile passed through the crisis of the so-called Great Depression of the 1880's and had now somewhat recovered. This implied an inevitable readjustment in the Spanish economy's progress, and it showed signs of profound uneasiness. Alterations in trade and production were very sharp, especially after the crisis of 1892 and the beginning of the last colonial war in Cuba.

For ten years the Restoration had lived an economic miracle: cyclical expansion in the midst of a general depression. When the depression was over, Spain's prosperity collapsed. This happened in 1892. In that year a notable crisis occurred, brought about by the collapse of the foreign market in wine and iron. The change was tremendously rapid, and this explains the drop in cotton import indexes (1889, 152; 1892, 129; 1897, 45) and in foreign trade (1889, 176; 1891, 195; 1893, 150). On the other hand, the protectionism established in 1891, which included the Antilles and the Philippines, permitted recovery of the cotton industry, development of the Basque iron and steel industry, the rise in agricultural prices (index rose from 78 in 1891 to 82 in 1897), and the slow introduction into the gamut of export products of oranges (after 1890) and canned fruits and vegetables (after 1887), in addition to the traditional dried fruits and olive oil.

The Spanish economy's worst failing at this moment of transition, when she was maneuvering to protect herself against an overwhelming invasion of foreign products, was the weakness of her currency. Depreciation of the peseta was a chronic phenomenon after 1881, and became more acute in 1892, when the pound sterling was worth 29.62 pesetas. It reached a tragic point with the colonial disaster of 1898 (average value of the pound sterling, 39.24 pesetas).

Reacting to the fluctuations of the economy and the currency situation, the Stock Exchange underwent a profound crisis in 1898. The downward movement of the curves was a reflection of the pessimism of the bourgeoisie, whose hopes of ending the century in peace, order, and prosperity had been frustrated. Hence the bourgeois element's affiliation with the political and social theories of regeneration which a few far-seeing intelligences had been preaching, and to which the unimaginative policies of the Restoration had paid no heed.

But the 19th century did not end with a lifeless Spain, either in the political or the economic field. On the contrary, a powerful, active, and dynamic generation arose in the economic sphere, which was responsible in the decade from 1900 to 1910 for three of the great 20th-century economic transformations: agrarian progress, through the use of chemical fertilizers and the spread of irrigation; the revolution in manufacturing industries by use of hydroelectrical power; and appearance of the modern banking system.

Bibliography

What follows is the bibliographical material which has served as a basis for this volume, and which we hope will be useful for further study. At the same time, we offer supplementary bibliographical lists representing a first attempt at a systematic bibliography of the economic history of Spain.

In general, works mentioned have to do with the chapter under which they appear. Books are listed with the usual bibliographical description. As for the articles, an abbreviated description of the review in which they are found is given. The chief abbreviations are as follows:

AAEPC: *Anales de la Asociación Española para el Progreso de las Ciencias.* Madrid.

AEArq: *Archivo español de Arqueología.* Madrid.

AdE: *Anales de Economía.* Madrid.

AHDEsp: *Anuario de Historia del Derecho Español.* Madrid.

AIA: *Archivo Ibero-Americano.* Madrid.

AIECat: *Anuari de l'Institut d'Estudis Catalans.* Barcelona.

AHisp: *Archivo Hispalense.* Seville.

AM: *Annales du Midi.* Toulouse.

Ant: *L'Anthropologie.* Paris.

ASI: *Archivio Storico Italiano.* Florence.

Amp: *Ampurias.* Barcelona.

BAH: *Boletín de la Real Academia de la Historia.* Madrid.

BAsCaAEP: *Butlletí de l'Associació Catalana d'Arqueologia, Etnologia i Prehistòria.* Barcelona.

BHi: *Bulletin Hispanique.* Bordeaux.

BArTar: *Butlletí Arqueològic de Tarragona.*

BIIH: *Boletín del Instituto de Investigaciones Históricas.* Buenos Aires.

BRACord: *Boletín de la Real Academia de Córdoba.*

BRAGallega: *Boletín de la Real Academia Gallega.* La Coruña.

BSAL: *Butlletí de la Societat Arqueològica Lulliana.* Palma.

BSCastEx: *Boletín de la Sociedad castellana de excursiones.* Valladolid.

BSEExc: *Boletín de la Sociedad española de excursiones.* Madrid.

BSCC: *Boletín de la Sociedad castellonense de cultura.* Castellón.

BUSC: *Boletín de la Universidad de Santiago de Compostela.*

CHEsp: *Cuadernos de Historia de España.* Buenos Aires.

CuE: *Cultura española.* Zaragoza.

DZGW: *Deutsche Zeitschrift für Geschichtswissenschaft.* Freiburg i. B.

EEMCA: *Estudios de Edad Media de la Corona de Aragón.* Zaragoza.

EG: *Estudios Geográficos.* Madrid.

EHM: *Estudios de Historia Moderna.* Barcelona.

EM: *La España Moderna.* Madrid.

EUC: *Estudis Universitaris Catalans.* Barcelona.

His: *Hispania.* Madrid.

IyP: *Investigación y Progreso.* Madrid.

NT: *Nuestro Tiempo.* Madrid.

PdV: *Príncipe de Viana.* Pamplona.

QE: *Quaderns d'Estudi.* Barcelona.

RABM: *Revista de Archivos, Bibliotecas y Museos.* Madrid.

RArch: *Revue Archéologique.* Paris.

RCC: *Revue des Cours et Conférences.* Paris.

RCa: *Revista Castellana.* Valladolid.

RCHLP: *Revista Crítica de His-* toria y Literatura española, portuguesa e hispanoamericana. Madrid.

RCo: *Revista Contemporánea.* Madrid.

REP: *Revista de Estudios Políticos.* Madrid.

REsp: *Revista de Filología Española.* Madrid.

RH: *Revue Historique.* Paris.

RHi: *Revue Hispanique.* Paris.

RHL: *Revista de Historia.* La Laguna.

RHV: *Revista Histórica.* Valladolid.

RIS: *Revista Internacional de Sociología.* Madrid.

RJC: *Revista Jurídica de Catalunya.* Barcelona.

RMen: *Revista de Menorca.* Mahón.

RNord: *Revue du Nord.* Lille-Paris.

ROcc: *Revista de Occidente.* Madrid.

RPHLH: *Revue de Philologie, de Littérature et d'Histoire anciennes.* Paris.

RSI: *Revista Storica Italiana.* Naples.

RUMadr: *Revista de la Universidad de Madrid.*

RUO: *Revista de la Universidad de Oviedo.*

Sef: *Sefarad.* Madrid.

SErud: *Semanario Erudito.* Madrid.

Univ: *Universidad.* Zaragoza.

The places of publication are also abbreviated in the more obvious cases: M (Madrid), B (Barcelona), P (Paris).

748

Chapter 1: General History of Spain

BIBLIOGRAPHIES

Bibliografía. "Nueva Revista de la Literatura Hispánica." M., 1950–1955. 4 vols.

Bibliografía Hispánica. "Revista Hispánica Moderna." New York.

Bibliografía Histórica de España e Hispanoamérica (Indice Histórico Español). B., 1953–1954, 1955–1956, 1957.

Boissonade, P. *Les études relatives à l'histoire économique de l'Espagne et ses résultats.* "Revue de Synthèse Historique," 1910–1912.

Handbook of Latin American Studies. Washington, 1939–1958. 18 vols.

Inter-American Review of Bibliography. Revista Interamericana de Bibliografía. Washington, D.C., Pan American Union.

Humphreys, R. A. *Latin American History.* Oxford University Press, 1958.

Sánchez Alonso, Benito. *Fuentes de la Historia de España e Hispano-América.* M., 1952. 3 vols.

Vives, José. *Bibliografía hispánica de Ciencias histórico-eclesiásticas.* "Analecta Sacra Tarraconnensia" and in "Hispania Sacra."

GENERAL WORKS

Aguado Bleye, Pedro. *Manual de Historia de España.* M., 1947–1956. 6th edn. 3 vols.

Ballesteros Beretta, Antonio. *Historia de España y su influencia en la Historia Universal.* B., 1918–1941. 10 vols. 2nd edn. B., 1943–1956.

———. *Historia de América y de los pueblos americanos.* B., 1936. 11 vols.

Castro, Américo. *España en su historia. Cristianos, moros y judíos.* Buenos Aires, 1948. 2nd edn.: *La realidad histórica de España.* Mexico, 1954.

Diccionario de Historia de España. M., 1952. 2 vols.

García de Valdeavellano, Luis. *Historia de España.* M., 1955. 2nd edn. 2 vols. (only up to the 12th century).

García Villada, Zacarías. *Historia eclesiástica de España.* M., 1929–1936. 5 vols. (up to the conquest of Toledo).

Menéndez Pidal, Ramón. General editor. *Historia de España.* M., 1935. 6 vols. (Volumes are referred to separately under the different chapter headings.)

Sánchez Albornoz, Claudio. *España. Un enigma histórico.* Buenos Aires, 1956. 2 vols.

BIBLIOGRAPHY

Soldevila, Fernando. *Historia de España*. B., 1947–1959. 8 vols.

Vicens Vives, Jaime. *Aproximación a la historia de España*. B., 1952.

Vilar, Pierre. *Histoire de l'Espagne*. P., 1947.

ECONOMIC HISTORY OF SPAIN

GENERAL SOURCES

Assó, I. de. *Historia de la economía política de Aragón*. Zaragoza, 1789 (modern edition with preface and indexes by J. M. Torres Casas. Zaragoza, 1947).

Canga-Argüelles, J. *Diccionario de Hacienda con aplicación a España*. 2nd edn. 2 vols. M., 1833–1834.

Colmeiro, M. *Biblioteca de los Economistas españoles de los siglos XVI, XVII y XVIII*. "Memorias de la Real Academia de Ciencias Morales y Políticas." T. I. Madrid, 1879 (privately printed 2nd edn. by "Biblioteca Carandell," B., 1947).

Gallardo, F. *Origen, progreso y estado de las rentas de la Corona de España, su gobierno y administración*. M., 1805. 7 vols.

Iparraguirre, Demetrio, S. J. *Las fuentes del pensamiento económico en España en los siglos XIII al XVI*. "Estudios de Deusto," II (1954).

Laporta, F. F. *Historia de la Agricultura española. Su origen, progreso y estado actual*. M., 1789. 2 vols.

Larruga, E. de. *Memorias políticas y económicas sobre los frutos, comercio, fábricas y minas de España*. M., 1787–1800. 45 vols.

Sempere y Guarinos, J. *Historia del luxo y de las leyes suntuarias en España*. M., 1788. 2 vols.

———. *Historia de las rentas de la Iglesia en España*. M., 1793.

———. *Biblioteca española económico-política*. M., 1801.

———. *Historia de los vínculos y mayorazgos*. 2nd edn., 1847.

GENERAL WORKS

Barceló, José Luis. *Historia económica de España*. (Very incomplete.)

Beneyto, Juan. *Historia Social de España e Hispanoamérica*. M., 1961.

Carrera Pujal, J. *Historia de la Economía española*. B., 1943–1947. 5 vols.

Colmeiro, M. *Historia de la economía política en España*. M., 1863. 2 vols.

Goury de Rosland, J. *Essai sur l'histoire économique de l'Espagne*. P., 1888.

Vicens Vives, Jaime. General editor. *Historia social y económica de España y América*. B., 1957–1959. 5 vols.

BIBLIOGRAPHY

POPULATION AND URBAN STUDIES

Fuster, Miguel. *La duración de la vida en la población española desde la prehistoria a nuestros días.* "Trabajos del Instituto Bernardino de Sahagún de Antropología y Etnografía," no. 3 (1954).

Lacarra, José M.ª. *Orientation des études d'histoire urbaine en Espagne entre 1940 et 1957.*

Mols, Roger, S. J. *Introduction à la démographie historique des villes d'Europe du XIVe au XVIIIe siècle.* Louvain, 1954–1956. 3 vols.

Russell, J. C. *Late Ancient and Medieval Population.* Philadelphia, 1958.

Torres Balbás, L.; L. Cervera; F. Chueca; P. Bidagor. *Resumen histórico del urbanismo en España.* M., 1954.

SOCIETY AND PROPERTY

Cárdenas, Francisco de. *Ensayo sobre la historia de la propiedad territorial en España.* M., 1873.

Caro Baroja, Julio. *Razas, pueblos y linajes.* M., 1957 (very interesting collection of articles for an overall view of Spanish cultural anthropology).

López Rodó, Laureano. *El Patrimonio Nacional.* M., 1955.

Mayer, Ernesto. *Historia de las instituciones sociales y políticas de España y Portugal desde los siglos V al XIV.* M., 1925–1926. 2 vols.

Rumeu de Armas, Antonio. *Historia de la previsión social en España. Gremios y Cofradías.* M., 1873.

AGRICULTURE

Camacho, A. M. *Historia jurídica del cultivo y de la ganadería en España.* M., 1912.

Caro Baroja, J. *La vida agraria tradicional reflejada en el arte español.* "Estudios de Historia Social," I (1949).

Costa, Joaquín. *Colectivismo agrario en España.* M., 1894.

Costa Martínez, Tomás. *Apuntes para la historia jurídica del cultivo de la ganadería en España.* M., 1918.

PRODUCTION AND TRANSPORT

Alzola, Pablo de. *Las obras públicas en España.* M., 1899.

Fernández Duro, C. *Armada española desde la unión de los reinos de Castilla y de Aragón.* M., 1895–1903. 9 vols.

BIBLIOGRAPHY

Menéndez Pidal, Gonzalo. *Los caminos en la historia de España.* M., 1951.

Salas, Francisco Xavier de. *Marina española de la Edad Media.* M., 1894. 2nd edn.: M., 1925–1927. 2 vols.

STATE AND LAW

Beneyto, Juan. *Historia de la administración española e hispanoamericana.* M., 1958.

García Gallo, A. *Curso de historia del Derecho español.* M., 1946–1950.

Torres López, M. *Lecciones de Historia del Derecho Español.* (2 vols. published so far.) 2nd edn.: Salamanca, 1935–1936.

MONEY AND BANKING

Mateu Llopis, Felipe. *La moneda española.* (Short monetary history of Spain.) B., 1946.

Vives, A. *La moneda hispánica.* M., 1926.

REGIONAL ECONOMIC HISTORY

Aguilera, J. *Historia de la industria catalana.* B., 1921.

Bofarull, F. de. *Antigua marina catalana.* B., 1901. (Memorias Ac. de B. L.)

Botet i Sisó, J. *Les monedes catalanes.* B., 1908.

Capmany, Antonio de. *Memorias históricas sobre la marina, comercio y artes de la antigua ciudad de Barcelona.* M., 1779–1792. 4 vols.

Carrera Pujal, J. *La Lonja del Mar y los Cuerpos de Comercio de Barcelona.* B., 1953.

Ciriquiain-Gaiztarro, M. *Los puertos marítimos vascongados.* San Sebastián, 1951.

Fernández Duro, C. *La marina de Castilla.* M., 1894.

Guiard, T. *La industria naval vizcaína.* Bilbao, 1917.

Romeva, Pau. *Historia de la industria catalana.* B., 1952. 2 vols.

Ventalló, L. *Historia de la industria lanera catalana.* Tarrasa, 1904.

———. *Cantabria y País vasco: Aportación al estudio de la historia económica de la Montaña.* Santander, 1957.

NOTE: to avoid unnecessary repetition in citing works, we have adopted as a general rule the practice of mentioning them only in the place where they belong, chronologically or in relation to their subject; and those of a general nature under the chapter where they should be consulted initially. We remind the reader that every bibliography is an organic whole, and must be known in its totality from the beginning.

CHAPTER 2: INFRASTRUCTURE OF SPANISH ECONOMIC HISTORY

FUNDAMENTAL WORKS

Dantín Cereceda, Juan. *Resumen fisiográfico de la Península Ibérica.* M., 1912.

Hernández Pacheco, E. *Síntesis fisiográfica y geológica de España.* M., 1932.

Huguet del Villar, E. *El valor geográfico de España.* M., 1921.

Perpiñá Grau, R. *De estructura económica y economía hispana.* M., 1952.

Terán, Manuel de. General editor. *Geografía de España y Portugal.* (2 vols. published so far.) B., 1952–1954.

SUPPLEMENTARY BIBLIOGRAPHY

Brunhes, Jean. *L'irrigation dans la Péninsule ibérique et dans l'Afrique du Nord.* P., 1902.

Dantín Cereceda, Juan, and Antonio Revenga Carbonell. *Las líneas y zonas isóxeras de España, según los índices termopluviométricos.* EG. (1941).

Hernández Pacheco, Eduardo. *El solar de la Historia hispana.* M., 1952.

Iñíguez, Francisco. *Clima de la Península Ibérica.* "Reseña Geográfica y Estadística de España." I.

Lautensach, H. *Die Niederschlagshöhen auf der iberischen Halbinsel.* "Pettermans Geograph. Mitteil." (Gotha) XCV. (1951).

Mallada, Lucas. *Los males de la patria y la futura revolución española.* M., 1890.

Martín Echevarría, L. *Geografía de España.* B., 1928. 3 vols.

Masachs Alavedra, Valentín. *El régimen de los ríos peninsulares.* B., 1948.

Puig, Ignacio. *Épocas de sequía y de lluvia en España.* "Ibérica." No. 167–169 (1949).

González Quijano, Pedro Manuel. *Mapa pluviométrico de España.* M., 1946.

Vicens Vives, J. *España. Geopolítica del Estado y del Imperio.* B., 1940.

BIBLIOGRAPHY

Chapter 3: Man in Spanish Economic Life

FUNDAMENTAL WORKS

Almagro, Martín. *Origen y formación del pueblo hispano*. B., 1958.
Bosch Gimpera, Pedro. *La formación de los pueblos de España*. Mexico, 1945.
Caro Baroja, Julio. *Los pueblos de España*. B., 1946.
López Ibor, Juan José. *El español y su complejo de inferioridad*. M., 1951.
Menéndez Pidal, R. *Los españoles en la Historia y en la Literatura*. Buenos Aires, 1951.
Pi Sunyer, C. *L'aptitud econòmica de Catalunya*. B., 1927. 2 vols.

SUPPLEMENTARY BIBLIOGRAPHY

Altamira, Rafael. *Psicología del pueblo español*. B., 1917.
"Azorín." *El alma castellana* (1600–1800). M., 1900.
Corominas, P. *El sentimiento de la riqueza en Castilla*. M., 1917.
Madariaga, Salvador de. *Ingleses, franceses, españoles. Ensayo de psicología colectiva comparada*. M., 1934.
Ortega y Gasset, J. *La España invertebrada*. 4th edn. M., 1934.
Vicens Vives, Jaime. *Noticia de Cataluña*. B., 1954.
―――. *Sobre la decadencia económica de España*. "De Economía" (número monográfico II), VI (1952).
―――. *Más en torno a la no decadencia económica de España*. "De Economía" (número monográfico III), VII (1954).

Chapter 4: Economy of Prehistoric Spain

FUNDAMENTAL WORKS

Bosch Gimpera, Pedro. *Etnología de la Península Ibérica*. B., 1932.
Camón Aznar, José. *Las artes y los pueblos de la España primitiva*. M., 1954.
Caro Baroja, Julio. *España primitiva y romana*. B., 1957.
Menéndez Pidal, R. General editor. "Historia de España." Vol. 1: *España prehistórica*. M., 1947. (M. Almagro, A. del Castillo, and J. Maluguer de Motes collaborated on this volume, writing respectively on the Paleolithic, Neo-Neolithic, and Bronze Age.)
Obermaier, H.; A. Garcia Bellido; and L. Pericot. *El hombre prehistórico y los orígenes de la humanidad*. 6th edn. M., 1957.
Pericot, Luis. *La España primitiva*. B., 1950.

BIBLIOGRAPHY

————. *Historia de España. Época primitiva y romana.* Ed. Gallach. Vol. I. 2nd edn. B., 1958.

Tarradell, Miquel. *Les arrels de Catalunya.* B., 1963.

SUPPLEMENTARY BIBLIOGRAPHY

Aoberg, N. *La civilisation enéolithique dans la Peninsule Ibérique.* Uppsala, 1920.

Bosch Gimpera, Pedro, and Luis Pericot. *Les civilisations de la Péninsule Ibérique pendant l'Enéolitique.* Ant. (1925).

————. *Las relaciones de los pueblos atlánticos en el Neolítico y en la Edad del Bronce.* I y P (1927).

————. *I rapporti fra le civiltà mediterranee nella fine dell'Età del Bronzo.* Reggio, 1929.

Castillo, Alberto del. *La cultura del vaso campaniforme.* B., 1928.

Childe, V. Gordon. *Prehistoric Migrations in Europe.* Oslo, 1950.

Clark, J. G. D. *L'Europe préhistorique. Les fondements de son économie.* P., 1955.

Fletcher Valls, Domingo. *Le Edad del Hierro en el Levante Español.* M., 1954.

Hawkes. *Las relaciones atlánticas al final de la Edad del Bronce.* Amp (1952).

Leisner, G. and V. *Die Megalithgräber der iberischen Halbinsel.* Berlin, 1943 and 1956.

López Cuevillas, Florentín. *La Edad del Hierro en la cuenca del Ebro y en la meseta central.* M., 1954.

Maluquer de Maluquer, J. *Las culturas hallstáticas en Cataluña.* Amp, VII–VII (1946–1947).

Martínez Santa Olalla, J. *Esquema paletnólogico de la Península Ibérica.* M., 1946.

Serra Ràfols, J. de C. *Els començos de la mineria i metal·lúrgica del coure a la Península Ibèrica.* BAsCatAEP, B (1942).

————. *El poblament prehistòric de Catalunya.* B., 1930.

Siret, E. and L. *Las primeras edades del metal en el Sudeste de España.* B., 1890.

Villaamil, J. *Productos de la metalurgia gallega en tiempos remotos,* Orense, 1907.

BIBLIOGRAPHY

Chapter 5: Economy of the Hispanic Colonizations

FUNDAMENTAL WORKS

Bosch Gimpera, Pedro. *Los iberos.* CHEsp. IX (1948).

Caro Baroja, Julio. *Regímenes sociales y económicos de la España pre-rromana.* RSI, I (1943).

Carpenter. *The Greeks in Spain.* London, 1925.

García Bellido, Antonio. *La Península Ibérica en los comienzos de su historia.* M., 1953.

Menéndez Pidal, R. General editor. "Historia de España." Tomo I, Vols. 2 and 3: *España Protohistórica y España Prerromana.* M., 1952, 1954. (The editors of these volumes are: García Bellido, A; Almagro, M.; Maluquer de Motes, J.; Taracena, Blas; and Caro Baroja, J. García Bellido's article on Tartessos and Maluquer's on Celts and Iberians are of special interest.)

Schulten, Adolf. *Tartessos.* Spanish edn. M., 1924.

Villard, François. *La céramique grecque de Marseille (VIe–IVe siècle) Essai d'histoire économique.* P., 1960.

SUPPLEMENTARY BIBLIOGRAPHY

Bonsor, J. *Les colonies agricoles pré-romaines de la vallée du Betis.* RArch, September 1899.

Bosch Gimpera, Pedro. *Problemas de la colonización fenicia de España y del Mediterráneo occidental.* ROcc., June, 1928.

———. *Problemas de la colonización griega en España.* ROcc., June 1929.

———. *Los celtas y la civilización céltica en la Península Ibérica.* BSEEx (1921).

Fletcher Valls, Domingo. *Problemas de la cultura ibérica.* "Servicio de Investigación Prehistórica." Valencia, 1960.

García Bellido, Antonio. *Fenicios y cartagineses en Occidente.* M., 1942.

———. *Las navegaciones ibéricas en la Antigüedad, según los textos clásicos y la arqueología.* EG, no. 16.

———. *Hispania Greca.* B., 1947. 3 vols.

Henzey, L. *Sur les relations de l'industrie phénicienne et carthaginoise avec la Péninsule ibérique.* (Comptes rendus des séances de l'Acad. des Inscriptions et Belles Lettres, P., 1900.)

Jáuregui, J. J. *La carrera del estaño en la Ora Maritima de Avieno.* M., 1953.

Ramos Loscertales, J. M. *Hospicio y clientela en la España céltica.* "Emérita" X (1942).

————. La "devotio ibérica." *Los soldurios* AHDEsp., I (1924).

Rodríguez Adrados, F. *La "fides" ibérica.* "Emérita," 14 (1946).

CHAPTER 6: THE ECONOMY OF ROMAN SPAIN (I)

FUNDAMENTAL BIBLIOGRAPHY

Beloch, J. *Die Bevölkerung der griechisch-römischen Welt.* Leipzig, 1896.

Bouchier, E. S. *Spain under the Roman Empire.* Oxford, 1914.

Rostovzeff, M. *The Social and Economic History of the Roman Empire.* Oxford, 1926.

Sánchez Albornoz, Claudio. *Proceso de romanización de España desde los Escipiones hasta Augusto.* "Anales de Historia Antigua y Media." Buenos Aires, 1949.

Serra Ràfols, J de C. *La Hispànica romana.* M., 1954.

Torres, Manuel de. *La península hispánica, provincia romana.* (Economic, social, and politico-administrative institutions.) In "Historia de España" edited by R. Menéndez Pidal, vol. II: *La España Romana.* M., 1935.

SUPPLEMENTARY BIBLIOGRAPHY

Albertini, E. *Les divisions administratives de l'Espagne romaine.* P., 1923.

Albertini, H. *Les étrangers résidants en Espagne à l'époque romaine.* P., 1913.

Bullón, E. *La política social de Trajano.* M., 1935.

Friedländer, L. *La sociedad romana. Historia de las costumbres en Roma desde Augusto hasta los Antoninos* (Spanish trans.). Mexico, 1947.

McElderby, Knox. "Vespasian's Reconstruction of Spain," *Journal of Roman Studies,* VIII (1919).

Mispoulet, J. B. *Transformations de l'Espagne pendant les trois premiers siècles de l'empire romain.* RPLH, October, 1910.

Rickard, T. A. "The Mining of the Romans in Spain." *Journal of Roman Studies,* XVIII (1928).

Rostovtzeff, M. *Studien zur Geschichte des römischen Kolonats.* "Archiv für Papyrusforschung" (Berlin-Leipzig), I (1910).

Schulten, Adolf. *Die römischen Grundherrschaften.* 1896.

Serra Ràfols, J. *La vida en España en la época romana.* B., 1944.

Sutherland, C. H. V. *The Romans in Spain. 217 B.C.–A.D. 117.* London, 1939.

Thouvenot, R. *Essai sur la province romaine de Bétique.* P., 1940.

Vendeure, J. *Contribution à l'étude du régime minier romain. Étude sur la table d'Aljustrel découverte en 1906.* Dijon, 1910.

Waltzing, J. P. *Étude historique sur les corporations professionelles chez les romains depuis les origines jusqu'à la chute de l'Empire d'Occident.* Brussels, 1895–1902. 4 vols.

CHAPTER 7: THE ECONOMY OF ROMAN SPAIN (II)

FUNDAMENTAL WORKS

Bury, J. B. *History of the Later Roman Empire (395–565).* London, 1923. 2nd edn. 2 vols.

Lot, F. *La fin du monde antique et le début du Moyen Âge.* P., 1927.

Seek, Otto. *Geschichte des Untergangs der antiken Welt.* Berlin, 1895–1921. 6 vols.

West, L. C. *Imperial Roman Spain: The Objects of Trade.* Oxford, 1929.

SUPPLEMENTARY WORKS

Bonsor, Jorge. *Los pueblos antiguos del Guadalquivir y las alfarerías romanas.* RABM (1901), 837.

Charlesworth, M. P. *Le vie commerciali dell'Impero Romano.* Milan, 1940.

Dressel, Enrique. *Ricerche sul monte Testaccio.* Anales del Instituto Arqueológico germánico. Rome, L (1878).

Molina, Victorio. *El puerto gaditano de la época romana.* Cádiz, 1904.

Thevenot, E. *Una familia de negociantes en aceite establecida en la Baetica en el siglo II: los Aelii Optati.* AEArq, XXV (1952).

CHAPTER 8: THE ECONOMY OF VISIGOTH HISPANIA

FUNDAMENTAL WORKS

Abadal y Vinyals, Ramón de. *Del reino de Tolosa al reino de Toledo.* Discurso de recepción en la Real Academia de la Historia. M., 1960.

Dopsch, A. *Fundamentos económicos y sociales de la cultura europea. De César a Carlomagno.* Buenos Aires, 1951. (Translation of *Die wirtschaftliche und soziale Grundlagen der europäischen Kulturentwicklung aus der Zeit von Caesar bis auf Karl der Grossen.* Vienna, 1923–1924.)

Pérez Pujol, E. *Historia de las instituciones sociales de la España goda.* (Valencia, 1896. 4 vols.

Torres, Manuel. *Las invasiones y los reinos germánicos de España (años 409–711),* in "Historia de España," edited by R. Menéndez Pidal, Vol. III, M., 1940. (The article on economic and social institutions was written in collaboration with Ramón Prieto Bances.)

SUPPLEMENTARY BIBLIOGRAPHY

Courtois, Christian. *Les vandales et l'Afrique.* P., 1955.

Dahn, F. *Über Handel und Handelsrecht der westgothen "Bausteine,"* II (1880).

García Gallo, A. *Notas sobre el reparto de tierras entre romanos y visigodos.* His, I (1941), 40.

Goubert, P. *Administration de l'Espagne byzantine.* "Revue des Études Byzantines," 4 (1946).

Havet, Julien. *Du partage des terres entre les romains et les barbares chez les burgondes et les wisigoths.* RH, VI (1878), 87.

Heiss, A. *Description générale des monnaies des rois wisigoths.* P., 1872.

Katz, S. *The Jews in the Visigothic and Frankish Kingdoms of Spain and Gaul.* Cambridge (Mass.), 1937.

Martínez Díez, Gonzalo, S.J. *El patrimonio eclesiástico en la España visigoda, Estudio histórico-jurídico.* Comillas, 1959.

Miles, George. *The Coinage of the Visigoths of Spain. Leovigild to Achilla II.* New York, 1952.

Reinhardt, Wilhelm. *El Reino hispánico de los suevos y sus monedas.* AEArq. No. 40 (1942).

———. *Sobre el establecimiento de los visigodos en la Península.* AEArq, XVIII (1945).

———. *Historia General del reino hispánico de los suevos.* M., 1952.

Sánchez Albornoz, Claudio. *Ruina y extinción del municipio romano en España e instituciones que le reemplazan.* Buenos Aires, 1943.

CHAPTER 9: FEUDAL AND SEIGNORIAL ECONOMY: GENERAL INDICATIONS

FUNDAMENTAL WORKS

Bloch, M. *La société féodale.* P., 1939–1940. 2 vols.

Calmette, Joseph, and Charles Higounet. *Le monde féodal.* 3rd edn. P., 1952.

Ganshof, F. L. *Qu'est-ce que la féodalité?* 3rd edn. Brussels, 1957. (Spanish trans. *El feudalismo,* with an important appendix *Las instituciones feudales en España,* by L. G. de Valdeavellano, B., 1963.)

Pirenne, Henri. *Historia económica y social de la Edad Media.* (Spanish trans.) Mexico, 1947.

Sánchez Albornoz, Claudio. *En torno a los orígenes del feudalismo.* Mendoza, 1942. 3 vols.

SUPPLEMENTARY BIBLIOGRAPHY

Calmette, J. *El feudalisme i els origens de la nació catalana.* QE, XIII (1921).

Dopsch, A. *Die Wirtschaftsentwicklung der Karolingerzeit.* 2nd edn. Weimar, 1921–1922. 2 vols.

Dubler, E. *Über das Wirtschaftsleben der iberischen Halbinsel vom XI zum XIII Jahrhundert.* Geneva-Zurich, 1943.

Font Rius, José M.ª. *Instituciones medievales españolas.*

García Gallo, A. *Las instituciones sociales en España, en la Alta Edad Media* (*siglos VIII–XII*). REP, Suplemento de Política Social (1945) nos. 1 and 2.

Herculano, A. *Da existência ou não-existência do feudalismo nos reinos de Leão, Castella e Portugal.* In "Opúsculos" 4th edn. Lisbon, vol. V. undated.

Merea, P. *Sobre a palavra "atondo." Contribução para a história das instituções feudais na Espanha.* AHEDsp (1924).

Sánchez Albornoz, Claudio. *Un documento de interés para la historia del vasallaje español.* "Logos" (Buenos Aires), 1942.

———. *El "stipendium" visigodo y los orígenes del beneficio prefeudal.* Buenos Aires, 1947.

———. *España y el feudalismo carolingio.* "Settimane di Studi del Centro Italiano di Studi sull'Alto Medievo," Spoleto, 1954.

CHAPTER 10: THE ECONOMY OF AL-ANDALUS

FUNDAMENTAL WORKS

Lévi-Provençal, É. *Histoire de l'Espagne musulmane.* 2nd edn. Paris-Leyden, 1950.

———. *L'Espagne musulmane au Xe siècle. Institutions et vie sociale.* P., 1932. (Spanish trans. in "Historia de España," edited by R. Menéndez Pidal, Vols. IV and V. M., 1950, 1957.)

SUPPLEMENTARY BIBLIOGRAPHY

Bellver, M., and V. del Cacho. *Influencia que ejerció la dominación de los árabes en la agricultura, industria y comercio de la provincia de Castellón.* Valencia, 1890.

Cagicas, Isidoro de las. *Los mozárabes.* M., 1947.

Carande, Ramón. *La huella económica de las capitales hispanomusulmanas.* "Moneda y Crédito" (1949), no. 29, 3.

Codera, F. *Tratado de numismática arábigo–española.* M., 1879.

García Maceira, A. *Apuntes y noticias sobre la agricultura de los árabes españoles.* Zamora, 1876.

Lévi-Provençal, É. *La vie économique de l'Espagne musulmane au Xe siècle.* RH (1931).

Madrazo, P. de, and J. A. de los Ricos. *Importancia histórica de las atarazanas árabes de Almería.* M., 1868.

Mas Latrie, Comte de. *Rélations et commerce de l'Afrique Septentrionale au Mogreb avec les nations chrétiennes du Moyen Âge,* 1886.

Sánchez Albornoz, Claudio. *La España musulmana según los autores islamitas y cristianos medievales,* I. Buenos Aires, 1946.

Simonet, F. J. *Historia de los mozárabes de España.* M., 1897–1903.

Torres Balbás, Leopoldo. *Estructura de las ciudades hispanomusulmanas: la medina, los arrabales y los barrios.* "Al-Ándalus" (1953), 149.

———. *Extensión y demografía de las ciudades hispanomusulmanas.* "Studia Islamica," III (1955).

———. *Plazas, zocos y tiendas en las ciudades hispano-musulmanas.* "Al Andalus" (1947).

CHAPTER 11: ECONOMY OF THE WESTERN HISPANIC KINGDOMS FROM THE 8TH TO THE 12TH CENTURIES

FUNDAMENTAL WORKS

García de Valdeavellano, Luis. *En Castilla durante la Edad Media.* AHDEsp (1931).

———. *Economía natural y monetaria en León y Castilla durante los siglos IX, X y XI.* "Moneda y Crédito" (1944), 28.

———. *Sobre los burgos y los burgueses de la España medieval (Notas para la historia de la burguesía).* M., 1960.

———. *La moneda y la economía de cambio en la Península Ibérica desde el siglo VI hasta mediados del siglo XI,* in "Settimane di Studio del Centro italiano di Studi sull'Alto Medioevo, VIII," Spoleto, 1961.

García Rives, A. *Clases sociales en León y Castilla, siglos X–XIII.* RABM (1920 y 1921).

Sánchez Albornoz, Claudio. *Estampas de la vida en Léon durante el siglo X.* 4th edn. Buenos Aires, 1947.

SUPPLEMENTARY BIBLIOGRAPHY

Amador de los Ríos, R. *Los fueros de los pobladores cristianos en la ciudad de Toledo.* EM, August, 1904.

Concha, I. de la. *La pressura.* AHDEsp, XV (1943).

Díaz Jiménez, J. E. *Inmigración mozárabe en el reino de León.* BAH, XVIII.

Fernández y González, Francisco. *Estado social y político de los mudéjares de Castilla.* M., 1866.

Gugliemi, Nilda. *El "Dominus Villae" en Castilla y León.* CHEsp (1953), 55

Hinojosa, Eduardo de. *Origen del régimen municipal en León y Castilla.* "Estudios sobre la historia del Derecho español." M., 1903.

Lacarra, Jose M.ª. *La repoblación del camino de Santiago.* In "La Reconquista española y la repoblación del país." Zaragoza, 1951.

Laguzzi, M. del P. *El precio de la vida en Portugal durante los siglos X y XI.* CHEsp (1946), 140.

López Ferreiro, A. *Fueros municipales de Santiago y de su tierra.* Santiago, 1895–1896. 2 vols.

López Peláez, A. *El señorío temporal de los obispos de Lugo.* La Coruña, 1897. 2 vols.

Mateu Llopis, Felipe. *Sobre la hipótesis del oro asturleonés anterior al maravedí.* AHDEsp (1947), p. 630–641.

Pérez de Urbel, J. *Reconquista y repoblación de Castilla y León durante los siglos IX y X.* In "La Reconquista española y la repoblación del país." Zaragoza, 1951.

Prieto Bances, R. *La explotación rural del dominio de San Vicente de Oviedo en los siglos X al XIII.* Coimbra, 1940.

Puyol, J. *Orígenes del reino de León y de sus instituciones políticas.* M., 1926.

Sáez, Emilio. *Nuevos datos sobre el coste de la vida en Galicia durante la Alta Edad Media.* ADHEsp (1946), 865.

Sánchez Albornoz, Claudio. *La repoblación del reino asturleonés.* "Humanidades" (Buenos Aires, 1936), no. 1.

———. *Los libertos en el reino asturleonés.* "Revista Portuguêsa de História" (1947).

―――. *Contratos de arrendamiento en el reino asturleonés.* CHEsp (1948), p. 142.

―――. *La primitiva organización monetaria de León y Castilla.* AHDEsp (1928), 301.

―――. *El precio de la vida en el reino asturleonés hace mil años.* "Logos" (Buenos Aires), III.

―――. *El "Tributum quadragesimale." Supervivencias fiscales en Galicia.* "Mélanges du Moyen Âge dédiés à la mémoire de Louis Halphen." P., 1951.

―――. *La potestad real y los señoríos en Asturias, León y Castilla en los siglos VIII al XIII.* RABM, XXX (1914), 263.

Sánchez de Ocaña, R. *Contribuciones e impuestos en León y Castilla.* M., 1896.

Sarmiento, P. *El origen de los villanos.* SErud, IV.

Soares de Sousa, T. *O repovoamento do Norte de Portugal no século IX.* "Biblos" XVIII (1942).

―――. *Les bourgs dans le Nord-Ouest de la Péninsule Ibérique. Contribution à l'étude des origines des institutions urbaines en Espagne et en Portugal.* "Bulletin des Études Portugaises" (1943).

Vázquez de Parga, Luis. *El fuero de Léon.* AHDEsp (1928).

Vázquez de Parga, Luis; José M.ª Lacarra; and Juan Uria. *Las peregrinaciones a Santiago de Compostela.* M., 1948–1949. 3 vols.

Villaamil, J. *Galicia en el siglo XII. (Estado de las personas. Infeudaciones. Fueros. Concejo. Enjuiciamiento. Autoridades. Iglesia.)* RCo, May–August, 1881.

CHAPTER 12: ECONOMY OF THE PYRENEAN KINGDOMS FROM THE 8TH TO THE 12TH CENTURIES

FUNDAMENTAL WORKS

Abadal, Ramón de. *Cataluña Carolingia.* B., 1925–1955. 4 vols.

―――. *Com neix i com creix un gran monestir pirenenc abans de l'any mil. Eixalada-Cuizà.* Montserrat, 1954.

Font y Rius, José María. *Origen y evolución del municipio en Cataluña.* M., 1946.

Hinojosa, Eduardo de. *El régimen señorial y la cuestión agraria en Cataluña durante la Edad Media.* M., 1905.

Lacarra, José M.ª. *La Reconquista y repoblación del valle el Ebro.* In "La Reconquista española y la repoblación del país." Zaragoza, 1951.

Torre, Antonio de la. *La reconquista en el Pirineo*. In "La Reconquista española y la repoblación del país." Zaragoza, 1951.

SUPPLEMENTARY WORKS

Abadal, Ramón de. *Els primers comtes catalans*. B., 1958.

Altamira, Rafael. *La servidumbre rural en Cataluña*. M., 1913.

Anzar, F. *Los señoríos aragoneses. Actos de posesión y homenaje*. CuE, November, 1905.

Brutails, J. A. *Étude sur la condition des populations rurales en Roussillon pendant le Moyen Âge*. P., 1891.

Carreras Candi, F. *La ciutat de Barcelona*. In "Geografia general de Catalunya." B., 1911.

Coroleu e Inglada, J. *El feudalismo y la servidumbre de la gleba en Cataluña*. B., 1879.

Dupont, André. *Les relations commerciales entre les cités méditerranéennes d'Espagne et d'Italie du Xe siècle*. Nîmes, 1942.

Hinojosa, Eduardo de. *La servidumbre de la gleba en Aragón*. EM (1904).

Lacarra, José María. *À propos de la colonisation "Franca" en Navarre et en Aragon*. AM (1953), 331.

———. *Un arancel de aduanas del siglo XI*. Zaragoza, 1950.

Lafuente, V. de. *Los señoríos en Aragón*. "Revista Hispanoamericana," Vol. VIII, 5 and 354.

Lafuente Poyanes, M. *Origen, progresos y estado actual de la fabricación del azúcar en nuestra costa del Mediterráneo*. Discrec. Ac. Hist., 1918.

Montsalvatge i Torres, F. *Els remenses*. Palafrugell, 1908.

Mundó, Dom Anscari, O. S. B. *El políptic dels bens i censos de Sant Pere de Vilamajor*. "Circular del Archivo Histórico y Museo Fidel Fita." Arenys de Mar, 1961.

Pericot, L.; A. del Castillo; J. Ainaud; and J. Vicens Vives. *Barcelona a través de los tiempos*. B., 1943.

Piskorski, Vladimir. *El problema de la significación y del origen de los seis "malos usos" en Cataluña*. Spanish trans. B., 1928.

———. *La servidumbre rural en Cataluña*. RCHLEF, 15 April, 1903.

Ramos Loscertales, J. H. *La formación del dominio y los privilegios de San Juan de la Peña entre 1035 y 1904* AHDEsp (1929), 6.

Serra i Vilaró, J. *Senyoria feudal sobre'l castell de Malgrat*. B., 1907.

Vilà Valentí, Joan. *Notes sobre el poblament català. El mercat*. "Miscel·lània Puig i Cadafalch." B., 1947–1951.

Vives, A. *La moneda aragonesa*. "Revista de Aragón," (1903), 49.

Chapter 13: Reconquest and Resettlement in the 12th and 13th Centuries

FUNDAMENTAL WORKS

Font y Rius, José María. *Reconquista y repoblación de Levante y Murcia.* In "La Reconquista española y la repoblación del país." Zaragoza, 1951

González, Julio. *La repoblación de la Extremadura leonesa.* His (1943).

—————. *Reconquista y repoblación de Castilla, León, Extremadura y Andalucía.* In "La Reconquista española y la repoblación del país." Zaragoza, 1951.

Lacarra, José María. *La repoblación de Zaragoza por Alfonso el Batallador.* Zaragoza, 1949.

Torres Fontes, Juan. *Repartimiento de Murcia.* M., 1960.

SUPPLEMENTARY BIBLIOGRAPHY

Aguiló, E. de K. *Actes de venda o de modificació de domini otorgats per primers grans porcioners de l'illa.* (D. 1232.) BSAL, 1911.

Aznar Navarro, F. *Los solariegos de León y Castilla.* CuE (1906).

Ballesteros Beretta, Antonio. *La reconquista de Murcia 1243–1493.* BAH, CXI (1924), 133–150.

Fita, F. *Repoblación de Fuencarral a mediados del siglo XIV. Datos inéditos.* BAH, XXXV (1899), 434.

Larragueta, Santos G. *El gran priorato de Navarra de la Orden de San Juan de Jerusalén. Siglos XII–XIII.* Pamplona, 1957. 2 vols.

Puyol y Alonso, J. *Una puebla en el siglo XIII* (Carta de población de El Espinar). RHi, XI (1944).

Sancho de Sopranis, Hipólito. *La repoblación y el repartimiento de Cádiz por Alfonso X.* His, XV (1955), 483–539.

Chapter 14: The Evolution of Urban Economy

FUNDAMENTAL WORKS

Lestocquoy, J. *Les villes de Flandre et d'Italie au Moyen-Âge.* P., 1952.

López, Robert S. "The Commercial Revolution." *The Cambridge Economic History of Europe.* Vol. II, 289–320. Cambridge, 1952.

—————. *Les Influences Orientales et l'éveil économique de l'Occident.* "Cahiers d'histoire mondiale," I (1954).

Luzzatto, Gino. *Breve storia economica d'Italia. Dalla caduta dell'Impero romano al principio del Cinquecento.* Turin, 1958.

Mollat, M.; P. Johansen; M. Postan; A. Sapori; and Ch. Verlinden. *L'économie européenne aux deux derniers siècles du Moyen-Âge.* In "Relazioni," the Tenth International Congress of Historical Sciences, Vol. VI, Florence, 1955.

Pirenne, H. *Les villes au Moyen-Âge.* P., 1927.

Sapori, Armando. *Studi di Storia Economica* (secoli XIII–XIV–XV). Florence, 1956. 2 vols.

Renouard, Yves. *Les hommes d'affaires italiens au Moyen-Âge.* P., 1949.

CHAPTER 15: ECONOMY OF THE CATALAN URBAN PATRICIATE. DEMOGRAPHY AND SOCIAL STRUCTURE

FUNDAMENTAL WORKS

Iglesies, José. *El fogaje de 1365–1370. Contribución al conocimiento de la población de Cataluña en la segunda mitad del siglo XV.* B., 1962.

Garulo Sancho, Julio. *La población de Aragón en el siglo XV.* "Actas y comunicaciones del IV Congreso de Historia de la Corona de Aragón," Palma de Mallorca, 1959 [1961].

Pons Gurí, J. M. *Documentos sobre fogatges de Montclús y de Montseny (s. XIV).* "Circular del Archivo Histórico y Museo Fidel Fita." Arenys de Mar, 1960.

Quadrado, J. *Forenses y ciudadanos. Historia de las disensiones civiles de Mallorca en el siglo XV.* 2nd edn. Palma de Mallorca, 1895.

Verlinden, Charles. *La Grande Peste de 1348 en Espagne. Contribution à l'étude de ses conséquences économiques et sociales.* RBPhH (1938), XVII.

Vicens Vives, Jaime. *Historia de los remensas en el siglo XV.* B., 1945.

SUPPLEMENTARY BIBLIOGRAPHY

Bofarull, P., *Censo de Cataluña ordenado en tiempo del rey Don Pedro el Ceremonioso.* B., 1856.

Gual Camarena, Miguel. *Los mudéjares valencianos en la época del Magnánimo.* "Actas y comunicaciones del IV Congreso de Historia de la Corona de Aragón," Palma de Mallorca, 1959 [1961].

López de Meneses, Amada. *Documentos acerca de la Peste Negra en los dominios de la Corona de Aragón.* EEMCA, VI (1935–1955 [1956]).

Macho y Ortega, Francisco. *Condición social de los mudéjares aragoneses (s. XV).* Zaragoza, 1922–1923.

Masía de Ros, Ángeles. *Contribución al conocimiento del censo de población musulmana en Cataluña.* "Tamuda," III (1955).

Paz, J. *Reclamaciones de los mallorquines llamados de "La Calle" sobre su condición social.* RABM (1907).

Piles Ros, Leopoldo. *Situación económica de las aljamas aragonesas a comienzos del siglo XV.* Sef, X (1950).

———. *La situation social de los moros de realengo en la Valencia del siglo XV.* M., 1949.

Richard, W. Emery. *The Jews of Perpignan in the Thirteenth Century. An Economic Study Based on Notarial Records.* New York, 1959.

Roca Traver, Francisco. *Un siglo de vida mudéjar en la Valencia medieval (1238–1338).* EEMCA, V (1952).

Rubió Balaguer, Jorge. *Vida española en la época gótica.* B., 1943.

Serrano Sanz, Manuel. *Notas acerca de los judíos aragoneses en los siglos XIV y XV.* RABM. XXXVII (1917).

Sobrequés Vidal, S. *Censo y profesión de los habitantes de Gerona en 1462.* "Anuario del Instituto de Estudios Gerundenses," VI (1951).

CHAPTER 16: ECONOMY OF THE CATALAN URBAN PATRICIATE. LABOR AND INDUSTRY

FUNDAMENTAL WORKS

Bonnassié, Pierre. *L'organisation du travail à Barcelone à la fin du XVe* (in course of publication in EHM).

Reglá, Juan. *El comercio entre Francia y la Corona de Aragón en los siglos XIII y XIV y sus relaciones con el desenvolvimiento de la industria textil catalana.* Zaragoza, 1950.

Vicens Vives, J.; L. Suárez Fernández; and Claude Carrère. *La economía de los países de la Corona de Aragón en la Baja Edad Media.* M., 1957.

SUPPLEMENTARY BIBLIOGRAPHY

Bafarull y Sans, F. de. *Ordenanzas de oficios y artes de los siglos XIV y XV.* B., 1910.

Bofarull, M. de. *Gremios y cofradías de la Antigua Corona de Aragón (ss. XIV y XV).* B., 1876.

Buades, A. *Per l'història dels gremis de Mallorca.* BSAL, December 1917–April 1918.

Codera, F. *Antiguos gremios de Huesca.* BAH, LX (1912).

Fajarnés, E. *Asociaciones gremiales de Mallorca durante la Edad Media.* BSAL, July–August, 1847.

González Sugrañes, M. *Contribució a la història dels antics gremis dels arts i oficis de la ciutat de Barcelona.* B., 1915–1918.

Madurell Marimón, José M.ª. *La contratación laboral judaica y conversa en Barcelona (1349–1416).* Documents. Sef, XIV (1956).

Sagarra, E. *Los gremios.* B., 1911.

Tramoyeres y Blasco, L. *Instituciones gremiales. Su origen y organización en Valencia.* Valencia, 1889.

————. *La cosecha de azúcar en el reino de Valencia.* "El Archivo," 1886.

CHAPTER 17: CATALONIAN TRADE

FUNDAMENTAL WORKS

Carrère, Claude. *Le droit d'ancrage et le mouvement du port de Barcelone au milieu du XVe siècle.* EHM, III (1953).

De Roover, Raymond. *L'évolution de la lettre de change: XIV–XVII siècles.* P., 1953.

Heyd, W. *Histoire du commerce du Levant au Moyen-Âge.* Leipzig, 1885.

Melis, Federigo. *Aspetti della vita economica medievale (Studi dell'Archivio Datini di Prato),* Vol. I. Siena, 1962.

Nicolau d'Olwer, Lluís. *L'expansió de Catalunya en la Mediterrània Oriental.* B., 1926.

Origo, Iris. *Le marchand de Prato. Francesco di Marco Datini.* P., 1959. (1st edn., in English, 1957.)

Reparaz, Gonzalo de. *Catalunya a les mars.* B., 1930.

Rubió i Lluch, A. *Diplomatari de l'Orient Català.* B., 1948.

Smith, R. S. *The Spanish Guild Merchant: A History of the Consulado, 1250–1700.* Durham, 1940.

Verlinden, Charles *L'esclavage dans l'Europe Médiévale. I. Péninsule Ibérique-France.* Bruges, 1955.

SUPPLEMENTARY BIBLIOGRAPHY

Chabás, R. *La esclavitud en Valencia.* "El Archivo," November–December 1890.

Coll Juliá, Nuria. *Aspectos del corso catalán y del comercio internacional en el siglo XV.* EHM, IV (1954).

De la Roncière, Charles. *La découverte de l'Afrique au Moyen-Âge.* Cairo, 1924–1925. 2 vols.

Dufourq, Ch. E. *La Couronne d'Aragon et les Hafsides au XIIIe siècle.* "Analecta Sacra Tarraconensia," XXV (1952).

―――. *Les activités politiques et économiques des catalans en Tunisie et en Algérie Orientale de 1262 à 1377.* "Boletín de la Real Academia de Buenas Letras." (Barcelona), XIX (1946).

Durliat, Marcel, and Joan Ponis i Marquès. *Recerques sobre el moviment del port de Mallorca en la primera meitat del segle XIV.* VI Congreso de la Corona de Aragón. M., 1959.

Font y Rius, José M.ª. *Las instituciones de la Corona de Aragón en la primera mitad del siglo XV.* (*reinados de Fernando de Antequera y Alfonso el Magnánimo*). Palma de Mallorca, 1955.

Giménez Soler, A. *Nota sobre relación comercial entre Cataluña e Italia en el siglo XIV.* AIEcat (1909–1910). 701.

―――. *El comercio en tierra de infieles durante la Edad Media.* "Boletín de la Real Academia de Buenas Letras." (Barcelona), 1909–1910.

Heers, Jacques. *Il commercio nel Mediterraneo alla fine del secolo XIV e nei primi anni del XV.* ASI, CXIII (1955).

López de Meneses, Amada. *Los consulados catalanes de Alejandría y Damasco en el reinado de Pedro el Ceremonioso.* EEMCA, VI (1956).

Maréchal, Joseph. *La colonie espagnole de Bruges du XIVe au XVIe siècle.* RN, XXXV (1953).

Miret y Sans, J. *La esclavitud en Cataluña en los últimos tiempos de la Edad Media.* RHI, XLI (1917).

Noguera, R. *La compañía mercantil en Barcelona durante los siglos XV y XVI.* "La Notaría," LXXIX (1944).

Piles Ros, Leopoldo. *El comercio valenciano a fines de la Edad Media.* AAEPC, XXI (1956).

Reparaz, G. de. *L'activité maritime et commerciale du royaume d'Aragon au XIIIe siècle et son influence sur le développement de l'école cartographique de Majorque.* BHi (1947).

Richard, W. Emery. "Flemish Cloth and Flemish Merchants in Perpignan in the Thirteenth Century." *Essays in Medieval Life and Thought Presented in Honor of Austin Patterson.* New York, 1955.

Sanç Capdevila, C. *El mercat d'esclaus a Tarragona a la primera dècada del segle XV.* BAr-Tarr, IV (1929–1924).

Sancho, P. A. *Suspensión del comercio entre los dominios del rey de Aragón y los del Soldán de Babilonia en 1386.* BSAL, Sep. 1900.

Sayous, André-E. *La technique des affaires: sa genèse.I.-Les origines de la commandite: Un contrat de société à Barcelone en 1336.* "Annales d'Histoire économique et Sociale." (Paris, 1934).

———. *Les méthodes commerciales de Barcelone au XIIIe Siècle. . . . au XIVe . . . au XVe . . .* EUC, XVI (1931); XVIII (1933), y "Revue de Droit Français et Étranger." Paris (1936).

Schulte, A. *Geschichte der grossen Ravensburger Handelsgesellschaft.* Stuttgart, 1923. 3 vols.

Serra Ráfols, E. *El descubrimiento y los viajes medievales de los catalanes a las Islas Afortunadas, 1926.*

———. *Els catalans de Mallorca a les Illes Canàries.* "Revista de Historia" (La Laguna), 54 and 55 (1941).

———. *Los mallorquines en Canarias.* "Revista de Historia" (La Luguna), 54 and 55 (1941).

Traselli, Carmelo. *Sull'esportazione di cereali dalla Sicilia nel 1407–1408.* "Atti dell'Academia di Scienze, Lettere e Arti di Palermo," XIV (1953–1954).

Tramoyeres Blasco, L. *Letras de cambio valencianas.* RABM, IV (1900).

Wolff, Philippe. *Commerces et marchands de Toulouse (1350–1450).* P., 1954.

CHAPTER 18: PRICES, MONEY, BANKING AND GENERAL ECONOMIC SITUATION IN THE CROWN OF ARAGON

FUNDAMENTAL WORKS

Hamilton, E. J. *Money, Prices and Wages in Valencia, Aragon and Navarre (1351–1500).* Cambridge, 1936.

Usher, A. P. *The Early History of Deposit Banking in Mediterranean Europe.* I. *Banking in Catalonia.* Cambridge, 1943.

Vicens Vives, J. *Evolución de la economía catalana durante la primera mitad del siglo XV.* Palma de Mallorca. 1955.

———. *Consideraciones sobre la historia de Cataluña en el siglo XV.* "Cuadernos de Historia Jerónimo Zurita" (1951).

Vilar, Pierre. *Le déclin catalan du Bas Moyen-Âge.* EHM, VI (1959).

SUPPLEMENTARY BIBLIOGRAPHY

Batlle, Carmen. *La ideología de la "Busca." La crisis municipal de Barcelona en el siglo XV.* EHM, V. (1955–[1957]).

Broussole, Jean. *Les impositions municipales de Barcelonne de 1328 à 1462.* EHM, V. (1955 [1957]).

Brutalis, J. A. *Note sur la valeur du sou de tern en 1298.* BHi, III (1901).

Carreres Zacares, Salvador. *La Taula de Cambis de València, 1408–1719.* Valencia, 1957.

García Sanz, Arcadio. *La banca en los siglos XIII y XIV según el Aureum Opus.* BSCC, XXXIII (1957).

López, Robert Sabatino. *Settecento anni fa: il ritorno all'oro nell'Occidente duecentesco.* "Quaderni della Rivista Storica Italiana," 4. Naples, 1955.

Rahola, F. *Los antiguos banqueros de Cataluña y la "Taula de Cambi," banco principal de Barcelona.* B., 1912.

Saleta, Honorata de. *Estado social del reino de Navarra bajo el gobierno de D. Sancho el Fuerte.* M., 1915.

CHAPTER 19: PUBLIC POWER AND FINANCIAL ORGANIZATION IN THE CROWN OF ARAGON

FUNDAMENTAL WORKS

Coroleu, J., and J. Pella Forga. *Los fueros de Cataluña.* B., 1878.

Roustit, Yvan. *La consolidation de la dette publique à Barcelone au milieu du XIVe siècle.* EHM, IV (1954).

Torre, A. de la. *Orígenes de la "Deputació" del General de Cataluña.* B., 1923.

SUPPLEMENTARY BIBLIOGRAPHY

García de Cáceres, F. *Impuestos de la ciudad de Valencia durante la época foral.* Valencia, 1909.

Marinesco, C. *Alfonse le Magnanime, Protecteur d'un rival du commerce catalan: Jacques Coeur.* EHM, III (1953).

Salavert, V. *Cerdeña y la expansión mediterránea de la Corona de Aragón.* M., 1956. 2 vols.

Sevillano Colom, F. *Préstamos de la ciudad de Valencia a los reyes Alfonso V y Juan II.* Valencia, 1951.

Torella Niubó, J. *El impuesto textil de "la bolla" en la Cataluña medieval.* His, XIV (1954).

CHAPTER 20: STRUCTURE AND EXPANSION OF THE
CASTILIAN HERDING AND AGRARIAN ECONOMY
FROM THE 13TH TO 15TH CENTURIES

FUNDAMENTAL WORKS

Amador de los Ríos, J. *Historia social, política y religiosa de los judíos de España y Portugal.* M., 1875–1876. 3 vols.

Baer, Fritz. *Die Juden in christlichen Spanien.* 1929–1936. 2 vols.

Bishko, Ch. *El castellano, hombre de llanura. La explotación ganadera en el área fronteriza de la Mancha y Extremadura durante la Edad Media.* (In course of publication in EHM.)

Ferrari Núñez, Ángel. *Castilla dividida en dominios según el Libro de las Behetrías.* M., 1958.

Klein, J. *The Mesta: A Study in Spanish Economic History 1273–1836.* Cambridge, 1920. (Spanish trans. 1936).

López, Robert S. *The Origin of the Merino Sheep.* New York, 1953. (Spanish trans. in EHM, IV [1954]).

Redonet, Luis. *El latifundio y su formación en la España medieval.* "Estudios de Historia Social." I (1949).

SUPPLEMENTARY BIBLIOGRAPHY

Cos Gayón, F. *La Mesta.* REsp, XI y X (1869–1870).

Escagedo Salmón, M. *La casa de la Vega, comentarios a las behetrías montañesas y al pleito de los valles.* Torrelavega, 1917.

Jimeno, Esther. *La población de Soria y su término en 1270 según el padrón que mandó hacer Alfonso X de sus vecinos y moradores.* BAH. CXLII (1958).

Klein, J. *Los privilegios de la Mesta de 1273 y 1276.* BAH, LXIV (1914).

———. *The Alcalde Entregador of the Mesta.* BHi April–June 1915.

CHAPTER 21: CASTILIAN INDUSTRY AND TRADE FROM
THE 13TH TO THE 15TH CENTURIES

FUNDAMENTAL WORKS

Ballesteros, A. *La marina cántabra y Juan de la Cosa.* Santander, 1954.

Caranda, Ramón. *Sevilla fortaleza y mercado. Algunas instituciones de la ciudad, en el siglo XIV especialmente, estudiadas en sus privilegios, ordenamientos y cuentas.* ADHE, II (1925).

BIBLIOGRAPHY

Carlé, María del Carmen. *Mercaderes en Castilla (1252–1512)*. CHEsp, XXI–XXII (1954).

Heers, J. *Le commerce des Basques en Méditerranée au XVe siècle*. BHis, LVII (1955).

López, Robert S. *Storia delle colonie genovesi nel Mediterraneo*. Bologna, 1938.

Rumeu de Armas, A. *España en el África Atlántica*. M., 1956–1958. 2 vols.

Suárez Fernández, Luis. *Navegación y comercio en el golfo de Vizcaya. Un estudio sobre la política marinera de la casa de Trastámara*. M., 1959.

Verlinden, Ch. "The Rise of Spanish Trade in the Middle Ages." *The Economic History Review*, X (1940).

———. *À propos de la politique économique des ducs de Bourgogne à l'égard de l'Espagne*. His, X (1950).

SUPPLEMENTARY BIBLIOGRAPHY

Ballesteros, A. *Sevilla en el siglo XIII*. M., 1913.

Beardwood, A. *Alien Merchants in England*. Cambridge, 1931.

De la Fosse, M. *Trafic rochelais aux XVe siècle. Marchands poitevins et laines d'Espagne*. "Annales" (Paris), 1952.

Espejo, C. *Documentos para ilustrar las ferias de Medina del Campo*. BSCastExc, 1908, 1909, 1910, 1912.

———. *Apuntes para la historia de las ferias de Alcalá de Henares*. BSCastExc, August 1910.

Espejo, Cristóbal, and Julián Paz. *Las antiguas ferias de Medina del Campo*. Valladolid, 1912.

Finot, J. *Étude historique sur les relations commerciales entre la Flandre et l'Espagne au Moyen-Âge*. P., 1899.

García Concellón, E. *La Universidad de mercaderes y consulado de Burgos*. 1906.

Gorosabel, P. de. *Ferias y mercados en Guipúzcoa*. "Euskal-Erria," 17 March 1907.

Guiard, J. *Historia de Bilbao*. Vol. I. Bilbao, 1905.

Häbler, K. *Der hansisch-spanische Konflikt von 1419 und die älteren spanischen Bestände*. "Hansische Geschichtsblätter" (1894).

Justi, C. *Los lombardos en Sevilla*. EM (1913).

Laurent, H. *La draperie des Pays-Bas en France et dans les pays méditerranéens (XIIe–XVe siècles)*. P., 1935.

Lecea y García, D. de. *Recuerdos de la antigua industria segoviana*. Segovia, 1897.

López, Robert S. *Alfonso el Sabio y el primer almirante genovés de Castilla.* CHEsp, XII (1950).

Lozoya, Marqués de. *Historia de las corporaciones menestrales en Segovia.* Segovia, 1921.

Martínez Guitián, L. *Naves y flotas de las Cuatro Villas de la Costa.* Santander, 1942.

Mollat, Michel. *Le commerce maritime normand aux XVe siècle et dans la première moitié du XVIe.* P., 1952.

Pérez Embid, F. *Los descubrimientos en el Atlántico hasta el tratado de Tordesillas.* Seville, 1947.

Salzmann, L. F. *English Trade in the Middle Ages.* Oxford, 1931.

Sancho de Sopranis, Hipólito. *Historia social de Jerez de la Frontera al fin de la Edad Media. I. La vida material. II. La vida espiritual. III. Anécdota.* Centro de Estudios Históricos Jerezanos. Jerez, 1959.

San Pelayo, Julián de. *Ordenanzas de Valverde, comunidad y tierra de Segovia, sobre la plata y paños de las bodas y otras cosas.* M., 1894.

Van Severen, Guillodts. *Cartulaire de l'Ancien Consulat d'Espagne à Bruges.* Bruges, 1901.

Verlinden, Ch. *Contribution à l'étude de l'expansion commerciale de la draperie flamande dans la Péninsule ibérique au XIIIe siècle.* RNord, XXII (1936).

———. *Draps des Pays-Bas et du Nord de la France en Espagne au XIVe siècle.* "Le Moyen-Âge" (1937).

Viñas Mey, Carmelo. *De la Edad Media a la Moderna. El Cantábrico y el estrecho de Gibraltar en la historia política (y económica) española.* His, I (1940–1941).

———. *Los Países Bajos en la política y en la economía mundial de España.* M., 1944.

Wilson, E. M. Carus. *The Overseas Trade of Bristol in the Middle Ages.* Bristol, 1937.

CHAPTER 22: MONEY, USURY AND PUBLIC FINANCE IN CASTILE

FUNDAMENTAL WORKS

Cantera, F. *Alvar Garcís de Santamaría: Historia de la judería de Burgos y de sus conversos más egregios.* M., 1952.

Castro, Américo. "Los judíos españoles." Ch. XII of *La realidad histórica de España.*

Melis, Federico. *Malaga sul sentiero economico del XIV e XV secolo.* "Economia e Storia." (Roma), II (1956).

Piskorski, V. *Las Cortes de Castilla desde 1188 a 1520.* Kiev, 1897. (Span. trans. B., 1930).

Vives Escudero, A. *La moneda castellana.* M., 1901.

SUPPLEMENTARY BIBLIOGRAPHY

Álvarez de la Braña, Ramón. *Igualación de pesos y medidas por Don Alfonso el Sabio.* BAH, XXXVIII (1901).

Jiménez de la Espada. *La guerra del moro a fines del siglo XV.* BAH, XXV. (1894).

López de Ayala Álvarez de Toledo y del Hierro, Jerónimo. *Contribuciones e impuestos en León y Castilla durante la Edad Media.* M., 1896.

López Martínez, Nicolás. *Los judaizantes castellanos y la Inquisición en tiempos de Isabel la Católica.* Burgos, 1954.

Sánchez de Ocaña, Ramón. *Contribuciones e impuestos en León y Castilla durante la Edad Media.* M., 1896.

Sancho de Sopranis, H. *Los genoveses en la región gaditano-xericiense de 1460 a 1500.* His, VIII (1948).

CHAPTER 23: THE ECONOMY OF
FERDINAND AND ISABELLA'S REIGN

FUNDAMENTAL WORKS

Ballesteros Gaibrois, M. *La obra de Isabel la Católica.* Segovia, 1953.

Clemencín, Diego. *Elogio de la reina Doña Isabel.* M., 1820.

Goris, J. A. *Étude sur les colonies marchandes méridionales (Portugais, Espagnols, Italiens) à Anvers de 1488 à 1567.* Louvain, 1925.

Hamilton, E. J. *El florecimiento del capitalismo y otros ensayos de historia económica.* M., 1948.

Ibarra y Rodríguez, E. *El problema cerealista en España durante el reinado de los Reyes Católicos.* "Anales de Economía," 1941, 1942.

Merriman, Roger B. *The Rise of the Spanish Empire,* Vol. II. New York, 1918.

Prescott, W. H. *History of the Reign of Ferdinand and Isabella.* London, 1838. 3 vols.

Vicens Vives, J. *Política del Rey Católico en Cataluña.* B., 1940.

SUPPLEMENTARY BIBLIOGRAPHY

Alcázar. Cayetano. *Las comunicaciones en la época de los Reyes Católicos.* "Curso de conferencias sobre la política africana de los Reyes
Católicos." V (1953).

Beneyto Pérez, J. *Regulación del trabajo en la Valencia del 1500.* M.,
1931.

Bosque Carceller, Rodolfo. *Murcia y los Reyes Católicos.* Murcia, 1953.

Espejo, C. *Renta de la aguela y habices de Granada.* RCa (1918).

Fajarnés, E. *El comercio de la sal de Ibiza en el reino de Nápoles
(1485).* BSAL, May, 1896.

Floristán Samanes, A. *Juntas y mestas ganaderas en las Bárdenas de
Navarra.* Zaragoza, 1952.

Fuertes Arias, Rafael. *Estudio histórico acerca de Alfonso de Quintanilla, contador mayor de los Reyes Católicos.* Oviedo, 1909.

Gonzales Yanes, Emma. *Importación y exportación en Tenerife durante
los primeros años de la conquista (1497–1503).* RHL, XIX, (1953).

Guiard, T. *Historia del Consulado y Casa de Contratación de Bilbao y
del Comercio de la villa (1511–1880).* Bilbao, 1913–1914. 2 vols.

López Orriols. *Política económica de los Reyes Católicos.* B., 1894.

Ibarra y Rodríguez, E. *Documentos de asunto económico correspon-
dientes al reinado de los Reyes Católicos (1475–1516).* M., 1917.

———. *El problema de las subsistencias en España al comenzar la
España moderna. La carne.* NT (1926).

Oliver, Bienvenido. *La universidad de mercaderes y consulado de Burgos.* BAH, L (1907).

Piles Ros, Leopoldo. *La expulsión de los judíos en Valencia. Repercusiones económicas.* Sef, XV (1955).

Sevillano Colom, Francisco. *Las empresas nacionales de los Reyes Católicos y la aportación económica de la ciudad de Valencia.* His, XIV
(1954).

Valladar, F. de P. *Las ordenanzas de Granada y las actas industriales
granadinas.* Granada, 1915.

Vicens Vives, Jaime. *Instituciones económicas, sociales y políticas de
la época fernandina.* Zaragoza, 1952.

———. *El "Redreç" de la economia catalana de 1481.* "Studi in onore
di A. Sapori," II, Milán, 1956.

———. *El Gran Sindicato remensa (1488–1508).* M., 1954.

Vives, A. *Reforma monetaria de los Reyes Católicos.* M., 1898.

Zabala Allende, M. *El Consulado y las ordenanzas de Comercio de
Bilbao.* Bilbao, 1907.

BIBLIOGRAPHY

CHAPTER 24: EXPANSION OF THE SPANISH ECONOMY
IN AMERICA AFTER THE DISCOVERY

FUNDAMENTAL WORKS

Bargallo, Modesto. *La minería y la metalurgia en la América española durante la época colonial.* Mexico, 1955.

Chaunu, Huguette and Pierre. *Séville et l'Atlantique (1504–1650).* P., 1955–1959. 9 vols.

Hanke, Lewis. *La lucha por la justicia en la conquista de América.* Buenos Aires, 1948.

Konetzke, R. *El Imperio español. Orígenes y fundamentos.* (Span. trans. M., 1946).

Manzano Manzano, Juan. *La incorporación de las Indias a la Corona de Castilla.* M., 1948.

Ots Capdequí, José. *El derecho de propiedad en la legislación de Indias.* AHDEsp, II (1925).

———. *Instituciones económicas durante el periodo colonial.* AHDEsp, XI (1943).

———. *Manual de Historia del Derecho español en las Indias.* Buenos Aires, 1945.

Schaefer, E. *El Consejo Real y Supremo de las Indias.* Seville, 1935–1947. 2 vols.

Verlinden, Ch. *Les influences médiévales dans la colonisation de l'Amérique.* "Revista de Historia de América" (1950).

———. *Le influenze italiane nella colonizzazione iberica (uomini e metodi).* "Nuova Rivista Storica," XXXVI (1952).

Zavala, Silvio. *La encomienda indiana.* M., 1935.

SUPPLEMENTARY BIBLIOGRAPHY

Alcalá Henke, A. *La villa imperial de Potosí.* Sucre, 1954.

Diffie, B. W. "Estimates of Potosí Mineral Production, 1541–1555." *Hispanic American Historical Review* (1940).

Friede, J. *Algunas observaciones sobre la realidad de la emigración española a América en la primera mitad del siglo XIV.* "Revista de Indias" (1952).

Häebler, K. *Die Angänge der Sklaverei in Amerika.* Weimar, 1896.

Ibot, I. *Los trabajadores del río Magdalena durante el siglo XVI.* B., 1933.

Konetzke, Richard. *Colección de documentos para la historia de la formación social de Hispanoamérica (1493–1810).* M., 1953. Vol. I.

Manzano Manzano, Juan. *La adquisición de Indias por los Reyes Católicos y su incorporación a los reinos castellanos.* AHDEsp, XXI–XXII (1951–1952), 5.

Moreno, Laudelino. *Los extranjeros y el ejercicio del comercio en Indias.* M., 1936.

Nesmith, R. S. *The Coinage of the First Mint of the Americas at Mexico City, 1536–1572.* New York, 1955.

Ots Capdequí, José. *Instituciones sociales de la América española durante el período colonial.* La Plata, 1934.

Pérez de Tudela, J. *Las armadas de Indias y los orígenes de la política de colonización (1492–1505).* M., 1956.

Saco, José A. *Historia de la esclavitud de la raza africana en el Nuevo Mundo.* Havana, 1938. 4 vols.

Sayous, André-E. *Les débuts du commerce de l'Espagne avec l'Amérique.* P., 1934.

———. *Les procédés de paiement et la monnaie dans l'Amérique espagnole pendant la première moitié du XVIe siècle.* "Revue Economique Internationale" 1927.

———. *Le rôle des genois, lors des premiers mouvements réguliers d'affaires entre l'Espagne et le Nouveau Monde (1505–1550).* "Boletín de la Sociedad Geográfica Nacional." LXXII (1932).

Scelle, Georges. *La traite négrière aux Indes de Castille.* P., 1906. 3 vols.

Serra Ràfols, Elías. *La colonización española en Canarias.* RHL (1946).

Wagner, H. F. "Early Silver Mining in New Spain." *Revista de Historia de América* (1942).

Zavala, Silvio. *Las instituciones jurídicas en la conquista de América.* M., 1935.

———. *La conquista de Canarias y América.* In "Estudios Indianos." Mexico, 1948.

CHAPTER 25: DEMOGRAPHIC AND SOCIAL STRUCTURE IN THE 16TH CENTURY

FUNDAMENTAL WORKS

Boronat, P. *Los moriscos españoles y su expulsión.* Valencia, 1901.

Braudel, Ferdinand. *La Méditerranée et le monde méditerranéen à l'époque de Philippe II.* P., 1949 (Span. trans. Mexico, 1953.)

Caro Baroja, Julio. *Los moriscos del reino de Granada.* M., 1957.

Domínguez Ortiz, Antonio. *La esclavitud en Castilla durante la Edad Moderna.* "Estudios de Historia Social de España," II (1952).

Girard, Albert. *La chiffre de la population d'Espagne dans les temps modernes.* "Revue d'Histoire Moderne," III (1928), IV (1929).

————. *La répartition de la population en Espagne dans les temps modernes, XVIe, XVIIe, XVIIIe Siècles.* "Revue d'Histoire Economique et sociale," XVII (1929).

Halperin Donghi, Tulio. *Un conflicto nacional: moriscos y cristianos viejos en Valencia.* CHEsp, XXIII–XXIV (1955–1957).

Iglèsies, Josep. *La població catalana en el segle XVI.* B., 1957.

Lapeyre, Henri. *Une famille de marchands: Les Ruiz. Contribution à l'étude du commerce entre la France et l'Espagne au temps de Philippe II.* P., 1955.

Nadal, J., and E. Giralt. *La population catalane de 1553 à 1717. L'immigration française.* P., 1960.

SUPPLEMENTARY BIBLIOGRAPHY

Basas Fernández, M. *Simón Ruiz burgalés.* Burgos, 1953.

Borrás, Antonio. *Contribución a los orígenes del bandolerismo en Cataluña. La pragmática de Carlos V de 1539.* EHM, III (1953).

Carriazo, Juan de M. *Negros, esclavos y extranjeros en el barrio sevillano de San Bernardo.* AHisp, XX (1954).

Caruana, José. *Los malteses en Valencia.* Valencia, 1911, and BAH, LX (1912).

Domínguez Ortiz, Antonio. *Los conversos de origen judío después de la expulsión.* "Estudios de Historia Social de España," III (1955).

Donnet, F. *Histoire de l'établissement des Anversois aux Canaries au XVIe siècle.* Antwerp, 1895.

García Valdecasas, A. *El hidalgo.* "Escorial," X (1943).

Giralt, E., and J. Nadal. *Ensayo metodológico para el estudio de la población catalana de 1553 a 1717.* EHM, III (1953).

Guzmán, A. *Los caballeros cuantiosos de la ciudad de Córdoba.* BRA Córd, XXIII (1952).

Halperin Donghi, Tulio. *Recouvrements de civilisations: Les morisques du royaume de Valence au XVIe siècle.* "Annales" (Paris), XI (1956).

Herrero Martínez de Aizcoitia, Guillermo. *La población palentina en los siglos XVI y XVII.* Institución "Tello Téllez de Meneses." Palencia, 1961.

Jiménez de Gregorio, Fernando. *Repoblación y poblamiento del campo murciano.* "Anales de la Facultad de Murcia. Facultad de Filosofía y Letras," XV (1956–1957).

————. *La población en la Jara Toledana.* EG, XIII (1952).

Morel Fatio, A. *Les Allemands en Espagne du XVe au XVIIIe siècle.* RFE (1922).

Piles Ros, Leopoldo. *Aspectos sociales de las germanías de Valencia.* M., 1952.

Poch, J. *El antiguo bandolerismo en el Pirineo catalán.* "Pallars," I (1953).

Prieto Bances. *Los hidalgos asturianos en el siglo XVI.* RUO, XIV (1953).

Ruiz Almansa, Javier. *Población de Galicia: 1500–1945.* M., 1948.

Salyer, John C. *La importancia económica de los moriscos en España.* AdE, IX (1949).

Sancho Sopranis, J. *Estructura y perfil demográfico de Cádiz en el siglo XVI.* "Estudios de Historia social de España," II (1952).

Serrahima Cirici, Enrique. *Hugonotes y bandidos en el Pirineo catalán. La actuación de San José de Calasanz en Urgel (1587–1589).* EHM, IV (1954).

Uria Riu, Juan. *Los Vaqueiros de Alzada en el Aspecto Social.* "Estudios de Historia Social de España," III (1955).

CHAPTER 26: LABOR AND PRODUCTION IN THE 16TH CENTURY

FUNDAMENTAL WORKS

Achilles, Walter. *Getreidepreise und Getreidehandelsbeziehungen europäischer Räume im 16. und 17. Jahrhundert.* Frankfurt, 1959.

Carrera Pujal, J. *Historia de la economía española.* (Especially the 16th, 17th, and 18th centuries.) B., 1943–1947. 5 vols.

———. *Historia política y econômica de Cataluña (siglos XVI–XVIII).* B., 1947–1949. 5 vols.

Häebler, Konrad. *Die wirtschaftliche Blüte Spaniens in 16. Jahrhundert und ihr Verfall.* Berlin, 1888.

Viñas Mey, Carmelo. *El problema de la tierra en la España del siglo XVI.* M., 1941.

SUPPLEMENTARY BIBLIOGRAPHY

Artiñono, Gervasio de. *La producción española en los siglos XVI y XVII.* Madrid científico, 1913.

Espejo, C. *Arbitrio sobre imposición tributaria en el trigo y en la cebada.* RABM, April-June (1923).

Garrad, K. *La industria sedera granadina en el siglo XVI.* "Miscelánea de estudios árabes y hebraicos." Univ. Granada, 1956.

Juliá, Eduardo. *Una nota sobre las contiendas de los gremios en Valencia. (1534)*. BSCC, May, 1920.

Lecea y García, C. *Recuerdos de la antigua industria segoviana*. Segovia, 1897.

Madurell Marimón, José M.ª, and Jorge Rubió Balaguer. *Documentos para la historia de la imprenta y librería en Barcelona (1470–1553)*. B., 1955.

Sancho Seral, Luis. *El gremio zaragozano*. Univ., Oct.–Nov.–Dec. 1925.

Usher, A. P. "Spanish Ships and Shipping in the Sixteenth and Seventeenth Centuries." *Facts and Factors in Economic History*. Cambridge, Mass., 1932.

CHAPTER 27: AMERICAN COLONIAL ECONOMY FROM 1550 TO 1700

FUNDAMENTAL WORKS

Carande, Ramón. *Carlos V y sus banqueros*. M., 1943–1949. 2 vols.

Hamilton, E. J. *American Treasure and the Price Revolution in Spain (1501–1650)*. Cambridge, Mass., 1934.

Kellenbenz, Hermann. *Unternehmerkräfte im hamburger, Portugal– und Spanienhandel (1590–1625)*. Hamburg, 1954.

Lapeyre, Henri, and Ramón Carande. *Relaciones comerciales en el Mediterráneo durante el siglo XVI*. M., 1957.

Larraz, José. *La época del mercantilismo en Castilla (1500–1700)*. M., 1943.

Nadal, Jorge. *La revolución de los precios españoles en el siglo XVI*. His, 1959.

Schick, León. *Jacobo Fúcar. Un gran hombre de negocios del siglo XVI*. M., 1961.

Ulloa, Modesto. *La hacienda real de Castilla en el reinado de Felipe II*. Rome, 1963.

Vilar, Pierre. *Les primitifs espagnols de la pensée économique. "Quantitativisme" et "Bullionisme."* In "Mélanges offerts à Marcel Bataillon," Bordeaux, 1963.

SUPPLEMENTARY BIBLIOGRAPHY

Bennassar, Bartolomé. *En Vieille-Castille: Les ventes de rentes perpétuelles. Première moitie du XVIe siècle.* "Annales. Économies. Sociétés. Civilisations." P., 1960.

Bennassar, Bartolomé. *Facteurs sévillans au XVIe siècle, d'après des lettres marchandes.* "Annales," 1957.

Carande, R. *El crédito de Castilla en el precio de la política imperial.* M., 1949.

———. *Un banquero de Felipe II en Medina del Campo.* "Moneda y Crédito," no. 49 (1954).

Chabod, Frederigo. *Note e documenti per la storia economico–finanziaria dell'impero di Carlo V.*

Coniglio, Giuseppe. *La política financiera española en Nápoles en la segunda mitad del siglo XVI.* "Moneda y Crédito," no. 56 (1956).

Espejo, C. *Precio de los principales artículos en San Sebastián y Valladolid en tiempo de Felipe II.* RABM (1907).

———. *La carestía de la vida en el siglo XVI y medios de abaratarla.* RABM (1920), XLI.

———. *Sobre organización de la Hacienda española en el siglo XVI.* CE, May–August 1907.

———. *El Consejo de Hacienda durante la presidencia del marqués de Poza.* M., 1924.

———. *Arbitrios propuestos por el bachiller Reina para amortizar los juros. Siglo XV.* Valladolid-Santarem, 1907.

———. *La renta de las salinas hasta la muerte de Felipe II.* RABM (1918).

Fernández Álvarez, Manuel. *El Memorial de Luis de Ortiz.* AdE, 1957.

García de Quevedo y Concellón, E. *Ordenanzas del Consulado de Burgos de 1538.* Burgos, 1905.

Girard, A. *Le commerce français à Seville et Cadix au temps des Hapsbourgs.* Bordeaux, 1932.

Giralt, Emilio. *En torno al precio del trigo en Barcelona durante el siglo XVI.* His, XVIII (1958).

Häebler, K. *Die Geschichte der Fugger'schen Handlung in Spanien.* Weimar, 1897.

Iglesia, F. de la. *La organización de la Hacienda en la primera mitad del siglo XVI.* NT, June 1906.

———. *Las rentas del Imperio en Castilla.* M., 1907.

———. *Las deudas del Imperio.* NT, November 1904.

———. *Los gastos de la corona en el Imperio.* M., 1907.

Kellenbenz, Hermann. *Spanien, die nördlichen Niederlande und der skandinavisch-baltische Raum in der Weltwirtschaft und Politik um 1600.* "Vierteljahrschift für Sozial– und Wirtschaftsgeschichte," XLI (1954).

———. *Autour de 1600: Le commerce du poivre des Fugger et le marché international du poivre.* "Annales," XI (1956).

Lapeyre, Henri. *Le commerce des laines en Espagne sous Philippe II.* "Bulletin de la Société d'Histoire Moderne," LIV (1955).

———. *La banque, les changes et le crédit au XVIe siècle.* "Revue d'Histoire Moderne et Contemporaine," III (1956).

———. *Simón Ruiz et les "asientos" de Philippe II.* P., 1953.

Llorente. *Crisis de la Hacienda en tiempo de Felipe II.* RE, I.

López de Peñalver, Juan. *Reflexiones sobre la variación del precio del trigo.* AdE, XIII–XV (1953–1956).

Madurell Marimon, José Maria. *Notas sobre el antiguo comercio de Barcelona con las islas Canarias y Santo Domingo.* "Anuario de Estudios Atlánticos," III (1957).

Mantilla, C. *Precios de algunos sueldos, jornales y artículos a mediados del siglo XVI.* RHV, January–March 1924.

Montañez, María. *El correo en la España de los Austrias.* M., 1953.

Ullastres, Alberto. *Martín de Azpilcueta y su comentario resolutorio de cambios.* AdE, I (1941).

Van der Essen, Léon. *Contribution à l'histoire du port d'Anvers et du commerce d'exportation des Pays-Bas vers l'Espagne et le Portugal à l'époque de Charles Quint, 1553–1544.* "Bulletin de l'Académie Royale d'Archéologie de Belgique," 1920.

Vázquez de Prada, V. *Lettres marchandes d'Anvers.* P., undated. 4 vols.

Verlinden, Ch.; J. Craeybeckz; and E. Scholliers. *Mouvements des prix et des salaires en Belgique au XVIe siècle.* "Annales," X (1955).

Viñas Mey, Carmelo. *Felipe II y el problema económico español.* "Revista Nacional de Economía," IX (1921).

CHAPTER 28: AMERICAN COLONIAL ECONOMY FROM 1550 TO 1700

FUNDAMENTAL WORKS

Artiñano, Gervasio de. *Historia del comercio con las Indias durante el dominio de los Austrias.* B., 1917.

Borah, Woodrow. *New Spain's Century of Depression.* Berkeley, 1951.

Borah, Woodrow, and S. F. Cook. *The Aboriginal Population of Central Mexico on the Eve of the Spanish Conquest.* Berkeley and Los Angeles, 1963.

Céspedes del Castillo, Guillermo. *La avería en el comercio de Indias.* Seville, 1945.

Chevalier, François. *La formación de los grandes latifundios en México. Tierra y sociedad en los siglos XVI y XVII.* (Span. trans.)

———. "Problemas agrícolas e industriales de México." VIII (1956).

Durand, José. *La transformación social del conquistador*. Mexico, 1953. 2 vols.

Haring, Clarence H. *Trade and Navigation between Spain and the Indies in the Time of the Hapsburgs*. New York, 1917. (Span. trans.: Mexico, 1939).

—————. *The Spanish Empire in America*. New York, 1947.

Konetzke, Richard. *La esclavitud de los indios como elemento de la estructura social de Hispanoamérica*. M., 1949.

Mauro, Frédéric. *Le Portugal et l'Atlantique au XIIIe siècle (1570–1670). Étude économique*. P., 1960.

Morales Padrón, F. *El comercio canario-americano (XVI–XVIII)*. Seville, 1955.

Rosenblat, A. *La población indígena y el mestizaje en América*. Buenos Aires, 1954. 2 vols.

Rumeu de Armas, A. *Piraterías y ataques navales contra las islas Canarias*. M., 1947–1950. 5 vols.

SUPPLEMENTARY BIBLIOGRAPHY

Bagú, Sergio. *Estructura social de la colonia*. Buenos Aires, 1952.

—————. *Economía de la sociedad colonial*. Buenos Aires, 1949.

—————. *Aportación de los colonizadores españoles a la prosperidad de América (1493–1516. . .)*. M., 1929.

Belaúnde, Manual. *La encomienda en el Perú*. Lima, 1945.

Benítez, Fernando. *La vida criolla en el siglo XVI*. Mexico, 1953.

Borah, Woodrow. *Early Colonial Trade between Mexico and Peru*. Berkeley, 1954.

Burzio, Humberto F. *La ceca de la villa imperial de Potosí y la moneda colonial*. Buenos Aires, 1945.

Castro y Bravo, F. *Las naos españolas en la carrera de Indias. Armadas y flotas en la segunda mitad del siglo XVI*. M., 1927.

Chaunu, P. *Le galéon de Manile*. "Annales," VI (1951).

Chevalier, François. *Les cargaisons de flottes de la Nouvelle Espagne vers 1600*. "Revista de Indias," IV (1943).

Cobb, G. B., "Supply and Transportation for the Potosí Mines (1545–1640)" HAMR (1940).

Connell-Smith, Gordon. *Forerunners of Drake: A Study of English Trade with Spain in the Early Tudor Period*. London, 1954.

Hussey, Roland H. "Antecedents of the Spanish Monopolistic Companies (1624–1728)." *Hispanic American Historical Review,* IX 1929).

Konetzke, Richard. *La formación de la nobleza en Indias.* "Estudios Americanos" (1951).

———. *La legislación sobre inmigración de extranjeros en América durante el reinado de Carlos V.* "Charles-Quint et son temps." P., 1959.

Leonard, Irving A. *Los libros del conquistador.* Mexico, 1953.

Miranda, José. *Notas sobre la introducción de la Mesta en Nueva España.* "Revista de Historia de América" (1944).

Moreyra, M. *La técnica de la moneda colonial.* "Revista de Historia de América" (1945).

Muñoz Pérez, José. *El comercio de Indias bajo los Austrias y los tratadistas españoles del siglo XVII.* "Revista de Indias, XVII (1957).

Peraza de Ayala, José. *El régimen comercial de Canarias con las Indias en los siglos XVI, XVII, XVIII.* La Laguna, 1952.

Reglà, Juan. *Los envíos de metales preciosos de España a Italia a través de la Corona de Aragón durante los Austrias y sus relaciones con el bandolerismo pirenaico.* EHM, IV (1954).

Rumeu de Armas, A. *Los viajes de John Hawkins a América (1562–1595).* Seville, 1947.

Schaefer, E. *Comunicaciones marítimas y terrestres de las Indias españolas.* "Anuario de Estudios Americanos," III (1946).

Schurz, William. *The Manila Galleon.* New York, 1939.

Simpson, Lesley B. *The Encomienda in New Spain.* Berkeley, 1950.

Whitaker, A. P. *The Huancavélica Mercury Mines.* Harvard, 1941.

CHAPTER 29: DEMOGRAPHIC, AGRICULTURAL AND INDUSTRIAL DECLINE OF SPAIN IN THE 17TH CENTURY

FUNDAMENTAL WORKS

Bermúdez Cañete, Antonio. *La decadencia económica de España en el siglo XVI. Ensayo de una interpretación.* "Revista de Economía Política." M., 1956.

Elliott, John. *The Revolt of the Catalans.* Cambridge, 1963.

———. "The Decline of Spain." *Past and Present,* no. 20, 1961.

Giralt, Emilio. *La colonia mercantil francesa de Barcelona a mediados del siglo XVII.* EHM, VI (1956–1959).

Lapeyre, Henri. *Géographie de l'Espagne morisque.* P., 1959.

Olagüe, Ignacio. *La decadencia española. San Sebastián,* 1939. 2 vols.

Palacio Atard, Vicente. *Derrota, agotamiento, decadencia en la España del siglo XVII.* M., 1949.

Reglà, Juan. *La expulsión de los moriscos y sus consecuencias. Contribución a su estudio.* His, XIII (1953).

Sainz Rodríguez, P. *Evolución de las ideas sobre la decadencia española.* M., 1924.

SUPPLEMENTARY BIBLIOGRAPHY

Bataller Bataller, Adelina. *La expulsión de los moriscos: su repercusión en la propiedad y la población de la zona de los riegos del Vernisa.* "Saitabi." Valencia, 1960.

Bonn. *Spaniens Niedergang während der Preisrevolution des 16. Jahrhunderts.* Stuttgart, 1906.

Elliott, John. "The Catalan Revolution of 1640. Some Suggestions for a Historical Revision." EHM, IV (1954).

Fajarnés, E. *Cosecha de granos en Mallorca en 1612.* BSAL, March 1895.

———. *La población ebusitana en los siglos XVII y XVIII.* "El Archivo," July, 1892.

Girard, A. *L'Espagne à la fin du XVIIe siècle.* RSH, P., 1931.

Juderías, J. *El territorio español a fines del siglo XVII.* RABM, January–June 1912.

Momblanch y González, Francisco de P. *Le segunda germanía del reino de Valencia.* Alicante, 1957.

Schwarzmann, Maurice. *Background Factors in Spanish Economic Decline.* "Exploration in Entrepreneurial History," III (1951). Sp. trans. in "Sobre la decadencia económica de España." "De Economía," VI (1953).

Ullastres, Alberto. *Notas sobre España y su economía en el siglo XVII.* AdE, VIII (1948).

Weis, Ch. *Des causes de la décadence de l'industrie et du commerce en Espagne depuis le règne de Philippe II.* Dunkirk, 1898.

CHAPTER 30: COMMERCIAL STAGNATION, TAX PRESSURE AND CURRENCY INFLATION IN THE 17TH CENTURY

FUNDAMENTAL WORKS

Capella, Miguel, and Antonio Matilla. *Los Cinco Gremios Mayores de Madrid. Estudio crítico-histórico.* M., 1957.

Domínguez Ortiz, Antonio. *Política y hacienda de Felipe IV.* M., 1960.

———. *Orto y ocaso de Sevilla.* Seville, 1946.

Grice-Hutchinson, Marjorie. *The School of Salamanca. Readings in Spanish Monetary Theory, 1544–1605.* Oxford, 1952.

Hamilton, E. J. *War and Prices in Spain, 1651–1800.* Cambridge, Mass. 1947.

Spooner, C. Frank. *L'économie mondiale et les frappes monétaires en France, 1493–1680.* P., 1956.

SUPPLEMENTARY BIBLIOGRAPHY

Bonnel de Ganges, E. *Los impuestos y la hacienda en España desde Felipe III a Carlos II.* EM, XCVIII (1897).

Bonnassié, Pierre. *Contrats d'affrètement et commerce maritime à Barcelone au XVIIe siècle.* "Revue d'Histoire Economique et Sociale," XXXV (1957).

Colmeiro y Penido, M. *Discurso sobre los políticos y arbitristas de los siglos XVI y XVII y su influencia en la gobernación del Estado.* M., 1857.

Coniglio, Giuseppe. *Il viceregno di Napoli nel secolo XVII. Notizie sulla vita commerciale e finanziaria secondo nuove ricerche negli archivi italiani e spagnoli.* Rome, 1955.

———. *El comercio de las especias en el segundo decenio del siglo XVII a través de documentos de Simancas y Livorno.* "Moneda y Crédito," 1957.

Domínguez Ortiz, A. *La desigualdad contributiva en Castilla durante el siglo XVII.* AHDEsp, XXI–XXII (1951–1952).

Espejo, C. *Las últimas ferias de Medina del Campo.* Valladolid, 1908.

Fontana Lázaro, José. *Sobre el comercio exterior de Barcelona en la segunda mitad del siglo XVII. Notas para una interpretación de la coyuntura catalana.* EHM, V (1955–1957).

Kellenbenz, Hermann. *Autour de 1600: le commerce du poivre des Fugger et le marché internacional du poivre.* "Annales," XI (1956).

———. *Oberdeutsche Portugal- und Spanienhandler in Hamburg um 1600.* "Städtewesen und Bürgertum als geschichtiche Kräfte." Lübeck, 1953.

———. *Spanien, die nördlichen Niederlande und der skandinavisch-baltische Raum in der Weltwirtschaft und Politik um 1600.* "Vierteljahrschift für Sozial- und Wirtschaftsgeschichte," XLI (1954).

Legrand, T. *El comercio de Bretaña con España a fines del siglo XVII.* RAMB, XXI.

Mathiez, J. *Trafic et prix de l'homme en Méditerranée.* "Revista de Historia," XVIII (1952).

Schaefer, Enst. *Apuntes sobre las dificultades financieras de España durante el reinado de Don Felipe IV, según los documentos del Consejo de Indias.* TyP, IX (1935).

CHAPTER 31: STUDY OF THE TRADE CYCLE
UNDER THE HAPSBURGS

BIBLIOGRAPHY

Chaunu, Huguette and Pierre. *À la recherche des fluctuations cycliques dans l'économie des XVe et XVIIe siècles. Crise de tonnage. Crise de fret.* "Eventail de l'Histoire vivante," II. P., 1953.

Hamilton, E. J. "Monetary Inflation in Castile, 1598–1600." *Journal of Economic and Business History,* II (1931).

Nef, John U. *La naissance de la civilisation industrielle et le monde contemporain.* P., 1954.

Salyer, John C. *La política económica de España en la época del mercantilismo.* AdE, VIII (1948).

Ugorri, Fernando. *Ideas sobre el gobierno económico de España en el siglo XVII. La crisis de 1627, la moneda de vellón y el intento de fundación de un banco nacional.* "Revista de la Biblioteca, Archivos y Museos del Ayuntamiento de Madrid," XIX (1950).

Van Klaveren, Jacob. *Europäische Wirtchaftsgeschichte Spaniens im 16. und 17. Jahrhundert.* Stuttgart, 1960 (with important additions by R. Konetzke. "Moneda y Crédito," 1961).

Vilar, Pierre. *Le temps du "Quichotte."* "Europe," XXXIV (1956).

CHAPTER 32: BOURBON REFORM POLICIES

FUNDAMENTAL WORKS

Carande, Ramón. *El Despotismo Ilustrado de los "Amigos del País."* (In "Curso de conferencias sobre cuestiones históricas y actuales de la economía española.") Bilbao, 1957.

Desdevises du Dézert, G. *L'Espagne de l'Ancien Régime (La société. Les institutions. La richesse et la civilisation).* P., 1897–1904. 3 vols.

Herr, Richard. *The Eighteenth-Century Revolution in Spain.* Princeton, 1958.

Menéndez Pelayo, M. *Historia de los heterodoxos españoles.* M., 1880–1881. 3 vols.

Palacio Atard, Vicente. *El Despotismo Ilustrado español.* "Arbor" (1947).

BIBLIOGRAPHY

Reglà, J., and S. Alcolea. *El siglo XVIII.* "Historia de la Cultura Española." B., 1957.
Sarrailh, Jean. *L'Espagne éclairée de la seconde moitié du XVIIIe siècle.* P., 1954.
Sánchez Agesta, Luis. *El pensamiento político del Despotismo Ilustrado.* M., 1953.
Shafer, R. J. *The Economic Societies in the Spanish World (1763–1821).* Syracuse, 1958.
Smith, Robert S. *Economists and the Enlightenment in Spain, 1750–1800.* Chicago, 1955.
Vilar, Pierre. *La Catalogne dans l'Espagne moderne. Recherches sur les fondements économiques des structures nationales.* P., 1962. 3 vols.

SUPPLEMENTARY BIBLIOGRAPHY

Alcázar, Cayetano. *Los hombres del Despotismo Ilustrado en España. El conde de Floridablanca, su vida y su obra.* Murcia, 1934.
———. *Los hombres del reinado de Carlos III. Don Pablo de Olavide, el colonizador de Sierra Morena.* M., 1927.
Aralar, José de. *El conde de Peñaflorida y los Caballeritos de Azcoitia.* Buenos Aires, 1942.
Bejarano, Francisco. *Historia del Consulado y de la Junta de Comercio de Málaga (1785–1859).* M., 1949.
Bonnet, B. *Los amigos del País en Canarias.* Tenerife, 1941.
Carrera Pujal, J. *La Escuela de Nobles Artes de Barcelona (1775–1901).* B., 1957.
———. *La Barcelona del segle XVIII.* B., 1951. 2 vols.
Casanovas, Ignasi. *Finestres.* B., 1932. (Sp. trans. *La Cultura Catalana en el siglo XVIII.* B., 1953.)
Cobos Cárdenas, Eduardo. *Joseph Galiel de Mora. Una nota para el estudio de las ideas sobre política industrial en el siglo XVIII.* AdE, January–March 1947.
Corona Baratech, Carlos. *Revolución y reacción en el reinado de Carlos IV.* M., 1949.
Delpy, G. *L'Espagne et l'esprit européen: l'oeuvre de Feijoo.* P., 1936.
Galí, A. *Rafael d'Amat, Baró de Maldà.* B., 1951.
Gómez Molleda, M.ª. *El pensamiento de Carvajal.* His (1955).
Labra, Rafael María de. *Las Sociedades Económicas de Amigos del País.* M., 1904.
Lesen Moreno, José. *Historia de la Sociedad Económica de Amigos del País de Madrid.* M., 1863.

Monbeig, Pierre. *La Real Sociedad Económica de los Amigos del País. Une source de l'histoire économique de Majorque au XVIIIe siècle.* AM., April 1953.

Peñalver, Patricio. *Modernidad tradicional en el pensamiento de Jovellanos.* Seville, 1953.

Pérez Bustamante, C., *El reinado de Fernando VI en el reformismo español del siglo XVIII.* RUMadr, III (1945).

Rodríguez Casado, Vicente. *Política interior de Carlos III.* "Simancas," I (1951).

Ruiz y Pablo, A. *Historia de la Real Junta Particular de Comercio de Barcelona (1758–1847).* B., 1919.

Smith, Robert S. *The "Wealth of Nations" in Spain and Hispanic America, 1780–1830.* Chicago, 1957.

Soldevila, F. *Barcelona sense Universitat i la Universitat de Barcelona a Cervera.* B., 1938.

Soraluce, Nicolás. *Historia compendiada de la Real Sociedad Vascongada de Amigos del País.* San Sebastián, 1880.

CHAPTER 33: POPULATION AND LABOR

FUNDAMENTAL WORKS

Caro Baroja, Julio. *Las "nuevas poblaciones" de Sierra Morena y Andalucía. Un experimento sociológico en tiempos de Carlos III.* "Clavileño," III (1952).

Domínguez Ortiz, Antonio. *La sociedad española en el siglo XVIII.* M., 1955.

Meijide Pardo, Antonio. *La emigración gallega intrapeninsular en el siglo XVIII.* "Instituto Balmes de Sociología," M., 1960.

Vicens Vives, J. *Coyuntura económica y reformismo burgués.* EHM, IV (1954).

Vilar, Pierre. *La formation de la bourgeoisíe catalane au XVIIIe siècle.* "X Congresso de Scienze Storiche," Vol. VII. Florence, 1955.

SUPPLEMENTARY BIBLIOGRAPHY

Alcázar Molina, C. *Las colonias alemanas de Sierra Morena.* M., 1930.

Amorós, León, O.F.M. *Estadística de los conventos y religiosos de las provincias franciscanas de España en el año 1768.* AIA, XVI (1956).

Castro, A. de. *Colonia de orientales en Cádiz en los siglos XVII y XVIII.* BAH, XI (1887).

Domínguez Ortiz, Antonio. *El ocaso del régimen señorial en la España del siglo XVIII*. RIS, X (1952).

Fajarnés Tur, E. *Demografía dinámica de Baleares*. Palma, 1901.

———. *Desarrollo de la población ebusitana en los tres últimos siglos*. Palma, 1928.

Fuentes, Francisco. *Estadística de Tudela en el año 1797*. PdV, XIV (1953).

García Ormaechea. *Supervivencias feudales en España*. M., 1932.

Giralt, E., and J. Nadal. *Barcelona en 1717–1718. Un modelo de sociedad pre-industrial*. "Homenaje a don Ramón Carande," Vol. II. M., 1963.

Goméz Pizarro, J.G. *El absentismo en España*. M., 1886.

Guerra y Peña, L.A. de la. *Memorias (Tenerife en la segunda mitad del siglo XVIII)*. M., 1951.

Herrera Oria, E. *La Real fábrica de tejidos de Avila*. Valladolid, 1922 (with information on labor unrest).

Jiménez de Gregorio, Fernando. *Incidencias en algunos gremios y cofradías de Murcia a finales del siglo XVIII*. Murcia, 1951.

Kaltofen, R. A. *Por trescientos reales (Florecimiento y desaparición de una colonia alemana de campesinos a fines del siglo XVIII)*. M., 1944.

Kany, Charles E. *Life and Manners in Madrid. 1750–1800*. Berkeley, 1932.

Lasso de la Vega, M. *La nobleza española en el siglo XVIII*. RABM, LX (1954).

Martínez Guitián, Luis. *La villa y la ciudad de Santander en el siglo XVIII*. M., 1950.

Matilla Tascón, Antonio. *El primer catastro de la Villa de Madrid*. RABM. M., 1961.

Nadal, Jorge. *Demografía y economía en los orígenes de la Cataluña moderna. Un ejemplo local: Palamós*.

Palacio Atard, Vicente. *Fin de la sociedad española del Antiguo Régimen*. M., 1952.

Quirós, Bernardo de. *Los reyes y la colonización de España desde el siglo XVI al XIX*. M., 1929.

Sánchez Agesta, Luis. *La apología de los gremios de Capmany*. "Archivo de Derecho Público," 1949.

San Román, Francisco de B. de. *El libro de las ordenanzas del Arte Mayor de la Seda*. "Revista de Toledo," January 1925.

Weiss, Joseph. *Die deutsche Kolonie an der Sierra Morena*. Cologne, 1907.

BIBLIOGRAPHY

Chapter 34: Agriculture and Livestock Production

FUNDAMENTAL WORKS

Anes, Gonzalo. *El informe sobre la Ley Agraria y la Real Sociedad matritense de Amigos del País.* "Homenaje a don Ramón Carande," Vol. I. M., 1963.

Carande, Ramón. *Informe de Olavide sobre la Ley Agraria.* BAA. CXXXIX (1956).

Defourneaux, Marcelin. *Le problème de la terre en Andalousie au XVIIIe siècle et les projets de réforme agraire.* RH (1957) CCXVII.

Helman, Edith F. *Some Consequences of the Publication of the "Informe de Ley Agraria" por Jovellanos.* "Estudios hispánicos." (Wellesley, Mass.) 1952: "Homenaje a Archer M. Huntington."

Leonhard, Rudolf. *Agrarpolitik und Agrarreform in Spanien unter Carl III.* Munich, 1909.

Vilar, Pierre. "Agricultural Progress and the Economic Background in Eighteenth-Century Catalonia." *The Economic History Review.* IX (1958).

SUPPLEMENTARY BIBLIOGRAPHY

Barceló Pons, Bartolomé. *Evolución de la estructura agraria del término de Ocaña.*

Cabo Alonso, Angel. *El colectivismo agrario en Tierra de Sayago.* EG, XVII (1956).

Huetz de Lemps, A. *Le vignoble de la "Tierra de Medina" au XVIIe et XVIIIe siècles.* "Annales." P., 1957.

Giménez Soler, A.; M. Gutiérrez del Arroyo; and A. Lasierra Purroy. *El Canal Imperial de Aragón.* (Undated.)

Giralt Raventós, E. *La viticultura y el comercio catalán del siglo XVIII.* EHM, II (1952).

Llobet, Salvador. *De geografía agraria de la comarca del Maresme (Barcelona).* EG, XVI (1955).

Monbeig, M. P. *Vie de relations et spécialisation agricole: les Baléares au XVIIIe siècle.* "Annales d'histoire économique et sociale." 1932.

Chapter 35: Industrial Revival

BIBLIOGRAPHY

Camos Cabruja, Luis, and José Viñes. *Destacado impulsor de la técnica de los tintes en el siglo XVIII.* Barcelona. Divulgación Histórica. VIII. (1951), 172–176.

Canellas López, Ángel. *La Real Compañía de Comercio y Fábricas de Zaragoza: Historia de su primer trienio.* Zaragoza, III (1952 [1954]) "J. Zurita."

Casariego, J. E. *El marqués de Sargadelos y los comienzos del industrialismo capitalista en España.* Oviedo, 1950.

Gálvez Cañero. *Fausto de Eluyar.* "Boletín del Instituto Geológico y minero de España." LIII, 1933.

Imbert, Erasmo de. *Erasmo de Gónima. 1746–1821. Apuntes para una biografía y estudio de su época.* B., 1952.

Lanza, F. *Apuntes sobre una fábrica de lienzos fundada en Ribadeo por Carlos III.* BRA Gallega, 1927–1928.

Rivera Manescau. *La Real Fábrica de tejidos de algodón estampados de Ávila y la reorganización nacional de esta industria en el siglo XVIII.* Valladolid, 1922.

CHAPTER 36: THE AMERICAN ECONOMY

FUNDAMENTAL WORKS

Céspedes del Castillo, Guillermo. *Lima y Buenos Aires. Repercusiones económicas y políticas de la creación del virreinato del Plata.* "Anuario de Estudios Americanos," III (1946).

Konetzke, R. *Die Politik des Grafen Aranda.* Berlin, 1929.

Lanning, J. T. *Academic Culture in the Spanish Colonies.* New York, 1940.

Levene, Ricardo. *Investigaciones acerca de la historia económica del Virreinato del Plata.* 2nd edn. Buenos Aires, 1952. 2 vols.

Lynch, John. *Spanish Colonial Administration. 1782–1810. The Intendant System in the Viceroyalty of the Río de la Plata.* L., 1958.

Moreyra, M. *El tribunal del Consulado de Lima.* Lima, 1956.

Motten, G. C. *Mexican Silver and the Enlightenment.* Philadelphia, 1950.

Tannenbaum, F. *Slave and Citizen. The Negro in the Americas.* New York, 1957.

Vidart, Daniel V. *La vida rural uruguaya.* Montevideo, 1955.

Vieillard-Baron, A. *L'établissement des intendants aux Indes par Charles III.* "Revista de Indias" (1952).

Whitaker, A. P. *La historia intelectual de Hispanoamérica en el siglo XVIII (1955).* "Revista de Historia de América" (1955).

SUPPLEMENTARY BIBLIOGRAPHY

Arcilla Farias, E. *El siglo ilustrado en América. Reformas económicas del siglo XVIII en Nueva España.* Caracas, 1955.

Chávez, L. *Documentos para la historia económica de México.* Mexico, since 1933. 9 vols.

Christelow, A. "Great Britain and the Trade from Cadiz and Lisbon to Spanish America and Brazil (1759–1783)." *American Hispanic Historical Review* (1947).

Helmer, M. *Commerce et industrie au Pérou à la fin du XVIIIe siècle.* "Revista de Indias" (1950).

Hernández Sánchez-Barba, M. *La población hispanoamericana y su distribución social en el siglo XVIII.* "Revista de Estudios Políticos" (1954).

Howe, W. *The Mining Guild of New Spain (1770–1821).* Cambridge, 1949.

Konezke, Richard. *El mestizaje y su importancia en el desarrollo de la población hispanoamericana durante la época colonial.* "Revista de Indias" (1946).

Pantaleão, Olga. *A penetração comercial de Inglaterra na America española de 1713 a 1783.* São Paolo, 1946.

Pares, R. *War Trade in the West Indies, 1739–1763.* Oxford, 1936.

Viñas Mey, Carmelo. *La sociedad americana y el acceso a la propiedad rural.* RIS (1943).

CHAPTER 37: COMMERCIAL DEVELOPMENT

BIBLIOGRAPHY

Brown, Vera L. *Anglo-French Rivalry for the Trade of the Spanish Peninsula.* "Studies in the History of Spain in the Second Half of the Eighteenth Century"; Smith College Studies in History, XV (1929–1930).

Cotrina, J. *Sobre la industria y comercio menorquines en el último período del siglo XVIII.* R. Men, April 1929.

Enciso, Luis M. *Nipho y el periodismo español del siglo XVIII.* Valladolid, 1956.

———. *Prensa económica española del siglo XVIII: El Correo Mercantil de España y sus Indias.* Valladolid, 1958.

Fernández Guillén Tato, Julio. *Índice de los papeles de la sección de corsos y presas 1784–1838.* M., 1953.

Lefèvre, J. *Étude sur le commerce de la Belgique avec l'Espagne au XVIIIe siècle.* Brussels, 1921.

Peuchet. *État des colonies et du commerce des Européens dans les deux Indes depuis 1773 jusqu'à 1821.* P., 1821.

Saltillo, Marqués de. *Un comerciante bilbaíno del siglo XVIII: el marqués de la Colonilla.* M., 1932.

See, Enrique. *Esbozo de la historia del comercio francés en Cádiz y en la América española en el siglo XVIII.* BIIH, VI (1927).

———. *Notas sobre el comercio francés en Cádiz y particularmente el comercio de las telas bretonas en el siglo XVIII.* AHDEsp, II (1925).

———. *Algunos documentos sobre las relaciones comerciales entre Francia y España en el siglo XVIII.* AHDEsp, V (1928).

———. *Bosquejo de las relaciones comerciales de Holanda con España y Portugal a fines del siglo XVIII.* AHDEsp, II (1925).

Vilar, Pierre. *Le "Manual de la Companya Nova" de Gibraltar (1709–1723).* P., 1962.

CHAPTER 38: ECONOMIC POLICY

FUNDAMENTAL WORKS

Bosher, W. *The Spanish Colonial System.* Cambridge, 1944.

Castedo, J. A. *Referencias históricas y comentarios sobre la economía arancelaria española.* (Particularly in the 18th and 19th centuries). M., 1958.

Defourneaux, Marcelin. *Pablo de Olavide ou l' "Afrancesado" ' (1725–1803).* P., 1959.

Rahola Trèmols, Federico. *Comercio de Cataluña con América en el siglo XVIII.* V., 1931.

Sureda, José L. *La política económica española del siglo XVIII.* AdE, VI (1946).

SUPPLEMENTARY BIBLIOGRAPHY

Basterra, Ramón de. *Una empresa en el siglo XVIII. Los navíos de la Ilustración. Gran Compañia Guipuzcoana de Caracas y su influencia en los destinos de América.* Caracas, 1925.

Hamilton, E. J. *The Mercantilism of Gerónimo de Uztáriz.* "Economics, Sociology and the Modern World" (1935).

Hussey, R. D. *The Caracas Company, 1728–1784.* Cambridge, 1934.

Mounier, André. *Les faits et la doctrine économique en Espagne sous Phillippe V. Jerónimo de Uztáriz (1670–1732).* Bordeaux, 1919.

Muñoz Pérez, José. *Mapa aduanero español.* EG, XVI (1955), 747.

Peraza de Ayala, José. *La Junta de Comercio de Canarias.* "Anuario de Estudios Atlánticos." Madrid-Las Palmas, 1959.

CHAPTER 39: MONEY AND FINANCE

BIBLIOGRAPHY

Hamilton, E. J. "Money and Economic Recovery in Spain under the First Bourbon, 1701–1746." *Journal of Modern History,* XV (1943), 192.

————. "The First Twenty Years of the Bank of Spain." *Journal of Political Economy,* LIV (1946), 17, 116.

————. "The Foundation of the Bank of Spain." *Journal of Political Economy,* 1945.

Matilla Tascón, A. *La única contribución y el Catastro de Ensenada* M., 1947.

————. *Catálogo de la colección de Órdenes generales de rentas.* (*Aportaciones para la historia de los tributos y del comercio españoles.*) T. I. M., 1950.

CHAPTER 40: SURVEY OF ECONOMIC FLUCTUATIONS IN THE 18TH CENTURY

BIBLIOGRAPHY

Hamilton, E. J. *War and Prices in Spain (1651–1800).* Cambridge, Mass., 1947.

Vilar, Pierre. *Dans Barcelone au XVIIIe siècle.* In "Estudios históricos y documentos de los archivos de Protocolos" (Barcelona), II (1950).

CHAPTER 41: 19TH CENTURY SPIRIT OF REFORM

BIBLIOGRAPHY

There are numerous works dealing with Spanish policies during the nineteenth century, from a political as well as a cultural and ideological point of view. Here we shall list only those which include the economic factor in historical development or those which serve as works of reference.

Brenan, G. *The Spanish Labyrinth: An Account of the Social and Political Background of the Civil War.* 2nd edn. Cambridge, 1950.

Bruguera, F. G. *Histoire contemporaine d'Espagne. 1789–1950.* P., 1954.

Carrera Pujal, Jaime. *La economía de Cataluña en el siglo XIX.* B., 1961. 4 vols.

Larraz López, José. (*Fases principales de la expansión de la economía española en el siglo XIX*), en F. de Lequerica. "La actividad económica de Vizcaya en la economía nacional." M., 1956.

Macías Picavea, R. *El problema nacional. Hechos, causas, remedios.* M., 1899.

Madariaga, Salvador de. *España.* 4th edn. Buenos Aires, 1944.

Miguel, Antonio de. *El potencial económico de España.* M., 1935.

Robert, Antonio. *Perspectivas de la economía española.* M., 1954.

Vicens Vives, Jaime, and Montserrat Llorens. *Industrials i polítics.* B., 1958.

Sánchez Agesta, L. *Historia del constitucionalismo español.* M., 1955.

Zabala Lera, P. *Historia de España. Edad Contemporánea.* B., 1930. 2 vols.

CHAPTER 42: POPULATION AND PROPERTY

FUNDAMENTAL WORKS

Caballero, Fermín. *Fomento de la población rural.* M., 1863.

Carrión, Pascual. *Los latifundios en España.* M., 1932.

Viñas Mey, Carmelo. *La reforma agraria en España en el siglo XIX.* Santiago, 1933.

SUPPLEMENTARY BIBLIOGRAPHY

Alzina Caules, Jaime. *Investigación analítica sobre el movimiento de población en Cataluña.* "Cuadernos de Información Económica y Sociológica." 1954–1956.

Azcárate, Gumersindo de. *Los latifundios.* M., 1905.

Aznar, Severino. *Despoblación y colonización.* M., 1929.

Camps y Arboix, J. *La propiedad de la tierra y su función social.* B., 1953.

Carcano, M. A. *Evolución histórica del régimen de la tierra pública, 1810–1916.* M., 1925.

Fernández, Felipe. *El más antiguo mapa de población de la Península Ibérica.* EG, XVII (1956), 704.

Fontana Lázaro, José. *La gran propiedad agraria de los conventos españoles a comienzos del siglo XIX.* "Première Conférence Internationale d'Histoire Économique," Paris–The Hague, 1960.

Fuentes Martiánez, Mariano. *Despoblación y repoblación de España (1842–1920).* M., 1929.

Hoyos Sainz, Luis de. *La densidad de población y su acrecentamiento en España.* M., 1933

Molina, Blas. *Bienes nacionales. Manual de compradores.* M., 1841.

Rodríguez Revilla. *El agro español y sus moradores. Política agraria.* M., 1931.

CHAPTER 43: AGRICULTURAL AND LIVESTOCK PRODUCTION

FUNDAMENTAL WORKS

Millet, Salvador. *Història de l'agricultura espanyola durante els segles XIX i XX.* (Unpublished. Ms awarded a prize by the "Institut d'Estudis Catalans.")

SUPPLEMENTARY BIBLIOGRAPHY

Aguilar, A. *Los riegos en España.* RIb, 20 October 1917.

Alburquerque, J. *La producción frutera de España.* B., 1914.

Aymard. *L'irrigation du Midi de l'Espagne.* P., 1862.

Camps, Marqués de. *La production forestière en Espagne.* B., 1914.

Carralero y Burgo, José. *Historia de las ganaderías bravas de ambas Castillas. Apuntes históricos y críticos.* B., 1907.

Codorníu, Ricardo. *Apuntes relativos a la repoblación forestal de la sierra de España, presentados al Congreso agrícola de Murcia.* Murcia, 1900.

Crespo y León, V. *El olivo en la cuenca del Ebro.* M., 1909.

Espejo, C. *Cultivo del olivo.* M., 1898.

Estelrich, P. *El almendro y su cultivo en España e islas Baleares.* M., 1907.

———. *La higuera y su cultivo en España.* Palma–., 1909.

Fribourg, A. *La transhumance en Espagne.* "Annales de la Géographie," XIX (1910).

Frontera, Marqués de la. *Estudios sobre la ganadería española.* Zaragoza, 1909.

Llauradó, A. *Tratado de aguas y riegos.* M., 1878.

Mallada, L. *Causas de la pobreza de nuestro suelo.* "Boletín de la Sociedad Geográfica de Madrid," XII (1882).

Manjarrés, R. de. *El cultivo del algodón en España.* Seville, 1919.

Mediavilla Sánchez, José. *Las aguas de la región murciana en relación con los antecedentes históricos del abastecimiento de la ciudad y campos de Cartagena, Base Naval y Puerto y otros aprovechamientos de los mismos.* Cartagena, 1927.

Monbeig, Pedro. *Les transformations économiques dans "las huertas" et la région entre Alicante et Murcie.* P., 1930.

Parrada y Borreto, Diego. *Noticias sobre la historia y estado actual del cultivo de la vid y del comercio vinatero de Jerez de la Frontera.* Jerez, 1868.

Quintanilla, G. *Cultivo cereal en Castilla la Nueva.* M., 1918.

Romaña, Barón de. *Riegos del Alto Aragón. Los recursos hidráulicos y la zona regable.* B., 1914.

Senador Gómez, Julio. *Castilla en Escombros. Las leyes. Las tierras, el trigo y el hambre.* Valladolid, 1915.

Suárez, S. *El cultivo de la caña dulce en España.* "Boletín de la Sociedad Geográfica" 4, XLV.

Toca, Marqués de. *La viticultura española.* M., 1900.

Valencia, Pedro de. *Discurso sobre el acrecentamiento de la labor de la tierra.* M., 1818–1819.

CHAPTER 44: INDUSTRY

FUNDAMENTAL WORKS

Graell, Guillermo. *Historia del Fomento del Trabajo Nacional.* B., 1911.

Lequerica, José Félix de. *La actividad económica de Vizcaya en la vida nacional.* M., 1956.

Medir Jofra, R. *Historia del gremio corchero.* M., 1953.

Sánchez Ramos. *La economía siderúrgica española.* M., 1945.

SUPPLEMENTARY BIBLIOGRAPHY

Beltrán Flórez, Lucas. *La industria algodonera española.* B., 1943.

Castañeda y Alcover, Vicente. *La industria abaniquera en Valencia.* BAH, April–June 1933.

Castillo, Alberto del. *La Maquinista Terrestre y Marítima, personaje histórico (1885–1955).* B., 1955.

Collado y Ardanuy, Benito del. *Apuntes para la historia contemporánea de la minería española en los años de 1825 a 1849.* M., 1865.

Cornet y Mas, J. M. *Influencia de la metalurgia en la prosperidad y po-*

derío de las naciones. (Acceptance speech at the Royal Academy of Science and Art. B., 1904.)

Escarrá, Edouard. *Le développement industriel de la Catalogne.* P., 1908.

Fontana i Lázaro, Josep. *Aribau i la indústria cotonera a Catalunya.* B., 1963.

Fontana y Tarrats, J. M. *La lucha por la industrialización de España.* M., 1953.

González, Tomás. *Registro y relación general de las minas de la corona de Castilla.* M., 1832. 2 vols.

Labra, Rafael M. de. *El Instituto de Agricultura, Industria y Comercio y las Sociedades Económicas de Amigos del País.* 1905.

Malo de Molina, Manuel. *Manual del minero español.* M., 1863.

Moral y Martínez, F. *La evolución de la industria en España.* In "Breve historia de la ingeniería en España." M., 1950.

Melgares, Ramón. *Memoria acerca del estado de la industria sericícola en España.* M., 1883.

Novo P. de Ortega, M. *La minería española.* In "Breve historia de la minería española." M., 1950.

Sanz Escartín, E.; Rafael Salillas; and Julio Puyol. *Informe referente a las minas de Vizcaya.* M., 1904.

Vilá Valentí, Juan. *El origen de la industria catalana moderna.* "Estudios geográficos." M., 1960.

CHAPTER 45: TRANSPORT AND TRADE

BIBLIOGRAPHY

Arrillaga, Manuel María. *Los iniciadores y promotores de los caminos de hierro en España (1830–1853). Datos recopilados.* M., 1930.

Barreda, F. *Viajes de navíos santanderinos a Filipinas en el siglo XIX.* Santander, 1933.

———. *La flota comercial santanderina desde 1800 a 1870.* Santander, 1932.

Becker, Jerónimo. *Relaciones comerciales entre España y Francia durante el siglo XIX.* M., 1910.

Cossío, Francisco de. *Cien años de vida sobre el mar. La Compañía. Transatlántica (1850–1950).* M., 1950.

Hillman, Adolphe. *Notes sur l'échange commercial entre l'Espagne et la Suède, 1875–1894.* Söderhamm, 1896

Marvaud, A. *Douze ans de relations économiques avec l'Espagne (1892–1904).* "Annales de Sciences politiques," May 1906.

Plaza Prieto, Juan. *El desarrollo del comercio exterior español desde principios del siglo XIX a la actualidad.* "Revista de Economía Política." M., VI (1955), 25–26.

Rué Dalmau, A. *El puerto de Barcelona.* B., 1931.

Wais, Francisco. *Origen y desarrollo de los ferrocarriles aragoneses.* "Zaragoza" (1956).

CHAPTER 46: ECONOMIC POLICY

BIBLIOGRAPHY

Castedo, J. A. *Referencias históricas y comentarios sobre la economía arancelaria española.* M., 1958.

Pugés, M. *Cómo triunfó el proteccionismo en España.* B., 1931.

Tallada, José M.ª. *La política comercial y arancelaria española en el siglo XIX.* AdE, III (1943).

Vicens Vives, J., and M. Llorens. *Industrials i Polítics (segle XIX).* B., 1958. (Spanish trans.: *Cataluña en el siglo XIX,* M., 1961).

CHAPTER 47: MONEY CREDIT, AND BANKING

FUNDAMENTAL WORKS

Pérez-Agote y Poveda, José María. *Orígenes del capitalismo en Vizcaya.* "Boletín de Estudios Económicos" (Deusto), XIII (1953), 23–48.

Sardá, Juan. *La política monetaria y las fluctuaciones de la economía española en el siglo XIX.* M., 1948.

Tallada, José M.ª. *Historia de las finanzas españolas del siglo XIX.* M., 1946.

SUPPLEMENTARY BIBLIOGRAPHY

El sistema monetario de España desde 1868. BAH, November 1921.

Ballesteros, Pío. *Medio siglo de Hacienda española.* AdE, VIII (1948).

Bernis, Francisco. *La Hacienda española.* B., 1916.

Canosa, Ramón. *Un siglo de banca privada (1845–1945).* M., 1945.

Galvarriato, J. A. *El Banco de España. Su historia en la centuria 1829–1929.* M., 1932.

Tallada, Josep M.ª. *Economia monetària espanyola.* B., 1930. (Spanish trans.: *El problema monetario español en el siglo XIX.* "Moneda y Crédito," no. 58, 1956).

BIBLIOGRAPHY

CHAPTER 48: SURVEY OF THE 19TH CENTURY BUSINESS CYCLE

FUNDAMENTAL WORKS

Sardá, J. *La política monetaria y las fluctuaciones de la economía española en el siglo XIX*. M., 1948.

SUPPLEMENTARY WORKS

Alfaya, M. Concepción. *Datos para la historia económica y social de España. Abastos y tasas (1800 a 1820)*. "Revista de Biblioteca, Archivo y Museo" (M.), III (1926).

Tallada, José M.ª. *Barcelona económica y financiera en el siglo XIX*. B., 1944.

Index of Names and Places

Aachen, 568
Abadal, Ramón de, 140, 141, 144
Abbas-ibn-Firnas, 114
Abbassids, 102
Abbeville, 273, 528
Abdera, 48, 51
Abderrahman I, 102, 103
Abderrahman II, 103, 121
Abderrahman III, 103, 113, 117, 118
Aben Alawanz, 109
Abraham de Barchilón, 284
Acapulco, 398, 400, 406, 408, 547, 551
Acre, 202, 213
Adaro, 660, 712
Adra, 739
Aelius Optatus (family), 64
Ágreda, Sister María de, 419
Aguado (banker), 720, 737
Aguirre, 568, 592
Agullana, 533
Akra Leuké, 50
Alagon (river), 18
Alalia, battle of, 49, 53
Álamos y Barrientos, Baltasar de, 451
Al-Andalus, 5, 102, 103, 104, 105, 106, 108, 110, 111, 112 113, 115, 116, 118, 121, 126, 139, 161, 163
Alar del Rey, 673, 674, 685
Alaric, 86
Álava, 492
Alavide, 473
Alba, counts of, 247, 277
Alba, dukes of, 363, 478, 493
Albacete, 15, 506, 637, 640
Albarracín, 517

Alberca, La, 413
Alberoni, Cardinal, 527
Albi, 178
Albolote, 515
Alburquerque, 246
Alburquerque, Leonor de, 246
Alcalá, Decree of, 275
Alcalá, dukedom of, 493
Alcalá de los Gazules, 165
Alcántara, military order of, 161, 165, 249, 295
Alcaraz, 276
Alcarria, 161, 247, 295, 528
Alcaudete, 165
Alcázar de Arriaza, 454
Alcira, 180, 515
Alcobé, Santiago, 21
Alcoy, 672
Aleppo, 292
Alexander Severus, 75
Alexandria, 77, 148, 178, 207, 212, 268, 292, 301, 363
Alfaques, Los, 365, 578
Alfonso I of Asturias, 123, 127, 146
Alfonso II ("the Chaste") of Asturias, 134, 152
Alfonso III, 123, 127
Alfonso V ("the Magnanimous") of Aragon, 182, 185, 186, 205, 217, 233, 238, 239, 287, 312
Alfonso VI, 123, 161, 162, 278, 279
Alfonso VIII, 150, 264, 278
Alfonso X ("the Wise") of Castile, 11, 131, 160, 245, 252, 253, 256, 261, 263, 275, 276, 278, 279, 280, 284, 285, 286, 288, 335, 348
Alfonso XI, 200, 243, 275, 279, 287

Alfonso XII, 655, 662, 710
Algarve, 13, 45, 157
Algeciras, 569
Algeria, 623, 723
Alghero, 204
Alhakcm I, 121
Alhakem II, 109
Alicante, 48, 50, 51, 52, 197, 357, 358, 360, 366, 487, 506, 554, 560, 569, 578, 623, 642, 650, 684, 685, 728
Aljustrel, 68
Almadén, 9, 68, 112, 114, 253, 262, 323, 529
Almansa, 685
Almansur, 103, 123, 139
Almería, 13, 14, 22, 43, 45, 47, 106, 113, 115, 116, 157, 185, 231, 282, 480, 522, 578, 623, 642, 661
Almodóvar del Río, Duke of, 709
Almuñécar, 480
Alonis, 50
Álora, 296
Alpujarras, revolt of, 334
Altamira, 22
Álvarez de Toledo (family), 246, 247, 295
Amadeus I of Savoy, 614
Amador de los Ríos, José, 243, 248
Amaya, 127, 128
Amelot, 598
Amiens, Peace of, 580, 604, 679
Ampolla, La, 365
Amposta, 515
Ampuero, 530
Ampurdán, 48, 144, 179, 365
Ampurias, 49, 52, 58, 65, 77, 147, 365; countship of, 493
Amsterdam, 422, 596
Anatolia, 206
Andalusia, 18, 22, 23, 26, 28, 39, 43, 44, 47, 51, 53, 56, 64, 86, 102, 103, 112, 114, 157, 158, 160, 162, 163, 165, 166, 199, 200, 210, 241, 242, 245, 246, 247, 250, 253, 260, 263, 269, 276, 281, 283, 286, 292,

295, 296, 297, 303, 312, 335, 345, 358, 359, 360, 413, 416, 420, 464, 485, 486, 490, 512, 513, 520, 534, 539, 555, 562, 570, 571, 589, 619, 620, 629, 636-7, 639, 660, 673, 682, 686, 702
Andrea Doria, 335, 361
Andrés Álvarez, V., 693
Andújar, 243
Angola, 390, 399
Antilles, 305, 316, 317, 318, 321, 322, 326, 327, 390, 393, 394, 396, 405, 409, 541, 543, 545, 546, 574, 599, 602, 612, 673, 674, 690, 691, 697, 745
Antillón, 484
Antioch, 77
Antonelli (engineer), 365
Antwerp, 209, 330, 354, 362, 363, 384, 397, 420, 438, 460
Aporoma, 395
Appert process, 653
Apulia, 270
Aquitaine, 151, 336, 337
Arabia, 108, 120
Aragon, 20, 113, 139, 140, 142, 150, 152, 155, 156, 157, 158, 160, 164, 166, 173, 176, 177, 179, 180, 181, 185, 187, 195, 196, 197, 198, 199, 201, 204, 208, 210, 211, 212, 214, 217, 218, 224, 226, 228, 231, 232, 233, 234, 235, 237, 242, 244, 246, 247, 255, 259, 260, 263, 269, 270, 279, 282, 286, 292, 293, 294, 296, 297, 298, 299, 301, 307, 308, 310, 313, 331, 334, 336, 337, 348, 352, 357, 362, 382, 409, 412, 413, 421, 423, 424, 444, 466, 476, 477, 485, 493, 496, 501, 509, 510, 512, 515, 517, 529, 534, 539, 553, 554, 576, 581, 582, 586, 591, 595, 619, 628, 652, 653, 660, 664, 674, 680, 682
Aranda, Count of, 473, 484, 519
Aranda de Duero, 255
Aranjuez, 526, 646, 653, 683, 684, 685

Aranzadi, 21
Archangel, 434
Arcos, dukes of, 295
Ardoin, 720
Arellano, Romualdo, 665
Arenys de Mar, 689
Arequipa, 576
Argantonios, 53
Argar, El, 43
Argentina, 541, 545, 689, 723
Arib-ibn-Saab, 108
Arica, 578
Aristotle, 320
Arles, 204, 360
Armenia, 206
Arnús (family), 744; Evaristo, 729, 732
Arras, 273
Artiñano, 326
Assó, Ignacio, 473, 478
Assyria, 46
Astigi, 64
Astopas, 56
Astorga, 73, 126, 127, 128
Asturias, 5, 9, 18, 43, 48, 61, 68, 101, 123, 124, 125, 126, 127, 131, 133, 134, 199, 367 482, 495, 511, 512, 529, 533, 623, 642, 656, 659, 664, 665, 666, 682, 711, 730, 739, 741
Atienza, 261
Attica, 50
Augsburg, 397
Augustus, 54, 58, 59, 62, 71, 73, 77, 125
Aurelian, 78
Ausona, 178
Australia, 6, 251
Austria, 466, 476, 560, 684
Autun, 64, 72
Avignon, 195, 204
Ávila, 26, 123, 127, 161, 250, 253, 258, 259, 262, 305, 360, 485, 503, 528
Avilés, 328, 370
Ayacucho, 612

Ayamonte, 522
Ayllón, 255
Ayres, L. P., 733
Azcárate, Gumersindo, 709
Azcoitia, 479
Aznar de la Sota, Eduardo, 691
Azores, 15, 327

Babylonia, 46
Babylonia, Sultanate of, 207
Badajoz, 243, 253, 276, 640, 650, 656
Badalona, 675
Baer, Fritz, 248, 291
Baetica, 51, 61, 62, 64, 66, 67, 68, 70, 81, 165
Baeza, 162, 243, 259, 354, 480, 490
Baghdad, 103, 117, 213
Bahía, 405
Bailén, 490
Bailon, 67
Balearic Islands, 47, 164, 175, 300, 620, 637, 642, 682
Balkans, 205
Ballesteros Gaibrois, M., 302
Bañolas, 200
Baracaldo, 665, 666, 667
Barbary Kingdoms, 198, 212, 213, 231, 281
Barcelona, 6, 13, 48, 63, 70, 139, 147, 148, 149, 170, 173, 174, 177, 179, 181, 183, 184, 185, 186, 189, 190, 191, 192, 194, 195, 196, 197, 198, 199, 200, 202, 205, 206, 207, 208, 209, 211, 212, 213, 214, 215, 216, 217, 218, 219, 220, 221, 222, 226, 227, 228, 229, 230, 237, 268, 269, 270, 277, 292, 293, 297, 300, 301, 307, 308, 330, 333, 335, 341, 351, 352, 354, 356, 361, 363, 364, 365, 368, 369, 376, 397, 410, 415, 421, 430, 433, 467, 478, 481, 485, 487, 495, 497, 498, 499, 500, 503, 504, 525, 528, 530, 535, 536, 537, 538, 539, 546, 547, 559, 560, 562, 563, 565, 569, 570, 574, 576, 578,

Barcelona (*continued*)
580, 589, 590, 595, 596, 600, 601,
602, 617, 620, 621, 622, 623, 650,
665, 668, 669, 670, 673, 675, 680,
683, 684, 685, 688, 689, 690, 691,
692, 693, 706, 707, 708, 710, 717,
725, 727, 728, 729, 730, 731, 732,
733, 734, 739, 741, 742, 744
Basas, Manuel, 433
Basque Provinces, 409, 476, 479,
553-54, 579, 591, 642, 655
Basque Country, 7, 30, 41, 48, 55,
126, 127, 241, 247, 264, 267, 359,
485, 495, 526, 554, 595, 623, 662,
663, 681
Battló (family), 669, 744
Bautier, Robert, 206
Bayonne, 216, 263, 270, 274, 328,
370, 581, 680
Baza, 165
Beauce, 364
Beirut, 207
Béjar, 253, 534, 570, 672; dukes of,
256, 295, 534
Belén, Pragmatic of, 427
Belgium, 559, 560, 609, 657, 666,
744
Belluga, Cardinal, 491
Bélmez, 725
Belo, 67
Beloch, Julius, 61, 412
Belorado, 246
Beltrán, Lucas, 535
Benavente, counts of, 247, 374; Duke
of, 307
Beneyto, Juan, 432
Benidorm, 50
Beni-Gania (dynasty), 208
Beni-Marin (family), 208
Benjamin de Tudela, 148
Berga, 200, 525
Bergamo, 368
Berlanga, 255
Bermeo, 265, 267, 362
Bertrán de Lis, 708, 713, 714, 717
Bertrand (family), 744

Besalú, 177
Besançon, 363
Bessemer process, 657, 661, 664
Bethancourt, Agustín de, 679
Bethencourts, 210
Betis (river), 68, 75
Bigot de Sainte-Croix, 500
Bilbao, 265, 266, 267, 268, 306, 307,
308, 327, 328, 330, 357, 360, 362,
364, 366, 370, 371, 372, 397, 410,
421, 438, 478, 485, 497, 558, 560,
563, 573, 622, 664, 665, 667, 668,
675, 680, 685, 690, 691, 712, 724,
725, 728, 729, 730, 732, 743
Bilbilis, 69, 70
Biscay, 10, 267, 271, 306, 311, 353,
364, 366, 436, 529, 530, 565, 657,
661, 664, 665, 666, 682, 706, 711,
739, 741
Blanes, 222, 689
Bloch, Marc, 91, 226
Blois, 273
Bolívar, Simón, 612
Bolivia, 541
Bologna, 374
Bolueta (company), 666
Bonaplata (family), 665; (company),
669, 705
Bonnassié, Pierre, 189, 191, 193
Borah, Woodrow, 385, 386
Bordeaux, 71, 72, 75, 202, 264, 265,
274, 364
Borrego, Andrés, 703
Bosch Gimpera, P., 21
Bosch y Labrús, P., 710, 712
Boston, 580
Bougie, 208, 209, 217, 301
Bourgoing, A., 528
Brabant, 352, 560
Bracara, *see* Braga
Braga, 61, 75
Braudel, Fernand, 339, 342, 348, 456
Bravo Murillo, Juan, 684, 721, 728
Brazil, 408, 598
Brielle, La, 363, 420
Brihuega, 527, 528, 534

Bristol, 533
Brittany, 45, 52, 71, 360
Bröens, 85
Bruges, 106, 200, 209, 210, 220, 221, 265, 266, 267, 271, 273, 306, 363
Bruil, Juan, 714
Brunhes, Jean, 13, 14
Brussels, 368, 421
Bücher, Karl, 129
Bueno (deputy), 634
Buenos Aires, 399, 406, 531, 545, 546, 548, 549, 550, 573, 577, 578, 580, 582
Buitrago, 255
Burgallal (minister), 731
Burgos, 73, 84, 127, 128, 132, 243, 249, 253, 262, 264, 265, 266, 267, 268, 271, 275, 276, 277, 280, 283, 301, 306, 307, 308, 327, 340, 357, 358, 364, 366, 368, 371, 372, 376, 377, 403, 428, 430, 433, 438, 439, 461, 485, 493, 558, 648, 680
Burgos, Javier, 737
Burgundy, 210, 271
Burriana, 180
Byzantium, 102, 116, 167

Caballero, Fermín, 618
Cabarrús, Francisco, 473, 516, 519, 526, 575, 576, 585, 596, 597
Cabero, Manuel, 682
Cabra, 112; counts of, 295
Cáceres, 253, 302, 368, 640, 643, 655, 656, 686
Cadalso, José, 473
Cadaqués, 365
Cádiz, 14, 48, 51, 53, 66, 67, 71, 73, 75, 157, 247, 264, 268, 275, 276, 282, 326, 328, 333, 337, 357, 361, 362, 363, 366, 370, 390, 398, 399, 403, 405, 408, 410, 420, 421, 422, 435, 437, 438, 440, 441, 467, 473, 478, 480, 485, 487, 495, 497, 521, 530, 547, 560, 567, 571, 572, 573, 575, 576, 577, 578, 579, 580, 600,

601, 611, 622, 625, 626, 629, 632, 640, 641, 644, 650, 655, 656, 673, 680, 688, 689, 691, 692, 727, 728
Caecili (family), 64
Caesar, Julius, 58, 59, 72, 79
Cagliari, 204
Cairo, 292
Calahorra, 63, 72, 259
Calatayud, 69, 113, 177, 431, 455
Calatrava, military order of, 161, 165, 256, 295
California, 317, 541, 717, 736
Callao, 400, 578, 580
Camacho (minister), 711, 722
Cambrai, 265, 273
Cameros, 253
Campania, 72
Campeche, 577, 578
Campillo, José, 554, 593, 598
Campins (factory), 536
Campo, Antonio del, 533
Campogiro, 673
Campomanes, Pedro Rodríguez de, 473, 474, 478, 480, 482, 483, 490, 492, 500, 501, 510, 516, 518, 519, 520, 521, 563
Camprodón, 198
Campuzano, 531
Canada, 602
Canals, Esteban, 536, 537
Canals, Juan (Baron of Vall Roja), 538, 539
Canary Islands, 210, 211, 268, 269, 273, 282, 327, 359, 370, 398, 404, 406, 407, 408, 421, 551, 570, 577, 578, 623, 637, 682
Candia (Crete), 206, 215
Canga Argüelles, 557, 579, 613, 669, 705
Cánovas del Castillo, Antonio, 712
Cantabria, 41, 48, 67, 69, 89, 101, 123, 127, 267, 330
Cantera Burgos, F., 249
Canton, 582
Capmany, Antonio de, 189, 199, 201, 216, 473, 478, 488, 500, 501, 567

Caracalla, 59, 77
Caracas, 545, 565, 572, 573, 576, 577, 578
Carande, Ramón de, 28, 247, 324, 328, 338, 349, 352, 377, 403, 418, 480
Carboneros, 491
Cardona, 69, 146; counts of, 186; dukedom of, 493
Cardoner (river), 670
Carlé, María del Carmen, 249
Carlota, La, 491
Carmona, 51, 75, 243, 490
Caro Baroja, J., 21, 53, 55, 56, 63
Carolina, La, 491
Carrera Pujal, J., 362, 509, 535
Carrère, Claude, 201, 216
Carrión, Pascual, 640
Carrión, princes of, 135
Cartagena, 10, 51, 67, 68, 69, 70, 75, 86, 157, 160, 264, 269, 275, 328, 357, 359, 365, 370, 487, 530, 554, 569, 578, 655, 657
Cartagena (Colombia), 401, 404, 405, 544, 578
Cartago Nova, *see* Cartagena
Carteia, 51
Carthage, 47, 50, 57, 90
Carvajal (chronicler), 293
Carvajal, José de, 515; Carvajal-Keene agreements, 568
Casal, 473
Caspe, 685
Castelar, Emilio, 709
Castellar de la Frontera, 641
Castellón de la Plana, 642
Castile, 5, 6, 12, 14, 15, 18, 20, 23, 26, 28, 30, 84, 98, 100, 101, 104, 110, 111, 118, 121, 122, 123, 124, 125, 126, 127, 129, 132, 133, 143, 144, 145, 146, 150, 156, 157, 158, 160, 161, 164, 165, 166, 177, 180, 186, 208, 210, 211, 217, 228, 233, 235, 240, 241, 242, 243, 244, 245, 246, 247, 248, 249, 250, 251, 252, 253, 255, 258, 259, 260, 261, 262, 263, 264, 265, 266, 267, 269, 271, 273, 275, 276, 277, 278, 279, 280, 281, 282, 283, 284, 285, 287, 291, 292, 293, 294, 295, 296, 297, 298, 299, 301, 302, 304, 307, 308, 309, 310, 311, 312, 313, 314, 315, 316, 319, 322, 328, 330, 331, 333, 334, 336, 338, 339, 349, 351, 352, 353, 354, 355, 357, 358, 359, 360, 361, 362, 363, 365, 369, 370, 372, 374, 376, 377, 382, 409, 412, 415, 418, 423, 428, 430, 438, 440, 441, 443, 444, 445, 446, 449, 451, 452, 453, 454, 458, 460, 461, 464, 465, 467, 474, 480, 483, 485, 486, 490, 492, 493, 494, 496, 499, 502, 505, 508, 511, 513, 516, 517, 518, 519, 531, 534, 538, 553, 554, 555, 583, 588, 589, 591, 593, 594, 598, 599, 609, 619, 620, 626, 628, 639, 642, 647, 655, 673, 682, 702, 711; Canal of, 515, 519, 673
Castillo, Álvaro del, 456
Castres, 178
Castro, Américo, 162, 248, 249, 298, 472
Castro, viscount of, 186
Castrojeriz, 127
Castro Urdiales, 264, 265
Catalonia, 6, 7, 18, 20, 22, 23, 24, 28, 30, 35, 43, 52, 99, 100, 118, 132, 138, 139, 140, 141, 142, 143, 144, 145, 146, 147, 149, 150, 151, 157, 164, 166, 173, 174, 175, 176, 177, 178, 179, 180, 181, 182, 183, 184, 185, 186, 187, 188, 191, 196, 197, 199, 200, 202, 206, 211, 213, 214, 218, 220, 223, 224, 227, 229, 230, 231, 234, 235, 236, 238, 239, 240, 242, 243, 262, 263, 286, 291, 292, 293, 294, 296, 299, 301, 309, 310, 312, 313, 330, 335, 336, 337, 340, 341, 342, 343, 356, 360, 361, 362, 365, 376, 409, 412, 413, 421, 426, 429, 430, 432, 435, 448, 464, 466, 467, 475, 476, 477, 485, 488,

496, 498, 508, 510, 511, 512, 513, 516, 519, 522, 525, 526, 528, 529, 530, 531, 532, 534, 535, 537, 538, 539, 553, 554, 555, 558, 562, 565, 569, 579, 582, 583, 589, 591, 592, 593, 595, 599, 601, 609, 620, 621, 628, 642, 647, 650, 652, 653, 658, 660, 661, 664, 667, 669, 670, 672, 673, 674, 675, 677, 680, 682, 693, 702, 703, 706, 709, 711, 712, 737, 738, 739, 743, 744

Catholic Monarchs, see Ferdinand and Isabella

Cavada, La, 428, 530

Cavanilles, A., 473

Caxa de Leruela, 452

Cazorla, 165

Cellorigo, Martín González de, 418, 452, 464

Celtiberia, 69

Cerda (family), 295

Cerdaña, 141, 145

Ceret, 200

Cervantes, Miguel de, 464

Cervera, 177

Céspedes del Castillo, G., 327, 329, 371, 403, 404

Ceuta, 208, 209

Chabert, 379

Chad (lake), 209

Chagres, 579

Chalcis, 49

Charlemagne, 143, 149, 279

Charles of Bourbon (Carlist pretender), 613

Charles of Hapsburg (archduke), 581

Charles V of France, 274

Charles VII of France, 212, 215

Charles III ("the Noble") of Navarre, 137

Charles II of Spain, 392, 412, 417, 428, 438, 449, 450, 465, 466, 475, 492, 567, 581, 598, 719

Charles III of Spain, 236, 348, 472, 474, 477, 488, 489, 490, 493, 502,

507, 511, 514, 515, 516, 519, 520, 528, 529, 530, 537, 540, 547, 561, 562, 563, 568, 569, 571, 573, 576, 581, 583, 584, 585, 586, 593, 594, 595, 596, 600, 601, 602, 610, 713, 725

Charles IV of Spain, 476, 488, 498, 516, 518, 521, 528, 569, 576, 580, 585, 590, 596, 602, 604, 610, 679, 705, 713, 719, 725

Charles V of Spain (Emperor Charles), 250, 305, 310, 328, 335, 336, 347, 348, 349, 350, 351, 361, 365, 370, 374, 377, 380, 382, 383, 390, 397, 398, 407, 409, 411, 420, 436, 445, 457, 459, 460, 561

Chaunu, Pierre, 326, 327, 385, 398, 399, 401, 404, 405, 406, 434, 456, 459, 460, 580

Chavarri, (family), 667

Cherchel, 72

Chevalier, François, 387

Chicago, 693

Chile, 541, 545, 548, 550, 578, 580

Chiloë, 546

China, 110, 114, 536, 547, 557, 570, 571, 576

Chios, 206

Ciempozuelos, 44

Cipolla, Carlo M., 456

Ciudad Real, 353, 640, 642

Ciudad Rodrigo, 480

Claudians (family), 58, 59

Clovis, 85

Clunia, 63, 127

Cockerill, (company), 662

Coeur, Jacques, 212, 215, 239

Coimbra, 127, 128

Coín, 296

Colliure, 212, 365

Colmeiro, Manuel, 259, 348, 427, 429, 432, 453, 454

Colmenar de Oreja, 348

Cologne, 279

Colombia, 322, 394, 458, 541, 548, 578, 612

Columbus, Christopher, 268, 316, 317, 328, 390, 409
Columella, 66
Comillas, 481
Compostela, *see* Santiago de Compostela
Concepción, 578
Conflent, 145, 356, 359
Consett (company), 662
Constantina, 112
Constantine, 78, 91
Constantine IX, 206
Constantinople, 178, 205, 206, 207, 292
Cook, Shelburne, 386
Copóns, 555
Cordova (Córdoba), 26, 68, 70, 75, 102, 106, 113, 115, 117, 134, 148, 162, 243, 247, 249, 250, 259, 275, 293, 352, 354, 368, 419, 427, 466, 490, 630, 637, 640, 641, 646, 650, 652, 653, 655, 656, 685
Cornet, Pedro, 539, 555
Córnide, José, 523
Cornwall, 45, 52, 71
Corominas, Joan, 583
Corsica, 204
Cortez, Hernán, 317, 386
Cortina, marquis of, 730
Corunna (La Coruña), 73, 75, 328, 370, 405, 478, 481, 514, 538, 563, 578, 623, 656
Cos Gayón, 719, 721, 722
Costa, Joaquín, 630, 647, 676
Costa Brava, 197, 533, 678
Crete, 206
Crimea, 205
Crimean War, 655, 694, 697, 721, 736, 738, 741, 742
Cromwell, Oliver, 435
Cros, Francisco, 675
Cuba, 403, 543, 545, 548, 578, 580, 619, 648, 670, 674, 689, 690, 721, 728, 730, 745
Cuenca, 110, 243, 252, 253, 259,

284, 352, 354, 355, 357, 375, 428, 496, 534, 576, 581, 620, 642, 648
Cuixá (monastery), 145
Cumae, 47, 49
Cumaná, 573, 577
Curaçao, 405
Curtius, Jean, 428
Cuzco, 549
Cyprus, 206

Dacia, 77
Dalmau y Xifré (company), 675
Dalrymple, 490
Damascus, 207
Dantín, Juan, 14
Danube, 16, 64
Danzig, 561
Darlington, 682
Daroca, 517
Datini (archive), 205, 369
Del Treppo, Mario, 201
Denain (company), 662
Denia, 49, 75, 148; marquisate of, 493, 569
Descaus (banker), 228
Díaz Imbretchts, José, 682
Dieppe, 274
Diocletian, 66, 78
Dodecanese Islands, 206
Dolfuss, Heinrich, 706
Dolores, 491
Domitian, 64, 73
Domínguez Ortiz, A., 335, 412, 413, 418, 437, 492, 495, 509
Don Benito, 255
Dopsch, Alfred, 97
Doria, Andrea, 335, 361
Dormer, Joseph, 466
Douai, 265, 273
Drake, Sir Francis, 405
Dublin, 480
Dueñas, Rodrigo de, 377
Duero (river), 14, 25, 30, 48, 56, 67, 68, 75, 85, 99, 100, 123, 127, 128, 131, 134, 138, 161, 245, 250, 642

Dufourcq, Charles A., 201
Durán, José, 555
Durán Sampere, A., 535
Durán y Blas, M., 708
Duró, Pedro, 665, 666

East Indies, 4, 110
Ebro (river), 10, 11, 12, 14, 15, 16, 17, 18, 43, 48, 51, 52, 55, 69, 73, 75, 138, 140, 142, 145, 146, 151, 158, 187, 196, 348, 358, 413, 533, 554, 653, 685
Echegaray, José, 658, 709, 716, 730, 743
Echevarría (family), 667
Écija, 64, 75, 348
Edison, Thomas, 675
Edward III of England, 266
Egelaste, 69
Egypt, 45, 71, 109, 112, 114, 116, 120, 121, 206, 207, 213, 231, 301, 558, 559
Eiximenis, 432
El Dorado, 322
Elhuyart, F., 658, 659
Elliott, 379
Eminente, Francisco, 435, 454, 568
England, 4, 7, 29, 172, 186, 209, 212, 213, 233, 250, 251, 252, 264, 265, 266, 268, 271, 273, 274, 301, 306, 363, 397, 408, 421, 428, 435, 456, 457, 478, 489, 517, 523, 524, 530, 531, 532, 537, 538, 540, 542, 548, 550, 551, 552, 555, 556, 558, 560, 564, 567, 568, 569, 572, 577, 579, 580, 584, 585, 596, 601, 602, 603, 609, 657, 658, 666, 667, 673, 679, 682, 684, 704, 727, 733, 735, 744. See also Great Britain
Enríquez (family), 247, 260, 374
Ensenada, marquis of, 489, 494, 522, 529, 568, 569, 574, 577, 593, 594, 598
Ericsson, 690
Erill, baron of, 186

Escalona, 132
Escombreras, 75
Escorial, El, 253, 256, 527
Esla (river), 247
Esparó, Valentín, 665
Espartero, Baldomero, 646, 653, 683
Esquerit, (banker), 228
Esquilache, marquis of, 516
Estella, 137, 159
Estepa, 165
Estúñiga (family), 247, 295
Euric, 86
Extremadura, 18, 27, 104, 111, 131, 157, 161, 166, 247, 276, 295, 303, 358, 485, 505, 512, 517, 519, 520, 574, 619, 620, 639, 656, 677, 682
Ezcaray, 527, 534, 576

Fabra, (family), 669
Fajardo (family), 295
Faroe Islands, 263
Fassio, Francisco, 682
Feijoo, Father Benito, 473, 474
Felguera, La, 665, 666
Feliu de la Penya, Narcis, 429, 467
Ferdinand I of Aragon, 205
Ferdinand II of Aragon and V of Castile ("the Catholic"), 184, 189, 208, 236, 240, 262, 294, 299, 300, 301, 305, 307, 308, 309, 313, 317, 335, 343, 407, 409, 457
Ferdinand I of Castile, 123
Ferdinand III ("the Saint") of Castile, 157, 160, 162, 166, 200, 247, 261, 263, 264, 275, 280, 335
Ferdinand IV of Castile, 280
Ferdinand VI, 483, 488, 489, 492, 515, 517, 527, 529, 530, 547, 549, 567, 568, 571, 581, 583, 593, 599
Ferdinand VII, 612, 625, 626, 629, 632, 680, 682, 699, 706, 720, 725, 731, 737, 738
Ferdinand and Isabella (Catholic Monarchs), 6, 24, 25, 32, 117, 158, 202, 207, 222, 242, 244, 246, 254,

Ferdinand and Isabella (*continued*)
255, 262, 274, 279, 280, 291, 292,
293, 294, 295, 296, 297, 298, 299,
300, 301, 302, 303, 304, 305, 306,
307, 309, 310, 311, 312, 313, 314,
315, 319, 326, 334, 338, 346, 348,
351, 352, 353, 365, 371, 374, 376,
430, 440, 445, 447, 464, 483, 517,
518, 561, 590–91
Feria, dukedom of, 493
Fernández de Córdoba (family),
246, 295
Fernández Duro, 263
Fernández Marco, Juan, 628
Fernández de Navarrete, Martín,
451, 452
Figuerola, Laureano, 658, 671, 709,
715, 743
Flanders, 106, 174, 209, 211, 213,
220, 250, 251, 252, 258, 266, 268,
271, 273, 274, 301, 306, 349, 352,
353, 359, 360, 362, 363, 372, 373,
377, 416, 418, 449, 513
Flavians (family), 58, 60, 68
Flix, 196, 675
Florence, 205, 216, 220, 221, 224,
306, 374, 416
Flores de Lemus, Antonio, 702
Flórez Estrada, Álvaro, 613, 705
Florida, 512
Floridablanca, count of, 473, 478,
484, 515, 519, 520, 521, 562, 585
Fluviá (river), 670
Foix, 356
Fonegra, Marcos, 560-61
Fontana, José, 425, 456, 466, 636
Font Rius, José María, 219
Formosa, 212
Foronda, 519
Fos, Joaquín Manuel, 535
Fraga, 554
France, 12, 20, 21, 22, 29, 52, 102,
106, 138, 143, 148, 156, 172, 178,
180, 181, 186, 199, 200, 210, 211,
212, 213, 220, 230, 231, 251, 265,
266, 268, 273, 274, 279, 307, 327,

356, 359, 360, 361, 363, 364, 368,
372, 408, 416, 421, 428, 435, 456,
457, 458, 466, 477, 478, 487, 489,
508, 513, 516, 517, 526, 535, 538,
540, 556, 558, 559, 560, 564, 565,
568, 585, 601, 602, 603, 609, 609,
611, 625, 633, 651, 657, 658, 666,
673, 679, 684, 685, 733, 735, 744
Franche Comté, 363
Frederick II of Sicily, 232
Freser (river), 198
Frías, dukes of, 493, 628
Fuenterrabía, 23, 265
Fugger (family), 335, 384

Gades, Gadir, *see* Cádiz
Gafsa, El, 22
Galen, 414
Galicia, 14, 18, 23, 43, 45, 48, 51,
84, 85, 89, 123, 124, 125, 126,
127, 247, 367, 414, 481, 485, 486,
495, 509, 510, 511, 513, 519, 522,
523, 528, 530, 533, 534, 555, 562,
572, 591, 623, 682, 730
Gálvez, Miguel, 568
Gandía, 569
García Barzanallana (minister), 719
García Bellido, A., 50
García, Roy, 264
Garí (banker), 228
Gascony, 151, 264
Gasset, R., 647
Gaul, 26, 61, 64, 70, 71, 72, 75, 81,
86, 102
Genil (river), 110, 653
Genoa, 116, 148, 167, 196, 197, 204,
205, 207, 210, 215, 224, 228, 231,
237, 251, 263, 268, 270, 275, 282,
283, 300, 330, 335, 353, 360, 361,
363, 367, 369, 375, 384, 397, 459
Genseric, 84
Gerion, 53
Germany, 29, 72, 182, 186, 307,
359, 363, 418, 532, 558, 559, 609,
657, 666, 673, 710
Gerona, 48, 63, 177, 179, 180, 191,

200, 219, 228, 229, 595, 675, 688
Ghent, 106, 265, 273
Gibraltar, 10, 39, 81, 263, 268, 275, 563, 586, 596, 601, 602, 727
Gijón, 478, 482, 485, 497, 530, 563, 578, 655, 659, 680, 683
Gil, Father, S.J., 365
Gimbernat, Antonio de, 473
Giralt, Emilio, 415, 456, 531
Girona, Manuel de, 667, 730; (family), 728
Gloria, Bernardo, 537
Godoy, Manuel, 484, 489, 514, 587
Goitia (family), 667
Gómez Fernández, Francisco, 629
Gónima, Erasmo de, 503
González, Julio, 163
González, Nazario, 439
Gormaz, 127
Graells, 365
Gramme machine, 675
Granada, 102, 106, 110, 117, 163, 165, 212, 244, 270, 281, 282, 283, 291, 293, 296, 299, 303, 305, 309, 310, 311, 312, 333, 334, 352, 357, 425, 427, 445, 466, 480, 485, 513, 534, 535, 569, 570, 574, 640, 642, 646, 653, 674, 685
Granja de San Ildefonso, La, 526, 527, 555
Granollers, 200
Grao, El, 684
Gravette, La, 21
Great Britain, 356, 359. *See also* England
Greece, 12, 46, 90, 148, 176, 559
Grice-Hutchinson M., 452
Guadalajara, 84, 496, 503, 527, 534, 561, 570, 637, 642, 661
Guadalcanal, 529, 658
Guadalete (river), 682
Guadalquivir (river), 10, 11, 12, 14, 44, 52, 75, 110, 112, 163, 345, 366, 437, 490, 515
Guadalupe, 253, 255; Sentence of, 183, 184, 294, 299

Guadiana (river), 157, 161, 679
Guadix, 75
Guaira, La, 580
Gual, Domenec, 211
Gual Villalbí, 712
Guardia, La, 523
Guatemala, 545, 550, 576, 578
Guayaquil, 578
Güell, Juan, 707, 708; (family), 669, 737, 744
Guetaria, 265
Guillemberg, count of, 514
Guillerías, 141, 343
Guillodts van Severen, L., 266
Guimarães, 259
Guinea, 209, 269, 335, 689
Guipúzcoa, 306, 479, 493, 522, 530, 664
Guizot, François, 739
Guriezo, 664, 665, 666, 667
Guzmán (family), 246, 295
Gwinner (banker), 730

Habana, marquis of La, 653
Hacha, (river), 573
Hafsids, 208
Haiti, 545
Hamburg, 420, 434, 487, 559, 560, 576
Hamilcar (Barca), 51
Hamilton, E. J., 223, 225, 304, 310, 323, 324, 345, 372, 378, 379, 380, 381, 396, 411, 412, 425, 443, 444, 445, 450, 456, 460, 462, 465, 547, 575, 582, 589, 597, 598, 599, 601
Hannibal (Barca), 51
Hanseatic League, 196, 209, 268, 273, 361, 420, 434
Harfleur, 274
Haring, C. H., 326, 406, 433
Haro, count of, 247
Hawkins, Sir John, 405
Havana, 399, 401, 543, 550, 573, 574, 576, 577, 578, 580, 689
Heers, 197, 201
Hemeroscopeion, 49, 50

Henry II of Castile, 246, 269, 280, 295
Henry III of Castile, 280, 287, 288
Henry IV of Castile, 259, 287, 288, 295, 302, 308
Henry the Navigator, 210, 269, 282
Henry of Trastamara, 257, 286
Heredia (company), 664
Hernández, M., 387, 389
Hernández Pacheco, Eduardo, 11
Herr, Richard, 509, 531, 535
Herrera, Alfonso de, 365
Herrier (banker), 596
Hesperia, 9
Highs machines, 525
Hinojosa, Eduardo de, 142
Hispalis, 75
Hispaniola, 403, 437, 458, 578
Holland, 4, 12, 352, 400, 408, 416, 420, 434, 435, 447, 513, 532, 558, 559, 560, 572, 609
Honduras, 572, 574
Hornachuelos, 641
Huancavélica, 323
Huelva, 9, 51, 112, 268, 640, 642, 650, 657, 664, 673, 724
Huesca, 44, 73, 77, 159, 177, 352, 637, 642
Hugh IV of Ampurias, 207
Humboldt, Alexander von, 541
Hungary, 205, 223, 226
Hurdes, Las, 413

Ibarra, Eduardo, 304
Ibiza, 49, 50, 197, 270
Iceland, 15
Ifriqa, 207, 208
Ignatius of Loyola, St., 35
Igual, Ramón, 528
India, 71, 212, 301, 422, 547, 572
Indies, 310, 314, 316, 318, 319, 320, 323, 325, 326, 328, 333, 336, 337, 339, 345, 346, 353, 357, 359, 360, 361, 362, 364, 367, 370, 371, 374, 377, 379, 385, 386, 387, 389, 397, 399, 400, 401, 402, 408, 409, 410, 413, 416, 418, 420, 421, 422, 434, 436, 437, 440, 452, 453, 456, 459, 460, 550, 574, 578, 713
Infantado, dukes of, 256, 295, 478, 493
Iol Cesarea, *see* Cherchel
Ireland, 45, 421, 489, 532
Irún, 368, 680, 685
Isabella I ("the Catholic"), 302, 303, 305, 307, 322, 333, 366, 374, 409
Isabella II, 613, 655, 680, 697, 709, 715, 743
Isidore, St., 11, 87, 89
Istúriz, 473
Itálica, 70
Italy, 12, 27, 47, 49, 50, 61, 64, 72, 79, 90, 114, 173, 174, 186, 199, 211, 213, 220, 232, 251, 270, 307, 311, 349, 352, 354, 356, 359, 360, 366, 368, 373, 397, 411, 416, 418, 434, 458, 525, 558, 559, 652

Jaca, 26, 159, 226, 480
Jaén, 162, 640, 652, 657
Jalón (river), 20, 43
Jamaica, 405, 545
James I ("the Conqueror"), 157, 160, 166, 208, 218, 219
James II, 204, 206, 208, 238
Játiva, 114, 684
Jaumeandreu, Eduardo, 703
Jenner, Edward, 617
Jerez de la Frontera, 243, 250, 275, 512, 532, 641, 682, 684
Jiloca (river), 48
John of Austria, Don, 429
John II' of Aragon, 179, 207, 239, 294, 299, 336
John II of Castile, 236, 249, 259, 280, 295
Joseph I (Bonaparte), 625, 632
Jovellanos, Gaspar Melchor, 472, 473, 474, 478, 482, 500, 501-502, 510, 519, 521, 530, 567, 629, 659
Juan, Jorge, 473, 482, 577
Júcar (river), 157, 515

Juglar, 734
Julius II, Pope, 442

Kastellorizo, 206
Keene (English diplomat), 568
Kerch, Strait of, 205
Keynes, M., 381
Kiev, 214
Klein, Julius, 130, 251, 255, 256, 303, 305, 348, 425, 427
Kolaios of Samos, 49
Kondratiev, Nikolai, 734
Kovalevsky, 214
Krupp (company), 662

Labande, Georges, 428
Labrousse, E., 508, 733
Lacarra, José Ma., 137, 146
Lafitte, House of, 728
Lagos, 356
Lancia, 127
Landes, Les, 151
Langreo, 659, 693
Languedoc, 202, 204, 337, 359
Lapeyre, Henri, 220, 221, 367, 368, 372, 423, 456
Lara, Pedro de, 683
Laredo, 264, 265, 328, 362, 370, 372, 397, 465
La Roncière, Charles de, 209, 217
Larrard (banker), 596
Larraz, José, 339, 428, 432, 433, 442, 444, 451, 452, 454, 647, 649, 652, 653, 738
Larruga, Eugenio, 528, 555, 573, 575
Las Casas, Father Bartolomé, 320
Law, John, 564
Leghorn, 360, 361, 434
León, 5, 12, 13, 14, 17, 18, 20, 48, 61, 100, 101, 121, 122, 123, 124, 127, 132, 133, 134, 135, 143, 144, 146, 243, 247, 252, 253, 409, 485, 493, 496, 513, 619, 620, 636, 639, 642, 650, 660, 667, 682, 730
León, Juan Francisco de, 573
Leovigild, 84, 91, 122

Lequerica, José Félix de, 663
Lérida, 73, 115, 138, 140, 228, 362, 514, 595, 653, 685
Liérgana, 428
Liérganes, 530
Liguria, 212
Lille, 273
Lima, 399, 408, 549, 550, 576, 577
Limoges, 265
Linares, 529
Lisbon, 73, 210, 268, 277, 328, 362, 363, 365, 433, 434, 467, 596
List, Friedrich, 710
Liverpool, 667
Llobera, Pablo, 665
Llobregat, (river), 189, 670
Lloret de Mar, 688, 689
Logroño, 75, 253, 306, 534, 653
Loire (river), 274, 364
Lombardy, 212, 672
London, 200, 266, 306, 416, 422, 560, 576, 582, 602, 692, 693, 728, 731, 742
López (family), 744
Lopez, Robert S., 226, 231, 251
López Ballesteros, Luis, 658, 659, 705, 720, 725, 737
López Ibor, Juan José, 29, 30, 31
López y López, Antonio, 690, 730
López de Meneses, Amada, 178
López de Reino, Pedro, 451
Lorca, 160, 515
Louisiana, 578
Low Countries, 363, 382, 420, 428, 560
Lozoya, marquis of, 259, 262
Lübeck, 273
Lucena, 480
Lucentum, 50. *See also* Alicante
Lucus Augusti, 61. *See also* Lugo
Lugo, 61, 656
Luna, Álvaro de, 286
Lusignan (family), 206; María of, 206
Lusitania, 61, 62, 68, 75, 89
Luzzato, Gino, 321, 324, 456

Lyons, 72, 360, 363, 364, 368, 672, 673

Madariaga, Salvador de, 12
Madoz, Pascual, 631, 634, 636, 638, 679, 703, 738
Madrid, 15, 18, 20, 84, 243, 342, 357, 368, 375, 376, 416, 421, 431, 438, 439, 440, 466, 475, 480, 482, 485, 487, 488, 491, 493, 495, 497, 498, 499, 502, 506, 515, 526, 527, 534, 535, 538, 540, 562, 576, 578, 581, 590, 592, 600, 610, 620, 621, 622, 637, 642, 665, 675, 676, 680, 683, 684, 685, 686, 707, 709, 712, 727, 728, 730, 731, 732, 737, 742
Madrigal, 259
Maestrazgo, 43, 48, 212, 416
Magarola (factory), 537
Mahón, 49
Mainaké, 49, 50
Majarrés, Ramón, 675
Majorca, 158, 163, 164, 176, 177, 179, 182, 184, 185, 200, 208, 214, 216, 218, 220, 226, 263, 270, 275, 292, 293, 358, 416, 476, 496, 589, 591, 595
Malaca, see Málaga
Malacca (Malay Peninsula), 212
Málaga, 48, 49, 67, 70, 71, 106, 150, 185, 270, 281, 282, 296, 328, 357, 370, 421, 422, 441, 478, 481, 485, 487, 512, 522, 532, 533, 560, 569, 570, 578, 622, 640, 650, 664, 673, 685, 688, 728
Mâle, Louis de, 271
Mallada, Lucas, 11, 12
Malta, 513, 537, 558, 571
Maluenda (family), 377
Mancha, La, 15, 18, 27, 30, 161, 247, 250, 253, 295, 413, 509, 520, 620, 650
Manila, 400, 481, 536, 550, 572, 576
Manzanares (river), 515
Manzanedo (bank), 728
Manzano, J., 313

Maracaibo, 405, 573
Marbella, 664
Marca Hispanica, see Spanish March
Marchena, 51
Maresme, 174, 189, 197, 422, 491
Margarita, 572, 574, 578
María, queen-regent of Aragon, 239
Marineo Sículo, Lucio, 296
Marinescu, Constantine, 201
Marseilles, 47, 49, 148, 196, 202, 204, 211, 212, 231, 270, 353, 361, 367, 369, 434, 558, 717
Martín I ("the Humane") of Aragon, 181
Martín Sánchez-Juliá, Fernando, 12, 640
Martínez de la Mata, 428, 451
Martínez de Rivas (family), 668
Martos, 165
Masías de Ros, Ángeles, 201
Masson de Morvilliers, 28
Matanzas, battle of, 399, 405
Mataró, 536, 683, 684
Mateu Llopis, Felipe, 118
Mauretania, 79
Mazarrón, 359
McAdam, John, 679
Mechlin, 273
Medina, Bartolomé de, 323
Medinaceli, duke of, 295, 493
Medina del Campo, 161, 243, 255, 276, 277, 283, 306, 307, 313, 330, 340, 354, 360, 362, 366, 373, 374, 375, 376, 377, 438, 445, 460, 461, 685
Medina de Ríoseco, 306, 307, 374, 375
Medina Sidonia, 165
Medinasidonia, dukes of, 247, 295
Medir (banker), 228
Mela, Pomponius, 49
Meléndez Valdés, Juan, 473
Mellaría, 67
Méndez de Cancio, Gonzalo, 512
Mendizábal, Juan Alvarez, 633
Mendoza (Argentina), 545

Mendoza (family), 246, 247, 295
Menéndez Pidal, Ramón, 124
Mercado, Tomás de, 345, 452
Mérida, 63, 71, 73, 75, 115, 253, 276, 679
Mesopotamia, 41, 109
Messina, 204
Meuvret, Jean, 414, 456
Mexico, 6, 316, 317, 321, 322, 326, 358, 359, 386, 395, 396, 399, 400, 406, 436, 458, 529, 530, 533, 541, 544, 546, 547, 548, 549, 579, 612
Mexico City, 576
Mieres, 665
Miguel, Antonio de, 676
Milan, 360, 364, 368, 382, 416, 449
Millares, Los, 43
Millás Vallicrosa, José María, 243
Millau, 178
Millet, Salvador, 626, 644, 645, 649, 652, 738
Miño (river), 85
Minorca, 49, 147, 476, 487, 601
Miqueloterena (family), 728
Mirambell, Juan, 689
Miranda del Rey, 491
Miravalles, count of, 665
Mitjá, Marina, 220
Módica, counts of, 186
Moghreb, 207, 208
Mohammed, 106, 112
Mohammed II, 206
Mohammed-ibn-Ubaid, 113
Mojados, 539
Molí de l'Ermentera, 365
Molins de Rey, 684
Moll, 583
Mon, Alejandro, 708, 721, 726, 727, 740
Moncada, Sancho de, 422, 433, 451
Mondoñedo, 512
Monfar, chronicle of, 185
Montalbán, 255
Montblanc, 177
Monteagudo, treaty of, 208
Montecristo, 578

Montevideo, 578
Montiel, battle of, 269
Montilla, lords of, 295
Montpellier, 204
Montseny, 18, 197
Montserrat, monastery of, 738
Monzón, Cortes of, 301, 310, 363, 382
Morales, Ambrosio de, 349
Moreau de Jonnès, 612, 623, 647, 663, 688, 693, 694, 738
Moret, Segismundo, 709
Morocco, 110, 116, 208, 269, 274, 281, 559
Morón, 165
Motril, 480, 677
Moyá, 217
Muchada, 647
Mula, 160
Muluya (river), 208
Muñoz Pérez, José, 569
Münster, treaty of, 435
Muntada (family), 669
Murcia, 14, 18, 28, 47, 110, 157, 158, 159, 160, 162, 176, 243, 253, 259, 260, 275, 278, 293, 295, 302, 357, 416, 425, 485, 493, 527, 535, 576, 623, 640, 650, 682
Muros, 523
Murrieta (family), 667
Musa, 103, 107

Nadal, J., 415, 456
Nalón (river), 530, 659
Nantes, 274, 306, 340, 360, 364, 372, 421
Naples, 47, 185, 204, 205, 213, 215, 238, 300, 301, 356, 359, 361, 382, 416, 596
Napoleon I (Bonaparte), 7, 559, 576
Narbonensis, 61, 79
Narbonne, 52, 71, 72
Narváez, Ramón María de, 708, 714
Nasrids, 212
Navarre, 137, 139, 142, 150, 155, 223, 224, 235, 259, 291, 311, 331,

Navarre (*continued*)
  409, 476, 492, 496, 529, 530, 553,
  591, 595, 619, 642, 655, 681
Navas de Tolosa, Las, 161, 491
Necker, Jacob, 514
Nef, John, 456, 524
Negro (river), 545
Nero, 77
Nervión (river), 364, 668, 675
Nevers, Louis de, 267, 271
Newfoundland, 355
New Orleans, 531
New Spain, 317, 320, 321, 322, 323,
  325, 387, 391, 393, 394, 395, 396,
  398, 399, 401, 403, 404, 549, 550,
  577, 579
New York, 205
Nice, 204, 300
Nicholas IV, Pope, 202
Nicolau d'Olwer, 201
Nile (river), 41, 110
Nîmes, 72
Nipho, Francisco Mariano, 564
Noguera, R. 220
Nombre de Dios, 399, 401
Normandy, 274
Nueva Granada, 323, 394, 404, 458,
  547-48, 549, 550
Nueva Santander, 541
Numantia, 48
Núñez de Balboa, Vasco, 307
Núñez de Castro, Alfonso, 417

Ocaña, 353, 359
Olano, Larrinaga (company), 667
Olavide, Pablo de, 473, 490, 491
Olivares, Count-Duke of, 399, 428,
  591
Olivella, de (banker), 228
Olisipo (Lisbon), 73, 76
Olot, 200
Omar (caliph), 106
Omar-ibn-Hafsún, 103
Omayyads, 102
Omoa, 578
Oporto, 128

Oran, 208, 301, 623,
Orconera (company), 744
Ordeig, Jaime, 503
Orduña, 554
Orense, 685
Orihuela, 491
Orinoco (river), 573
Orlando (minister), 708
Oropesa, count of, 428, 455, 466
Orry, Jean, 598
Ortiz, Luis, 451
Osma, 51, 63, 123, 127, 259
Ostende, 560
Osuna, 51, 480
Ots Capdequí, José María, 391
Oviedo, 480, 530, 622, 656

Pacheco (family), 247
Pachuca, 395
Padrón, 75
Palafrugell, 533, 677
Palamós, 365, 533, 677
Palata, marquis of, 392
Palencia, 73, 84, 253, 259, 276, 333,
  496, 643
Palermo, 204, 215
Palestine, 46, 167, 206
Pallars, 139, 140, 145; marquisate
  of, 493; counts of, 186
Palma de Mallorca, 177, 222, 480,
  578
Pamplona, 26, 75, 159, 685
Panadés, 139, 422
Panamá, 307, 399, 400, 401
Paraguay, 392, 541, 550, 573
Paris, 106, 560, 576, 596, 674, 685,
  692, 693, 727, 728, 731
Pasajes, 573
Pasco, 395
Pasqual (banker), 228
Passegno (family), 268
Pasteur, Louis, 672
Pastor, Luis Ma., 709
Patagonia, 546
Patiño, José, 438, 474, 522, 572,
  592, 598

Paynó, Vicente, 518, 519
Payta, 400, 549
Pedregal, 709
Peñaflorida, count of, 478, 479
Peñarroya (company), 724, 744
Pera (Constantinople), 205
Pereire (family), 684, 721, 724, 742
Pericot, Louis, 21
Perpignan, 177, 180, 200, 202, 219, 226, 228, 293, 352, 680
Peru, 6, 316, 317, 320, 321, 323, 325, 391, 393, 394, 395, 399, 404, 406, 436, 530, 541, 542, 548, 549, 550, 578
Peter III ("the Great") of Aragon, 160, 183, 207, 234
Peter IV ("the Ceremonious") of Aragon, 215, 220, 226, 228, 233, 235, 238, 269
Peter I ("the Cruel") of Castile, 246, 251, 269, 280
Peter I of Cyprus, 206, 207
Pez, Andrés de, 438
Pfandl, Ludwig, 419
Philadelphia, 693
Philip II, 31, 336, 340, 347, 348, 349, 354, 363, 366, 375, 377, 382, 383, 391, 394, 397, 407, 412, 436, 441, 442, 446, 453, 459, 460, 461, 462, 464, 471
Philip III, 157, 338, 391, 394, 413, 424, 427, 436, 443, 446, 454, 461, 462, 463, 598
Philip IV, 400, 419, 435, 443, 449, 461, 462, 463
Philip V, 6, 410, 475, 492, 526, 529, 533, 536, 553, 554, 561, 566, 572, 573, 577, 581, 582, 583, 590, 591, 596, 598, 599
Philip the Good (duke), 267
Philip the Handsome, 368
Philippine Islands, 400, 406, 408, 547, 548, 565, 572, 576, 586, 596, 612, 619, 690, 697, 730, 744, 745
Piacenza, 363
Pi y Sunyer, Carlos, 35

Piedmont, 517
Pimentel (family), 246, 247, 374
Pinillos, Saez (company), 691
Piquer, Andrés, 502
Pirenne, Henri, 97
Pisa, 116, 147, 148, 167, 204, 220
Pius IV, Pope, 442
Pius V, Pope, 442
Plá, Simón, 525
Pla de Llobregat, 174
Plasencia, 253; counts of, 247
Plata, La (river region), 395, 399, 408, 444, 540, 544, 545, 546, 550, 561, 577, 599, 612; viceroyalty of, 548, 549, 550, 580, 689
Pliny, 61, 69
Po (river), 16
Poitiers, battle of, 102
Poland, 461
Polybius, 56, 69
Pompey, 72
Ponce de León (family), 246, 295
Ponçgem, Juan, 503
Pons, Antonio, 473
Pontevedra, 623
Pontus (Black Sea region), 67
Ponza, battle of, 205
Poperinghe, 273
Portal, 682
Port-Bou, 685
Portobello, 401, 405, 406, 544, 579
Portugal, 13, 14, 18, 20, 23, 45, 48, 55, 68, 84, 157, 222, 246, 259, 260, 269, 274, 282, 307, 331, 354, 409, 412, 414, 420, 426, 433, 448, 463, 464, 513, 516, 555, 574, 603, 686
Portugalete, 364, 371
Port-Vendres, 365
Posidonius, 53
Potosí, 321, 323, 395, 396, 444, 546, 549
Poval ironworks, 664
Poza de la Sal, 262
Prades, countship of, 186, 493
Pradt (abbot), 579

Prato, 205, 210, 369
Presa, Francisco de la, 340, 360
Priego, counts of, 295; marquisate of, 493
Prieto Bances, Ramón, 417
Probus, 64
Provence, 202, 204
Prussia, 489, 517, 684
Puerto Deseado, 546
Puerto de Santa María, 358, 421, 422, 562, 569, 675, 682, 684
Puerto Rico, 403, 437, 574, 577, 578, 648, 670
Puertollano, 9, 725
Puigcerdá, 200
Puteoli, 72

Quintanilla, Alonso de, 291, 312
Quito, 325, 549

Ragusa, 205, 367
Ramón Berenguer I, 150
Ramón Berenguer III, 147, 149
Ramón Berenguer IV, 149
Reccared, 84
Recceswinth, Code of, 84
Reglá, Juan de, 424
Regomir, 216
Reims, 106
Reinosa, 531
Remisa, Gaspar, 658, 727, 737
Renieblas, 51
Reparaz, Gonzalo de, 201
Requesens de Soler (family), 186, 230
Reus, 365, 531, 653, 682
Revenga, Antonio, 14
Rheinhardt, W., 84
Rhine (river), 16, 23, 167, 271,
Rhineland, 560
Rhodes, 49, 206
Rhodesia, 657
Rhône (river), 16
Riaza, 255
Ribagorza, 139, 140
Ribas, 198

Ricard, Robert, 209
Riga, 561
Río, Antonio del, 560
Río de la Hacha, 578-79
Río Grande (river), 317
Río de Oro, 211
Rioja, 48, 130, 246, 247, 250, 478, 650
Ríotinto, 69, 529, 530, 657, 658, 663, 724, 744
Ripoll, 140, 141, 198, 200, 530
Ripollés, 178
Riperdá, baron of, 527
Roa, 123
Robert of Flanders, 271
Robla, La, 667
Roca y Roca, J., 683
Roca Traver, F. 180
Rochelle, La, 273, 274, 306
Rocroi, battle of, 464
Rodhae, 49, 77
Roger de Flor, 205
Romá, Francisco, 555
Romano, Ruggiero, 456, 556
Rome, 4, 25, 33, 50, 51, 57, 58, 59, 60, 61, 62, 63, 64, 68, 69, 72, 75, 76, 81, 102, 110, 368, 521, 596
Romero Robledo, F., 647
Romeva, P., 535
Roncesvalles, 75
Ronda, 296
Roover, Raymond de, 220, 374
Rosario, 545, 550
Rosas, 49, 365
Rosenblat, Ángel, 387, 389, 390, 541
Rostow, W., 733
Rothschild (family), 685, 721, 728, 742
Roucher, 567
Rouen, 106, 274, 363, 364
Roussillon, 139, 145, 197, 200, 356, 359, 413, 533
Rozier, 514
Rubió y Lluch, A., 201
Ruiz (archive), 367, 368, 369
Ruiz, Simón, 340, 360, 377

Ruiz Almansa, Jaime, 331, 412, 414
Ruiz y Pablo, Ángel, 535
Rumania, 213
Rumeu de Armas, Antonio, 499
Russia, 205, 335, 434

Saavedra Fajardo, Diego, 464
Sabadell, 200, 430, 534, 621, 671, 672, 744
Sacedón, 491
Sacramento, 550
Saetabis, 70
Sagasta, Práxedes, 711
Saguntum, 51
Sahagún, 132, 276
Sahara, 43, 209, 217, 282
St. John of Jerusalem, military order of, 206
St. Petersburg, 582
Sainz (bank), 728
Sainz de Andino, Pedro, 725
Salamanca, 73, 123, 127, 243, 247, 253, 262, 293, 295, 452, 453, 485, 516, 636, 637, 648, 655, 656, 677, 685
Salamanca, José, 683, 684, 685, 714, 726, 727, 740
Salaverría, Pedro, 715, 718
Salonica, 292
Salou, 365
Saltacaballo, 667
Sama, 683
San Felipe Neri (Alicante), 491
San Feliu de Guixols, 209, 533, 677
San Fernando, 527, 528, 538, 576, 706
San Fulgencio (Alicante), 491
San Ildefonso (see La Granja.)
San José (Argentina), 546
San Juan de las Abadesas, 141, 200, 658
San Juan (Puerto Rico), 401, 409
San Juan del Oro, 395
San Mateo (Castellón), 212
San Pedro, Ramón de, 732, 744
San Pedro Pescador, 365

San Sebastián, 263, 265, 276, 328, 370, 573, 579, 675
San Vicente de la Barquera, 264, 265, 362
Sánchez Agesta, Luis, 623
Sánchez Albornoz, Claudio, 98, 99, 122, 125, 127, 131, 132, 144, 284
Sánchez Ramos, F., 530, 660, 663, 664, 706, 709
Sancho IV of Castile, 200, 263, 269, 276, 280, 284, 285, 286
Sancho III ("the Great") of Navarre, 139, 145
Sancho VI ("the Wise"), 263
Sancho de Moncada, 422, 433, 451
Sangüesa, 159
Sanlúcar de Barrameda, 363, 366, 399, 400, 421, 437, 480, 538, 682, 689
Sant Joan de Fábregues, 145
Santa Cruz, (engineer), 683
Santa Cruz de Mudela, 490
Santa Cruz de Tenerife, 578
Santa Elena, 491
Santa María de Gamonal, 267
Santa María del Paular, 256
Santa María de Santoña, 264
Santa María, Alvaro de, 249
Santa Marta, 578
Santa Olalla, count of, 726
Santander, 18, 75, 125, 241, 264, 265, 267, 306, 307, 362, 364, 372, 422, 428, 438, 464, 465, 480, 481, 485, 486, 495, 522, 527, 530, 531, 533, 554, 558, 561, 563, 578, 623, 642, 661, 664, 673, 674, 685, 728, 729
Santiago de Compostela, 136, 137, 275, 276, 487, 494
Santiago (Cuba), 578, 690
Santiago, military order of, 161, 165, 249, 257, 286, 295, 304
Santo Domingo, 401, 405, 574, 577, 578
Santoña, see Santa María de Santoña
Santo Tomás de Castilla, 578

Saragossa (Zaragoza), 18, 48, 63, 73, 106, 138, 140, 146, 159, 177, 218, 292, 293, 297, 352, 368, 430, 466, 480, 485, 494, 534, 570, 612, 646, 656, 676, 680, 684, 685, 728

Sardá, F. 584, 697, 714, 716, 721, 722, 733, 734

Sardinia, 47, 49, 61, 164, 176, 185, 186, 197, 200, 204, 213, 235, 300, 301, 356, 360, 416

Sarmiento, 251

Sarrailh, Jean, 482

Sarriera, Juan, 301

Satrústegui, Patricio de, 690

Savona, 204

Savoy, 204

Saxony, 517

Sayous, André, 220

Sayró, Esteban, 670

Scheldt (river), 363

Scotland, 39, 421

See, Henri, 433

Segorbe, dukedom of, 493

Segovia, 84, 131, 161, 243, 252, 253, 255, 256, 258, 259, 260, 261, 276, 305, 306, 308, 352, 354, 358, 428, 480, 485, 534, 570, 581

Segre (river), 112, 413

Segura (river), 14, 47, 165

Seine (river), 274

Sempere Guarinos, Juan, 519

Senegal, 211, 282

Septimania, 90, 143

Sepulveda, 123, 127

Sepúlveda, Ginés de, 320

Serena, count of, 597

Serna, Antolín de la, 454

Serra (family), 689, 728

Sert (family), 669

Sesa, dukes of, 295

Sestao, 668

Seville, 75, 109, 110, 115, 116, 157, 162, 198, 210, 243, 247, 249, 251, 258, 260, 261, 262, 264, 265, 267, 268, 269, 270, 275, 276, 277, 282, 283, 293, 297, 308, 309, 312, 323,

325, 326, 327, 328, 329, 333, 335, 337, 345, 353, 357, 358, 359, 361, 362, 363, 364, 367, 368, 370, 371, 372, 373, 374, 390, 396, 398, 399, 400, 401, 402, 403, 404, 406, 407, 408, 409, 410, 419, 420, 421, 422, 427, 433, 434, 435, 436, 437, 438, 440, 456, 459, 466, 467, 480, 485, 487, 494, 495, 496, 527, 530, 538, 560, 574, 577, 578, 581, 622, 629, 637, 640, 642, 646, 655, 658, 664, 685, 689, 725, 728

Sexi, 48, 51

Shafer, 479

Siberia, 15

Sicily, 47, 50, 61, 79, 97, 148, 164, 176, 185, 186, 196, 200, 204, 211, 213, 235, 238, 270, 300, 301, 356, 360, 361, 363, 382, 433, 461, 558

Siemens process, 664

Sigüenza, 253, 259

Silesia, 223, 226

Simancas, 123, 127

Simiand, André, 733

Siret, Luis, 45

Siruela, 255

Sisapo (Almadén), 69

Sisternes Feliu, Manuel, 519

Sit, Pedro, 555

Smith, Adam, 552, 567

Smith, Robert S., 433, 467

Smyrna, 559

So, viscounts of, 186

Sobradiel, counts of, 628

Sobrarbe, 139

Soetbeer, 547

Soissons, 106

Soldevila, F. 482

Soler, Juan, 559

Solórzano, Juan, 409

Sombart, Werner, 24, 129

Somorrostro, 69, 356, 662, 744

Somoza de Monsorín, Francisco, 523

Soria, 51, 89, 110, 131, 252, 253, 259, 261, 305, 480, 493, 496, 555, 643, 648, 656

Sota y Aznar (company), 691
Sota y Llano, Ramón, 691
Sotomayor, Enrique de, 246
Spanish March, 99, 139, 149
Spice Islands, 301
Spínola, Lorenzo de, 384
Spooner, Frank C., 397, 445
Stephenson, George, 679
Stockton, 682
Strabo, 49, 66, 67, 71
Struzzi, Alberto, 452, 453
Suárez Fernández, Luis, 269
Suárez de Figueroa (family), 246, 295
Subercase (engineer), 683
Sudan, 148, 209, 217, 281
Sudetenland, 487
Suero, 530
Sultepec, 395
Suñer II of Ampurias, 147
Sureda Blanes, J., 440
Sweden, 461, 517
Swinthila, 86
Switzerland, 12, 204
Syracuse, 204
Syria, 45, 109, 114, 116, 206, 213, 292, 558

Taberner (family), 744
Taberner y Tintorer, Domingo, 729
Tader (river), 68
Tagus, (river), 14, 56, 67, 68, 75, 85, 112, 161, 245, 348, 365, 515
Taifa Kingdoms, 102. 117. 118. 148. 150
Talavera de la Reina, 253, 255, 262, 276, 365, 480, 527. 535. 576
Tallada, 35, 733
Tamerlane, 270
Tanais, 205
Tarapaca, 396
Tarazona, 69, 159, 177
Tarazona de la Mancha, 480
Tarifa, 368, 563
Tarik, 103, 107
Tarraco, *see* Tarragona

Tarraconensis, 61, 62, 89
Tarragona, 18, 48, 63, 70, 73, 75, 77, 81, 191, 563, 650, 653, 682, 685
Tarrasa, 200, 621, 671, 672, 744
Tárrega, 480
Tartessos, 49, 50, 52, 53, 56, 102
Tassis (family), 307, 368; Francesco de, 368; Leonardo de, 368
Tauste, canal of, 515, 586
Tavira, 157
Tendilla, counts of, 295
Ter (river), 145, 198, 670
Termantia, 63
Teruel, 292, 517, 534, 570, 637, 642, 656, 661
Theodoric, 86
Theodosius, 76
Thomas process, 661, 664
Thürriegel (baron), 490, 491
Tibelein (banker), 596
Tierra Firme, 401, 404, 548
Tierra del Fuego, 317
Tlalpujahua, 395
Tlemçen, 208, 209, 217, 281, 282
Toledo, 20, 26, 69, 73, 84, 89, 106, 113, 114, 115, 123, 161, 162, 165, 198, 243, 249, 258, 259, 260, 262, 263, 267, 275, 276, 277, 278, 293, 294, 295, 297, 305, 352, 354, 357, 359, 368, 427, 428, 430, 451, 466, 485, 494, 530, 535, 570, 574, 637, 640, 642, 648
Toledo (viceroy), 321
Tolosa, 530
Toreno, count of, 716, 720
Toro, 128, 250, 296, 337
Torres Balbás, L., 105, 106, 125
Torres Fontes, Juan, 302
Tortosa, 75, 138, 140, 148, 149, 177, 181, 187, 196, 219, 228, 358, 554
Tortuga, 405
Toulouse, 202
Tournai, 273
Tours, 359
Tous, Nicolás, 665

Townsend, 535
Toynbee, Arnold, 95
Trafalgar, 603
Transylvania, 77
Trápani, 204
Trasmiera, 464
Trasselli, C., 200, 210
Trastamara (dynasty), 246, 286
Triano, 662
Trinidad, 573, 577, 578
Tripoli (Libya), 301
Tripoli (Syria), 292
Troeltsch, Ernst, 32
Trubia, 664
Tucumán, 549, 573
Tudela, 138, 159, 480, 685
Tuir, 200
Tunis, 208, 209, 217
Tunisia, 22
Turia (river), 535
Turiaso, 69
Tuscany, 210, 212, 369
Tyre, 48, 49

Úbeda, 162, 243, 345
Uganda, 209
Ujíjar, 515
Ulloa, Antonio de, 577
United Kingdom, 559. *See also* England; Great Britain
United States of America, 29, 506, 561, 580, 602, 609, 666, 670, 710, 733
Urdaneta, Andrés de, 400
Urgel, 148, 187, 191, 196, 343; canal of, 515, 653
Uribarren (family), 667
Urrutia, Juan, 675
Uruguay, 541
Usher, A. P., 220, 227
Usón, Matías, 295
Utrecht, peace of, 540, 572; treaty of, 483, 486, 522, 535, 542, 550, 559, 567, 568, 572, 598
Uztáriz, Jerónimo, 454, 483, 486, 566, 567, 572

Uztáriz brothers, 575

Valdeavellano, Luis, 133
Valencia, 18, 22, 28, 48, 106, 115, 148, 157, 158, 159, 166, 175, 176, 177, 179, 180, 181, 182, 184, 187, 188, 195, 196, 199, 200, 211, 212, 214, 216, 218, 221, 224, 227, 228, 229, 231, 235, 242, 263, 268, 270, 277, 283, 293, 297, 300, 309, 310, 334, 335, 352, 357, 360, 368, 413, 416, 421, 424, 425, 427, 430, 432, 465, 466, 476, 478, 480, 485, 488, 494, 496, 497, 513, 531, 532, 534, 535, 538, 539, 553, 558, 560, 562, 563, 569, 570, 574, 575, 576, 582, 589, 591, 595, 596, 620, 622, 637, 642, 646, 647, 650, 672, 680, 682, 684, 685, 725, 728
Valencia, Pedro de, 452
Valenciennes, 265
Valentinian III, 76
Valerian, 81
Valers, Francesc dez, 211
Valladolid, 15, 73, 84, 161, 243, 250, 262, 276, 277, 293, 302, 306, 308, 330, 354, 357, 367, 368, 374, 439, 480, 493, 513, 514, 530, 534, 538, 539, 555, 637, 646, 648, 685, 728
Valldemosa, 570
Valle de la Cerda, Luis, 345, 346, 454
Vallés, 200
Vall-Ferrera, 145
Vall Roja, baron of, 538
Valls (family), 669, 744
Valmaseda, 554, 683
Valparaíso, 578
Vega, Lope de, 360
Vejer, 165
Vélez Málaga, 480
Vendramin, 336
Venezuela, 394, 545, 572, 573, 579, 599, 612
Venice, 167, 205, 207, 215, 237, 360, 367, 368, 372

Ventalló, 199
Vera (Almería), 480
Veracruz, 399, 401, 544, 576, 580
Vergara, 479, 482
Verlinden, Charles, 201, 210, 213, 214, 224, 456
Vespasian, 58, 59, 80
Viada, Miguel de, 682
Vich, 48, 140, 141, 200
Vienna, 490
Vigo, 485, 622, 655, 685
Vilamarí (admiral), 206, 216
Vilanova, A., 119
Vilar, Pierre, 178, 411, 423, 464, 508, 512, 535, 536, 589, 590, 599, 601
Villacastín, 360
Villafranca del Panadés, 531
Villalón, 307, 374, 375
Villalonga (family), 667
Villanueva, Jaime, 473
Villanueva de la Serena, 255
Villars, marquis of, 486
Villaviciosa, 560
Villena, marquises of, 247, 295
Vilumara (bank), 729
Viñas Mey, C., 241, 419, 475
Vinent (bankers), 730
Vipasca, 68, 69
Virgili, Pedro, 473
Viriatus, 56
Vitoria, 262, 265, 306, 554
Vitoria, Francisco de, 319

Vitré, 421
Volga (river), 16

Ward, Bernard, 480, 483, 489, 501, 567
Watt, James, 525
Weber, 32
Welser (family), 335
Westphalia, peace of, 420
Windward Islands, 407, 578

Xifré (family), 737

Ybarra (family), 664, 665, 666, 691; José María, 662, 691
Yllas y Vidal, 708
Young, Arthur, 725
Ypres, 265, 272
Yucatan, 578

Zaccarías (family), 263
Zacatecas, 444
Zag de la Maleha (family), 284
Zamora, 13, 14, 17, 73, 123, 126, 127, 250, 253, 259, 262, 480, 538, 642
Zaracondegui, 712
Zaragoza, *see* Saragossa
Zarza la Mayor (company), 565, 574
Zavala, Silvio, 541
Zuloaga, Antonio de, 531
Zuloaga, José de, 533